John Curwen

The Standard Course of Lessons and Exercises

in the tonic sol-fa method of teaching music : (founded in Miss Glover's Scheme for rendering psalmody congregational, 1835). With additional exercises

John Curwen

The Standard Course of Lessons and Exercises
in the tonic sol-fa method of teaching music : (founded in Miss Glover's Scheme for rendering psalmody congregational, 1835). With additional exercises

ISBN/EAN: 9783337465940

Printed in Europe, USA, Canada, Australia, Japan

Cover: Foto ©Paul-Georg Meister /pixelio.de

More available books at **www.hansebooks.com**

THE

STANDARD COURSE

OF LESSONS AND EXERCISES

IN THE

Tonic Sol-fa Method of Teaching Music

(FOUNDED ON MISS GLOVER'S "SCHEME FOR RENDERING PSALMODY CONGREGATIONAL," 1835).

WITH

ADDITIONAL EXERCISES.

BY

JOHN CURWEN.

ELEVENTH EDITION.

London:
J. CURWEN & SONS, 8 & 9 WARWICK LANE, E.C.

PRICE THREE SHILLINGS AND SIXPENCE.

1895.

J·CURWEN·AND·SONS·
OLD NOTATION
TONIC SOL-FA

NOTICE.

Several friends have said to me "why do you not arrange your book in lessons? It would be so convenient for us, every time we go to our class, to know exactly how much and how little we have to teach." I would gladly have done this; but the different capacities, tastes, and circumstances of our pupils make it impossible. A School lesson and a lesson to an Evening class, a Reformatory lesson and a College lesson, differ exceedingly both in the manner of teaching and in the number of things which can be taught. I can only provide a general method, some points of which are essential and some non-essential, leaving the teacher to adapt this method to the particular class he has to deal with. Such topics as Harmony, Pronunciation, Musical Form, Voice Training, and the difficult parts of Time, Tune, and Expression may, however important, be reckoned as non-essentials, and will have to be omitted in many classes.

Although I could not fix the exact amount of instruction and exercise which every class can receive lesson by lesson, I have divided the method into Steps. By a step I mean a certain stage of the pupil's progress at which he is expected to stop and examine himself, and bring the different divisions of his labours (tune, time and expression) abreast of one another. This is what is called, in the counting house, "taking stock," in the House of Commons, "Reporting progress." It is ascertained that ordinary students do learn a certain proportion of each branch of the subject *concurrently*, and this proportion is given as nearly as possible in each step. One-sidedness of study is most dangerous and miserable to the student. A clever reader of *tune* who cannot keep *time* is constantly finding himself wrong, and annoying his neighbours, and a good *timeist* who is often singing out of *tune* feels himself to be unsatisfactory, and often stops the class to get his errors corrected. The steps, with their amplitude of questions at the end, enable all the members of a class to march together,—to keep step.

But the Lesson is a different thing from the Step. A very dull class may require three or four lessons before they finish the first stage of progress and bring themselves up to the mark distinctly drawn by the examination at the close of the first step. Rarely have we found classes so quick and ready that they can accomplish the first step at a single lesson. The teacher studies the kind of class he is about to teach, and draws out the plan of his lessons accordingly. Until he knows his class more perfectly he will seldom be able to do in a lesson exactly what he had planned to do, but be always goes to his class with a plan,—having chosen the exercises to be done, and having anticipated in his own mind and pictured to his imagination, the blunders he will be required to correct, and the brief verbal explanations he will be expected to make.

When a *new* topic is introduced, it occupies a larger portion of time than the other topics, and may at first do this even to the exclusion of others. But directly a subject has reached the "wearying point" in a class it must stop, even if it has occupied only a short time. At first the chief care will be given to the subject of *tune*, and not until the attention of the class *gets near* the wearying point, does the teacher introduce the first elements of time, as a variety. When the association of syllable and interval in **d m s** is fully established, and not till then, will *much* attention be given to the earlier time names. It is not wise to introduce a great number of *new* topics in one lesson. The Voice exercises should occupy a brief portion of each lesson at its opening. On all teachers, taking up our Method, I urge faithful attention from the beginning to three things—the Pattern—the Mental Effects, and the preparation for Certificates. The experienced teacher knows how to arrange the topics of his class, how to pass promptly from one to the other, how to keep up the interest, and how to secure an even progress in all the branches of study. For the inexperienced teacher, I have gathered together all the helps I could think of, in the "Teacher's Manual of the Tonic Sol-fa method."*

JOHN CURWEN.

Plaistow, *2nd July*, 1872.

* Price Five Shillings.

INDEX OF TOPICS.

TUNE.

TIME.

EXPRESSION.

PRONUNCIATION.

VOICE TRAINING.

HARMONY.

MUSICAL FORM.

NOTATION.

FINGER-SIGNS FOR TIME,

AS SEEN FROM THE PUPIL'S (NOT THE TEACHER'S) POINT OF VIEW.

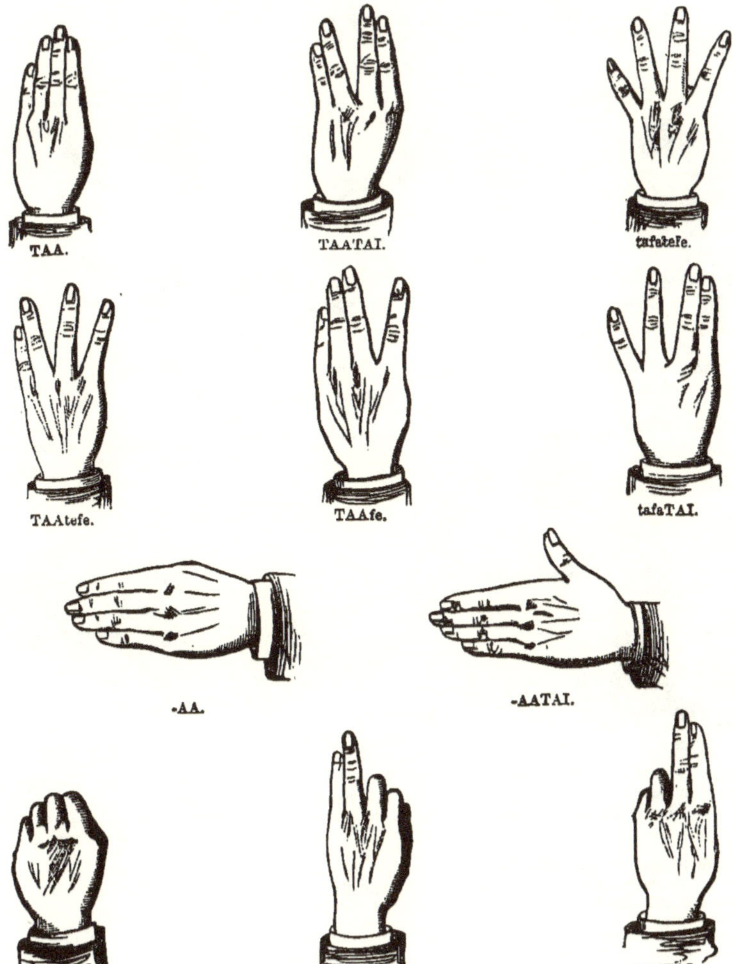

MENTAL EFFECTS AND MANUAL SIGNS OF TONES IN KEY.

Note.—*These diagrams show the hand as seen by pupils sitting on the left-hand side of the teacher. The teacher makes his signs in front of his ribs, chest, face, and head, rising a little as the tones go up, and falling as they go down.*

FIRST STEP.

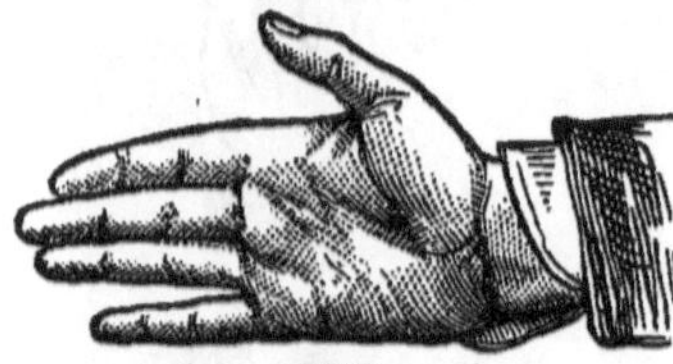

SOH.

The Grand or *bright* tone,—the Major Dominant, making with *Te* and *Ray* the Dominant Chord,—the Chord S, and with *Fah* also the Chord ^{7}S.

ME.

The Steady or *calm* tone,—the Major Mediant, making with *Soh* and *Te* the rarely used Chord M.

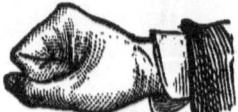

DOH.

The Strong or *firm* tone,—the Major Tonic, making with *Me* and *Soh* the Tonic Chord, the Chord D.

SECOND STEP.

TE.

The Piercing or *sensitive* tone,—the Major Leading Tone, making with *Ray* and *Fah* the weak Chord T.

RAY.

The Rousing or *hopeful* tone,—the Major Supertonic, making with *Fah* and *Lah* the Chord R,—in which case it is naturally sung a comma flatter, and may be distinguished as *Rah.*

THIRD STEP.

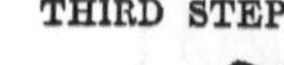

LAH.

The Sad or *weeping* tone,—the Major Submediant, making with *Doh* and *Me* the Chord L.

FAH.

The Desolate or *awe-inspiring* tone,—the Major Subdominant, making with *Lah* and *Doh*, the Subdominant Chord,—the Chord F.

⁂ For **fe** let the teacher point his first finger horizontally to the left. For **ta** ditto to the right. When seen by the class these positions will be reversed, and will correspond with the Modulator. For **se** let the teacher point his forefinger straight towards the class.

Note.—*These proximate verbal descriptions of mental effect are only true of the tones of the scale when sung slowly—when the ear is filled with the key, and when the effect is not modified by harmony.*

SECOND STEP.

TE.

The PIERCING or *sensitive* tone — the Major LEADING TONE, making with *Ray* and *Fah*, the weak Chord T.

RAY.

The ROUSING or *hopeful* tone —the Major SUPERTONIC, making with *Fah* and *Lah* the Chord R—in which case it is naturally sung a komma flatter, and may be distinguished as *Rah*.

FIRST STEP.

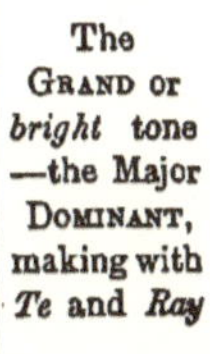

The GRAND or *bright* tone —the Major DOMINANT, making with *Te* and *Ray* the Dominant Chord —the Chord S, and with *Fah* also the Chord ^{7}S.

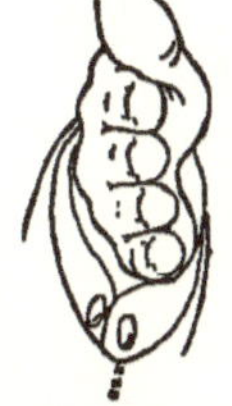

SOH.

ME.

The STEADY or *calm* tone—the Major MEDIANT, making with *Soh* and *Te* the rarely used Chord M.

DOH.

The STRONG or *firm* tone—the Major TONIC, making with *Me* and *Soh*, the Tonic Chord, the Chord D.

THIRD STEP.

LAH.

The SAD or *weeping* tone—the Major SUBMEDIANT, making with *Doh* and *Me*, the Chord L.

FAH.

The DESOLATE or *awe-inspiring* tone—the Major SUBDOMINANT, making with *Lah* and *Doh*, the Subdominant Chord—the Chord F.

TA.

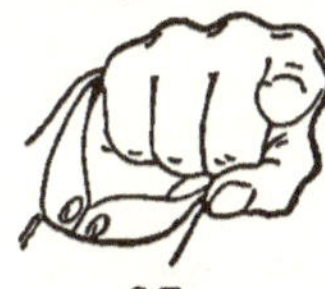

SE.

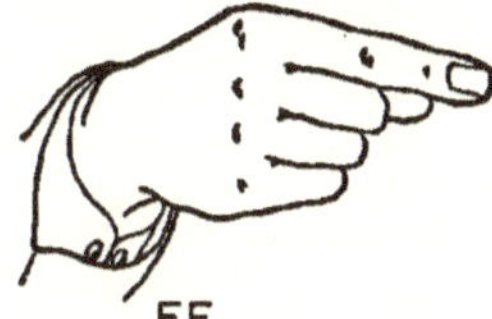

FE.

NOTE.—*These diagrams show the hand as seen by the pupil, standing in front of the teacher. The proximate verbal description of mental effect are only true of the tones of the scale when sung slowly—when the ear is filled with the key, and when the effect is not modified by harmony.*

TONIC SOL-FA TIME CHART.

By JOHN CURWEN.

(Copyright.)

Wholes. Halves.	Quarters.	Thirds.
:1 TAA	:1 ,1 .1 ,1 tafatefe	:1 ,1 ,1 taataitee
:— -AA	:1 .1 ,1 TAAtefe	:1 ,– ,1 TAAtee
: *SAA*	:1 ,1 TAAfe	:1 ,1 ,– taatai-ee
:1 .1 TAATAI	:1 ,1 .1 tafaTAI	: ,1 ,1 *sai*taitee
:- .1 -AATAI	: ,1 .1 ,1 *sa*fatefe	:1 ,– , TAA*see*
: .1 *SAA*TAI	:1 ,1 .1 , tafate*se*	:1 , , taa*sai-ee*
:1 . TAA*SAI*	:1 . ,1 TAA*se*fe	:1 , ,1 taa*sai*tee

Eighths.	:11,11.11,11 tanafanatenefene	**Sixths.** 3 accents.	:11,11,1.1 tafatefetifi
Ninths.	:111,111,111 taralatereletirili	**Sixths.** 2 accents.	:111.111 taralaterele

NOTE.—"Ai" is pronounced as in m*ai*d, f*ai*l, &c. "Aa" is pronounced as in f*a*ther, "a" as in m*a*d, "e" as in l*e*d, and "i" as in l*i*d. These time-names are copied from M. Paris's "Langue des durées." The minute divisions are seldom used except in instrumental music. In the Tonic Sol-fa notation we often write *two* measures in the place of *one* in the common notation, thus expressing the accent more truly.

The flats of the scale, ta, la, ma, ra, are pronounced *taw, law,* &c.; and the sharps, de, re, fe, le, are pronounced *dee, ree,* &c. Ba (the sharp sixth of the minor scale) is pronounced *bay.*

St. Co.

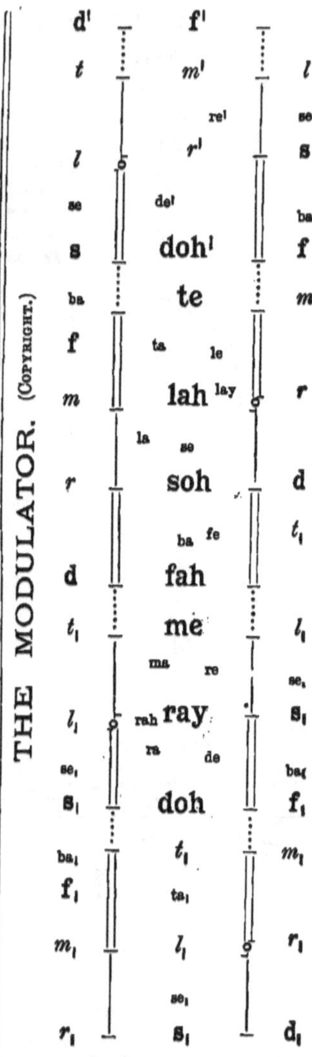

THE EXTENDED MODULATOR.

DOH=G♭ / Lah=E♭	D♭ / B♭	A♭ / F	E♭ / C	B♭ / G	F / D		C / A		G / E	D / B	A / F♯	E / C♯	B / G♯	F♯ / D♯
se		ba	t	m	l	D'	r' r'	D'	s	d'	f			se
s	d'	f			se	♭		♯	ba	t	m	l	r r'	s
ba	t	m	l	r r'	s	C'	DOH'	C'	f			se		ba
f			se		ba	B	TE	B	m	l	r r'	s	d	f
m	l	r r'	s	d	f	♭	ta le	♯		se		ba	t,	m
	se		ba	t,	m	A	LAH	A	r r'	s	d	f		
r r'	s	d	f			♭	la se	♯		ba	t,	m	l,	r r'
	ba	t,	m	l,	r r'	G	SOH	G	d	f			se,	
d	f			se,		♭	ba fe	♯	t,	m	l,	r r'	s,	d
t,	m	l.	r r'	s,	d	F	FAH	F			se,		ba,	t,
		se,		ba,	t,	E	ME	E	l,	r r'	s,	d	f,	
l,	r r'	s,	d	f,		♭	ma re	♯	se,		ba,	t,	m,	l,
se,		ba,	t,	m,	l,	D	RAY r'	D	s,	d	f,			se,
s,	d	f,			se,	♭	ra de	♯	ba,	t,	m,	l,	r, r'	s,
ba,	t,	m,	l,	r, r'	s,	C	DOH	C	f,			se,		ba,
f,			se,		ba,	B,	t,	B,	m,	l,	r, r'	s,	d,	f,

THE STANDARD COURSE

OF THE

TONIC SOL-FA METHOD OF TEACHING TO SING.

FIRST STEP.

To produce a good tone. To train the muscles which rule the lungs. Given a key tone, to recognize and produce its fifth and third. To recognize and produce its upper octave and the lower octave of its fifth. To recognize and produce the simplest divisions of time.

Voice Training

A singing lesson is a calisthenic exercise, and should be preceded, where possible, by such gymnastic movements of the arms and shoulders as will exercise and strengthen the muscles of the chest.

Good Tone.—From the earliest exercise, the pupil should try to produce *a good tone*, that is, a tone clear and pure (without any admixture of breathiness), and of a pleasant quality. For this purpose constant, if possible, *daily* attention must be directed to three things: 1st, the "shock of the *glottis*;" 2nd, the throwing *forward* of the voice; and 3rd, the *control* of the breath. *Purity* of tone depends on the first and third of these, *quality* on the second and third. The lump in our throat called the *larynx* or "Adam's apple," is the instrument of voice. The *glottis* is the slit between those lips of the larynx (or vocal cords), which form its lower opening. When Garcia and other voice-trainers speak of the "shock of the glottis;" and when Dr. Rush, Mr. Melville Bell, and other elocutionists speak of the clear "explosion" of vowel sounds, they refer to the *firm closing*, followed by the *distinct opening* of these lips of the larynx. The action of the lips of the mouth, in pronouncing strongly the letter *p*, in *papa*, will illustrate this; and the "shock of the glottis" may be *felt* in a slight cough, or in pronouncing clearly the letter *g*, as in *game*; or *k*, as in *keep*. This "shock" does not require force, but only *definiteness* of action. It must also be delivered with *as little breath* as possible. The word *skaalaa*, (*aa* as in father) which many voice-trainers use for their exercises, has this advantage, that its first syllable *necessitates* that clearly marked "explosion" of the vowel of which we speak; but in using it, the *s* must be scarcely heard, and the *k* must be delivered sharply.

Quality of voice (*timbre*, that which makes the difference between a hard wiry voice, a soft clear voice, a full rich voice, &c.) depends chiefly on *the habit* of throwing the air-stream *forward* in the mouth. Professor Helmholtz' experiments, as well as the practice of Garcia and others, support this view. The stream of vocalized air should strike against the palate as near as possible to the root of the upper teeth. Some vowels naturally favour this habit more than others. In English, *ee*, *ai* (as in *fail*, *maid*, &c.), *oa* (as in *oar*, *coat*, &c.), and *oo*, are all "forward" vowels, as any one may know by a few experiments with his own voice. The frequent use of these vowels, in vocalizing, in connection with a proper management of the breath, enables the voice-trainer "to form," says Madame Seiler, "out of a sharp, hard, and disagreeable voice, a voice sweet and pleasing." The open vowel *aa* (as in f*a*ther) is commonly formed, by the English, the French, and the Germans, far *back* in the mouth; but "the Italians," says Madame Seiler, "form no vowel so far *front* as their clear-sounding beautiful *aa*." When we copy the old Italian voice-trainers in employing this vowel—so useful in vocalizing, because it opens the mouth properly—let us take care to throw it forward, and so give it the soft round Italian quality. It is unfortunate that our *ee*, *ai*, *oa*, and *oo*, do not, like the Italian *aa*, promote the proper opening of the mouth.

The proper management of breath promotes a correct striking of the tones, as well as their purity and quality. Insufficient breath causes flatness of pitch, at the same time with thin and poor quality. The slightest *unnecessary* force of breath makes itself heard along with the vocal klang, and causes mixture and *impurity* of tone. "Every tone," says Madame Seiler, "requires, for its greatest possible perfection, only a certain quantity of breath, which cannot be diminished or increased without injury." As the breath has to be received into the lungs by the same channel through which it leaves them, it is obvious that the regular action of breathing must be interrupted when we speak or sing. Hence the necessity of care and management. Elocutionists as well as voice-trainers recommend that the lungs should be *kept* fairly full. Mrs. Blaine Hunt says: "Accustom yourself to take breath *wherever you can*, although you may not feel the necessity for it at the time. This is important *to beginners*, as it teaches them soon to take it without exertion, and less perceptibly to the hearer." Of course the sensible singer *cannot* take breath in any place in which his doing so would spoil the sense and continuity of the words, or of the musical phrases. There is no need of noisy effort to draw in the breath; the nose and mouth being open, it is only necessary to expand the ribs and the lungs *are* filled. In the beginning of his studies the singer should take breath at the end, and at some convenient place in the middle of each line of poetry. Gradually the muscles which *hold* the ribs distended sideways, as well as those *underneath* the lungs, by which alone the breath should be expelled, or rather *expended*, will gain strength. A long sustained tone should not be expected at first; and *the swell* upon such tones, properly delivered, is, as Garcia, Bassini, and others shew, among the *last* attainments of vocal power. Exercise steadily pursued, and nothing else can give to the muscles the requisite power of control. Voice exercises should, for a long time, be sung, as the old Italian masters required, *only softly*. The effort to sing softly (or *piano*), with a full but not overcrowded chest, *compels* attention to the control of the muscles; it also the better enables the pupil to *perceive for himself* what is meant by purity and beautiful quality of tone. Until this perception is formed nothing is done. The pupil in a popular evening class, must, in this matter, rely chiefly on himself and his daily practice. It is but little study of individual voices which a class-teacher can give. Much, however, is done in classes by imitation and sympathy. We have noticed that every teacher who himself understands what "a good tone" is, *will* have it in his class; and when once the right habit is established there, new comers naturally and easily fall into it.

Position.—The singer should (*a*) *stand* with heels together or in the soldiers posture of "stand at ease;" (*b*) with head erect, but not thrown back; (*c*) with shoulders held back, but not up; (*d*) with lungs kept naturally filled—not with raised chest, except on extraordinary occasions—but with the ribs, never allowed to collapse, pressing against the clothes at each side, and the lower muscles of the abdomen drawn in; (*e*) with the mouth freely open, but not in the fish-mouth shape 0,—the lips being pressed upon the teeth, and drawn somewhat away from the opening, so as not to deaden the sound,—the lower jaw falling,—the palate so raised as to *catch* on its front-part the stream of air from the lungs,—and the tongue flat, its tip just touching the lower teeth. These rules have to be carefully studied by the singer, and, at first, they will make him stiff and self-conscious; but soon, and with care, the proper position will *grow into a habit*. Everything will be most easy, and the motto of the old masters will be realized—"Pleasant face makes pleasant tone." The teacher "calls his pupils into position" by giving out as words of command—"*a*," "*b*," "*c*," "*d*," "*e*." At each order, the pupils take the position indicated by those letters as above, and the teacher watches to make sure that they do so properly. He makes a sign—a motion—with the fingers of his left hand to those who do not open the mouth sideways as much as he wishes, and another sign to those who do not keep their teeth about two finger-breadths apart. He shakes his head at those who do not make a "pleasant face," and so on. Garcia says: "Open mouths of an oval shape, like those of fishes, produce tones of a sorrowful and grumbling character; those of which the lips project, in the form of a funnel, give a hard barking voice; very wide mouths, which exhibit the teeth *too* much, render the tone rough; those which have the teeth too close, form shrivelled tones." These points must be attended to at the commencement and in the course of every early lesson. There is no other way in which the pupil can be saved from slovenly habits and coarse flat singing.

Ex. 1.—*To train the muscles at the sides of the lungs and under them.*—To be repeated at the opening of each lesson of the first step.

The pupils standing, if possible, in single file, round the room (so that the teacher may approach each one and quietly signify any defect of position while the exercise is going on), the teacher raises his hand while the pupils take in breath slowly, and without noise. The pupils *hold**their breath while the hand remains high, and let out the breath again through the mouth, and *gradually* as the teacher lowers his hand. The teacher counts "one," "two," "three," &c (at the rate of M. 60, or as slowly as a common eight-day clock ticks), while he lowers his hand. The pupils say, by holding up hands, who held out as far as "three," "four," "six," &c. The teacher is well satisfied with "four" at first, and does not require even that from weak lungs.

Ex. 2.—*To train the larynx for the production of pure vocal klang.* To be repeated at the opening of each lesson in the first step.

The teacher sings on the syllable *ai* (as in g*ai*n, p*ai*l, &c.) a middle tone of the voice, say G or A. The pupils imitate that tone, commencing immediately the teacher opens his hand, and cutting it off sharply the instant the teacher closes his hand. This done, he gives the vowel *ai* again, but immediately changes it into the more open and pleasant *aa*; changing, however, as little as possible the *ai* position of the tongue, so as to secure the "forward" Italian *aa*. The pupils imitate, attention being given exclusively to the position and to purity of the voice. This is done with various tones—say with D, with F, and with A.

First Exercises in Tune.

Pitch.—By "pitch," we mean the *highness* or *lowness* of sounds; the difference between the sounds produced towards the right hand on the piano and those towards the left, or between a squeak and a growl. We are not anxious, at present, to teach the *absolute pitch* of sounds. Our first and chief work is to teach the *relation* of sounds in a tune to what is called the key-sound of that tune.

Key Tone.—Everything in a tune depends on a certain "given" sound called its governing, or key-tone, from which all the other tones measure their places. At present the teacher will pitch the key-tone for the pupil. The modulator represents this key-tone with its six related tones, in the way in which they are commonly used. The pupil will learn to sing them by first learning to perceive their effects on the mind, and *not* by noticing their relative distances from each other.

Pattern.—The teacher never sings *with* his pupils, but sings them a brief and soft "pattern." The first art of the pupil is to *listen well* to the pattern, and then to imitate it exactly. He that listens best, sings best. When it is the pupil's turn to sing let him strike the tones firmly, and hold them as long as the teacher pleases. As soon as the modulator is used, the teacher points on it while he sets the pattern, and also while the pupil imitates.

Ex. 3.—The Teacher asks his pupils for a rather *low* sound of their voice. He gets them to sing it clearly, and well drawn out, to the open syllable *aa*. He takes it for the *key tone* of a tune. He sings it, and immediately adds to it what is known as the fifth above. The pupils try to imitate the "pattern," singing (still to *aa*) the key tone and its nearest related tone. When, by patient pattern and imitation, this is done,—

Ex. 4. The Teacher gives a *different* low sound of the voice for the key tone, and asks the pupils to give him that other related tone again. This he does several times, always changing the key tone.

Names and Signs.—Immediately that a thing is understood it is important to have a *name* for it, and sometimes a *sign* also. Any name or sign which is agreed upon between Teacher and pupil, will answer the purpose. But it is convenient to use the same names which others use. On our modulator and in our notation we call the key tone just given *Doh*, and the other nearly related sound *Soh*. For voice Exercises, in which the Teacher has to look at pupils while he gives them signals to guide their singing, it will be useful to employ the closed hand as a sign for *Doh*, and the open hand, pointing outwards, with the thumb upwards, for *Soh*.

* By means of the ribs, not the throat.

Ex. 5. The Teacher gives *Doh* and *Soh* (to the open *aa*) and, immediately after, another sound, different from *Soh*, which he knows as the third of the scale. The pupils imitate his pattern. The Tonic Solfa *name* for this sound is *Me*, and the *sign* is the open hand with the palm downwards,

Ex. 6. The Teacher, by the above named manual signs, causes the pupils to sing (while he watches their position and the opening of their mouths,) to the open sound *aa* such phrases as the following, *Doh, Soh, Me, Soh, Doh.—Doh, Me, Soh.—Soh, Me, Doh, Me*, &c., &c. The Teacher changes his key tone with nearly every new Exercise, lest the pupils should be tempted to try and sing by *absolute pitch*, instead of directing their attention to the *relation* of sounds.

Mental Effect.—The effect felt by the mind as it listens to these three tones, arises first from their difference in pitch, one being higher or lower than the other, and secondly and chiefly from their *agreeing* well with each other,—so that it is pleasant to hear them one immediately after the other, and pleasant to hear them sounded together. The science of sound shows how closely and beautifully these three tones are related to each other, in the number of their vibrations. Their agreement may be shewn by sounding together 1st *Doh* and *Soh*, 2nd *Doh* and *Me*, 3rd *Me* and *Soh*, and 4th *Doh Me Soh*. When three tones are thus related, and sounded together, they are called a *Chord*. The pupils will be led to notice the different *effect on their minds* of the three tones of this Chord. As they form the Chord of the key tone, they are the bold, strong, pillar tones of the scale, on which the others lean, but they differ in the *manner* of their boldness, one being brighter, another stronger and more restful, another more peaceful, &c. The Teacher, having brought his pupils to a clear conception of these tones, apart from syllabic association, now attaches to each of them its singing syllable,—teaching by pattern, and pointing on the modulator the six following exercises. For the sake of solitary students, who cannot be thus taught, these exercises are printed, in the form of diagrams, with skeleton modulators at the side. The first letters of the syllables on the modulator are used to indicate the notes, and so point to the modulator in the mind's eye. A narrower type and somewhat altered form is given to the letter m (m), for convenience in printing.

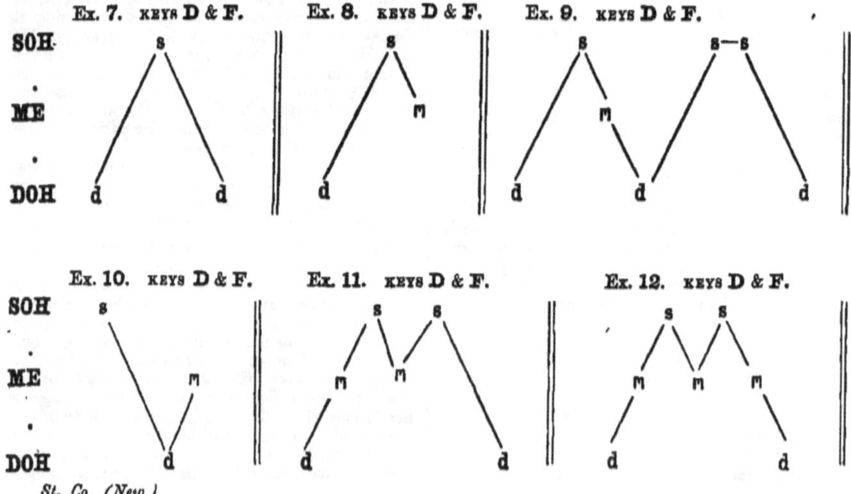

Octaves or Replicates.—It is in the nature of music, that tones, which vibrate twice as fast or twice as slow as some other tone, should sound so like that other tone, and blend so perfectly with it, that they are treated as the same tone and receive the same name. They are *the same* in Relative position and mental effect,—the difference of pitch being the *only* difference between them. Thus every sound has its "replicate" or repetition above and below. The two sounds are called octaves one to another, because if you count the tones of a scale from any sound to its replicate (including the tones at both ends) you count *eight* or an octave of sounds. We put a figure one upward thus—(ˡ), as a mark for the upper octave, and downward thus—(ˌ), as a mark for the lower octave. If we wish to indicate higher or lower octaves still, we use the figure (²). The *sign* for a higher octave would be given by raising the hand which gives the sign, and for a lower octave by lowering it.

Ex. 13. The Teacher gives a *low* sound of the voice for *Doh*, and patterns to the open syllable *aa*, **d, m, s, dˡ**. The pupils imitate. Again, by manual signs, the Teacher requires the pupils to sing which ever of these notes he pleases, while he watches the position and the opening of the mouth,—in each exercise varying the key.

Ex. 14. The Teacher gives a *middle* sound of the voice for *Doh*, and then patterns to the open *aa*, **d, m, s, sˌ, d.** The pupils imitate. Again, watching his pupils, he requires them, by manual signs, to make any of these tones he pleases, in each exercise varying the key.

The Teacher sets for each of the following Exercises a Solfa pattern on the modulator.

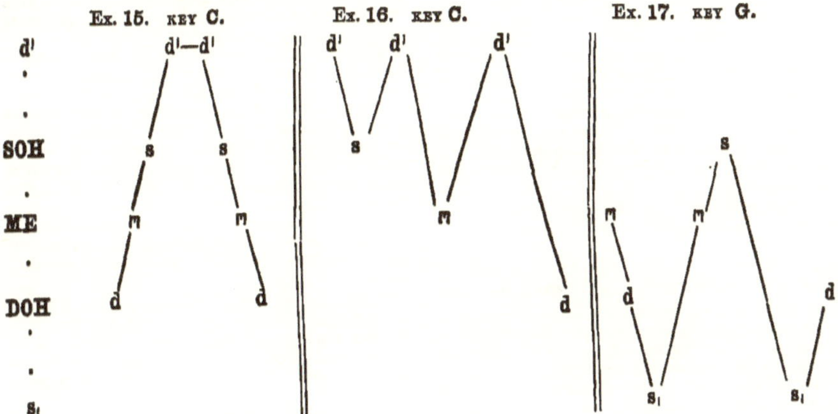

FIRST EXERCISES IN NOTATION.

In the following Exercises, "Key G," "Key C," "Key A," tell the Teacher where to pitch his *Doh*. The letters point on the *modulator in the mind's eye*. The Teacher pitches the key tone. The pupils "sound the chord," singing (when they have a middle sound of the voice for *Doh*,) *Doh, Sohˌ, Me, Doh*, and when they have a low sound, *Doh, Me, Soh*. As there is no indication of time, the tones may be made as long or as short as the Teacher likes. A gentle tap on the desk will tell the pupils when to begin each tone. During this Exercise it may be well to let the large modulator hang before the pupils, that they may glance at it when their mental modulator fails them.

Ex. 18. KEY G.

s_1 d m s m s m d

Ex. 19. KEY C.

s d^1 s m s m s d

Ex. 20. KEY A.

d s_1 d m s m d

Ex. 21. KEY C.

s m s d d^1 m s d

Ex. 22. KEY A.

m d m s s s_1 d

Ex. 23. KEY C.

s m d^1 m s d m

First Exercises in Time.

Time and Rhythm. The word time is commonly used in three different senses. Sometimes it means the *degree of speed* at which the music is sung, as when we speak of quick time, slow time, etc. This we call "The Rate of Movement." Sometimes it means the arrangement of accents in a tune, as when we say "common time," "triple time," etc. This we call "The Measure." Sometimes it means the varied lengths of a set of notes standing together, as when we speak of "keeping the time" in a certain phrase. These time-arrangements of brief musical phrases we call "Rhythms." The word Rhythm is also used in a general sense to express the larger relations of time and accent, such as the number and kind of measures in a tune, and the proportion which is given to each "section" of the tune.

Accent or Stress. The Teacher, by singing on one tone such an exercise as the following,

KEY G.

d :d	d :d ‖	:d	d :d	d ‖
aw - *ful*	dawn-*ing*	*a* -	wake, *a*-	rise.

leads his pupils to distinguish the difference between a *weak* and a **strong** accent both in words and music. The Teacher will be careful not to let his pupils exaggerate the strong accent, so as to make a jerked tone instead of simply an accented tone. Accent is produced by the combined use of *distinctness* (or abruptness) and *force*—in their various degrees, and it differs in quality as one or the other element predominates. An upright bar (|) shews that the note which follows it is to be sung with the stronger accent. Two dots, thus, (:) shew that the note which follows them is to be sung with the weak accent.

Pulses.—It will be noticed that in music the voice is naturally delivered in successive beats or impulses, some having the strong and some the weak accent. These we call *Pulses*. The Teacher illustrates this. The pulses move faster in some cases and slower in others, but the pulses of the same tune are equal in length one to the other. The Teacher illustrates this. The beginning of a pulse of time is indicated by an accent mark as above, and its end is shown by the next accent mark. In Tonic Solfa printing we place the accent marks in each line of the music, at equal distances, so as to measure time pictorially.

Measure.—In music the accents recur in regular order,—that is, if they begin thus,—STRONG. *weak*, they go on in the same way,—if they begin STRONG, *weak*, *weak*, they continue to recur in that order and so on. The Teacher illustrates this by singing tunes to his pupils, and requiring them to tell him which *order of accents* he uses. The *time* which extends from one *strong* accent to the next is called a *measure*. It is the *primary* form of a measure. If the tune begins on a weak accent the measure is reckoned from that, and extends till the same accent recurs again. This is the *secondary* form of a measure.

Two-pulse measure.—When the accents of a tune recur in the following regular order, STRONG, *weak*, STRONG, *weak*, and so on, or *weak*, STRONG, *weak*, STRONG, and so on, that tune is said to be in *two pulse measure*. The primary form of two pulse

measure would be represented thus {| : {

and the secondary form thus {: | {

Time Names.—We call a single pulse (whatever be the rate of movement) TAA.

Ex. 24. The Teacher causes his pupils to sing a number of primary two-pulse measures on one tone to the time-names, while he beats the time steadily. He does this till all have "got into the swing" of the rhythm (TAA, TAA, TAA, TAA, &c.), so that all the voices strike the beginning of each pulse perfectly together. *Alternate* measures are then sung by teacher and pupils, maintaining the same rate. They do this again with an entirely different rate of movement, only taking care to keep up the rate of movement when once begun. In this exercise let the pupils be careful to sing each pulse fully to the end. The second vowel AI is often added to make him do so.*

Ex. **25**. The teacher in the same manner makes his pupils practise secondary two-pulse measures TAA, TAA, TAA, TAA, &c.

Ex. **26**. Sing Exs. 20, 22, and 23, beginning with the strong accent, and again beginning with the weak.

Ex. **27**. Sing Exs. 18, 19, and 21, beginning with the weak accent, and again beginning with the strong.

Three-pulse Measure.—When the accents of a tune recur at regular intervals thus, STRONG, *weak*, *weak*, STRONG, *weak*, *weak*, and so on (that is like the accents in the words "**heav***enly*," "**hap***piness*," and so on) or *weak*, STRONG, *weak*, *weak*, STRONG, *weak*, and so on, (that is like the accents in the words "*a***maz***ing*," "*a***bun***dant*," and so on) the tune is said to be in *three pulse measure*. The primary form of three pulse measure is this | : : ‖ and the secondary this : | : ‖ In the three pulse measure, *when sung slowly*, the *second* accent is not weak, but often nearly as strong as the first. For convenience, however, we always write this measure as above.

Ex. **28**. The Teacher will make his pupils sing TAA, TAA, TAA (primary three-pulse measure) on a single tone, while he beats time, first at one rate of movement and then at another rate, always sustaining, in each exercise, the rate at which he commences it.

Ex. **29**. The teacher will do the same with TAA, TAA, TAA (secondary three-pulse measure).

Ex. **30**. Sing exercises 20 and 22 in the primary three-pulse measure, making two measures, and the first pulse of the next, to each exercise.

Ex. **31**. Sing exercises 18 and 19 in secondary three-pulse measure, making for each exercise, two measures and two pulses of a third measure.

Continued Tones.—When a tone is continued from one pulse into the next, we mark the continuation by a horizontal line, thus (—). The time-name for continuations is always obtained by dropping the consonant, thus, TAA, -AA, &c. Pupils are apt to fail in giving their full length to prolonged tones.

Half-pulses.—When a pulse (TAA) is equally divided into two parts, we give it the name TAATAI. The sign for an equally divided pulse is a dot in the middle, thus (| . :), and thus (| **d** .**m** :).

Beating Time.—Pupils should never be allowed to "beat" time till they have gained *a sense of time*.

Speaking in Time.—The value of the Time-names depends on their being habitually used *in time*—each syllable having its true proportion.

Taatai-ing.—We propose to use this as a short word for the phrase "singing on one tone to the time names," just as we use "Solfaa-ing" to save the circumlocution "singing with the use of the Solfa syllables." In the early steps of any art it is better to learn each element separately. As the pupil has first learnt tune separately from time on the Modulator, so now, with the help of the Time Chart, he studies time separately from tune. The rule of good teaching that, at the first introduction of any distinct topic, that topic should occupy much more than its ordinary proportion of each lesson, will strongly apply in this case; for we have to establish in the *memory* an association of syllable and *rhythm*, just as, in teaching tune, we have already begun to establish a mnemonic association of syllable and *interval* through mental effect. 1st. The teacher patterns and points on the Time Chart (just as he patterns and points on the Modulator) and the pupils imitate (taatai-ing on one tone) the first *half* of one of the time exercises. The Teacher's pointer will sufficiently well beat time as it strikes on the Chart. 2nd. Teacher and pupils Taatai the time-phrase *alternately*, the teacher singing softly, with clear accent and very exact and well filled time, but only pointing or tapping on the Time Chart when the pupils take their turn. This is done till the pupils "get into the swing," striking the accent well together and giving each tone its full length. 3rd. The second half of the exercise is taught in the same way by pattern and alternating repetition. 4th. The two parts are put together and patterned and alternated as above, but at a quicker rate, without pointing,—the teacher beating time only when it is the pupils turn to sing. 5th. The pupils Taatai from the book as directed in Ex. 32. The other processes of Time-laaing, of Tuning, the time-forms and of Taatai-ing in tune, are introduced a little later, when the time-names are familiar. Each process is only continued till the exercise is

* **Later on (p. 18) the AI may be omitted.**

perfect. These many processes, each increasing in difficulty, give variety to the work of the learner and keep his attention fixed on an otherwise uninteresting but most important subject.

Ex. 32. *First slowly*—repeated so at least three times—*and then quickly*, and repeated so six times.

|1	:1	|1	:—	|1	:—	|1	:1	‖
TAA	TAA	TAA	-AA	TAA	-AA	TAA	TAA	

Ex. 33. *Slowly—and quickly.*

|1	:1	|1	:1	|1	:—	|—	:—	‖
TAA	TAA	TAA	TAA	TAA	-AA	-AA	-AA	

Ex. 34. *Slowly—and quickly.*

:1	|1	:—	|—	:1	|1	:1	|1	‖
TAA	TAA	-AA	-AA	TAA	TAA	TAA	TAA	

Ex. 35. *Slowly—and quickly.*

|1	:1	:1	|1	:—	:1	|1	:1	:1	‖
TAA	TAA	TAA	TAA	-AA	TAA	TAA	TAA	TAA	

Ex. 36. *Slowly—and quickly.*

:1	|1	:1	:1	|1	:—	:—	|1	:1	‖
TAA	TAA	TAA	TAA	TAA	-AA	-AA	TAA	TAA	

Time Laa-ing.—The Teacher when *all* the above exercises have been properly learnt, with time names, will cause them to be sung again in the same way, but to the open syllable *Laa*. The time syllables are, like the Solfa syllables, valuable as mnemonics, and must be much used, especially in the early steps. But they must not be too exclusively used, lest our pupils should be able to sing correct time to nothing else.

Ex. 37. *Laa* Exs. 32 to 36.

Tune.

Tune Laa-ing.—As soon as the memory-helping Solfa syllables have been rendered familiar, every tune should be *Laad* from *the book*. Some teachers make a habit of *Laa-ing* from *the modulator*, directly after the Solfa pattern has been learnt. One study should be always before the teacher's mind while his pupils are *Laa-ing*,—that of the blending and tuning of the voices. As all are using the same syllable *Laa* (not *law* or *lōa*) it is more easy to notice whether *in unison* (that is when all sing the same tones) the tones *blend* as into one voice,—and whether, in *harmony* (that is when several melodies are sung together) the tones *tune* well with each other.

Two-part Singing.—It is at first very difficult for pupils to sing independently one of another. The simplest form of two-part singing is that in which one set of voices repeatedly strikes the same tone ("tolls the bell"), while the other set sings the tune, as in exercises 38 to 41. These exercises should first be taught by pattern from the modulator, and then sung from the books, the Teacher beating the pulses by gentle taps on the desk. If the long tones are not held the proper length, they must be sung to the time names.

{ **Brackets** are used both at the beginning and ending of lines to shew what parts of the music may be sung together.

Double Bars (‖) are used to shew the end of a tune, or the end of what is called a musical "section," generally corresponding to a line of poetry. Where the double bar occurs, the regular accent mark, whether strong or weak, is omitted. But it must nevertheless be understood and observed.

Exchanging Parts.—The exercises of this and the second step do not go too high for low voices, or too low for high voices. All kinds of voices can sing both the upper and the lower parts. At these two steps, therefore, as soon as an exercise is sung, and without a moments pause, it should be sung over again,—those who have sung the higher part taking the lower, and those who have sung the lower taking the higher. It is obvious that these early exercises are best fitted for those classes in which the voices are all of the same sort, that is, all men's voices, or else all women's and children's voices. If, however, the class is a mixed one, the exercises can well be used, although they will not be so pleasant. It is better in this case to let the voices be mixed for both of the parts; for variety, however, the teacher may occasionally give the higher part to the ladies, and the lower to the gentlemen.

Breathing Places.—It will be soon felt that music naturally divides itself into short portions or *phrases*. *Just before the opening of a phrase* is, musically considered, always the best breathing place. The pupil will soon learn to select breathing places for himself; but at the present step we have marked the most convenient breathing places by means of a dagger thus †. The endings of lines, however, are not marked, as breath should *always* be taken there. The pupil who sings on till his ribs collapse and his lungs are empty, *and then* takes breath, produces a flat tone, and feels uncomfortable.

Ex. 38. KEY D. †

```
|d  :—  |m  :—  |s  :—  |d'  :—  †|d'  :—  |s  :—  †|m  :—  |d  :—  ||
|d  :d  |d  :d  |d  :d  |d   :d   |d   :d  |d  :d   |d  :d  |d  :d  ||
```

Ex. 39. KEY D. †

```
|d  :d  |m  :m  |s  :s  |d'  :d'  †|d'  :d'  |s  :s  †|m  :m  |d  :—  ||
|d  :—  |d  :—  |d  :—  |d   :—    |d   :—   |d  :—   |d  :—  |d  :—  ||
```

Ex. 40. KEY F. †

```
|d  :—  |s  :—  |m  :—  |d  :—  †|s  :—  |s  :—  †|d  :—  |—  :—  ||
|d  :d  |d  :d  |d  :d  |d  :d   |d  :d  |d  :d   |d  :d  |d  :—  ||
```

Ex. 41. KEY D. †

```
|d  :m  |s  :m  |s  :m  |d'  :—  †|d'  :s  |m  :s  †|s  :m  |d  :—  ||
|d  :d  |d  :d  |d  :d  |d   :—   |d   :d  |d  :d   |d  :d  |d  :—  ||
```

Ex. 42. KEY D. *Quickly.*

```
|d  :m  |m  :s  |s  :d'  |d'  :—  †|d'  :s  |s  :m  |m  :d  |d  :—  ||
|d  :—  |—  :—  |m  :—   |—   :—   |m   :—  |—  :—  |d  :—  |—  :—  ||
```

Ex. 43. KEY B. †

```
|d   :—   |s,  :—   |m   :—   |d   :—  †|m  :—   |d   :—  †|s,  :—   |d   :—  ||
|m,  :m,  |m,  :m,  |s,  :s,  |m,  :—   |d  :s,  |m,  :d,  |m,  :s,  |d,  :—  ||
```

Ex. 44. KEY F. *Quickly.*

```
|d  :m  |s,  :m  |d  :m  |s  :m  †|d  :m  |s  :m  |s  :s  |s  :—  |
|d  :—  |s,  :—  |d  :—  |m  :—   |d  :—  |s  :—  |m  :—  |—  :—  |

|s  :m  |d  :m  |s  :m  |d  :m  †|s   :m  |d  :m  |d  :d  |d  :—  ||
|m  :—  |d  :—  |m  :—  |d  :—   |s,  :—  |—  :—  |d  :—  |—  :—  ||
```

d'
.
.
SOH
.
ME
.
DOH
.
.
s,

Ex. **45.** *Slowly,—and quickly.*

```
||l         :l  .l  |l        :l  .l  |l  .l   :l  .l  |l        :—   ||
  TAA       TAATAI   TAA      TAATAI   TAATAI  TAATAI   TAA      -AA

KEY C.                                   KEY G.
|d  :m.s|d'  :s.m|s.m:s.m|d  :— ||       |d  :s,.d|m  :d.d|m.d:m.d|s  :— ||
KEY C.                                   KEY G.
|d'  :s.m|d  :m.s|d'.s:d'.s|m  :— ||     |d  :s,.s,|d  :s,.m|d.d:s,.m|d  :— ||
```

Ex. **46.** *Slowly,—and quickly.*

```
||l         :l       |l  .l   :l      |l  .l   :l  .l  |l  .l   :l      ||
  TAA       TAA       TAATAI  TAA      TAATAI  TAATAI   TAATAI  TAA

|d  :m  |s.m:d  |s.m:s.m|s.m:d ||   |d'  :s  |m.s:d'  |d'.s:m.s|m.s:d  ||
|m  :d  |d.m:s  |d.m:s.m|d.m:s ||   |d  :s,  |d.m:d  |d.s,:d.s,|d.m:d  ||
```

Taatai-ing in Tune.—*Laa-ing* on *one* tone helps to form that *abstract* idea of a rhythm which is desired. But such an idea is never truly established until the ear can recognize a rhythm as *the same*, through all the various *disguises* which different tune-forms put upon it. To learn the abstract, you must recognize it in *many* concretes,—the abstract idea "round" in the concretes—wheel, plate, full moon, penny, &c., &c.; of "crimson" in a shawl, a feather, a flower, a punctured finger, &c., &c. If we saw nothing round but a wheel, we could not form an *abstract* idea of "roundness." As a help to this distinct conception of rhythm, it is useful to *taatai* each time exercise on *various* tune forms. The Teacher 1st, *tunes* the time-form, solfaa-ing and teaching, by pattern, one of the phrases printed under the time exercises,—2nd, patterns the same from the Modulator, as before, but *taatai-ing*, as he points, instead of solfaa-ing. The pupils imitate. The time-names shew them the sameness of the rhythm, while the modulator points them to the difference in tune,—3rd, causes his pupils to sing the same from the book.

Ex. 47.—*Taatai in tune*, all the tune-forms printed below Ex. 45 and 46, and any others, the Teacher may invent.

The following exercises (introducing three-pulse measure without divided pulses, and *taatai* in two-pulse measure), should now be solfaad by pattern, from the modulator, *taataid* from the book, *solfaad* from the book, and *laad* from the book. Let each "part" be taught separately before the two parts are sung together.

Ex. **48.** KEY **D.** *Quickly,—and slowly.*

```
|d   :d   :d   |m   :—   :—   |m   :m   :m   |s   :—   :—
|d   :—   :d   |d   :—   :—   |d   :—   :d   |m   :—   :—

|s   :s   :s   |d'  :d'  :d'  |s   :s   :s   |d   :—   :—   ||
|m   :—   :m   |m   :—   :—   |m   :—   :m   |d   :—   :—   ||
```

St. Co. (New.)

Ex. 49. KEY D. *Quickly,—and slowly.*

| d :m :s | d^1 :— :— | d^1 :s :m | d :— :— |
| d :— :d | m :— :— | m :— :d | d :— :— |

| m :s :d^1 | s :— :— | s :m :s | d :— :— ||
| m :— :m | m :— :— | m :— :m | d :— :— ||

d^1

SOH

ME

DOH

s_1

Ex. 50 KEY G. *Slowly,—and quickly.* †

:s_1 | d :— :d | m :d :m | s :— :s | m :— |
:s_1 | m_1 :— :s_1 | d :— :d | m :— :m | d :— |

:d | s_1 :d :m | s_1 :d †:m | s :— :s_1 | d :— ||
:m_1 | m_1 :— :s_1 | m_1 :s_1 :d | m_1 :— :s_1 | m_1 :— ||

Ex. 51. KEY C. *Slowly,—and quickly.*

| d :m | s :s †| d .m :s .d^1 | s :— †| m :s | d^1 :d^1 †| d^1.s :d^1.s | m :— ||
| d :d | m :m | d .d :m .s | m :— | d :m | m :m | m .m :m .m | d :— ||

Ex. 52. KEY G. *Slowly,—and quickly.*

:s_1 | d :m .d | s_1 †:d | m :d †| s :m | d :s_1.d †| m :d | s :s_1 | d ||
:s_1 | m_1 :m_1.m_1 | m_1.m_1 :m_1 | s_1 :d | s_1 :s_1 | m_1 :m_1.s_1 | d .d :d | m_1 :s_1 | m_1 ||

Ex. 53. KEY D. *Slowly,—and quickly.*

| d .m :m | d .m :m †| s :s | m :— †| m .s :s | m .s :s †| d^1 :s | d^1 :— ||
| d :d | d :d | d .m :m | d :— | m :m | m :m | m .s :s | m :— ||

Modulator Voluntaries.

At every lesson, the pupils will be exercised in following the Teacher's pointing on the modulator, *without a pattern*. The difficulty of this is, that the pointer cannot shew accent,—but, in cases of difficulty, by means of the time names the teacher can explain any rhythm he wants. The pupils will learn to follow promptly, and to form the habit of holding the tones as long as the pointer stays on a note. The movements of the pointer are most visible when it passes from note to note with a curve sideways. The Teacher can invent his voluntaries or take them from other Courses. But they should never include greater difficulties than belong to the step which the class has reached. See the "Hints for Voluntaries." These Exercises will prepare for the next.

Ear Exercises.

The Teacher will now give his pupils short musical phrases, sung to figures, and ask them to tell him to which figure or figures **d** fell?—to which **m**?—to which **s**?—to which **d'**?—to which **s,**? He will also give them a key tone and chord, singing immediately to the sharply opening syllable *skaa*, either **d**, **m**, **s**, **d'**, or **s,**, and requiring the pupils to tell him *what* tone he has sung. The answers to these exercises should not come from a few only of the class, but the Teacher will contrive (by subdividing the class or otherwise), that *all shall feel the responsibility* of thinking and preparing an answer, and all will be interested. See "Hints for Ear Exercises." It is a great advantage when the answers to these ear exercises can be written by the pupil, and afterwards examined and registered by the teacher or his assistants.

Pointing from Memory.

At the close of each lesson the pupils should take a pride in shewing their teacher how many of the previous exercises they can point and Sol-fa from memory. These Exercises should be registered in favour of each pupil. Musical memory should be cultivated from the first, because it will greatly facilitate the progress of the pupil in future steps, and will be of constant service to him in after life.

Writing Exercises.

Notation is best taught by writing, and the thing *noted* is more quickly and easily practised when the notation is clear and familiar to the mind. Hence the value of writing exercises. For the first step the teacher should bid his pupils draw on slate or paper four (or eight or sixteen) two pulse measures, in the primary (or secondary) form. The teacher may do the same on a black board to *shew* his pupils what is meant. When the measures are properly drawn out, the teacher will *dictate* the notes to be written in each pulse, or he will write them on the blackboard for his pupils to copy. These notes he may invent for himself, or copy from other courses, but they must always belong to the same "step."

Dictation.

Dictation has always been difficult as soon as the *time* became at all complicated, but the time names give us a means of dictating, by very brief orders, *one pulse at a time*, "Rhythm," "Accent," and "Tune," at once. Thus, if we were dictating Ex. 52, we should first say to our pupils "secondary two-pulse measure." "Prepare for 8 measures." "TAA lower **s,**," "TAA **d**," "TAATAI **m d**," &c., or in Ex. 53 "TAATAI **d m**," "TAA **m**," &c.

The Tonic Sol-fa music paper will be found very useful for dictation. By this means a whole class may be permanently supplied with copies of a tune, while in the process of writing they make a thorough acquaintance with the tune, and are thus prepared to sing it. The Sol-fa music paper is so ruled that the copyist can keep his pulses of equal lengths throughout the tune. He can allow one compartment to a pulse, or two. In either case he will not find it necessary to mark *with the pen* or pencil more than the strong accents.

Writing from Memory.

Pupils should also be well practised in writing tunes from memory. Even where it is difficult for a whole class to point on their modulators from memory at the same moment, so as to be seen by the teacher, it is not difficult to engage a whole class at the same moment, in writing with closed books from memory, the tunes they have learnt. If every pupil has his number, and writes that number on the right hand upper corner of the exercise, instead of his name, assistants can be employed to correct the exercises, and to register a mark for every *pulse* properly written.

Supplementary Exercises.

The Teacher naturally desires to see that all the members of his class (except the careless and inattentive who have no claim upon him) have mastered the topics of each step before that step is left. Some classes require longer practice on one topic, and some on others. For this purpose as well as with the view of gathering all eyes to one point in his elementary explanations, he is recommended to make good use of the black board, and the "Standard Charts," pp. 1 to 5 (Tonic Sol-fa Agency). The "Wall Sheets," No. 1 (for time exercises), and Nos. 7 and 8 (for tune) may also be used as supplementary to the exercises of this step.

QUESTIONS FOR WRITTEN OR ORAL EXAMINATION.

DOCTRINE.

1 To what three practices must the pupil give daily attention in order to produce a *pure* and *pleasant* tone?

2 What two habits improve the *purity* of tone?

3 What two habits improve the *quality* of tone?

4 Which are the forward vowels in the English language?

5 What three things are promoted by a proper management of the breath?

6 What mismanagement of the breathing causes flatness of pitch?

7 What effect on a tone arises from the use of too much breath?

8 Where should a beginner regularly take breath?

9 Where should we not take breath?

10 By the action of which set of muscles should the breath be expended?

11 What are the two reasons for singing the early voice exercises softly?

12 Describe the best position for the body in singing—for the head—for the shoulders—for the chest—for the mouth—the lips—the lower jaw—the palate—the tongue.

13 Describe the bad effects of any wrong positions of mouth or body.

14 What do we mean by the "pitch" of sounds?

15 What is your idea of a key tone?

16 Why is it important to listen well to the pattern?

17 What is the name for the key tone of a tune, and what is its manual sign?

18 What are the names and signs (1) for the tone which is commonly known as the fifth above the key tone, and (2) for that which is known as the third above it?

19 From what two causes arise the different effects of the related tones *Doh*, *Me*, and *Soh* on the mind?

20 What is the name given to a set of three tones thus related?

21 What is an octave or replicate, and its sign?

22 We can tell pupils what tones of the scale to sing, either by pointing on the modulator, or by giving them manual signs. What other way have we of doing so?

23 What do "Key G," "Key C," "Key A" mean at the beginning of a tune?

24 What are the three common uses of the word "Time," and what distinct name do we give to each of the three things?

25 How is "Accent" produced?

26 What is the sign for a strong accent, and what for a weak?

27 What is the name we give to the time which extends between one accent (of either sort) and the next?

28 What is the time name for a one-pulse tone?

29 In what cases may pulses be different in length one from the other?

30 In what circumstances are pulses the same in length one with the other?

31 What is the order of accents in the primary form of two-pulse measure? What in its secondary form?

32 What is the order of accents in the primary form of three-pulse measure? What in its secondary form?

33 Give the time names which represent a primary two-pulse measure, and a secondary three-pulse measure?

34 How do you mark a two-pulse tone, and how do you name it?

35 How do you mark and name a three-pulse tone?

36 Why is it important, in elementary teaching, to use distinct names for continuations?

37 What educational principle distinguishes the early steps of any art?

38 How long should the pupils repeat the first time exercises?

39 What is the difficult thing which the teacher has to *maintain* in the time exercises?

40 Why are the pupils at first not to *beat* time?

41 How is it that the Sol-fa syllables come to be mnemonics (or memory-helps) of tune, and the time syllables mnemonics of time?

42 What is the use of Laa-ing?

43 What is the meaning of a bracket?

44 What is the meaning of a double bar?

45 What are the best breathing-places when music only is considered?

46 What is the sign for a pulse equally divided into two-parts? What is its time name?

47 What do you mean by taatai-ing?

48 What is meant by taatai-ing in tune?

49 How does the practice of taatai-ing help the mind to individualize—to form a distinct conception of—a rhythm?

50 In the practice of modulator voluntaries, what two habits must the pupil form?

51 What difficulties must not be included in voluntaries?

52 Describe the two forms in which ear exercises can be presented?

53 Why should musical memory be cultivated?

54 What is the best way of teaching notation?

55 What advantage does the singer get from the practice of writing music?

56 How would you dictate the air of the first four measures of Ex. 53?

PRACTICE.

57 Hold a *steady* tone, without taking breath, for five seconds.

58 Sing any two of the exercises 38 to 44, and 48 to 53, chosen by the teacher, to the open syllable *Laa*, correctly and *without breathiness of tone.*

59 Sing to the open syllable *Laa*, the *Soh* to any *Doh* the teacher gives you.

60 Sing in the same manner the lower *Soh*$_1$.

61 Sing in the same manner the upper *Doh*'.

62 Sing in the same manner the *Me*.

63 Sing in the same manner the lower *Me*$_1$.

64 Taatai the upper "part" in one of the Exs. 51, 52, or 53, chosen by the teacher.

65 Taatai in tune one of the Exs. 51, 52, or 53, but not the same as in the last requirement, chosen by the teacher.

66 Point on the modulator from memory any one of the Exs. 46 to 51, chosen by the teacher.

67 Write down from memory another of these exercises.

68 From any phrase (belonging to this stage) sung to figures, tell your teacher, or write down, which figure was sung to *Me*.

69 Ditto *Soh*.

70 Ditto *Doh*.

71 Ditto *Doh*'.

72 Ditto *Soh*$_1$.

73 Having heard the chord, tell, or write down which tone of the scale was sung to *Skaa*. Do this with two different tones belonging to this step.

74 Follow to the teacher's pointing on the modulator in a new voluntary, containing *Doh*, *Me*, *Soh*, *Doh*', and *Soh*$_1$. TAA, TAA-AA, and TAATAI.

75 Write from dictation, and afterwards sing a similar exercise.

St. Co. (New).

SECOND STEP.

To train the voice in purity, beauty, and good accord. To distinguish the mental effects of **d, m, s, t** *and* **r.** *To produce them. To distinguish and produce the medium accent and the four-pulse and six-pulse measures,—also the whole-pulse silence, the half-pulse sounds in three pulse measure, and the fourths of a pulse in their simplest form. To observe the reasons for breathing places. To commence the study of chords, intervals, discords, and passing tones.*

VOICE TRAINING.

The teacher calls his pupils into position just as he did at the beginning of every lesson in the first step. Every lesson of the present step should open with the following three exercises. It is exceedingly important that the pupils should *cultivate for themselves* a good position in singing. It will then become an easy habit.

Ex. 54. CHEST EXERCISE, to strengthen the muscles under the lungs and on its sides, and give them control over the slow emission of breath. The same as Ex. 1, except that the breath should be breathed out more slowly, and that a sound may accompany it. Some will now be able to continue the tone while the teacher slowly counts ten, say for ten seconds. The weak-chested must not be discouraged. This exercise daily practised will be life and health to them.

Ex. 55. VOCAL KLANG EXERCISE.—The same as Ex. 2, except that instead of using only one tone the pupils will sing the Tonic chord. They will sing, in obedience to the teacher's manual signs **d m s d' d' s m d.** The manual signs enable the teacher to watch the posture of his pupils, and the pupils to watch the commands and intimations of the teacher. This exercise will be sung slowly (say at M. 60) and also *softly*, for the sake of studying beauty in the quality of tone. When in any exercise, the teacher feels that he has secured that good quality, he occasionally ventures on a *middle* force of voice, but always strives to maintain the same good quality. In mixed classes of men and women this exercise will, of course, be sung in octaves, as the voices of men and women are naturally an octave apart. The importance of this simple exercise, and the difficulty of obtaining a perfect and pure unison of voices in it are strongly enforced by Fetis (see "Choir and Chorus Singing," page 9).

The exercise is 1st, sol-faad *once*, 2nd, sung *once* to the forward syllable *lai*, 3rd, sung *three* times to the forward and pleasant Italian syllable *laa*, and 4th, sung *once* to the best English syllable for the sharp accented delivery of tones—*koo*, striking four sharp *koos* to each tone. The first step of this process puts the ear in tune: the second places the tongue properly, and so prepares the mouth for the real Italian *aa*: the third gives the best form of mouth for the production of a beautiful sound: and the fourth strengthens the voice by vigorous (not *forced*) action, and favours that downward motion of the larynx on the delivery of short and accented (though not loud) tones which has to be formed into a habit for after use. The exercise, having been thus *six* times sung in Key C, the same process will be repeated in Key D.

Tuning Exercises can now be added for the purpose of teaching voices singing different parts *to study one another*, and to chord well together. To some extent this is done in every exercise, but it requires also separate study. The teacher divides his women's and children's voices into three "parts," (1st, 2nd, and 3rd) and causes them first to sol-faa and then to *lai* and *laa*, the following exercise. When this is done to the teacher's satisfaction he utters the word "change" and those who have sung the first part take the second, the second the third, and the third the first. At the word "change" again the same process is repeated. The teacher then divides his men's voices in a similar manner and carries them through the same six-fold exercise. The teacher, in this exercise, watches his pupils—*first*, to ensure the holding of their books easily, not cramping the chest, as high as possible (so as just to see their conductor over the top) and without bending the head,—*second*, to secure a uniformly clear, *soft* tone, making a signal to anyone whose voice is so prominent as to stand out from the rest, —and *third*, to maintain the perfect *tuning into each other* of all the parts of the chord. The distinct entry of each "part" is meant to assist the perception of "just" or exactly true intonation. See Fetis, page 9. It is not every class that has the thoughtfulness and courage to take this exercise at *the beginning* of the second step, but it should be attempted. The division of voices is a severe test of independence, and therefore useful. Some singers will never be independent till you compel them to try. For some time the accord of the voices will be very rough and imperfect, but soft singing and listening will amend the fault.

Ex. 56. KEYS F and G. [Silent pulse, see p. 18.]

1st.	:	:	s :—	m :—	s :—	— :—	m :s	s :— ‖
2nd	:	m :—	m :m	d :—	:	m :—	d :s	m :— ‖
3rd.	d :—	— :—	d :d	d :—	:	:	d :s_1	d :— ‖

TUNE.

Mental Effects.—It is of small importance *what* names the pupil gives to the mental effect of the different tones, but it is all-important that he himself (not his teacher, nor his class-mates) should give those names, or if he cannot find a name, that he should at least form for himself a *distinct* idea of each mental effect. Let him listen carefully, therefore, while his teacher sings to the class such "exercises for ascertaining the mental effect" as those below. (*a*) The teacher first sings the exercise to consecutive figures, telling his pupils that he is about to introduce a new tone (that is, one *not* d m or s) and asking them to tell him on which figure it falls. (*b*) When they have distinguished the new tone, he sings the exercise again—laa-ing it—and asks them to tell him how that tone "makes them feel." Those who can *describe* the feeling hold up their hands, and the teacher asks one for the description. But others, who are not satisfied with words, may also perceive and feel. The teacher can tell by their eyes whether they have done so. He multiplies examples (like those in "Studies," &c., which he may point on the modulator) until *all* the class have their attention fully awakened to the effect of the new tone. (*c*) This done he tells his pupils the Sol-fa name and the manual sign for the new tone, and guides them by the signs to Sol-fa the exercise, and themselves produce the proper effect. The signs are better, in this case, than the modulator or the notation, because with them the teacher can best *command the attention* of every eye, and ear, and voice, and at the first introduction of a tone, attention should be acute.

The manual sign for *ray* is the upturned hand, open, and shewing the palm; that for *te* is the upturned hand, pointing with the forefinger.

Ex. 57. KEY B♭. Effect of *Ray*, high in pitch.

| d :s_1 | m :d | r :— | d :— ‖

Ex. 58. KEY B♭. Ditto.

:s_1 | d :— :m | r :— :s_1 | d :— ‖

Ex. 59. KEY F. Effect of *Ray*, low in pitch.

:s_1 | d :m :d | r :— :m | d :— ‖

Ex. 60. KEY D. Ditto.

| d :s | m :d | r :— | m :— ‖

Ex. 61. KEY D. Effect of *Te*, high in pitch.

| d :m | s :t | t :— | d^1 :— ‖

Ex. 62. KEY D. Ditto.

| d :m | s :t | t :s | d^1 :— ‖

Ex. 63. KEY F. Effect of *Te*, low in pitch.

| d :s | m :t_1 | t_1 :— | d :— ‖

Ex. 64. KEY F. Ditto.

:s_1 | d :m | s :— | t_1 :— | d ‖

Collective Reading.—The following exercises 65 to 70 (including leaps of r and t without any new difficulties of time) will now be taught, in the same manner and with the same processes as Ex. 48 to 53. with this addition, that after the tune has been *Laad* correctly and easily, *the words* will be studied. The Teacher reads the portion of words *from one breathing place to another*, giving clear vowels and sharp consonants, the pupils imitate collectively. Vowels are ways of emitting the breath; consonants ways of interrupting it. Both require *definite* positions and movements of the lip and tongue. Many uneducated persons are lazy in their use of both organs. The object of the teacher will be to shew *by pattern* that marked and clear utterance which is the beauty of speech. Musical tones cannot be prolonged on consonants; the vowels are therefore the more important to the singer. The elocutionary studies of "accent," and "inflection," need not occupy the time of the class, because there is no inflection in a musical tone, and the music necessarily decides the accent. A simple monotonous delivery of vowels and consonants will therefore be sufficient for the teacher's present purpose. The pupils will enjoy this exercise in proportion as their teacher criticises their pronunciation with care. A closer study of the subject will follow in the fourth step.

Breathing Places have, thus far been chosen to suit the natural division of a line of music into "phrases." But the sense of the words is more important than the marked distinction of phrases. It therefore over-rules all. Let the pupil notice that in Ex. 65, we take breath before each cry of "fire." This is a case of "breathing for emphasis," and illustrates an important rule for taking breath. In Ex. 67 let him notice that the *musical* phrasing would place the breathing place between "I" and "love," but the poetic phrasing does not allow us to disconnect any parts of a word or any two closely related words. "Morning bells I" would not sound well, therefore the division "Morning bells" † "I love to hear." This is a case of "breathing for sense." In Ex. 69, the musical phrases of the first line naturally divide between m and r, each being two measures in length. This breathing place is quite suitable for the first and third verses, but it would cut a word in two if it were used for the second or the fourth. In the third line the musical division suits the first and second verses, but if adopted for the third and fourth verses would make the nonsense "Shall foster and" † "mature the grain," and "The angel reap-" † "ers shall descend." The practice of dividing the "announcements" for Collective Reading at the breathing places, is of great use in calling attention to this important subject. In every exercise of this step there should be with the collective reading a discussion on the correctness or doubtfulness of the breathing places here marked,—but the teacher will decide for the whole class, so that the breathing may be with one consent. A delightful effect of unity and clear expression is produced by this unanimity of breathing.

Rounds.—Ex. 65, is a Round for four "parts." The first "part" commences the Round alone, and goes on steadily repeating it until stopped. When the *first* "part" is going to strike the note under the asterisk (*) the *second* "part" strikes the first note of the Round, and so on. The *third* "part" follows the second, as the second imitated the first. A clap or some other signal of the teacher's hand tells you when to stop a Round. It should first be learnt from the modulator by the whole class as one part, and should not be sung as a "round" till the third step, unless the class has been very well practised in *maintaining* the rate of movement. When the whole class can sol-fa it "by heart," watching the teacher's beat and keeping most exact time with the stroke of his hand,—let the class be divided into four parts, and each part tested in the power to sing separately. Even when this is fairly done, the parts will still find it difficult to "hold their own," as soon as the other parts enter. The difficulty of maintaining the rate of movement is very much increased when the Round is in three-pulse measure or contains divided pulses. It is this difficulty which makes the Round so valuable an exercise in time keeping.

Da Capo pronounced Daa Caapoa [oa as in *coal*] and abbreviated D.C. means "return to the beginning."

m' r' d' t . s . m r d t_1 . s_1

Ex. 65. KEY G. A round for four parts.

s_1 : s_1	d : d †	s_1 : s_1	d : d †	* > r : —	m : — †	> r : —	m : — †
Scot-land's	burn - ing,	Scot-land's	burn - ing,	Look	out,	Look	out,

> s : — †	> s : — †	> s : — †	> s : — †	t_1 : r	d : d †	t_1 : r	d : d D.C. ‖
Fire!	Fire!	Fire!	Fire!	Pour on	wa - ter,	pour on	wa - ter.

Ex. 66. KEY D. A round for four parts.

d : r	m : d †	* m : s	s : — †	d'.d' : t .t	d'.s : m.d †	s : s	d : — D.C. ‖
Sing it	o - ver	with your	might,	Never leave it,	Never leave it	till 'tis	right.

St. Co. (New.)

Ex. 67. KEY C. A round for four parts. D.C.

d :s	s :s	m :s	d' :—	d' :r'	m'.d': d'	s :t	d' :—	
Morn-ing	bells I	love to	hear,	Ring-ing	merri-ly,	loud and	clear.

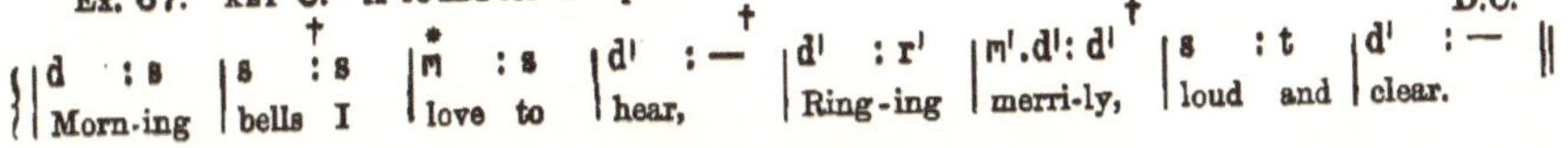

"GONE IS THE HOUR OF SONG."

Ex. 68. KEY E. Round for four parts. *J. C.*

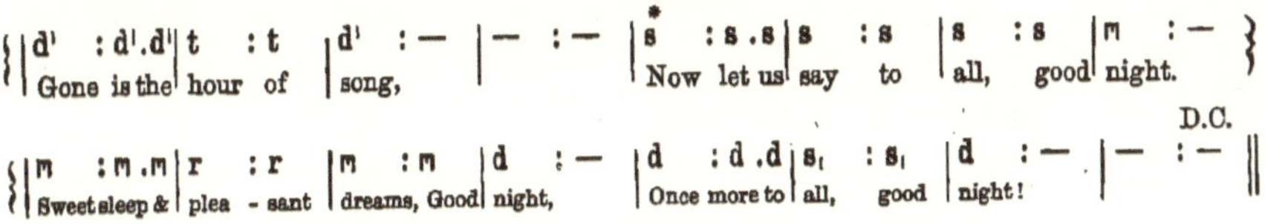

d' :d'.d'	t :t	d' :—	— :—	s :s .s	s :s	s :s	m :—
Gone is the	hour of	song,		Now let us	say to	all, good	night.

D.C.

m :m .m	r :r	m :m	d :—	d :d .d	s_1 :s_1	d :—	— :—	
Sweet sleep &	plea - sant	dreams, Good	night,	Once more to	all, good	night!	

"SOW IN THE MORN THY SEED."

A. L. C.

Ex. 69. KEY G. Words by *James Montgomery.*

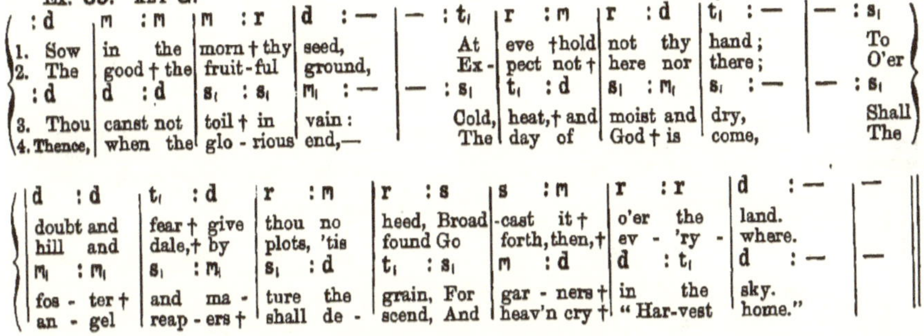

:d	m :m	m :r	d :—	— :t_1	r :m	r :d	t_1 :—	— :s_1
1. Sow	in the	morn † thy	seed,	At	eve †hold	not thy	hand;	To
2. The	good † the	fruit-ful	ground,	Ex-	pect not †	here nor	there;	O'er
:d	d :d	s_1 :s_1	m_1 :—	— :s_1	t_1 :d	s_1 :m_1	s_1 :—	— :s_1
3. Thou	canst not	toil † in	vain:	Cold,	heat,† and	moist and	dry,	Shall
4. Thence,	when the	glo - rious	end,—	The	day of	God † is	come,	The

d :d	t_1 :d	r :m	r :s	s :m	r :r	d :—	—	
doubt and	fear † give	thou no	heed, Broad	-cast it †	o'er the	land.	
hill and	dale,† by	plots, 'tis	found Go	forth, then,†	ev - 'ry -	where.	
m_1 :m_1	s_1 :m_1	s_1 :d	t_1 :s_1	m :d	d :t_1	d :—	—
fos - ter †	and ma -	ture the	grain, For	gar - ners †	in the	sky.	
an - gel	reap - ers †	shall de -	scend, And	heav'n cry †	"Har-vest	home."	

"FRET NOT THYSELF."

Ex. 70. KEY B. *R. P.*

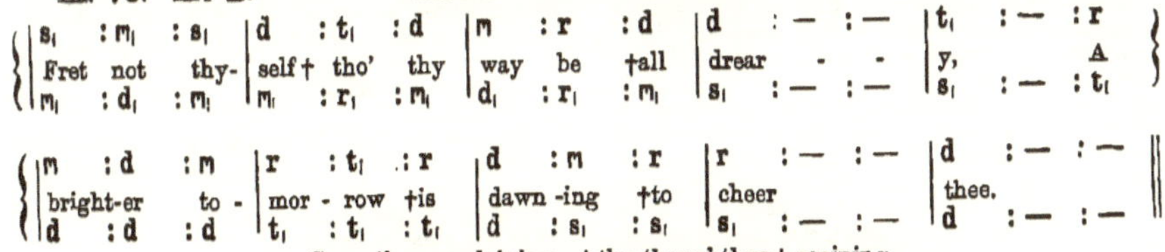

s_1 :m_1 :s_1	d :t_1 :d	m :r :d	d :— :—	t_1 :— :r
Fret not thy-	self † tho' thy	way be †all	drear - -	y, A
m_1 :d_1 :m_1	m_1 :r_1 :m_1	d_1 :r_1 :m_1	s_1 :— :—	s_1 :— :t_1

m :d :m	r :t_1 :r	d :m :r	r :— :—	d :— :—	
bright-er to -	mor - row †is	dawn -ing †to	cheer	thee.
d :d :d	t_1 :t_1 :t_1	d :s_1 :s_1	s_1 :— :—	d :— :—

Cease thy complaining—† thy thoughtless † repining,
The clouds may be black,† but the sun is still † shining.
Though thou art hemm'd in † by mountains † of sorrow,
Stand still—† a broad path † may be open'd † to-morrow.

TIME.

The Medium Accent.—Pupils will easily be brought by examples and illustrations to notice that in addition to the strong and weak accent, there is also a medium accent to many tunes. The introduction of the medium accent makes two two-pulse measures into a four-pulse measure, and two three-pulse measures into a six-pulse measure. This mark | is used for the medium accent.

It will be noticed that several of the exercises already sung, require (when not sung slowly) this medium accent, in place of every alternate strong accent. Let the pupils try Ex. 65 and 69, singing them quickly and lightly. They will soon perceive the natural necessity for a medium accent. The teacher, however, must not expect too great a nicety of distinction at first. The finer points, both of time and tune, require much practice.

Four-pulse Measure.—When the accents of a tune are arranged in the order **strong**, *weak*, MEDIUM, *weak* (as in the words "**mo**men**TA**ry," "**plan**e**TA**ry"), and so on, it is said to be in the four-pulse measure. The pupils will taatai on one tone, as below, while the teacher beats, first slowly, then quickly.

NOTE.—When the pupil has learnt to hold his tones to their full length, and where nearly all the pulses are undivided, it will be sufficient to call a pulse TAA, omitting the AI.

A primary four-pulse measure.

1	:1	¦1	:1	‖
TAA	TAA	TAA	TAA	

A secondary form.

:1	|1	:1	¦1	‖
TAA	TAA	TAA	TAA	

Another form.

:1	¦1	:1	|1	‖
TAA	TAA	TAA	TAA	

Another form.

¦1	:1	|1	:1	‖
TAA	TAA	TAA	TAA	

Six-pulse Measure.—When the accents of a tune are arranged in the order **strong**, *weak*, *weak*, MEDIUM, *weak*, *weak* (as in the words "**spi**ri*tu*AL*i*ty," "**im**mu*ta*BIL*i*ty"), and so on, it is said to be in six-pulse measure. The pupils will taatai on one tone, as below, while the teacher beats slowly.

A primary six-pulse measure.

1	:1	:1	¦1	:1	:1	‖
TAA	TAA	TAA	TAA	TAA	TAA	

A secondary form.

:1	|1	:1	:1	¦1	:1	‖
TAA	TAA	TAA	TAA	TAA	TAA	

Another form.

:1	¦1	:1	:1	|1	:1	‖
TAA	TAA	TAA	TAA	TAA	TAA	

Another form.

¦1	:1	:1	|1	:1	:1	‖
TAA	TAA	TAA	TAA	TAA	TAA	

Silent Pulse.—It is more difficult for pupils to appreciate time in silences than in sounds. Therefore the silent pulse was not introduced in the first step. The name for a silent pulse is *SAA*. In taatai-ing, after the first time of going through an exercise, or as soon as the rhythm is perfectly learnt, the silence-syllables should be less and less heard. M. Paris uses only the one word "Hush" for all the silences. In dictation, as well as for the purpose of first marking and measuring them distinctly to the mind, we find the advantage of a separate name for each silence corresponding with the names we use for sound. Silences are denoted in the Tonic Sol-fa notation, by the simple absence of any name for sound. Even if an accent mark is placed at the end of a line, a silent pulse is supposed to follow it.

Pulse and a half Tones are very common and easily learnt. They are named and written as below.

Quarter Pulse Tones are more easily learnt when the pulse is divided into four distinct quarters than when it is divided into a half and two quarters—two quarters and a half—or a three-quarter tone and a quarter tone. Therefore the "four quarters" are introduced in this early step. They are thus named, *tafatefe* [*a* is the *short* vowel for *aa*, and *e* is the short vowel for *ai*.] Thus the vowels still divide the pulse as before. If the time-names are to become aids to the memory, we must again repeat that even in *speaking* both teachers and pupils should *form the careful habit* of uttering them in their proper time. Thus, TAA should be as long as TAATAI, and "tafatefe" should occupy no more time than either; neither TAA nor TAI should have longer utterance one than the other; and *tafatefe* should form four exactly equal lengths. In the Tonic Sol-fa notation a comma divides a half pulse into quarters.

Let the Exercises 71 to 75 be (*a*) taught by pattern and repeated, see page 7. The exercise may be divided into two patterns if necessary. It should be sung at at least two distinct rates. (*b*) Alternated, see p. 7. (*c*) Laad, see p. 8. (*d*) Taataid in tune, see p. 10.

Ex. 71.

||1 TAA : SAA |1 TAA : SAA |1 TAA :1 .1 TAATAI |1 TAA :1 TAA ||

KEY G. |d : |d : |d :d .r |m :d ||
KEY F. |s : |s : |s :m .r |d :m ||
KEY A. |d : |r : |m :t, .r |d :s, ||

KEY A. |s, : |t, : |d :s, .t, |d :r ||
KEY F. |s : |m : |r :t, .d |r :m ||
KEY F. |m : |s : |m :r .t, |r :d ||

Ex. 72.

||1 TAA :1 TAA | SAA :1 .1 TAATAI |1 TAA :– .1 -AATAI |1 .1 TAATAI :1 TAA ||

KEY G. |d :s, | :d .r |m :– .d |t, .d :r ||
KEY F. |m :d | :r .d |s :– .m |r .d :t, ||
KEY G. |r :s | :r .t, |s, :– .t, |d .r :m ||

KEY B. |d :t, | :r .d |s, :– .d |m .r :d ||
KEY F. |m :r | :d .m |s :– .t, |r .d :d ||
KEY F. |m :d | :s .m |m :– .r |m .s :s ||

Ex. 73.

||1 TAA :– .1 -AATAI :1 .1 TAATAI |1 .1 TAATAI :1 TAA : SAA |1 .1 TAATAI :1 TAA :1 TAA ||

KEY G.
|d :– .t, :d .r |m .r :d : |m .r :d :s, ||

KEY F.
|d :– .r :m .s |t, .r :d : |t, .r :d :s, ||

KEY A.
|m :– .r :d .t, |r .d :d : |r .d :t, :d ||
St. Co. (New.)

KEY A.
|d :– .s :m .d |s, .t, :r : |s, .t, :r :t, ||

KEY A.
|m :– .d :t, .d |m .r :m : |d .t, :d :s, ||

KEY G.
|s, :– .t, :r .t, |d .m :m : |m .s :s :m ||

Ex. 74.

| 1 :1 | 1 .1 :1 | 1 .1 :1 .1 | 1 .1 :1 |
TAA TAA | TAATAI TAA | TAATAI TAATAI | TAATAI TAA

| 1,1.1,1 :1 .1 | 1,1.1,1 :1 .1 | 1,1.1,1 :1 .1 | 1 .1 :1 ||
tafatefe TAATAI | tafatefe TAATAI | tafatefe TAATAI | TAATAI TAA

KEY G.

| s_1 :s_1 | s_1 .m :d | s_1 .m :d .s_1 | s_1 .m :d |

| s_1,s_1.s_1,s_1 :s_1 .t_1 | t_1,t_1.t_1,t_1 :t_1 .r | d,d.d,d :d .m | r .t_1 :s_1 ||

KEY G.

| s :s | s .m :d | s .m :d .m | s .m :d |

| s,s.s,s :s .m | m,m.m,m :m .d | r,r.r,r :r .t_1 | d .m :s ||

Ex. 75.

| 1 :1 .1 | 1 :1 | 1 .1 :1 .1 | 1 :1 |
TAA TAATAI | TAA TAA | TAATAI TAATAI | TAA TAA

| 1 :1,1.1,1 | 1 .1 :1 | 1,1.1,1 :1,1.1,1 | 1 .1 :1 ||
TAA tafatefe | TAATAI TAA | tafatefe tafatefe | TAATAI TAA

KEY G.
| d :m .d | m :d | r .t_1 :r .t_1 | r :s_1 | d :m,r.d,r | m .d :d | r,d.t_2,d :r,d.t_2,d | r .t_1 :s_1 ||

KEY E.
| d :t_1.r | d :m | t_1 .r :d .m | r :s | d :t_2,d.r,t_1 | d .m :m | t_2,d.r,t_1 :d,r.m,d | r .s :s ||

TUNE.

The Two Principal Chords.—As the tones **d m** and **s**, sung together form a chord, so do the tones **s t** and **r'**. The first we call the chord of *Doh*, the second the chord of *Soh*. We always write chord-names in capital letters, D, S. These two chords considered separately and in themselves, are exactly alike. Their tones are precisely at the same distances of pitch one from the other, and if the chord S, or the successive tones **s t r'** were heard without the sound of any previous chord of D, or succession of **d m s**, they would produce precisely the same effect upon the mind. But as soon as we place two such chords at a certain interval one from the other we establish a new set of relations, and so enrich the mental effect. It is no longer *one* chord and its interval relations which the ear perceives, but *two* chords and their relations to each other,—so strong and rapid is the power of mental association. That chord, in a tune, which is the *first* to occupy the ear, rules the chords which follow. Thus in Exercises 57 to 64 we were careful to "establish the key" by making **d m s** heard before we could make the mental effects of **t** and **r** felt. This relation between D and S, that is between any chord and that other which starts from its own highest tone, is a peculiar and very important one. It is called the relation between Tonic (D) and Dominant (S). It is the chief element in key-relationship. These two chords alone are sufficient to make music. Many a single page of brilliant classic music consists of the chords D and S.

Thirds, Sixths, and Tenths.—Most classes and all self-teaching pupils will be glad to study the harmony (or the sounding together of tones) as they sing, and they will sing the better for doing so. Intervals or distances between tones, are generally counted step-wise on the scale—always including the two extremes. Thus the distances between **d** and **r** or **m** and **f** are called a second, those between **d** and **m** or **r** and **f** are called a third, and so on. By counting, in this way, on the modulator, it will be seen that from **d** to the **m** next above is a *third*,—from **d** to the **m** next below (m_1) is an *inverted* third, or a *sixth*,—and from **d** to the higher octave of its **m** above (m^1) is a *tenth*. So also from l_1 to **d** is a third (a *minor* or lesser third) from **l** to **d** is a sixth, and from l_1 to d^1 is a tenth. What are the intervals between **m** and **s**? —**m** and s_1?—**m** and s^1? These intervals (which are the third in various positions) form the *sweetness* of all harmony, and are therefore, abundantly used. In Exercise 69 find twelve thirds and six sixths. In Exercise 80 find a sixth followed by a tenth.

Octaves and Unisons.—Exercise 69 has its first tone and its last, in both parts, *the same*, that is *in identical unison*. At the beginning of the last line of words it has an octave between the parts. These unisons and octaves do not give the true feeling of harmony, —that is, separateness with agreement, and they are seldom used on a strong pulse where they would be much noticed, but they are useful in the flow of the harmony—allowing the parts to pass through them to something sweeter or stronger, or bringing them to a close on the key tone. Two such intervals, one following the other, would make the harmony disappear. Therefore, such a succession is, as the pupil will notice, carefully avoided. In speaking of unison above, we have referred to *absolute* unison, but the word unison is also commonly used to indicate the singing of the same tones, by male and female voices, an octave apart, as in our "Vocal Klang Exercises."

Fifths and Fourths.—In Exercise 69 there are two fifths (s_1 to **r** in both cases) and in Exercise 70 there is a fourth s_1 to **d**. The two tones of a fifth agree with one another more *perfectly* than those of any other interval except the octave, but they have not the sweetness of the thirds. Their agreement is somewhat hard and cold, though strong and sure. They are, therefore, not very much used in two-part harmony, and *two* of them in succession are the dread of all composers. Fourths are the *inversions* of fifths (as sixths are of thirds) but are very much less acceptable to the ear. They have neither the *perfect* agreement of the fifths, nor the *sweet* agreement of the thirds, and are much avoided in two-part harmony; even bald unisons and octaves being prefered to them. Where used they are found on a weak (and therefore, less observed) pulse or on a strong pulse in places where they suggest to the mind certain familiar habits of chords to be hereafter explained.

Discords.—Octaves, fifths, fourths, and thirds are *concords*. Seconds, as **f** against **s**, or **d** against **r**, whether close together or separated by octaves (that is, whether seconds, or sevenths, or ninths) are *discords*. They sound harshly together. But a Discord may be so sweetly introduced, and so pleasantly brought to a close, and the "part" which contains it may move so smoothly that it is made agreeable. This is because the ear naturally notices *the motion of the two melodies* as well as the actual consonance or dissonance of the moment. Thus, in Exercise 69, we have, on the fifth pulse counting from the last, or the fifth-last pulse, **d** dissonating against **r**, but it is so "prepared" by its own previous "sweet" consonance with **m**, and so smoothly "resolved" by going down step-wise to t_1, and there satisfying the ear with another sweet consonance, that it cannot be called unpleasant. It is only unpleasant when singers are afraid of it, and so put themselves out of tune. Hence the advantage of *knowing* what you sing. Find a similar discord at the close of Exercise 78. A note undergoes preparation when it is heard in a previous chord as a consonance; it undergoes resolution when (being a discord) it moves down one step.

Passing Tones.—As we have observed that the weak pulse is less noticed by the ear than the strong pulse, so is the second or weak *part* of a pulse less noticed than the first part. Therefore, things may be allowed there which the ear objects to elsewhere. Thus in Exercise 79, second score, third measure, second pulse, we find an apology for the dissonant **r**, because it is on the weak part of a pulse, and because it moves *smoothly* step-wise from one tone of the scale to the next. Find other examples of the same "part-pulse passing tone" in the same Exercise 79

Ex. **76.**—Name, pulse by pulse, the harmonic intervals of Exercises 69, 70, 77, 78, 79, and 80.

Let the Exercises which follow, be taught with the same process of Pattern from the Modulator, first one part and then the other—taatai-ing in tune every difficult rhythm—Sol-faa-ing from the book—laa-ing from the book—collective reading of words—study of breathing places—and singing to words, as before. Before each exercise, when the key-tone is pitched, let the pupils sol-faa by the manual signs the *two* chords, thus—**d m s, s t r' d'**, or in middle keys **d s, m, s, t, r d.**

Ex. 77. KEY **A.** **WHEN LANDS ARE GONE.** *R. P.*

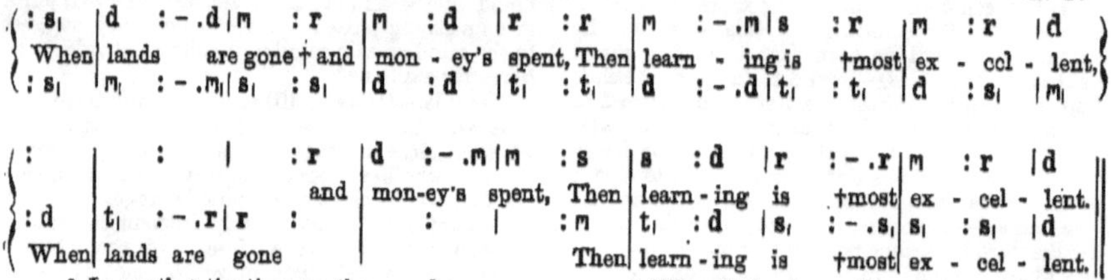

:s,	d :-.d | m :r	m :d | r :r	m :-.m | s :r	m :r | d
When	lands are gone † and	mon - ey's spent, Then	learn - ing is †most	ex - cel - lent,
:s,	m, :-.m, | s, :s,	d :d | t, :t,	d :-.d | t, :t,	d :s, | m,

:	: | :r	d :-.m | m :s	s :d | r :-.r	m :r | d
	and	mon-ey's spent, Then	learn - ing is †most	ex - cel - lent.
:d	t, :-.r | r :	: | :m	t, :d | s, :-.s,	s, :s, | d
When	lands are gone	Then	learn - ing is †most	ex - cel - lent.

2 In youth † the time we thus employ,
Is counted as † the richest joy.

3 When little else † old age can cheer,
These harvests are † most rich and rare.

Ex. 78. KEY **B♭.** **M. 72.** **FARMER JOHN.** *A. L. C.*

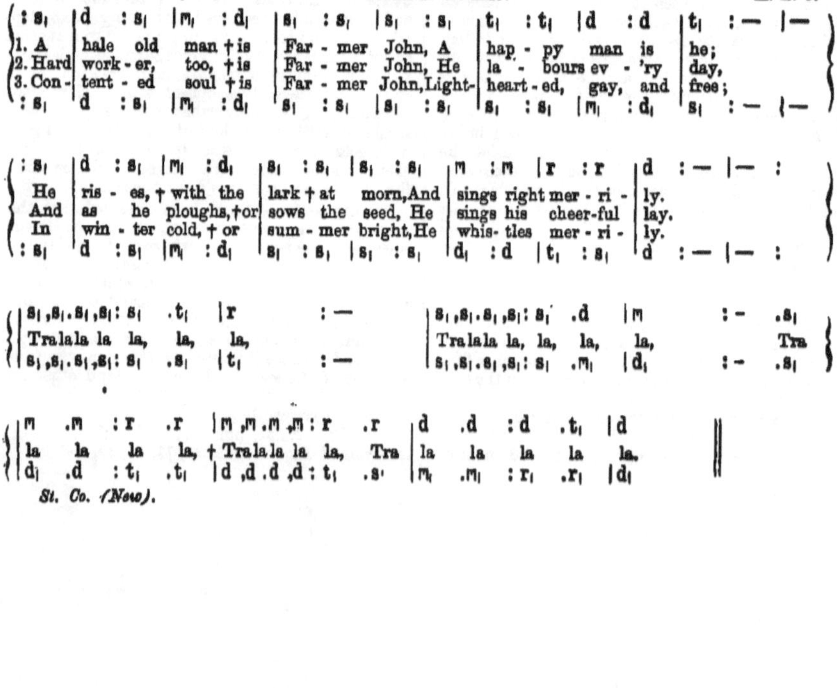

:s,	d :s, | m, :d,	s, :s, | s, :s,	t, :t, | d :d	t, :— | —
1. A	hale old man † is	Far - mer John, A	hap - py man is	he;
2. Hard	work - er, too, † is	Far - mer John, He	la - bours ev - 'ry	day,
3. Con -	tent - ed soul † is	Far - mer John, Light-	heart - ed, gay, and	free;
:s,	d :s, | m, :d,	s, :s, | s, :s,	s, :s, | m, :d,	s, :— | —

:s,	d :s, | m, :d,	s, :s, | s, :s,	m :m | r :r	d :— | — :
He	ris - es, † with the	lark † at morn, And	sings right mer - ri -	ly.
And	as he ploughs, † or	sows the seed, He	sings his cheer-ful	lay.
In	win - ter cold, † or	sum - mer bright, He	whis- tles mer - ri -	ly.
:s,	d :s, | m, :d,	s, :s, | s, :s,	d, :d | t, :s,	d :— | — :

s,.s,.s,.s, : s, .t, | r :—	s,.s,.s,.s, : s, .d | m :- .s,
Tralala la la, la, la,	Tralala la, la, la, la, Tra
s,.s,.s,.s, : s, .s, | t, :—	s,.s,.s,.s, : s, .m, | d, :- .s,

m .m :r .r | m.m.m.m : r .r	d .d :d .t, | d
la la la la, † Tralala la la, Tra	la la la la la.
d, .d :t, .t, | d.d.d.d : t, .s,	m, .m, :r, .r, | d,

St. Co. (New).

THE DAISY.

Ex. 79. KEY F. M. 76. Words by *Fletcher*. *A. L. C.*

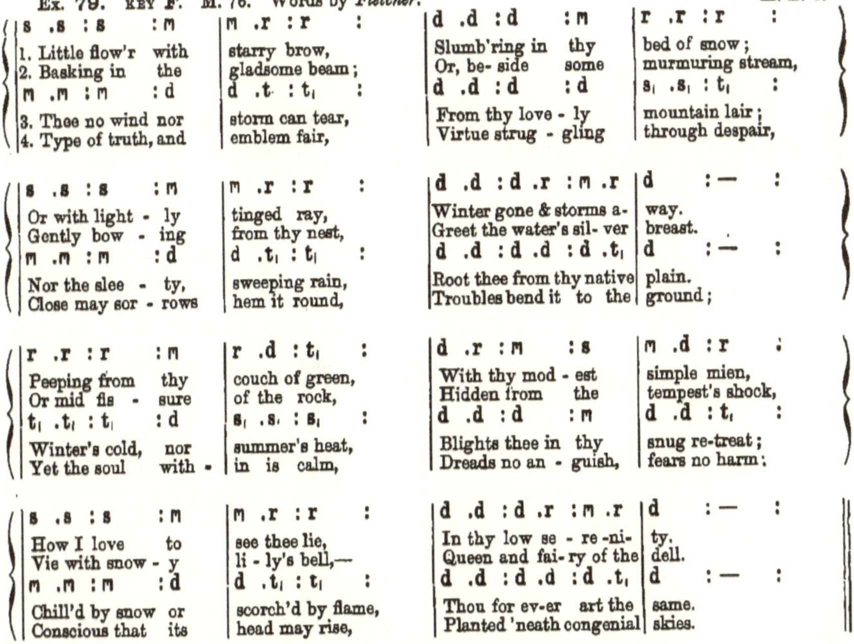

s .s : s : m	m .r : r :	d .d : d : m	r .r : r :
1. Little flow'r with	starry brow,	Slumb'ring in thy	bed of snow;
2. Basking in the	gladsome beam;	Or, be- side some	murmuring stream,
m .m : m : d	d .t, : t, :	d .d : d : d	s, .s, : t, :
3. Thee no wind nor	storm can tear,	From thy love - ly	mountain lair;
4. Type of truth, and	emblem fair,	Virtue strug - gling	through despair,

s .s : s : m	m .r : r :	d .d : d .r : m .r	d : — :
Or with light - ly	tinged ray,	Winter gone & storms a-	way.
Gently bow - ing	from thy nest,	Greet the water's sil- ver	breast.
m .m : m : d	d .t, : t, :	d .d : d .d : d .t,	d : — :
Nor the slee - ty,	sweeping rain,	Root thee from thy native	plain.
Close may sor - rows	hem it round,	Troubles bend it to the	ground;

r .r : r : m	r .d : t, :	d .r : m : s	m .d : r :
Peeping from thy	couch of green,	With thy mod - est	simple mien,
Or mid fis - sure	of the rock,	Hidden from the	tempest's shock,
t, .t, : t, : d	s, .s, : s, :	d .d : d : m	d .d : t, :
Winter's cold, nor	summer's heat,	Blights thee in thy	snug re-treat;
Yet the soul with -	in is calm,	Dreads no an - guish,	fears no harm;

s .s : s : m	m .r : r :	d .d : d .r : m .r	d : — :
How I love to	see thee lie,	In thy low se - re -ni-	ty.
Vie with snow - y	li - ly's bell,—	Queen and fai- ry of the	dell.
m .m : m : d	d .t, : t, :	d .d : d .d : d .t,	d : — :
Chill'd by snow or	scorch'd by flame,	Thou for ev-er art the	same.
Conscious that its	head may rise,	Planted 'neath congenial	skies.

COME, GENTLE MAY.

Ex. 80. KEY D. M. 60, twice. *A. L. C.*

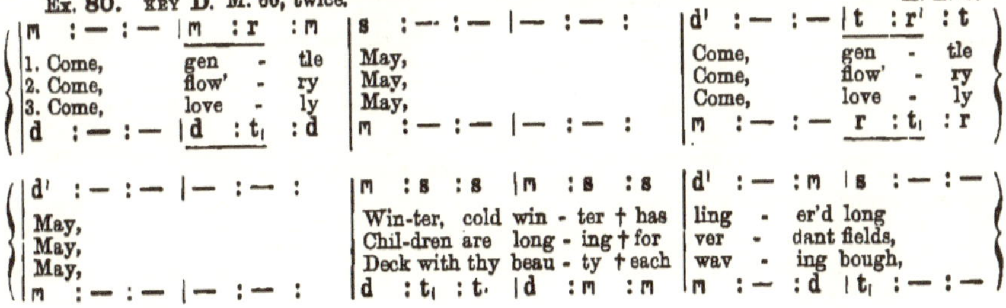

m : — : —	m : r : m	s : — : —	— : — :	d' : — : —	t : r' : t
1. Come,	gen - tle	May,		Come,	gen - tle
2. Come,	flow' - ry	May,		Come,	flow' - ry
3. Come,	love - ly	May,		Come,	love - ly
d : — : —	d : t, : d	m : — : —	— : — :	m : — : —	r : t, : r

d' : — : —	— : — :	m : s : s	m : s : s	d' : — : m	s : — : —
May,		Win-ter, cold	win - ter † has	ling - er'd	long
May,		Chil-dren are	long - ing † for	ver - dant	fields,
May,		Deck with thy	beau - ty † each	wav - ing	bough,
m : — : —	— : — :	d : t, : t,	d : m : m	m : — : d	t, : — : —

t t :t	d' :— :s	s :— :m	r :— :—	m :s :s	m :s :s
Now let thy balm - y†		breez - es play;		Fill all the woods† with the	
Deck'd with thy flow'rs † so		bright and gay,		Longing for plea-sure † thy	
Bring us the haw - thorn's†		whit - en'd spray;		Beau-ti - ful May-time,† why	
r :r :r	m :— :m	m :— :d	t_1 :— :—	d :t_1 :t_1	d :m :m

d' :— :m	s :— :—	m :— :—	m :r :m	s :— :—	— :— :
birds' sweet song:		Come,	gen - tle	May.	
pres - ence yields;		Come,	flow' - ry	May.	
ling - 'rest thou?		Come,	lov - ly	May.	
m :— :d	t_1 :— :—	d :— :—	d :t_1 :d	m :— :—	— :— :

Beating twice to the measure.—Let Ex. 80 be patiently *taataid,* while the teacher beats every pulse, never pausing and never hurrying. Only thus can the exact lengths of sound and silence be appreciated. But when six-pulse measure moves more quickly than this should do, each pulse is regarded by the ear as a third of a pulse, and the whole measure as a two-pulse measure with ample use of "thirds." In this case the conductor beats only twice in a measure.

Modulator Voluntaries are used at every lesson.

Ear Exercises, like those in "Hints for Ear Exercises," and if possible, ear exercises in which the pupil writes the answer, will also be as constant as the lesson hour. If the teacher finds that the pupils do not discover which is **r** easily, he does not either tell them or let them guess, but he reminds them again of the mental effect of **r**, and illustrates over again the high rousing **r** and the low prayerful **r**, and then again tests them. After the Sol-fa prelude, the pupils must be very careful to note to which tone figure one falls. They do not possess a sufficient clue unless they catch the *first note.* The teacher should be very careful to make his own pattern clear. One way in which a teacher keeps all his class at work is to cause all that can answer to hold up their hands, and then to select those whose answers he wishes. Another way is to give the proper answer and ask all who were right to hold up hands.

In *time* ear exercises the teacher 1st *taatais* with accent two plain measures, then continuously *laas* a rhythm of two measures on one tone, which he requires his pupils to write or *taatai.* 2nd, he *sol-faas* a short rhythm, and requires his pupils to *taatai* it *in tune.* Many of the old exercises and some of the "Hints for Ear Exercises" will give him ready materials.

St. Co. (New.)

Dictation.—Notation, and with it, clear perception, will be cultivated by Dictation Exercises. The second part of Ex. 77, second score (or line), fifth measure (always counting the first part of a measure as one) would be dictated thus:—"TAA lower t_1" "-AA-TAI r" "TAA r" "*SAA*" "*SAA*" &c. Ex. 78, third score, first measure, would be dictated thus:—"tafatefe lower s_1 s_1 s_1 s_1" "TAATAI lower s_1 lower t_1" "TAA -AA r."

Pointing from Memory and Writing from Memory will still be practised diligently, as recommended at page 12. The teacher who can appoint half an hour before or after the regular class meeting for memory pointing, memory writing, and dictation exercises finds the interest of his class and the accuracy of its knowledge ten folded. At the close of every lesson, one or two of the exercises should be chosen for the memory exercises of the next meeting. The pupil should copy that exercise six or ten times from the book, until he finds by testing himself that he can write it from memory. In the presence of the teacher, even at first, ten minutes is sufficient for writing from memory on clear paper without book. Meantime the teacher may walk about his class to give advice or information In less than five minutes the quickest have their exercises ready. The teacher glances over them and marks them as suggested at page 12, and the secretary credits the marks in favour of each pupil, in the class book. The teacher can make remarks on the common errors, or shew them on the black board.

Elementary Certificate.—Pupils now begin to make up their list of six tunes for the Elementary Certificate. See Preface.

SUPPLEMENTARY EXERCISES for this step may be found in Wall Sheets

QUESTIONS FOR WRITTEN OR ORAL EXAMINATION.

DOCTRINE.

1 Is the watchfulness of a Class-teacher sufficient to form in his pupils *habits* of position, &c.? Who must form them?

2 What is the object of the "Chest Exercises?"

3 In the "Vocal Klang Exercises" what are the chief points of the pupil's study?

4 Describe the four steps of this exercise and the reasons for each?

5 What is the special purpose of the "Tuning Exercises," and what are the three points to which the teacher will give attention during these exercises?

6 When the tonic chord is established in the ear, what do you yourself feel to be the mental effect of a high *Ray* when sung somewhat slowly? Describe the effect in your own words, as nearly as you can describe it, but be careful to describe only your own perceptions not those of others.

7 In the same way, describe the effect of a low *Ray*.

8 What mental impression do you receive from a high *Te*?

9 What feeling is produced by a low *Te*?

10 How do you distinguish vowels and consonants?

11 What kind of persons are commonly *lazy* in their use of lip and tongue, and consequently *indefinite* in their vowels and consonants?

12 Why is the clear and marked delivery of *vowels* so important to the singer?

13 In choosing breathing-places, what consideration is more important than that of the natural division of the musical line or section into phrases?

14 Give an example (different from those referred to above) in which "breathing for sense" would contradict the "breathing for phrase."

15 Give an illustration of "breathing for emphasis."

16 Describe the "musical form" called a Round.

17 What is the chief difficulty in singing a Round?

18 Describe the Four-pulse Measure.

19 Describe the Six-pulse Measure.

20 What sign is used for the medium accent?

21 What is the time name for a silent pulse?

22 What is the name for a tone a pulse-and-a-half long?

23 How do we name that quarter of a pulse which occurs at the end of the first half?—that, at the end of the second half?—that, at the beginning of the first half?—that, at the beginning of the second half?

24 How would you dictate the last three measures of Ex 79.

25 When tones related to one another as *Doh*, *Me*, and *Soh* are, or as *Soh*,, *Te*,, and *Ray* are, are sung together or in succession, what is such a combination called?

26 When one such chord has been first heard and has pre-occupied the ear, if another such chord starts from the highest tone of the first what can you say of the relationship between them?

27 Name or write a third,—a sixth,—a tenth.

28 How are sixths related to thirds? How are tenths related to thirds?

29 What is the quality in these intervals which makes them so much used in Harmony.

30 What is the difference between a common unison and an identical unison?

31 Where are octaves and identical unisons useful in two-part harmony?

32 What effect on the harmony would *consecutive* octaves and unisons produce?

33 Name or write two fifths, and two fourths.

34 How are fourths related to fifths?

35 Of fifths, fourth, and thirds, which contain the nearest or most *perfect* agreement of vibrations? Which the *sweetest*?

36 In what case are fifths avoided by composers?

37 Why are they not very much used in two-part harmony?

38 How are fourths regarded in relation to harmony?

39 Name or write four different sorts of Concords.

40 Name or write several Discords.

41 Describe how the Discords you have heard are prepared and resolved.

42 Describe the passing tones you have noticed on the weak part of a pulse.

PRACTICE.

43 Hold a steady tone without taking breath for ten seconds.

44 Sing *Doh, Me, Soh, Doh', Doh', Soh, Me, Doh*, in Keys D or C, to the "forward" Italian *Laa*, as softly and as pleasantly as you can.

45 Sol-fa any example you please shewing the Mental Effect of high *Ray'*,—of low *Ray*,—of high *Te*,—of low *Te*.

46 Sing to words the upper part of any *one* of the Exs. 65 to 70, chosen by the examiner. Sing correctly as to Time Tune and Pronunciation, without breathiness of tone and with proper breathing places. Marks should be given for each of these four points.

47 Ditto with Ex. 77 to 80.

48 Sing to *Laa* the *Ray* and the *Te*, to any *Doh* the teacher gives.

49 Sing to *Laa* the *Ray'* and the *Te* to any *Doh* the teacher gives you.

50 Taatai from memory any one of the Exs. 71 to 75, chosen by the examiner.

51 Taatai the upper part of one of the Exs. 77 or 78, chosen by the teacher.

52 Taatai-in-tune the upper part of one of the Exs. 79 or 80, chosen by the examiner.

53 Point on the modulator from memory (sol-faaing) any one of the following four Exs. 65, 66, 67, 69, chosen by the examiner.

54 Follow the examiner's pointing in a new "voluntary," containing *Doh, Me, Soh, Te* and *Ray*, but no difficulties of time.

55 Write, from memory, any other of these exercises chosen by the examiner.

56 From any phrase (belonging to this stage) sung to figures, tell your examiner (or write down) which figure was sung to *Ray*,—to *Ray'*,—to *Te*,,—to *Te*.

57 Having heard the tonic chord, tell your examiner (or write down) which tone of the scale (*Doh, Me, Soh, Te* or *Ray*) was immediately sung to *skaa*. Do this with two different tones.

58 Taatai any Rhythm of at least two measures belonging to this step which the examiner shall *laa* to you. He will first give you the measure and the rate of movement by taatai-ing two plain measures and marking the accents without beating time, but the two measures you have to copy he will simply *laa* on one tone.

59 Taatai-in-tune any Rhythm of at least two measures, belonging to this step, which, after giving the measure and rate as above, the examiner may sol-faa to you.

THIRD STEP.

To execute more difficult Chest, Klang and Tuning Exercises. To recognize the a *and* b *positions, and the various constitutions of Chords,—the resolution of the "Major Dominant,"—and the dissonance* d *against* r *in* S. *To recognize and produce the Fourth and Sixth of the Scale. To observe the relation of speed of movement to mental effect. To recognize the different sorts of voices. To recognize and produce one tone in absolute pitch and one rate of movement. To pitch tunes. To select breathing places. To gain first ideas of Expression. To become conscious of the great break from the thick or first to the thin or second register. To strengthen in men the thin or second register. To recognize and produce half-pulse silences, various divisions of sound produced by combinations of quarter-pulse and syncopations. To study the elements of Chanting. To recognize the partial dissonance* t f, *and the unprepared dissonance* f *against* s. *To recognize the relative motion of two parts.*

Ex. 81. Chest Exercise. The same as Ex. 54, except that 15 seconds may now be expected from all instead of ten. If the teacher is not quite sure of being able to count M. 60, he will use at least a string metronome.

Ex. 82. Vocal Klang Exercise. To be used with Manual Signs and with the same processes as Ex. 55. After exercising in each key, let the teacher test the pitch. There should be no flattening in these chordal exercises.

KEY C, B and D. Vocal Klang Exercise.

```
|d  :m  :s  |d  :m  :s  |s  :t  :r' |s  :t  :r' |d' :—  :—  ||
```

Ex. 83. Tuning Exercise. To be used with the same processes as Ex. 56, taking care to secure a soft tone, each part listening for the others and learning to enjoy the perfect blending of the voices. Ex. 85 and 86 to be used in the same way, without words.

KEY D. Tuning Exercise for three "equal" voices.

```
|d' :—  |s  :d' |t  :   |   :   |r' :—  |s  :t  |d' :—  |—  :—  ||
|m  :—  |s  :m  |s  :   |t  :—  |—  :—  |s  :r  |m  :—  |—  :—  ||
|d  :—  |m  :d  |s  :—  |—  :—  |s, :—  |t, :s, |d  :—  |—  :—  ||
```

Positions of Chords.—In connexion with the tuning exercises, a study of the "positions" and "constitutions" of chords will promote thoughtful, and therefore sure singing. Only the more intelligent classes, or the more intelligent members of classes will be expected to pursue this study. When the tones of a chord stand one above the other as closely as possible (as D when it stands in the order **d**, **m**, **s** counting upwards,—or S when it stands in the order **s**, **t**, **r**) they are said to be in their *normal* position, the lowest tone being called the *Root*, the middle tone its *Third*, and the highest its *Fifth*. In Ex. 56, measures 3 and 8 D is in its "normal" position. In Ex. 83, measure 3, pulses 1 and 2 S is in its normal position. Let the pupils listen to them afresh, and feel their *strength*. In Ex. 83, measure 3, pulse 4, S has its root in the lowest part, but is not in its normal position. When the *root* is in the lowest part the chord, even if not in its close normal form, the chord is in the *a* position. When the *third* is in the lowest part, the chord is in its *b* position See D*b* in Ex. 85, measure 2, pulse 1, and S*b* in Ex. 83, measure 3, pulse 3. Let the pupils listen to them afresh and mark their comparative weakness. When the *fifth* is in the lowest part. the chord is in its *c* position. This will be illustrated at the next step. The *a* position is best and most used. The *b* position is much used to make the melody of the lowest part smoother or more pleasant. The *c* position is only used in special cases, to be afterwards noted, but chiefly in the close of a section, as in Ex. 85.

Constitution of Chords.—One or more of the constituent parts of a chord may be omitted or doubled. In Ex. 56, measures 3 and 8 D is complete. *Completeness* we mark (when we wish to mark constitutions) by a figure 1, thus D*a*1. See S*a*1 in Ex. 83, measure 3, pulses 1, 2, and 4. The root (the most important tone of the chord) is often and freely doubled. The *trebling* of the root (not uncommon in four-part harmony) is marked by 2. In Ex. 56 measure 7, pulse 2, the root is trebled,—indeed, the *chord* has to be *supposed*. If, however, a third or fifth were added to this trebled root we should call it the chord S*a*2. The *third*, the source of sweetness, is rarely omitted. Its *omission* would be indicated by 3. The third is doubled frequently in D*a*, D*c*, F*a*, and F*c*; but in D*b* and F*b*, where the third is already made prominent by being in the lowest part, its doubling (too much sweetness) is avoided (See Minor Chords, page 46) except for the sake of better melody in the parts; and in S the third cannot be doubled because its **t** always goes to **d'** of the next chord, and we should then have the bald effect of two t's going to two **d'**'s—consecutive octaves. See page 21. The *doubled* third is marked by 4. It is quite common to omit the fifth. Being so like the root, its presence or absence is less noticed than that of the third. Its *omission* is marked 5, its *doubling* 6. See D*a*5 in Ex. 56, measures 4 and 7, and Ex. 83, measures 1 and 4. See S*a*5 in Ex. 83, measure 2, and S*b*5 in measure 3. Omitted roots—omitted foundations—are marked *om*, but we only interpret a chord as having its root omitted when the habits of the ear make it absolutely necessary for us *to think* of the absent root *in such a place*. See Ex. 83, measure 1.

Progression of S.—Notice that S seldom moves to any other chord than D, its t going to **d'**, its **r** to **m** or **d**, and its **s** to **d** or **s** or more rarely to **m**. See the close of Ex. 83, and Exs. 85 and 86. Thus these two chords, which are in their own internal structure the same, acknowledge a relationship to one another. S proves itself the clinging dependent on D. But, like other dependents, it is said to dominate—that is to rule the key,—and is called the Dominant. In fact, its clear declaration of allegiance to D decides the key. Wherever, in the region of pitch, two such chords *thus* cling together *there* is a key. Let the pupils listen afresh to the softly *laad* close of Ex. 83.

The Chord Four Soh.—Notice, at the close of Ex. 86, the dissonance **d** against **r** occurring in the chord of S, the third of the chord being omitted to make room for it. It would be counted as a fourth in this chord. We call the chord "Four Soh," and write it thus ^{4}S. In this case the position is *a* and the constitution 3.

Ex. **84**. Name, pulse by pulse, the chords, with their positions and constitutions, of Ex. 85 and 86. Thus D*a*5, S*a*1, &c.

Ex. **85**. KEY C. Tuning Exercise, as above.

d'	d' : d'	t : – ‖	t	d' : d'	d' : t	d' : – ‖
m	s : m	s : – ‖	s	s : m	m : r	m : – ‖
d	m : d	s : – ‖	s	m : d	s_1 : s_1	d : – ‖

Ex. **86**. KEY G. Tuning Exercise, as above.

m	m : r	m : – ‖	m	r : d	r : r	m : – ‖
d	d : t_1	d : – ‖	d	t_1 : d	d : t_1	d : – ‖
d	d : s_1	d : – ‖	d	s_1 : m_1	s_1 : s_1	d : – ‖

Words to Ex. 85 *to be taught at Ex.* 110.

'From all-that dwell-be | low the skies —
Let the-Cre | a tor's praise a rise —
Let the-Re deem er's | name be sung —
Through every | land by ev' ry tongue —
'E ternal are-thy | mer cies Lord —
'E ter nal | truth at tends thy word —
'Thy praise-shall sound 'from | shore to shore —
'Till suns-shall | rise and set no more —

Words to Ex. 86 *to be taught at Ex.* 110.

Glory-to thee-my God-this night 'for all-the blessings | of the light —
Keep-me-O keep-me King-of Kings 'be neath-thine | own Al might y wings —
For give-me Lord-for thy-dear Son 'the ill-that I-this | day have done —
'That with-the world-my self and thee I ere-I | sleep at peace may be —
Teach-me-to live-that I-may dread 'the grave-as little | as my bed —
Teach-me-to die-that so-I may . rise glorious | at the judg ment day —
'O may-my soul-on thee-re pose 'and with-sweet sleep-mine | eye lids close —
Sleep-that-may me-more vigorous make 'to serve-my | God when I a wake —

St. Co. (New.)

The Hold (⌒) signifies that the note below it may be held as long as the conductor or singer pleases.

Mental Effects of Fah and Lah.—The mental effects of these tones are developed with the same process which was used for t and r, page 15.

The manual sign for *fah* is the hand firmly pointing downwards. The manual sign for *lah* is the hand hanging down from the wrist.

Ex. 87. KEY A. Effect of high *Fah.*

| d .t_1 :d .r | m :d | f :— ||

Ex. 88. KEY A. Effect of high *Fah.*

| d :m | t_1 :s_1 | f :f | m :— ||

Ex. 89. KEY A. Effect of low *Fah.*

| d .t_1 :d .r | m :d | f_1 :— ||

Ex. 90. KEY A. Effect of low *Fah.*

| d :t_1.d | m.r :d | f_1 :f_1 | s_1 :— ||

Ex. 91. KEY G. Effect of low *Lah.*

| d.r :m.t_1 | r :l_1 | d :t_1 | l_1 :— ||

Ex. 92. KEY F. Effect of low *Lah.*

:s_1 | d :m :d | l_1 :— :t_1 | d :— ||

Ex. 93. KEY D. Effect of high *Lah.*

:d | m .:s | t :l | l :— | d' ||

Ex. 94. KEY D. Ditto.

| d :m | s :m | l :— | s :— ||

Ex. 95. KEY A. Effect of *Fah* and *Lah.*

| d :s_1 | m :d | l_1 :f | m :— ||

Ex. 96. KEY D. Ditto.

| d :s | m :l | f :s | d :— ||

Speed of movement and mental effect.—Hitherto we have studied the mental effect of tones when sung slowly. Let the pupils sing any exercise containing *lah* and *fah* very slowly indeed, and notice how their mental effects are brought out. Then let them sol-faa the same piece as quickly as they can, keeping the time and observing the change. *Lah* and *fah* are now gay and abandoned instead of weeping and desolate in their effect, and the other tones undergo a similar modification. Let the pupils try in the same way any other tunes which are deemed most characteristic. They will thus discover for themselves that great speed of movement makes the bold tones (**d m s**) sharper in their effect, though still firm; and makes the emotional tones (**r f l t**) more bright and lively, but leaves them still the emotional tones of the scale. Handel in his songs calls "to arms" chiefly by the use of **d m s**, but he also employs **d m s** with great rapidity of movement to express the abandonment of jolly laughter. *Emotional* laughter, however, he expresses by the rapid use of **t r f l**. It is also well known how effectively his songs employ these emotional tones in their slow and more serious moods. Ex. 113 includes good illustrations of **f** and **l** in both aspects. In measure 3, pulse 2, and measure 4. pulse 2 we have the quick *fah* in its lively, abandoned spirit. In measure 5, pulses 1 and 2 we have the slower *fah* in its more solemn effect. In measure 7, pulse 1 we have the quick *lah* in its brilliant emotion. In the second-last measure we have the slower *lah* in its loving, earnest, serious emotion.

The Scale.—We have now studied a key-tone with its six related tones. Seven tones thus related to each other are called a scale. The successive tones of the scale ascending in pitch are, **d r m f s l t d'** descending, **d' t l s f m r d.** The pupil must now practise himself in repeating the names of the notes, *in their successive order* both in ascending and descending. **d m** and **s** are readily classified as the bold and strong tones of the scale, and **t r f l** as the leaning tones. Of these last **t** and **f** have the strongest leaning or *leading* tendency, **t** leading upward to **d'**, and **f** downward to **m.** Of the intervals of this scale and its harmonic structure, more at the next step.

d'
t
l
s
f
m
r
d

The Standard Scale of Pitch.—Hitherto the teacher has fixed the pitch of the key-tone. The pupils themselves should now learn to do it in turn. Any conceivable sound can be taken as a key-tone, and the relationships of chord and scale, which we have already studied, will spring out of it. But,—it is found convenient to have one standard scale of pitch tones by which others may be gauged. For this purpose a certain tone called tenor or middle C, which stands high in a man's voice—low in a woman's, and is producible by a stretched string giving 256 complete vibrations in a second, is fixed upon as the standard, and its scale is called the "standard scale." This is given at the side. The octave of this tone C' (512 vibrations) is usually given in tuning-forks for vocal purposes.

C'
B
A
G
F
E
D
C

Pitching Tunes.—The pupil strikes the C' tuning-fork, and runs down to the tone he wants. That tone he swells out, and then repeats it to the syllable *doh*. At first it will help the pupil's memory to notice that he has to spell the words "bag" and "fed" in running down this scale, thus:—

|d' :- |t :l |s :f |m :r |d :- ||
C' *B A G* *F E D* C

Remembering C'.—It is much more easy to fix on the memory *one* tone in absolute pitch than is commonly thought, and it is a great advantage to be able to do so. *Frequently* the teacher asks his pupils to sound C' (which in a man's voice is really C) and then tests them with the tuning-fork. In this way the power of recollection is soon developed. In estimating the chances of certainty, however, we should always bear in mind that any bodily or mental depression has a tendency to flatten even our recollections.

Classification of Voices.—In the following exercises the parts are not kept within so close a range as before. It will not now be possible to "exchange parts." It is therefore necessary that the teacher should (either himself or by his assistants) examine every voice in his class and divide them into higher and lower voices. The female and children's voices are naturally pitched about an octave higher than the men's. The pitch tone G stands at about the middle of the range of female and children's voices. In examining these voices, the teacher pitches this tone as a key tone and requires the pupil to sol-faa, first upward and then downward from it. If the fuller—more beautiful—and more easily produced tones of the voice lie above G it may be classed as a high voice If the best tones of the voice lie below G, it may be called a low voice. Cultivation may afterwards make a difference, but this simple mode of classification answers our present purpose. The high voices of women and children are called Soprano (pronounced Sopraano); the low voices, Contralto. The G_{1} an octave lower than the last, serves to divide the men's voices in the same way. It is the *quality* of the tones above and below G or G_{1}, not the present reach of the voice, which decides the question. The high voices of men are called Tenor; the low voices, Bass.

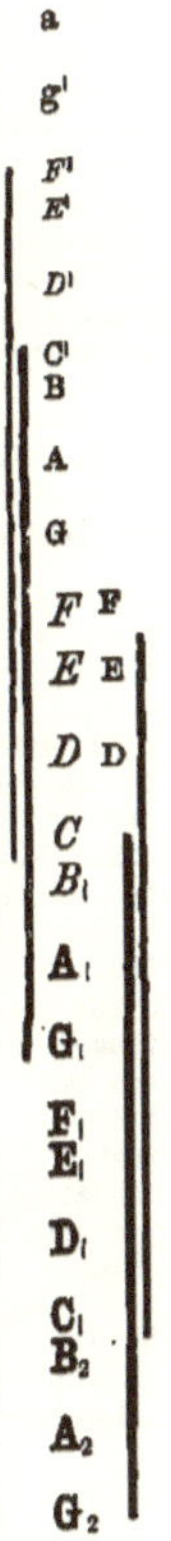

The Compass of Voices upward and downward *varies greatly*, and is not a sufficient test of their fitness for the high or low "part" in the music, but it is useful to bear in memory that the *easy* compass of most voices is about an octave and a half. Basses and Contraltos easily compass—one from G_2 to C, the other from G_1 to C'. Tenors and Sopranos *easily* compass—one from C_1 to F, and the other from C to F'. Voice trainers commonly give the name Mezzo- (pronounced Metso) Soprano to voices which seem to be between Contralto and Soprano, and Baritone to voices which are neither Bass nor Tenor. But the most scientific of them have reached the conclusion that true medium voices are comparatively rare, and that those which seem so are commonly only uncultivated Tenors or Contraltos,—the high part of a man's voice and the low part of a woman's being the most liable to neglect. The diagram, at the side, shows the common easy compass of voices as given above. The difference of the type in the letters and the double printing of F, E, D is explained under the heading "Registers," p. 32.

a
g'
F'
E'
D'
C'
B
A
G
F F
E E
D D
C
B_1
A_1
G_1
F_1
E_1
D_1
C_1
B_2
A_2
G_2

Octave Marks.—The pitch of *doh* is always taken from the unmarked octave of the Standard Scale, and this d with the scale above it are without octave marks. But, to save the unnecessary multiplicity of octave marks both in writing and printing, the Tenor and Bass part are always written an octave higher than they really are. In quoting octave marks, as in dictation, it may be useful to distinguish the higher octave marks by naming them before the note, and the lower by naming them after,—thus D^2 "two-D"—D_2 "D-two"—G^3 "three G" C_1 "C-one," &c. It will help the memory to notice that the higher comes first. Thus, we say that the easy Bass compass is, as above, "from G-two to unmarked C," that of the Contralto "from G-one to one-C," that of the Tenor "from C-one to unmarked F," that of the Soprano "from unmarked C to one-F."

Men's and Women's Voices.—Ask a man to sound the same note as a woman, girl, or boy, or ask them to sing together the air of a tune, and they will sing an octave apart. If you doubt this, get the woman, girl, or boy, after sounding what is commonly called the same note, to sing down the scale an octave; the man then resounds the note he first struck. The ear will then feel that these two sounds last struck are really in unison, and that what commonly goes by the name of unison is really octaves.

Naming of Parts—In the titles of tunes the initial-letters are used to name the parts, thus:—S for *Soprano*, C for *Contralto*, T for *Tenor*, and B for *Bass*.

Breathing Places.—After Ex. 113, the breathing places are no longer marked, but if the markings already given have been carefully studied, the pupils will be able to mark breathing places for themselves. Before the words are read collectively the class should do this under the guidance of the teacher, who will often remind them of the principles laid down, page 16. In addition, it may be noticed that if one wishes to take breath before a strong pulse, the time of the breath must be taken from the end of the previous weak pulse; but that if one wishes to take breath before a weak pulse, the time of it may be taken away from the beginning of the same pulse; that it is not only convenient but necessary to take a good breath before all long sustained tones or long connected passages. In sol-faaing or laaing breath should still be taken "for phrasing." This will lead to a study of the musical phrases. The importance of taking breath for clear soft "emphasis" will appear in such Exercises as 97, where the purity of the tone on the first $d^{\prime}$ will be wonderfully improved by requiring a breath to be taken before it.

Expression is such a use of *loudness* and *softness* in singing as tends to make the music more expressive. Even in the earliest steps, pupils enjoy thus embellishing their music. In the fifth step the subject is more fully treated. Here it is enough to draw attention occasionally to what is indeed the chief part of expression—that which is suggested by the words. In our Tonic Sol-fa books we early adopted the plan of using type-marks for this kind of expression. First, there must be fixed the *medium* or normal degree of force proper to the *general sentiment* of the piece to be sung; then whatever words are printed in the common type are to be sung with that appropriate medium force, whatever words are printed in small CAPITALS are to be sung louder, and whatever words are printed in *italics* are to be sung more *softly*. In writing, a single line is drawn under the words for italics, and a double line for small capitals. These marks of the pen can be easily added by the student to his printed copy. In Ex. 97, the general sentiment of the words is subdued and prayerful; therefore the common type indicates soft singing, but in the last two lines the spirit of earnestness rises to a climax, and demands greater force of voice. The general spirit of Ex. 100 is soft and gentle, but it should begin *very* softly—increasing in force as the phrase *ascends*. Ex. 101 and 102 also open with ascending phrases to be treated in a similar way. Continuous or *repeated* tones, as in the second line of Ex. 103 and in Ex. 65, suggest the same treatment. Notice that any tunes like Ex. 102 and 103 which require a light and tripping style, require also a *soft* voice Observe, in all these cases, how useful this distinction of loud and soft is in marking out the musical phrases or in "phrasing."

Ex. 97 to 103 should now be taught in the same manner as before, except that previous to each exercise, the teacher will put the voices in tune by causing his pupils to sing, after his manual signs, for a low key-tone, **d m s—f l $d^{\prime}$—s t $r^{\prime}$ $d^{\prime}$.**—and for a middle key-tone **d s_1 m d—f_1 l_1 d—s_1 t_1 r d.**

SUN OF MY SOUL.

Ex. 97. KEY C. *Mainzer.*

:s	s :s	$d^{\prime}$:t	l :l	s :l	f :s	m :$d^{\prime}$	t :l	s
1.Sun	of my	soul,† thou	Sa - viour	dear, It	is not	night† if	thou be	near:
2.When	the soft	dews† of	kind - ly	sleep My	wear-ied	eye - lids†	gen - tly	steep,
:m	m :m	d :r	f :f	m :d	r :t_1	d :m	r :d	t_1
3.A -	bide with	me† from	morn till	eve, For	with-out	thee† I	can - not	live:
4.Come	near† and	bless us	when we	wake, Ere	thro' the	world† our	way we	take:

St. Co. (New).

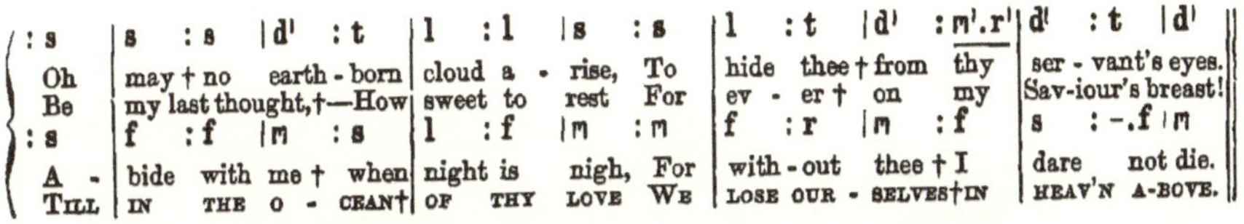

: s | s : s | d' : t | l : l | s : s | l : t | d' : m'.r' | d' : t | d' ||
Oh | may † no earth - born | cloud a - rise, To | hide thee † from thy | ser - vant's eyes.
Be | my last thought, †—How | sweet to rest For | ev - er † on my | Sav-iour's breast!
: s | f : f | m : s | l : f | m : m | f : r | m : f | s : -.f | m ||
A - | bide with me † when | night is nigh, For | with - out thee † I | dare not die.
TILL | IN THE O - CEAN† | OF THY LOVE WE | LOSE OUR - SELVES†IN | HEAV'N A-BOVE.

LABOUR'S STRONG AND MERRY CHILDREN.

Ex. 98. KEY G. Round for two parts.

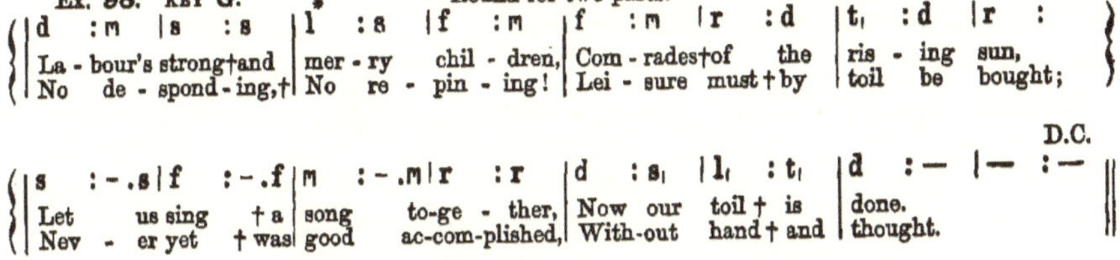

| d : m | s : s | *l : s | f : m | f : m | r : d | t, : d | r : |
La - bour's strong†and | mer - ry chil - dren, | Com - rades†of the | ris - ing sun,
No de - spond - ing,† | No re - pin - ing! | Lei - sure must † by | toil be bought;

D.C.

| s : -.s | f : -.f | m : -.m | r : r | d : s, | l, : t, | d : — | — : — ||
Let us sing † a | song to-ge - ther, | Now our toil † is | done.
Nev - er yet † was | good ac-com-plished, | With-out hand † and | thought.

ALL THE SPRINGING FLOWERS.

Ex. 99. KEY F. Round for two parts.

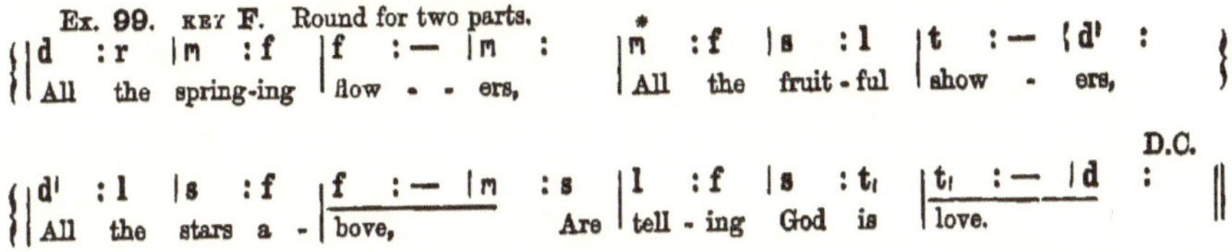

| d : r | m : f | f : — | m : | *m : f | s : l | t : — | d' : |
All the spring-ing | flow - - ers, | All the fruit - ful | show - ers,

D.C.

| d' : l | s : f | f : — | m : s | l : f | s : t, | t, : — | d : ||
All the stars a - | bove, Are | tell - ing God is | love.

LULLABY.

Ex. 100. KEY D. Round for two parts.

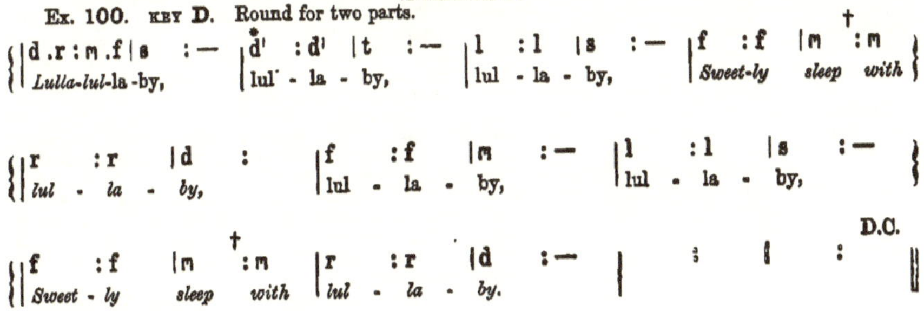

| d .r : m .f | s : — | *d' : d' | t : — | l : l | s : — | †f : f | m : m |
Lulla-lul-la - by, | lul - la - by, | lul - la - by, | *Sweet-ly sleep with*

| r : r | d : | f : f | m : — | l : l | s : — |
lul - la - by, | lul - la - by, | lul - la - by,

D.C.

| f : f | m †: m | r : r | d : — | : | : ||
Sweet - ly sleep with | *lul - la - by.*

St. Co. (New.)

DOH, RAY, ME.

Ex. 101. KEY G. Round for four parts.

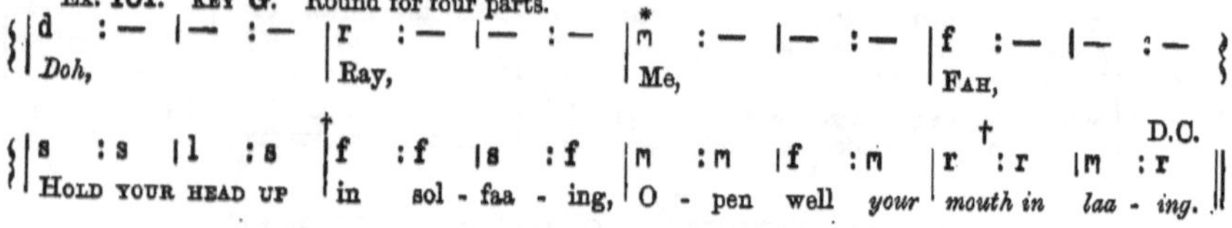

| d :— |— :— | r :— |— :— | *m :— |— :— | f :— |— :— |
| *Doh,* | Ray, | Me, | FAH, |

| s :s |l :s | †f :f |s :f | m :m |f :m | †r :r |m :r ‖ D.C.
| HOLD YOUR HEAD UP | in sol - faa - ing, | O - pen well *your* | *mouth in laa - ing.* |

WHO COMES LAUGHING?

Ex. 102. KEY E♭. Round for three parts.

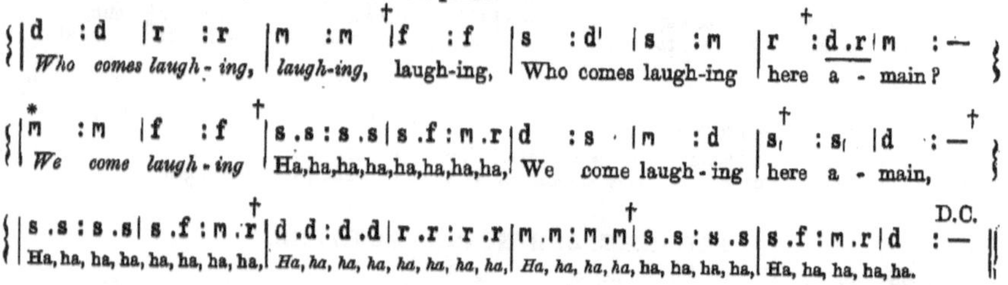

| d :d |r :r | m :m |†f :f | s :d' |s :m | †r :d.r|m :— |
| *Who comes laugh - ing,* | *laugh-ing,* laugh-ing, | Who comes laugh-ing | here a - main? |

| *m :m |f :f | †s.s:s.s|s.f:m.r | d :s |m :d | †s, :s, |d :— † |
| *We come laugh - ing* | Ha,ha,ha,ha,ha,ha,ha,ha, | We come laugh - ing | here a - main, |

| s.s:s.s|s.f:m.†r | d.d:d.d|r.r:r.r | m.m:m.†m|s.s:s.s | s.f:m.r|d :— ‖ D.C.
| Ha, ha, ha, ha, ha, ha, ha, ha, | *Ha, ha, ha, ha, ha, ha, ha, ha,* | *Ha, ha, ha, ha,* ha, ha, ha, ha, | Ha, ha, ha, ha, ha. |

GLAD HEARTS AND FREE.

Ex. 103. KEY A. Round for four parts,

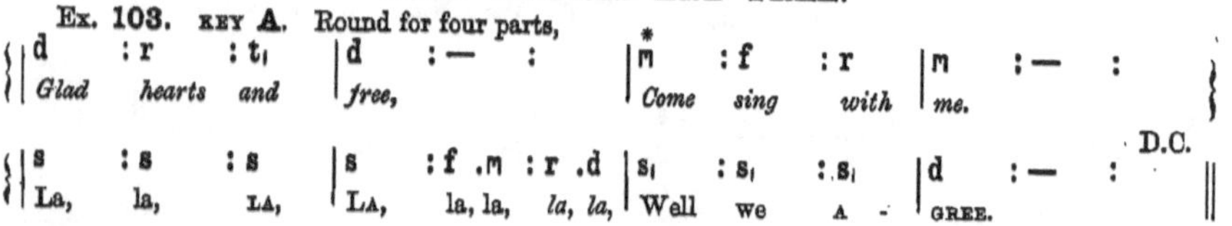

| d :r :t, | d :— : | *m :f :r | m :— : |
| *Glad hearts and* | *free,* | *Come sing with* | *me.* |

| s :s :s | s :f.m :r.d | s, :s, :s, | d :— : ‖ D.C.
| La, la, LA, | LA, la, la, *la, la,* | Well we A - | GREE. |

Registers.—In the highest part of the compass of men's voices, and in the lowest part of the compass of women's voices, may be noticed a remarkable change in the quality of the tones. The place where this change occurs is called "the great break." It is in all voices between F and G. The break arises from the different way in which the tones are produced in the larynx. Below the break the tones are produced by what we may call the first or thick register of the voice, above the break by the second or thin register. In women's voices there is a yet higher register, beginning with g', which we may call the third or small register. These registers of the voice are indicated on page 29, the "thick" register being shown by large capital letters, the "thin" by ordinary small capitals, and the "small" by common letters.*

Optional Tones.—Although the lower registers cannot be forced upward, beyond the limits mentioned, without injury to the voice, the higher registers can in all cases be used some way below their proper limit. So much is this the case with the thin register, that the three tones F, E, and D are called optional tones, and the pupil is advised to exercise his voice in order to equalise the quality and power of these three tones, and to use either register interchangeably. In women's voices it is this thick register at the bottom which is commonly found to be uncultivated, and in men's voices it is the thin register at the top which is commonly left untrained.

* Italic capitals shew the *Upper* thick and thin registers.

Recognition of the Lower Thin Register.—It will be seen from the scale, p. 29, that women naturally use this register in the middle of their voices and have no difficulty in recognising it,—that, among men, Basses have little need for it except for solo singing and for any part-music which demands an uncommon compass of voice,—but that Tenors require a careful cultivation of this register and of the "optional tones." It may also be noticed that Contraltos require a special cultivation of the first or thick register, but that is deferred till the next step. In order to enable men to discover and recognise the thin register, the teacher causes them to take a loud tone for *doh* (say D), which is decidedly within the thick register, and then guides them by his manual signs to sing the chord slowly, thus, **d m s**. If he allows them to sing the *soh* softly, they will instinctively produce it in the thin register. Having once found that register, it will not be difficult for them to continue the same quality of tone in a downward phrase like the following, **s f m r d**. Having got back to the *doh* in the thin register they may then take breath and sing it again in the thick. Of course the pupils can take A_1 or G_1 for their key-tone. They will then have to follow the manual signs thus, **d m s d^1**; —d' will be delivered softly in the thin register, and the descending passage in the same register would be **d^1 t l s f m r d**. It is better that *all* the men's voices should go through this experiment.

Strengthening of the Lower Thin Register.—Exercise—regular exercise—strengthens the tones of this register so as to make them blend easily into the tones of the stronger register. Like all other exercises intended to strengthen the muscles, it must have something of force and violence in it, a marked shock of the glottis (see p. 1), but must not be over-strained. For strengthening the legs a run is better than a walk, but *over*-exertion does more harm than good. Therefore the necessity in the following exercise of using well the *forceful* staccato syllable *koo*. It will be remembered that a new combination of the delicate muscles of the larynx is required for every conceivable sound which it produces and that all these muscles and combinations of muscles have to be exercised. Hence, the necessity of using this exercise in various keys, so as to bring intervening tones into play. Ex. 104 should be first sol-faad with the manual signs; second, sung to *koo* five or more times, much more quickly and forcefully; third, sol-faad again. On sol-faaing the second time the quality of the tone will be found to be very much improved. But care must be taken not to fatigue the voices. At first five *koo-ings* will do this, and there must be a rest before the exercise is used in another key. The first and second keys will be quite fatiguing enough at first. The keys are so arranged that without the use of the tuning-fork the teacher can pass from one to another. For example, after exercising in key B, he strikes *ray*, calls it *doh*, strikes the chord and proceeds with the exercise again. After thus using what is called the key of C sharp, he strikes *te_1*, calls it *doh*, strikes the chord and proceeds with the exercise in key C. In the same way the *ray* of key C will give him key D. This exercise should be used for a very short time, at every future lesson of this step. If the class is a mixed one, women should join in this exercise, which lies in the lower compass of their voices. and is easy to them. They will encourage the men's voices, and prepare themselves for a blending of the thick and thin registers at the next step.

Ex. 104. To strengthen the Lower Thin Register. To be sung in the highest part of men's voices, and the lower part of women's voices.

KEYS B, C♯, C, D.

{ :s |m :f |r :m |d :r |t_1 :— |d ||

TIME.

The Metronome (pronounced *metronoam*) is an instrument for regulating the rate of movement in a piece of music. It is a pendulum which can be made to swing at various rates per minute. M. 60 placed at the beginning of a tune in the Tonic Sol-fa notation means "Let the *pulses* of this tune move at the rate of 60 in a minute." The *stroke* of the metronome is the moment when it passes the lowest point of its arc. In the case of very quick six-pulse measure, the metronome rate is made to correspond not with pulses but with half measures—"beating twice in the measure."

Sustaining the rate of Movement.—When a tune, as in psalmody, is intended to be sung to several verses, the singers may vary the rate of movement according to the sense of the words, and in simple songs this rate of movement may be occasionally accelerated or retarded to suit the sentiment. But even this power of *varying* the rate of movement with any good effect depends upon a previously gained power of *sustaining* the rate of movement uniformly. Exercises for the cultivation and testing of this power are *frequently* introduced. The teacher causes his pupils to taatai on one tone a simple measure, thus, TRAA TAA TLAA TAA, repeating it steadily, say six times *with* the metronome, so as to get into the swing. He then stops the metronome and they continue holding the rhythm steadily for another six measures. Just at the stroke of the first pulse in the next measure he lets his metronome go, and then the class immediately see whether they have sustained the rate. Accomplished musicians say that this power of sustaining a uniform speed is one of the first and most important musical elements. The irregular and ever-varying speed of movement, without any apology, on the ground of Expression, which many organists and precentors indulge in, is very painful to practised ears.

Remembering M. 60.—It is quite common among Tonic Sol-faists to be able by habit to form a conception in their own minds of the rate of movement given in the title of a tune, without referring to a metronome. This power is gained by first fixing in the mind the rate of M. 60 as a standard of comparison. Then, twice that speed, M. 120, or a speed half as fast again, M. 90, are easily conceived. Even some intermediate rates are recollected with considerable precision. To fix M. 60 in the mind, the teacher *frequently* asks his pupils to begin *taatai-ing* at what they conceive to be that rate, and then tests them well with his metronome. The recollection of rate of movement is, like the recollection of pitch, affected by temperament of body and mood of mind. But these difficulties can be conquered, so that depression of either kind shall not make us sing too slowly.

The silent half-pulse is indicated by the absence of any note between the dot which divides the pulse in two and the accent mark. It is named *SAA* on the accented and *SAI* on the unaccented part of the pulse. See Exs. 105, 106, 107.

The three-quarter-pulse tone is indicated by a comma placed close after a dot, leaving a quarter to fill up the pulse. It is named as below, TAAfe. With lighter accent and quicker speed TAAfe is the same thing as TAA-AA-TAI. And this is the same thing in small as TAA-AA-AA TAA. The teacher causes such an exercise as 71 to be sung quickly and lightly.

Two quarters and a half are indicated by the use of the comma and dot, as below, Ex. 106. This pulse-form is called tafaTAI. It is the same thing in its nature with the larger and more strongly accented time-forms TAATAI TAA and TAA TAA TAA -AA. The teacher causes such exercises as 72 to be sung rapidly.

A half and two quarters are indicated as below, Ex. 107, and are called TAAtefe. This pulse-form is the same in its nature as TAA TAATAI and TAA-AA TAA TAA. See Ex. 75

Syncopation is the anticipation of accent. It requires an accent to be struck before its regularly recurring time—changing a *weak* pulse or weak part of pulse into a *strong* one and the immediately *following* strong pulse or part of a pulse into a *weak* one. Its effect in time is like that of a discord in tune. It is a contradiction of the usual and expected. Both the discord and the syncopation should be boldly attacked and firmly held by the voice,—just as one grasps a stinging nettle to master it. Insufficient definitions of syncopation have led many singers to strike the new accent, indeed, but also to retain the original strong accent on the immediately following pulse. This common misunderstanding entirely destroys the intended effect. In Ex. 108 the first line shews how syncopations are commonly written, and the second line shews the real alteration of accent which they create and the manner in which they should be sung. Note that it is difficult to "beat the measure" in the ordinary way (see preface) during syncopations, because they seem to contradict the beating. It is easier to beat simply pulse by pulse.

Exs. 105 to 109 should be taught as above, pp. 7, 8, and 19, especially with "time-laa-ing," p. 8.

Ex. **105.** *Slowly,—and quickly.*

|l .l : .l |l .l : |
TAATAI *SAA*TAI TAATAI *SAA*

KEY F.
|m.r : .d|r.d : |s.f : m. |m.r : d. ||

KEY G.
|s,.d : .t,|d.m : |f.r : t,. |s.m : d. ||

St. Co. (New).

|l .l : l . |l .l : l . ||
TAATAI TAA*SAI* TAATAI TAA*SAI*

KEY F.
|s.m : .l|s.m : |s.f : r |f.m : d ||

KEY F.
|m.s : .s|f.l : |f.r : f. |m.d : m. ||

Ex. 106. *Slowly,—and quickly.*

| l .l ,l : l .l | .l : l | l,l.l : l .l | l . : l ||
TAAtefe TAATAI *SAA*TAI TAA tafaTAI TAATAI TAA*SAI* TAA

KEY G.
| d .r,m : d .s,| .l, : t, | d,r.m : f .m | r. : d ||

KEY F.
| s .f,m : r .m | .f : m | m,r.d : t,.d | m. : r ||

KEY G.
| m .s,f : m.d | .f : r | m,s.f : m.d | t,. : d |

KEY C.
| s .l,t : d'.s | .l : s | l,t.d' : t.s | f. : m ||

Ex. 107. *Slowly—and quickly.*

| l .l ,l : l .,l | l ,l.l ,l : l | l .,l : l .,l | l .l : l .l ||
TAAtefe TAAfe tafatefe TAA TAAfe TAAfe TAATAI TAATAI

KEY D.
| d .r,m : f .,m | r,m.f,s : l | s .,f : m .,r | s .f : m .r ||

KEY D.
| m .f,s : l .,t | d',l.s,m : r | d .,m : r .,f | m .s : f .l ||

KEY F.
| s .f,m : r .,d | t,,d.r,m : f | l .,f : s .,m | l .f : s .m ||

KEY F.
| s .m,d : s .,d | s,f.m,r : m | r .,f : m .,d | f .l : s .m ||

Ex. 108. *Slowly—and quickly.*

| l : l | l : l | — : l | l : l | — : — | l : l ||
TAA TAA TAA TAA -AA TAA TAA TAA -AA -AA TAA TAA
| l : l | l | l : — : l | l | l : — : — | l : l ||

Ex. 109. *Slowly—and quickly.*

| l : l | l : l | l .l : l .l | l .l : – .l | – .l : l .l | l : l ||
TAA TAA TAA TAA TAATAA TAATAI TAATAI -AATAI -AATAI TAATAI TAA TAA

Chanting is the recitation of words on a single tone with a musical close or cadence at the end. The chant of English origin, called the Anglican Chant, has either *two* reciting tones with cadences, in which case it is called a "*single* chant," or *four* recitations with cadences and is called a "double chant." The most important rule in reference to chanting is that the music should be well learnt "by heart" before any attempt to apply words to it. The chant is commonly and properly applied to prose words (see next step), but the chanting of hymns is not out of place when the hymns are very long. It also forms a good exercise preparatory to the art of prose-recitation. The rhythms are so simple and admit of so little variation that attention can be almost exclusively given to distinct and sharp utterance.

The division of words for Chanting is commonly made simply by placing a single bar where the cadence begins and a double bar where the cadence ends. In addition to this there have been many contrivances for guiding the manner of the recitation so as to secure appropriate breathing places and to prevent confusion. Our Tonic Sol-fa teachings naturally suggest the division of the whole into pulses. Our simple rules are that the syllables which *stand together*—whether joined by hyphens or otherwise—are to be sung in one pulse,—*that* this mark ' before a syllable denotes a silence on the first half of a pulse and a convenient breathing place,—that this mark . denotes a silent pulse, and this — the continuation of a sound. In Ex. 85 notice the rhythms to the short recitations TAA TAATAI twice, *SAA*TAI TAA TAA once, and *SAA*TAI TAATAI once, and the rhythms to the longer recitations *SAA*TAI TAATAI TAATAI twice, TAA TAATAI TAA TAA once, and *SAA*TAI TAATAI TAA *SAA*TAI once. Verify each of these rhythms and study the reasons for their differences of rhythmic form. Why will not one form do for all the short recitations, and another for all the long ones? It is important to notice that the pulses of the cadence and of the recitation move at the same rate although it is customary and also natural to put more syllables into each pulse of the recitation than into those of the cadence.

In **teaching Chanting** the teacher causes his pupils (*a*) to *taatai* a line by pattern, (*b*) to recite it by pattern, clearly and distinctly, and (*c*) to sing it to the chant already learnt by heart.

Ex. 110. Chant the words to Exs. 85 and 86.

New Consonances.—Hitherto we have had for thirds and sixths and fifths and fourths (See p. 21):

m s t r' AND s r'
d m s t d s

Now, there are added

l d' f AND d' l m'
f l r f m l

The harmony student will find and *mark* cases of each new consonance, and listen to them while the music is sung.

The Partial Dissonance.—The very peculiar interval of the scale f to t with its inversion f to t, is not a discord according to the description at p. 21. But its effect on the ear forbids it to be called a concord. The ear requires rest and sweetness after it, and therefore expects f to go to m and t, to d. We call it the partial dissonance. See and *hear* Ex. 116, *l* 4, *m* 1, *p* 4.—NOTE.—*l* stands for *line* or score, *m* for *measure*, and *p* for *pulse*,—Ex. 119, *l* 1, *m* 4, *p* 4. But the effect of the partial dissonance is specially illustrated in the cadences of Ex. 99.

New dissonances.—We have hitherto studied (see p. 21) *one* dissonance, d against r. It is *the model* of those dissonances which occur on *the strong* pulse and are regularly "prepared" and "resolved." We now have other dissonances of the same kind. In Ex. 114, in addition to d against r in *m* 3 and 6, we have s against l in *m* 4, and f against s in *m* 2. In Ex. 116, in addition to the ordinary d against r, *l* 5, *m* 1, we have the same dissonance with *delayed* resolution *l* 4, *m* 1, and m against f with the less common *interrupted* resolution,—the consonance l "interrupting" the resolution of m' upon r', and f against s in *l* 1, *m* 2.

f against s.—Although this dissonance *is* used on the *strong* pulse, and with the same kind of preparation as above, it is far more commonly used on the *weak* pulse and often without any sort of preparation. Its favourite form of melodic preparation, however, is when the f comes down stepwise from s and goes on as it always must to m. See and *listen* to Ex. 97, *l* 2, *m* 2, *p* 1, 2,—Ex. 111, *m* 7, *p* 1—where f is unprepared and has an interrupted resolution,—and Ex. 118, *m* 5, *p* 2. This dissonance f against s is the *model* of unprepared discords.

Relative Motion of Parts.—Two parts may follow each other upward or downward at the same time. This is called *similar* motion, and is generally sweet and pleasant, as in Ex. 97, *m* 5, and in Ex. 99, when the first two measures are sung with the second two. Two parts may move upward and downward in opposite directions. This is called *contrary* motion, and is exceedingly gratifying to the ear. See and listen to Ex. 97, pulses 3 to 6 and 9 to 12, and Ex. 99, when the third and fourth measures are sung with the fifth and sixth. In the last case, indeed, the parts cross one another. The crossing of parts is common in Rounds, but not in other compositions. Anything which tends to confuse one part with another is objected to in modern music. *Oblique* motion is that in which one part "stands"—that is, continues the same sound, while the other part moves downwards or upwards. See Ex. 117, *m* 6, 7, and Ex. 97, beginning of line 2. Very much of the relative motion of parts cannot be described by these simple terms. The ear could not be satisfied with one sort of relative motion only. It requires variety; but that which satisfies longest is the *similar* motion.

Imitation.—The music-student cannot fail to notice that every kind of imitation is agreeable to the ear. It is a great help to the singer to notice such cases. Imitations in the waving of the melody—or *melodic figure*—such as that simple one in Ex. 70, *l* 2, where the air of the second measure imitates, in figure, that of the first,—or that in Ex. 98, between the two parts at the opening of line 2,—or those in Ex. 101, *l* 2, are easily perceived. The imitations in Ex. 116 are interesting. In the opening, the second part is imitated by the first, for a measure and a half, starting a *fifth* above. In the second line the music of "grief of heart" is replied to, a fifth above, by that of "killing care;" then, the second part repeats "grief of heart" a small step higher and is again replied to by the air a fifth higher. Let the student carefully verify observations like these; it will teach him to see more in a piece of music than most others see. When the imitation is in two or more parts simultaneously, as in Ex. 97, pulses 9, 10, with 11, 12, it is called a harmonic *sequence*. The study of *rhythmic* imitation is very interesting. See in Ex. 113, *l* 2, tafaTAI tafaTAI TAA quickly replied to by the same rhythm with contrary motion. See TAA TAATAI TAA in Ex. 116. Find other examples.

"Elementary Rhythms," containing passages selected from popular songs, and published separately, will now make good home practice and prepare for the elementary certificate.

Laa Voluntaries.—When once the use of the Sol-fa syllables is fixed in the ear and has obtained mnemonic power, it becomes very important to prevent that otherwise useful power satisfying the pupil. The practice of *laa-ing* every tune which has already been *sol-faad* is a step towards liberty, but *laa-ing* the Modulator voluntaries is a step further still towards that ready perception of the mental effects of the tones, *apart from associated syllables*, which is desired. This practice, therefore, of *laa-ing* at first sight from the teacher's pointing should be constantly used.

The Pupil's Pointing on the Modulator while he sol-faas must still be encouraged. Where it is possible for the pupils to point in class—each using a mounted "Home Modulator," and holding it up, while the teacher passes along the rows behind or stands on a chair or table so as to overlook all—that is the best plan. It makes all work.

The "*Standard Additional Exercises*" appended to this book, introduce four-part pieces at this step.

The "*Standard Mixed-Voice Exercises*" and the "*Standard Men's Voice Exercises*" introduce four-part music in the course of this step.

OH! GIVE THANKS.

Ex. 111. KEY **A.** Round for four parts.

d :r	† m :d .,d	r :t_1	d :s_1	* m :f	s :m .,† m	f :r .,r	m :d
Oh! give	thanks to the	God of	hea - ven,	For his	mer- cy en-	dur- eth for	ev - er.

:	:	s_1 :s_1	s_1 :d	:	:	s :s	s :m D.C.
		Hal - le -	lu - jah,			Hal - le -	lu - jah.

PEACE, LOVELY PEACE.

Ex. 112. KEY **E♭.** Round for four parts.

d :r .r	m :– † .r	* m .m :f .f	s : † .s
Peace, love - ly	peace a -	gain re - news her	youth, Hur-

s † .,d' :t .,r'	d' .s :s .f	m † :r	d : D.C.
rah, hur- rah for	peace and lib - er -	ty and	truth.

St. Co. (New.)

PRAISE YE THE LORD.

Ex. 113. KEY A. *A. L. C.*

```
|s,   :- .s, |d    :- .s, |m    :r    |d    :   .s |s,f.m :f,m.r |m     :  .s
 Praise the Lord  † with   cheer - ful  voice,  † Re- joice,              † re-
|m,   :- .m, |m,   :- .s, |d    :s,   |m,   :      |      :  .t, |d     :
                                                           Re-joice,

|s,f.m :f,m.r |m   :      |f       :- .f    |m    :- .m  |r       :f
 joice,                    Praise  the Lord    † with      cheer -  ful
|      :  .t, |d   :  .s, |l,,t,.d :t,,d.r  |d    :  .s, |l,,t,.d :t,,d.r
        re - joice,   re-  joice,                   re-   joice,    -

|m    :  .s |l,s.f :m  .s |f,m.r :d  .m |r   :- .r  |d    :
 voice,  re-  joice,  -    -   -    -     -   re - joice.
|d    :     |l, .t, :d .s, |l, .t, :d .s, |f,  :- .f, |m,   :
 -            Praise  the   Lord,   re-    joice, re - joice.

|t,   :- .d  |r .d  :t, .d  |r     :m    |f     :—  |m    :- .f  |s    :d
 1. In his   tem  -  ple   † joy - ful    raise        To  our  God    † the
|r,   :- .m, |f, .m, :r, .m, |f,   :s,   |l,    :—  |s,   :- .f, |m,   :m,
 2. Now his  migh  -  ty    acts † re -  cord,        Sing the great - ness
 3. Now to   praise  † the  name  di  -  vine,        Ev  - 'ry liv  - ing

|r .m  :r .d  |t,   :—  |s,   :- .s, |d    :- .s, |m     :r    |d    :—
 song   of     praise,   While the fir  -  ma-      ment † on   high,
|f, .s, :f, .m, |r,  :— |m,   :- .m, |m,   :- .s, |d     :s,   |m,   :—
 † of   our    Lord,     Trum - pet, harp, † and   psal - t'ry  bring,
 † crea - ture join,     Bring your sweet  - est,  † no - blest  song,

|s    :- .f  |m .r  :m .f |m    r    |d    :  .r |m,r.d :r,d.t, |d .r :m .s
 Sing  his   pow'r  † and  ma - jes - ty.  † Re-  joice,   -    -     † re-
|m    :- .r  |d .t, :d .l, |s,  :f,  |m,   :     |       :  .s,  |d    :- .m
 Sound his   praise † with tune - ful  string.           Re-joice,
 Swell the   chor  - rus†  loud  and   long,

|s,f.m :f,m.r |m .f :s  |l     :- .l |s     :- .d |t,    :r    |d    :—   ||
 joice,                  Praise the Lord   † with  cheer - ful  voice.
|m,r.d :r,d.t, |d .r :m |f     :- .f, |m,   :- .m, |s,   :- .f, |m,   :—   ||
```

St. Co. (New.)

AMEN.

Ex. 114. KEY C. *Mainzer.*

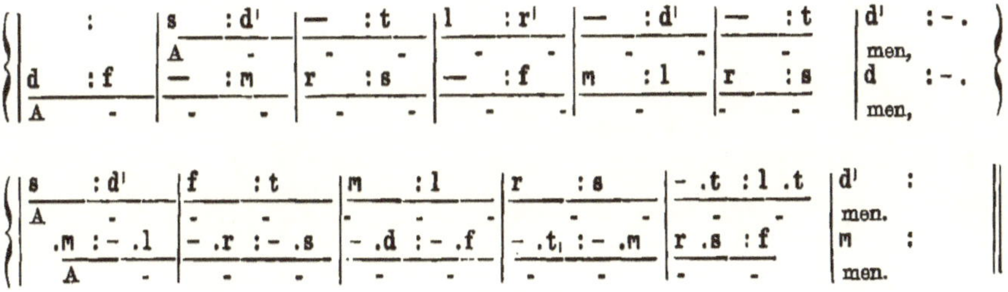

:	s :d'	— :t	l :r'	— :d'	— :t	d' :–.
	A -	- -	- -	- -	-	men,
d :f	— :m	r :s	— :f	m :l	r :s	d :–.
A -	- -	- -	- -	-	- -	men,

s :d'	f :t	m :l	r :s	– .t :l .t	d' :
A -	- -	- - -	- -	- -	men.
.m :– .l	– .r :– .s	– .d :– .f	– .t, :– .m	r .s :f	m :
A -	- -	- -	- -	- -	men.

THE SKYLARK.

Ex. 115. KEY E♭. Words by *Hogg.* M. 96. *A. L. C.*

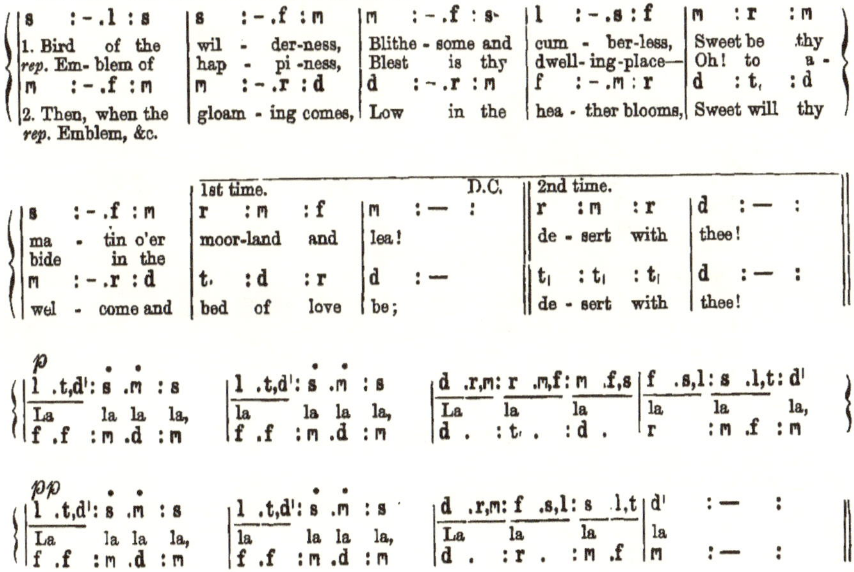

s :– .l :s	s :– .f :m	m :– .f :s	l :– .s :f	m :r :m
1. Bird of the	wil - der-ness,	Blithe - some and	cum - ber-less,	Sweet be thy
rep. Em- blem of	hap - pi -ness,	Blest is thy	dwell- ing-place—	Oh! to a -
m :– .f :m	m :– .r :d	d :– .r :m	f :– .m :r	d :t, :d
2. Then, when the *rep.* Emblem, &c.	gloam - ing comes,	Low in the	hea - ther blooms,	Sweet will thy

	1st time.	D.C.	2nd time.	
s :– .f :m	r :m :f	m :— :	r :m :r	d :— :
ma - tin o'er	moor-land and	lea!	de - sert with	thee!
bide in the				
m :– .r :d	t, :d :r	d :—	t, :t, :t,	d :— :
wel - come and	bed of love	be;	de - sert with	thee!

p

l .t,d' :s .m :s	l .t,d' :s .m :s	d .r,m :r .m,f :m .f,s	f .s,l :s .l,t :d'
La la la la,	la la la la,	La la la	la la la,
f .f :m .d :m	f .f :m .d :m	d . :t, . :d .	r :m .f :m

pp

l .t,d' :s .m :s	l .t,d' :s .m :s	d .r,m :f .s,l :s .l,t	d' :— :
La la la la,	la la la la,	La la la	la
f .f :m .d :m	f .f :m .d :m	d . :r . :m .f	m :— :

St. Co. (New.)

IN SWEET MUSIC.

Ex. 116. KEY C. *Gebhardi.*

| : | : | s :l .t | d' :d' | d' :t .l | s :— | l :s .f | m :
| In sweet mu - sic | is such art, | is such art,
| d :r .m | f :f | f :m .r | m :d | l :s .f | m :— | f :m .r | d :
| In sweet mu - sic,

| r :— | r :f | m : | : | : | t :s | r' :— | — :—
| Kill - ing | care, | kill - ing | care,
| t, :— | t, :r | d : .m | m :d | s :— | — :— | — :s | f :r
| and grief of | heart, | and grief of

| — :— | d' :l | m' :— | — :— | — :l | r' :— | — :s | d' :—
| kill - ing | care, | and grief | of heart,
| l :— | — :— | — :— | s :l .s | f :— | f :s .f | m :— | m :f .m
| heart, | Fall a - | sleep, fall a - | sleep, fall a -

| — :d' | t :t | d' :— | | l :— | s :f | m :— | m :—
| and grief of | heart, | Fall a - | sleep or
| r :m .f | s :f | m :— | : | f :— | m :r | d :— | d :—
| sleep, or hear - ing | die,

| r :— | r :— | d :— | : ||
| hear - ing | die.
| d :— | t, :— | d :— | : ||

HALLELUJAH.

Ex. 117. KEY D. *Mainzer.*

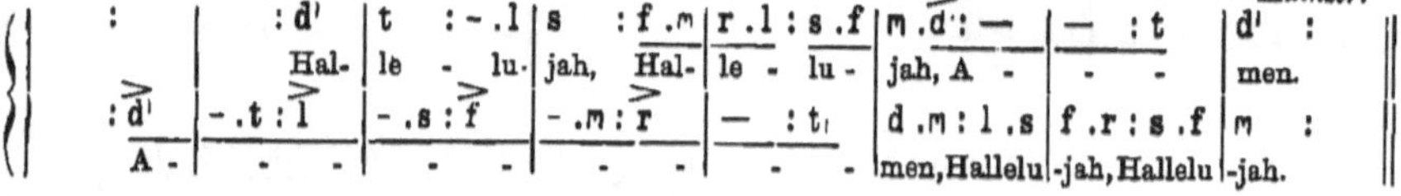

:	:d'	t :- .l	s :f .m	r .l :s .f	m .d' :—	— :t	d' :	
Hal-	le - lu-	jah, Hal-	le - lu -	jah, A -	- -	men.	
:d'	- .t :l	- .s :f	- .m :r	— :t,	d .m :l .s	f .r :s .f	m :	
A -	- -	- -	- -	- -	men, Hallelu	-jah, Hallelu	-jah.	

HALLELUJAH, AMEN.

Ex. 118. KEY A. *Mainzer.*

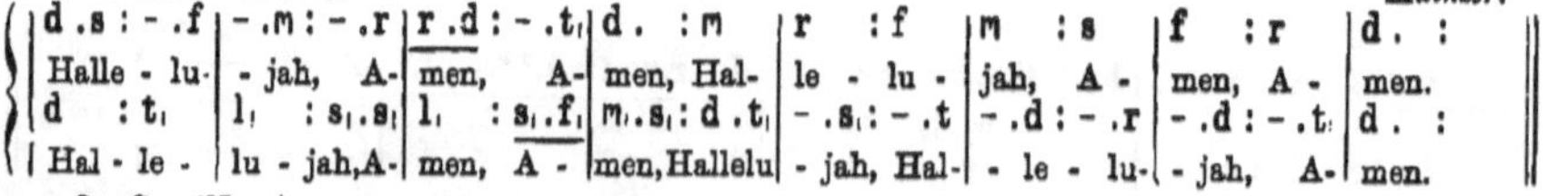

d .s :- .f	- .m :- .r	r .d :- .t,	d . :m	r :f	m :s	f :r	d . :	
Halle - lu-	- jah, A-	men, A-	men, Hal-	le - lu -	jah, A -	men, A -	men.	
d :t,	l, :s, .s,	l, :s, .f,	m, .s, :d .t,	- .s, :- .t	- .d :- .r	- .d :- .t,	d . :	
Hal - le -	lu - jah, A-	men, A -	men, Hallelu	- jah, Hal-	- le - lu-	- jah, A-	men.	

St. Co. (New.)

ART THOU POOR.

Ex. 119. KEY A. *F. L. R.*

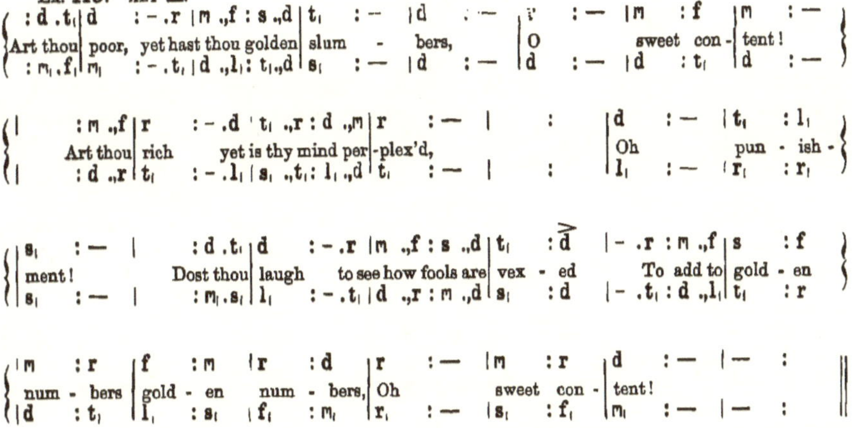

:d .t, |d :- .r |m .,f :s .,d |t, :- |d :- |r :- |m :f |m :-
Art thou poor, yet hast thou golden slum - bers, O sweet con - tent!
:m,.f, |m, :- .t, |d .,l, :t, .,d |s, :- |d :- |d :- |d :t, |d :-

| :m .,f |r :- .d |t, .,r :d .,m |r :- | : |d :- |t, :l,
Art thou rich yet is thy mind per -plex'd, Oh pun - ish -
| :d .,r |t, :- .l, |s, .,t, :l, .,d |t, :- | : |l, :- |r, :r,

|s, :- | :d .t, |d :- .r |m .,f :s .,d |t, :d |- .r :m .,f |s :f
ment! Dost thou laugh to see how fools are vex - ed To add to gold - en
|s, :- | :m,.s, |l, :- .t, |d .,r :m .,d |s, :d |- .t, :d .,l, |t, :r

|m :r |f :m |r :d |r :- |m :r |d :- |- :
num - bers gold - en num - bers, Oh sweet con - tent!
|d :t, |l, :s, |f, :m, |r, :- |s, :f, |m, :- |- :

WHERE DO THE FAIRIES DWELL?

Ex. 120. KEY C. *A. L. C.*

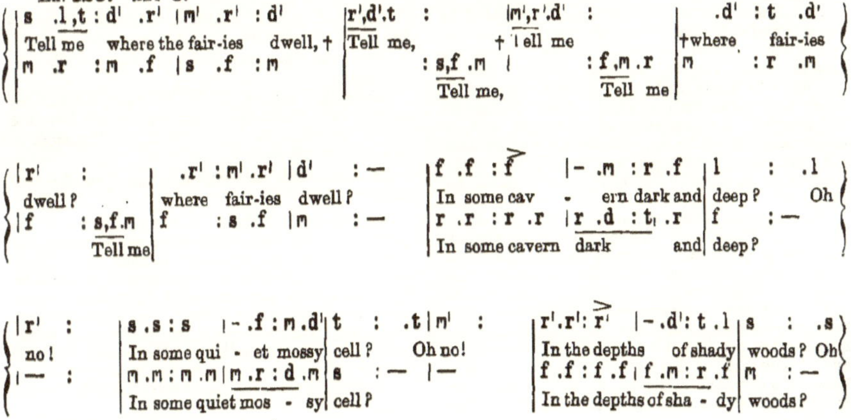

|s .l ,t :d' .r' |m' .r' :d' |r',d'.t : |m',r'.d' : | .d' :t .d'
Tell me where the fair-ies dwell, † Tell me, † Tell me †where fair-ies
|m .r :m .f |s .f :m | :s,f .m | :f ,m .r |m :r .m
Tell me, Tell me

|r' : | .r' :m' .r' |d' :- |f .f :f |- .m :r .f |l : .l
dwell? where fair-ies dwell? In some cav - ern dark and deep? Oh
|f :s,f.m |f :s .f |m :- |r .r :r .r |r .d :t, .r |f :-
Tell me In some cavern dark and deep?

|r' : |s .s :s |- .f :m .d' |t : .t |m' : |r'.r' :r' |- .d' :t .l |s : .s
no! In some qui - et mossy cell? Oh no! In the depths of shady woods? Oh
|- : |m .m :m .m |m .r :d .m |s :- |- |f .f :f .f |f .m :r .f |m :-
In some quiet mos - sy cell? In the depths of sha - dy woods?

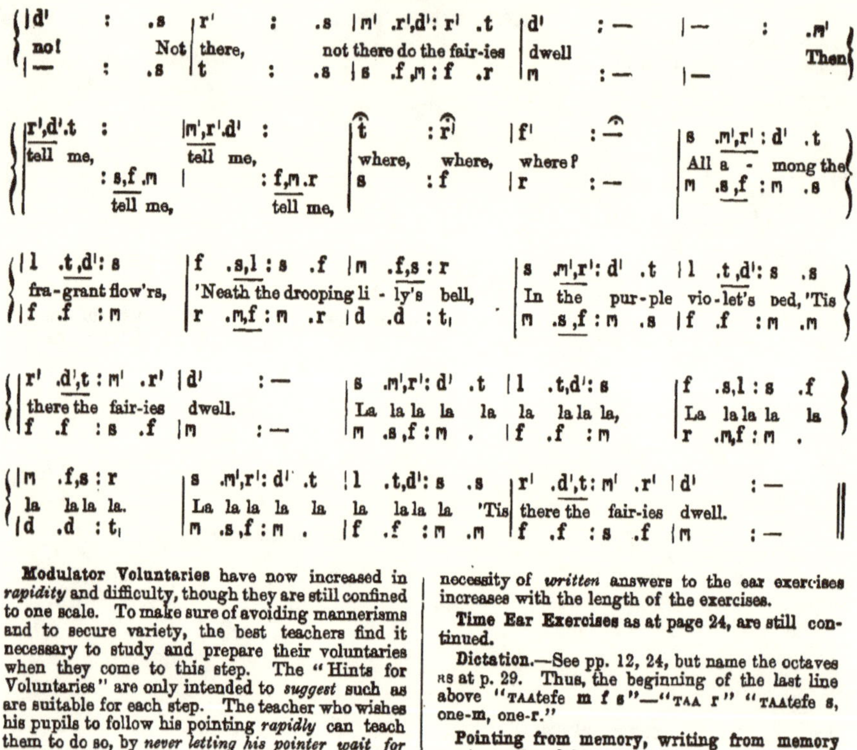

|d' : .s |r' : .s |m' .r',d' : r' .t |d' :— |— : .m'
no! Not there, not there do the fair-ies dwell Then
|— : .s |t : .s |s .f,m : f .r |m :— |—

|r',d'.t : |m',r'.d' : |t : r' |f' :— |s .m',r' : d' .t
tell me, tell me, where, where, where? All a - mong the
: s,f .m | : f,m .r |s : f |r :— |m .s,f : m .s
tell me, tell me,

|l .t,d' : s |f .s,l : s .f |m .f,s : r |s .m',r' : d' .t |l .t,d' : s .s
fra-grant flow'rs, 'Neath the drooping li - ly's bell, In the pur-ple vio-let's bed, 'Tis
|f .f : m |r .m,f : m .r |d .d : t, |m .s,f : m .s |f .f : m .m

|r' .d',t : m' .r' |d' :— |s .m',r' : d' .t |l .t,d' : s |f .s,l : s .f
there the fair-ies dwell. La la la la la la la la la, La la la la la
|f .f : s .f |m :— |m .s,f : m . |f .f : m |r .m,f : m .

|m .f,s : r |s .m',r' : d' .t |l .t,d' : s .s |r' .d',t : m' .r' |d' :— ||
la la la la. La la la la la la la la la 'Tis there the fair-ies dwell.
|d .d : t, |m .s,f : m . |f .f : m .m |f .f : s .f |m :— ||

Modulator Voluntaries have now increased in *rapidity* and difficulty, though they are still confined to one scale. To make sure of avoiding mannerisms and to secure variety, the best teachers find it necessary to study and prepare their voluntaries when they come to this step. The "Hints for Voluntaries" are only intended to *suggest* such as are suitable for each step. The teacher who wishes his pupils to follow his pointing *rapidly* can teach them to do so, by *never letting his pointer wait for them.*

Ear Exercises.—A few two-part Ear Exercises, as in the "Hints," can now be wisely introduced, but only to quick and observant classes. To others each "part" of the exercise will serve as a separate exercise. When the great majority of the class do not follow the ear exercises with pleasure, the teacher goes back to earlier steps,—continually reminding his pupils, not by words, but by examples and illustrations, of the *mental effects* of particular tones, and continually urging them to notice the *first* tone of the exercise after the "prelude." The necessity of *written* answers to the ear exercises increases with the length of the exercises.

Time Ear Exercises as at page 24, are still continued.

Dictation.—See pp. 12, 24, but name the octaves as at p. 29. Thus, the beginning of the last line above "TAAtefe **m f s**"—"TAA **r**" "TAAtefe **s**, one-**m**, one-**r**."

Pointing from memory, writing from memory as at pp. 12 and 24.

Elementary Certificate Slips being given to the pupils, they are *now*,—that is six weeks before the close of the class,—constantly coming up for individual examination in one requirement or the other, first passing the examination of the assistants, and then that of the teacher himself. The examination is conducted sometimes before the whole class, sometimes privately, according to the convenience of teacher and pupils. All the requirements must be done within six weeks, else the examination begins again.

QUESTIONS FOR WRITTEN OR ORAL EXAMINATION.

DOCTRINE.

1 What is a "hold"—What does it signify?

2 What is the advantage of a knowledge of chords to the singer?

3 Describe the normal position of a chord?

4 What are the root—the third—and fifth of a chord?

5 What is the difference between the *a* position and the normal position of a chord?

6 What is the *b* position of a chord?—the *c* position?

7 Which of these positions is the most acceptable to the ear? and how are the other positions used?

8 What does the name "Constitution" of chords refer to?

9 How do we figure the *omission* of the third?—of the fifth?—of the root?

10 How do we figure the *doubling* of the third?—and fifth?—and *trebling* of the root?

11 Which of the three tones of a chord is most easily *omitted* without notice?

12 What quality of a chord is lost by omitting the third?—the root?

13 Which tone of a chord can be easily doubled because it is the least noticed?—and which because it is the most characteristic and important?

14 In the resolution of S into D where does *te* go?—*soh*?—*ray*?

15 Why is S called the Dominant?

16 Describe the chord ⁴S

17 What do you yourselves feel to be the mental effect of low *lah*?—of high *lah*?

18 What is the effect of high *fah*? of low *fah*?

19 How does greater speed of movement modify the mental effect of *doh*, *me*, and *soh*?—of *ray*, *fah*, *lah*, *te*? Mention any examples that occur to you.

20 Which are the strong tones of the scale, and which the leaning tones? Which have the strongest leaning tendency?

21 What are the successive tones of the scale descending in pitch?—What are they ascending?

22 How many vibrations in a second give the standard pitch tone, middle C?—In what part of men's voices is this C? Where is it in women's voices?

23 Describe the manner in which tunes are pitched from the standard scale.

24 What variable circumstances affect our power of recollecting a tone in absolute pitch?

25 What pitch tone stands at about the middle range of female and children's voices?—of male voices?

26 How do we judge whether an uncultivated voice belongs to the contralto or bass class of voices, or to the soprano or tenor?

27 What is the easy compass of the soprano voice?—of the contralto?

28 What is the easy compass of the tenor voice?—of the bass?

29 Among uncultivated voices, which part of a man's voice is most commonly found to be neglected?—of a woman's?

30 The octave marks of a tune being taken from *doh*, how do we know which *doh* is to be without an octave mark? In key G how would the *lah* below the key-tone corresponding with the pitch E be marked? In key C how would the *me* above the key-tone corresponding with the pitch E be marked?

31 With what octave marks are the bass and tenor parts written?

32 In speaking of octave marks for the purposes of dictation, how do you distinguish the lower *doh* from the higher *doh*?—the lower C_2 from the higher C^i.

33 If we want fresh breath on a strong pulse, where do we take away the time of the breathing? And if on a weak pulse?

34 Write down all the rules for breathing places which you can remember.

35 What is meant by "Expression" in music?—and what are the elements of tone chiefly employed in it?

36 In using the type-marks for expression of words what has to be first settled in the mind before those marks obtain their true meaning?

37 What, *then*, is the meaning of common type?—*Italic* type?—SMALL CAPITALS?

38 What is the *writing* mark for Italics?—for small capitals?

39 How are ascending passages and continuous or repeated tones naturally treated for expression?

40 What other means are there, besides taking breath, of separating and distinguishing musical phrases one from the other while one sings?

41 What is the "great break of register" in the voice?

42 Where does it occur in men's voices?—in women's? Between what tones in absolute pitch is it always found?

43 Where does the "small register," peculiar to women's voices, commence?

44 What are the three commonly used "optional tones" between the thick and thin registers?

45 Describe or write the exercise by by means of which men come to perceive their thin register.

46 Why is forceful action of the larynx necessary to the strengthening of the thin register? What syllable puts the organs of voice into the best position for this kind of vigorous effort?

47 Why is it necessary to employ the strengthening exercise in various keys?

48 Describe the process of using the strengthening exercise, Ex. 104.

49 What is a metronome?

50 What is the meaning of M. 60. placed in the title of a tune?

51 How is the rate of very quick six-pulse measure marked?

52 Why is it necessary to have exercises for sustaining a uniform rate of movement?

53 Describe the exercises for attaining this power.

54 Why should the rate indicated by M. 60 be fixed in the mind?

55 Describe the exercise for teaching this.

56 What is the name for a silence on the first half of a pulse?—for the second half?

57 How is a three-quarter-pulse tone indicated in the Sol-fa notation?

58 How is the pulse divided into three-quarters-and-a-quarter indicated in the time-names? What are its two larger relatives?

59 How is the pulse divided into two quarters-and-a-half indicated in the Tonic Sol-fa notation and in the time-names; What are its larger relatives?

60 How is the pulse divided into a half-and-two-quarters indicated in the Tonic Sol-fa notation and the time names? What are its larger relatives?

61 What is syncopation? How does it affect the next following strong pulse?

62 What is there in *tune* like syncopation in Time? In what style should syncopation be sung?

63 What is chanting?

64 Describe an Anglican single chant—a double chant.

65 What is the most important rule in chanting?

66 Why should a student of chanting begin by chanting hymns?

67 By what marks are the words divided for chanting, so as to separate the words of the reciting-tone from those of the cadence? How is TAA or any division of TAA indicated in the printing of the words? How is *SAA* indicated? *SAATAI*?

68 What relation is there between the rate at which the pulses of the cadence move and those of the recitation?

69 What is the process of teaching chanting recitations?

70 What are the new Consonances introduced at this step, distinguishing the thirds from the fifths?

71 What is the partial-dissonance, and its effect upon the mind?

72 What new prepared dissonance have we in this step?

73 What dissonance is considered the model of unprepared discords? On what kind of pulse does it most commonly occur, and what is its favourite melodic preparation?

74 Describe what is meant by the similar motion of two parts in relation to each other,—by contrary motion,—by oblique motion.

75 Which kind of relative motion is the least wearying to the ear? Which is the most exciting?

76 What is meant by imitations of melodic figure?

77 What is meant by imitation of rhythmic form?

78 What is meant by harmonic sequence.

PRACTICE.

79 Hold a steady tone with one breath for a quarter of a minute.

80 Sing, softly and pleasantly, to the Italian *Laa*, Ex. 82 in keys B and D.

81 Name, pulse by pulse, the chords with positions and constitutions in Exs. 85 and 86.

82 Sol-faa from memory any example you please, shewing the mental effect of high *fah*,—low *fah*,—low *lah*,—high *lah*.

83 Give from memory an example of the manner in which speed of movement modifies mental effect.

84 Repeat the names of the scale tones upward, — downward, — repeat the strong tones upward and downward,—repeat the leaning tones upward and downward.

85 Strike, by the help of a tuning-fork, the pitch tone C' (for women's voices C', for men's voices unmarked C,) and run down the standard scale of pitch.

86 Pitch the key D,—G,—A,—F.

87 Strike from memory the pitch note C' (for women) and C unmarked (for men).

88 Are the best tones of your voice *above* G (for women and children) or G, (for men) or are they below that tone?

89 What is the easy compass of your voice?

90 For which of the four common parts in music is your voice best fitted?

91 Write the Soprano of a tune in key C with the proper octave marks. Do the same in key B.

92 Write down "three G" — "G three" — "two *ray*" — "*ray* two" — "unmarked G."

93 Write the letters by which you would indicate in the title of a tune that it is to be sung by two Sopranos and a Contralto,—by Soprano, Tenor, and Bass,—by Soprano, Contralto, and Tenor.

94 Mark breathing places, considering the phrasing only, to Exs. 100, 101, 98, and 115.

95 Mark breathing places for emphasis in Exs. 115 and 120.

96 Mark breathing places to correspond with the sense of the words in Ex. 116.

97 Mark with your pen underneath the words the style of "expression" you think it best to give to them in Exs. 112, 119, and 120.

98 Sing to words any one of the exercises from 97 to 103 as required, page 25, question 46.

99 Ditto with exercises 110 to 120.

100 Sing to *laa* the *lah* and the *lah*, to any *doh* the teacher gives you.

101 Sing to *laa* the *fah* and the *fah*, to any *doh* the teacher gives

102 Sing A in the thin register of your voice,—in the thick register.

103 In the key of C what are the Sol-fa names of your three principal optional tones?—in the key of G?—in the key of D?—in the key of A?

104 Sing to *koo* Ex. 104 with your thin register in key D.

105 Taatai with accent a four-pulse measure, at the rate of M. 60 from memory,—at the rate of M. 120,—at the rate of M. 90.

106 Taatai with accent *eight* four-pulse measures, sustaining the rate of M. 60,—the rate of M. 90.

107 Taatai from memory any one of the Exs. 105 to 107 chosen by the examiner, the 1st measure being named.

108 Taatai the upper part of any one of the Exs. 113, 115, or 120 chosen by the examiner.

109 Taatai in tune the upper part of any one of the Exs. 111, 112, 114, 116, 117, 118, or 119 chosen by the examiner.

110 Recite in correct time any two of the recitations in the words to Ex. 86 chosen by the examiner.

111 Show examples of the new consonances introduced at this step.

112 Ditto of the semi-dissonance.

113 Ditto of the new prepared dissonances.

114 Ditto of *fah* against *soh* unprepared.

115 Shew an example of similar motion between parts, — of contrary motion,—of oblique motion.

116 Shew an example of rhythmic imitation,—of melodic imitation, — of harmonic sequence.

117 Follow the examiner's pointing in a new voluntary containing all the tones of the common scale but no difficulties of time greater than those of the *second* step.

118 Point and sol-faa on the modulator from memory any one of the following seven exercises, 97, 98, 99, 100, 103, 111, 112, chosen by the examiner.

119 Write from memory any other of these seven exercises chosen by the examiner.

120 Tell which is *lah*,—which is *fah*, as directed, page 25, question 56.

121 Tell what tone of all the scale is *skaa*, as at page 25, question 57.

122 Taatai any rhythm of two four-pulse measures belonging to this step, which the examiner shall laa to you, see page 25, question 58.

123 Taatai-in-tune any rhythm of two four-pulse measures belonging to this step, which the examiner sol-faas to you, see page 25, question 59.

FOURTH STEP.

To perform Exercises for Strengthening the Chest, securing Purity of Tone, and perfect Blending of "Parts." To know by ear the Chords of the Subdominant, Dominant-Seventh, Supertonic, Leading-tone, Submediant, and Mediant in the Major Mode. To observe Cadences. To remember the structure of the Scale in its conjunct intervals. To perceive Transition to the First Sharp and the First Flat Keys, its mechanism and its mental effect. To perceive Chromatic Resolution. To distinguish Cadence, Passing, and Extended Transition. To Pitch Tunes. To learn correct Recitation, with special regard to the consonants. To learn the art of Chanting. To become familiar with the silent quarter-pulse and the sounding thirds of a pulse. To learn the art of Beating Time. To strengthen the Thin Register in Men. To recognise and strengthen the Thick Register in Women. To Blend the Registers. To understand Part-pulse Dissonances. To observe various points of Musical Form.

Ex. 121. Chest and Klang. These exercises are now united. The lower part is to be sung as a chest exercise, always to the word "skaa-laa," and on one breath. When taken at the rate of M. 50 the pupil will have to economise his breath for 20 seconds. Those who sing the upper part may take breath at the places marked. They must deliver the first measure very softly *(pp)*, the second measure softly *(p)*, the third measure with a medium force of voice *(m)*, and the fourth measure with full force of voice *(f)*. As soon as the exercise is thus sung, the singers must change parts for the sake of rest and variety, and this is reckoned one performance of the exercise. Let the exercise be performed thus: *first time* in key C, the upper voices "slurring" each measure to the forward Italian "laa," at the rate of M. 60. *Second time*, the same in key D. The teacher will pass from key to key as directed, p. 33. *Third time*, in key C♯, the upper voices singing to the staccato "koo," at M. 50. *Fourth time*, the same in key D♯. *Fifth time*, in key D, the upper voices laa-ing as above, at M. 50. Laa-ing is used here as a rest before the last effort. *Sixth time*, in key E, the upper voices sol-faaing, at M. 70. Sol-faaing is used here to make sure of correctness of tune in the highest tones. The teacher will be careful not to carry the voices any higher than is here indicated, for, especially in an exercise with increasing force, he may cause the first or thick register of men to be strained, and unfit them for changing the register on the optional tones. It is remarkable that the woman's voice changes into the small register just where, an octave lower, the man's voice changes into the thin register. But women do not commonly use optional tones below the G'. Their voices, however, require equal care to avoid straining. Basses may use this thin register for d' in keys D♯, D, and E.

KEYS C, D, C♯, D♯, D, E. Chest and Klang Exercise. M. 70, 60, and 50.*

```
pp                        †p                         †m                          f
|d .m :s .m |d .m :s .m |f .l :d'.l |f .l :d'.l |s .t :r'.t |s .t :r'.t |d'  :—  |—  :—  ||
 Skaa   -     -     -     -    -    -    -    -    -    -    -    -    -     laa.
|d    :—    |—    :—    |f    :—    |—    :—    |s    :—    |—    :—    |d'  :—  |—  :—  ||
```

Ex. 122. Tuning Exercise. To be used with the same processes as described at p. 14, except that the parts cannot be changed. Exs. 123 to 126 are to be employed in the same way, without words.

KEY E. Tuning Exercise for three equal voices.

```
|d'  :t   |d'  .—  |     :    |     :    |d'  :—  |t   :—  |d'  :—  |—  :—  ||
|m   :r   |m   :—  |     :    |l    :—   |—   :—  |f   :—  |m   :—  |—  :—  ||
|d   :s,  |d   :—  |f    :—   |—    :—   |f,  :—  |s,  :—  |d   :—  |—  :—  ||
```

The Chord Fah.—The tones f, l, and d sung together form the chord of *Fah*. This chord considered separately and in itself is exactly the same as the chords D and S. But when placed in relation with those chords,—that is, when starting from the fifth *below* the first or leading chord D, just as the chord S starts from the fifth *above*,—it obtains a distinct mental effect. See p. 20. In Ex. 123 there

* As to style of rendering, see page 81, close of first paragraph.

are two cases of F in its *a* position. Let the exercise be softly laad, F being dwelt upon longer than its proper time, and let the pupils decide its mental effect. If D is called the *Resting* chord and S the *Moving* chord, F may perhaps be called the *Serious* chord. When D is called the Tonic and S the Dominant, F is called the Subdominant. It is much used before these chords in the Tonic close or cadence. See Ex. 123. It is also much used in its *b* position. See Exs. 124, 125, and 126.

The Chord Seven-Soh.—When **f** intrudes as a dissonance into the chord of *Soh*, the chord thus modified is called *Seven-Soh*, and written ⁷S. The figure 7 is used because the **f** commonly occurs at the interval of a seventh above the **s**; but it may occur at the interval of a second beneath the s. There is often an additional octave (making a fourteenth or a ninth) between the dissonance **f** and its resisting tone **s**. When this is the case the dissonant effect is very slight. The dissonant **f** follows, both in its preparation and resolution, the rules named in the paragraph "**f** against **s**," page 36. Let the pupils softly *laa* again Ex. 123, lingering and listening on ⁷S and its resolution.

Ambiguity of Chords.—Observe that there is nothing in the structure and intervals of the first phrase of Ex. 123 to prevent the ear interpreting the chords as : S | S : D | S. But according to the principle named at page 20, the ear naturally prefers to regard the first chord which rules it as a principal chord, and has, therefore, no difficulty in interpreting the first phrase as : D | D : F | D. Except for this pre-occupation of the ear by the first chord which is emphatically struck, D, S, and F are ambiguous. But there is no ambiguity in ⁷S. It cannot be mistaken for any other chord. It decides the key with an absolute certainty which S does not possess.

Major, Minor, and Diminished Chords. — The chords hitherto described have a major or larger third at the bottom. Chords of this kind are by far the most acceptable to the ear. Their tones have a perfect agreement in every respect—a full sonorousness. But for contrast and for variety of mental effect, chords which have a lesser or minor third at the bottom are necessary. The minor chords of the scale are R, L, and M. Let the pupil point them out upon the modulator. They are glad of doubled thirds, even in the *b* position, p. 27. Far less sonorous than even the minor chords is the chord *Te*, for it has an imperfect or diminished fifth.

The Grave Ray.—When the tone **r** is required to tune with **f** (as **m** tunes with **s**, and **l** with **d**'), and when it is required to tune with **l** (as **d** tunes with **s**, and **f** with **d**'), the ear of singers, and of quartet players on stringed instruments, naturally seeks to produce the **r** a little lower than when it is required to tune with **s** and **t**. When we wish to distinguish this lower or "grave" form of **r** from its commoner form we call it *Rah*,—to make it correspond, in its vowel sound, with *Fah* and *Lah*. The interval between *rah* and *ray* is called a komma. General Thompson, who first drew attention to this point in his "Just Intonation," says that in the chord ⁷S the acute form of ray is used because it is more important that it should agree with the root and third of a chord than with the dissonant seventh. His "Enharmonic Organ" proves this.

The Chord Ray, r, f, l, (more properly called *Rah*) is the most used of the minor chords. It frequently occurs in its *a* position when the bass moves thus— | **r** : **s**, | **d** ‖ But it is most commonly found in its *b* position. See Ex. 124. Let the pupils laa this exercise, dwelling on R*b*, and listening to it. When F is called the "Serious" chord, R, from its similarity of effect, especially in its *b* position, is called the *semi-serious* chord.

The Chord Te, t,, r, f.—The root and fifth of this chord form the "Partial-dissonance" described at page 36, and follow the rule of "Resolution" there described. This chord is much used as a "Substitutional Chord" for ⁷S. In many places in which there is not room for ⁷S, or where ⁷S does not allow so pleasant a melodic flow in the parts, this much weaker chord is substituted. It is chiefly used in its *b* position, which is less harsh than the *a* position. Listen well to T*b* in Ex. 125. See T*a* in Ex. 126. T, in its relation to S and ⁷S, is called the *weak moving* chord.

The Chord Lah, l,, d, m, has its chief use in the minor mode, which will be described in the next step. *Apart from this*, it is used almost exclusively in its *a* position, L*b* being seldom seen, and L*c* never. L*a* is used, interchangeably with F*b*, when the tone **l** is wanted in the bass, and when a minor chord is required to set off the clearer sonorousness of the major. Let Ex. 126 be laad and the L dwelt upon. Notice that S can resolve into L, as can also ⁷S and T,—for special effect. L, from its proper mental effect, is called the *sorrowful* chord.

The Chord M, m, s, t, though in itself as good as any other minor chord, for some reason not yet sufficiently explained is rarely used in Modern Music.

Perhaps the mental effect of its fifth contradicts too strongly the mental effects of its root and third. The tone f in ^7S also contradicts the mental effect of the rest of the chord, but it is a decided dissonance, and is easily resolved downwards. M is called the *unmeaning* chord.

The Chord ^7R has, in it, the dissonance d against r with which we are already familiar in the less-used chord ^4S. See pp. 21, 27. The dissonating d is prepared and resolved in the same way, in this chord also. ^7R*b* is much used in closes, as a "substitutional chord" for F. Listen to it in Ex. 126.

For fuller explanations of the habits of these chords, reference should be made to "The Commonplaces of Music" and "How to observe Harmony." We can only attempt here to awaken such an interest in the subject, as will lead the singer to further study. A thorough knowledge of the nature and meaning of the music he sings, both heightens the pleasure of the singer, and gives him confidence in striking his tones. This *intelligent* singing is what we are most anxious to promote.*

The Mental Effects of Chords are much governed by the natural effect of that tone which is heard in the bass, especially if it is doubled. But the chief source of mental effect in a chord is its root. It follows therefore that the clearest mental effect of a chord is that which it gives in its *a* position. It then best developes the proper mental effect of its root. This should be shown by experiment.

Ex. 123. KEY **G.** Tuning Exercise, as above.

```
|s  |m :l  |s  :- ||s  |m :l  |r  :f  |m :- ||
|m  |d :f  |m  :- ||t, |d :d  |t  :r  |d :- ||
|d  |d :f, |d  :- ||s, |d :f, |s, :s, |d :- ||
```

'Be hold-how good-and HOW | PLEASANT IT IS — || 'For brethren-to dwell 'to | gether in u ni ty —

As the | dew of Hermon — || And-as-the dew-that-de scendod-up on 'the | moun — tains of Zion —

. 'For there-the Lord 'com | manded the blessing — || Ev en | life for ev er more —

. 'The grace-of-our Lord — | Je sus Christ — || Be — | with you all A men —

Ex. 124. KEY **A.** Tuning Exercise, as above.

```
|m  |f  :r  |t, :- ||d  |l, :f  |m  :r  |d :- ||
|d  |l, :l, |s, :- ||s, |l, :d  |d  :t, |d :- ||
|d  |f, :f, |s, :- ||m, |f, :l, |s, :s, |d :- ||
```

'The Lord — | bless — thee — || And — | keep — — — thee —

. 'The Lord make-his face . | shine up on-thee — || And be | gra cious un to thee —

. 'The Lord-lift up-his counte nance-up | on — thee — || and — | give — thee — peace —

Ex. 125. KEY **A.** Tuning Exercise, as above.

```
|m  |m :f  |s  :- ||s  |f  .m.r|m  :r  |d :- ||
|d  |d :d  |t, :- ||d  |t, :d   |d  :t, |d :- ||
|d  |d :l, |s, :- ||m, |r, :d,  |s, :s, |d :- ||
```

Ho every one-that thirsteth 'come | ye to-the waters — || . And he-that hath-no money . | come ye buy and eat — || . Yea come buy | wine and milk — || without — | money and-with out — price —

. . Wherefore do-ye spend money 'for that-which | is not bread — || . and-your labour for | that which satis fieth not — || . . Hearken diligently unto me 'and eat-ye | that-which is good — || 'and let-your soul 'de | light it self in fatness —

. 'In cline-your ear 'and | come unto me — || Hear — | and your soul shall live — || Seek-ye-the Lord . while-He | may be found — || Call ye-up | on Him while He-is near —

Ex. 126. KEY **A.** Tuning Exercise, as before.

```
|m  |s :f  |m  :- ||f  |f  :m  |r  :r  |d :- ||
|d  |m :r  |d  :- ||d  |r  :d  |d  :t, |d :- ||
|d  |d :s, |l, :- ||l, |t, :d  |f, :s, |d :- |
```

Now unto | him-that is able — || . 'to do-exceeding-A BUNDANT LY 'a bove | all-that we ask or think —

. 'Ac cording to-the power 'that | worketh in us — || . 'unto him-be glory-in-the church . | by Christ Je — sus —

THROUGH — | OUT ALL AGES — || world-with out | end — A — men —

* For dogmatic summary of the subject see "Mus. Theory," Book V.

Ex 127. Name, pulse by pulse, the chords with their positions and constitutions, of Exs 122 to 126.

Cadences.—It has already been noticed (p. 9) that music naturally divides itself into short portions or phrases. No one can sing over a tune without also observing that several such phrases together naturally form a larger divison of the melody, and that these larger divisions close in such a manner as conveys to the mind with more or less completeness, a feeling of rest. These resting points in a tune are called cadences. The teacher can sol-faa several melodies, and ask his pupils to hold up their hands, or make some other signal, when he comes to the natural points of rest. These cadences *cut* the tune into larger portions which we call *Sections*. These Sections correspond with lines in poetry. When harmony is added to melody, the cadences become more marked and decisive, and the chords move towards these points of rest in a very clear and marked manner. Properly speaking a cadence in harmony consists of the two last chords, but other chords approaching such a cadence are very carefully marshalled. The principal cadence is that of the Tonic. Listen to it in its various approaches in both cadences of Ex. 86, and 123, and in the second cadence of Exs. 85, 124, 125, and 126. Notice that the chords F, S, D, contain all the tones of the scale, so that when these three chords proceed to a cadence it is as though the whole scale were summoned to do homage to its Tonic. Among these Tonic cadences however is one in which the Dominant (S) is omitted, and there is nothing but the progression of the Sub-dominant (F) to the Tonic. This is called a plagal cadence. It produces a very solemn effect when the key is well established in the ear. See Ex. 123. The cadence next in importance to the Tonic is that on the Dominant. Listen to it with its various approaches in Exs. 85, 124, and 125. This cadence is felt to be one of expectancy as well as of rest. The only other cadence to be here noticed is that on L, just where from the common habits of cadences D would be expected. This we call the Surprise cadence. Listen to it in Ex. 126.

C Positions.—The *c* position (p. 26) of chords is chiefly used in D*c*, as the third-last chord of a cadence. See Exs. 85, and 124. There is this great peculiarity about the third position of D, that it asserts the key very strongly, for while the chord itself is the Tonic, the Dominant of the key is allowed the emphasis and importance which belongs to the bass tone of a chord. When the cadence moves thus, F, D*c*, S, D, it is as though the music in coming to a close swung like a pendulum from Sub-dominant to Dominant, passing through the point of rest—the Tonic—to which it finally returns. The *c* position of chords is in its own nature unsonorous and partially dissonant, the ear is not satisfied that any other chords should use it except those on the Tonic, Dominant, and Sub-dominant, It commonly has some apology in the melodic motion of the bass. It is either "passing," or "continuing," or "accented and moving stepwise."

Constitution of ^{7}S and Minor Chords.—(Compare p. 27.) Differing from consonant major chords, ^{7}S allows its third to be *omitted*, because by the help of its seventh, there still remains a third in the chord. Minor chords also differ from major chords in allowing their third to be doubled in the *b* position, because as the minor chords are in themselves somewhat harsh and unsonorous, additional sweetness improves them.

The Steps of the Scale.—We have now learnt the complete *common scale of music*, and have seen that these seven *peculiarly related* tones produce certain effects on the mind *by virtue* of that relationship. We have seen also that these mental effects repeat themselves in "Replicates" or Octaves.*

The pupils should now be led to observe the Steps, from one tone to the next, of this scale. The teacher may laa the scale and ask his pupils to tell by ear where the tones lie closest to each other. They will quickly see that the two *Little Steps*, are between **m f** and **t, d.** They will not be able to perceive by ear but they may be told, as a mathematical and musical truth, that there is a difference among the other steps of the scale,—that the three *Greater Steps* are between **d r, f s** and **l t**, and that the two *Smaller Steps* are between **r m** and **s l.** The difference between *ray* and *rah* called a komma, is the difference between a greater and a smaller step. The scale may therefore be described as consisting of two little steps, separated one way by a *couple* of steps, and the other way by a *triplet* of steps. One little step has a "major third" (couple of steps) above it, and the other has what is called a "tritone" (triplet of steps) above it. Doh may be defined as that tone of the scale which stands on a little step with two steps and a little step above. The great characteristics of **d** are, first, that one little step *leads up* to it, and second, that the other little step *leads down* to its third above. From **t,** up to **f** we have a major third with little steps above and below

* See fuller analysis of Scale "Mus. Theory," Book I., pp. 5 to 10.

it. From f up to t we have the peculiar interval called a tritone.

Thus t and f become the most marked characteristic tones of the scale. From their mental effects t may be called the *sharp* tone of the scale, and f the *flat* tone of the scale. We shall presently see how the whole aspect of the scale changes whenever t is substituted for a f, or f for a t. It may be worth notice that the interval from t_1 to f is slightly greater than the true Tritone from f to t. Both contain a major third, but one has, in addition, to a *major third* two little steps, and the other one greater step,—and two little steps are larger than one greater step.

Perception of Transition. — Transition is the "passing over" of the music from one key into another. Sometimes, in the course of a tune, the music seems to have elected a new governing or key-tone; and the tones gather, for a time, around this new key-tone in the same relationship and order as around the first. For this purpose one or more new tones are commonly required, and the tones, which do not change their absolute pitch, change, nevertheless, their "mental effect" with the change of key-relationship. To those who have studied the mental effect of each tone, the study of "transition" becomes very interesting. At the call of some single new tone characteristically heard as it enters the music, the other sounds are seen to acknowledge their new ruler, and, suddenly assuming the new offices he requires, to minister in their places around him.

The musical *fact*, thus dogmatically stated, may be set before the minds of pupils in some such such way as the following:—

"Listen to me while I sing to you a tune. I shall 'figure' the first line, and you will tell me what tone that is on which the figure 'eight' falls. The tune begins on s. What is 'eight?'" Teacher sings to figures as below:—

KEY **F.**

:s	s	:f	m	:r	d	:l	s
1.	2.	3.	4.	5.	6.	7.	8.

"Yes, the 'eight' was s. What is the mental effect of s?" The grand or clear note. "Can you tell by your ears, the difference between s and d? Which gives the fullest feeling of *repose*,—is the stronger *resting tone*?" d. I will sing the second line of the tune. Tell me the effect on your minds of the tone which *now* falls to the syllable 'eight.'" Teacher sings as follows:—

:s	d^1	:t	l	:s	s	:fe	s
1.	2.	3.	4.	5.	6.	7.	8.

"Was that s—the grand, clear trumpet-tone, or d the firm, final resting-tone? . . Listen again, while I sing *both* lines, and you compare the two 'eights.'" Teacher sings. "What was the difference between them? . . Yes, the first was s and the second sounded more like d. And yet, let me tell you, the two sounds were exactly the same in pitch. How came the second 'eight' to produce so different an effect on our minds? What made it so much a tone of rest and conclusiveness? . . Let us take the Modulator, and you shall sol-faa the two lines you have heard as I point to them." The teacher points while the pupils sing, but gives the f of the original key where the accidental occurs. Thus:—

:s	d^1	:t	l	:s	s	:f	s

"Was that as before?" No. "But try it thus again. . . Did the s sound like d then? Was it any way different from the other s?" No. "Then what do we want to make s sound like d?" A new tone instead of f. "Very well. Then we will call the new sound fe, and sing it properly. They sol-faa it from the centre column of the Modulator. "You feel that you have *passed over* into a new key."

The same musical fact, in another transition, may be shewn thus:—

"I will *figure* two lines. Tell me what is the mental effect of the first *nine* and of the second *nine*? Each line begins on d. What is *nine*?" The teacher figures without the modulator—

KEY **A.**

:d	f	:m	:r	d	:-	:	t_1	:l_1	:s_1	f_1	:-
1.	2.	3.	4.	5.			6.	7.	8.	9.	

:d	f	:m	:r	d	:-	:	ta_1	:l_1	:s_1	f_1	:-
1.	2.	3.	4.	5.			6.	7.	8.	9.	

The first *nine* had strongly the effect of f; the second had the repose of d. "Yes, but they are both exactly the same tone in absolute pitch! What has altered the mental effect of the second?" You introduced a new tone instead of t_1. "Yes, it was the new tone which changed the effect of f. Then let us call that new tone tau (spelt ta) and sol-faa these two lines from the modulator." They sol-faa. "You feel that we have, as before, *passed over* into a new key, but into a *different* new key."

Distinguishing tones of transition.—When transition is made by means of a new tone instead of f, the mental effect of the new tone is felt to be in contrast with that of the tone blotted out. The desolate tone is changed for a piercing tone, and the *flat* tone of the old key is thrown out to make room for the *sharp* tone of the new. We therefore call fe the sharp distinguishing tone. When transition is made by the introduction of another tone instead of t, it is felt that the sharp piercing tone of the old key has been exchanged for the flat desolate tone of the new key. *Taw* is therefore called the flat distinguishing tone. The teacher will know how to make this evident to the ear of the pupil.

Melodic tendency to transition.—Let the pupils *laa* (*not* sol-faa) from the modulator such a passage as this:—

KEY D.

| d :m.f | s :d' | t.l :s | t.l :s |

| t :— | l :— | s :— | f :— | s |

and they will *feel* that the f sounds unnatural. It is more natural to sing a sound which is "under-leading-tone to s, as t, is to d, a sound which we should call fe. Let them sing it again, using fe, and they will feel that the mental effect of t l s has become that of m r d. The reason is that our ears are so much accustomed to the *two full* "steps" m r and r d leading down to a key-tone, that whenever they perceive similar intervals accented in a similar manner they prefer to interpret them as m r d.

Try the only other interval of two full steps in the scale, l s f, and you will find the same habit of ear, the same tendency of mind to interpret this interval as m r d. Deal with this example as with the other.

KEY D.

| d :m | s :t | d' :l | f :— |

| f.s :l | f.s :l | f :— | s :— |

| l :— | t :— | l ||

St. Co. (New.)

Here t is felt to be the unnatural tone. You want an "over-leading-tone" to l, as f is to m. The ear naturally interprets the constantly repeated f s l as d r m, and desires to make the last three tones m f m. Indeed it may be noticed that the "tritone," as a melodic progression (with its three long steps) is not loved by the ear, and that the lower part of the scale is much preferred to the upper.

Adjacent keys in transition.—Such transitions as have just been studied are called transitions of one remove, because only one change is made in the pitch tones used. When s becomes d the music is said to go into *the first sharp key*. When f becomes d we say that a transition is made into *the first flat key*. Eighty per cent. of all the transitions of music are to one or the other of these two keys, and of them the first sharp key is the one chiefly used in "principal transition," or transition from the principal key of the music. The relation of these two adjacent keys should be very clearly understood by the pupil, and he should be led to notice how the pitch tones change their mental effect. This may be proximately described by the table below.

Piercing	t	*becomes*	Calm	m.
Sorrowful	l	,,	Rousing	r.
Grand	s	,,	Strong	d.
Desolate	f	*is changed for*	Piercing	t.
Calm	m	*becomes*	Sorrowful	l.
Rousing	r	,,	Grand	s.
Strong	d	,,	Desolate	f.

If the teacher has a black-board, it will be well for him to let his pupils construct the new key by the side of the old one in some such way as this:—

d'	f
te	m
lah	r
soh—	d
fah	t,
me	l,
ray	s,
doh	f,

"I have drawn the scale [as at side] and you will see that I have observed carefully the shorter distances between m f and t d'. Let us suppose that our s is changed into d. To represent this I write d on the right of s. What change now takes place in the mental effect of s?" * * "In that case what will l become, and what will be the change of mental effect?" * * "What will t become, and how will it change its effect?" * * "What of m?" * * "What of r?" * * "What of d?" * * "What becomes of f? Is there a Step or a Little Step between d and the tone below it?" * * "What is there between s and f?" . . "Then f is not near enough to the new d to form a proper 'leaning tone.' We therefore banish f from the new key, and use fe instead. This is the principal change of mental effect which occurs. How will you describe it?" Again the teacher may say "Let us suppose that f has become a new d. I will write d on the left hand of f. What shall I write on the left hand of m?—r?—d?—s?—l? What becomes of t?" . . "Yes, the new flat tone is put in its stead."†

Returning Transition.—As a rule all tunes go back again to their principal key, but the returning transition is not always taken in so marked a manner as the principal transition, because the principal key has already a hold on the mind, and the ear easily accepts the slightest hint of a return to it. Commonly also it is in the principal transition that the composer wishes to produce his effect, and in which he therefore makes his chords decisive, and his distinguishing tones emphatic. It is not always so, however, and in hymn-tunes the returning transition is often as beautiful and effective as the principal transition. Let it be carefully noticed that the return to the original key is the same thing in its nature as going to the first flat key, so that a study of the mutual relation of these two keys is the groundwork of all studies of transition. For convenience of memory it is well for the student to draw a diagram of a principal key with its first sharp and first flat keys, and to learn by rote the relations of their notes. Thus let him say aloud "d f, d s; r s, r l; m l, m t; f to t, f d; s d, s r; l r, l m; t to f, t m. It may be interesting to mention that in passing to the first sharp key, the new t requires the old l to be raised a komma to make it into a new r. If it were necessary, this form of the tone might be called *Lay*.

s	d^1	f
	t	m
f—*ta*		
m	l	r
r	s	d
	fe—t_1	
d	f	
t_1	m	l_1
l_1	r	s_1
s_1	d	f_1

Notation of Transition.—Tonic Sol-fa pupils always prefer that their notes should correspond with the mental effects of the tones they represent. We therefore adopt the plan of giving to some tone closely preceding the distinguishing tone, *a double name.* We call it by its name in the old key as well as by that which it assumes in the new, pronouncing the old name slightly and the new name emphatically, thus *M'Lah*, *S'Ray*, *D'Fah*, &c. These we call *bridge-tones*, and write them thus—^{m}l, ^{s}r, ^{d}f. We call this the *Perfect Method* of indicating transition. But when the transition is very brief we write the new t as fe, and the new f as ta. This is called the *Imperfect Method*. The teacher will point on the modulator and teach by pattern such phrases as

|d :m |s :d^1 |^{s}d :t_1 |d
or |d :m |s :d^1 |s :fe |s
and |d :m |s :$^{d^1}$s |f :m |r
or |d :m |s :d^1 |ta :l |s

making the pupils sol-faa in both ways. Occasionally the transition is taken as in Ex. 129 and 123 on a bridge-tone which is *not* common to the two keys. In these cases we write the "better" notation of transition thus:—

|f :$^{fe}t_1$ |d or |t :^{ta}f |m

Signature of Transition.—The signature of the new key is placed over every transition when written according to the perfect method. If it is a sharp key (*i.e.* to the *right* on the modulator) the new tones are named on *the right* of the key name, thus, **A.** t., or (if two removes) **A.** t.m. If it is a flat key (*i.e.* to the *left* on the modulator) the new tones are placed to *the left*, thus, f. **B♭.**, or d.f. **B♭.**, and so on. By this the singer knows that he has a new f or a new t to expect. More distant removes would have their two or three other distinguishing notes similarly placed.

Mental effects of Transition.—The most marked effects of transition arise from the distinguishing tones which are used. Transition to the first sharp key naturally expresses excitement and elevation; that to the first flat key depression and seriousness.

Manual Signs.—It is not advisable to use manual signs in teaching transition, because they are apt to distract attention from the modulator with its beautiful "trinity of keys." The greatest effort should be made to fix the three keys of the modulator in the mind's eye. But if, on occasion, it is wished to indicate transition by manual signs, the teacher may, to indicate transition *to the right* on the modulator, use his *left* hand (which will be to the pupils' right) thus. When with the right hand he reaches a bridge-tone, let him place his left hand close under it, making the sign proper to the new

† See other "presentations of Transition" in "Teacher's Manual," pp. 130 to 133.

key, then withdrawing his right hand, let him proceed to signal the music with his left. He can use the reverse process in the flat transition. Signs could easily be invented for fe, ta, etc., but we do not advise their use.

Chromatic Effects.—The ear forms such a habit of expecting t to move to d^1 and f to move to m, especially in cadences and other phrases meant to decide the key, that a new effect arises when the ear is disappointed of its expected gratification. This is markedly the case when a new t or a new f threaten to decide for us a *new* key. Some of the most startling and a few of the most beautiful effects of modern music are thus obtained. See more on "Chromatic Resolution of Chords" in "How to Observe Harmony."

Such exercises as the following should be carefully taught by *pattern* from the modulator. Let them be first sol-faad and afterwards laad, the voices lingering on the distinguishing tone. But let the voices carefully mark the resolution (or "progression") of that tone, because on the resolution it depends whether the effect will be transitional or chromatic.

Ex. 127*b*. KEY E. Effect of the new t.

B. t.
:d |m :d |s :t_1 |f :— |m :$^m l_1$ |t_1 :d |r :t_1 |f :— |m ||

Ex. 128. KEY A. E. t.
:d |t_1 :d |m :s |f :— |m :^{r}s |l :t |d^1 :r^1 |t :— |d^1 ||

Ex. 129. KEY E♭. Effect of fe chromatic.
|d :r |m :d |f :fe |s :— |d^1 :s |l :s |fe :f |m :— ||

Ex. 130. KEY B♭. Effect of the new f.
f. E♭.
:d |s_1 :d |t_1 :f |m :r |d :^{d}s |f :m |r :f |m :r |d ||

Ex. 131. KEY F. f. B♭.
:d |m :d |s :d^1 |t :— |d^1 :^{f}d |m :d |s :d |f :— |m ||

Ex. 132. KEY B. Effect of ta chromatic.
:m |r :d |t_1 :ta_1 |l_1 :t_1 |d :s_1 |l_1 :ta_1 |t_1 :d |m :r |d ||

s d^1 *f*
t *m*
f
m l *r*
r s—*d*
t.
d—f
t, m *l*,
l, r *s*,
s, d *f*,
t, *m*,
f,
m, *l*, *r*,
r, *s*, *d*,

Cadence Transition.—The commonest form of transition to the first *sharp* key is that in which it gives life and beauty to a cadence. See Exs. 133, and 134. When a transition does not begin before the second-last measure* of a line, and does not continue beyond the cadence, we call it cadence-transition. The first *flat* key is seldom used thus, but see Ex. 141. We write cadence-transition in the "Imperfect" manner—that is, with fe or ta.

The Cadential Movement of the Bass.—|d :r |s, or |r :r |s_1 sounds like |f :s |d or |s :s |d of the first sharp key, and suggests transition to the mind even without the fe.

LORD, WHILE FOR ALL.

Ex. 133. KEY A. *Firmly.* *Dr. Croft.*

:d	m :r	m :d	r :t_1	d :d	s :r	m :fe	s
1. Lord,	while for	all man -	kind we	pray, In	ev - 'ry	clime and	coast,
:d	d :t_1	d :m_1	f_1 :s_1 .f_1	m_1 :d	t_1 :t_1	d .t_1 :l_1	s_1
2. O	guard our	shores from	ev - 'ry	foe, *With*	*peace our*	*bor - ders*	*bless;*

St. Co. (New.)

* Or the third last accent.

: s	f : r	m : d	f : m	r : t₁	r : s	f : r	d
O	HEAR US	FOR OUR	NA - TIVE	LAND,—The	land we	love the	most.
: m	r : t₁	d : m₁	l₁ . t₁ : d	t₁ : s₁	f₁ : m₁	f₁ : s₁ . f₁	m₁
With	pros - p'rous	times our	cit - ies	crown, OUR	FIELDS WITH	PLEN-TEOUS-	NESS.

3 Unite us in the sacred love
Of knowledge, truth, and Thee,
And let our hills and valleys shout
THE SONGS OF LIBERTY.

4 *Lord of the nations! thus to Thee*
Our country we commend;
Be thou her refuge and her trust,
HER EVERLASTING FRIEND!

PRAISE TO GOD.

Ex. 134. KEY A. *Joyfully.* *German Chorale.*

m : r	d : m	s : f	m : —	l₁ : t₁	d : r	t₁ : l₁	s₁ : —
1. Praise to	God! O	let us	raise,	From our	hearts a	song of	praise;
d : t₁	l₁ : d	t₁ . s₁ : l₁ . t₁	d : —	f₁ : f₁	m₁ : fe₁	s₁ : fe₁	s₁ : —
2. Praise to	him who	made the	light,	Praise to	him who	gave us	sight;

d : t₁	l₁ : d	f : m	r : —	s : f	m : r	d : t₁	d : —
Of that	good- ness	let us	sing,	Whence our	lives and	bless - ings	spring.
m₁ : s₁	f₁ : l₁	t₁ . r : d . l₁	t₁ : —	m : r	d : f₁	s₁ : - . f₁	m₁ : —
Praise to	him who	form'd the	ear;	Will he	not his	chil - dren	hear?

3 Praise him for our happy hours;
Praise him for our varied powers;
For these thoughts that rise above,
For these hearts he made for love.

4 Praise his mercy that did send
Jesus for our guide and friend:
Praise him every heart and voice,
HIM WHO MAKES ALL WORLDS REJOICE.

Passing Transition.—The commonest form of the transition to the first *flat* key is that in which it makes a *passing* harmonic ornament, not in a cadence, but in the middle of a line or near the beginning. See Ex. 142, 144. The first sharp key is seldom used thus, but see Ex. 170, 171. We write Passing transition in the "improper" manner.

Extended Transition is that which is carried beyond a cadence. The first sharp key is much used in this way in hymn-tunes, often occupying the second or the third lines, and sometimes the greater part of both. See Ex. 135, 136, 137, 140.

St. Co. (New).

The first *flat* key is seldom thus employed in tunes which are in popular use. It is rare to find such an example of it as Handel gives in Ex. 143.

The Exercises.—All the early transitions, and all the more difficult transitions which follow, should be well taught from the modulator. If this is not done transition will become a confusion instead of a beauty and a pleasure to the learner.

Missed Transitions.—If one "part" is silent while another changes key *twice*—when it enters *both* bridge-tones are given in some old music, thus [rs]d, but this plan is not now adopted. When a part enters after others which are already in the new key the bridge-note is placed in brackets ([d]).

O SAVIOUR, GO BESIDE US.

Ex. 135. KEY E. *Gently.* M. 60.

:d	m :r | m :l	s :f | m :l	s :f | m :r	m :— | —
1. *O*	*Sa - viour, go be -*	*side us, Wher-*	*ev - er we may*	*go ;*
:d	d :t_1 | d :f	m :r | d :f	m :r | d :t_1	d :— | —
2. O	Shep- herd, go be -	side us, And	lead thy faint - ing	flock ;

B. t. f. E.

:^{s}d	r :m | f :m	r :— | d :$^l{}_1$m	f :m | r :r	d :— | —
And	*let no harm be -*	*tide us, From*	*ma - lice of the*	*foe.*
:$^s{}_1$$d_1$	t_2 :d_1 | l_1 :s_1	f_1 :— | m_1 :$^f{}_1$d	t_1 :d | f_1 :s_1	d :— | —
With	pas - tures green pro-	vide us, And	well- springs from the	rock.

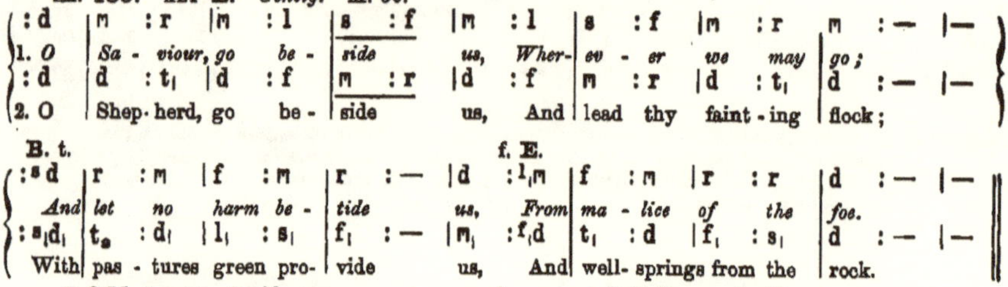

3 O Master, stay beside us,
Our hearts with wisdom store;
Be strength and grace supplied us,
To grow for evermore.

4 O Father, go beside us,
Till all our wand'rings end;
LET WEAL NOR WOE DIVIDE US
FROM THEE, OUR FAITHFUL FRIEND.

LO! MY SHEPHERD'S HAND.

Ex. 136. KEY F. C. t. *A. Stone.*

d :r	m :m	f :m	r :—	^{m}l :t	d' :r'	m' :r'	d' :—
1. Lo! my	Shep-herd's	hand di -	vine!	Want shall	nev - er	more be	mine;
d :t_1	d :d	l_1 :d	t_1 :—	^{d}f :r	m :f	s :f	m :—
2. When I	faint with	sum - mer's	heat,	He shall	lead my	wea - ry	feet

f. F.

^{l}m :m	f :f	r :r	m :—	s :f	m :r	d :t_1	d :—
In a	pas - ture	fair and	large,	He shall	feed his	hap - py	charge.
^{f}d :d	r :r	t_1 :s_1	d :—	m :r	d :f_1	s_1 :- .f_1	m_1 :—
To the	*streams that*	*still and*	*slow,*	*Through the*	*ver - dant*	*mea - dows*	*flow.*

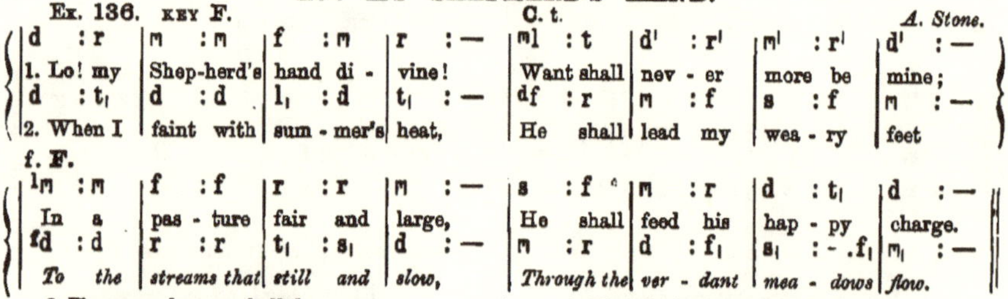

3 He my soul anew shall frame;
And his mercies to proclaim,
When thro' devious paths I stray,
Teach my steps the better way.

4 *Though the dreary vale I tread,*
By the shades of death o'erspread,
There I walk from terror free,
STILL PROTECTED, LORD, BY THEE.

Words by *Tupper.* Music by *A. L. C.*

COURAGE!

Ex. 137. KEY B♭. *Boldly.* M. 112.

s_1 :- .s_1 | s_1 :l_1.t_1	d :— | t_1 :	s_1 :- .s_1 | l_1.t_1 :d .r	m :— | r :
Dan - gers do not	dare me,	Ter - rors do not	scare me,
s_1 :- .f_1 | m_1 :r_1	d_1 :m_1 | s_1 :	f_1 :- .f_1 | f_1 :m_1.r_1	d_1 :d | t_1 :

F. t.

r :- .d | t_1.d :r .m	f :— | f :	^{fe}t :- .t | t :t	d' :— | d :—
God, my guide, I'll	bear me	Man - ful-ly for	ev - er.
t_1 :- .l_1 | s_1 :f_1.m_1	r_1 :— | r :	^{r}s :- .s | s :f	m :— | d :—

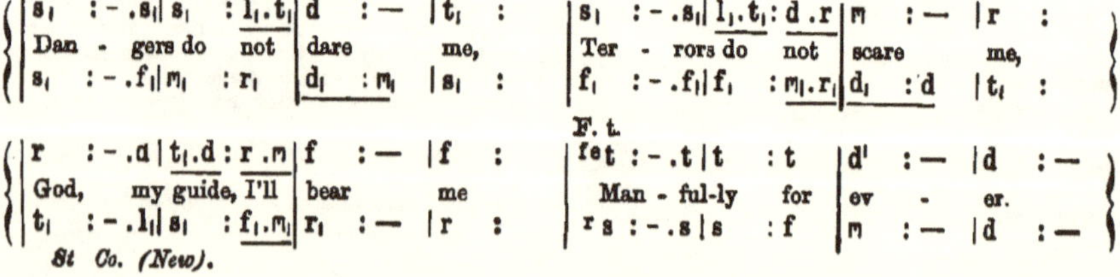

St Co. (New).

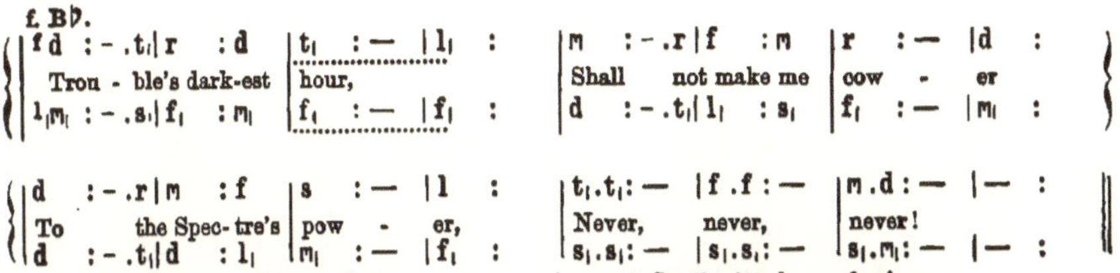

f. B♭.

| fd :-.t₁\|r :d \|t₁ :— \|l₁ : \|m :-.r\|f :m \|r :— \|d :
Trou - ble's dark-est hour, Shall not make me cow - er
l₁m₁ :-.s₁\|f₁ :m₁ \|f₁ :— \|f₁ : \|d :-.t₁\|l₁ :s₁ \|f₁ :— \|m₁ :

d :-.r\|m :f \|s :— \|l : \|t₁.t₁:— \|f .f :— \|m .d :— \|— :
To the Spec- tre's pow - er, Never, never, never!
d :-.t₁\|d :l₁ \|m₁ :— \|f₁ : \|s₁.s₁:— \|s₁.s₁:— \|s₁.m₁:— \|— :

2 Up, my heart, and brace thee,
While the perils face thee,
In thyself encase thee
Manfully for ever.
Foes may howl around me,
Fears may hunt and hound me,—
Shall their yells confound me?
Never, never, never!

3 Constant, calm, unfearing,
Boldly persevering,
In good conscience steering
Manfully for ever.
Winds and waves defying
And on God relying,
Shall he find me flying?
Never, never, never!

Ex. 138. Let this be practised until each *syllable* (*A* - and *men*) can be taken with one breath.

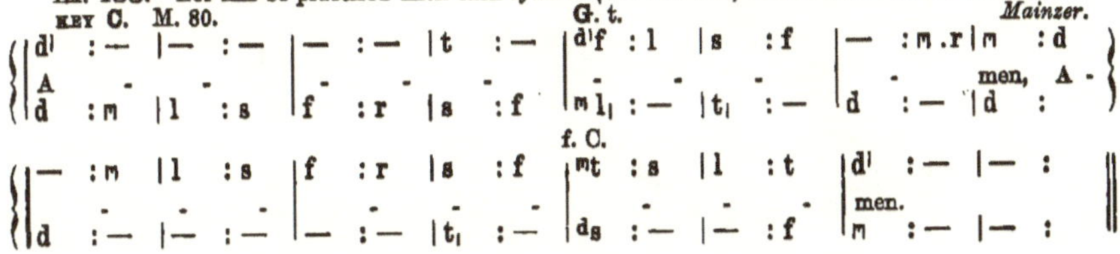

KEY C. M. 80. G. t. *Mainzer.*

d¹ :— \|— :— \|— :— \|t :— \|d¹f :l \|s :f \|— :m .r\|m :d
A - - - - - - - - - - men, A -
d :m \|l :s \|f :r \|s :f \|m l₁ :— \|t₁ :— \|d :— \|d :

f. C.

— :m \|l :s \|f :r \|s :f \|ᵐt :s \|l :t \|d¹ :— \|— :
- - - - - - - - - men.
d :— \|— :— \|— :— \|t₁ :— \|ᵈs :— \|— :f \|m :— \|— :

O LITTLE CHILD, LIE STILL.

Words from the "Lamp of Love." *A. L. C.*

Ex. 139. KEY D. *Softly.* M. 96.

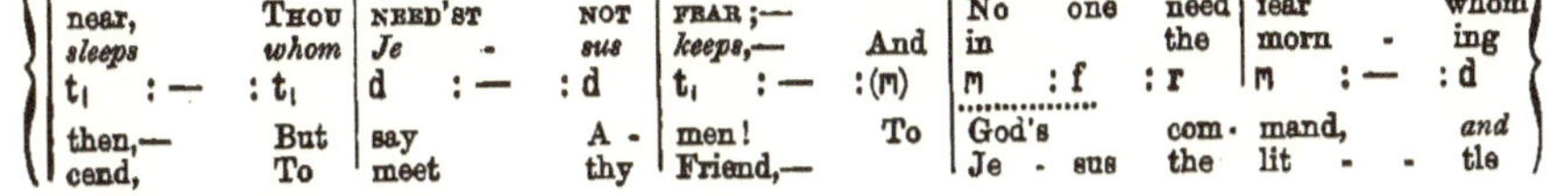

:m \|m :r :m \|s :— :f \|m :— :r \|r :— :— \|d :r :m
1. *O lit - tle child, lie still and sleep!* Je - sus is
2. *O lit - tle child, lie still and rest,—* *He sweet - ly*
:d \|d :t₁ :d \|m :— :r \|d :— :t₁ \|t₁ :— :— \|d :d :d
3. *O lit - tle child, when thou must die,* Fear no - thing
4. Then with thy an - - gel wings quick grown, Shalt thou as -

r :— :r \|r :m :fe \|s :— :(s) \|s :l :t \|d¹ :— :m
near, THOU NEED'ST NOT FEAR;— No one need fear whom
sleeps whom Je - sus keeps,— And in the morn - ing
t₁ :— :t₁ \|d :— :d \|t₁ :— :(m) \|m :f :r \|m :— :d
then,— But say A - men! To God's com - mand, *and*
cend, To meet thy Friend,— Je - sus the lit - - tle

St. Co. (New).

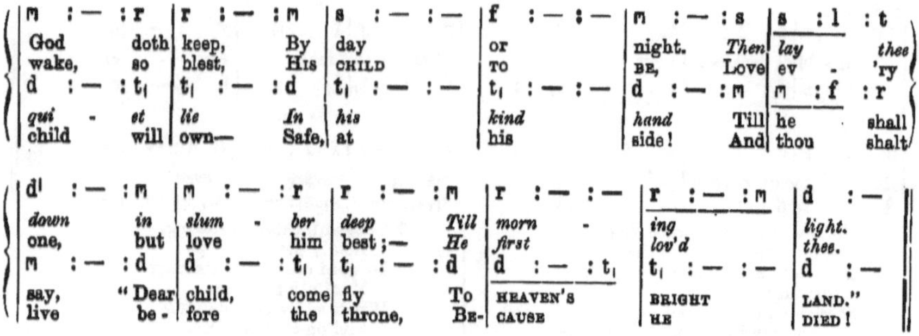

m :— :r	r :— :m	s :— :—	f :— :—	m :— :s	s :l :t
God doth	keep, By	day	or	night. *Then*	*lay thee*
wake, so	blest, His	CHILD	TO	BE, Love	ev - 'ry
d :— :t_1	t_1 :— :d	t_1 :— :—	t_1 :— :—	d :— :m	m :f :r
qui - et	*lie In*	*his*	*kind*	*hand* Till	he shall
child will	own— Safe,	at	his	side! And	thou shalt

d' :— :m	m :— :r	r :— :m	r :— :—	r :— :m	d :—
down in	*slum - ber*	*deep Till*	*morn -*	*ing*	*light.*
one, but	love him	best;— *He*	*first*	*lov'd*	*thee.*
m :— :d	d :— :t_1	t_1 :— :d	d :— :t_1	t_1 :— :—	d :—
say, "Dear	child, come	fly To	HEAVEN'S	BRIGHT	LAND."
live be -	fore the	throne, BE-	CAUSE	HE	DIED!

BLEST BE THE HOUR.

Ex. 140. KEY G. Tune "Dublin."

:m	m :s :f	m :r :d	r :l_1 :t_1	d :— :^{r}s (D. t.)
1. Blest	be the	hour when	friends shall	meet, Shall
:d	d :t_1 :l_1	s_1 :— :l_1	f_1 :— :f_1	m_1 :— :t_1m
2. Sweet	hope, deep	cher - ish'd,	not in	vain, Now

l :t :d'	f :m :r	d :— :^{f}d (f. G.)	r :— :m	f :— :m
meet to	part no	more, And	with ce -	les - tial
f :— :m	r :d :t_1	d :— :^{l}m_1	s_1 :— :d	l_1 :t_1 :d
thou art	rich - ly	crown'd, All	that was	dead re -

r :m :d	d :t_1 :s_1	s :f :m	r :l_1 :t_1	d :—
wel - come	greet, On	an im -	mor - tal	shore.
s_1 :— :l_1	s_1 :— :s_1	t_1 :— :d	f_1 :— :f_1	m_1 .—
vives a -	gain; All	that was	lost is	found.

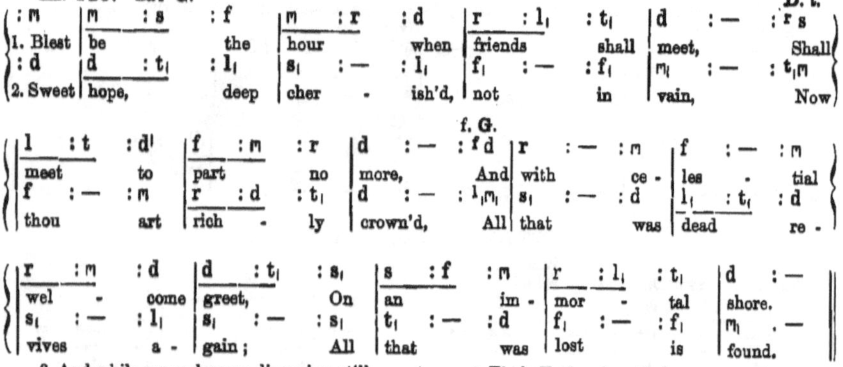

3 And while remembrance, lingering still,
Draws joy from sorrowing hours,
New prospects rise, new pleasures fill
The soul's capacious powers.

4 Their Father fans their generous flame,
And looks complacent down;
The smile that owns their filial claim
Is THEIR IMMORTAL CROWN.

HALLELUJAH.

Ex. 141. KEY C. M. 72. *Natorp.*

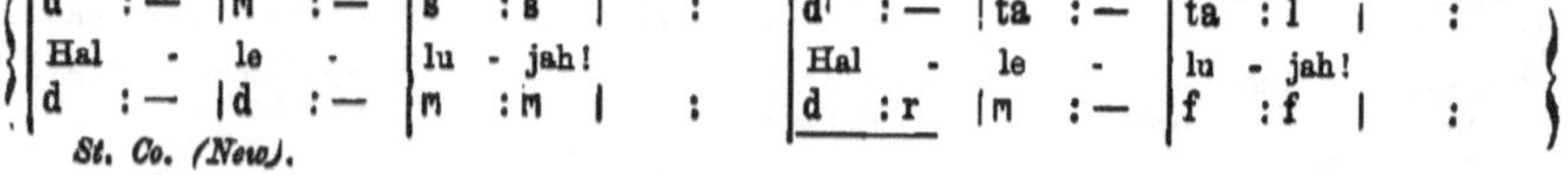

d :—	m :—	s :s	:	d' :—	ta :—	ta :l	:
Hal -	le -	lu - jah!		Hal -	le -	lu - jah!	
d :—	d :—	m :m	:	d :r	m :—	f :f	:

St. Co. (New).

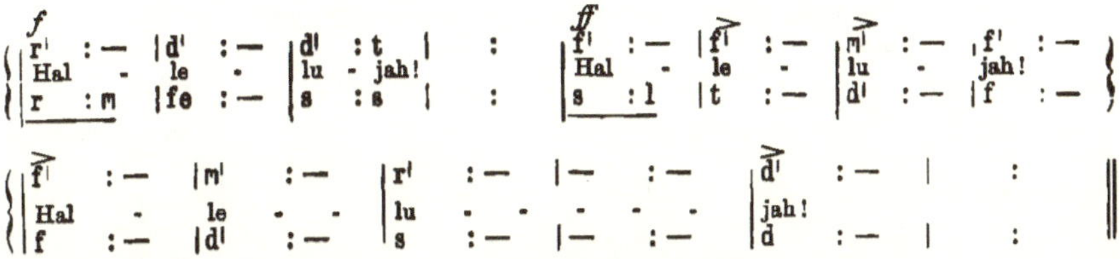

f r' :—	d' :—	d' :t	:	*ff* f' :—	f' :—	m' :—	f' :—
Hal -	le -	lu - jah!		Hal -	le -	lu -	jah!
r :m	fe :—	s :s	:	s :l	t :—	d' :—	f :—

f' :—	m' :—	r' :—	— :—	d' :—	:
Hal -	le - -	lu - -	- - -	jah!	
f :—	d' :—	s :—	— :—	d :—	:

Ex. 142. KEY B♭. M. 58. **THROUGH THE DAY.**

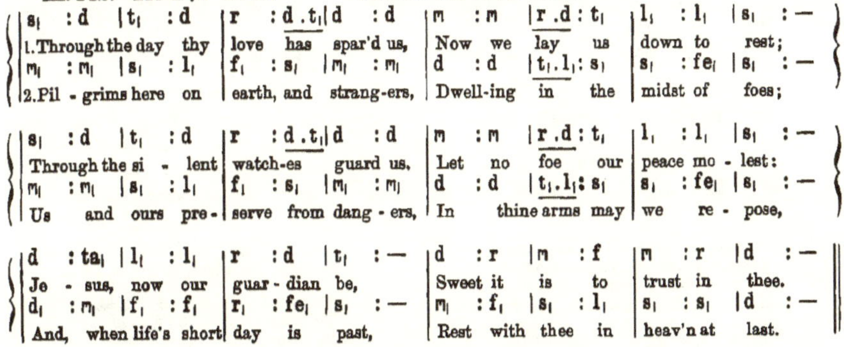

s, :d | t, :d	r :d .t,| d :d	m :m | r .d : t,	l, :l, | s, :—
1.Through the day thy	love has spar'd us,	Now we lay us	down to rest;
m, :m, | s, :l,	f, :s, | m, :m,	d :d | t,.l,: s,	s, :fe, | s, :—
2.Pil - grims here on	earth, and strang-ers,	Dwell-ing in the	midst of foes;
s, :d | t, :d	r :d .t,| d :d	m :m | r .d : t,	l, :l, | s, :—
Through the si - lent	watch-es guard us,	Let no foe our	peace mo - lest:
m, :m, | s, :l,	f, :s, | m, :m,	d :d | t,.l,: s,	s, :fe, | s, :—
Us and ours pre-	serve from dang - ers,	In thine arms may	we re - pose,
d :ta, | l, :l,	r :d | t, :—	d :r | m :f	m :r | d :—
Je - sus, now our	guar - dian be,	Sweet it is to	trust in thee.
d, :m, | f, :f,	r, :fe, | s, :—	m, :f, | s, :l,	s, :s, | d :—
And, when life's short	day is past,	Rest with thee in	heav'n at last.

Ex. 143. KEY F. f. B♭. **GREAT IS THE LORD.** *Handel.*

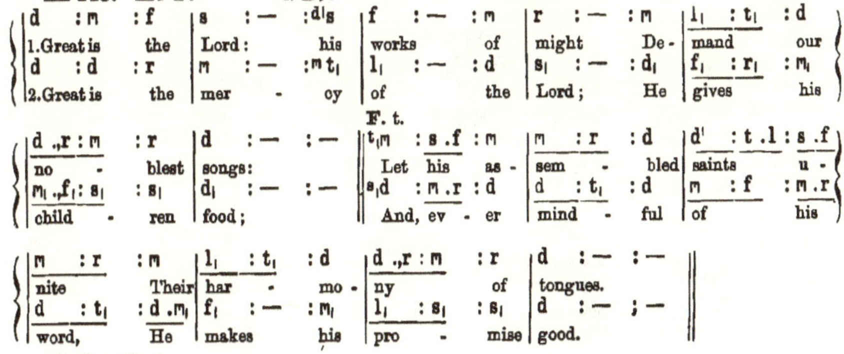

d :m :f	s :— :d's	f :— :m	r :— :m	l, :t, :d
1.Great is the	Lord: his	works of	might De-	mand our
d :d :r	m :— :m t,	l, :— :d	s, :— :d,	f, :r, :m,
2.Great is the	mer - cy	of the	Lord; He	gives his

d .,r :m :r	d :— :—	F. t. t,m :s .f :m	m :r :d	d' :t .l :s .f
no - blest	songs:	Let his as -	sem - bled	saints u -
m, .,f,: s, :s,	d, :— :—	s,d :m .r :d	d :t, :d	m :f :m .r
child - ren	food;	And, ev - er	mind - ful	of his

m :r :m	l, :t, :d	d .,r :m :r	d :— :—
nite Their	har - mo-	ny of	tongues.
d :t, :d .m,	f, :— :m,	l, :s, :s,	d :— ;—
word, He	makes his	pro - mise	good.

"O'ER THE DARK WAVE OF GALILEE."

Ex. 144. KEY B♭. M. 72. Words by *Russell*. *A. L. C.*

```
|m  :r  :d     |t,  :l,  :s,    |l,  :—  :t,     |d  :—  :—   |s,  :l  :ta,
 1.O'er the dark wave of           Gal - i -         lee          The gloom of
|d, :r, :m,    |f,  :—   :m,    |f,  :—  :s,.f,  |m, :—  :—   |m,  :f, :s,
 2.The wea - ry bird hath          left  the         air,         And sunk in -

|l,  :—  :r    |l,  :t,  :d     |t,  :—  :—      |m  :r  :d    |t,  :l,  :s,
 twi - light    ga  -  thers      fast,            And on the     wa - ters
|f,  :—  :f,   |se, :s,  :l,    |s,  :—  :—      |d, :r, :m,   |f,  :—  :m,
 to  his        shel - ter'd      nest;            The wand-'ring beast hath

|l,  :—  :t,   |d  :—  :—  |r  :m  :f     |m  :d  :r     |d  :—  :t,   |d  :—  :—  ||
 drear - i -    ly           De - scends the  fit - ful      ev - 'ning     blast.
|f,  :—  :s,.f,|m, :—  :—  |f, :m, :r,    |d, :m, :f,    |m, :—  :r,   |d, :—  :—  ||
 sought his     lair,        And laid him     down to        wel - come     rest.
```

3 Still, near the lake, with weary tread,
  Lingers a form of human kind;
And, from his lone, unsheltered head,
  Flows the chill night-damp on the wind.

4 Why seeks not he a home of rest?
  Why seeks not he the pillowed bed?
Beasts have their dens, the bird its nest;—
  He hath not where to lay his head.

5 Such was the lot he freely chose,
  To bless, to save, the human race;
And, through his poverty, there flows
  A rich, full stream of heavenly grace.

I LOVE MY LOVE.

Ex. 145. KEY C. M. 88, twice. Words by *Charles Mackay*. *A. L. C.*

```
|s  :m  :s  |l  :-  :s  |s  :-  :f  |m  :-  :d'  |d'  :t  :d'  |m'  :-  :d'  |t  :-  :-
 1.What is the mean - ing  of   the song That    rings  so clear  and           loud,
|m  :d  :m  |f  :-  :m  |m  :-  :r  |d  :-  :m   |m   :r  :m   |d   :-  :m   |s  :-  :-
 2.What is the mean - ing  of   thy thought, O    maid - en fair  and           young?
 3.O hap - py words! at    Beau - ty's feet We     sing  them ere  our           prime;

|-  :   :t    |d'  :-  :m  |s   :-  :t    |d'  :-  :m  |s   :-  :m'  |m'  :f'  :m'  |r'  :d'  :t
        Thou   night - in - gale  a -       mid   the copse,—Thou    lark   a - bove   the
|-  :   :s.f  |m   :-  :d  |t,  :-  :s.f  |m   :-  :d  |t,  :-  :d   |s   :l   :s   |f   :m   :r
        There  is   such plea - sure        in    thine eyes, Such   mu - sic on       thy
        And    when  the ear - ly           sum - mers pass, And     care comes on      with
```

St. Co. (New).

G. t

d' :- :- |- : :d'f |m :- :m |m :- :r |d :- :t_1 |d :- :(s)
cloud? What says thy song, thou joy - ous thrush,
m :- :- |- : :ml_1.t_1 |d :- :s_1 |s_1 :- :f_1 |m_1 :- :r_1 |m_1 :- :(m_1)
tongue; There is such glo - ry on thy face—
Time, Still be it ours, in care's des - pite, To

f. C.

s :s_1 :s_1 |t_1 :- :s_1 |d :- :- |- : :ds |s :l :s |l :- :t
Up in the wal - nut tree? "I love my love be-
m_1 :m_1 :m_1 |f_1 :- :f_1 |m_1 :- :- |- : :l_1m |m :f :m |f :- :r
What can the mean - ing be?
join in the cho - rus free—

d' :- :d' |t :- :t |d' :- :- |r' :- :- |m' :- :- |- : :s |s :l :s
cause I know My love loves me, I love my
m :- :d.m |s :- :f |m :- :- |s :- :- |d' :- :- |- : :m |m :f :m

l :- :t |d' :- :d' |t :- :s |m' :- :- |r' :- :- |d' :- :- |- :- :
love be- cause I know My love loves me."
f :- :r |m :- :d.m |s :- :s |s :- :- |f :- :- |m :- :- |- :- :

Pitching Tunes.—By this time the pupil is probably possessed of a C' tuning fork, but that should not prevent (it should rather promote) his constantly exercising himself to remember "one C" (C') as recommended p. 29. In pitching the key F, it is useful to suppose your C' s, and *fall* on your key-note thus, s m d. The pupil will not now find it necessary to run down to G, but will fall upon it at once from his C'. E may be pitched by falling to m, thus, C'd' s m - ^{m}d. A may be pitched by falling on l, thus, C'd' l - ^{l}d. D may be pitched thus C'd' r' - ^{r}d'. The key may be pitched a little higher (sharper) or a little lower (flatter) than any tone of the "standard scale of pitch," p. 29. The tones thus required are named "F sharp," "E flat," &c., and the sign ♭ is used for "flat," and ♯ for "sharp." A sharp bears no relation to the tone below it and after which, for convenience, it is named, but its relation is to the tone above it. To that tone it is an under-little-step, as t_1 to d. It is like the f, in transition, changed into fe. In order to strike it correctly we sing the tone above and then smoothly descend a little step to it. A flat bears no relation to the tone above it and after which it is named. It is an over-little-step (as f to m) to the tone below it. It is like the t, in transition, changed into ta. To pitch it correctly in the cases of A♭, G♭, and D♭, we should sing the tone below and then rise to it a little step. But in the more commonly used keys of B♭ and E♭ it is easier and surer to pitch thus:—For B♭ suppose your C' to be s and sing s f - ^{f}d. For E♭, suppose it to be l and rise stepwise to d', thus, C'l - t d'.

Recitation.—The art of reciting well on one tone is a very difficult but exceedingly beautiful one. A pure and exact enunciation, making every word stand out as it were in bright colours before you, is a wonderful charm even in common speech, but when one listens to the clear utterance of some great singer, words seem like old friends arrayed in startling beauty and inspired with new power. A good elocutionary recitation depends on the study and practice of the most suitable rhythms, emphases, and pauses for expressing well the meaning of the words, and on a thorough mastery and careful practice of the articulations and vowels of speech. The emphasis of words belongs to elocution rather than to singing. The choice of accent also, in words set to music, belongs to the composer rather than to the performer. Varieties of rhythm the pupil will learn in the study of chanting. But the consonants and vowels, the articulations and continuations of voice, are proper objects of the singer's study. Of these, the vowels or continuations are the more important to the singer, because on them alone can a good tone be prolonged, and every fault a man has in speaking vowels is greatly magnified the moment he begins to sing. But the vowels have already been practised to some extent in connexion with the voice exercises, and will be studied more fully in the next step. Besides, in first attracting the attention of the pupil to the action of his vocal organs it is easier to begin with the consonants. In preparing the scheme of exercises on consonants and vowels, the author has been greatly aided by old studies of Dr. Rush on the Voice, and by Mr. Melville Bell's "Visible Speech" and "Dictionary of Sounds." But his chief help has come from the generous and patient personal assistance of Mr. Alexander J. Ellis, author of "English Phonetics," "Early English Pronunciation," and other works.

An Articulation is a joint. A joint implies in this case both a separation and a connexion of spoken sounds. The lips may come into contact with one another, or the lip touch the upper teeth, or the tongue touch teeth or palate. There may be thus an absolute or nearly absolute stopping of the vowel sounds. And these points of separation are also made points of junction. They are joints or articulations.

Qualities of articulation.—If the student produces strongly P and B, without any distinct vowel following them, as in *la-p*, *tu-b*, he will soon notice that P has a hard quality and gives nothing but breath; that B has a softer quality and something of *voice* in it. In fact the larynx takes part in the act of articulation. The same differences may be easily noticed between the Tip-tongue articulations T as in *pe-t*, and D as in *mai-d*, and between the Back-tongue articulations K as in *seek*, and G as in *plag(ue)*. These we propose to call *the two qualities* of articulation,—the Breath quality, and the Voice quality.

Modes of Articulation. — If the student pronounces carefully the Lip-articulations P as in *shee-p*, WH as in *wh-ile*, and with the use of the teeth F as in *li-f(e)*, he will soon notice that in producing P the lips *shut* the passage of the breath; that in WH they give it a narrow *central* opening; and that in F they oblige the breath to force its way through chinks on *both sides* of the point of junction. It is easy to notice the same difference of passage in producing the Tip-tongue articulations T (with shut passage) as in *be-t*, S (with central opening) as in *la-ss*, SH (central) as in *la-sh*, and TH (with side openings) as in *wra-th*; and in the Back-tongue articulation K (shut) as in *la-k(e)*, and Mid-tongue Y (central) as in *y-oung*. Again, there is the trill or tremulous motion of the tip of the tongue for the rough R (written R') as in *herring*,—and a peculiar mode of articulation called nasal, in which the voice resounds within the nose, as for M, N, and NG. These we propose to call the five Modes of articulation: shut, central, side, trilled, and nasal.

Organs of Articulation.—The muscles of articulation reside chiefly in the lips and the tongue, for the teeth and the palate are comparatively stationary. The work has to be done by the Lips, or by the Tip, the Middle or the Back of the tongue. We may call the Lips, the Tip, Middle, and Back of the tongue *the four organs* of articulation. These Organs, Modes, and Qualities produce the following:—

The Lip articulations, P, B, WH, W, and M, are easily understood. But it will be seen that in F and V the upper teeth act with the lower lips in making the articulation.

The Tip-tongue articulations, T, D, L, N, and the trilled R' are also quickly understood. For TH, DH it will be seen that the tip of the tongue acts against the teeth. S, Z, and SH, ZH require both the tip and middle of the tongue, the teeth and lips also usually acting. S, Z use the tip more decidedly than SH, ZH. The letters DH, ZH, are commonly used by elocutionists to represent the soft forms of TH, SH.

The trilled R' occurs only before vowels. When not before a vowel, R is vocal and modifies the preceeding vowel, forming diphthongs. See pp. 143, 144.

YH and Y require no explanation.

CH and J are double articulations, or consonantal diphthongs, and might be spelt TSH and DZH. Hence they are not included in the table.

The Aspirate H is simply the sound of breath driven sharply through the open larynx. Its impulse comes from the muscular floor on which the lungs rest. See p. 96.

TABLE OF ENGLISH ARTICULATIONS.*

	LIPS.			TIP-TONGUE.				BACK-TONGUE.
	Lips.	Teeth.		Palate.	Mid-tongue.			
SHUT.								
Breath.	P *pea*	—	—	T *toe*	—	—	—	K *keen*
Voice	B *bee*	—	—	D *doe*	—	—	—	G *gain*
CENTRAL.								
Breath.	WH *wheel*	F *feel*	TH *thin*	— —	S *seal*	SH *rush*	YH *hew (yheu)*	—
Voice.	W *weal*	V *veal*	DH *then*	— —	Z *zeal*	ZH *rouge (roozh)*	Y *you*	—
SIDE.								
Breath.	—	—	—	—	—	—	—	—
Voice.	—	—	—	L *lay*	—	—	—	—
TRILLED.								
Voice.	—	—	—	R' *ray*	—	—	—	—
NASAL.								
Voice.	M *sum*	—	—	N *sun*	—	—	—	NG *sung*

How to sing a consonant.—A study of the above table will shew how little there is in any of the consonants which can be sung. The breath articulations with shut posture, P, T, K, have positively no sound; the hisses WH, F, TH, S, SH, YH, cannot be sung at all, and should be made as short as possible; the buzzes W, V, DH, Z, ZH, Y, are very disagreeable when continued, although it is just possible to sing them; the voice articulations with shut posture B, D, G, are far too smothered for singing; and although L, R, M, N, and NG may be more or less murmured or hummed, they cannot be properly sung. In passing, however, from consonant to vowel and vowel to consonant, that is from one fixed position to another, the organs necessarily assume an endless number of intermediate positions, and voice being uttered during the time of this change, there results a varying sound, which may be called a Glide. This is not a glide in pitch, but in vowel qualities. The organs do not change much, and there is comparatively little glide between *b* and *oo*, but there is a great change in the organs, and therefore a considerable glide between *b* and *ee*. A similar difference may be observed between the Glides *k* to *ai*, and *k* to *oa*. It should be noticed that as long as any two sounds, for example *m* and *ee*, are kept separate, however closely they are put together, there is no syllable. It is the glide which makes sounds into syllables. Indeed the only part of a consonantal effect which can be really sung is the glide. The exercise of singing a consonant, therefore, consists of making this glide conspicuous by *opening the mouth well* for the vowel and closing it smartly for the consonant. All real intelligibility in singing depends upon the manner in which the singer brings out the glide, taking care not to introduce puffs, or to prolong hisses or buzzes. On this exercise he will then concentrate his attention.

Ex. 146. Enunciation Exercises on the Lip articulations. Let the following lines be sung as in a chant, on the tone G, the pupils taking extreme care to make the requisite distinctions of articulation and to bring out the glide. When an exercise has been sung to the open *aa* it should be practised with the other principal vowels *ai*, *ee*, *au*, *oa*, *oo*; for each vowel will introduce a new glide.

: . The | lips-pro : duce-with | shut : passage | p*aa* : b*aa* | m*aa* : | *aa*p : *aa*b | *aa*m : | *aa*p+ : p*aa* |

: . The | lips-pro : duce-with | central : passage | wh*aa* : w*aa* | wh*aa* : w*aa* | &c.

: . The | lips-pro : duce-with | central : passage | f*aa* : v*aa* | f*aa* : v*aa* | *aa*f : *aa*v‡ | *aa*f : f*aa* | *aa*v : v*aa* |

St. Co. (New.)

* For Diagrams see "Teacher's Manual," p. 198. + Don't open lips. ‡ Note, p. 62.

Ex. **147.** Enunciation Exercises on the Tip-tongue articulations.

: . The | Tip : tongue-pro | duces : . with | shut : passage | *taa* : d*aa* | n*aa* : | *aa*t : *aa*d | *aa*n :
| *aa*t : t*aa* | *aa*d : d*aa* |

: . The | Tip : tongue-pro | duces : . with | central : passage | s*aa* : z*aa* | s*aa* : &c.*

: . The | Tip : tongue-pro | duces : . with | central : passage | th*aa* : dh*aa* | l*aa* : | *aa*th : *aa*dh | *aa*.
: | *aa*th : th*aa* | *aa*dh : dh*aa* | &c.

Ex. **148.** Enunciation Exercises on the Mid, Back, and trilled-Tip-tongue articulations.

: . The | Mid : tongue-pro | duces : . with | central : passage | sh*aa* : zh*aa* | *aa*sh : *aa*zh |

: . The | Back : tongue-pro | duces : . with | shut : passage | k*aa* : g*aa* | ng*aa* : | *aa*k : *aa*g | *aa*ng :

: . The | Tip : tongue | trilled : . pro | duces : with | central : passage | r*aa* : r*aa* | *aa*r*aa* : *aa*r*aa* |

Ex. **149.** Pronunciation of the Lip articulations. Recite on one tone (G) paying exact attention to the thick letters. This will require close attention to a careful pattern. Where the pronunciation varies from the spelling, the proper phonetic letters are introduced. The ending articulations and the double articulations are very difficult in singing. They must be delivered very *distinctly* but very *quickly*.

Cap, *cab*, pull, bull, *cup*, *cub*, pet, bet, mop, mob, babe, babble, bump, peep, *stopcock*, upmost, leapt, map, member, *film*, minimum, mumble, triumph.

When. wen, where, ware, while, wile, whither, wither, whim, whip, wharf, whelm, whimper, whiffle, whiff.

Fain, vain, fault, vault, fear, veer, foist, voiced, fife, five, serf, serve, safe, save, muff, puff, move, love.

Ex. **150.** Pronunciation of the Tip-tongue articulations.

Bet, *bed*, tire, dire, neat, need, troll, droll, colt, cold, batch, badge, writer, rider, tight, tied, titilate, tetrapon, tittletattle, tantalize, avidity, oddity, meditate, paint, pained, painless, nap, map, son, some, muttn, saddn.

Moss, moth, *face*, *faith*, seal, zeal, ice, eyes, base, baize, sport, store, skope, sere, smile, swear, sue, suit, jezuit, spazms, feasts, fifths, desks, zest, assassin, sashes.

Death, deaf, loth, loaf, thew, few, thrill, frill, path, padhs, oath, oadhz, mouth, moudhz, lath, ladhs, clodhz, close, ladhe, lave, owez, loathsome, loadheth, fair, fair'er, near, near'er, err, err'ing, fir, mirr'or, br'ide, thr'ce, ver'ily, r'evelr'y, pr'uder'y, litter'ally, liter'ar'y, holily, worldlily, listlessly, jollily, blidhely, boldly, falsely, foully, eel-like, ill-look, play, flame, glass, slave, saddle, kettle.

Ex. **151.** Pronunciation of the Mid and Back-tongue articulations.

Kape, gape, klass, glass, karter, garter, krate, grate, back, bag, duck, dug, peck, peg, pick, pig, frock, frog packt, akt, sekt, strikt, picknick, quikset, klik-klak, kricket, clang, clan, thing, thin, dinging, dinning, singing, sinning, angktious, compungktion, congkord, ungktuous, fungktion, longest, long-gest, rung, run.

Ashes, asses, shine, sign, Greeshian, adhezhion, shaises, incizhion, speshial, seizhure, Rushian, treazhure, shrewed, vizhion, suspishious, intruzhion, batch, baj, bats, etch, lej, frets, leech, liej, beats.

Ear, year, ooze, yeuz, booty, byuty, do, deu (dew, due), pyure, tyune.

Ex. **152.** Error exercises on the articulations.

"Foller," follow, window, sorrow, pillow, shallow. "Runnin," running, writing, speaking, walking, singing. "Laud," lord, storm, worm, far, first, smart, worst. "Gwacious," gracious, great, green, rich, rest, rough, right. "'appy," happy, heaven, hymn, hail, when, why, which, while. "Hone," own, and, air, ill, eve.

St. Co. (New.)

* Don't let *final* dh run into dhth, nor z into zs, nor v into vf.

"The soldier's steer," the soldier's tear.
"That lasts till night," that last still night.
"Study deceit," studied deceit.
"A languid aim," a languid dame.
"His cry moved on," his crime moved on.

"Luxurious oil," luxurious soil.
"Pray to nobody," prate to nobody.
"Make lean your heart," make clean your heart.
"Proof of utility," proof of futility.
"Beer descending," beard descending on his breast.

Collective Reading.—This practice, commenced in the second step, p. 15, should now be revived with great care and constancy.

Pulses and Accents in Public Speaking.—Any one who listens to a good public speaker may notice that the *pulses* of his speech are of equal length and constant recurrence, like those of music,—but that he has a greater liberty of *accent*. His accents sometimes fall so as to divide the pulses into three-pulse measure, but more commonly into two-pulse measure. Some public speakers even beat time with their hands while they speak, and nothing interrupts the regularity of their movement but this occasional introduction of a three-pulse measure. Both in poetry and in music if we begin in three-pulse measure or in two-pulse measure, we must continue in it. But in prose the two-pulse and three-pulse measures are continually intermixed in the same line. Let the pupil try to speak, in a clear declamatory tone, and with proper emphasis, the following words, and to mark the pulses and accents of his voice as he does so. He will then soon understand our meaning:—"And suddenly there was with the angel a multitude of the heavenly host." The words "heavenly host" we may, for the moment, leave out of consideration, because in chanting they would belong to the cadence, and the cadence is rhythmical music—not recitation.

If we recite these words on a single musical tone, and then write down the rhythms we have used, they will probably have the following appearance:—

```
          | Two-pulse Measure.  | Two-pulse Measure.
{ :l      | l  .l   :l   .l     | l        :l   .l   }
   And    | sudden   ly-there   | was       with-the }

{ | Three-pulse Measure.     | Three-pulse Measure.
{ | l    :l      :   .l     | l .l  :l     :l .l ||
{ | an - gel          'a    | multi  tude   of-the||
```

Here you notice that the first and second measures are of two beats, while the third and fourth are of three beats. Some of the old church chants had three-pulse cadences or closes, but in the recitations the frequent occurrence of three-pulse measures is recognised by all who observe with care. Even the following well-known musical responses shew the natural tendency to the mixed-measures of *speech* in distinction from the unchanging measures of song. They are here given in various rhythmic forms, as we find them in the "uses" of different cathedrals. In the three-pulse forms we may notice the *heaviness* of the second pulse when this measure is sung slowly. Let each example be sung in exact time and accent.

```
    KEY F.
{ |d      :—    |l,     :t,    |d      :—    ||
{ |Spare        |us      good  |Lord.        ||

    KEY F.
{ |d      :l,      :t,     |d       :—     ||
{ |Spare   us       good   |Lord.          ||

    KEY A.
{ |d .d :d   |d    :- .d |l,.l,:t,     |d   :—  ||
{ |We beseech|thee     to|hear us good |Lord.   ||

    KEY A.
{ :d .d |d  :d.d       |d    :l,   :t,   |d   :—  ||
{ We be-|seech thee to |hear  us    good |Lord.   ||

    KEY G.
{ |    :d  |d   :d .d      |d   :-.l,|l,   :—   ||
{ |    And bless thine in- |her  -   i - tance.  ||

    KEY G.
{ :d   |d     :d      :- .t, |l, .l, :l,      ||
{  And |bless  thine     in- |her-i - tance.  ||
```

And, in reciting "Thou art the everlasting Son," every one will admit that it is better to use the three-pulse measure, thus—

| Thou : art-the : ever | last : ing | Son—

than to sing thus—

| Thou : art-the | ever : lasting | Son—

Chanting.—The chant is intended to aid the united recitation of prose words by many people. It supplies, therefore, a single tone for the *recitation*, and a short musical phrase for the *cadence* of each line of the words. A melodic cadence at the end of sentences, is natural to public speakers when they rise into an excited state of mind: whether they be fishwomen quarrelling in Billingsgate, or preachers closing their discourses among the mountains of Wales or of Scotland, or even ministers of the Society of Friends speaking or praying under strong emotion. The reciting tone may be as long or as short as the words require. It is indicated by a Hold 𝄐 placed over the note. This elasticity of the reciting tone should always be kept in mind by the accompanist as well as the singer. The music of a chant should always be learnt *familiarly* and by rote, before it is sung to words. Then the words should be taken *line by line*, and *taataid* by pattern, clearly recited by pattern, and sung to the music. At the present step the pupil must obey exactly the marking of the recitations. Afterwards he may learn to make "markings" of his own. The present labour will be repaid not only by the great enjoyment there is in a freely delivered chant, but also by marked and valuable improvement in Rhythmical Perception. The teacher can beat time in pulses, or better still, use a metronome. If he uses a baton let it move simply from left to right and back again; he will then have his accent sometimes on one side and sometimes on the other.

Ex. 153. Learn as above the rhythms of Ex. 123. Notice cases of three-pulse measures in the recitations *next before* the first cadence of the first verse, the second cadence of the second verse, the first cadence of the third, and the first cadence of the last verse. Two-pulse measures are much more common in this position.

Ex. 154. Learn as above the rhythms of Ex. 124.

Ex. 155. Ditto Ex. 125. Notice three-pulse measures from the beginning of the first recitation of the first verse, of the first recitation of the third verse, of the first recitation of the fourth verse, and of the first recitation of the fifth verse.

Ex. 156. Learn as above the rhythms of Ex. 126.

TIME.

The silent quarter-pulse is indicated, like the other silences, by a vacant space among the pulse-divisions. It is named *sa* on the accented and *se* on the unaccented part of the pulse. The time exercises should be taught as directed, p. 19.

Ex. 157.

| l :l .l | ,l .l ,l :l .l ||
TAA TAA-TAI *sa*fatefe TAA-TAI

St. Co. (New).

KEY G.
| d :m .s | ,f .m ,r :d d ||
KEY G.
| m :r .d | ,t, .d ,r :m .m ||
KEY D.
| s :m .f | ,r .m ,f :s .s ||
KEY D.
| s :m .d | ,l .s ,f :m .d ||

Ex. 158.

| l ,l .l ,l :l .l | l ,l .l , :l ,l .l , ||
tafatefe TAATAI tafate*se* tafate*se*

KEY F.
| d ,r .m ,f :s .s | s ,f .m , :m ,r .d , ||
KEY F.
| m ,r .d ,t, :d .d | f ,f .f , :m ,m .m , ||
KEY D.
| s ,m .d ,m :s .m | r ,m .f , :m ,f .s , ||
KEY D.
| m ,s .m ,d :m .s | f ,r .t,, :s ,m .d , ||

Thirds of a pulse are indicated by a comma turned to the right, thus— : , , ||. The first third of a pulse is named TAA, the second third TAI, the third third TEE, and the silences and continuations are named in the same manner as before.

Ex. 159.

| l :l ,l ,l | l ,,l :l . ||
TAA taataitee TAAfe TAA*SAI*

KEY F.
| d :r ,m ,f | m ,,s :s ||
KEY F.
| m :f ,m ,r | m ,,d :d . ||
KEY A.
| s :m ,d ,m | s ,,s :s ||
KEY A.
| m :d ,l, ,t, | d ,,d :d ||

Ex. 160.

| l .l :l ,,l | l ,l ,l :l .l ||
TAATAI TAAfe tataitee TAATAI

KEY F.
| d .r :m ,,f | m ,r ,d :r .d ||
KEY F.
| m .r :d ,,r | m ,f ,s :f .m ||
KEY A.
| d .s, :m ,,r | d ,t, ,d :m .r ||
KEY A.
| m .d :s ,,l | s ,f ,m :r .d ||

Ex. 161.

```
|l ,l ,l :l ,- ,l |l,l .l,l :l   .l   ||
 taataitee taa-aitee tafatefe TAATAI
KEY F.
|d ,m ,s :m ,- ,d |d ,r .m ,f :s  .s  ||
KEY F.
|s ,m ,d :m ,- ,s |s ,f .m ,r :d  .d  ||
KEY A.
|d ,t, ,d :m ,- ,d |r ,d .r ,m :d  .s, ||
KEY A.
|m ,f ,m :r ,- ,m |s ,l .s ,f :m  .d  ||
```

What is a pulse?—It will be noticed that the six-pulse exercises in this step move more quickly than Ex. 80, and that the time is most easily indicated by "beating twice to the measure," as directed p. 24, and might have been written accordingly in two-pulse measure. Ex. 175 might have been written thus—

```
{      : , ,s |s    :-,-,s |s    :-,-,s |s,-,s :m',-,r' }
{|d'   : -,- , |l ,- ,t :d',- ,l |s       : d'          }
```

The present plan is only adopted for the sake of greater clearness to the eye in the time divisions. All such rapidly moving tunes should be *taataid* as "Two-pulse measure abounding in thirds." It will also be noticed that many of the rhythms, given in our time-exercises might be written out more fully by making one measure into two. Tunes are differently written in this respect in the common notation as well as in the Tonic Sol-fa notation. Even Handel in one copy of a tune puts into two measures the music which in another copy he puts into one measure and in yet another into four measures. The principle which seems to guide composers is this. The quicker they wish the music to be sung the fewer measures they give it, and the slower they wish it sung the more measures they divide it into. They know that singing quickly makes the accents slighter and less observable, and that singing slowly developes accents which would otherwise have been scarcely noticed. As in common life it is only by occurrences that we can mark the flight of time, so in music it is only by accents that we can measure out our tones. The accents of a musical passage may be distinguished as the principal and the subordinate ones. The principal accents should be marked by the divisions of a measure, and the subordinate accents by the divisions of a pulse. Whether any particular accent is principal or subordinate depends much on the rate at which the music is sung, and is always a matter of judgment. A pulse or beat we define as a unit of the principal and regularly recurring accents of a tune, but a pulse is not in all cases an absolute, undeniable, unmistakeable unit. It is "a measure of estimation." The composer sings or plays or *feels* his music, and where, in his estimation, the principal accents fall, there he writes the great pulses of his measure, the subordinate accents falling into their places *within* those pulses. But if the subordinate accents are numerous and regularly recurring, it is often better for the clear reading of his music that he should treat them as principal accents. Unfortunately in the common notation there is no certainty which note (crotchet, quaver, or minim) the composer means for a "beat." If writers made it a law that the crotchet (for example) should always stand for what they mean to be *a beat* of their music, we should have no difficulty in understanding them, but even the same composer represents a pulse at different times in different ways; so that the Tonic Sol-fa translator is obliged to *listen* to the music, *feel* the accents, and write accordingly.

Beating Time.—Hitherto the pupil has not been allowed to beat time. He has only learnt to *sing* in time. Because no one can well learn two things at once, and, consequently, those who try to do so are constantly found beating to their singing instead of singing to an independent, steady beat. There are some, however, to whom the swing of the hand or the motion of the foot easily becomes instinctive. The beating goes on without need of thought or attention—like the swing of a pendulum. Such persons and such only can use *beating* in time as a criterion of *singing* in time. Hitherto the teacher has been the standard of time for his pupils. He has infused into them by watchfulness, by criticism, by decision, his own feeling of time. He is striving throughout to make his pupil's sense of *hearing* appreciate time; but when that failed, there was always his beating (communicating time through another sense, the sense of sight) to correct them. If he wishes, now, to give them a criterion of their own, he may proceed as follows. The teacher says, "Watch my beating, and do as I do."

He beats the four-pulse measure at the rate of M. 60. The pupils imitate him. This should be done by one hand, silently, chiefly by the motion of the wrist (the thumb being always upwards), and with very little motion of the arm. The finger should pass swiftly and decidedly from one *point* of the beating to the next, and it should be held steadily at each point as long as the "pulse" lasts. When this is properly done, the teacher will say, "Now, you shall beat one measure, I the next, and so on." This not-easy exercise accomplished, a more difficult one is proposed. Let each pupil beat one measure, in turn, all taking care that there is no pause nor variation in the rate of movement. A more difficult exercise still—but most useful for establishing the sense of time in both ear and mind—will be for the teacher and pupils to beat time together for a few measures, and then at a given signal to drop the hand, and pause for one, two, three, or more measures (as the teacher may have fixed beforehand), *and to begin beating again at the right moment.* In this exercise you will soon notice how fast time goes with the ardent temperaments, how slow with the heavy-minded, and how difficult it is for any one to attain an exact sense of time. The same series of exercises will be pursued in three-pulse measure, in two-pulse measure, and in six-pulse measure. A metronome may be introduced as a test, instead of the teacher's own judgment. There are various ways of beating time. We recommend the following as the most appropriate and the most clearly visible. The direction of the motion is from the thinner to the thicker end of each dash. The thick end of each dash shows the "point of rest" for each pulse.

TWO-PULSE MEASURE. THREE-PULSE MEASURE. FOUR-PULSE MEASURE. SIX-PULSE MEASURE.

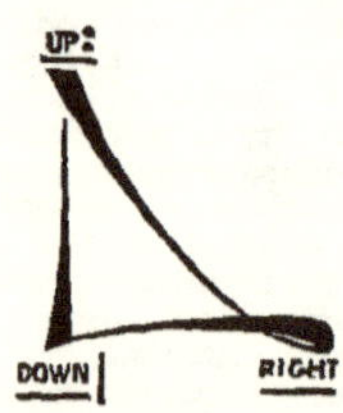

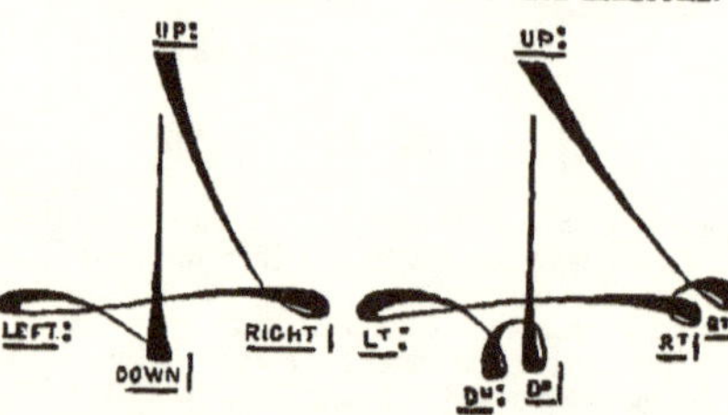

NOTE.—It is better to beat the second pulse of "three-pulse measure" towards the right, than (as some do it) towards the left, because it thus corresponds with the medium beat of the "four-pulse measure," and the second pulse of three-pulse measure is *like* a medium pulse. It is commonly treated (both rhythmically and harmonically) as a continuation of the *first* pulse. Similar reasons show a propriety in the mode of beating recommended for "six-pulse measure;" but when this measure moves *very* quickly, it is beaten like the "two-pulse measure," giving a beat on each accented pulse.

M. 60.—Efforts to remember this rate and twice as fast, M. 120, and about *half* as fast again, M. 92, and between that and 60 *two* rates, M. 80 and M. 72, and between that and 120 *one* rate, M. 106, should be frequently made, as recommended, p. 34. By self discipline this can be done.

The Registers.—It has been shewn that the human voices make together one great organ—running through its various registers from the lowest bass to the highest soprano—so that the voices of a class containing men and women could run up one grand homogeneous scale of three or four octaves. See pp. 29 and 32. The compass of each particular voice is only a portion cut out of this great scale and taking the registers as they come. It should be carefully noted that the difference of male and female voices, as soprano, contralto, tenor, bass, does not necessarily make any difference of quality on identical tones. Thus a contralto, a tenor, and a bass, when naturally trained, do not generally differ in quality on $G_,$, $A_,$, and $B_,$, and a soprano, contralto, and tenor singing the identical tones *C*, *D*, *E*, could not be distinguished from one another except by the shades of difference which naturally mark individual voices.

or the more marked differences introduced by false training. Uncultivated male singers are commonly much ashamed of their weak Thin register until they have made it strong by practice. Already some progress has been made in strengthening it by means of Ex. 104, p. 33. This *staccato* koo-ing exercise must not be discontinued. It may, however, now be varied after the manner of the two exercises which follow.

*Ex. 162. KEYS **F, G, F♯, G♯.**

| m'.d' : r'.t | d'.l : t .s | l : t | d' : — ||
koo, &c.

Ex. 163. KEYS **A, B, A♯, C.**

: d' | t.,t : l.,l | s.,s : f.,f | s : s | d' ||
koo, | &c.

Recognition of the first or Thick Register.—As the Thin register was found to be neglected by men and commonly used by women, so the Thick register is neglected by women and commonly used by men. Many soprano singers do not know what it is, and even contraltos are afraid to employ what they think is a man's voice. Mdme. Seiler says it is quite common for voice-trainers to encourage women to ignore altogether the *upper* Thick register using the Thin instead; so that when on A, they do at last enter the Thick register it is on its fully vibrated tones, and the change of quality is unpleasantly marked. To enable female pupils to *recognise* the Thick register, place the scale (p. 29) or the Voice Modulator (p. 106) before them, and then, beginning with a tone (B, A, or G) decidedly within the Thin (their easy) register, let them sing *downwards* (guided by the manual signs) **d' s m d**, and *with increased force* on the lowest tone. This last tone will certainly be in the Thick register. Having got that quality of tone let them run up, *retaining the same quality*, to **F**. This is the converse of the process by which the tenors and basses learnt to recognise the Thin register, p. 33.

Strengthening of the Thick register.—Contraltos and sopranos will require the same *staccato* koo-ing exercise to strengthen the lower part of their voices, which tenors and basses required (p. 33) for the *higher* part of *their* voices. The process of strengthening must be upwards from the undoubted territory of the Thick register towards the borderland of Thick and Thin. Be careful not to *force* this register too much, for the registers cannot be made to overlap *upwards* without injury. Male voices may join with the female voices in this exercise, for it is easy to them, and they may encourage the sopranos and contraltos, but they must sing softly lest the voices which need the exercise should be unheard. Let the following exercises be used after the manner described p. 33. The men will have to suppose the notes an octave higher than they are written.

Ex. 164. KEYS **A, B, A♯.**

: d, | m, : r, | f, : m, | s, : s, | d, ||
koo, | &c.

Ex. 165. KEYS **G, A, G♯, A♯.**

| d,.m, : r,.f, | m,.s, : f,.l, | s, : s, | d, : — ||
koo, &c.

†Ex. 166. KEYS **G, A, G♯, A♯.**

: d, | r,.,r, : m,.,m, | f,.,f, : s,.,s, | l, : s, | d, ||
koo, | &c.

Blending of Registers.—A good singer should be able to pass from one register to another without allowing the difference to be noticed. With this view the voice trainer strengthens on the "optional tones" (p. 32) the weaker of the two registers (in men the Thin—in women the Thick) till it equals, in volume, in quality, and in ease of production, the stronger one. He then tests the power of the singer in producing one or the other register at will, as in the following exercises imitated from Garcia. The notes in common type are to be sung in the Thick, and those in italics in the Thin registers. The effort will be to make the two tones as similar as possible. Let the pupil take no breath in passing from one register to the other, and let him sing each exercise quicker and quicker. Male voices will sing these exercises in the higher part of their range, and female voices in the lower part of their range. Men and women will sing identical tones. None of the keys must be omitted, because we have to give exercise to *all* the small Laryngeal muscles, through the whole range of the optional tones. This is a case in which class teaching is insufficient. It can only set the pupil in the right way. He must judge his own progress. The effort to do so will make him eager to enjoy the advantage of individual teaching.

* This Exercise can be used for the "Upper Thick," in key C, and for the "Upper Thin" in keys C', D', E', &c. It may be adapted for the "Small" in keys B', C', &c.

† Be careful not to carry the "Lower Thick" above B (or A, for men), but to change into the "Upper Thick."

Ex. 167. KEYS C, D, C♯, D♯.

| d' :m' | d' :m' | d' :m' | d' :— ||
| koo, &c.

Ex. 168. KEYS C, D, C♯, D♯, D, E.

| d' :r' | d' :r' | d' :r' | d' :— ||
| koo, &c.

Ex. 169. KEYS C, D, C♯, D♯, D, E, D♯, F, E, F♯.

| d' :d' | d' :d' | d' :d' | d' :— ||
| koo, &c.

Recognition and Management of Optional Tones.—Tenor singers should now systematically study the best use of their optional tones. First, before commencing any tune they should notice the key, and from that ascertain to what Sol-fa notes their optional tones will fall. The Voice Modulator p. 106 will at first assist them in this. Second, they should study the phrasing of each passage in which the optional tones are employed. Third, in cases in which a *piano* or *forte* is required they will remember that they can obtain a stronger tone with the Thick than with the Thin register. Some persons habitually change the register at a certain pitch, whatever the passage sung. Others try to avoid changing the register within any single musical phrase, as much as possible. Descending from the thin register, they keep it as far as they can. Ascending into the thin register, they begin their phrase, if possible, in that register. In Exercises 170 to 173 a thin horizontal mark is placed over the tone in which, for various reasons, it is thought best that a tenor voice should change into the thin register, and a double horizontal mark is placed where it is thought better to change into the thick register. Let the pupil be required to find the reasons for each of these changes, and be encouraged to suggest other and better changes.

A Knowledge of Dissonances is useful to the singer in making him fearless. If he does not recognise the fact that he is striking a dissonance, he feels as though something were wrong, and is tempted to sing falsely. But if he knows what he is doing he strikes his tone with courage, looks well to the resolution, and makes it beautiful. Notice the definition of dissonances, p. 21.

Part-pulse Dissonances.—At p. 21 there is an explanation of the commonest sort of dissonance which appears on the weak part of a pulse,—*the part-pulse passing tone.* Four other apologies are also accepted by the ear for dissonances on the weak part of a pulse. When, like **s** in the following — | r .,s : s || they simply *anticipate* the tone which follows them,—when like l or t in the following — | d' .t : d' | s .l : s || they *wave* upward or downward, or when, like **f** and **m** in the following — | s .f : r .m | d || they *hang* upward or downward from the proper tone of the chord, or when, like t and l in the following — | m .t, : d .l, | t, || they *guide*, generally by an upward step, to the tone which follows. All these melodic relations are accepted as an occasional apology for dissonances. In addition to these dissonances on the weak part of a pulse, dissonances are also allowed, though less frequently, on the first or *strong* part of a pulse. These are all called *Forestrokes.* They nearly all "resolve" (see p. 21) by going a step downwards. The smoothest "preparation" for these discords is when, like **r** in the following — : r | r .d || the dissonance has just been heard as a consonance in the previous chord. This will be called a *Horizontal* forestroke. The preparation which stands next in acceptance with the ear is when, as **s** in the following — : l | s . f || the dissonance comes down from the tone above,—like a passing tone, but on the strong part of a pulse. This is called an *Oblique* forestroke. A less common apology is when, like **f** in the following— | .m : f .m || we have a *Waving* forestroke. Less frequently still we may have, like **m** in the following — | d .r : m .f | s || an under oblique forestroke resolving upward. But when the composer wishes not to apologize for a forestroke, but to *assert* it for the sake of a certain tart effect he leaves it *Unprepared*, like l in the following— : m | l .s : f ||. Advanced pupils only will have time to study these points. They may do so privately by marking beforehand, in the exercises, the cases they wish to notice, and, when the time for singing comes, *listening* for the effects. Or, if the whole class is sufficiently skilful and attentive, the teacher may lead the class to examine each of the following cases and then to sing the phrase softly to *laa* two or three times. See Examples of Part-pulse *Passing* tones in Ex. 133, *l.* 1, *m.* 4, *p.* 2; and *m.* 7, *p.* 1; and *l.* 2, *m.* 4, *p.* 1; and Ex. 172, *l.* 3, *m.* 3, *p.* 2, a peculiar case. See Anticipation tones, Ex. 174, *l.* 4, *m.* 2, *p.* 2. See Waving tones, Ex. 125, *m.* 5, *p.* 2; Ex. 171, *l.* 2, *m.* 3, *p.* 3; Ex. 174, *l.* 3, *m.* 3, *p.* 1, 2, 3; and *l.* 4, *m.* 1, *p.* 1, 2, 3. See Horizontal Forestrokes in Ex. 172, *l.* 2, *m.* 1, *p.* 2 and 3; and *l.* 2, *m.* 3, *p.* 3; and *m.* 4, *p.* 1 and 2;

Ex. 174, *l.* 5, *m.* 1, *p.* 3. See Oblique Forestrokes, Ex. 170, *l.* 1, *m.* 1, *p.* 4; and *m.* 2, *p.* 4; and *m.* 3, *p.* 4; and *m.* 5, *p.* 4; and *m.* 6, *p.* 4.

Full-pulse Dissonances.—All the apologies above described are also accepted by the ear as excusing full-pulse dissonances. If the music moves very quickly, Passing tones and other dissonances so common on the weak *part* of a pulse are freely used on the weak *pulse*, the strong and weak pulse being treated harmonically as though they were one pulse. But when the music moves slowly the ear is not so content with these slight apologies; and only the "passing tone" is much used. On the strong pulse, however, as on the strong *part* of a pulse, the various forestrokes are often employed. When prepared they are employed for the smoothness of melody, when unprepared for the sake of effect.

See examples of quick moving dissonances in Ex. 141, *l.* 1, *m.* 3, *p.* 2; and *l.* 2, *m.* 1, *p.* 2; Ex. 192, *l.* 1, *m.* 3, *p.* 2 and 6; *l.* 6, *m.* 4, *p.* 2 and 6; *l.* 10, *m.* 2, *p.* 5; Ex. 174, *l.* 7, *m.* 3, *p.* 2. See the partial dissonance (explained p. 36). Ex. 140, *l.* 2, *m.* 1, *p.* 2; and *l.* 3, *m.* 3, *p.* 2; and Ex. 143, *l.* 3, *m.* 2, *p.* 2; and "disguised" (d for f and fe for t), Ex. 174, *l.* 7, *m.* 3, *p.* 4; and also Ex. 144, *l.* 1, *m.* 2, *p.* 1, in which last case the t not being resolved on d sounds more like a forestroke. See Horizontal forestrokes in Ex. 170, *l.* 1, *m.* 4, *p.* 4, in which f, horizontally prepared, continues two pulses and then resolves on m. It is the same with m in the next measure and with r in the measure following. The waving fe in *l.* 1, *m.* 4, *p.* 4, waving against a dissonance is curious and harsh. Also in Ex. 174, *l.* 7, *m.* 1, *p.* 1; and Ex. 142, *l.* 1, *m.* 4, *p.* 1. See a case of "delayed resolution" in Ex. 137, *l.* 1, *m.* 3, where f passes through a consonance before it is resolved; and Ex. 141, *l.* 2, *m.* 3, *p.* 1, where it passes through consonance and partial dissonance to its resolution. See an *Un*prepared dissonance "l against t" introduced for its own touching effect in Ex. 174, *l.* 7, *m.* 1, *p.* 3. See d and s (Tonic and Dominant) exercising the privilege of long holding (or pedal) tones, in spite of dissonance, because of their relation to the key, in Ex. 138, *l.* 1, *m.* 2, *p.* 2; and *l.* 2, *m.* 2, *p.* 2; and *m.* 3, *p.* 3.

New Cadences.—In two-part music the full chords cannot be given. But, for reasons given in the "Common-places of Music" two-part consonances always *suggest* the chords of which they form a part. Thus, s, with d above it suggests the chord D*o*; m with s above it suggests, not the "unmeaning" and seldom used chord M*a*, but D*b*; t, with r above it suggests, not the "weak" chord T, but S*b*; l with f above it suggests F*b*, and so on. Thus interpreted, the exercises in this step introduce us to two new cadences in addition to those (the D, the S, the F D, and the L cadences) which are named on p. 48. See the uncommon cadences on F and R in Ex. 137. See what we call [S]D cadences in Ex. 142, and a [F]D cadence in Ex. 143. See what we call a "weak-pulse cadence" in Ex. 141, *l.* 2, *m.* 2, *p.* 2; and a "[F]D weak-pulse cadence" in *l.* 1, *m.* 4, *p.* 2.

Phrases, Sections, Periods.—The nature of a cadence has been explained at p. 48. There it has been shewn that the cadence naturally *cuts* the melody into parts, and that these parts are called "Sections." "Phrases" are divisions of melody *within* a Section. "Periods" are divisions of melody including two or more Sections. In extended pieces of music we use the word "strain" to represent several periods combined in one melodic whole. A Section, which is two measures in length, we call a Duain, one of three measures a Triain, and one of four a Quadrain.

Musical Form.—A good form in house or ornament or animal must be symmetrical and varied and adapted, in all its parts, to its chief purpose. So, in music, a well-formed tune has symmetry and proportion in the length of its principal parts or "lines;" it has both symmetry and variety in the rhythms and melodic replies of its musical phrases; and its harmony as well as the style of its melody combine together to express the general sentiment desired. A disjointed, ill-formed tune would be like a picture in which a number of men and women beautiful and ugly, should be thrown together "any how." A well-formed tune is like those men and women artistically grouped in one picture — where the beautiful are placed forward and the ugly kindly put in the shade, and the colours and postures all arranged for some unity of effect. It is pleasant when one sees a house or an ornament or an animal, to "know its points" of excellence, but we can receive much enjoyment from them without so intelligent an eyesight. In *listening* to music the case is similar. But in *singing* music the case is different. For the singer is an Artist. The sculptor and the painter can present their own works to the public view. But the musical composer is dependent on another artist—the singer or the player

—to present his works. By singing loudly or softly, quickly or slowly, in various places and various degrees, the singer can make or mar the handiwork of the helpless composer. Every intelligent singer will therefore feel it his duty to study his music beforehand, and to fix in his mind how, by the art of Expression (p. 30), its various rhythmical divisions and melodic ideas are to be distinguished and "set off' one from the other, how he can change a bare outline into a coloured picture. The main principles of Melodic Relation have already been suggested under the headings "Relative motion of parts" and "Imitation," pp. 36, 37. Some ideas of "phrasing"—or marking out of melodic divisions are suggested under the heading "Breathing-places," pp. 9, 30. Other principles of Rhythmic Proportion may be easily apprehended, and then an examination of a few examples will shew the pupil how to *begin* this enjoyable study. A fuller development of it is found in "Musical Theory," Book III.

Parsing or Analysis of Musical Form.—The practice of requiring a pupil to make a written or verbal analysis of the tune about to be sung is very useful. Even elementary pupils should answer the first and second questions,—

1st. What is the Form—as Psalm-tune, Song, Dance, March, etc.

2nd. What are the Key, the Measure, the Rate, and the Style?

3rd. What is the Rhythmical Division? (That is, does it divide itself into two principal parts, or into three? Is it Two-fold or Three-fold?) And what is its Cadence design? The *first* "Cadence design" makes its principal dividing cadence (the most important cadence next to the final one) on the first sharp key (^{S}D), or in a minor mode tune on the relative major (D); the *second*, on the Dominant S (or ^{S}E*M*); the *third*, on the Tonic generally, with its Third or Fifth in the air (D^{3} D^{5} D or L^{3} L^{5} L); and the *fourth* must have some other Cadence in that place.

4th. What is the Structural Plan? That is, describe or mark the place where the Periods and Sections (p. 69) of the Tune begin, using the Roman figures, I, II, etc., to indicate Periods, and the small capitals, A, B, etc., to indicate Sections. Thus IA means First Section of First Period.

St. Co. (New.)

5th. What are the Transitions or Modulations most worthy of note?

6th. What are the Principal Responses? That is, first, (or Pds.), what are the *principal* Melodic or Rhythmic replies (see Imitation, pp. 36, 37), of Period to Period? Second (or Sec.), What are the principal Melodic or Rhythmic replies of Section to Section within each Period? Third (or Har.), What are the principal points in the relation of "Parts" in the Harmony? (See above, p. 36).

7th. What are the most interesting devices, that is, Sequence, Fugal Imitations, etc.?

8th. What is the Emotional Development and Point? That is, describe how, in the successive Sections, the "feeling" of the tune rises and falls; and say which in your opinion is the most remarkable and effective point (whether of elevation or depression) in all the tune.

Examples of Parsing.—The following examples should be tested by singing over and over again, and comparing one with another the various Sections and Periods of the tune. The teacher will find useful examples of Parsing *from the Charts* in "Teacher's Manual," p. 194.

Ex. 133 is—

1st. A Psalm-tune.

2nd. In key A, in two-pulse measure, of firm and prayerful style, about M. 80.

3rd. Is Two-fold, and of the first cadence design.

4th. IA a Quadrain, IB a Triain, lengthened by the "hold" to a Quadrain; IIA a Quadrain, IIB Triain, sung as a Quadrain.

5th. IB First Sharp Cadence.

6th. (Pds.) IIA contrasts with IA by setting of **f** against **m**: otherwise it imitates it. IIB contrasts the **r s** against the **s r** of IB, and has contrary motion in its second phrase. (Har.) contrary motion of parts at the end of IB, and similar motion at the beginning of IIA.

7th. None.

8th. IA seems to make a quiet assertion with a double emphasis on **m**. IB seems to give an exciting reply; IIA the assertion made more solemn by **f** twice emphasized. IIB, the joyful sure decision leaping up to the brilliant **s** and making the "point" of the tune by falling on the solemn **f**.

Exercise **137** is—1st. A song for S and C.

2nd. In key B♭, in four-pulse measure, in a bold style, at M. 112.

3rd. Is Two-fold, and of the first cadence design.

4th. IA, a Duain, IB, Duain, IC, Duain, ID, Duain; IIA, Duain, IIB, Duain, IIC, Duain, IID, Duain.

5th. First sharp extended in ID.

6th. (Pds.) IIA B has contrasted motion to IA B. (Sec.) IB is a rising imitation of IA, and ID similarly rises out of IC. IIB imitates IIA a third higher, IIC again returns strongly to the rising motion which sets off the wide intervals and the elegant rhythm of IID. Rhythmical unity in the beginning and ending of every Section till the last which makes the rhythm of the last more effective. (Har.) I has principally contrary motion between parts; IIA opens with contrary motion, IIB has chiefly similar motion, IIC has contrary motion, IID has oblique and similar motion.

7th. A melodic sequence in IIA and B.

8th. IA, a resolute thought (with TAA -AATAI and accented s and d), IB, repeated more earnestly, IC, a rising feeling, ID, passionate resolution; IIA, quieter counsels, IIB, repeated in loftier strain. IIC, return of the passion bringing the tune to its "point" of greatest energy, IID, the subsidence of passion in settled resolve.

When a systematic course is pursued, the exercises of the 3rd and 4th Steps can be taken in the following order:—97, 115, 134, 136, 140, 141, 142, 143, 144, 145, 113, 119, 120, 174, 175. Some of the exercises with fugal imitations are too difficult for the present step. For a fuller course, apply to the Secretary of the Tonic Sol-fa College.

HOSANNA.

Ex. 170. KEY C. *Optional Tones,* d' r' m' f' * *Mainzer.*

s :l .t | d' :—	– .l :t .d' | r' :—	– .t :d' .r' | m' :—	– .d' :r' .m' | f' :—
Ho - san - na,	Ho-san - na,	Ho-san - na,	Ho-san - na,
: | .d :r .m	f :— | – .r :m .fe	s :— | – .m :f .s	l :— | – .l :s .fe
Hallelu-	jah! Hallelu-	jah! Hallelu-	jah! Hallelu-

– .f' :m' .r' | m' :—	– .m' :r' .d' | r' :—	– .r' :d' .t | l :s .f	m :— | — :—
Ho-san - na,	Ho-san - na,	Ho - san -	na.
s :— | – .s :f .m	f :— | – .f :m .r	m :— | – .f :m .r	d :— | — :—
jah! Hallelu-	jah! Hallelu-	jah! Hallelu-	jah!

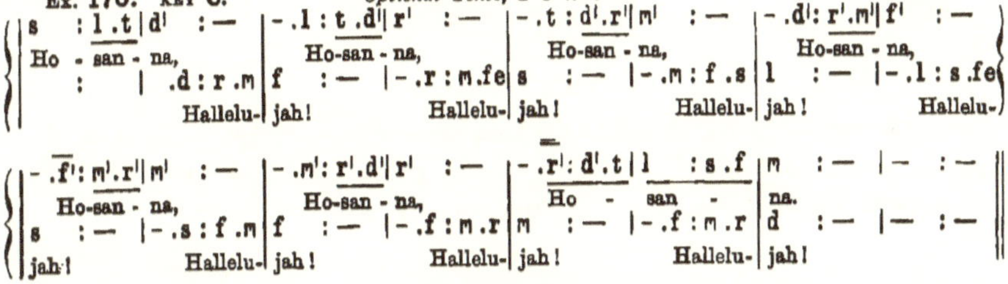

HALLELUJAH.

Ex. 171. KEY C. *Optional Tones,* d' r' m' f' *Mainzer.*

s :l .t | d' :—	l :t .d' | r' :—	t :d' .r' | m' .s' :f' .m'	f' :— | – .f' :m' .r'
Hal - le-lu-jah!	Hal - le -lu -jah!	Hal - le -lu-jah! A -	men, A -
m :— | – .s :f .m	f :— | – .l :s .fe	s :— | – .t :l .s	l :r' .d' | t .l :s .f
A - - -	men, A -	men, A -	men, Hal - le - lu -

m' :— | – .m' :r' .d'	r' :— | – .r' :d' .t	d' :— | t :—	d' :— | — :—
men, A -	men, A -	men, A -	men.
m :d' .t | l .s :f .m	r :t .l | s .f :m .r	m .f :m .r | s .l :s .f	m :— | — :—
jah! Hal - le - lu -	jah! Hal - le - lu -	jah! A - -	men.

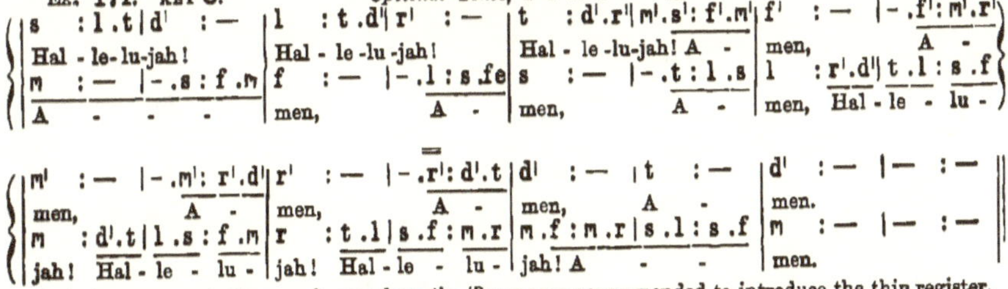

* A stroke over a note thus — shews where the Tenors are recommended to introduce the thin register. and a double stroke thus ═ shews where they are advised to use the thick register.

Ex. 172. KEY G. **AMEN.** *Optional Tones,* m f s l *Albrechtsberger.*

.d :r .m :f .s,f	m .d' :t .d' :l .t	d' .s,f :m .d :r .t,	d : .l :f .s,f
A - -	men, A - -	men, A - -	men, A -
: :	.d :r .m :f .s,f	m : .m :f .r	m .s,f :m .d :r .t,
	A - -	men, A -	men, A - -

D. t.

m .d' :- .t :- .l	l r' .d' :- .t,l :t .d',r'	m' .r',d' :t .d' :f	m .l :r :s
men, A - -	- - -	men, A - men,	A - -
d .m :r .s :d	t, m :r :s	d .f :- .m :- .r	- .d :- .t,,l, :t, .d,r
men, A - men,	A - -	men, A - -	- - - -

f. G.

d :m t, .d :r .t,	d .s :r .m :f .s,f	m,s .l,t :d' :- .t	d' :— :
men, A -	men, A - -	men, A - -	men.
m .d' :s r .m :f .s,f	m :t, .d :r .s,	d : ,m .r,d :r	d :— :
men, A - -	men, A -	men, A -	men.

THE CUCKOO.

Ex. 173. KEY C. M. 112. Round for four parts. *Optional Tones,* d' r' m' *A. L. C.*

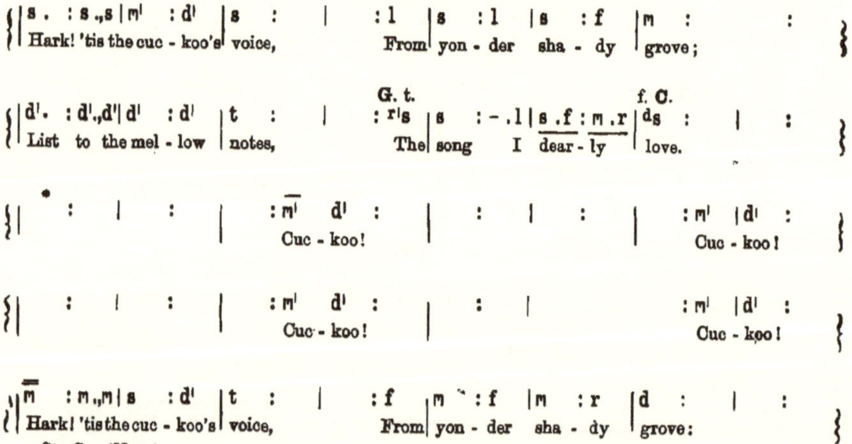

s . :s .,s | m' :d'	s : | :l	s :l | s :f	m : :
Hark! 'tis the cuc - koo's	voice, From	yon - der sha - dy	grove;

G. t. f. C.

d' . :d' .,d' | d' :d'	t : | :r's	s :- .l | s .f :m .r	ds : | :
List to the mel - low	notes, The	song I dear - ly	love.

: | :	:m' d' :	: | :	:m' | d' :
	Cuc - koo!		Cuc - koo!

: | :	:m' d' :	: |	:m' | d' :
	Cuc - koo!		Cuc - koo!

m :m .,m | s :d'	t : | :f	m :f | m :r	d : | :
Hark! 'tis the cuc - koo's	voice, From	yon - der sha - dy	grove:

St Co. (New.)

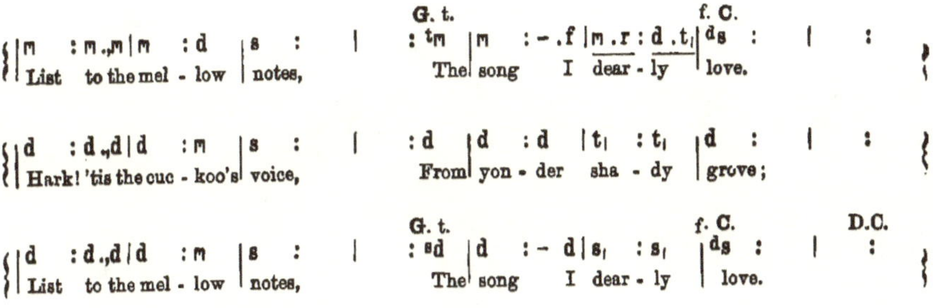

G. t. f. C.
| m :m.,m | m :d | s : | :tm | m :-.f | m.r :d.t, | ds : | : |
List to the mel - low notes, The song I dear - ly love.

| d :d.,d | d :m | s : | :d | d :d | t, :t, | d : | : |
Hark! 'tis the cuc - koo's voice, From yon - der sha - dy grove;

G. t. f. C. D.C.
| d :d.,d | d :m | s : | :sd | d :- d | s, :s, | ds : | : |
List to the mel - low notes, The song I dear - ly love.

CODA. To be sung by all together.

f= m p— pp
| :m' | d' : | :m' | d' : | :m' | d' : | :m' | d' : ||
Cu - koo! Cuc - koo! Cuc - koo! Cuc - koo!

THE MAYTIME.

Ex. 174. KEY G. WORDS BY J. S. STALLYBRASS. *A. L. C.*

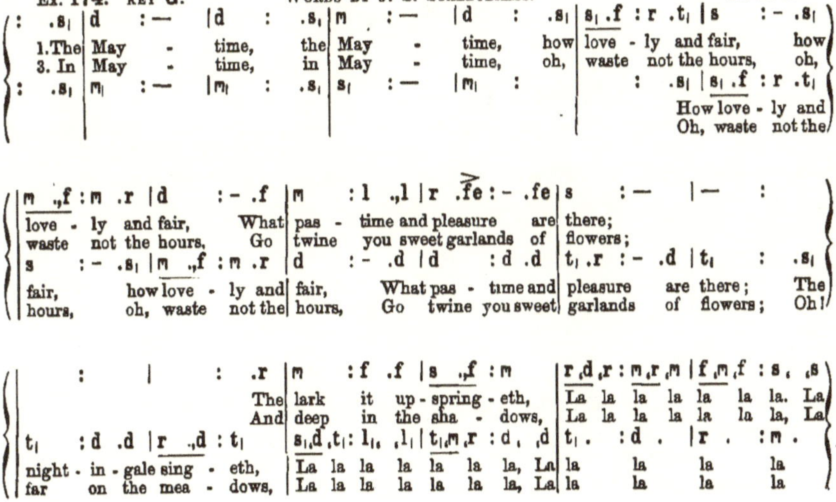

: .s, | d :— | d : .s, | m :— | d : .s, | s,.f :r .t, | s :- .s, |
1. The May - time, the May - time, how love - ly and fair, how
3. In May - time, in May - time, oh, waste not the hours, oh,
: .s, | m, :— | m, : .s, | s, :— | m, : | : .s, | s,.f :r .t, |
How love - ly and
Oh, waste not the

| m .,f :m .r | d :- .f | m :l .,l | r .fe :- .fe | s :— | — : |
love - ly and fair, What pas - time and pleasure are there;
waste not the hours, Go twine you sweet garlands of flowers;
| s :- .s, | m .,f :m .r | d :- .d | d :d .d | t, .r :- .d | t, : .s, |
fair, how love - ly and fair, What pas - time and pleasure are there; The
hours, oh, waste not the hours, Go twine you sweet garlands of flowers; Oh!

| : | : .r | m :f .f | s .,f :m | r,d,r :m,r,m | f,m,f :s, ,s |
The lark it up - spring - eth, La la la la la la la. La
And deep in the sha - dows, La la la la la la la, La
| t, :d .d | r .,d :t, | s,,d,t, :l,,l, | t,,m,r :d, ,d | t, . :d . | r . :m . |
night - in - gale sing - eth, La la la la la la la, La la la la la
far on the mea - dows, La la la la la la la, La la la la la

l . :s .	f . :m .r	d .r :- .r	m :- .f	s :—	— :s .f
la la la, O - ver	field and hill and	dale, O - ver
la la la, There is	fulness of life and	joy, And there
f ,s ,f :m ,f ,m	r ,m ,r :d .	.t₁ :t₁ .d	- .s₁ :d .r	m :—	— :
La la la la la la,	O'er field and hill and	dale,
La la la la la la,	Is fulness of life and	joy,

m .f :- .m	r :- .r	d :—	— : .s	s :—	m : .m	m :—	d : .d
field and hill and	dale. The	May - time, the	May - time, the
reacheth us no an-	noy.
.r :r .d	- .d :t₁ .s₁	d :—	— : .m	m :—	d : .d	s₁ :—	m₁ : .m₁
O'er field and hill and	dale. The	May - time, the	May - time, the
There reacheth us no an	-noy.

FINE. D. t.

t₁ :r	— :f	m :—	d ‖	:	:	:	: .sd¹
love - - ly	May - time. ‖ The
s₁ :t₁	— :t₁	d :s₁	m₁ ‖ .d	d :t₁ .l₁	ml :s .f	m .f :m .r	d :d
love - - ly	May - time. ‖ 2 The	gates of the earth that were	lock'd up so fast, Let

f. G.

d¹ :t .l	r¹l :s .f	m .f :m .r	d :t₁	d .,d :r	m :fe .,fe
gates of the earth that were	lock'd up so fast, Let	out their poor pris - 'ners at
r .,r :r	m t₁ :t₁ .,t₁	d :- .s₁	m₁ :s₁	d :d	d :—
out their poor pris - 'ners at	last, Let out their	pris - 'ners at

s :—	— : .f	m .f :- .f	m .,r :d .m	s .s :l .l	s .f :m .r
last, As	li - lies, and ro - ses, And	vi - o - lets for po - sies, And the
t₁ :—	— : .t₁	d .r :- .r	d .,t₁ :d .d	m .m :f .f	m .,r :d .
last, As	li - lies, and ro - ses, And	vi - o - lets for po - sies,

D.C.

| d .r :- .r | m :m .f | s :— | s :s .f | m .f :- .m | r :- .r | d :— | — ‖
| pinks, and the bunch-es of | blue - bells, And the | little red pim - per- | nels. ‖
| .t₁ :t₁ .d | - .s₁ :d .r | m :— | m : | .r :r .d | - .d :t₁ .s₁ | d :— | — ‖
| The pinks and bunches of | blue - bells, | The little red pimper- | nels. ‖

St. Co. (New.)

THE SEA FOR ME.

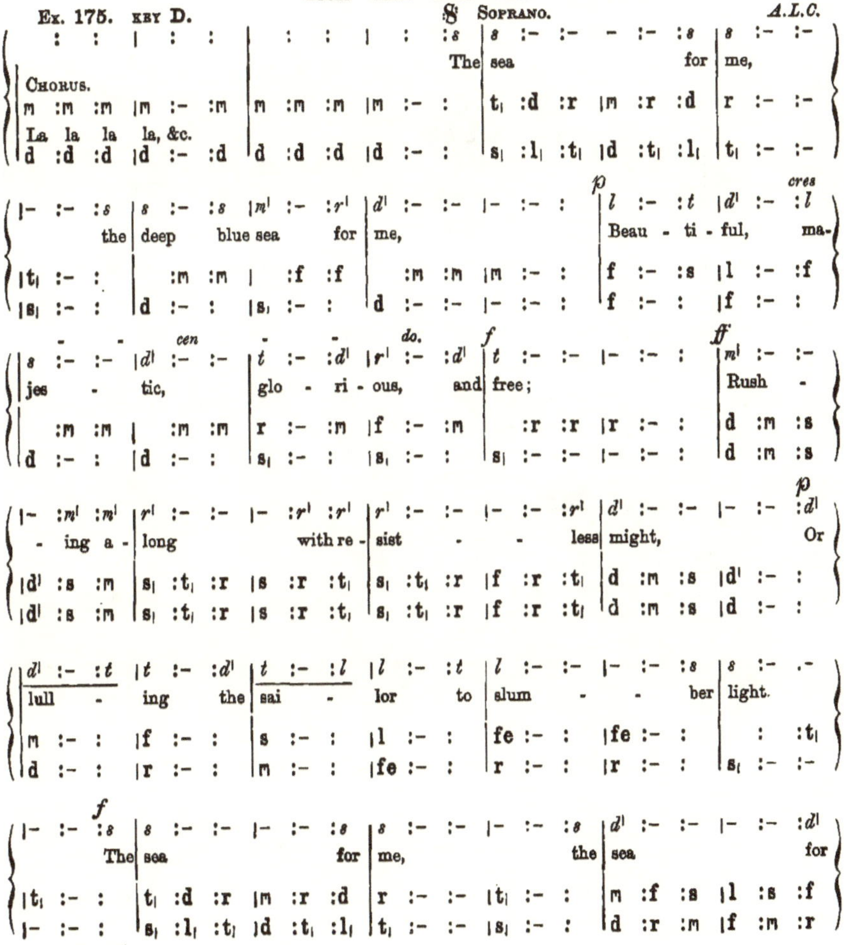

Ex. 175. KEY D. 𝄋 SOPRANO. *A.L.C.*

: : | : : | : : | : :s | s :- :- | - :- :s | s :- :-

The | sea for | me,

CHORUS.

m :m :m |m :- :m | m :m :m |m :- : | t_1 :d :r |m :r :d | r :- :-

La la la la, &c.

d :d :d |d :- :d | d :d :d |d :- : | s_1 :l_1 :t_1 |d :t_1 :l_1 | t_1 :- :-

p *cres*

|- :- :s | s :- :s |m^1 :- :r^1 | d^1 :- :- |- :- : | l :- :t |d^1 :- :l

the | deep blue sea for | me, | Beau - ti - ful, ma-

|t_1 :- : | :m :m | :f :f | :m :m |m :- : | f :- :s |l :- :f

|s_1 :- : | d :- : |s_1 :- : | d :- :- |- :- : | f :- : |f :- :

\- - *cen* - - *do.* *f* *ff*

| s :- :- |d^1 :- :- | t :- :d^1 |r^1 :- :d^1 | t :- :- |- :- : | m^1 :- :-

jes - tic, | glo - ri - ous, and | free; | Rush -

| :m :m | :m :m | r :- :m |f :- :m | :r :r |r :- : | d :m :s

| d :- : |d :- : | s_1 :- : |s_1 :- : | s_1 :- :- |- :- : | d :m :s

p

|- :m^1 :m^1 | r^1 :- :- |- :r^1 :r^1 | r^1 :- :- |- :- :r^1 | d^1 :- :- |- :- :d^1

\- ing a - | long with re - | sist - - less | might, Or

|d^1 :s :m | s_1 :t_1 :r |s :r :t_1 | s_1 :t_1 :r |f :r :t_1 | d :m :s |d^1 :- :

|d^1 :s :m | s_1 :t_1 :r |s :r :t_1 | s_1 :t_1 :r |f :r :t_1 | d :m :s |d :- :

| d^1 :- :t |t :- :d^1 | t :- :l |l :- :t | l :- :- |- :- :s | s :- .-

lull - ing the | sai - lor to | slum - - ber | light.

| m :- : |f :- : | s :- : |l :- : | fe :- : |fe :- : | : :t_1

| d :- : |r :- : | m :- : |fe :- : | r :- : |r :- : | s_1 :- :-

f

|- :- :s | s :- :- |- :- :s | s :- :- |- :- :s | d^1 :- :- |- :- :d^1

The | sea for | me, the | sea for

|t_1 :- : | t_1 :d :r |m :r :d | r :- :- |t_1 :- : | m :f :s |l :s :f

|- :- : | s_1 :l_1 :t_1 |d :t_1 :l_1 | t_1 :- :- |s_1 :- : | d :r :m |f :m :r

| d' :- :- | - :- :s | s :- :- | s :- :- | m' :- :- | - .- :r' | d' :- :- |
me, the | deep blue | sea for | me,
| s :- :- | m :- : | :m :m | :m :m | :s :s | :f :f | :m :s |
| m :- :- | d :- : | d :- : | d :- : | s_1 :- : | s_1 :- : | d :- : |

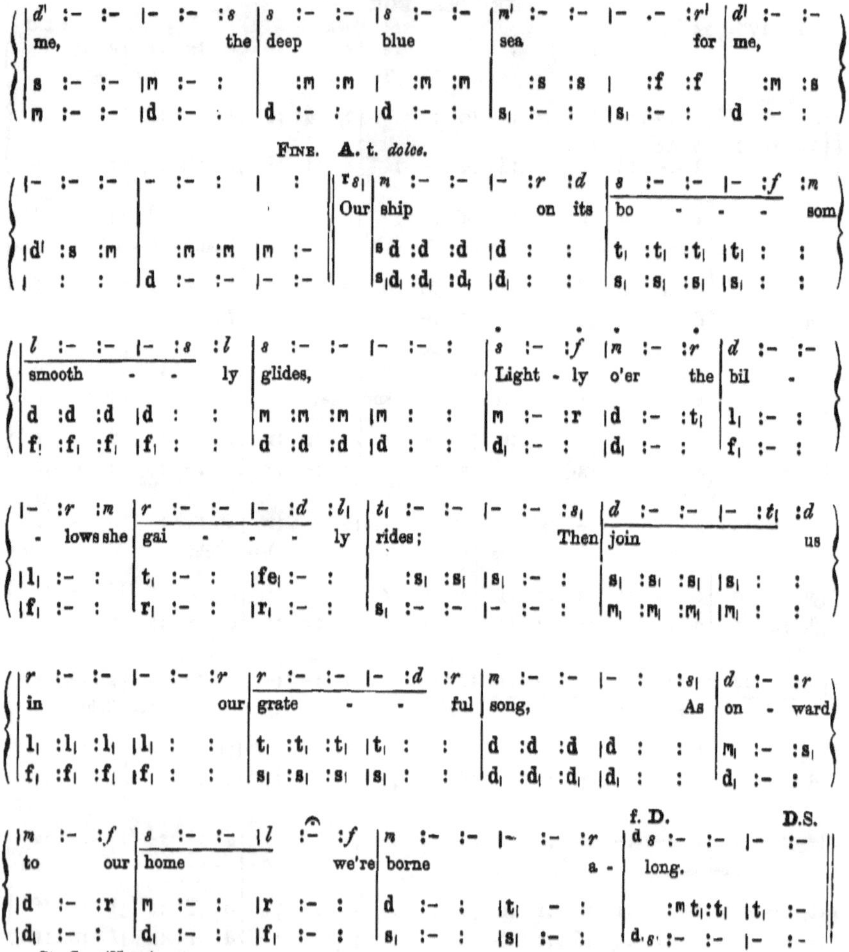

FINE. A. t. *dolce.*

| - :- :- | - :- : | : || rs_1 | m :- :- | - :r :d | s :- :- | - :f :m |
Our | ship on its | bo - - - som
| d' :s :m | :m :m | m :- || s d :d :d | d : : | t_1 :t_1 :t_1 | t_1 : : |
| : : | d :- :- | - :- || s_1d_1 :d_1 :d_1 | d_1 : : | s_1 :s_1 :s_1 | s_1 : : |

| l :- :- | - :s :l | s :- :- | - :- : | s :- :f | m :- :r | d :- :- |
smooth - - ly | glides, | Light - ly o'er the | bil -
| d :d :d | d : : | m :m :m | m : : | m :- :r | d :- :t_1 | l_1 :- : |
| f_1 :f_1 :f_1 | f_1 : : | d :d :d | d : : | d_1 :- : | d_1 :- : | f_1 :- : |

| - :r :m | r :- :- | - :d :l_1 | t_1 :- :- | - :- :s_1 | d :- :- | - :t_1 :d |
- lows she | gai - - - ly | rides; Then | join us
| l_1 :- : | t_1 :- : | fe_1 :- : | :s_1 :s_1 | s_1 :- : | s_1 :s_1 :s_1 | s_1 : : |
| f_1 :- : | r_1 :- : | r_1 :- : | s_1 :- :- | - :- : | m_1 :m_1 :m_1 | m_1 : : |

| r :- :- | - :- :r | r :- :- | - :d :r | m :- :- | - : :s_1 | d :- :r |
in our | grate - - ful | song, As | on - ward
| l_1 :l_1 :l_1 | l_1 : : | t_1 :t_1 :t_1 | t_1 : : | d :d :d | d : : | m_1 :- :s_1 |
| f_1 :f_1 :f_1 | f_1 : : | s_1 :s_1 :s_1 | s_1 : : | d_1 :d_1 :d_1 | d_1 : : | d_1 :- : |

f. D. D.S.

| m :- :f | s :- :- | l :- :f | m :- :- | - :- :r | d s :- :- | - :- ||
to our | home we're | borne a - | long.
| d :- :r | m :- : | r :- : | d :- : | t_1 - : | :m t_1 :t_1 | t_1 :- ||
| d_1 :- : | d_1 :- : | f_1 :- : | s_1 :- : | s_1 :- : | d_1s_1 :- :- | - :- ||

St. Co. (New.)

Modulator Voluntaries now include transition of one remove. These should not be made too difficult by wide and unexpected leaps on to the distinguishing tone; nor too easy by always approaching the distinguishing tone stepwise. While the effects of transition are in process of being learnt these exercises may be *solfaad*, but the teacher cannot now be *content* with solfaa-ing. Every exercise should also be *laad*, p. 37, and that to the *Italian laa*, p. 2.

Two-part Modulator Voluntaries interest the pupils much and form good voice exercises when sung to the pure and open *skaalaa*, and the simpler they are the better for this purpose. But if they are made difficult to the pupil they become difficult to the teacher and his attention is so taken up with the music he is making that he forgets to listen for the proper quality of voice. The teacher who would use only good two-part music should prepare such exercises carefully.

Sight-laa-ing.—The laa-voluntaries are really sight-singing exercises, if the teacher does not get into self-repeating habits of pointing. See p. 42. But, at their best, they give no practice in reading *time* at sight. Therefore the absolute necessity of sight-laa-ing from new music (as the monthly *Reporter*) or the black-board.

Memorizing the three keys.—The pupils should now know from memory, not only what is above any one note on the modulator and what below it, but what is on its right and what on its left. The one key no longer stands alone on the mind's modulator. It has an elder brother on the right and a younger on the left, and each of its tones bears cousinship to the other two families and may be called to enter them. Therefore at all the later lessons of this step exercises should be given in committing to memory this relationship. p. 51. The pupils must learn to say these relations, collectively and each one for himself, *without* the modulator.

Memory Patterns.—It is difficult to indicate divisions of time by the motions of the pointer on the modulator with sufficient nicety to *guide* the singer in following a voluntary, and it is important to exercise the memory of tune and rhythm. For these reasons our teachers give *long patterns*—extending to two or more sections—including some of the more delicate rhythms. These patterns are given laa-ing but pointing on the modulator. The pupils imitate them, *without* the teacher's pointing, first solfaa-ing and then laa-ing.

St. Co. (New.)

Memory Singing.—The practice of singing whole pieces to words from memory,—in obedience to the order "Close books: eyes on the baton,"—is a very enjoyable one. The singer enjoys the exercise of subordination to his conductor along with a sense of companionship in that subordination, and delights in the effects which are thus produced. This practice is very needful at the present stage in order to *form a habit*, in the singer, of *looking up* from his book. This should now be his normal position. But, as from necessity, the learner's eyes have hitherto been much engaged with his book, he will have to make a conscious effort to form "the habit of looking up." Occasional "Memory Singing" will make him feel the use and pleasure of this.

Ear Exercises, as at pp. 24, 42, will fasten on the mind the mental effects of **fe** and **ta**.

Time Ear Exercises, as at p. 24, should still be continued with the new difficulties of time.

Dictation, as at pp. 12, 24, with the new language of time just introduced, will now be carried to a much greater extent. Copies of tunes belonging to this step from other courses, or original compositions, or pieces for special occasions, can thus be rapidly multiplied. When once the practice of Dictation and the use of the "Tonic Sol-fa Copy Books" has got into familiar use in school or class many things can be done by it. Some schools are taught entirely by a Modulator, a set of Wall Sheets and Copy Books. The further we go in Dictation the more useful the time-names become. The "announcements" for Ex. 174, *l.* 3, *m.* 2, &c., would be as follows:—"TAA **m**"—"TAATAI **f f**"—"TAAfe **s f**"—"TAA **m**"—"taataitee **r d r**"—"taataitee **m r m**"—taataitee **f m f**"—taa*sai*tee **s s**"—"TAA*SAI* **l**"—"TAA*SAI* **s**"—TAA*SAI* **f**"—"TAATAI **d r**"—"-AATAI **r**" &c. The third measure of the same tune would be announced thus "TAATAI **s**-one **f**"—"TAATAI **r t**-one."

Pointing from memory and **Writing from memory**, as at pp. 12, 24, should still be practised. The second does not at all take the place of the first. We have known pupils who could write from memory, but could not point the same tunes on the modulator. It is important to establish in the memory that pictorial view of key relationship which the modulator gives, especially now that the study of Transition is added to that of the scale.

QUESTIONS FOR WRITTEN OR ORAL EXAMINATION.

DOCTRINE.

1 Name the tones of the chord of F. Say in what respect it is like the chords D and S? How is it related to the chord D, and how would you describe its mental effect?

2 Describe the chord 7S. In what case is the dissonant effect of *fah* against *soh* more slightly felt? How is the *fah* in this chord commonly prepared, and how is it always resolved?

3 What is meant by "ambiguity of chords," and which of the chords cannot be imagined to belong to more than one key?

4 What is a major chord?—A minor chord?—a diminished chord?—and which of these are in themselves the most acceptable to the ear?

5 What is the difference between the tones *ray* and *rah*? Which tones of the scale require *rah* to tune with them, and which *ray*?

6 What are the tones of the chord RAH? In what position is it most commonly found? And how would you describe its mental effect?

7 What are the tones of the chord T? How are its root and fifth usually resolved? In what position and under what circumstances is it commonly employed, and what is its mental effect?

8 What are the tones of the chord L? In what position is it used apart from the minor mode? And what chord is used interchangeably with it? What is its mental effect?

9 What are the tones of the chord M? Can it be easily substituted for the dominant or sub-dominant like the chords T and R? Is it much used?

10 What dissonance is there in the chord 7R? And how is it prepared and resolved? For what chord, in cadences, do modern writers often substitute 7R*b*?

11 What is the chief source of mental effect in a chord? And in what position is that mental effect best developed?

12 What is a cadence? Name the last three or four chords of a tonic cadence.—Of a dominant cadence.—Of a plagal cadence.—Of a surprise cadence.

13 What is the principal case in which a chord is used in its *c* position, and what is the peculiarity of this case? In what other cases is the *c* position allowed, and what are its three principal apologies?

14 Can you remember any peculiarity in the doubling or omission of the third which belongs to the chord 7S? Or any other peculiarity which belongs to minor chords generally?

15 Where are the little steps of the scale?—The greater steps?—The smaller steps? By what intervals are the two little steps of the scale separated from one another? How can you define *doh*?

16 Which are the most markedly characteristic tones of the scale? And how may they be described?

17 What is transition? In what respect are those tones of a tune changed which do not change their pitch?

18 What is the sharp distinguishing tone, and what is its effect on the ear? What is the flat distinguishing tone and its mental effect?

19 From the ear's dislike to the tritone as a melodic progression, what melodic phrases, often repeated, naturally suggest transition?

20 What is meant by the first sharp key?—The first flat key?—In going to the first sharp key, beside the substitution of the piercing tone for the desolate tone, what change of effect takes place in the tone a third above the distinguishing tone? Does any other change besides that of effect take place on the *lah*? (see "Grave *ray*" p. 46) In going to the first flat key, besides the change of a piercing for a desolate tone, what change of effect, and what other change takes place in the third above the new distinguishing tone?

21 What is the difference between the principal and a returning transition?

22 What is a bridge tone? Give examples of a bridge tone making transition through the distinguishing tone of the new key.

23 What is the meaning of the little notes placed to the right or left of the key signature in transition?

24 What are the general mental effects of transition to the first sharp key;—And to the first flat key?

25 How would you indicate transition by the manual signs?

26 What kind of effect is produced on the mind when *fe* does not move to *soh* in the next chord, or when *ta* does not go to *lah*?—And by what name is that effect called?

27 What is the commonest case of transition to the first sharp key, and by what name is it called? What is the difference between the flat and sharp keys in this respect?

28 What is the commonest case of transition to the first flat key, and by what name is it called? How does the use of the first sharp key differ from that of the flat in this respect?

29 How do you define extended transition? Which of the two transitions is more used in this way?

30 What is a sharp?—And what relation does it bear to the tones which stand below and above it in the scale? What is a flat?—And what relation does it bear to the tones above and below it in the scale?

31 On what particulars of knowledge and skill does a good musical recitation depend? What are other words for the articulations and continuations of voice? Which of these two is the more important?—And why? Why is the other of the two to be first studied?

32 Name and illustrate, by example, all the five lip articulations.

33 Name and illustrate the two articulations of lip and teeth.

34 Name and illustrate the two articulations of Tip-tongue and teeth.

35 Name and illustrate the five articulations of Tip-tongue and palate.

36 Name and illustrate the two articulations of the Mid-tongue with the Palate, in which the Tip-tongue takes a very decided part, the two in which it takes a less decided part, and the two in which it takes no part.

37 Name and illustrate the three Back-tongue articulations.

38 Name the six articulations with shut passage, placing the two qualities (breath and voice) together in couples.

39 Name, as above, the eight articulations with central passage.

40 Name, as above, the five articulations with side passages.

41 Name the three articulations with nasal passage.

42 Describe the aspirate *H*. In the articulations what organs of speech come in contact and separate?

43 Which are the consonants least capable of being sung? Which are the six Hisses? Which are the six Buzzes? How far are the Hisses and Buzzes capable of being sung? Which are the three smothered consonants? Which are the five which can be murmured or hummed. What is a Glide? What is the difference between the Glide joining *b* and *oo* and that joining *b* and *ee*? If two sounds are kept distinct, but pronounced rapidly one after the other, what *more* do they want to make them into a syllable? As scarcely any of the consonants are pleasant when sounded alone, what part of a consonantal effect

is it that can be really sounded? And what habit in the management of the organs of voice is it therefore important for the singer to form?

44 Describe in writing ten common errors in the use of consonants.

45 What is the difference between the recurrence of accent among the pulses of music and among the pulses of public speech? Give illustrations of the "mixed measures" of speech.

46 What is the purpose of a chant, and into what principal parts is it divided? What governs the length of the reciting tone? In teaching the music and words of a chant, which should be learnt by heart throughout the whole? How should the recitation of words be studied?

47 What is the name for a silent quarter of a pulse, when it comes within the accented half?—When within the unaccented half?—How is it indicated in the notation?

48 By what vowel is the first third of a pulse indicated?—the second?—the last? How are thirds of a pulse written in the notation?

49 What different sorts of accent are there in a musical passage, and how do you define a pulse? What must the Tonic Sol-fa translator do when he wishes to know whether crotchet, quaver, or minim, are treated as the pulse in a common notation tune? How should quickly moving six-pulse measure be taa-taid?

50 Why is the pupil not taught to beat time in the early steps?

51 Describe the kind of exercises by which the teacher endeavours to infuse into his pupils a sense of time.

52 Describe the most clearly visible ways of beating two-pulse measure—three-pulse—four-pulse—six-pulse.

53 The beat to the right being associated in four-pulse measure with a medium accent, why is it also suitable to the second pulse of three-pulse measure?

54 Does the quality of tone in the lower part of a woman's voice differ in any respect from that of the same tone when produced by the higher part of a man's voice? What register of their voices are male singers commonly ashamed of before their voices are cultivated?

55 What register is most neglected in uncultivated women's voices? Describe the means by which the teacher leads his female pupils to recognise their thick register.

56 Describe the process by which the thick register in women is strengthened.

57 What is meant by the blending of the registers? Describe the exercises by which the thick and thin registers are equalized.

58 What are the Sol-fa names of the optional tones of a tenor voice in key C?—G?—B♭?—F?—A?—D? If a group of tones commencing on an optional tone ascends above G, in which register would you begin it? If such a group commencing below the optional tones ascends to F, in which register would you begin? If such a group beginning above G descends into the optional tones, what register would you use? If other things are equal, which register would you prefer on the optional tones for a *forte* passage?—for a *piano* passage?

59 What is the advantage of a knowledge of dissonances to the singer?

60 What are the five principal apologies for a part-pulse dissonance on the weak part of a pulse? What is the common resolution of part-pulse dissonances on the strong part of the pulse? What are the three preparations for such dissonances? And the names for those preparations? Why does a composer sometimes leave a dissonance unprepared?

61 When a class is competent to study this subject of dissonances, how does the teacher introduce it practically to their attention?

62 Among full-pulse dissonances, which of them are used more freely when the pulses move quickly than when they move slowly? How are forestrokes used when smoothness of melody is the object, and how when dissonant effect is desired?

63 Describe the six additional cadences introduced in the two-part exercises of this step.

64 What is a section? What is a phrase? What is a period? What is a section of two measures called?—One of three measures?—One of four?

65 What are the three principal elements of good Form? Why is it more important for the singer to study the principles of musical form than for the listener?

66 What are the three questions which even elementary pupils should answer in respect to every tune, before it is sung? What are the other questions which pupils should answer in a complete parsing of musical form?

67 How should modulator voluntaries at this step be conducted?

68 Whence the necessity of sight-laaing from books?

69 Whence the importance of memorizing the modulator?

70 Why are memory patterns of use?

71 Give reasons for the practice of memory singing.

72 What new powers of dictation do the time exercises of this step bring to us?

73 Why should pointing from memory as well as writing be continued?

PRACTICE.

74 Hold a steady tone with one breath for twenty seconds.

75 Sing with a beautiful forward quality of voice each part of Ex. 121 in key E, M. 70.

76 Name pulse by pulse the chords in the first and third measures of Ex. 122, p. 45.

77 Laa in perfect tune the second part of Ex. 122, while your teacher or some other person, with correct voice, laas the first or third part. p. 45.

78 The teacher having caused to be sung to figures consecutively, chord by chord, Ex. 122, omitting the second measure, let the pupils say to which figures the chord *Da* was sung; the same with Exs. 123 to 126. Even elementary pupils should know by ear the mental effects of the principal chords in their *a* position. pp. 45 to 47.

79 In the same manner let the pupil distinguish the chord of *Sa* in Exs. 122 to 126.

80 In the same manner let the pupil distinguish *Fa* in Exs. 122, 123, and 124.

81 In the same manner let the pupil distinguish ⁷*Sa* in Exs. 122 & 123.

82 In the same manner let the pupil distinguish *La* in Ex. 126.

83 Listen to the laaing of Exs. 123 to 126 and name the cadences. p. 48.

84 In the same manner as question 78 let the pupil distinguish the chord D♭ in Exs. 124 and 125. This and the following four questions (to 88) may be answered by the more advanced pupils.

85 In the same manner let the pupil distinguish Dc in Exs. 124 and 125.

86 In the same manner let the pupil name F♭ in Exs. 124, 125, and 126, carefully distinguishing it from *La*.

87 In the same manner let the pupil name R*b* in Ex. 124, and ^{7}R*b* in Ex. 126, carefully distinguishing them from *Fa*.

88 In the same manner let the pupil name T*a* in Ex. 126, and T*b* in Ex. 125, carefully distinguishing them from ^{7}S*b* and ^{7}S*c*.

89 The teacher singing or causing to be sung to figures (one to seven twice) Ex. 127*b*, let the pupil decide on what figure the distinguishing tone of the first sharp key was heard. The same with Ex. 128. p. 50.

90 In the same manner let the pupil name the distinguishing tone of the first flat key in Exs. 130, and 131.

91 The teacher singing or causing to be sung to figures (eight to one line, six to the next) Ex. 133, let the pupil name by its figure first the distinguishing tone of transition, and second that of returning transition.

92 The same with Ex. 136. Sevens metre.

93 The same with Ex. 140. Common metre, or eight-sixes.

94 The same with Ex. 143.

95 Signal by manual signs and from memory, so that quick pupils could sing from your signalling, Exs. 65, 99, and the air of 97. p. 51 and preface.

96 Signal, as above, the first and third parts together of Exs. 85, 86, and 123.

97 Signal, as above, the first and third parts of Exs. 124, 125, and 126.

98 Mark the best breathing places (to suit the phrasing and the sense) for the first and second verses of Ex. 133, second line of the poetry, and Ex. 134, third line of the poetry.

99 Add any marks of expression (p. 30) which occur to you in Exs. 140, 142, 143, 144, and 145.

100 Pitch without a tuning-fork the keys B, B flat, E, E flat, and A flat. The pupil has not satisfied this requirement, if when tested he is found to be wrong so much as a step.

101 Sing to words any one of Exs. 133 to 145 as required, p. 25, question 46.

102 Enunciate, with freely moving jaw, Ex. 146, first with the vowel *aa*, next with the vowel *oo*. (p. 61.)

103 Enunciate Ex. 147, first with the vowel *ai*, and then with the vowel *oa*.

104 Enunciate Ex. 148, first with the vowel *ee*, and then with the *au*.

105 Sing correctly on a single tone any three words from each paragraph of Ex. 149 which the teacher points to.

106 The same with Ex. 150.

107 The same with Ex. 151.

108 The same with Ex. 152.

109 Recite, in exact time, the examples in the second column, p. 63.

110 Taatai on a single tone, exactly as marked, the rhythms of Exs. 123, and 125.

111 Taatai from memory any one of the Exs. 157 to 161,—the first pulse being named.

112 Taatai the upper part of any one of the Exs. 170 to 174.

113 Beat, as directed (p. 66) four two-pulse measures at the rate of M. 60, pause for two measures, and continue the beating *at the right moment* for two measures more. A silent metronome not seen by the pupil is the best test of this exercise.

114 The same, with four-pulse measure, M. 90.

115 The same, with three-pulse measure, M. 60.

116 The same, with six-pulse measure, M. 120.

117 Sing to *koo* with the thin register Exs. 162 or 163 whichever the teacher chooses. p. 66.

118 Sing to *koo* with the thick register Exs. 164, 165, & 166, whichever the teacher chooses.

119 Sing to *koo* Exs. 168, and 169, whichever the teacher chooses, making the registers of the same loudness and quality.

120 Mark, for the Tenor singer, in Ex. 133 first, the optional tones, and next the places at which it is most advisable to change register, as is done in Exs. 170 to 173, and as suggested, p. 68 and question 58 above.

121 The same, with Exs. 135, 136, 137, 138, 143, and 145.

122 Without, at the time, referring to pp. 68 and 69, turn to examples of the part-pulse passing tone—anticipation tone—waving tone—hanging tone—guiding tone—horizontal forestroke—oblique forestroke—waving forestroke—unprepared forestroke.

123 Without, at the time, referring to p. 69, turn to examples of the full horizontal forestroke—the oblique forestroke and the unprepared forestroke.

124 Without, at the time referring to p. 69, find examples of the following cadences, F,—R,—^{s}D,—^{r}D—weak pulse S—weak pulse ^{r}D.

125 Parse any one of Exs. 97, 115, 134, 136, and 140, which the teacher may select.

126 The same with Exs. 141 to 145.

127 The same with Exs. 113, 119, 120, 174, 175.

128 Mark the best breathing places in each part of Exs. 170 to 172, so as to sustain the voice, shew off the musical phrases, and not interfere with the sense of the words.

129 Add any marks of expression (see p. 30) which occur to you to Exs. 170 to 174.

130 Sing to words any one of Exs. 170 to 174, as required, p. 25, question 46, which the teacher may select.

131 Follow the examiner's pointing in a new voluntary, striking the disguishing tones both of the first sharp and the first flat keys by leaps, and singing to *laa*.

132 Point and sol-faa on the modulator, from memory, any one of Exs. 133 to 144, chosen by the examiner.

133 Write, from memory, any other of these twelve exercises chosen by the examiner.

134 *Laa*, at first-sight, any exercise not more difficult than these twelve.

135 Say aloud or write down, without looking at modulator or book, the bridge tones, to right and to left of each scale tone, as directed, p. 51.

136 Tell which is *fe* and which is *ta*, as directed, p. 25, question 56.

137 Tell what tone (*fe* or *ta*) is *skaa*, as directed, p. 25, question 57.

138 Taatai any rhythm of two or three four-pulse measures, belonging to this step, which the examiner shall *laa* to you. See p. 25, question 58.

139 Taatai in tune any rhythm of two or three four-pulse measures, belonging to this step, which the examiner shall *sol-faa* to you.

140 Sing to words, from memory, any one of Exs. 133 to 145 chosen by the examiner, singing either part, but taking the *last* verse of the words.

141 Write correctly the three musical phrases which would be dictated as follows: — 1st, "TAATAI *me doh*"—"*sa*fatefe *me ray doh*"—"TAAfe te_1 *doh*" — "TAA *ray*." 2nd, "tafatese *doh ray me*" — "TAATAI *me doh*" "tafatefe *me ray doh* te_1" — "TAA *doh*." 3rd, "taataitee *doh me soh*" — "Taa-aitee *fah ray*" — "TAATAI *fah me*"— "TAATAI *ray doh*" — "TAA te_1."

FIFTH STEP.

To practise more advanced Chest Klang and tuning exercises. To read chords disguised by notation. To recognise chromatic chords. To perceive the power of cadence and emphasis in developing the mental effect of a tone. To distinguish the various Modes of the Common Scale. To recognise and produce the characteristic cadences, and distinguishing tones of the Modern Minor. To recognise and produce Modulation and Transitional Modulation. To recite correctly. To arrange words for Chanting. Perception of the various modes of delivering tones,—attack and release. To practise the degrees of Musical Force and Speed. To apply them to the various requirements of Melodic and Harmonic Expression. Parsing Musical Passages. The small Register. The lesser Breaks. Perception of Registers. Scales of Registers. Classification of voices. Management of optional tones. Agility of voice. Sixths, Eighths, and Ninths of a pulse. Rare divisions of Time.

Chest and Klang.—For each key the singers change parts. At M. 60 the lower voices will have to economise their breath for 24 seconds. Key E♭, the upper voices slurring each Phrase of six tones to the forward Italian *laa*, M. 80. Key F, *koo-ing*, M. 72. Key E, *laa-ing* as above, M. 60. Key F♯, Sol-faing, M. 92. In all these keys Basses may use the thin register for d'. Tenors should not need to do so. This exercise is not to be sung *staccato*. The notes must not be detached, but on the other hand they must not be slurred into one another. There must be a clear stepping from note to note.

Ex. 176. KEYS E♭, F, E, and F♯ Chest and Klang Exercises.

:d ,m ,s	d' ,s ,m :d ,m ,s	d' ,s ,m :d ,m ,s (†)	d' ,s ,m :d ,m ,s	d' :d ,f ,l (†)	d' ,l ,f :d ,f ,l	d' ,l ,f
Skaa -	- - - -	- - - -	- - - -	la, Skaa -	- - - -	-
:d	— :—	— :—	— :—	— :f	— :—	—
Skaa -	- - - -	- - - -	- - - -	- - - -	- - - -	-

:d ,f ,l (†)	d' ,l ,f :d ,f ,l	d' :ds ,t ,r (†)	f ,r ,t :s ,t ,r	f ,r ,t :s ,t ,r (†)	f ,r ,t :s ,t ,r	D.C. sd'
- -	- - - -	la, Skaa	- - - -	- - - -	- - - -	la.
:—	— :—	— :ds	— :—	— :—	— :—	•d
-	- - - -	- - - -	- - - -	- - - -	- - - -	la.

Examination of Voices.—Since the proximate classification of voices, at the third step, p. 29, many voices will have changed. Cultivation will have developed new capacities. Each voice should therefore be examined afresh, and a report of its present physical condition drawn out, shewing its easy Compass, and its Quality and Volume in each register. The teacher will know, by its Best Region, whether it should be called First or Second Soprano, First or Second Contralto, First or Second Tenor, or, First or Second Bass. In large classes, and in ordinary evening classes, the teacher will not have time to go through this important process, unless he can command competent assistance. But, wherever it can be done, every pupil should, several times in the Course, receive advice about the character and management of his voice. He should in fact be "put in charge" of his own voice, and expected to present it in improved condition at the next examination.*

TUNING EXERCISES, for the purpose described at p. 14, can now be continued, and with the same process—except that there can be no changing of parts. When the men's voices are practised, the parts marked for first and second Soprano, should be sung by first and second Tenors, and those marked first and second Contralto, by first and second Basses.

* See p. 108, and the "Voice Report Book," 1s.

Ex. 177. KEY G. S.S.C.C., or T.T.B.B.

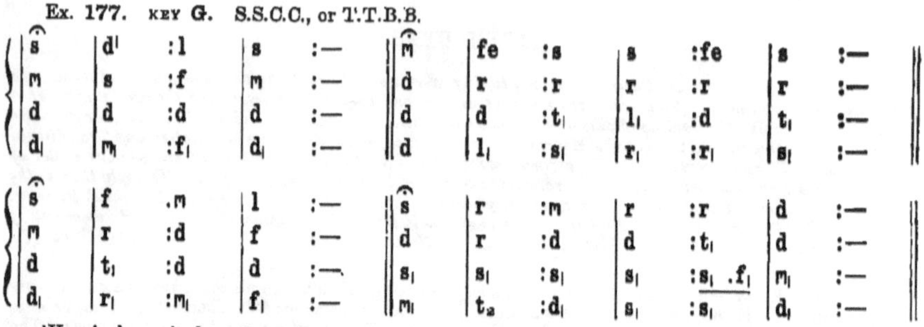

s	d' :l	s :—	m	fe :s	s :fe	s :—
m	s :f	m :—	d	r :r	r :r	r :—
d	d :d	d :—	d	d :t,	l, :d	t, :—
d,	m, :f,	d, :—	d	l, :s,	r, :r,	s, :—

s	f .m	l :—	s	r :m	r :r	d :—
m	r :d	f :—	d	r :d	d :t,	d :—
d	t, :d	d :—	s,	s, :s,	s, :s, .f,	m, :—
d,	r, :m,	f, :—	m,	t,, :d,	s, :s,	d, :—

'He is-de spised and-re | jected of men — ‖ 'A man-of sorrows — | and ac quainted with grief — ‖ . And-we hid-as-it were-our | fa ces from-him — ‖ . He-was-de spised 'and | we es teemed him not —

. . Surely he-hath | borne our griefs — ‖ And — | car ried our sor rows — ‖ Yet-we did-es | teem him stricken — ‖ Smitten of | God and af flic ted —

. 'But he-was wounded 'for | our trans gressions — ‖ . He-was bruised for | our in i qui ties — ‖ . 'The chastis ment-of our peace | was-up on him — ‖ And with | his stripes we are healed —

. . All we-like sheep 'have | gone a stray — ‖ . we-have turned every | one to his own way — ‖ . And-the Lord hath | laid on him — ‖ The in | iqui ty of us all —

. . He-was-op pressed 'and he-was | af flic ted — ‖ Yet he | op' ned not his mouth — ‖ . He-was brought as-a | lamb to-the slaughter — ‖ . And-as-a sheep-be fore-her shearers 'is dumb . so he | op' ned not his mouth —

Ex. 178. KEY G. D. t.

d	r :f	m :—	r s	l .t :d'	d' :t	d' :—
s,	r :t,	d :—	t, m	f :s	s :- .f	m :—
m,	s, :s,	s, :—	s, d	d .r :m	r :r	d :—
d,	t,, :s,	d, :—	s, d	f, :m, .f,	s, :s,	d :—

f. G.

d' s	s :ta	l :—	l	f :m	r :r	d :—
s r	s :m	f :—	d	t, :d	d :t,	d :—
m t,	d :d	d :—	f,	f, :s,	s, :s,	m, :—
d s,	m, :d,	f, :—	f,	r, :d,	s, :s,	d, :—

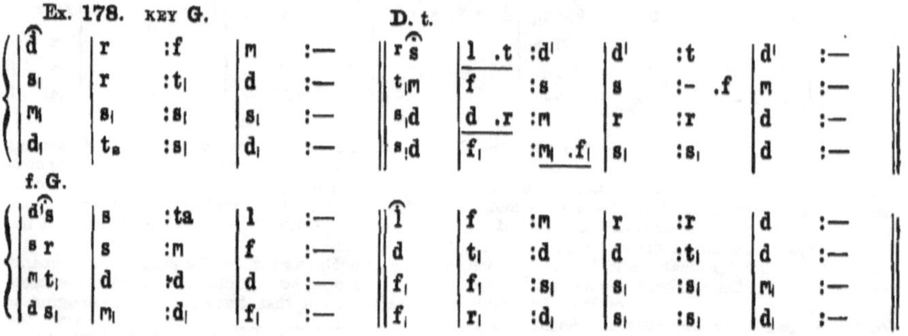

And-I heard-a great voice out-of | heaven — saying — ‖ 'Be hold-the Taberna cle-of | God — is with men —

'And he-will dwell-with them-and they-shall | be his people — ‖ And God-him self-shall be-with | them and be their God —

St. Co. (New.)

. 'And God-shall wipe-a way-all tears — | from their eyes — ‖ . 'And there-shall-be no-more death — | nei ther sorrow nor cry ing —
. . Neither shall-there be — | any more pain — ‖ . For-the for mer | things are passed a way —
. . . *What-are these-which are-ar rayed 'in | white — robes* — ‖ And — | whence — came — they —
. . These-are they-which came out-of | great tribu lation — ‖ . And-have washed-their robes 'and made-them | white in-the blood of-the Lamb —
. They-shall hunger-no more . neither | thirst any more — ‖ . Neither-shall-the sun light-on them . | nor — an y heat —
. For-the Lamb-which is-in-the midst-of-the throne 'shall | feed — them — ‖
. And-shall lead-them unto | liv ing fountains of waters —
‖: . 'And God 'shall | wipe a way — ‖ All — | tears — from their eyes — :‖

Disguised and Chromatic Chords.—In Ex. 177 the chord on the 7th pulse may at first be read ^{7fe}R*c*, but a little study of the modulator, and a quiet listening to the progression of the chord, show it to be ^{7}S*c*. It is disguised by what is called the improper notation of transition. (See pp. 52, 51). In analysing disguised chords we write the true name of the chord, and its resolution in parenthesis thus :—(^{7}S*c* D.)

Chromatic Resolution.—The same chord at the 12th pulse of Ex. 179 is *not* a disguised transition chord, because it is resolved chromatically. (See p. 52). Instead of moving to S, which would make a real (S D), it moves to D*c*, a chord which, like ^{7}S and D*b*, has a peculiar power of deciding the key. D*c*, while it is itself the very Tonic of the key, puts also the very dominant tone of the key in the most prominent position,—the Bass. Thus the chord ^{7fe}R, threatened a transition only to show how fast it clung to the original key. In the same way we notice that ^{ta}D in the 15th pulse of Ex. 178 is only ^{7}S disguised. It makes the transition which we express thus, (^{7}S D). But, the same chord in Ex. 179—4th pulse, is not a disguised transition chord, because it is resolved on ^{7}S, the deciding chord of the original key.

Ex. 179. KEY C. *W. G. M'N.*

|s :s	d' :*ta.ta |t :d'	r' :r'.r' |m' :m'	f' :*r' |m' :r'	d' :—	‖
Lord, have	mer - cy up- on	us, And incline our	hearts to keep this	law.	
|m :m	s :s .s |s :—	s :s .s |s :s	l :l |s :- .f	m :—	‖
|d' :d'	d' :d'.d' |r' :d'	t :t .t |d' :d'	d' :d' |d' :t	d' :—	‖
Lord, have	mer - cy up -on	us, And incline our	hearts to keep this	law.	
|d :d	m :m .m |f :m	s :s .s |d' :d'	f :fe |s :s,	d :—	‖

Ex. 180. Name all the chords in Exs. 177 to 179.

Effect of Accent, Cadence, and the Over-fifth in developing the mental effect of tones. It is easy to understand how the placing of any particular tone under the strong accent of a tune, will necessarily bring its proper mental effect into notice. It is also easy to understand how those resting points in a tune, called Cadences, p. 48, must give emphasis and importance to the tone on which they close. A close implies a pause to follow, and even in Elocution, a pause *after* a word gives it emphasis. In these Rhythmic closes there is also, very commonly, a descending motion of the Melody which gives weight to the tone it falls upon. The very name—"Cadence," springs from this idea. But another source of emphasis is more easily felt than explained. It is the influence on any tone of its over-fifth, or what is the same thing, of its under-fourth. Though we cannot give *reasons* for the power of the over-fifth in music, it may be interesting to observe that, in the order of consonances, the Fifth is, next to the Octave, the most perfect, and that the Fourth is next to it in truth of accord; that when a musical sound is resolved into its constituent parts, the

Fifth is the third part or "partial," the First after the Octave of the Fundamental Tone,—that in Harmony, which is only Closer Melody, the Fifth soon came to be called the Dominant on account of its acknowledged power in deciding the key, and that *Consecutive* Fifths in Harmony are felt to be hard and disagreeable, probably because they suggest the idea of two tones with Dominants where one only is wanted. In the first line of a well-known tune, "St. Bride's," we have l made emphatic and predominant.—1st, by the cadence upon it, and—2nd, by the motion to and from its under-fourth :—

:l |m :l .,t |d :t |l :— |— ||

By precisely the same means, in its next line, d is made predominant :—

:d' |s :d'.,r' |m' :r' |d' :— |— ||

In the third line no one tone is made to predominate in the melody :—

:m' |r' :d' |t :l |s :f |m ||

But in the last line, by the influence of its over-fifth, by accent and by cadence, l again predominates :—

:m' |l :r' |d' :t |l :— |— ||

Another example is afforded by the old tune. "Martyrs." When written according to the oldest copies, those which correspond with the present singing of the tune in the Highlands of Scotland, the tone r is made to predominate, in the first line by its twice rising to its over-fifth, and making a cadence on it :—

:r |f :r |l :f |m :r |l ||

In the second line by its cadence on the under-fourth :—

:l |d' :l |t :r' |l :- |- ||

In the third line by its cadence :—

:l |d' :s |l :f |m :r |l ||

And in the last line, after three cadences on the fifth of r, by a very decided cadence on r itself falling from its over-fifth :—

:d' |t :s |t :l |r :- |- ||

The Modes.—This power of making any one tone of the Scale so prominent as to stamp its own character on the whole or any part of a tune, was early understood among all nations, long before what we now call harmony was known. In the old Greek and Latin music there were as many *Modes* of doing this as there are tones in the Scale. In each mode special predominance was given to some one tone. Even to the present day the great eastern nations of Persia, India, and China, who dislike our harmony, are exceedingly exact about the correct intonation of the various modes of melody. (See examples in the "Historical Specimens" of my "Common Places of Music"). Much of the old music of Scotland, Ireland, Wales, and England, cannot be written as still traditionally sung, except by the use of these modes; and when (as in the case of "Martyrs" in Scotland, "Bangor" in Wales, and other well-known tunes) musical men, seeking to be wiser than Bach and Handel (who recognized the modes), altered the melody to suit the supposed requirements of modern harmony, and printed these altered melodies, the consequence was that the people either ceased to use the tune or continued to sing it differently from the printed copy.

The Modes are called by various names; by the Greek, the Latin, the Indian, and the Chinese writers on music. It will be sufficient for us to call them by the name of the Scale-tone, whose mental effect pervades them. Thus we have three modes with a major-third above the principal tone or Tonic—three major modes—those of *Doh*, *Fah*, and *Soh*, and three minor modes, those of *Lah*, *Ray*, and *Me*. The mode of *Te* with its diminished fifth, is but little used. Of the major modes, that of *Doh* is almost exclusively used in modern times and among the western nations. It was called, in ancient times, the Secular Mode—the mode of the dance and the song rather than of Ecclesiastical solemnity. No other mode suits modern harmony so well. Of the minor modes, the *Lah* mode has come to be the only one used among the nations of modern Europe, in connection with harmony. It could not be adapted to harmony, however, without alterations; and these so much modified the pure effect of the old mode, that we prefer calling the modified form "the Modern Minor" instead of "the Lah Mode." The history of the tune "Dundee" or "Windsor" will illustrate this. In its original form, and also as copied from ear by Dr. Mainzer, in his "Gælic Psalm Tunes," it is a *Ray* mode tune, and cleared from Gælic flourishes, reads thus :—

:r |r :m |f :m |r .:r |d ||f |l :s |f :m |f ||
:f |l :s |f :m |r :r |d ||f |m :r |r :d |r ||

This melody could have been written so as to begin on l instead of r, without altering the intervals. Melody alone would not decide which mode it is in. When harmony began to meddle with it, a "leading tone" to the r was wanted, and the three d's were changed in some printed copies into de—which is a little step beneath r. In this form the tune appears in Este's "Whole Book of Psalms," A.D. 1592. But, so strong was the resistance of the popular ear to such an alteration of the melody that, forty years later the tune appears in John Knox's Psalter with the first and second d's unaltered, and only the last made into de. Later still, harmonists found the *Ray* mode, for other reasons (See "Construction Exercises," p. 90.) unfavourable to their purpose, and wrote the tune in the *Lah* mode, altering the three notes as before, thus :—

:l | l :t | d' :t | l :l | se || d' | m' :r' | d' :t | d' ||

:d' | m' :r' | d' :t | l :l | se || d' | t :l | l :se | l ||

But the alteration of the *notes* in the books did not necessarily alter the tones of the people's singing, and wherever books and instruments do not dominate, there may still be heard the clear, firm, solemn cadences of the old melodic mode, | l :l | s or in its older form | r :r | d, and | l :s | l or | r :d | r. Thus, in the Highlands of Scotland, this tune is still sung. Even in England the modern version of the tune is seldom used, except where there is an organ or some other instrument to *make* the voices sing according to book. It is felt by all that se introduces a wierd unsettled effect, and greatly alters the whole spirit of the tune. It creates also a difficulty in striking the d' with which the next line begins. The ear naturally regards se as a new t, and can easily strike after it, t or r', because they have something to correspond with them in the supposed new key; but is puzzled to find d'. (See the diagram at the side). So, in the history of this tune, a curious thing happened. When musicians began to alter its melody, the people in the churches of Scotland, without presuming to resist the demands of harmony, or to contend against a learned Precentor or a Choir, fell instinctively into the expedient of striking some other tone *of the same chord*, which was *easier* than the uncertain se, and from which they could more easily rise to d'. A new tune called "Coleshill"—not interfering with the harmonies of Dundee, was the result. It reads thus :—

f' r'
m'
—d'
r' t
d' l
t se

:l | l :s | d' :s | l :l | m ||

:d' | m' :r' | d' :s | d' || d' | m' :r' | d' :s

| l :l | m || d' | s :l | r'.d' :t | l ||

The Doric or Ray Mode.—Before the introduction of modern harmony, this mode was the principal one used for worship. Throwing its emphasis on the earnest "prayer-tone" r, it was *strong* and *hopeful* as well as *sad*. The softer *Lah* mode cannot take its place. Much less can the modern minor with its sense of restless unhappiness. In Wales, both North and South, this mode is much preferred to the *Lah* mode, and popular tunes, printed in one mode, are sung in the other. The difference is easily observed, because (in addition to the question of the artifical leading tone) the expressive cadence d' t l in the *Ray* mode, becomes s f m in the *Lah* mode. It is like transition to the first-flat key. (See diagram). Let the pupils notice and describe the changes of melody, which would be necessary to put the tune "Martyrs" above into the *Lah* mode. Let them do the same with the following old *Ray* mode tunes—singing them in both modes. The first is the burden or chorus of an ancient Christmas Carol "Nowell, nowell," which Mr. Chappell ascribes to A.D. 1460 :—

l r
s d
t
f
m l
r s
d f
t m
l r

:r | r :- :f | m :- :d | m :-.r:d.t,

| l, :- :l, | d :- :d | r :- :r | m :- :m

| d :- :- | r :f :m | r :- :d | r :- ||

The next—"Bangor," is a tune of the ancient British Church, as it may now be heard in the churches of Wales and Scotland whenever sung without book or instrument :—

:l | f :m | r :l | r' :d'.t | l ||

:l | l :d'.t | l :s | l ||

:l |r' :d' |r' :f' |r' :d'.t |l ||
:l |r' :l .s |f :m |r ||

These studies are not mere matters of curiosity, or of history, for by far the largest part of the population of the world, at the present moment, makes use of these various modes in singing. Missionaries, above all others, should study this subject well.

The Modern Minor is built on the ancient *Lah* mode with adaptations to modern harmony. The relation of tones to one another is more strongly felt when they are sounded together in harmony than when they are merely heard successively in melody. Harmony, therefore, introduces new principles. The chief principle of modern harmony is that which chooses a particular chord, called the Tonic Chord, makes it preoccupy the ear, and then makes the chord on its over-fifth, its dominant, and that on its under-fifth, its subdominant, minister to it. The meanings and uses of these terms are given on pp. 20, 27, and 46, and at p. 48, this principle of "Chord Relation" is illustrated by the cadences. Those who not only see, but *listen* to these cadences, will understand what is meant. In the common, bright, clear *Doh* mode the chord relationship was satisfactory and pleasant. Two strong major chords, S and F, two-fifths apart, yielded and ascribed superiority to the chord D, which stood equidistant between them. The modern minor is an attempt to apply the same chord relation to the *Lah* mode. But in no other mode, except that of *Doh*, are the Tonic, Dominant, and Sub-dominant all major chords,—and the ear naturally dislikes two unsonorous minor chords (See p. 46,) together, especially in a cadence.

SE.—In the *Lah* mode, *L* the Tonic, *M* the Dominant, and *R* the Sub-dominant are all minor. The first harmonists sharpened the third of the Tonic *L*, making the chord l de m, and this is still done sometimes in slow music, but the most satisfactory artificial arrangement is that which sharpens the third of the Dominant *M*, making m se t, whenever it is wanted as a dominant. Occasionally, however, s is still used, especially in descending stepwise passages. **Se** is related to l as t is to d'.

l
se
(s)
f
m
r
d
t
l

St. Co. (New).

Bay.—The use of se, instead of s, makes a great unpleasant gap in stepwise passages, between se and f. Therefore, in such passages the composer often introduces another tone which he uses in place of f. It is related to se as l is related to t. We call it *bay* and write it ba. :l |se :ba sounds much like :d' |t :l and :m |ba :se |l sounds like :s |l :t |d'. There are, therefore, two "alternative tones" in the modern minor, one introduced for harmony's sake, the other for the sake of melody. *Bay*, however, is not so often substituted for f as se is for s.

l
se
(s)
(ba)
f
m
r
d
t
l

Difficulties of the Singer.—These arise from the modern minor, with its altered notes, being so like, and yet so unlike, the major of the same Tonic. See diagram at the side. The ear is drawn away from the key and confused. To prevent this it is best to train the singer to imitate the *relative* major, not the *Tonic* major, and so to keep the Doh in mind. Thus the teacher patterns on the modulator | m' : d' | t : d' || and immediately follows it by | d' : l | se : l ||. After a time he will give any major phrase and *ask* for the corresponding minor. The difficulty, already noticed, of striking d' after se is increased by the introduction of ba, because ba strengthens *the feeling* of a change of key. This feeling also makes it difficult to strike f, (especially by leap) as is seen by the diagram at the side, and felt by all singers. It will be easily seen from the diagram, and has often been felt by the teacher, that in singing such a phrase as this :m | ba : se | l :t | d' :— the pupils will sing de' instead of d', and even in singing such a passage as this :m | ba : se | l :— | m :— the pupils, instead of falling upon the same note with which they began, sometimes sing de as though it were the m of the major key drawn at the side. Such exercises as the following should be constantly practised from the Modulator, first *sol-faaing* and then *laaing*, always singing its relative major before each minor phrase.

l
f— m s
r f
—m
d—
t r
l d
se t
ba l
f—
m s
r f
m
d

D.C.
|d' :m' |r' :t |d' :— || l :d' |t :se |l :— ||

D.C.
|d' :t |l :t |d' :- || l :se |ba :se |l :- ||
D.C.
|m' :d' |s :l |t :d' || d' :l |m :ba |se :l ||
D.C.
|m' :d' |t :l |s :- || d' :l |se :ba |m :- ||
D.C.
|s :l |t :s |m' :- || m :ba |se :m |d' :- ||

The teacher patterns the relative major.

|m :se |t :m |d' :l |se :l |m :se |l :- ||

|d' :t |l :se |l :ba |se :l |m :se |l :- ||

But few composers understand about this. They therefore sometimes introduce tones which give great trouble to the singer, without adding, in the least degree to the beauty of the music. When composers write for a hired theatre-chorus (who dare not say that anything is difficult—much less hint that it is unnatural), we cannot wonder at their mistake. Even Handel has sometimes thus erred, and his notes to the phrase "Till thy people pass over, O Lord," are seldom correctly sung even by the Handel Festival chorus at the Crystal Palace. Tonic Sol-faists, after this warning, will know the difficulty and master it. Modern composers for the voice ought to know the difficulty and, except when it adds beauty to the music, avoid it.

The Exercises.—As the modern minor is so much the creature of harmony, it should be first studied in such exercises as the following six. They are simply previous Tuning Exercises changed into the modern minor:—

Ex. 181. KEY **E.** *L* is *C*♯. Compare Ex. 85.

l	l :l	se :-	se	l :l	l :se	l :-
d	m :d	m :-	m	m :d	d :t,	d :-
l,	d :l,	m :-	m	d :l,	m, :m,	l, :-

Ex. 182. KEY **B♭.** *L* is *G.* Compare Ex. 86.

d	d :t,	d :-	d	t, :l,	t, :t,	d :-
l,	l, :se,	l, :-	l,	se, :l,	l, :se,	l, :-
l,	l, :m,	l, :-	l,	m, :d,	m, :m,	l, :-

St. Co. (New).

Ex. 183. KEY **B♭.** *L* is *G.* Compare Ex. 123.

m	d :f	m :-	m	d :f	t, :r	d :-
d	l, :r	d :-	se,	l, :l,	se, :t,	l, :-
l,	l, :r,	l, :-	m,	l, :r,	m, :m,	l, :-

Ex. 184. KEY **C.** *L* is *A.* Compare Ex. 124.

d'	r' :t	se :-	l	f :r'	d' :t	l :-
l	f :f	m :-	m	f :l	l :se	l :-
l	r :r	m :-	d	r :f	m :m	l :-

Ex. 185. KEY **C.** *L* is *A.* Compare Ex. 125.

d'	d' :r'	m' :-	m'	r' :d'.t	d' :t	l :-
l	l :l	se :-	l	se :l	l :se	l :-
l	l :f	m :-	d	t, :l,	m :m	l :-

Ex. 186. KEY **C.** *L* is *A.* Compare Ex. 126.

d'	m' :r'	d' :-	r'	r' :d'	t :t	l :-
l	d' :t	l :-	l	se :l	l :se	l :-
l	l :m	f :-	f	m :l	r :m	l :-

Chord Relation in the modern minor. *L* is the Tonic of the minor mode as D is of the major. Therefore *M*, or with its commonly-sharpened third ^{se}M, is the Dominant, and *R* the Sub-dominant. What is said of the relations and habits of D, S, and F (pp. 21, 26, 27), applies almost equally to *L*, ^{se}M, and *R* in the minor. What is said of ^{7}S (p. 46), applies to ^{7se}M, and the habits of ^{7}R (p. 47), are imitated, as far as possible, by ^{7}T, and so on. For exacter particulars—See "Construction Exercises" p. 90 to 101. The chord M (p. 46) is called the "Mediant" in the Major, and *D* is called "Mediant" in the Minor. "Minor *D*" (that is *D* in the minor mode) is as little used as Major M. R is called the "Super-tonic" in the Major, and *T* in the Minor. "Minor *T*," and "Minor ^{7}T," are used like R and ^{7}R (pp. 46, 47). L is called the "Sub-mediant" in the Major, and both *F* and *BA* are Sub-mediants in the Minor. T is the chord of the "Leading Tone" in the Major, and *SE* in the Minor. No chord on the flat-seventh of the Minor (*S*) is used in distinctively Minor passages. It will be noticed that we write the chord-names for the minor mode in Italic Capitals to distinguish them from the same chords when influenced by the habits of the major mode; for the same purpose of distinction *in speaking* we say "Minor *L*," "Minor *T*," &c. The student should compare the above six chants in every respect with their major-prototypes. To make the comparison one of ear as well as eye, the two versions should be *laud* softly, the student *looking* at the major while the minor is sung, and at the minor while the major is sung.

Ex. **187.** Name all the chords in Exs. 181 to 186.

Modulation originally meant singing in mode. We use it for a change of mode, as from the D mode to the *L* mode—from the major to the minor, or from minor to major. Major *tunes* frequently introduce touching cadences in their *Lah* mode or "Relative Minor." (See Exs. 195, Meas. 23. 212, Meas. 14). And, it is almost a necessity for a minor tune, that some large portion of it should be brightened by modulation to the relative major. (See Exs. 189,—5th Meas., 190,—11th Meas., 191,—5th Meas., 192,—4th Meas., 193,—10th Meas). And even in 188 and 194 there are short phrases of major, with f and s to distinguish it.

d f
t m

l r
se–de
d
ba– t

Transitional Modulation.—When the music changes both its key and its mode, at the same time, some beautiful effects are introduced. The commonest change of this kind is that from the major mode to the relative minor of its first flat key. This originates a new "distinguishing tone" which we call (on the "improper method of notation) **de**. The **bay** is often used, disguised as t. The phrase :r | de : t_1 : de | r is really : l | se : ba : se | l. (See Ex. 234, Meas. 5). This "transitional modulation" is more frequently used in Passing than in Cadence modulation. (See Exs. 233, 245, and 236.) Additional Exercises, —p. 33, 3rd score; p. 47, 4th score; p. 49, 1st score; p. 52, 1st score; p. 54, 2nd, 3rd, and 5th scores; p. 80, 4th score; p. 88, 2nd score, and p. 60, 1st score. Another, though not a frequent Transitional Modulation, is that from the major to the relative minor of the first sharp key. This originates another distinguishing tone which we call **re**. The **bah**, in this case, is rarely used, but it would be called in passing modulation **de**. The transitional modulation of the first remove—minor to major is more common. Cases may be found moving to the first flat key in Add. Exs. p. 60, 3rd score; p. 69, 1st score; p. 88. 4th score,—and to the first sharp key in Add. Exs. p. 33, 3rd score; p. 59, 1st score; p. 60, 4th score; p. 79, 3rd score; p. 87, end of second score; p. 96, 1st score.

s d
t
f
m l
re–se
r
–ba
d

Accidentals.—Properly speaking, nothing is accidental in music, but this word is frequently used to indicate any tones which are out of the common scale. It will be the student's business to judge whether these tones indicate transition *from* the key, or lead to a chromatic effect *in* the key, or are merely brief ornamental passing or waving tones. In the Tonic Sol-fa notation we indicate a sharpened note by altering its vowel into *ee*, thus d, *dee*, (written to save space de) and a flattened note by altering its vowel into *au* as in *caught*, thus m, *mau*, l, *lau*, s, *sau*, and r, *rau*. To save space these are written—**ma, la, sa, ra.** See Ex. 247.

Rare Accidentals.—In uncommon cases like those in Ex. 247, the sharp of l is introduced. It is called **le**. It seldom has any very traceable key-relationship, but is introduced as an accompanying third to **de**. In the same way, but in exceedingly rare cases, **bay** is sharpened generally to accompany **le**. It is called **be**. In even rarer cases still, the sharps of m and t are required. They could not be properly written respectively f and d, because that would make them slightly too high. The sharp of any tone bears a fixed relation—that of a little step to the tone above. Its relation to the tone from which it is named, varies slightly according as it is taken from a greater or a smaller step of the scale; but it is always less than a little step. The sharp of m may be called **my**, that of t may be called **ty**. If in similar out-of-the-way cases, the flats of d and f were required, the flat of d would be called **du**, and that of f would be **called fu**. See "Staff Notation," p. 31.

FAREWELL, MY OWN NATIVE LAND.

Ex. **188.** KEY B♭. *L* is *G*. *Rather slow.* AIR "The Shepherd's Daughter."

:m_1	l_1 :– .l_1	t_1 .d :r .t_1	d :– .r	d :m	r :– .d	t_1 .d :r .t_1
1.Fare -	well my	own dear	na - tive	land, Dear	friends a	long fare -
:m_1 .r_1	d_1 :– .l_1	se_1.l_1 :t_1 .se_1	l_1 :– .t_1	l_1 :d	t_1 :– .l_1	se_1.l_1 :t_1 .se_1
2 Fare -	well to	all my	kin - dred	dear, My	child -	hood's home, fare -

St. Co. (New.)

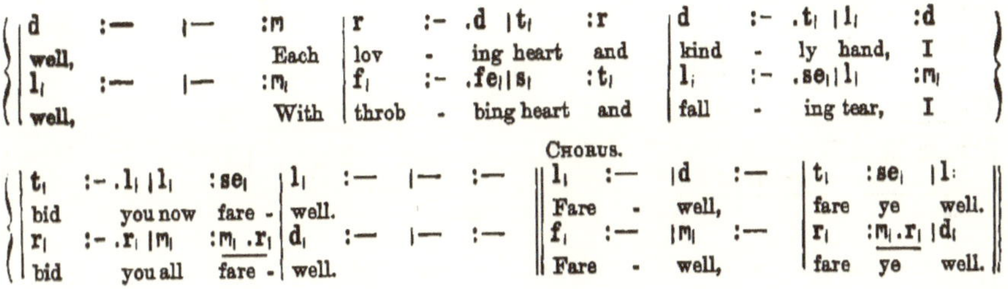

d :— |— :m	r :- .d | t, :r	d :- .t, | l, :d
well, Each	lov - ing heart and	kind - ly hand, I
l, :— |— :m,	f, :- .fe, | s, :t,	l, :- .se, | l, :m,
well, With	throb - bing heart and	fall - ing tear, I

t, :- .l, | l, :se,	l, :— |— :—	**Chorus.** l, :— | d :—	t, :se, | l,
bid you now fare -	well.	Fare - well,	fare ye well.
r, :- .r, | m, :m, .r,	d, :— |— :—	f, :— | m, :—	r, :m, .r, | d,
bid you all fare -	well.	Fare - well,	fare ye well.

OUR LIFE IS EVER.

Note.—Sing it firmly, with the "pressure form" more or less marked on every second pulse of the measure

Ex. 189. KEY C. *L* is *A*. M. 66. *Graun.*

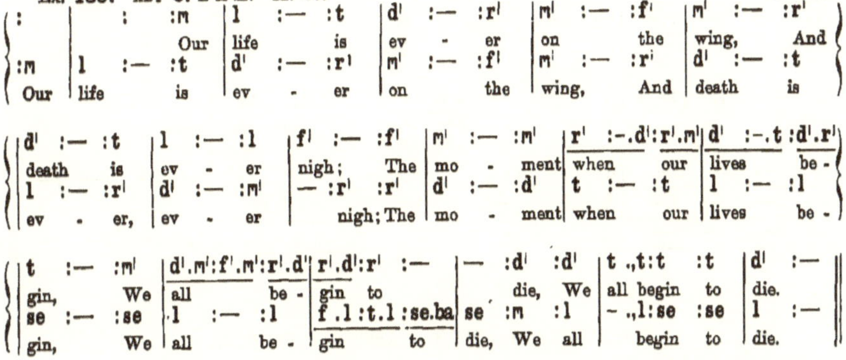

: | : :m	l :— :t	d' :— :r'	m' :— :f'	m' :— :r'
Our	life is	ev - er	on the	wing, And
:m | l :— :t	d' :— :r'	m' :— :f'	m' :— :r'	d' :— :t
Our | life is	ev - er	on the	wing, And	death is

d' :— :t	l :— :l	f' :— :f'	m' :— :m'	r' :-.d' :r'.m'	d' :-.t :d'.r'
death is	ev - er	nigh; The	mo - ment	when our	lives be -
l :— :r'	d' :— :m'	— :r' :r'	d' :— :d'	t :— :t	l :— :l
ev - er,	ev - er	nigh; The	mo - ment	when our	lives be -

t :— :m'	d'.m' :f'.m' :r'.d'	r'.d' :r' :—	— :d' :d'	t .,t :t :t	d' :—
gin, We	all be -	gin to	die, We	all begin to	die.
se :— :se	l :— :l	f .l :t.l :se.ba	se :m :l	— .,l :se :se	l :—
gin, We	all be -	gin to	die, We all	begin to	die.

SUMMER IS GONE.

Ex. 190. KEY B♭. *L* is *G*. *Slow.* Air, "Fortune, my foe."

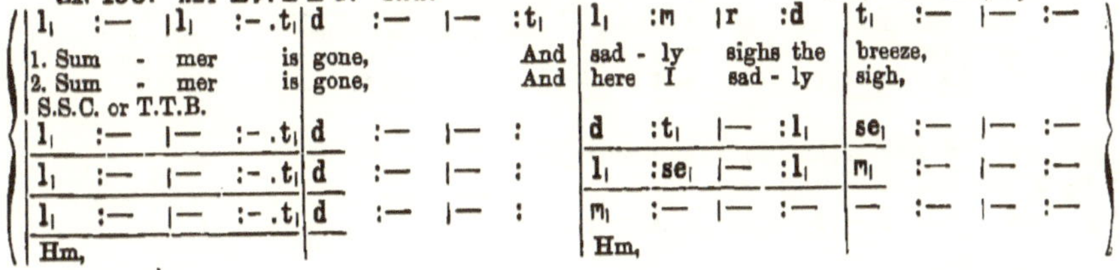

l, :— | l, :- .t,	d :— |— :t,	l, :m | r :d	t, :— |— :—
1. Sum - mer is 2. Sum - mer is	gone, And gone, And	sad - ly sighs the here I sad - ly	breeze, sigh,
S.S.C. or T.T.B.			
l, :— |— :- .t,	d :— |— :	d :t, |— :l,	se, :— |— :—
l, :— |— :- .t,	d :— |— :	l, :se, |— :l,	m, :— |— :—
l, :— |— :- .t,	d :— |— :	m, :— |— :—	— :— |— :—
Hm,		Hm,	

| l, :— | l, :- t, | d :— | — :t, | l, :m | r :d | t, :— | — :— |
Moan - ing it goes Through bare and leaf - less trees,
All, all a - lone, Not one dear friend is nigh;
l, :—	— :-.t,	d :—	— :	d :t,	— :l,	se, :—	— :—
l, :—	— :-.t,	d :—	— :	l, :se,	— :l,	m, :—	— :—
l, :—	— :-.t,	d :—	— :	m, :—	— :—	— :—	— :—
Hm, Hm,

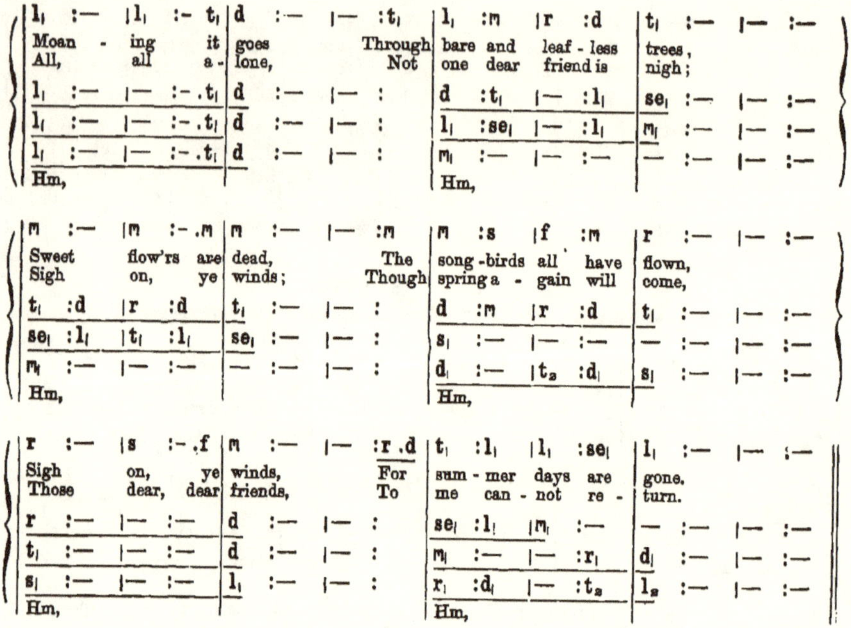

| m :— | m :-.m | m :— | — :m | m :s | f :m | r :— | — :— |
Sweet flow'rs are dead, The song-birds all have flown,
Sigh on, ye winds; Though spring a - gain will come,
t, :d	r :d	t, :—	— :	d :m	r :d	t, :—	— :—
se, :l,	t, :l,	se, :—	— :	s, :—	— :—	— :—	— :—
m, :—	— :—	— :—	— :	d, :—	t,, :d,	s, :—	— :—
Hm, Hm,

| r :— | s :-.f | m :— | — :r .d | t, :l, | l, :se, | l, :— | — :— ||
Sigh on, ye winds, For sum - mer days are gone.
Those dear, dear friends, To me can - not re - turn.
r :—	— :—	d :—	— :	se, :l,	m, :—	— :—	— :—
t, :—	— :—	d :—	— :	m, :—	— :r,	d, :—	— :—
s, :—	— :—	l, :—	— :	r, :d,	— :t,,	l,, :—	— :—	
Hm, Hm,

THE CHRISTIAN'S PARTING WORDS.

Words by *James Montgomery.* *Russian Air*

Ex. 101. KEY C. *L* is *A*. M. 50. D.C.

| l :l | l .d':t .l | se :se | se.t :l .se | l :l | l .d':t .l | m' :se | l :— |
1.Let me go, the day is break-ing, Dear com - pan - ions, let me go;
r.We have spent a night of wak - ing, In the wil - der - ness be - low.
| d :d | d .m :r .d | t, :t, | t,.r :d .t, | d :d | d .m :r .d | d :t, | d :— |

| d' :d' | d'.m':r'.d' | t :t | t .r':d'.t | l :l | l .d':t .l | m' :se | l :— ||
Up - ward now I bend my way. Part we here at break of day.
| m :m | m .s :f .m | r :r | r .f :m .r | d :d | d .m :r .d | d :t, | d :— ||

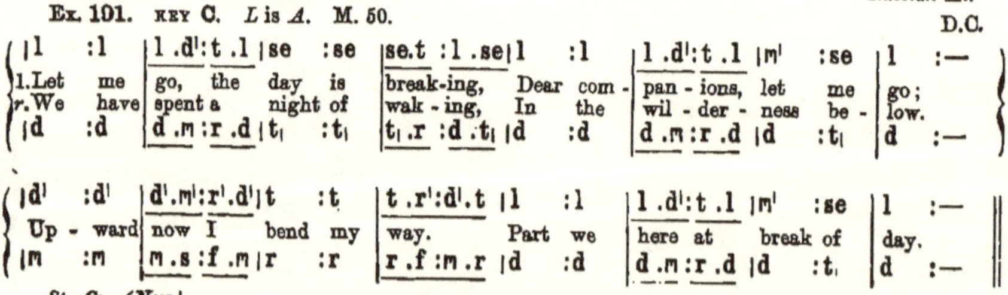

St. Co. (New).

2 Let me go—I may not tarry,
Wrestling thus with doubts and fears;
Angels wait my soul to carry
Where my risen Lord appears;
Friends and kindred, weep not so,
If ye love me, let me go.

3 Heaven's broad day hath o'er me broken
Far beyond earth's span of sky;
Am I dead?—Nay, by this token
Know that I have ceased to die.
Would you solve the mystery?
Come up hither, come and see.

DRIVE DULL CARE AWAY.

Ex. 192. KEY G. *L* is *E*. AIR.—"We be soldiers three."

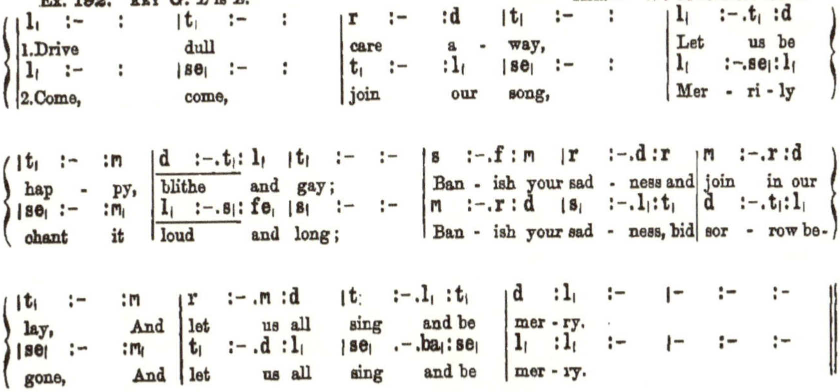

l, :- :	t, :- :	r :- :d	t, :- :	l, :-.t, :d
1.Drive	dull	care a -	way,	Let us be
l, :- :	se, :- :	t, :- :l,	se, :- :	l, :-.se,:l,
2.Come,	come,	join our	song,	Mer - ri - ly

t, :- :m	d :-.t,: l,	t, :- :-	s :-.f : m	r :-.d :r	m :-.r :d
hap - py,	blithe and	gay;	Ban - ish your	sad - ness and	join in our
se, :- :m,	l, :-.s,: fe,	s, :- :-	m :-.r : d	s, :-.l,:t,	d :-.t,:l,
chant it	loud and	long;	Ban - ish your	sad - ness, bid	sor - row be-

t, :- :m	r :-.m :d	t, :-.l, :t,	d :l, :-	- :- :-
lay, And	let us all	sing and be	mer - ry.	
se, :- :m,	t, :-.d :l,	se, .-.ba,:se,	l, :l, :-	- :- :-
gone, And	let us all	sing and be	mer - ry.	

THE DESTRUCTION OF SENNACHERIB.

Words by *Byron.* Music by *A. L. C.*

Ex. 193. KEY F. *L* is *D*.

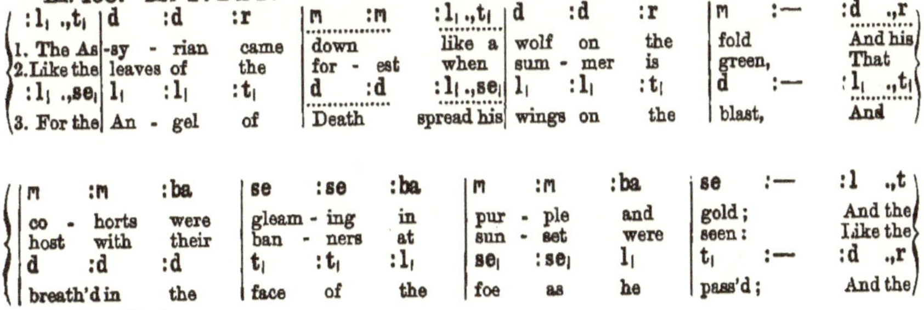

:l, .,t,	d :d :r	m :m :l, .,t,	d :d :r	m :— :d .,r
1. The As	-sy - rian came	down like a	wolf on the	fold And his
2. Like the	leaves of the	for - est when	sum - mer is	green, That
:l, .,se,	l, :l, :t,	d :d :l, .,se,	l, :l, :t,	d :— :l, .,t,
3. For the	An - gel of	Death spread his	wings on the	blast, And

m :m :ba	se :se :ba	m :m :ba	se :— :l .,t
co - horts were	gleam - ing in	pur - ple and	gold; And the
host with their	ban - ners at	sun - set were	seen: Like the
d :d :d	t, :t, :l,	se, :se, l,	t, :— :d .,r
breath'd in the	face of the	foe as he	pass'd; And the

St. Co. (New).

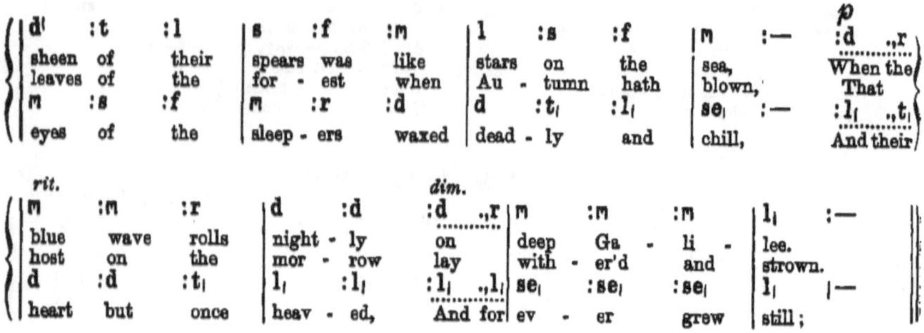

d' :t :l	s :f :m	l :s :f	m :— *p* :d .,r
sheen of their	spears was like	stars on the	sea, When the
leaves of the	for - est when	Au - tumn hath	blown, That
m :s :f	m :r :d	d :t, :l,	se, :— :l, .,t,
eyes of the	sleep - ers waxed	dead - ly and	chill, And their

rit. m :m :r	d :d *dim.* :d .,r	m :m :m	l, :—
blue wave rolls	night - ly on	deep Ga - li -	lee.
host on the	mor - row lay	with - er'd and	strown.
d :d :t,	l, :l, :l, .,l,	se, :se, :se,	l, :—
heart but once	heav - ed, And for	ev - er grew	still;

THE JEWISH CAPTIVES.

Ex. 194. KEY A. *L* is F♯. *Slow.* *A. L. C.*

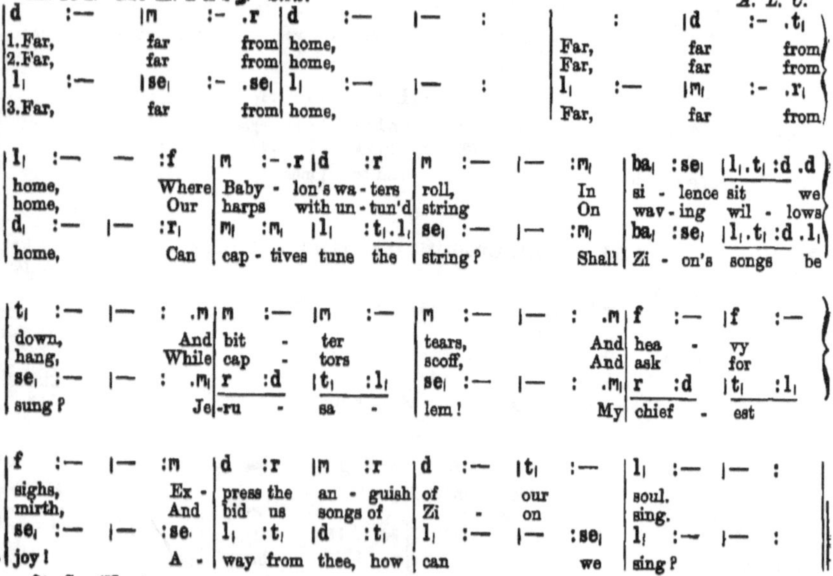

d :— | m :- .r	d :— | — :	: | d :- .t,
1.Far, far from	home,	Far, far from
2.Far, far from	home,	Far, far from
l, :— | se, :- .se,	l, :— | — :	l, :— | m, :- .r,
3.Far, far from	home,	Far, far from

l, :— | — :f	m :- .r | d :r	m :— | — :m,	ba, :se, | l, .t, :d .d
home, Where	Baby - lon's wa - ters	roll, In	si - lence sit we
home, Our	harps with un - tun'd	string On	wav - ing wil - lows
d, :— | — :r,	m, :m, | l, :t, .l,	se, :— | — :m,	ba, :se, | l, .t, :d .l,
home, Can	cap - tives tune the	string? Shall	Zi - on's songs be

t, :— | — : .m	m :— | m :—	m :— | — : .m	f :— | f :—
down, And	bit - ter	tears, And	hea - vy
hang, While	cap - tors	scoff, And	ask for
se, :— | — : .m,	r :d | t, :l,	se, :— | — : .m,	r :d | t, :l,
sung? Je	-ru - sa -	lem! My	chief - est

f :— | — :m	d :r | m :r	d :— | t, :—	l, :— | — :
sighs, Ex -	press the an - guish	of our	soul.
mirth, And	bid us songs of	Zi - on	sing.
se, :— | — :se,	l, :t, | d :t,	l, :— | — :se,	l, :— | — :
joy! A -	way from thee, how	can we	sing?

St. Co. (New).

FORGIVE THINE ENEMY.

Ex. 195. KEY G. D. t. *Fuchs.*

| : | : | : |ˢd' :— |t :s |l :t
For - give thine en - e -
|d :— |t, :s, |l, :t, |ᵈf :l |l .s :m .s |f :m .r
For - give thine en - e - my, thine en - e - my, thine

|d' :s' |— .f' :m' |— .r' :d' .t |l .t :d' |— :t |d' :—
my, thine en - e - my, thine en - - e - my,
|m :— .r |d :— .t, |l, :l .s |f :— .m |r :— |d .r :m
en - e - - my, thine en - - e - - my,

| |:f |m :d |r :m |f :l |— :s .f
For - give thine en - e - my, thine en - e -
|— .f :s .d |r :— .r |d : | :d |l, :f, |l, :t,
Forgive thine en - e - my, For - give thine en - e -

|m :d' |— :t .l |se :— |l .m :l |— :se |l :— | :
my, thine en - e - my, thine en - e - my,
|d :t, .l, |f :— |— :m .r |d :— .r,d |t, :— .t, |l, :— |f :—
my, thine en - e - my, thine en - e - my, For -

|d' :— |t :s |l :t |d' :t .l |t .m :m' |— .r' :l .t |d' :—
For - give thine en - e - my, thine en-e - my, thine ene - my,
|m :d |r :m |f :m .r |m .l, :l |— :s |f :— |— .m :d .m
give thine en - e - my, thine en-e - my, thine ene -

f. G.
|ᵈ's.f :r .f |m :d' |— .t :l |— .s :f |— :m |r :— .r |d :— ||
thine en - e - my, For - give thine, thine en - e - my.
|ʳl, :t, |d .t, :l, .m |f :— .m |r :— .d |t, .s, :d |— :t, |d :— ||
my, thine en - e - my, thine en - e - my, thine en - e - my.

Chanting.—The pupil will now learn the recitations of Exs. 177 and 178, paying special attention to the Consonants as taught at the last Step.

Ex. **196.** Sing to words Exs. 177—178, having first learnt the music by heart.

Arranging Recitations.—In connection with the study of Chanting, it will be well for the Teacher to give out a portion of a Psalm or some other passage of Scripture; to be fully marked for Chanting, with Cadence bars, Pulse divisions, Accent marks, and Type-expression. (See pp. 35, 36, 59). The comparison of these various plans, before the class at its next meeting, will prove both a fine exercise of taste, and an interesting study of the sense and meaning of the words. Besides, the Tonic Sol-faist should give himself the trouble of mastering all these principles of recitation practically, for he may some day have the duty and happiness of leading a congregation, and then, whether he uses a book marked for recitation like our exercises or not, he will require a practical mastery of our principles, unless he is content with tasteless, sinful "gabbling" instead of chanting.

In commencing such exercises, the student will first cut off the cadences. He will naturally try to arrange these so that the musical accent may correspond with the sense of the words. This cannot always be done. The attempt to do it, in difficult cases, often leads the marker to put too many syllables into the pulses of the cadence—so, that when it is sung quickly, as cadences should be sung, an irreverent dancing effect is produced, and when the cadence is sung slowly, it naturally makes the recitation also both heavy and jerky. The practice of putting *several* syllables into the pulses of a cadence, compels the reciter to put *many* syllables into the pulses of his recitation.*It is certainly better in the cadence—as far as sense will allow—to keep only one syllable for a pulse. Compare: ": . *Which* | *stilleth the* : *noise of the* | *seas* : . *the* : *noise of their* ‖ *waves* : *and the* | *tumult* : *of the* | *people*" with ": . *Which* | *stilleth the* : *noise of the* | *seas* : . *the* | *noise* : *of their* | *waves* : *and the* ‖ *tu* : *mult* | *of* : *the* | *people.*" The last can be sung quickly; the first must be slow and heavy, and still jerky.

In preparing the Recitation, let the student first make sure of its beginning and ending. For he must remember that the chant is a mixture of Speech and Song. The Recitation is Speech; the Cadence is Song. This necessitates some compromise, at least some "management" at the points (before and after the cadence) where Speech and Song meet. As an accent comes at the *beginning* of every cadence, there must always be *before* it either an unaccented pulse, or a *pause* of a pulse supposed to be unaccented. As we cannot well have two strong pulses together, it is unnatural to make any other than a weak pulse between the reciting tone and the cadence. Thus, if in the following sentence we feel the necessity of emphasising both "martyrs" and "praise," we should not attempt to write—": . *The* | *noble* : *army of* | *martyrs* | *praise*" but ": . *the* | *noble* : *army of* | *martyrs* : | *praise*, &c. As every cadence *closes* with a soft pulse the mind naturally expects the strong pulse to *follow*, and if the words will not bear this, you must give a *pause* to let the accent pass by. Thus "| *Thee* :— ‖ : . *The* | *holy* : *Church* : *throughout* | *all* " or better thus ": . *The* : *holy* | *Church.*"

Another hint is this. It is important that the student should use a metronome for his recitation, else he will find himself continually varying his rate of movement, and that cannot be done by a great congregation. It is very unnatural to *hurry* the pulses of the reciting tone and *slacken* those of the cadence. They should all move at the same *rapid* rate. If you chant slowly it is impossible to make the pauses indicated by the dots.

In further studying the reciting tone, the careful marker will observe that the two-pulse rhythm is the most common and easy, but the best speech contains a well-arranged variety. As a general rule, the rhythms in which a passage is best *said* are those in which, for chanting, it should be sung. Chanting, however, is not private *talk;* it is public speaking. Public speaking differs from private *talking* in this—that the *pulses* in public speaking are necessarily more regular, in order that the voice may carry further. The student, moreover, must not despair if he finds it, in some cases, extremely difficult to reconcile sense and rhythm. Prose is often written more for the reader than the speaker. The prose style of a Bolingbroke, a Brougham, a Gladstone, or a Bright, is quite different from that of a student or a learned translator, who seldom speaks further than across a table, and it is altogether more rhythmical. It was not all the translators of the Bible who studied the rhythmical structure of their sentences. While the student is thus recommended to exercise his judgment and taste in deciding which plan best expresses the sentiments of the words and best draws out the voice of the whole people,—he should be always ready to unite cheerfully in the "use" which he finds established in the church in which he worships.

The following hints are for the Precentor. *First*, avoid chants with high reciting-tones out of the reach of ordinary voices. Long recitations on a high tone are screaming impossibilities to a congregation. *Second*, avoid chants with wide intervals in the cadence. Such cadences are not like the natural cadences of an excited public speaker. They are almost necessarily slow and heavy when a congregation sings them, and "slow" cadence makes jerky recitation.

Expression.—At page 30, a brief and superficial reference to this subject is made. The pupil being

 * Because the pulses of recitation and cadence should move at the same rate.

now well grounded in the doctrine and practice of time and tune, is free to give full attention to expression. The subject is one of great intellectual and artistic interest, and both voice and mind should go through a thorough training in expression. The chief elements of expression are speed and force. How speed of movement influences the emotional effect of tones has been shown—p. 28. How the various Degrees of Force can influence expression is never known until the pupil has really learnt to control his own singing in this respect. It is one of the simplest, easiest, most effective, and *most neglected* of all the contrivances of music. Ordinary singers employ either an uniform weak drawl, or an equally uniform shout. They have never cultivated a *medium force* of voice, and they can never give that light and shade of sound, which, like the varied distances and lights in a painting, throw such a charm over the musical picture. The first thing to be secured—the foundation of all the rest—is a good delivery of each tone, both for the sake of *quality* and *clearness of impulse.*

Delivery of the Voice.—In singing, the student must remember that he is not singing to the top of his head or the bottom of his throat, or to the inside of his mouth, but to an audience in front of him. He will, therefore, direct his breath outwards, in a steady, well-regulated stream, keeping his teeth always wide apart—even when he has to round his lips. By this means he will avoid shrill bird-warbling, bass growling, and vague humming, and will produce a *rich, round tone,* without discordant upper "partials."

Attack and Release.—Closely connected with a good *quality* of sound, and essential to its production is that clear striking of every tone—that "good attack," as M. Fétis calls it—that "shock of the glottis," as Garcia describes it—that firm, but light and elastic "touch" as Mdme. Seiler speaks of it—which should become a habit of the singer. Every tone should have a sharp confident opening as well as a distinct close. It should be like a newly cut coin. "Any one," says Dr. Lowell Mason, "who gives attention to the production of tones by a good instrumentalist, or to the manner in which they strike the ear when the 'attack' is made upon them (or when they are first brought forth by a skilful player), cannot fail to observe their great superiority in promptness and energy of delivery, to those usually heard in singing. Indeed, choir or chorus singing can hardly be heard without revealing the fact that whatever proficiency may have been made in reading music, so far as it relates to time and tune, the proper use of the vocal organs in the enunciation or emission of tone has been sadly neglected." Any one who, in the Crystal Palace or elsewhere, has heard some great artist singing with the accompaniment of a vast chorus, must have been filled with wonder to notice how easily the artist's voice was heard above the thousands of uncultivated voices. It was greatly because the artist had formed the habit of good attack, and made his voice reach the ear more quickly and more truly. The increasing habit in singing classes (when time, tune, and words are learnt) of studying delivery and expression, *with closed books,* under the guidance of the leader and his bâton, have done much in England to remove this defect,—of bad attack.

Mr. F. Kingsbury, in his sensible pamphlet on the voice says:—Pass the breath in a small stream letting it commence *suddenly,* as if produced by the sudden opening of a valve, but without any further effort. Unnatural forcing of the breath must be avoided, while care is taken not to let it *ooze* out. By this prompt attack, after a few experiments the singer will positively *feel* the back of the throat and mouth *simultaneously* filled, as it were, with a solid body. The muscular power of these parts is felt to grasp or lay hold of the sound. This sensation of laying hold of the tone should always be present to the singer. He will then be conscious of a power to mould and shape the sound at his will.

The following hints from Mr. Ellis will assist the teacher in observing, and the pupil in learning the proper mode of attack. Only, that which he calls the "clear attack," forms the true action of the glottis to be practised by every singer. In this, the vocal membranes are brought into contact exactly at the moment when the breath is made to act upon them. In the "gradual" attack, the vocal membranes are brought together *while* the breath is being emitted, so that the passage *through* whisper to voice (whisper being speech without the vocal membranes) is unpleasantly audible. As this attack is common in speech, it is the more necessary to guard against it in song. It causes what we call "breathiness." In the "check" of the voice, the vocal membranes are brought tightly together *before* the breath acts upon them, and are separated with a sensation of a click in the throat. Only for an extreme *staccato* effect should this be used. In the "jerk," the *proper clear attack* is made with the addition of a sudden jerk of the breath, produced by the diaphram or muscular floor on which the lungs rest. This jerk can be easily felt by the hand. It is the proper form of the aspirate H for the singer—that is H without "breathiness." But, care must be taken not to allow a *puff* of wind to escape before the vocal membranes are brought close enough together to make the clear attack. In the "slurred" attack (that is the attack on the second vowel, or the continued vowel in a slur) there is a simple *relaxation* in the emission of breath between the two vowel impulses. So that no very sensible sound is heard between the two vowels, and no "clear" attack is heard on the second. The distinction between the slur and the glide (p. 61.) is this: In the glide the voice continues in full force while the organs are passing from one vocal position to another, and in the slur the voice is continued, but with greatly lessened force. This is true—both in music, when we pass from one tone to another, and in speech when, without change of tone, we pass from one vocal position to another.

The "release" of the vowel by a clear action of the glottis, leaving no ragged ends to the sound, should be very carefully practised. It produces as beautiful an effect as the clear attack itself. The teacher will make his pupils *try all* the various modes of attack, but *practise* only the clear attack. The power of recognizing *bad* execution helps the pupil to understand and enjoy that which is *good*.

Degrees of Force.—To give his pupils a proper command of their voices, in this respect, the teacher will find distinct and frequent practice necessary. *The degrees of force* he may introduce in the following manner:—

"Sing me a tone to the open LAH, at an easy pitch of your voice, which shall be neither *loud* nor *soft*. . . What shall we call it, if neither *loud* nor *soft*?" Medium. "Yes, it is called a medium, or, to use the Italian word (which has been adopted into all languages for this musical purpose) a *mezzo* (med·zoa)* sound of the voice. Let us write *m* in the middle of the black board, for *mezzo*, and you can sing with your medium force, whenever I point there. Let each one try to fix in his mind what is his own medium force of voice, and learn to produce it at command. Sing it now, as I point. . . Again. . . &c."

"Sing the same sound *louder*." . . For the loud sound we use the word *forte* (for·tai) or the letter *f*. We will write *f* to the right of *m*, on the black board. . . "Now sing as I point." (*m. f. f. m.* &c.)

"Sing the same sound *softly*. For the soft sound we use the Italian word *piano* (pyaa·noa), and the letter *p*. We will write *p*, to the left of the *m*, thus:—

p. *m.* *f.*

"Now sing with 'medium,' 'weak,' or 'strong' (mezzo, piano, or forte) power of voice, as I point to one or the other of these letters." The teacher points sometimes slowly, sometimes quickly, sometimes in one order, sometimes in another, and the pupils sing accordingly.

When these rough outlines of vocal force have been ascertained, and a good command of them secured, the teacher may proceed to develop, in a similar manner, the *intermediate* and the *extreme* degrees of force, using the marks *m.p. (mezzo-piano)*, and *m.f. (mezzo-forte)*, for the intermediate degrees, and *ff. (fortissimo)*, and *pp. (pianissimo)*, for the extreme degrees, *very* loud and *very* soft. Let the teacher show, by example, that it is possible to give a very loud tone without *screaming*:—

The black board will now have the following signs marked on it:—

pp. *p.* *mp.* *m.* *mf.* *f.* *ff.*

The teacher will exercise his pupils in passing from one part of this scale of strength to another. A really *gradual* (not a jerking) passage from one end of this scale to the other, and then back again, is one of the most difficult feats in music. The pupil must take a good breath before he begins, and use his breath economically. The exercise is of first importance.

Ex. 197.

| *f* *f* *f* *f* | *p* *p* *p* *p* | *f* *p* *f* *p* | *p* *f* *f* *p* ||
| l :l |l :l | l .l |l :l | l :l |l :l | l :l |l :l ||

Ex. 198.

| *p* *p* *p* | *f* *f* *f* | *p* *p* *f* | *f* *f* *p* ||
| l :l :l | l :l :l | l :l :l | l :l :l ||

St. Co. (New). *The inverted full point marks an accent on the preceding syllable.

Ex. 199.

```
|pp   p    f    ff  |ff   f    p    pp  |ff   f    p    pp  |pp   pp   pp       ||
|l   :l   |l   :l   |l   :—   |—   :—   |l   :l   |l   :l   |l   :l   |l   :    ||
```

Ex. 200.

```
|pp   p    mp   m   |mf   f    ff   ff  |ff   ff   f    mf  |m    mp   p    pp  ||
|l   :—   |—   :—   |—   :—   |—   :—   |—   :—   |—   :—   |—   :—   |—   :—   ||
```

Ex. 201.

```
|ff   f    mf   m   |mp   p    pp   pp  |pp   pp   p    mp  |m    mf   f    ff  |ff  ||
|l   :—   |—   :—   |—   :—   |—   :—   |—   :—   |—   :—   |—   :—   |—   :—   |—   ||
```

Crescendo (Kreshen·doa),*&c.—A long tone or a succession of tones passing gradually from the *piano* or *pianissimo*, to the *forte* or *fortissimo* is called a *crescendo* tone or passage. A long tone or a succession of tones passing from the *forte* or *fortissimo*, to the *piano* or *pianissimo* is called a *decrescendo* or *diminuendo* tone or passage. The gradual passing from *pianissimo* to *fortissimo* and back again to *pianissimo* is called a *swell*.

The *crescendo* is indicated thus, <

The *diminuendo* thus, >

The *swell* thus, <>

For the development thus far of the subject of force in music, the Editor is indebted to Dr. Lowell Mason, of America, who was the first to reproduce, in the English language, the Pestalozzian principles of music teaching, by which Nägeli and others had created a musical revolution in Germany. —See his "Boston Academy Manual of Vocal Music."

Pressure and Explosive Tones.—Pointing on the "scale of force," as above, let the teacher cause his pupils to perform a *very* rapid *crescendo*. A tone delivered in that manner is called a "pressure tone." It is indicated thus (<). In the same manner a quick or sharp diminuendo will produce the "explosive tone" marked thus (>). This manner of delivering a tone is also called *sforzando*, and marked *sf*. A combination of the two last modes of delivery on one short tone should be expressed thus (/\). This musical ornament is very elegant, but difficult to perform. A tone delivered with *equal* force, from beginning to end, is called an "organ tone," and may be indicated thus (=).

Ex. 202. KEY D.

```
|=    <    >        |>         =    >   |^    ^    ^    ^   |=         =    =   ||
|d   :r   |m   :f   |s   :l   |t   :d'  |d'  :t   |l   :s   |f   :m   |r   :d   ||
```

Staccato and Detached Tones.—When a tone is meant to be sung only half its proper length, and in a *marked* (not loud) manner, this is indicated by means of a small dash thus (') placed over the note. This mode of singing is called *staccato* (stakkaa·toa). When a tone is meant to be sung about three-quarters of its proper length, this is indicated by a *dot* placed over the note. These tones would be called "half staccato" or "*detached*" tones.

Legato.—When it is intended that the tones should glide gently and easily one into the other (the degree of *force* with which the first tone *ends* being the same as that with which the second *begins*), a slur ⁀ or the word *legato* (legaa·toa) is written over the note. Sing the following, first with *staccato*, next with *detached*, and lastly with *legato* tones. Do not make the *legato* dull and heavy, but smooth and elegant.

Ex. 203. KEY F.

```
:s |s   :f   |m   :r   |d   :l   |s   ||
```

Application of Force.—The application of the various degrees of force to the sense of the words is deferred to the last step. But, the use of force, as suggested by peculiarities in the musical phrases which are sung (apart from any modification which words may suggest), is now to be studied. Of course the words cannot be neglected at any step.

* For pronunciation, see Teacher's Manual, p. 202.

Already some hints on the subject have been given at p. 30, and the teacher will add more as he comes to the cases in each tune sung. It is only the *systematic* study of verbal expression which is deferred to the next step; musical expression alone will now be systematically studied.

"Additional Exercises."—We shall, from this place freely use the Additional Exercises (Pts. 1, 2, and 3) for the illustration of various points in musical and verbal expression, in musical Form and in the Analysis of Harmony. Our illustrations will be principally taken from the earlier numbers, but for the Exs. all three numbers will be required. It is very important that the pupil should, as far as possible, not only see but "hear" the illustrations. When the class cannot sing the piece, a quartet should sing it to them. Pains have been taken—not only to suit these exercises to the progressive steps of this book, and to select them from the best composers, but also to secure in them as great a variety of style as possible. It is quite common for a class to sing a large quantity of music without really learning anything, because they are always singing the same sort of music. There is, however, always something new to learn in each of these Additional Exercises.

Normal Force.—By this is meant not the force of certain *passages*, but the general—the prevailing force of the whole tune. Some pieces of music by their bold character, evidently demand loud singing to bring out their proper effect.—See "God speed the right," p. 1. "Freedom's sons," p. 13. "Time for joy," p. 15, &c. Others, equally by their gentle motion, suggest soft singing. "Hear me," p. 17. "Jackson," p. 2. "Hope," p. 12. "My Lady," p. 21, &c. Of course the sense of the words, and the character of certain phrases will introduce modifications in the course of the tune, but the "normal force" is that principally used. The pupil should endeavour to obtain full command of the Medium force *of his own* voice. The teacher should give out a tone, and require his pupils to sing it in various degrees of force as he demands them. Mezzo! piano! forte! piano! mezzo, &c. He should then require his pupils to judge from the musical style, speed of movement, &c., of various tunes, which of these three degrees of force should be the normal or general one given to the piece.

Piano Passages.—A true *piano* is sung, not with laxity, but with effort. To keep a *piano* passage from flattening in pitch, and to deliver it with clear and just intonation is very difficult. Echoes are commonly sung by a few select voices in another room, but, for the *practice of pianissimo*, it is better that they should be sung by all. When a true blended and real *pianissimo of many voices* can be obtained, it is far finer than the *piano* of a few. Illustrations of piano and pianissimo, for simple musical effect, may be found in "The Waits" when sung the last time,—in the imitations of the "Cuckoo" and the "Quail,"—pp. 9 and 14, —at the change of measure in "Swiftly," p. 29; and again at the change of measure, p. 31, &c.

Forte Passages should be sung with a very clear vocal *klang*, and should be perfectly free from the sound of breath. Such a *forte* is very heart-stirring. But the rude, coarse forte produced by strong lungs and harsh voice is only deafening. Illustrations of this may be shown in the manner of singing "God Speed the Right," p. 1. "The Waits," p. 8,—when sung the third time. The close of "Freedom's Sons," p. 13; close of "Hear Me," p. 19, and several closing parts of "Swiftly," p. 32, &c.

Melodic Phrasing is the art of dividing a melody into its natural parts, and showing by the manner of delivery that the singer himself distinguishes these parts, and wishes his hearers to distinguish them also. It is as important that these phrases should be distinctly marked by the good singer, as that the various members of a sentence (as indicated by the stops) should be marked by the good reader. This can be done by singing one phrase piano, another mezzo or forte and *vice versa*, by commencing a phrase forte and ending it piano and *vice versa*, by delivering the last tone of a phrase staccato, and shortening the first tone of the next phrase so as to allow a momentary silence before it, and so on. The proper choice of breathing places has a great effect in marking off the phrases. In some cases the phrasing of all the "parts" will be simultaneous; in other cases each "part" will have its separate phrasing. The phrases in "God Speed the Right" (p. 1.) are sufficiently marked out by the lines of the words. Each of the long lines is easily divided into two, however, if more breathing places are required.*

Ex. **204**. Mark the phrases and breathing places, on the supposition that there are no words to modify your judgment, in "God Speed the Right," (p. 1.) and as the two opening periods consist of the same music, mark how you would distinguish them in musical expression.

* For phrasing see further "Musical Theory," Book IV, pp. 244 & 261

Ex. 205. Mark in a similar way "Jackson," p. 2.

Ex. 206. Mark in the same way "The Waits," p. 8.

Ex. 207. Mark in the same way "Freedom's Sons," p. 13.

Ex. 208. Mark the phrases and breathing places in the Contralto and Tenor of "Spring Life," p. 3.

Ex. 209. Mark in the same way the Soprano and Bass of "May-time," p. 5.

Ex. 210. Mark in the same way all the parts of "Thou shalt show me," p. 7.

Ascending Passages.*—Passages which *ascend* by the steps of the scale (or otherwise) should, as a general rule, be delivered *crescendo.* Each tone should run into the next with regularly increasing force. We naturally associate height of pitch with ideas of energy and spirit. Full force of sound also naturally suggests the same ideas, and (except where it would interfere with some greater effect) should always accompany ascent. The *gradual* nature of the ascent also tends to "set off" the wider skips of interval in the other parts. It is difficult to make the crescendo *gradual,* each tone running into the next with a steady and not jerked increase of force, neglecting for the moment the common accents of the measure. It is generally necessary to commence *piano,* in order that the singer may have breath and strength to spare for the end. The slightest signs of fatigue in a crescendo, would utterly and miserably kill its musical effect. Imitative illustrations may be presented in the opening of "The Fortune Hunter," p. 4, where there is an ascent of an octave from $s_{,}$ to s, —in the opening of "The Waits," p. 8, where there is an ascent of a fifth. *Ascending imitative phrases,* as in the last four measures of "Swiftly," p. 32, should be sung with a crescendo effect; notice also the ascending bass.—See also Standard Course Exercise 137. As a general rule, such passages as these should be commenced more or less *piano* in order to get the *crescendo.* For the same reason, it is almost always necessary to take breath before commencing such a passage.

Descending Passages should *commonly* be delivered *diminuendo,* because an idea of quiet and rest is naturally connected with descent of sound. *Descending imitative phrases* follow the same rule. Find examples in "Going Home," p. 2; "May Time," top of p. 6. But where the character of the tune or the character of the words requires energy and power, this rule must be broken. See the bass—"Awake Æolian Lyre," p. 64, 1st score.

When an ascending passage, in one "part," comes into contrast with a descending passage in another, and both passages are properly delivered, the effect is very beautiful. See—"The Quail Call," p. 14, soprano and bass; "How Lovely," p. 60 (S. against C., and T. or S. and C. against T. and B.), three times in two scores to the words "Gone forth the sound of their." As a general rule, such passages as these must be commenced more or less *forte,* in order to get the *diminuendo.*

Repeated Tones.—The repetition of a tone, if it has any meaning, is intended to impress that tone upon the ear with cumulative force. To assist this purpose a repeated tone should be delivered crescendo, partly because the singer thus compensates the ear for want of variety in interval by variety in the degrees of force, and partly because he thus "sets off," by contrast, the *movement* of other parts, just as the line of the horizon "sets off" a varied landscape, and a quiet rock the rolling sea. The steadily increasing power also shows that the singer is not weary; and it is among the rules of art never to show weariness or exhaustion in the artist. See examples in 2nd score, "Going Home," p. 2; 2nd score, "Cuckoo," p. 9, and 1st score, "O, Saviour," p. 86. Repeated *phrases* and passages should be treated in the same way as repeated tones. See Standard Course Ex. 113; air, meas. 3 and 4, and contralto meas. 5 and 6. Ex. 115; meas. 11 and 12,—and "repeated passage," Ex. 120, last four measures.

Prolonged Single Tones.—Lifeless monotony is unbearable in music, and therefore every tone should take some form. It will be found by experiment that the form most suitable for holding tones is the swell, and this swell should be full and strong rather than soft and insignificant. The composer commonly means that the other parts should be covered with a flood of sound from the holding tones. "The greatest difficulty of this form of tone," says Fétis, "consists in employing an equal time in the increase of power and its diminution." A perfectly simultaneous and equal (not jerking) delivery of this "tone form" by a chorus is very difficult to attain. Only practising without book, but with the signal of the *gradually* outstretching and *gradually* returning hands of the

* "Musical Theory," Book IV., treats the subject of Expression with new illustrations.

teacher, can lead to this attainment. See the close of "Hallelujah Amen," p. 28; "Swiftly from," three cases, pp. 29, 30. In the case of repeated tones running into a prolonged tone, or a prolonged tone breaking into repeated tones, the two should be treated as one, and the crescendo extended through both the prolonged and the repeated tones. See the bass in the close of "Cuckoo," p. 10; "Harvest Home," p. 39, two cases; "Theme Sublime," p. 68, 3rd score, and p. 70, 2nd score. See also Standard Course Ex. 138.

Melodic Imitations.—When a composer makes one section or period of a melody imitate another, he designs that the singer should, by his manner, draw attention to the imitation. The best way of doing this is to make a *contrast* of force between the two. One must be more or less loud and the other soft. The pupils must study "the points" of a tune in order to know which of the passages must be loud and which soft. In "Jackson's," p. 2, the second section imitates the first chiefly in its rhythm. As it is a "rising" imitation, it is natural that it should be sung louder than the phrase it imitates. In the "Quail Call," p. 14, the section beginning "Look at her" imitates the first section, and is itself imitated by the section which follows. As the imitations are all "rising," the first section must be delivered very *piano* to get anything like a *forte* on the last imitation. A striking rising imitation is in "Hear me," p. 18, 1st score. A falling imitation, which would naturally be softer, is in "Nearer," p. 35, 2nd score. In "Where the Gay," p. 65, we have a descending rhythmic imitation, preparing by its *diminuendo* for the striking succession of ascending imitations which immediately follow. See Standard Course Ex. 113, 6th score, at "Rejoice, rejoice." Ex. 188, meas. 5 to 9. Ex. 233, on "and in" to "me live."

Marked Entrance.—When (as in much of the old sacred music, in the old English Madrigal, &c., &c.) each "part" in turn, takes *the lead* in announcing (in fugal style) the principal melodial theme, that "part" should assume its passing office with dignity, decision, and expressive clearness. The other "parts" should, at the same time, "give way," and hold themselves subordinate. It is plainly the composer's intention, that the entrance of these phrases into the music should be *distinctly marked*, like the entrance of some distinguished guest into a drawing-room, when all conversation is hushed and all eyes are intent. Study examples in "Thou shalt show me," pp. 7, 8, in which all the parts hush, to listen to "thou shalt show me;" "Bon Accord," p. 11, where the same thing should take place on the words "O, Grant us by," or "Thy goodness more." Marked entrance is often effective when there is no fugal imitation, as in "Going Home," p. 2, second score; "Hear me," p. 18, 4th score; "Spring Life," pp. 3, 4; "May Time," pp. 5 to 7. See also Standard Course Ex. 116, scores, 1 and 2; and Ex. 113, scores, 1, 2, 6, —contralto, "Rejoice."

Subordination of Parts.—As in the rule of "marked entry" the other parts were kept subordinate to the part which was entering the music, so in many other cases this hushing of several parts for the better display of some principal part has to be observed sometimes, as in "Gipsies Tent," p. 36, end of 1st score; during part of the tune the melody is evidently given to the soprano, and the contralto, tenor, and bass sing a subdued accompaniment, like the soft accompaniment of a piano or organ. Sometimes, as in "O, the Joy of Spring," p. 57,—this is the case throughout the tune. Sometimes, as in "Saviour, Breathe," p. 92, the principal melodies are given at one time to the soprano and contralto, and at another time to the tenor and bass. When the chorus is only an accompaniment to the melody, the harmony should be delivered in careful accordance with the joyous or the saddened *spirit* of the ruling melody, and always so as to let that melody be well heard. An unsympathetic accompaniment disgusts the mind of the listener. Let it be understood however, that whenever the part accompanied is silent, the accompaniment itself may speak out in fuller force and claim the attention of the listener. See—"Gipsies Tent," p. 35.

Humming Accompaniment.—Humming accompaniments may be produced in several ways.—First, by tightening and vibrating the lips without any voice from the larynx, the lips vibrating all round and not on one side. This should only be done when something of a reedy buzzing effect is wanted. —Second, by a soft voice from the larynx with only a slight opening of the lips.—Third, by a soft voice from the larynx, resounding in the nose, the lips being closed. In this case the singer must be careful not to contract the muscles of the nose so as to produce a nasal quality of tone. Care should also be taken to secure an exact and unanimous striking of the tones, so as to imitate the effect of stringed or reed instruments. See—"Night around," p. 22, and "Angel of Hope," p. 48. In these cases the third plan should be adopted. See also Standard Course Ex. 190.

Imitative Sounds.—When it is desired to imitate the rippling of water, the sighing of wind, or the sound of the drum or horn, the syllables commonly written under the notes, cannot be a sufficient guide to the singer; he must try to imitate the sounds intended, without caring to pronounce the exact syllables which dimly intimate them. The effect of nearness or distance is conveyed by loudness or softness of sound. Thus when the Christmas waits (p. 8) are supposed to be at a distance they sing softly; as they approach their singing sounds louder, and as they retire again their music dies away in the distance. The same remark applies to the sound of the drum, or any marching instruments. In a similar way the sound of distant bells, wafted by gusts of wind, may be imitated. See—"Come, let us all," pp. 24, 25. In imitating laughter we must remember that it has two characters; it is either light and trifling, or heavy and bold. Such a passage as "Fortune Hunter," p. 5, first score, may be treated in either way according to the spirit of the verses; if in the latter way it will contradict, but worthily, the natural diminuendo of a descending passage.

Ex. **211.** What musical expression would you give to the air in "May Time," from end of p. 5, to first line p. 6?

Ex. **212.** What musical expression would you give in "God Speed the Right," p. 1, to the air in first part of 3rd score,—to the air and bass in first part of 4th score,—to tenor and bass in 3rd score, —and to what part of this piece does the rule of subordination of parts apply?

Ex. **213.** What musical expression would you give to "Harvest Home," p. 41, end of second and first part of 3rd score,—also to soprano and contralto, 2nd score,—also to tenor and bass, p. 40, first part of 2nd score,—and also, tenor and bass beginning with second part of 2nd score, ending at the top of p. 41?

Ex. **214.** What musical expression would you give in "Loud the Storm-wind," p. 95, to the air of chorus, 2nd and 3rd scores?

Ex. **215.** What musical expression would you give to the air of the first line in "Father," p. 34, and to the air of the first line in "If I had," p. 45?

Ex. **216.** What musical expression would you give to the tenor and bass in the first eight measures of "Saviour, breathe," p. 91?

Ex. **217.** What expression would you give to the music in "Hear me," p. 19, 2nd score, where each of the parts in turn utters the words—"It is thou;" and to the 1st and 2nd scores on p. 26; and to the 3rd and 4th scores of "Swiftly," on p. 31, and to the 3rd and 4th scores of p. 30; and to the first three scores of "We fly," on p. 20?

Ex. **218.** How should the accompaniment be sung in "Home," p. 76?

Ex. **219.** What expression would you give to the music in all the four parts, of "How Lovely," p. 61; scores, 3 and 4?

Ex. **220.** What musical expression would you give to Standard Course Exercise 170, 1st score, both parts; Ex. 115, 3rd score, third and fourth measures; Ex. 170, 2nd score, both parts; Ex. 171, Amens in air, Hallelujahs, in contralto; Ex. 194, air in 9th and 10th measures, and 11th and 12th; Ex. 145, last eight measures; Ex. 193, first section, ditto second section; Ex. 190. first and second sections?

Ex. **221.** What musical expression would you give to Ex. 136, air,—1st score; Ex. 195, 1st and 3rd scores; Ex. 195, contralto, fourth measure, from *lah* to third *me*; Ex. 116, contralto, half second, and whole of third score?

Congenial Tones.*—As every tune has its own proper character, (bold and spirited, cheerful, didactic, solemn, &c.) it is natural that the Tonic Sol-faist should give clearest force to those tones of the scale which correspond best with the general sentiment of the piece, are "congenial" with that sentiment. Thus, in a quick and stirring tune, he would naturally emphasize the *trumpet tone* Soh, the *rousing* Ray, the *strong* Doh, &c.; and in a slow and solemn tune, the *sorrowful* Lah, the *desolate* Fah, &c. With this idea in the singers' minds, the tune will immediately become a new thing. The pupils will soon discover that they possess the power of making this, or any other peculiar effect prominent in the general harmony, very much in proportion to the height, in their own voice, of the tone which gives that effect. Thus a high tenor tone will *tell* better than a low one. A high contralto tone will also command attention, because energy and spirit is implied in the very effort of the voice to rise above its medium compass, and the more piercing sounds are better heard. *Low*

* See "Musical Theory," Book IV, p. 259.

sounds (in contralto and bass) also imply energy and force, and they are capable of yielding a good effect, especially when the harmony is "dispersed," and no other sound lies near. Some composers have great skill in setting the congenial tones of the music to that register, in each voice which is the most distinctive and the most beautiful.

Any high sound, or any favourably situated low sound which is *not* "congenial" with the general effect, the instructed singer will, therefore, deliver as lightly as possible. On the other hand, when the congenial tone occurs in a favourable position, he will never let it miss of its effect. With these principles to guide him, every singer may know where the strength of his "part" lies, and where it can best contribute to the general harmony. Psalm tunes, of the "didactic and variable" style, will thus be very differently treated according to the character of the words sung. If we were singing "The Fortune Hunter," (p. 4) we should notice that it was a very lively and playful tune, meant to be sung in a light staccato style—that, therefore, the quickly uttered emotional tones of the scale, would produce an effect congenial with the general character of the music. The sopranos would find an opportunity of developing congenial tones with bright explosive force on the first r of their part, and the second l and the second f. To contrast with these and give force to the jollity, the first s and the second d' would be similarly delivered. The l being in the high part of the voice should be brilliantly attacked; and the piquant effect of f against the t, and s below it, should be brought out with sharp accent. The contraltos have nothing very effective till the two bursts of bright sounds under the soprano l and d'. The greatest power of the tenor lies in the delivery of t under the soprano f; and the best point of the bass is in the s of the same chord. "Rise my Soul" (p. 33) is naturally a tune of joy, changing into meditative mood on the last section. The sopranos will, therefore, find congenial tones in their first bright s, in the stirring t and the triumphant d', for the change of character in the tune their returning f can be well given. The contraltos have a good $se_{|}$ in that full part of their voices, which best distinguishes them from other voices; they can help the excitement in the beginning of the second score by delivering their s, which is in the upper part of their voice, clearly and lightly. The tenors can set their mark on this tune by a prompt delivery of s in the first chord: their l at the beginning of the last section is also in a characteristic part of their voice. The basses have a fine effect in the full part of their voice in the first cadence, and they can well employ the high part of their voice in the second cadence, where l for a joyful effect should be delivered curtly; the returning f which follows will be naturally well marked. But, if to suit the words this tune has to be sung with a solemn or mournful effect—everything is changed—each voice must then strive to bring out f and l wherever they occur, and to lessen the force of the brighter tones. In "Come, let us all," (pp. 24, 25) the bell ringing (which is heard as a distant subdued accompaniment to the cuckoo), is given to two parts. But of these two subdued parts, the most distinct and bell-like are first the tenor, afterwards the bass,—because the tones are thrown by change of key into the higher parts of those voices; and of the two subdued parts, these must always have the pre-eminence. —See also congenial *me* and *fah* in a tune which expresses at once solemnity and repose in Standard Course Ex. 136; the congenial *doh, me, soh,* in a tune of great boldness, Ex. 137, and the congenial *lah* and *fah* in a tune which expresses soft and tender feelings, Ex. 140.

Ex. **222.** Describe the general character of "Jackson's," p. 2, and its congenial tones; name those congenial tones in each "part" which lie in the full characteristic region, or in the higher or more marked part of each voice.

Ex. **223.** Describe "The Waits," p. 8, as above.

Ex. **224.** "Father," p. 34, as above.

Ex. **225.** "Nearer my God," as above.

Rapid Passages.—The composer would never give the singer a rapid passage or run if he meant the notes to be blotched, and blurred and run into one another, so as to be little better than an indefinite and disagreeable single tone. He designs them to stand as distinctly united and as distinctly apart "as the pearls of a necklace, resting on a black velvet dress." The singers must give them the clearest articulation, and there must be perfect unanimity of attack. In order to secure this effect the pupil should always take breath at the beginning of a long run, and economise it carefully so that there be no appearance of fatigue at the end. In some choruses it will be necessary to "smuggle in" the breath even in the middle of the run. Illustrations can be found in "Thou shalt show me ' (p. 7) on the first syllable of the word "presence." An exact delivery of the TAA-efe, with unanimity of attack, will make this little run bright and beautiful. In "We fly by night" (p. 20) there are runs which will require careful forethought for the management of the breath. In "Hallelujah" (p. 27), unanimous and perfect delivery of TAA-efe, TAA-tefe, tafa-TAI will be re-required. In "Swiftly" (p. 32) we very seldom hear "universal song" sung with pearl-like clearness; it is more like a skuttering upstairs of many irregular feet. Handel's runs should be cultivated with great care as exercises in flexibility. See also rapid passages in Standard Course Exs. 102, 120, 174, and 247.

Form of Single Tones.—The explosive tone naturally expresses vigour and decision of feeling. See pp. 12, 39, 42, 45, 57, and Standard Course Ex. 141.

When a composer alters the accent by syncopation for a moment, he wishes the syncopation to be noticed by the hearer. The singer must, therefore, give it the explosive tone. Syncopation generally expresses restless force or impatient desire. See p. 87, 4th score. See also "Ye spotted," p. 81, a case of piano-explosive tones, in tenor s, end of 1st score; contralto d, with soprano r, at beginning of 2nd score. See also Standard Course Ex. 114.

The pressure tone naturally suggests deepening emotion. In any touching three-pulse measure to deliver the second pulse with this tone, at least occasionally, produces a beautiful effect. See "Jackson's," p. 3; notice also "The Woods," p. 72, second score. See also Standard Course Ex. 139, and Ex. 140.

Pressure tones on a weak pulse, swelling into explosive tones on the next strong pulse, are often very effective. A good solo singer would often instinctively use them in slowly moving psalm-tones, on the last pulse of a measure moving to the next accent. See p. 57, 3rd score, and p. 17, last score. See also Standard Course Ex. 193.

The legato style of singing is a modification of the pressure tone. It gives a smooth, gliding effect to the tones, and lessens the distinctions of accent. See p. 63, 3rd and 4th scores; and p. 82, 1st and 2nd scores.

The staccato style of singing is a modification of the explosive tone. It gives an abrupt, forceful effect to the tones, and necessarily lessens to a considerable extent the distinctions of accent. See tenor and bass, p. 40, and p. 42, first and last scores. See also a piano-staccato, immediately following a legato passage on p. 82, third score.

Unison Passages.—Passages in which all four parts strike either the same tones or their octaves together, should be sung with great care, so as to produce a perfect and clear blending of the voices. The voices should feel for one another, but not timidly, for such passages are generally meant to be very firm and strong. They should sing with conscious sympathy. See "God Speed," p. 1; "Fortune Hunter," p. 4; "O, Saviour," p. 87; "Harvest Home," p. 41, 2nd and 3rd scores; and "Stout Limbed Oak," p. 78, first and last scores.

Cadences.—Few things are more painful to a listener than to think that a singer is tired, few things more inspiring than to feel that he closes without fatigue. Even when the cadence is downward and diminuendo it should be firm, but in ascending cadences a sustained crescendo is absolutely requisite. See close of "Harvest Home," p. 41; and "Quail Call," p. 15, 1st and 2nd scores. Notice a vigorous descending cadence in "God Speed," p. 1; and others in "Theme Sublime," p. 71; "Rise my Soul," p. 33; "Stout Limbed Oak," p. 77, 4th score. See also contrasted cadences, Standard Course Ex. 145, last two scores.

Distinguishing Tones of transition of the minor mode and of chromatic resolution (except when occurring in some subordinate part, and evidently introduced more for the convenience of the harmonizer than for any effect upon the harmony), should always be delivered with marked emphasis; for they have an important meaning. They change the mental effect of all the other tones.. For the voices, in whose part the accidental occurs, not to deliver it firmly is to rob the whole music of its meaning. The tones of "returning transition" should also be emphasized. But, if the transition itself were carelessly given, this second effect would be lost.

Those movements of the bass which mark the tonic cadence of a new key, as | d : r | s, and | r : r | s, : or of the relative minor, as | r : m | l, and | m : m | l should be markedly delivered, because they help to certify the transition or modulation. See p. 52.

Chromatic resolutions should also be firmly shown, because they are intended to reassert the key. Special attention should be given to those tones of the chord which would be quite differently resolved if a transition were meant. In "Hope will banish," p. 12; 2nd score, the **fe** in the air is not in a favourable position for accent, but that in the bass should be well delivered. In "How beautiful," p. 12, at the end of the 1st score, the cadence is made to change key, more by the movement of the bass than by the very light distinguishing tone in the contralto; therefore, let the bass move firmly. In the next score the distinguishing tone of returning transition, which in this case is **f**, although it does not appear till the end of the section, comes out then with effect, and should be clearly delivered by contralto and bass. The same voices have the "returning **f**" at the top of p. 13. In "Hallelujah," p. 26, the sopranos have a very effective returning **f**. In "Lord, in this," p. 33, of course, the **se** will be well marked, because it is the distinguishing tone of the minor. In the second line of words there is a modulation to the major, which should be strongly marked by the cadential movement of the bass, and by the tenors' clear use of **s** instead of the preceding **se**. In "Ye spotted Snakes," p. 81, the tenors have a returning **f** at the end of the 1st score, and the contralto a transitional **f** at the beginning of the next score. In "Saviour, Breathe," p. 91 and 93, the chromatic resolution of **fe** into **f** should be clearly marked by the voice. In this piece, as well as at pp. 79, 94, 95, and 96, the manner in which such tones as **de, re, ma,** &c., flow into the tones which follow them should be clearly and lovingly marked.

Dissonances.—In all cases of dissonance there is a "resisting" tone, and a "dissonating" tone. Every singer should know which of the two belongs to his part,—the strong resisting tone or the smoothly moving dissonance. See pp. 21, 36, &c. It is difficult for pupils with uncultured ears to sing either of these tones steadily. But they *must* be sung without any "giving way." Else, their purpose is lost, and their beauty gone. Where would be the beauty of a cataract if the resisting rock gave way to the struggling current which strikes against its side and then flows on? The resisting tone should be sung in a firm, almost "explosive" style, and the dissonating tone (which springs from its "preparation," and flows forward to its "resolution") should be delivered as part of a short melodic phrase in a very smooth-connected manner. Let the pupils test their power of delivering dissonances well by singing "Jackson's" p. 3, where on the word "through" the contraltos have **d** dissonating against **r** of the soprano, and on the word "day" **r** against **m**, where also on the word "led" the sopranos have **t** dissonating against the tenor **d'**, and on the syllable "vin" **m** slightly dissonating against **f,** in the bass; while, on the same syllable the tenors have **s**, not only dissonating against this low **f**, but beating as a second against the **l** of the contraltos. This study of the dissonances will not only give the singer courage but great enjoyment, and will wonderfully add to the beauty of the effect. See also Standard Course Exs. 114, 141, 244.

Ex. 226. What is the style in which you would sing the passage in "Harvest Home," p. 40, "O'er them the wavy wealth;" and "Theme Sublime," pp. 69, 71; and the "Stout limbed oak," pp. 77, 78?

Ex. 227. What form of expression would you apply to the following tones on p. 67. Bass **f**, 1st score; 2nd score, tenor **d**, followed by bass **s** and **f**?

Ex. 228. What form of musical expression would you give to the two *lahs* of contralto, p. 85, 3rd score?

Ex. 229. What style of expression would you give generally to the tones of Standard Course Ex. 140?

Ex. 230. In singing the *p.* passage, "Morning Prayer," p. 79, 1st score, what special care will be required from the singers in all the parts?

Ex. 231. Why should the contralto and bass in "Come, Freedom's," p. 13, 2nd score, third and fourth measures be firmly delivered; and what note, soon following in the same voices, should be specially emphasized? In "Rise, my soul," p. 33, what are the most noticeable distinguishing tones, and how should they be sung?

Ex. 232. What musical expression would you give to Standard Course Ex. 142, third score, *ta,* and *fe,*; Ex. 189, third score, *se*; Ex. 193, second score, *ba*?

Parsing Fugal Passages.—The practice of parsing, described at the last step, becomes more difficult, but also more interesting when we have to analyse fugal imitations, or those in which one part seems to *fly* after another. In these cases the great rhythmical divisions of the melody are not so regular. One musical idea is made to interlace with another—thus, in Ex. 234, before the first section is complete the second voice commences a section of its own, and it is so very frequently throughout this and other pieces. We are therefore obliged to describe the passages and sections in such manner as the following:—Ex. 234 consists first of a subject of one measure and a half, started by the upper part, and imitated at the interval of a *fourth below* by the lower part *after one measure*. This also, after one measure, is imitated in the fourth above with a varied cadence. This again, after one measure, is imitated in the fifth below; and again, after one measure, in the sixth above, and again in the sixth below. After two measures the original theme with the old cadence is taken up by the higher voice for two measures, while the lower voice ornaments it. Then follows a sequence of two measures, each portion of which contains an internal imitation. The piece is concluded by four measures of ornamental cadence. Ex. 195 opens with a subject in the lower part of three measures and a half which is imitated in the higher part, after three measures in the fourth above, the lower part supplying a soft and light accompaniment. Then follows eight measures of what may be called contrapuntal symphony—that is, a play of the parts one against the other without special meaning. One measure before this is concluded, the higher part starts the old three-measure theme, which is indefinitely imitated after two measures, and then for six measures more there is another contrapuntal symphony. Again the lower part starts its first theme with a varied cadence extending to five measures, and this is imitated again in the fifth above, not as before—after three measures, but after one measure. This *coming closer* of an imitation is called a Stretto. After a brief ornamental, fugal imitation, the piece closes with five and a half measures of contrapuntal symphony. The singer should mark with pencil the exact length of the fugal subjects. When the other part or parts merely accompany the fugal subject they will, of course, be kept subdued. In the interludes and symphonies the parts may be of equal force. In the stretto the entries should be strongly marked, but the parts may be of equal force till the first which entered has finished the imitated subject, leaving the second to be well heard in its close. These observations will show the importance of this study. Let the student be now required to write out analyses of such exercises as 233, 235, and 246. It will be difficult to do so by sight, they should sing the exercises with a friend several times over.*

The Small Register is in the highest range of the human voice, and belongs to females and boys alone. They naturally pass into it on one-F♯ (F♯'), or one-G (G'). It is remarkable that the change of breakage into this register should be just an octave higher than that into the thin register. It is this fact on which early students of the voice built the false theory, that the registers of the male and female voices were the same—only, an octave apart. The distinction in quality between the small register and the thin is not so marked as that between the thin and the thick. The small muscles by which the voice is produced in this register are very delicate, and Garcia recommends that they should not be overstrained by too much practice. Some deep contralto voices, though weak and breathy in the thin register, produce many tones of this highest register. Their larger larynx and stronger chest enable them to force these tones more easily than many sopranos; but, though the volume is greater the quality is inferior, and ordinary singers should be advised not to cultivate a useless and unpleasant part of their voice. Specially gifted solo singers, like Alboni and others, have had opportunities of cultivating and using every register of their voices in a manner which, to most contraltos, would be impossible.

For ordinary choral singing the tones of this register, except one-G (G'), are little used; but Bach, Handel, Haydn, Mozart, Beethoven, and Mendelssohn all use one-A (A') in some of their choruses, so that every choral society should be able to command full, clear and unstrained force on this tone. This can be best obtained by cultivating the small register of the sopranos. It is sweeter and brighter than that of the contraltos above referred to—and besides, it is continuous, in them, with a good thin register (which such contraltos generally lack), so that passages running across the "break" can be sung with an even quality of voice. The classic composers expect their *solo* singers to go much higher. Beethoven in *Engedi* requires two-D (D^2); such things must be done by voices professionally trained. In psalm tunes written for trained choirs one-G (G') may be used even on holding tones; but, psalm tunes written for congregations should not even touch the small register, because the mass of women's voices in a congregation are not trained to its use.

* See further "Musical Theory," Book III, p. 105.

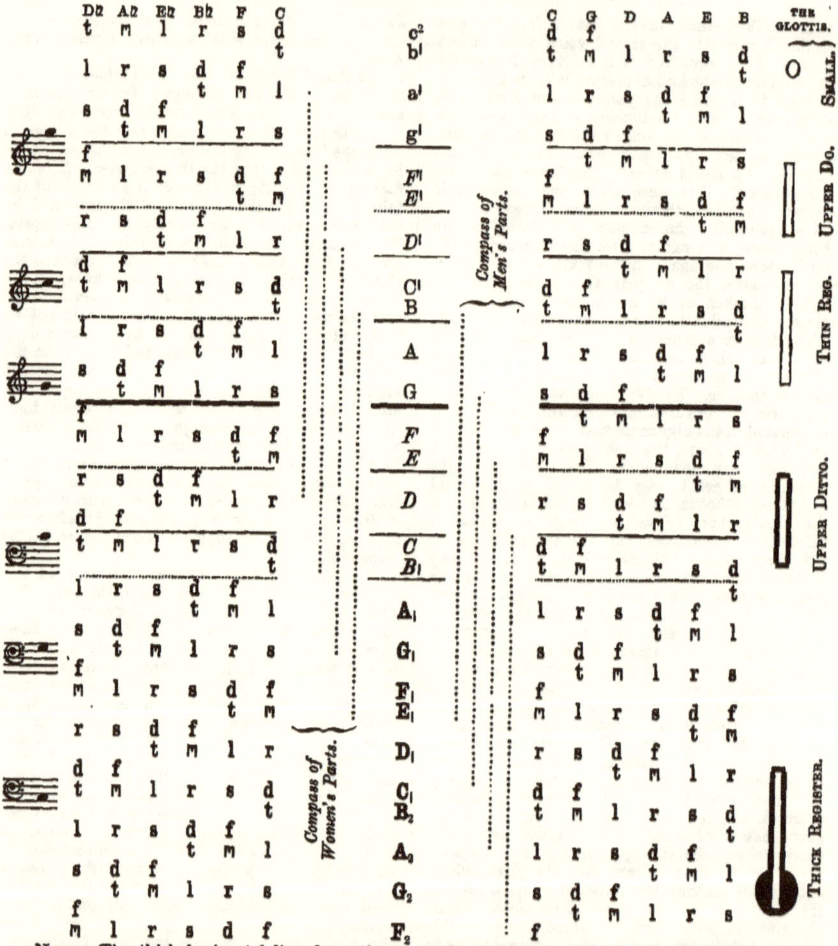

D♮ A♮ E♮ B♮ F C
t m l r s d
t
l r s d f
t m l
s d f
t m l r s
f
m l r s d f
t m
r s d f
t m l r
d f
t m l r s d
t
l r s d f
t m l
s d f
t m l r s
f
m l r s d f
t m
r s d f
t m l r
d f
t m l r s d
t
l r s d f
t m l
s d f
t m l r s
f
m l r s d f
t m
r s d f
t m l r
d f
t m l r s d
t
l r s d f
t m l
s d f
t m l r s
f
m l r s d f

Compass of Women's Parts.

c²
b'
a'
g'
F'
E'
D'
C'
B
A
G
F
E
D
C
B_1
A_1
G_1
F_1
E_1
D_1
C_1
B_2
A_2
G_2
F_2

Compass of Men's Parts.

C G D A E B
d f
t m l r s d
t
l r s d f
t m l
s d f
t m l r s
f
m l r s d f
t m
r s d f
t m l r
d f
t m l r s d
t
l r s d f
t m l
s d f
t m l r s
f
m l r s d f
t m
r s d f
t m l r
d f
t m l r s d
t
l r s d f
t m l
s d f
t m l r s
f
m l r s d f
t m
r s d f
t m l r
d f
t m l r s d
t
l r s d f
t m l
s d f
t m l r s
f

THE GLOTTIS.
SMALL.
UPPER DO.
THIN REG.
UPPER DITTO.
THICK REGISTER.

NOTE.—The thick horizontal line shews the "great break" between the Thick and Thin Registers, below G. The thin line, an octave above, shews the "small break" between the Thin and Small Registers. The dotted lines shew the *average* place of break, the other lines the *highest* place that is safe.

St Co. (New.)

The small register, like the other registers, can overlap downwards; but it does not so frequently do so as the thin register in men's voices. It may often be of advantage and a relief, especially to a second soprano, to take one-F (F') habitually in the small register.

The Lesser Breaks of the voice divide both the thick and the thin registers into upper and lower parts. The break between the upper and lower thin register, is quite manifest in ordinary soprano voices between one-C (C') and one-D (D'). The upper thin *may* overlap downward, but does not commonly do so. The break between the upper and lower thick registers is easily noticed in male voices between A-one ($A_{|}$) and B-one ($B_{|}$). The upper thick register *may* overlap downwards, but seldom does so in male voices. Madame Seiler says that in *women's voices* this break occurs one-third higher, between C and D; but we have noticed that many women habitually make the upper thick register overlap downwards, so that they change into the lower thick, just where the men do, on A-one ($A_{|}$).

Speaking Registers.—Men commonly speak in their thick register. Tenor voices, however, use the pleasant higher thick register. Very rarely a man may be heard speaking in his thin register, with a thin squeaking quality. Those who have to do with partially deaf persons ought to know that men are better heard when they speak gently at a high pitch of their voice, than loudly at a low pitch. This constant speaking in the thick register is the reason why men are tempted in singing to strain their voices too much upward, and to neglect the cultivation of their thin register. Women commonly speak in their thin register; but some contraltos use their rich upper thick tones, and occasionally a woman may be heard to speak in the rough lower thick register. It is this common habit of using the thin register in speech which tempts them, in singing, to employ it downward more than is necessary—and so, to neglect and ignore the better tones of the upper thick register.

Mechanism and Feeling of the Registers.—In the lower thick register, the whole length and the whole substance of the vocal membranes are thrown into full vibration. (See the Diagram at the side of the Voice Modulator). The air must, therefore, press upon the membranes with a greater volume than in the other registers. We *feel* the air passing into the windpipe from all parts of the lungs. This widens the rings of the windpipe, and as a consequence, draws down the larynx. "One thus has a sensation," says Madame Seiler, "as if the whole body took part in this formation of sound."

In the upper thick register, while the whole thickness of the membranes is still in vibration, their *length* is greatly shortened. "The sensation," says Madame Seiler, "is as if the tones came from the upper part of the chest." These physical sensations do not show how the sounds are generated, but what parts of the nervous system are excited in the process. They help us, however, to recognize the distinctions of register, and they account for some of the conflicting names by which the registers have hitherto been known.

In the lower thin register the whole length of the membranes is again employed; but only their thin edges vibrate. "The feeling is as if they had their origin in the throat."

In the upper thin register the membranes are again shortened, and the feeling is "as if the throat had nothing to do with the tones—as if they were formed above in the mouth."

In the small register only a small part of the glottis to the front of the larynx is opened, and "one has the feeling," says Madame Seiler, "that the tones come from the forehead." Thus the singer is like the violin player who sometimes uses a thin string, sometimes a thick one, sometimes a short string, sometimes a long one. These points of information will help to fix the pupil's attention on the various changes of his voice.

Boys' Voices we find to be much the same, in their various registers, as women's voices, but they are commonly used more roughly and coarsely. The practice of permitting boys to shout against an instrument in village schools and churches, not only tears the voice to pieces, but destroys that tenderness and fineness of feeling which music ought to promote. It is this coarse use of boys' voices which has produced the impression that they are different in quality from those of women and girls, and incapable of gentle training; but of course the greater physical strength of boys gives a greater *volume* to their voices than girls possess. It is a great mistake to set all the boys in a school to sing the contralto, and all the girls soprano. The soprano and contralto voices are found in about equal proportions among both boys and girls. When the time of the "change of voice" comes, the practice of singing should, for a time, not be even attempted, and should be only gradually and carefully resumed. Many voices have been ruined by the neglect of this precept.

Voices and "Parts."—The four principal "parts" of choral music are marked at p. 29; but for glees, anthems, and men's voice music, we require a more minute classification, and as the cultivation of the thin register has probably made some good tenors, and that of the thick register some good contraltos, the teacher should now advise each of his pupils as to the part or parts for which his voice is adapted. The "parts" which women have to sing are often divided into first soprano, second soprano, and contralto, Occasionally we meet with four-part women's music requiring the contraltos to be divided into first and second. The "parts" which men have to sing are frequently marked—first tenor, second tenor, and bass; an additional part being sometimes written for a first or second bass. Those who have analysed a great number of voices know that there is an almost boundless variety. Nothing should satisfy a teacher who wishes to use his class for the higher kinds of music, but an individual examination of each voice,—on the plan of the "Voice Report Book."

The process of examination is simple but needs to be conducted with deliberate care. The teacher gives in the case of women and boys, the pitch of G, and in the case of men G-one (G_1). If only a tuning-fork is used, the greatest care is necessary to secure the *exact* pitch. Beginning with G or G-one (G_1), the pupil *laas* downwards, (in long tones, taking breath before each), s, f, m, &c., while the teacher points on the "Voice Modulator."* The teacher takes notes or dictates them to an assistant. Doubtful tones should be tested over again. The various "breaks" should be crossed both upwards and downwards. When this has been done, the pupil, starting again from G or G-one (G_1), *laas* upwards, s, l, t, d', &c., while the teacher again studies and records the present condition of his pupil's voice. The teacher can bracket together several tones of the scale at the side of his Voice Report, and mark either by words or by figures (1 for fair, 2 for good, 3 for very good), first the quality then the volume; or, he can mark the tones singly in the same way. Figures showing degrees of excellence in the blending of the registers should be given in each case. The most useful men's optional tones should be named, and the place at which a woman's voice breaks, between the upper and lower thick registers, should be marked. After this it will be easy to mark the full compass of the voice and its best region. These considerations will decide the name to be given to it, as first or second soprano, &c., first or second contralto, &c. A faithful "Voice Report Book" will be invaluable to the teacher when he wishes to select singers for any particular purpose, and it will lead the pupil to study and cultivate his own voice.

A first Soprano cannot easily be mistaken; she possesses in addition to a good thin register, a few tones of the small register which easily blend with it. *A second Soprano* is distinguished by the possession of a good upper thick register, along with a good thin register, even if she cannot command more than a tone or two of the small.

A Contralto voice is that which possesses good full tones in the distinguishing region of the contralto "part"—the upper and lower thick registers. The teacher must not be misled by the great compass upward which some of these voices possess, for their thin register is commonly weak and tuneless; whilst their small register, though strong, is hard. When first contraltos are wanted, the teacher will naturally select those which are weaker in the lower thick, and better in the upper thick registers than the rest. This last voice is sometimes called *mezzo* (med·zoa), soprano.

A first Tenor (as it is now called in Germany and France), or an old English "counter tenor," cannot be easily mistaken. He has a light and pleasant quality of voice in the upper thick and lower thin registers. Well-trained counter tenors can give good tones up to one-F (F^1) at the top of the upper thin register; but such a range is not common. The *highest* reach of men's voice "parts" in Palestrina's time was one-C (C^1), or one-D (D^1); the counter-tenor in Tallis and Morley's music reaches A and B♭, and the first tenor in German men's voice music does not often go above B♭. It is quite common for tenors to force their upper thick register as high as this tone, but it is the distinctive quality of the *first* tenor that he uses with pleasure his thin register, and produces with it *bright, yet soft and flute-like tones.* This first tenor, counter tenor, or tenor alto was used in England for the highest parts in men's voice music throughout the famous Elizabethan and Madrigalian age. But at the restoration of Charles II., the Italian Opera brought along with it the Eunuch singers, whose rich, strong contralto voices suggested to bass singers the employment of their equally powerful, but not rich, upper thin registers.

* Large "Voice Modulator," 1s.

This unfortunate discovery led to the neglect of the softer and brighter counter-tenor, and all the contralto music through Handel's period was written for the hard-toned bass-alto, and the same voice is still used instead of the richer female contralto, in cathedrals and choral societies, in which eighteenth-century traditions are preserved. It has been observed above (See "Small Register") that contralto, as well as bass singers, possess the power through their larger larynx and stronger chest of *forcing* the highest register of their voices. Like them the bass-altos are weak and breathy in the next register below, so that there is no continuity and equality of voice across the break at G, and the change of register is marked and unpleasant. This peculiar, unsympathetic voice, is often uncertain and out of tune, and its cultivation is very undesirable. The Tyrolese basses use this thin voice in their Jodl songs; but do not attempt to employ the region of voice lying between. The true counter-tenor or tenor-alto is no more wanted to take the place occupied in modern times by the contralto than is the bass-alto. But, for men's voice music, and for solo singing, it is very valuable. The teacher will notice that many tenors have of late been misled by the false talk of a chest G or a chest A, so as to force their thick voice upwards, leaving the beautiful tones of their thin voice entirely uncultivated. The practice of men's voice music, either separately or for half an hour after a mixed-voice class, will remedy this, and restore to England her long lost counter-tenors. *The second Tenors* are known by the excellence of their lower tones; they have but little use for their thin register except on G. There, however, it should be truly cultivated if not also, as an optional register, on F. E. D. Tenors of both kinds, of the highest eminence, habitually change to the thin register on D or E. The shouting of the tenor part on a forced upper thick register is most painful to the ear, and a fruitful source of flattening.

The First Bass, or Baritone Voice may be distinguished from the second bass by its not possessing fulness below C-one (C_1), or B-two (B_2). Such voices seldom have the proper tones of the thin register, but they often find it a relief to employ that register as an optional one, instead of the higher two or three tones of the upper thick register; it saves them from straining and flattening. *The second Bass* is distinguished by its full robust tones on A-two (A_2), G-two (G_2), F-two (F_2), and even lower. In the upper part of the voice it is not very dissimilar to the baritone. Those basses which have the so-called bass-alto or "head-voice" generally (though not always) of a shrill and screamy character, are advised not to use it. The examination of voices, here recommended, cannot occupy less than from fifteen to thirty minutes for each person, and should be regarded as a separate private lesson of great value to each pupil.

Compass.—It will be noticed that in these instructions for the classification of voices, we have avoided any reference to *compass* as a criterion of judgment. This is not only because we are thus free to secure the best quality and the best volume for each "part," but because of the great injury done to voices by the habit of singing beyond the range of their proper part. Teachers and psalmody conductors are specially exposed to this danger. They wish to show other people the right tones and are careless of the manner in which they produce them. Previous teaching by quiet *pattern* is really a quicker, as well as a better way, of reaching the desired result. Some highly trained solo singers may with impunity cultivate a great range of voice, but others are found to injure the tones of their proper compass by going much out of it. When the more minute classification of "parts" is required (each of the ordinary *four* parts being divided into first and second), it may be useful to note that few composers go beyond the limits marked on "The Voice Modulator," p. 106. The highest men's voice, the counter-tenor, and the lowest women's voice, the second contralto, coincide; they sing the same part. From this point upwards and downwards the *common* compass of parts rises and falls by thirds.

The Causes of Flattening are—1st, Physical Weakness. In this case the singer should restrain his enthusiasm for the sake of others, and sing softly, and listen.—2nd, The forcing of the Upper Thick Register in the higher part of men's voices which is immediately cured by the cultivation of the thin.—3rd, Breathiness of Tone and other defects in various parts of particular voices.—4th, Defects of Ear, to be cured by long and attentive listening, and by study of mental effects. —5th, Careless and lax-delivery of *Piano* or violent and coarse delivery of *Forte*, which can easily be avoided.—6th, Habitually singing with "tempered" instruments, with their flat fifths and sharp thirds, putting the ear out of tune.—7th, Sympathy with bad singers who are near, and inattention to the leader.—8th, Bad posture in singing.—9th, Neglect of breathing places, and the consequent exhaustion, and—10th, Worst and commonest of all—*want of interest*, and its consequent drawling delivery. The teacher should make the maintenance of pitch a distinct object of his care, and should call the attention af his pupils to it, often testing them at the end of a piece. The close of one verse and the beginning of another is the commonest place for inattention and, therefore, for flattening. Let the teacher beware of it. If he is acting as a precentor, let him make his voice heard on its effective tones, especially at the starting of the lines. An organist may maintain the pitch without playing loudly, by a skilful management of the more piercing stops. A cadence (⁷S to D) delivered at a high pitch in an interlude, will impress the ear better than the loud roaring of the lowest tones.

Solfaa-ing the Break.—Tenor singers should, at this stage, be required to mark the places at which it is most advisable to change from the thick to the thin, and from the thin to the thick registers. See p. 68; but note that when the registers are well equalised, so that the change from the one to the other can scarcely be noticed by the hearer, it *may* be better always to change at one point of absolute pitch, instead of trying to suit the musical phrase; this is done by some of our best singers. Each pupil should study the capabilities of his own voice. Other voices, as well as the tenors, should form a habit of "Solfaa-ing their breaks" as soon as the key is pitched. Thus, for example, a second soprano, with a bad "upper thin" tone on one-F (F¹), who is advised to cultivate her "small" register on that tone, should learn to calculate the Sol-fa note on which it will fall. While Key C is being pitched, she calls to mind that the note she has to watch is **f**; while D is pitched, she thinks of her **re** and **m**; while E is pitched, she reminds herself of **de** and **r**, and so on. Mark the optional tones, and the places of change in the manner adopted in Exs. 170 to 175.—See questions at close of this step —No. 73.

Sixths, Eighths, and Ninths of a Pulse are very little used except in instrumental music. The *Eighths* of a pulse are thus named, *tanafanatenefene*, :l l,l l.l l,l l|. The Exercise of singing them to the teacher's beating, quicker and quicker, will be very amusing to the pupils, and will greatly help to refine their sense of time divisions. There are two ways in which a pulse may be divided into *Sixths*. It may first be divided into thirds and then the thirds into halves thus—taataitee, *tafatefetifi*, :l l ,l l ,l l| which we may call thirds-sixes," or it may be first divided into halves, and then the halves into thirds thus—TAATAI, *taralaterele*, :l l l .l l l | which we may call "halves-sixes." The *Ninths* suppose the pulse to be divided into thirds, and then each third into thirds again, thus —taataitee, *taralatereletirili*, :l l l ,l l l ,l l l|. It will be a useful exercise for the teacher while beating time to call for "halves," "quarters," "eighths," "thirds," "thirds-sixes," "ninths," "halves," "halves-sixes," and so on.

Rare Divisions of Time.—It will be useful here to give the notation for some of the less common rhythms. When a pulse is divided into a quarter tone, a half tone, and a quarter tone, it is written thus | t ,l .,s : or better thus | t ,l .–,s : When a pulse is divided into a three-quarter tone and two-eighths, it is written | r .,mf : When a pulse is divided into a three-eighths tone, an eighth-tone, and a half tone, it is written | d,–r.m : When a pulse is divided into a half-pulse continuation, and three halves-sixths, it is written :– .fmr | (3 over m) In instrumental music, especially for strings, it is sometimes necessary to divide a pulse into less than an eighth when the same tone has to be very rapidly repeated; in this case we place as many dots over a note as the parts into which it is to be divided. In the instrumental score of "Hallelujah to the Father," from Beethoven's *Mount of Olives* we find a half-pulse divided into six and another into nine; they would be written as follows:—

: .s l t d¹ r¹ m¹ | .m¹ r¹ d¹ t l s f m r ||

These exceedingly rare cases of rhythmical division require careful examination before they are sung, in the Common Notation as well as ours. It will be perceived that the Tonic Sol-fa Notation does not make any lower division of the pulse than that into eighths, and that division it indicates by the simple absence of a mark. The occasional practice of writing, in the Established Notation, two measures as though they were one (See—"What is a pulse?" p. 65), makes it necessary, *in that Notation*, to have a more minute subdivision of pulse. In the Tonic Sol-fa Notation we, in such pieces, put two measures for each one of the Established Notation. We find, practically, that this mode of writing secures a more ready appreciation, and a more exact execution of the time.

GIVE UNTO ME.

Ex. 233. KEY E♭. M. 96. *Gebhardi.*

| s :— | l :- .t | d' :— | — :t | l :t .d' | r' .d' :t .l | s :l .t |
Give un - to me, made low - - ly wise, The
| : | : | : | : | : | : | :

| d' :— | — :— | t :— | B♭. t. d f :d | — :f | — :m | s :— |
spi - - - rit of self - sac - - ri - fice;
| : | : | : | d f, :— | l, :- .t, | d :— | — :t, |
Give un - to me, made

| — :— | f :— | — :— | m :f .m | r :m .f | s :f |
- - The con - fi - dence of free - dom
| l, :t, .d | r .d :t, .l, | s, :l, .t, | d :— | — :— | .t, :— |
low - - - ly wise, The spi - - - rit

f. E♭.
| m t :s | d' :— | — :d' | t :t | t :d' | l :— | — :l |
give, And in the light of truth, Thy bonds - - man
| d s :s | s :m | r :m .f | s .f :m .r | d :— | — :d | t, :d .r |
of self - sac - ri - fice, self - sac - ri - fice, self - sac -

| se :se | l :- .l | d' :- .r' | m' :— | — :m' | f :- .f | l :- .t |
let me live, And in the light, And in the light of
| m .r :d .t, | l, : | l :— | s :- .f | m :m | f :— | f :— |
- ri - fice; And in the light of truth And

| d' :— | — :d' | — :t | l :r' | — :d' | t :m' | l :r' |
truth, In the light, In the light of truth, Thy
| m :- .r | d :d | r :s | s :f | m :l | — :s | — :f |
in the light of truth, Thy bonds - man let me live

| s :d' | d' :— | t :— | d' :— | — :s | l :l | l :m |
bonds - man let me live, And in the light of
| — :m | r :l | s :f | m :— | — :m | de :— | — :de |
Thy bonds-man let me live. And in the

St. Co. (New.)

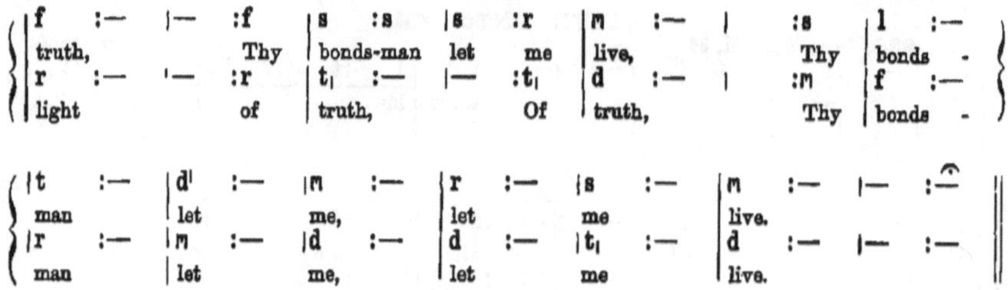

f :—	— :f	s :s	s :r	m :—	:s	l :—
truth, Thy	bonds-man let me	live, Thy	bonds -
r :—	— :r	t, :—	— :t,	d :—	:m	f :—
light of	truth, Of	truth, Thy	bonds -

t :—	d' :—	m :—	r :—	s :—	m :—	— :—	
man	let	me,	let	me	live.	
r :—	m :—	d :—	d :—	t, :—	d :—	— :—	
man	let	me,	let	me	live.	

PRAISE TO OUR GOD.

Ex. 234. KEY D. M. 96. *Rinck.*

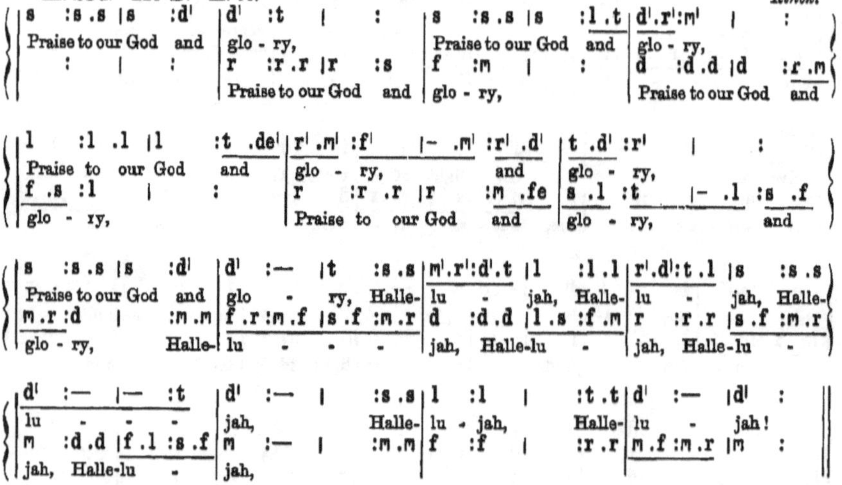

s :s .s	s :d'	d' :t	:	s :s .s	s :l .t	d'.r':m'	:
Praise to our God and	glo - ry,	Praise to our God and	glo - ry,
:	:	r :r .r	r :s	f :m	:	d :d .d	d :r .m
	Praise to our God and	glo - ry,	Praise to our God and

l :l .l	l :t .de'	r'.m' :f'	— .m' :r' .d'	t .d' :r'	:
Praise to our God and	glo - ry, and	glo - ry,
f .s :l	:	r :r .r	r :m .fe	s .l :t	— .l :s .f
glo - ry,	Praise to our God and	glo - ry, and

s :s .s	s :d'	d' :—	t :s .s	m'.r':d'.t	l :l .l	r'.d':t .l	s :s .s
Praise to our God and	glo - ry, Halle-	lu - jah, Halle-	lu - jah, Halle-
m .r :d	:m .m	f .r :m .f	s .f :m .r	d :d .d	l .s :f .m	r :r .r	s .f :m .r
glo - ry, Halle-	lu - - -	jah, Halle-lu -	jah, Halle-lu -

d' :—	— :t	d' :—	:s .s	l :l	:t .t	d' :—	d' :	
lu - - -	jah, Halle-	lu - jah, Halle-	lu - jah!	
m :d .d	f .l :s .f	m :—	:m .m	f :f	:r .r	m .f :m .r	m :	
jah, Halle-lu -	jah,			

LOVE THY NEIGHBOUR.

Ex. 235. KEY B♭. M. 96. *J. Mainzer.*

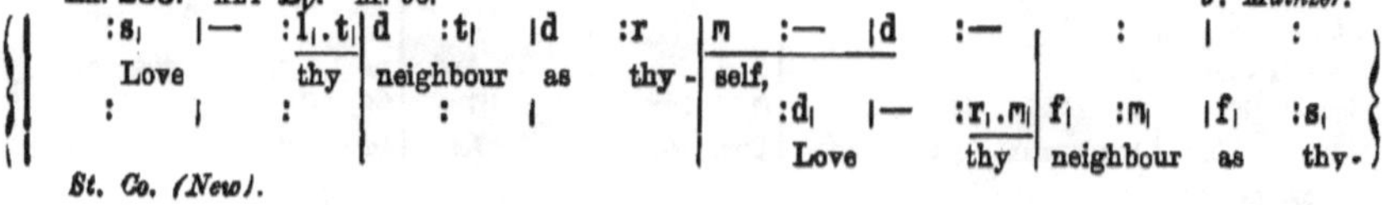

:s,	— :l, .t,	d :t,	d :r	m :—	d :—	:	:
Love thy	neighbour as thy -	self,	
:	:	:		:d,	— :r, .m,	f, :m,	f, :s,
		Love thy	neighbour as thy-

St. Co. (New).

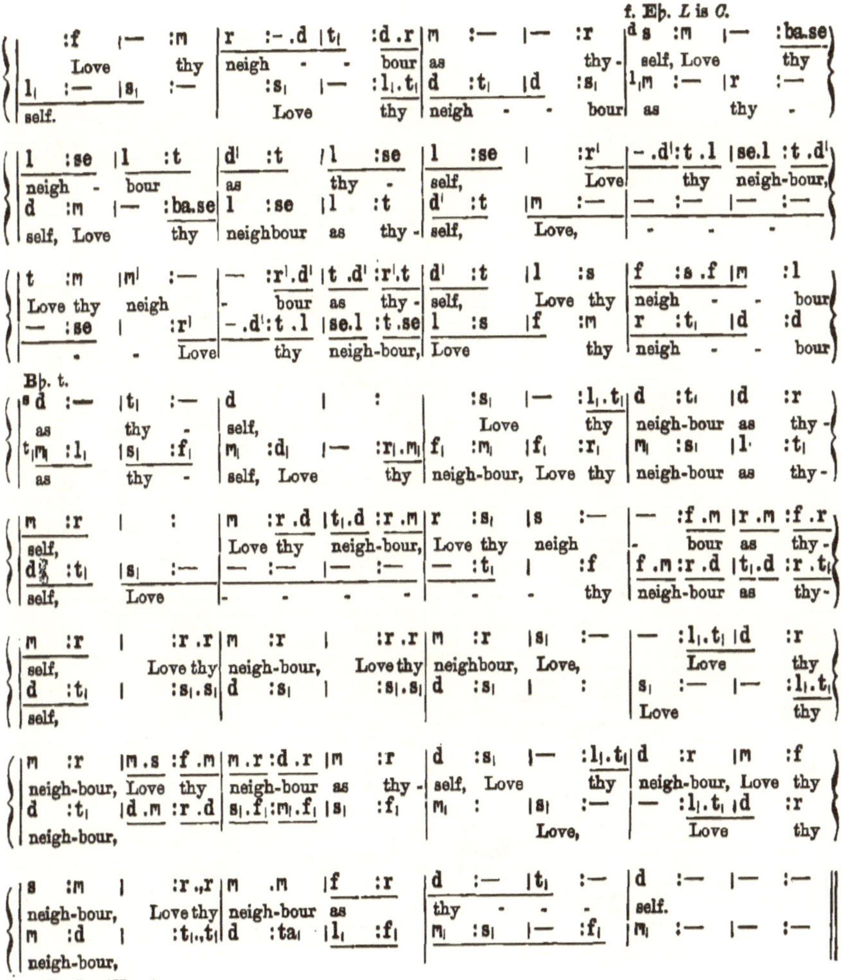

f. E♭. *L* is *C*.

| :f |— :m |r :-.d |t₁ :d.r |m :— |— :r |ᵈs :m |— :ba.se |
Love thy neigh - - bour as thy - self, Love thy
| l₁ :— |s₁ :— | :s₁ |— :l₁.t₁ |d :t₁ |d :s₁ |ˡ₁m :— |r :— |
self. Love thy neigh - - bour as thy -

| l :se |l :t |dˡ :t |l :se |l :se | :rˡ |-.dˡ:t.l |se.l :t.dˡ |
neigh - bour as thy - self, Love thy neigh-bour,
| d :m |— :ba.se |l :se |l :t |dˡ :t |m :— |— :— |— :— |
self, Love thy neighbour as thy - self, Love, - - -

| t :m |mˡ :— |— :rˡ.dˡ |t.dˡ :rˡ.t |dˡ :t |l :s |f :s.f |m :l |
Love thy neigh - bour as thy - self, Love thy neigh - - bour
| — :se | :rˡ |-.dˡ:t.l |se.l :t.se |l :s |f :m |r :t₁ |d :d |
- - Love thy neigh-bour, Love thy neigh - - bour

B♭. t.

| ˢd :— |t₁ :— |d | : | :s₁ |— :l₁.t₁ |d :t₁ |d :r |
as thy - self, Love thy neigh-bour as thy -
| ᵗ₁m₁ :l₁ |s₁ :f₁ |m₁ :d₁ |— :r₁.m₁ |f₁ :m₁ |f₁ :r₁ |m₁ :s₁ |l₁ :t₁ |
as thy - self, Love thy neigh-bour, Love thy neigh-bour as thy -

| m :r | : |m :r.d |t₁.d :r.m |r :s₁ |s :— |— :f.m |r.m :f.r |
self, Love thy neigh-bour, Love thy neigh - bour as thy -
| dᶠ :t₁ |s₁ :— |— :— |— :— |— :t₁ | :f |f.m :r.d |t₁.d :r.t₁ |
self, Love - - - - - - thy neigh-bour as thy -

| m :r | :r.r |m :r | :r.r |m :r |s₁ :— |— :l₁.t₁ |d :r |
self, Love thy neigh-bour, Love thy neighbour, Love, Love thy
| d :t₁ | :s₁.s₁ |d :s₁ | :s₁.s₁ |d :s₁ | : |s₁ :— |— :l₁.t₁ |
self, Love thy

| m :r |m.s :f.m |m.r :d.r |m :r |d :s₁ |— :l₁.t₁ |d :r |m :f |
neigh-bour, Love thy neigh-bour as thy - self, Love thy neigh-bour, Love thy
| d :t₁ |d.m :r.d |s₁.f₁ :m₁.f₁ |s₁ :f₁ |m₁ : |s₁ :— |— :l₁.t₁ |d :r |
neigh-bour, Love, Love thy

| s :m | :r.,r |m .m |f :r |d :— |t₁ :— |d :— |— :— ‖
neigh-bour, Love thy neigh-bour as thy - - - self.
| m :d | :t₁.,t₁ |d :ta₁ |l₁ :f₁ |m₁ :s₁ |— :f₁ |m₁ :— |— :— ‖
neigh-bour,

St. Co. (New.)

QUESTIONS FOR WRITTEN OR ORAL EXAMINATION.

DOCTRINE.

1. Describe your own voice. What is its easy compass—its quality and volume in each register—its best region? By what name is it called? —p. 81.

2. Under what name is the chord ⁷S disguised, by notation, in cadence transition to the first sharp key? How is the same chord disguised in passing transition to the first flat key? How do you know when the chords ⁷ᶠᵉR, and ᵗᵃD are transitional, and when they are chromatic?—p. 83.

3. What are the three principal things which intensify the mental effect of particular tones in a tune?—p. 83.

4. When any particular tone of the scale is strongly emphasised throughout a tune or part of a tune,—how is this fact described in words, and in what parts of the world is modal music still used in the greatest variety.

5. Which are the modes with a major third above their principal tone or tonic—which are those with a minor third? Of the major modes which is the one almost exclusively used among Western nations? Of the minor modes which is the one exclusively used in connection with modern harmony? Describe the historical changes through which the tune Dundee or Windsor has passed. What is the mental effect of the introduction of *se*?—and what is the difficulty which, especially in this tune, it occasions the singer?

6. Why is the Ray mode peculiarly suited for worship?—what is the peculiar cadence which distinguishes the Ray mode from the Lah mode?—p. 85.

7. What is the chief principle of modern harmony? In what respect has the Doh mode better chords for its Tonic, Dominant, and Sub-dominant than any other mode? What kind of chord does the ear object to when two such chords occur consecutively among the last four chords of a cadence?

8. How did the first harmonists overcome the difficulty of three minor chords in a cadence of the Lah mode? What is now found the most satisfactory arrangement for introducing variety in this cadence?—p. 86.

9. Where does the tone *bah* stand, and how is it related to *se*? Why is it introduced? How many alternative tones are there in the modern minor,—and which of them is most used?

10. Describe the six chief difficulties which arise to the singer from the introduction of *se* and *bah* in the minor mode.—p. 86.

11. Using the words Tonic, Dominant, Super-tonic, &c., as indicating the "Chord Relation," what is the chord relation of minor *L*?—of minor *D*?—of ˢᵉ*M*?—of minor *T*?—of *SE*? —of *BAH* and *F*?—of minor *R*? How do we distinguish the chord names of the major from those of the minor, mode in writing, and how do we distinguish them in speech?

12. What is meant by the word Modulation? What are the commonest modulations from major to minor, and from minor to major?—p. 88.

13. What is meant by Transitional Modulation? What is the commonest change of this kind, and what new distinguishing tone does it introduce? What other change of this kind is common, and what distinguishing tone does it introduce?

14. What is the meaning of the word Accidental, and how are accidentals expressed in the Tonic Sol-fa Notation?—p. 88.

15. Describe six cases of very rarely occurring sharps and flats with the names given to them.

16. What is the practice chiefly to be avoided in chanting?—p. 94.

17. In marking passages for recitation what is the first thing which the student should do, and what are the faults he has to avoid in doing it?

18. What is the great distinction between the recitation and the cadence of a chant? What kind of pulse should always come before the beginning of a cadence? What kind of pulse should always come after the end of a cadence? What relation should there be between the speed of the reciting tone and that of the cadence?

19. What is the difference between the rhythms of public speaking and private talk?

20. In choosing chants, what are the two blemishes which should lead a precentor to reject some?

21. What are the principal elements of expression in music? What are the common defects of singers who do not study expression?—p. 94.

22. What is the principal habit to be formed in the delivery of tones?—and for what quality of tone should we listen in our own voice?

23. By what other names is a good "attack" of the tones described? Give illustrations of its importance. Describe generally the sensations which accompany it both in the larynx and the mouth.—p. 95.

24. How do the breath and glottis act together in the clear attack?—in the gradual or breathing attack?—in the check?—in the jerk?—in the slur? What is the difference between a slur and a glide?

25. What is meant by a clear Release of the Tone,—and what is its importance?

26. Describe the manner in which a teacher should introduce his first exercises on the degrees of force.—p. 96.

27. What are the names and signs for a long tone, or a phrase increasing in force?—diminishing in force?—first increasing and then diminishing?

28. Describe the Pressure and Explosive tones.

29. Describe the Staccato, the Detached, and the Legato styles.

30. What are the two considerations which principally guide us in applying various degrees of force to music?

31. How is it that it is possible for classes to go on singing a large quantity of music without really *learning* anything?

32. What points in a tune have to be considered with the view of deciding whether it should be sung loudly or softly, or with a moderate degree of force?—p. 98.

33. How should a true *piano* be sung?

34. How should a real vibrating *forte* be sung?

35. What is "phrasing"? Show its importance. Mention three or four ways in which musical phrases can be marked off, and distinguished by the singer.

36. What is usually the best form of force in ascending passages, and why?

37. What is usually the best form of force in descending passages, and why?

38. How should Repeated tones be delivered, and why?

39. How should prolonged single tones be delivered, and why?

40. What is the best way of "setting off" the musical imitations in a melody?—p. 100.

41. How should the entrance of a "part" previously silent be treated?
42. In what two cases should any of the parts, in music, be subdued and subordinate?
43. How should accompaniment be delivered?
44. Describe the three ways of producing what is called a humming accompaniment. What should be specially noticed in the imitation of natural sounds?
45. What are the tones of the scale most congenial to a quick and stirring tune, and what to a slow and solemn tune? In what ranges of his voice is each singer able to make his tones most effectively heard in the midst of the harmony?—p. 101.
46. If in the harmony a singer finds a tone placed in an effective part of his voice, which is congenial with the sentiment he is singing,—how should he deliver it?
47. How should rapid passages and runs be sung, and when such pieces are sung in chorus, what point is it important to notice? In the management of the breath for a run, what point has the singer to notice at the beginning, and what at the end?
48. What kind of feeling is naturally expressed by the explosive tone, and what by the pressure tone? Which of these forms of tones is the exaggeration of the *legato* style, and into which of them does the *staccato* naturally break out?—p. 103.
49. In what manner should unison passages be sung, and what should each singer strive to do?
50. In what style should cadences be sung, and why?
51. How should distinguishing tones be sung, and why?
52. In cases of dissonances, what should every singer know in reference to his own part? How should the resisting tone be sung, and how the phrase which contains the dissonating tone?—p. 104.
53. Why is it difficult to parse the rhythm of pieces in which there are fugal imitations? What is the name given to a fugal imitation which has been heard before, but which now follows its leader sooner?—p. 104.
54. Describe the highest register of female voices. State the pitch at which they pass into it. What is the name of this register? Why should contraltos generally refrain from using it? p. 105.
55. What is the highest pitch which classic choruses require the first Sopranos to sing? What is the highest pitch which should be used in church choirs where the congregation does not join? What is the highest pitch that can be expected from congregations?
56. What kind of voice will sometimes find it a relief to sing one-F (F') in the small register?
57. Describe the lesser breaks of the voice. How, and at what pitch-sound are these manifested in female voices? How in male voices?
58. What registers are commonly used by men in ordinary speaking, and what by women? What is the consequence of these habits on the singing voice?
59. What is the mechanism of the Lower Thick register, and what are the physical sensations felt in producing it?
60. What is the mechanism and sensation of the Upper Thick register?
61. What is the mechanism and sensation of the Lower Thin?
62. What is the mechanism and sensation of the Upper Thin?
63. What is the mechanism and sensation of the Small?
64. What points are noticeable in boys' voices when compared with voices of women? What course should be taken at the "change of voice?"
65. Name the four "principal parts" into which voices are most commonly classified. What other "parts" are sometimes required? p. 108.
66. Describe the manner in which voices are examined and recorded.
67. What are the characteristics of a first Soprano? What of a second Soprano?
68. What are the characteristics of a first Contralto? What of a second?
69. What are the characteristics of a first Tenor? What of a second? From what class of men's voices do we get the most agreeable tones in the upper thin register? Give two powerful reasons why basses should not use this register.
70. What are the characteristics of a first Bass? What of a second?
71. What are the two reasons why in classifying voices you do not take compass for your guide? In what choral part, as in Handel's choruses, do the voices of men and women coincide, singing identical tones? In men's voice music, what is commonly the highest tone of first Tenor, and the lowest of second Bass? In women's voice music, what is commonly the highest tone of first Soprano, and lowest of second Contralto?
72. State all the causes within your knowledge of "flattening." Mention anything you think likely to prevent, arrest, or correct it. p. 109.
73. Mark in the heading of Exs. 188 to 191, 193, 195, the Sol-fa names of the optional tones, at the command of a tenor voice,—mark also the places at which you think it desirable to change the register.
74. In what cases may singers form the habit of changing the register always on the same tone in absolute pitch? In what cases should other than tenor voices study carefully their optional tones?
75. What are the chief uses of sixths, eighths, and ninths of a pulse in music? How are eighths of a pulse named and written? How are third-sixths of a pulse named and written? How are half-sixths of a pulse named and written? How are ninths of a pulse named and written? p. 110.
76. Give the Time names for the following:—

:t ,l .-,s ‖ :r . ,m f ‖

3
:d ,-r .m ‖ :- .f m r ‖

PRACTICE.

77. Hold a steady tone with one breath for twenty-four seconds.
78. Sing with a beautiful forward quality of tone, to the Italian *lah*. Ex. 176.
79. Analyse the harmony of one of the Exs. 177 to 179—whichever the teacher chooses.
80. Give an example different from those quoted of increased intensity given to the mental effect of a tone by accent—by cadence—by the interval of a fifth or under fourth.
81. Write from memory or sing the three versions of the tune Dundee or Windsor.—p. 84.
82. Draw from memory the diagram which shows the difference between the

Lah mode and the Ray mode. Write and sing the tune Nowell in the Ray mode and also in the Lah mode.

83. Laa from the teacher's pointing on the modulator all the exercises given in the paragraph "Difficulties of the singer."—p. 86.

84. Name the tones of the minor mode which belong to the following chord relations: Tonic,—Sub-dominant, —Dominant,—Super-tonic,—Leading Tone,—Sub-mediant,—Mediant.

85. Analyse any one of the chants, Exs. 181 to 186, which the teacher may require.

86. Point out examples, without having to look for them, of modulation to the relative minor, and of modulation to the relative major.—p. 88.

87. Point out examples, without having to look for them, of transitional modulation to the relative minor of the first flat key, and to the relative minor of the first sharp key.

88. Sing with correct time, tune, and expression, one of the Exs. 188 to 195, selected by the teacher.

89. Taa-tai on one tone the recitations of Exs. 177 and 178.

90. Mark the following passages of scripture for cadence and recitation. —Psalm 1, 8, 20, 84, 93, 98, 149. Isaiah. 12.

91. Deliver the vowels *aa*, *ai*, and *ee*, as forward in the mouth as possible, and with the best quality of voice you can produce.—p. 95.

92. Deliver the vowel *aa*, with clear attack,—with breathy or gradual attack, —with the check,—with the jerk,—with the slurred attack.

93. Sing the vowel *aa*, and end it with a clear release.—p. 96.

94. Perform any one of the Exs. 197 to 201, which the teacher may select.

95. Select from memory and sing a crescendo passage,—a diminuendo passage,—a swell passage.—p. 97

96. Sing Ex. 202.

97. Select and sing a passage with staccato tones,—with detached tones.

98. Select and sing a legato passage.

99. Sing a tone with medium force of your voice,—forte,—piano; with which degree of force should the following pieces be sung through the greater part of their extent?—Ex. 134, 141, 144, 188, 192, 194.

100. Select and sing a passage with true vigorous piano.—p. 98.

101. Select and sing a passage with clear vibrating forte.

102. Perform in the presence of the teacher any one of the Exs. 204 to 210, which he may select.

103. Select and sing an ascending passage in the proper manner.—p. 99.

104. Select and sing a descending passage with proper expression.

105. Select and sing with proper expression a good example of repeated tones.

106. Select and sing a good example of the prolonged single tone.

107. Select and sing a good example of imitations in melody.

108. Select and sing a good example in which the marked entrance of a "part" is required.

109. Select illustrations of subordination of parts, humming accompaniment, and imitative sounds.

110. Perform in the presence of the examiner one of the Exs. 211 to 214, chosen by him.

111. Perform any one of the exercises 222—225 which the examiner may select.

112. Perform any one (chosen by the examiner) of the runs named in the paragraph "Rapid Passages," with proper delivery and proper management of breath.

113. Select and sing a good example of the Explosive tone,—of the Pressure tone.

114. Sing a Unison passage with some other voice in perfect blending and unanimity of attack.

115. Select and sing a cadence in a proper manner.

116. Select and sing three different examples of distinguishing tones.

117. Select and sing two different examples of dissonances, your teacher holding the resisting tone.

118. Describe or parse Exs. 194, 196, or 197, which ever the examiner chooses.

119. If your voice is soprano sing two tones, at least, in the Small Register.

120. Show, by singing, the place of the lesser break or breaks in your own voice, and what part or parts of the music you can sing best.

121. If you are a tenor or contralto singer mark, in presence of the examiner, the optional tones and the best places of change in any one of the Exs. 174, 175, which he may select.

122. Tell your examiner what are the Sol-fa names of your optional tones in key C,—F,—B flat,—E flat,—G,—D. —A.

DICTATION EXERCISES.

NOTE, that TAA standing alone may be used to indicate a whole pulse, and that after the first measure the accents are not necessarily marked by R and L. Observe also octave marks, p. 29.

Ex. 236. Write in correct time TAAtefe d, r, m —TAATAI f m,—TAA r,—TAA d; and tafaTAI d, r, m —tafaTAI r, m, f,—TAATAI m, r,—TAA d.

Ex. 237. TAAfe s, f, — TAAfe m, r, — TAA d, —TAA t-one — TAAfe l-one, r—TAAtefe d, t-one, d —TAA r—TAA d.

Ex. 238. tafatefe d, r, m, f—TAATAI s, m— TAATAI l, s—TAA one-d—tafatefe one-d, t, l, s— tafatefe f, m, r, d— TAATAI s, s-one—TAA d.

Ex. 239. TAATAI d, r — TAA*SAI* m — TAATAI f, s—TAA*SAI* l—*SAA*TAI s—TAATAI s, s— TAA d.

Ex. 240. TAA s — *sa*fatefe l, s, l — tafatefe f, s, f, s—tafaTAI m, r, d; and TAATAI d, m— taataitee r, m, f—TAATAI m, d—*saa*taitee s, f— taataitee m, r, d—TAATAI r, d.

Ex. 241. *SAA*TAI s — tafaTAI m, f, s — *SAA*TAI s—tafaTAI l, t, one-d — *SAA*TAI s— TAATAI f, m—TAAfe r, d—TAA d.

Ex. 242. *SAA*TAI d — taa-aitee m, r — taa-aitee d, t-one — taataitee l-one, t-one, d— TAA -AA s.

SIXTH STEP.

Continuation of Chest, Klang, and Tuning Exercises. To perceive the Physical Facts and Mental Effects of Two Removes in Transition, and to sing such a Transition. To perceive the Physical Facts and Mental Effects of Three Removes and to sing such a Transition. To understand Principles on which various degrees of Force and Speed are applied to Words, and to make use of them. To practise the Phrasing of Words. To exercise the Organs in sustaining vowel sounds clearly and correctly. To understand the Principal Forms of Vocal Music. To understand the Resonances and their use. To exercise the Voice for Strength and Agility.

Chest, Klang, and Tuning Exercises.—Exercises for strengthening the chest, for the cultivation of a pure and beautiful klang and for the exact tuning of the voices one with the other, should still be pursued, at the opening of every lesson. The various voice exercises in the beginning of the last step and the minor mode chants in three parts will answer the purpose well. The teacher will choose the kind of exercise which he finds his class requires. "Wall Sheets" will enable the teacher to use more complex voice exercises, while leaving him at liberty to walk among the ranks of his class and superintend the posture and vocal delivery of each pupil. See Nos. 21, 22, 23.

```
m l r' s d
        t
r s d' f
    t m l
d f
t m l r s
l r s d f
      t m
s d f
  t m l r
f
m l r s d
        t
r s d f
   t, m l
d f
```

Two Removes.—Transitions to the first sharp key or to the first flat key (p. 50) are transitions of *one remove.* But the music often passes over the key of the first remove to the key of *its* first remove; this we call a transition of *two removes.* The teacher will first lead his pupils to observe the physical facts connected with these removes. First, they will notice, that the second *sharp* key raises the key tone and with it the whole music a fullstep,—that it blots out f and d of the old key and introduces in their place m and t of the new key as marked in the signature,—and that, of the two distinguishing tones, t is the more important because it distinguishes the *second* sharp remove from the *first.* Second, they will notice, that the second *flat* key depresses the key tone and with it the whole music a full step,—that it blots out the tones (which the sharp remove introduced) t and m,—and it introduces, for the new key, the tones (which the sharp remove blotted out) d and f,—and that of these two distinguishing tones, the f is the more important as distinguishing the second flat remove from the first.

These physical facts will prepare the mind for observing in the exercises which follow,—that the second sharp remove with its raised d and its effective t is even more expressive of rising emotion than the first sharp key,—that the second flat remove with its depressed d and its effective f, is even more expressive of seriousness and depression than the first flat remove. Compare p. 51. A transition of two removes from the principal key (a principal transition) is seldom used except for imitation and sequence. A transition of two removes from a subordinate (not principal) key of the piece is not uncommon and if the transition is from the key of the dominant to that of the sub-dominant or *vice versa* it is generally quite easy to sing. This kind of "oscillation" across the original key keeps that key in mind, and lessens the violent effect of the two removes. See "How to Observe Harmony," p. 54, and the "Common-places of Music," p. 111.

The Exercises.—The following three exercise should be done with great care, every transition passage being taught by pattern from the modulator. No words are provided, in order that attention may be given exclusively to the various points of difficulty in the transitions. Each part should be (1) first sol-faad (2) and then clearly laad. (3) If, in teaching the parts any difficulty arises, it is a good plan to teach the first phrase of the *new key* separately before the transition is attempted; for when the pupil knows what is on the other side of the bridge he crosses more boldly. This plan of introducing transition is even more important when the parts are sung together. Great assistance may be given to the pupils by shewing them on the modulator the first difficult interval or intervals which the new distinguishing tones create, and by likening these intervals to some others with which the ear is more familiar. The pupil must not begrudge any amount of patient care required in mastering these transitions, for such transitions occur in every classic work and sometimes very frequently. A good study of the modulator with a thoughtful exercise of his voice will not only teach him these particular tunes, but will shew him the way to master similar difficulties in other music.

In Ex. 243 the transition to the second sharp key becomes comparatively easy when the pupils realize the exact imitation there is in all the parts. As mentioned above, **t** is the more important of the two distinguishing tones. If the third part strikes it firmly and promptly the second part will have little difficulty. In teaching the parts separately, the ear is not assisted by harmony to establish the new key; it will therefore be useful to show on the modulator what the notes would have been in the old key. Thus the third part would have been **de l, r** and the second part would have been **m de r**. The second distinguishing tone **m** is felt to be a little sharp but is seldom a difficulty. This should be traced on the modulator.

In Ex. 244 the difficulty of the "principal" transition of two removes is again lessened by imitation. The second distinguishing tone comes in first, and then the second part strikes the first and more important distinguishing tone. When the second distinguishing tone is heard first the transition is easier to sing. It is something like taking one remove at a time. But the second case, that of a subordinate and "oscillating" two removes, at measure 9, is more difficult to sing because there is not the same help from imitation and second because the first distinguishing tone is first introduced. The next transition has a perfect imitation note for note in its second part, and in its first part there is an exact imitation of the melodial waving of the previous phrase one step lower. This last phrase would be **r f m r** (two more flat removes) if it were not harmonised chromatically, and so retained in the original key.

Other examples will be found in "Additional Exercises," p. 65 for imitation,—pp. 68 & 72 for oscillation and to give effect to the next transition,—and p. 83 a transitional modulation to the minor for special effect, also to prepare effect.

Ex. 243. KEY F.

m :m .f	s :s	d :r	m :—	l :t	d' :m	r :—	d :—
d :d	t, .r :d .t,	l, .d :— .t,	d :—	f :f	s :d	d :t,	d :—
d :d .l,	s, :m,	f, .l, :s,	d :—	f .m :r	m .r :d	s, :—	d :—

s :r	m :—	G. t. m. l s :r	m :—	f. C. f d' :s	l .t :d'
r :t,	d :—	m r :t,	d :—	d s :m	f :s .m
t, :s,	d :—	de t, :s,	d :—	l, m .r :d	f .r :m .d

r' :—	d' :—	f. F. r' l :t	d' :m	r :—	d :—
f :—	m :—	ta f :f	s :d	d :t,	d :—
s, :—	d :—	ta f :r	m :d	s, :—	d :—

Ex. 244. KEY F. M. 70. *W. G. M'N.*

p

d :r	m :s	s :m	m :r	m :s	s :f
d :t,	d :d	t, :d	d :t,	d :d .ta,	l, :l,
d :s,	d :m,	s, :d	s, :s,	d :m,	f, :f,

St. Co. (New.)

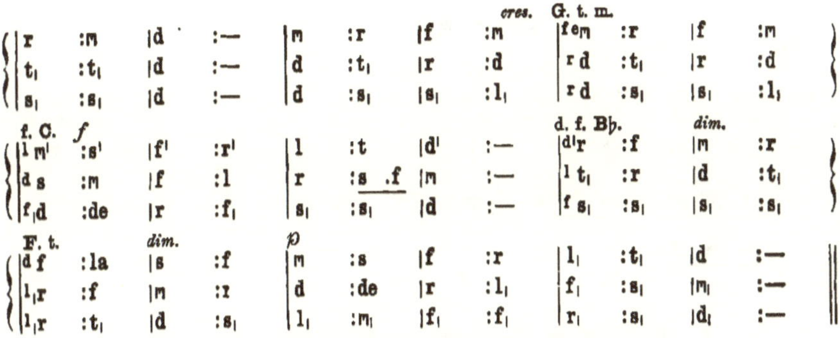

cres. G. t. m.

r :m	d :—	m :r	f :m	fem :r	f :m
t, :t,	d :—	d :t,	r :d	rd :t,	r :d
s, :s,	d :—	d :s,	s, :l,	rd :s,	s, :l,

f. C. *f* d. f. B♭. *dim.*

lm' :s'	f' :r'	l :t	d' :—	d'r :f	m :r
ds :m	f :l	r :s .f	m :—	lt, :r	d :t,
f,d :de	r :f,	s, :s,	d :—	fs, :s,	s, :s,

F. t. *dim.* *p*

| df :la | s :f | m :s | f :r | l, :t, | d :— ‖
| l,r :f | m :r | d :de | r :l, | f, :s, | m, :— ‖
| l,r :t, | d :s, | l, :m, | f, :f, | r, :s, | d, :— ‖

OH, I'M THE BOY 'O THE MOUNTAIN.

Ex. 245. M. 80, twice. (Words adapted from UHLAND, by J. S. STALLYBRASS.) *A. L. C.*

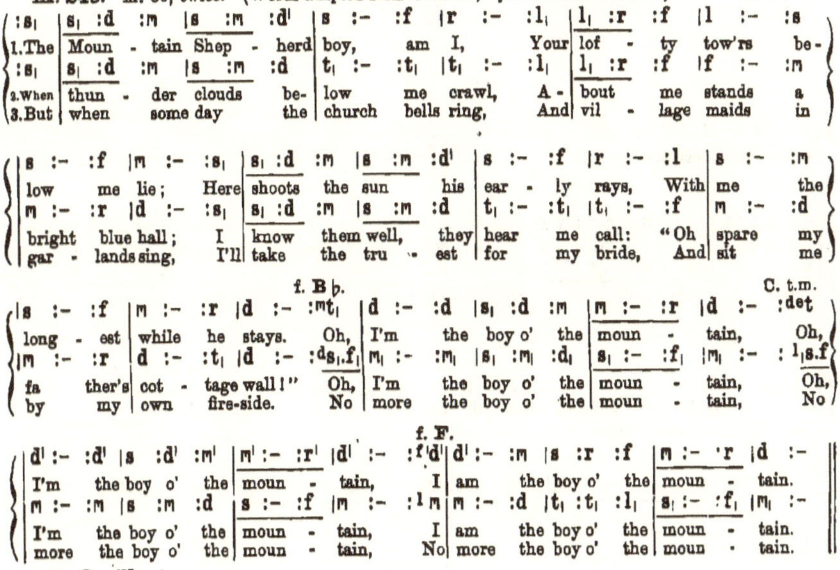

:s, | s, :d :m | s :m :d' | s :- :f | r :- :l, | l, :r :f | l :- :s
1.The | Moun - tain Shep - herd | boy, am I, Your | lof - ty tow'rs be-
:s, | s, :d :m | s :m :d | t, :- :t, | t, :- :l, | l, :r :f | f :- :m
2.When | thun - der clouds be- | low me crawl, A - | bout me stands a
3.But | when some day the | church bells ring, And | vil - lage maids in

| s :- :f | m :- :s, | s, :d :m | s :m :d' | s :- :f | r :- :l | s :- :m
low me lie; Here | shoots the sun his | ear - ly rays, With | me the
| m :- :r | d :- :s, | s, :d :m | s :m :d | t, :- :t, | t, :- :f | m :- :d
bright blue hall; I | know them well, they | hear me call: "Oh | spare my
gar - lands sing, I'll | take the tru - est | for my bride, And | sit me

f. B♭. C. t.m.

| s :- :f | m :- :r | d :- :mt, | d :- :d | s, :d :m | m :- :r | d :- :det
long - est | while he stays. Oh, | I'm the boy o' the | moun - tain, Oh,
| m :- :r | d :- :t, | d :- :ds,.f, | m, :- :m, | s, :m, :d, | s, :- :f, | m, :- :l,s.f
fa ther's | cot - tage wall!" Oh, | I'm the boy o' the | moun - tain, Oh,
by my | own fire-side. No | more the boy o' the | moun - tain, No

f. F.

| d' :- :d' | s :d' :m' | m' :- :r' | d' :- :f'd' | d' :- :m | s :r :f | m :- :r | d :- ‖
I'm the boy o' the | moun - tain, I | am the boy o' the | moun - tain.
| m :- :m | s :m :d | s :- :f | m :- :lm | m :- :d | t, :t, :l, | s, :- :f, | m, :- ‖
I'm the boy o' the | moun - tain, I | am the boy o' the | moun - tain.
more the boy o' the | moun - tain, No | more the boy o' the | moun - tain.

St. Co. (New.)

HOLY, HOLY, HOLY.

Ex. 246. KEY C. *Telemann* (1750)

s :— :s	l :— :l	ta :— :l	s :— :d'
Ho - ly,	ho - - ly,	ho - - -	ly, Lord
:m :d	f :— :f	s :m :f	— :m .r :m .d
Ho - ly,	ho - - ly,	ho - - ly,	ho - ly,

— :t .d' :r'	r' :d' :m'	m' :r' :d'	t :s :d'
	God of	Sa - - ba -	oth, Ho - ly,
r :— .m :f	m :— :s	f :— :fe	s : :l
Lord	God of	Sa - - ba -	oth, Lord

| d' :— .t :d' | r' .m' :f' :m' | r' :— : || :
| God of | Sa - - ba - | oth! ||
| s :f :m | t, :— :d | s :— : || :s .s,s
| God of | Sa - - ba - | oth! || Heaven and

G. t.

:	:	:	:d'f .s,s	l .s,l :t .l,t	d' .s :d'
			Heaven and	earth are full of thy	glo - ry, full,
l .s,l :t .l,t	d' .s :d'	— .t,l :s .f	m :	:d'f	— .m,r :m .r,d
earth are full of thy	glo - ry full	of thy glo -	ry,	Hea -	- ven and earth and

f. C. f. F. *L* is *D*.

— .t,l :s .f	m .m,f :s r',m'.d',r'	t .d',r' :m',f'.r',m'	d' . :l m .m,m	ba .m,ba :se .ba,se
of thy glo -	ry. Ho - san -	na! Ho - san -	na! Heaven and	earth are full of thy
r :— .r	d .,r :m t .l	s .l,t :d' .t	l .m :l m	— :r
full, are	full, are	full of thy glo -	ry. Ho - san	- - -

G. t.m. f. C.

l .m :l s	— :f .f	m .m :d s .s,s	l .s,l :t .l,t	d' .s :d'
glo - ry, full	of thy	glo - ry, Heaven and	earth are full of thy	glo - ry, full
d :l ,s, .s,,s,	l, .s,,l, :t, .l,,t,	d .s, :d s	— :f .f	m :— .f,s
na! Heaven and	earth are full of thy	glo - ry, full	of thy	glo - - -

— .r',m' :f'	m' .d',r' :m',f' .m',f'	r' .t ,d' :r',m' .r',m'	d' .l ,t :d',r' .d',r'
are full	of thy glo -	ry, Ho - san -	na! Ho - san -
l :— .t	d' :d'	t .s ,l :t	l :— .l
- - - - -	ry Ho -	san - - -	na! Ho -

St. Co. (New.)

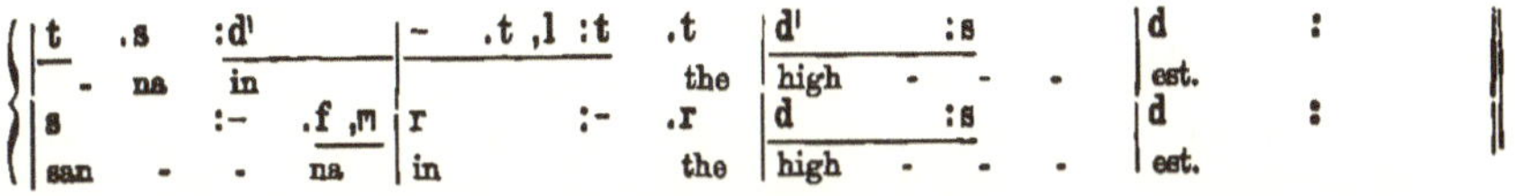

t .s :d^1	– .t ,l :t .t	d^1 :s	d :	
– na in	the	high - - -	est.	
s :– .f ,m	r :– .r	d :s	d :	
san - - na	in the	high - - -	est.	

GOOD NIGHT.

Words translated by J. S. Stallybrass. *A. L. C.*

Ex. 247. KEY A. [To illustrate chromatics.]

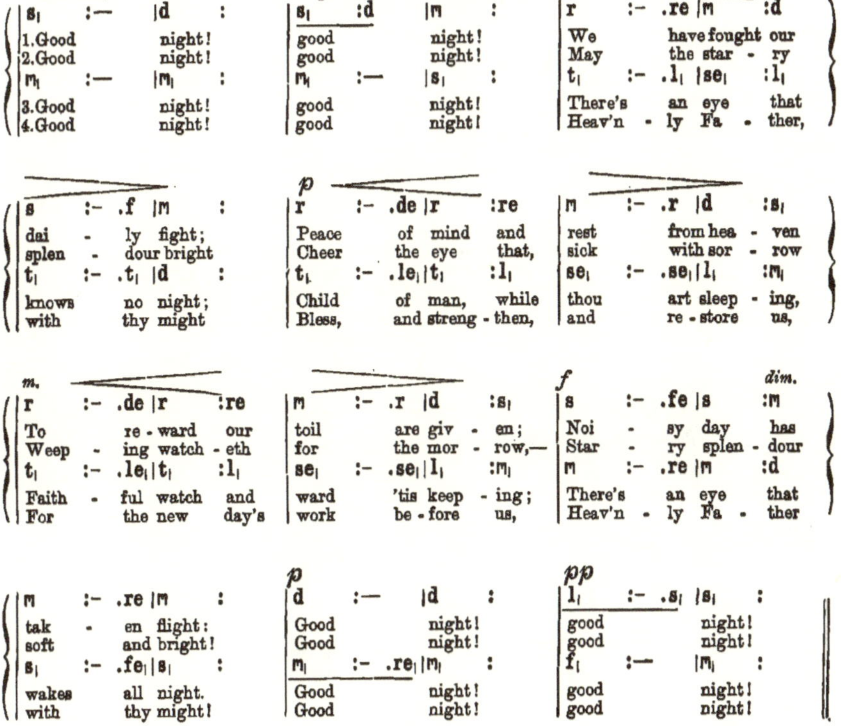

s_1 :– |d :	s_1 :d |m :	r :– .re |m :d
1.Good night!	good night!	We have fought our
2.Good night!	good night!	May the star - ry
m_1 :– |m_1 :	m_1 :– |s_1 :	t_1 :– .l_1 |se_1 :l_1
3.Good night!	good night!	There's an eye that
4.Good night!	good night!	Heav'n - ly Fa - ther,

s :– .f |m :	*p* r :– .de |r :re	m :– .r |d :s_1
dai - ly fight;	Peace of mind and	rest from hea - ven
splen - dour bright	Cheer the eye that,	sick with sor - row
t_1 :– .t_1 |d :	t_1 :– .le_1 |t_1 :l_1	se_1 :– .se_1 |l_1 :m_1
knows no night;	Child of man, while	thou art sleep - ing,
with thy might	Bless, and streng - then,	and re - store us,

m. r :– .de |r :re	m :– .r |d :s_1	*f* s :– .fe |s :m *dim.*
To re - ward our	toil are giv - en;	Noi - sy day has
Weep - ing watch - eth	for the mor - row,—	Star - ry splen - dour
t_1 :– .le_1 |t_1 :l_1	se_1 :– .se_1 |l_1 :m_1	m :– .re |m :d
Faith - ful watch and	ward 'tis keep - ing;	There's an eye that
For the new day's	work be - fore us,	Heav'n - ly Fa - ther

m :– .re |m :	*p* d :– |d :	*pp* l_1 :– .s_1 |s_1 :	
tak - en flight:	Good night!	good night!	
soft and bright!	Good night!	good night!	
s_1 :– .fe_1 |s_1 :	m_1 :– .re_1 |m_1 :	f_1 :– |m_1 :	
wakes all night.	Good night!	good night!	
with thy might!	Good night!	good night!	

St. Co. (New.)

NIGHT SONG.

p Ex. 248. KEY B♭. *A.L.C.*

: | : | : | s :f | m :— | m :r | d :— | :m | m :—
1. On the | woods there broods | Deep re - pose, | deep re - pose, | Not one / No pain
:m .r | d :t, | l, :— | t, :t, | d :— | s, :f, | m, :— | : | :d
2. In the | heav'nly land | An - gels sing, | an - gels sing, | Not / No

m :— | m :r | d .t, :d .l, | se, :— | — .se, :l, .t, | d :t,
breath / or | stirs / care | A - / Can | mong the / en - ter | firs, / there, | And no / But sweet | ze - phyr / voi - ces
d .t, :d .l, | se, :— .se, | l, .se, :l, .f, | m, :— .m, | m, :f, | m, :r,
one breath stirs A- / pain or care Can | mong the firs, And / en - ter there, But | no ze - phyr / sweet voi - ces

F. t. d.f. E♭.
l, :— | — : .fe,t, | d .,r :m | s :— .f,m | r :— | — :
blows. / ring. | The / On | birds have all end - ed their / earth we must soon end our | song, / song,
d, :— | — : | : .s,d | m .m :m .r,d | t, :— | — : .l,t,
blows. / ring. | The birds have ended their / On earth we soon end our | song, / song, | The / On

: .ta d' | d' .d' :d' .t,l | se :— | — : | *mf* s :— .m,d'
The birds have ended their / On earth we soon end our | song, / song, | Wait a-
d .,r :m | m :— .r,d | t, :— | — : | t, :— .d,m
birds have all end - ed their / earth we must soon end our | song, / song, | Wait a-

s : | f :— .m,f | r : | *f* F. t.m. s :— .m,d' | s :
while, | ere long, | Wait a - while,
m : | r :— .d,r | t, : | de t, :— .d,m | m :
while, | ere long, | Wait a - while,

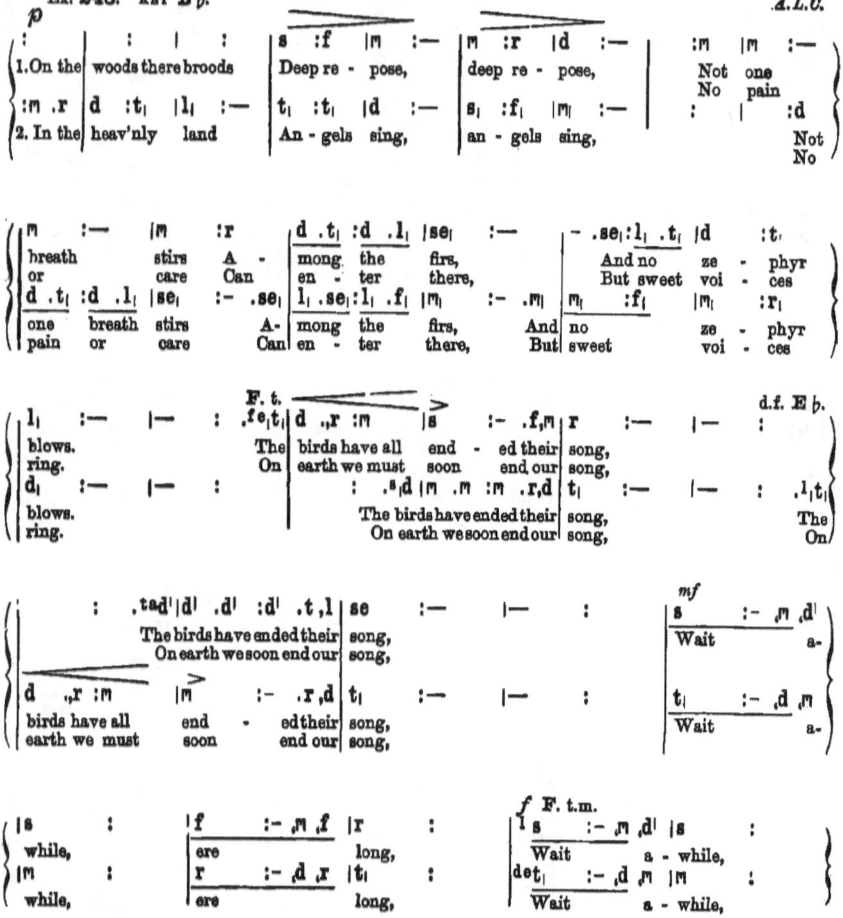

St. Co. (New.)

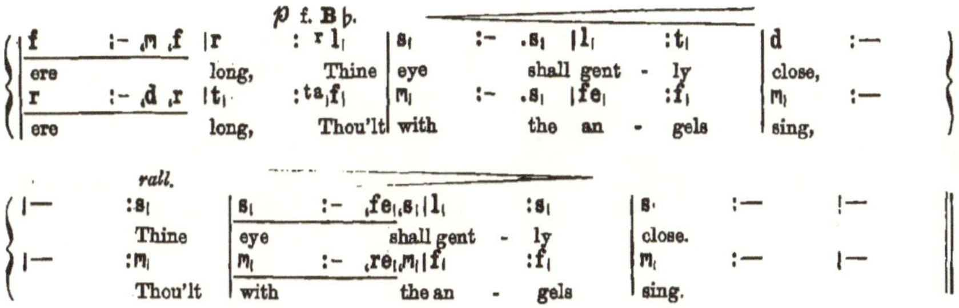

p f. B♭.

f :- .m .f	r : r l,	s, :- .s, | l, :t,	d :—
ere	long, Thine	eye shall gent - ly	close,
r :- .d .r	t, :ta, f,	m, :- .s, | fe, :f,	m, :—
ere	long, Thou'lt	with the an - gels	sing,

rall.

|— :s,	s, :- .fe,.s, | l, :s,	s, :— |—
Thine	eye shall gent - ly	close.
|— :m,	m, :- .re,.m, | f, :f,	m, :— |—
Thou'lt	with the an - gels	sing.

Three Removes.—Almost the only cases of three removes are those of three *flat* removes with modulation to the *minor*, or of three *sharp* removes with modulation to the *major*. In these cases the similarity of the upper part of the two modes (m ba se l and s l t d') assists the ear in passing over from one key into the other, especially if that form of the minor mode containing *bah* is used. The third flat remove is the more difficult to sing simply because the minor mode into which it enters is itself artificial and difficult. The third sharp remove is the less difficult, because the major mode into which it enters is more natural to the ear. The *Physical Changes*, therefore, made in three removes, vary with the varying use of *bah* and *se*. They may be greater or smaller than those of two removes. The *Mental Effects* are obvious,—for a modulation from major to minor and a flat remove together naturally produce a gloomy depression of feeling, and a modulation from minor to major combines with a sharp remove to produce a strange kind of excitement.

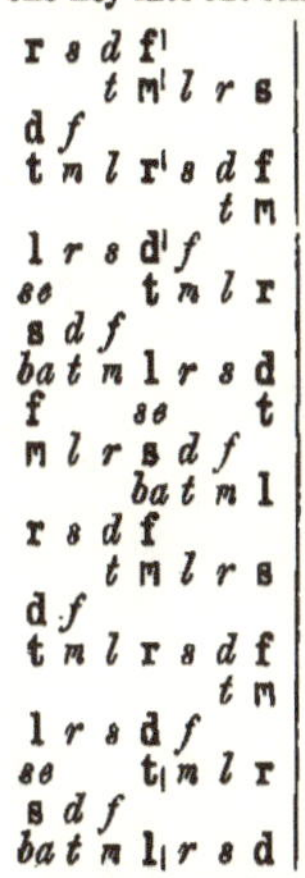

r *s d* f'
t m' *l r* s
d *f*
t *m l* r' *s d* f
t m
l *r s* d' *f*
se t *m l* r
s *d f*
ba t m l *r s* d
f *se* t
m *l r* s *d f*
ba t m l
r *s d* f
t m *l r* s
d *f*
t *m l* r *s d* f
t m
l *r s* d *f*
se t, *m l* r
s *d f*
ba t m l, *r s* d

THE EXERCISES.—In the same manner as above the teacher will shew his pupils on the modulator that in Ex. 249 the transition to the third sharp key is not very difficult, first, because it moves to the more familiar and more natural major mode, and second, because the *second* distinguishing tone (m) enters first, after that the *third* (l) and the most difficult (t) last of all. In teaching each part separately it may be well for the third part to remember that f m is the same thing as r de of the the preceding key,—and for the second part to notice d' fe is the same as f t,. All three parts should hold out the d its full length in order to get it well into the ear before taking the new transition. The section in key C should be practised separately before it is united to the previous section in E♭. This also should be the case with the section in key B♭, which is difficult, being a sudden remove from the major to the artificial minor. Although the distinguishing tone of the second remove (f) comes late, it is only an alternative tone with *bah*, and so is awkward to sing. This tune contrasts very plainly the natural boldness of the "relative major" and the cold brightness of the "tonic major." In Ex. 250 the transition to the minor of the third flat key is very difficult to sing, first, because it is to the minor, and, second, because it introduces the "alternative tone" (f) so early. If the third part sings f, f correctly and boldly, the second part will have no difficulty. In learning the third part separately it may be well to remember that :l, | f, :f .m | r is like :m | d :d'.t | l of another key. It may scarcely be necessary to note that, in the second part, d r f is like ma f la of the previous key,—and in the first part m l is like s d'.

Other examples may be found in "Additional Exercises," pp. 78 & 94 for special effect,—p. 86 for subordinate transition and return,—and pp. 79, 84 & 92 for returning transition.

Ex. 249. KEY E♭. *W. G. M'N.*

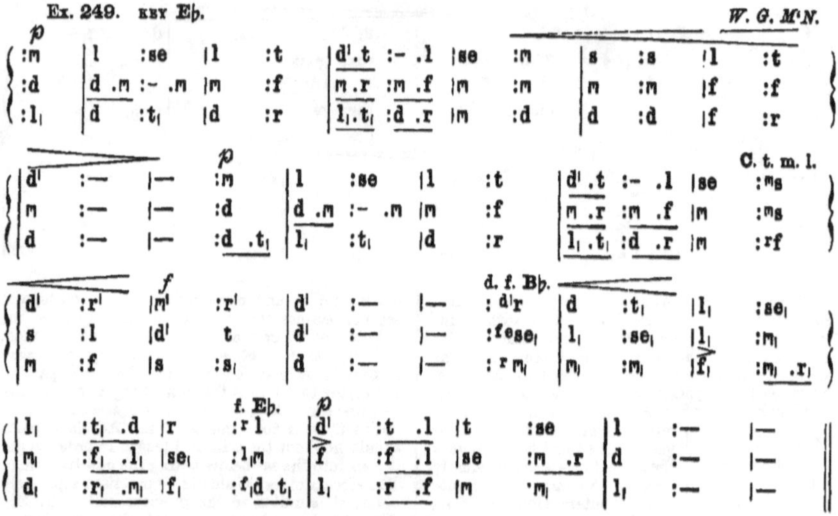

p

:m	l :se | l :t	d'.t :- .l | se :m	s :s | l :t
:d	d .m :- .m | m :f	m .r :m .f | m :m	m :m | f :f
:l,	d :t, | d :r	l,.t, :d .r | m :d	d :d | f :r

p — C. t. m. l.

d' :— | — :m	l :se | l :t	d'.t :- .l | se :ᵐs
m :— | — :d	d .m :- .m | m :f	m .r :m .f | m :ᵐs
d :— | — :d .t,	l, :t, | d :r	l,.t, :d .r | m :ʳf

f — d. f. B♭.

d' :r' | m' :r'	d' :— | — :ᵈ'r	d :t, | l, :se,
s :l | d' t	d' :— | — :ᶠese,	l, :se, | l, :m,
m :f | s :s,	d :— | — :ʳm,	m, :m, | f, :m, .r,

f. E♭. *p*

l, :t, .d | r :ʳl	d' :t .l | t :se	l :— | —
m, :f, .l, | se, :ˡm	f :f .l | se :m .r	d :— | —
d, :r, .m, | f, :ᶠd .t,	l, :r .f | m :m,	l, :— | —

Ex. 250. KEY C. *W. G. M'N.*

s. d. f. E♭. *L is C.* — C. t. m. l. — *dim.*

s :s .s | l :d'	s :s | s :ˢm	l :l .se | l :d'	t :— | ᵐs :—
m :m .m | f :m	r :m .f | m :ᵐᵃd	r :f | f :m .l	se :— | ᵐs :f
d :d .d | f :d	t, :d .r | d :ᵈl,	f, :f .m | r :l,	m :— | ᵐs, :-

s :s .s | l :d'	s :s | s :se	l :m'.r' | d' :t	d' :— | — :—
m :m .m | f :m	r :m .f | m :m	f :l | s :- .f	m :— | — :—
d :d .d | f :d	t, :d .r | d :d	f :fe | s :s,	d :— | — :—

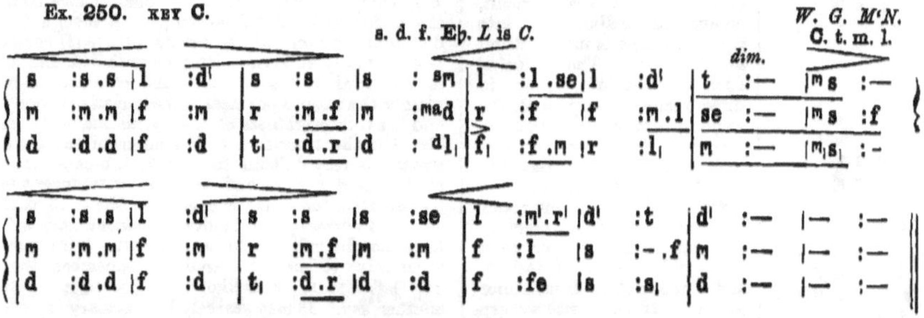

Ex. 251. KEY C. *Andante.* **THE LULLABY.** *A. L. C.*

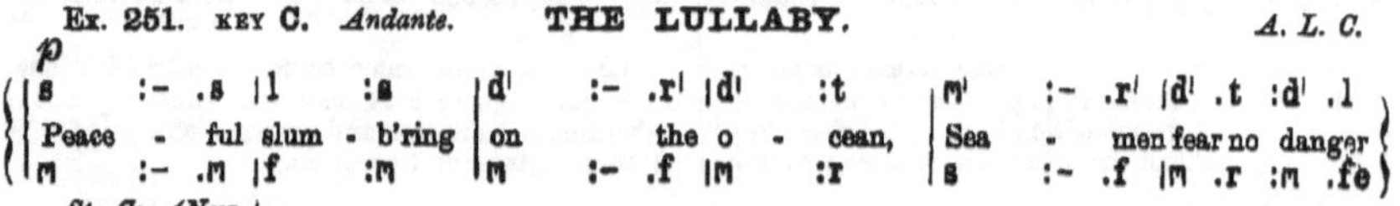

p

s :- .s | l :s	d' :- .r' | d' :t	m' :- .r' | d' .t :d' .l
Peace - ful slum - b'ring	on the o - cean,	Sea - men fear no danger
m :- .m | f :m	m :- .f | m :r	s :- .f | m .r :m .fe

St. Co. (New.)

s :— |— : |s :- .s |l :s |d' :- .r' |m' :d'
nigh, Winds and waves in gen - tle mo - tion,
s :— |- .f :m .r |m :— |f :— |m :- .f |s, :m
The winds and waves in gen - tle mo - tion.

p *rit.* *pp*
s :- .m |l .l :s .fe |s :— |f .m :f .s |m :— |— :
Soothe them with their lu-la- by, lul -la, lul -la- by.
m :- .d |f .f :m .re |m :— |r .d :r .t, |d :— |— :

s.d.f. E♭. *f*
sm :- .m |f :m |d' :- .t |l :se |m :- .r |d .t, :d .r
1. When the wind tem - pest - uous blow - ing, Rolls the billows mountains
md :- .d |r :d |m :- .r |d :t, |m :- .r |d .t, :d .r
2.'Neath a hea - ven black and scowl - ing, Trust - ing One a - bove the

C. t.m.l. *p*
ms :— |— : |s :- .s |l :s |d' :- .r' |m' :d'
high, Still no fear of dan - ger know - ing,
They in hor - rid tem - pest's how - ling,
ms :— |- .f :m .r |m :— |f :— |m :- .f |s :m
sky, E'en then no fear of dan - ger know - ing,
They in the hor - rid tem - pest's how - ling,

rit. *pp*
s :- .m |l .l :s .fe |s :— |f .m :f .s |m :— |— :
They in storms hear lulla- by, lul -la, lul -la- by.
m :- .d |f .f :m .re |m :— |r .d :r .t, |d :— |— :
Hear a mo-ther's lul-la- by, lul -la, lul -la- by.

MUSIC OF THE SPHERES.

Ex. 252. KEY A. Words translated from BESSELD, by J. S. STALLYBRASS. *A. L. C.*

d :- .d |d :s, .d |m :- .r |r :d |d .t, :l, .se, |l, :l, .t,
1.Stars are giv'n us our life to bright - en, And our dim earthly
m, :- .m, |m, :m, .m, |s, :- .f, |f, :m, |m, :f, |f, :f, .f,
2.See yon star written con - so - la - tion; "Here is past all

d :d .l, |l, :s, |m :m |m ..d :f .m |r :d |t, :- .(s,)
path - way to light - en; They can sweet - en the scourg - ing rod, They
m, :l, .f, |f, :m, |s, :s, |s, ..m, :l, .s, |fe, :fe, |s, :- .(s,)
earth's tri - bu - la - tion; Pil - grim, keep your cour - age high,

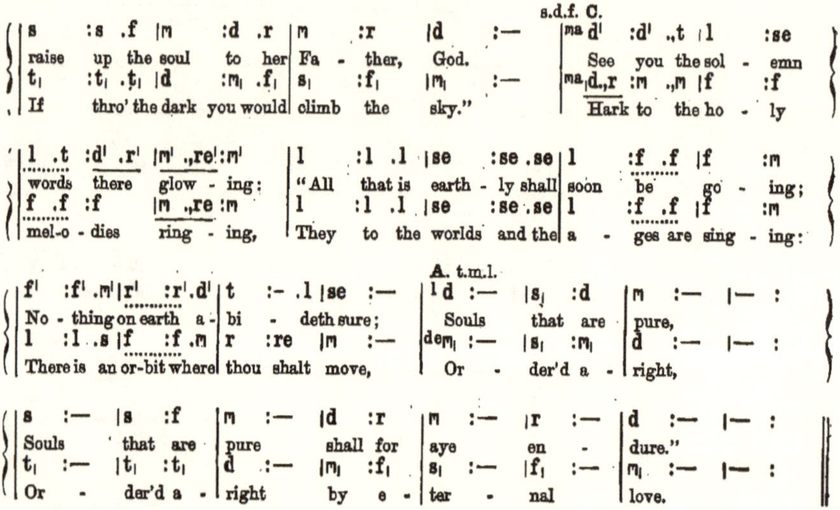

s.d.f. C.

s :s .f	m :d .r	m :r	d :—	ma d' :d' .,t	l :se
raise up the soul to her	Fa - ther,	God.		See you the sol - emn
t_1 :t_1 .t_1	d :m_1 .f_1	s_1 :f_1	m_1 :—	ma d.,r :m .,m	f :f
If thro' the dark you would	climb the	sky."		Hark to the ho - ly

l .t :d' .r'	m' .,re' :m'	l :l .l	se :se .se	l :f .f	f :m
words there glow - ing:	"All that is earth - ly shall	soon be go - ing;
f .f :f	m .,re :m	l :l .l	se :se .se	l :f .f	f :m
mel-o - dies ring - ing,	They to the worlds and the	a - ges are sing - ing:

A. t.m.l.

f' :f' .m'	r' :r' .d'	t :- .l	se :—	l d :—	s_1 :d	m :—	— :
No - thing on earth a -	bi - deth sure;	Souls that are	pure,
l :l .s	f :f .m	r :re	m :—	de m_1 :—	s_1 :m_1	d :—	— :
There is an or-bit where	thou shalt move,	Or - der'd a -	right,

s :—	s :f	m :—	d :r	m :—	r :—	d :—	— :	
Souls that are	pure shall for	aye en -	dure."
t_1 :—	t_1 :t_1	d :—	m_1 :f_1	s_1 :—	f_1 :—	m_1 :—	— :	
Or - der'd a -	right by e -	ter - nal	love.

SOUND THE LOUD TIMBREL.

Ex. 253. KEY C. Words by MOORE. *A. L. C.*

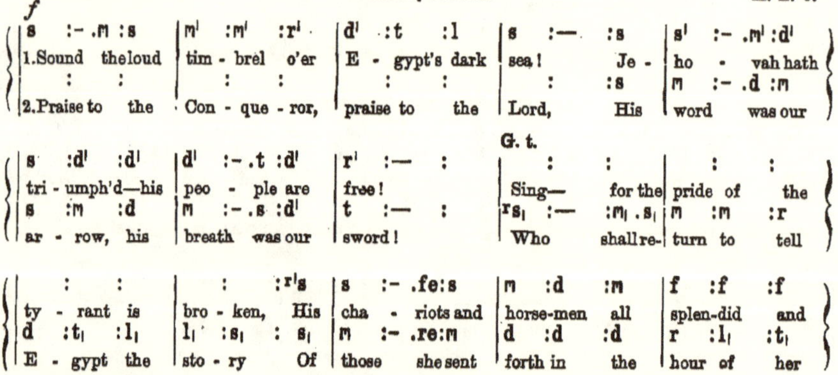

f

s :- .m :s	m' :m' :r'	d' :t :l	s :— :s	s' :- .m' :d'
1.Sound the loud	tim - brel o'er	E - gypt's dark	sea! Je -	ho - vah hath
: :	: :	: :	: :s	m :- .d :m
2.Praise to the	Con - que - ror,	praise to the	Lord, His	word was our

G. t.

s :d' :d'	d' :- .t :d'	r' :— :	: :	: :
tri - umph'd—his	peo - ple are	free!	Sing— for the	pride of the
s :m :d	m :- .s :d'	t :— :	r s_1 :— :m_1 .s_1	m :m :r
ar - row, his	breath was our	sword!	Who shall re-	turn to tell

: :	: :r's	s :- .fe :s	m :d :m	f :f :f
ty - rant is	bro - ken, His	cha - riots and	horse-men all	splen-did and
d :t_1 :l_1	l_1 :s_1 : s_1	m :- .re :m	d :d :d	r :l_1 :t_1
E - gypt the	sto - ry Of	those she sent	forth in the	hour of her

St. Co. (New.)

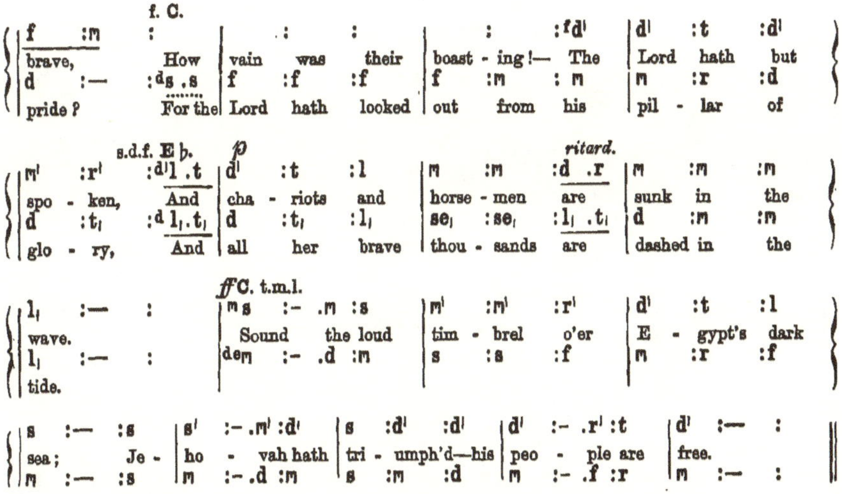

f. C.

f :m :	.: :	: :ᶠd'	d' :t :d'
brave, How	vain was their	boast - ing!— The	Lord hath but
d :— :ᵈs .s	f :f :f	f :m :m	m :r :d
pride? For the	Lord hath looked	out from his	pil - lar of

s.d.f. E♭. *p* *ritard.*

m' :r' :ᵈ'l .t	d' :t :l	m :m :d .r	m :m :m
spo - ken, And	cha - riots and	horse - men are	sunk in the
d :t, :ᵈl,.t,	d :t, :l,	se, :se, :l, .t,	d :m :m
glo - ry, And	all her brave	thou - sands are	dashed in the

ff C. t.m.l.

l, :— :	ᵐs :- .m :s	m' :m' :r'	d' :t :l
wave.	Sound the loud	tim - brel o'er	E - gypt's dark
l, :— :	ᵈᵉm :- .d :m	s :s :f	m :r :f
tide.			

s :— :s	s' :- .m' :d'	s :d' :d'	d' :- .r' :t	d' :— :	
sea; Je -	ho - vah hath	tri - umph'd—his	peo - ple are	free.	
m :— :s	m :- .d :m	s :m :d	m :- .f :r	m :— :	

TRUE LOVE.

Ex. 254. KEY G. *A. L. C.*

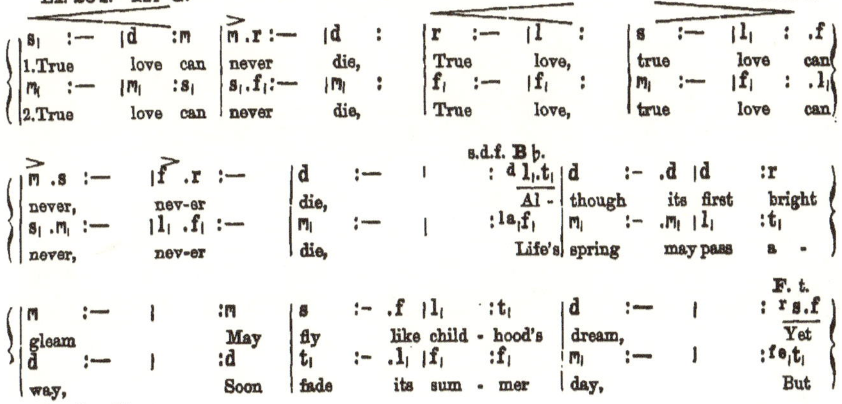

s, :— | d :m	m .r :— | d :	r :— | l :	s :— | l, : .f
1.True love can	never die,	True love,	true love can
m, :— | m, :s,	s,.f,:— | m, :	f, :— | f, :	m, :— | f, : .l,
2.True love can	never die,	True love,	true love can

s.d.f. B♭.

m .s :— | f .r :—	d :— | :ᵈl,.t,	d :- .d | d :r
never, nev-er	die, Al -	though its first bright
s, .m, :— | l, .f, :—	m, :— | :ˡᵃf,	m, :- .m, | l, :t,
never, nev-er	die, Life's	spring may pass a -

F. t.

m :— | :m	s :- .f | l, :t,	d :— | :ʳs.f
gleam May	fly like child - hood's	dream, Yet
d :— | :d	t, :- .l, | f, :f,	m, :— | :ᶠᵉt,
way, Soon	fade its sum - mer	day, But

St. Co. (New.)

cres. | | G. t.m. *cres.*

| m :r .m | s :f .m | l :— | — : | fe m :r .m | s :f .m |
burns its se - cret fire, Till life it - self ex-
| d :t_1 .d | l_1 .t_1 :t_1 .d | f :— | — : | r d :t_1 .d | l_1 .t_1 :t_1 .d |
bright 'mid win - try gloom, True love will ev - er

f *cres.*

| l :— | — :s .,fe | s :— | m :l .,t | d^1 :— | s : |
pire: Ev - er glow - ing, Ev - er grow - ing,
| f :— | — :m .,re | m :— | d :f .,f | m :— | m : |
bloom, Still un- dy - - ing, Time de- fy - - ing,

p *pp*

| m :— | — :r | d :— | — : | s_1 :— | l_1 :t_1 | d :— | — : ||
Till we die, Till we die.
| d :— | s_1 :f_1 | m_1 :— | — : | f_1 :— | f_1 :— | m_1 :— | — : ||

COME, FAYS AND FAIRIES.

Ex. 255. KEY D. *A. L. C.*

| d^1 . :s .,fe | s :— | m : | : | s . :m^1 .,re^1 |
Come, fays and fair - - ies, Come, fays and
| m . :m .,re | m :— | d :m .,m | m :— | m . :s .,fe |
Come, Come a - way, Come,
| d . : | : | :d .,d | d :— | d . : |

| m^1 :— | d^1 : | :s | s .d^1 :m^1 .,r^1 | d^1 .t :l ,t.d^1 |
fair - - ies, Yes, Come,a - way ye fays and fair -ies
| s :— | m :m .,m | m :f | m .m :s .,f | m .r :f .m |
Come a - way, Yes,
| : | :d .,d | d :t_1 | d . :d . | d . :d . |
Come, come, come, come,

| s .s :s,fe.s,l | s .f :r . | s .d^1 :m^1 .,r^1 | d^1 .t :l ,t.d^1 | r^1 .r^1 :r^1,d^1.t ,d^1 |
While the moon is shin - ing bright, Now for - sake the wood's deep sha-dows, Come and dance in her
| m .m :m,re.m,f | m .r :t_1 . | m .m :s .,f | m .r :f .m | t .t :t ,l .s ,l |
| d . :d . | s_1 . :s_1 . | d :d . | d . :d . | s . :s . |
Come, come, come, come, Come, come, come, come, Come, come,

St. Co. (New.)

t .l :s .s	s .d' :m' .,r'	d' .t :l ,t.d'	s .s :s,fe.s ,l	s .f :r .
sil - ver light,yes,	Come a - way, ye	fays and fair -ies,	While the moon is	shin-ing bright,
s .fe :s .f	m .m :s .,f	m .r :f .m	m .m :m,re.m ,f	m .r :t, .
r .r :s .t,	d . :d .	d . :d .	d . :d .	s, . :s, .
come a - way,yes,	Come, come,	come, come,	Come, come,	come, come,

FINE.

s .d' :m' .,r'	d' .t :l ,t .d'	r' .t :s .l ,t	m' .r' :d' .
Now for - sake the	woods' deep sha - dows,	Come and dance in her	sil - ver light.
m .m :s .,f	m .r :f .m	f .f :f .f ,f	f .f :m .
d . :d .	d . :d .	t, . :t, .	s, .s, :d .
Come, come,	come, come,	Come, come,	come a - way.

d.f. C. *f*

.s l,t	d' .d' :d' ,r'.m'	r' .t :s	*p* r' .d',d' :t .l	s .f :m .
Come,	trip it merri-ly	ho, ho, ho,	List to the li - ly	bell's sweet sound,
.maf	m .m :m ,f .s	s .s :s	r' .d',d' :t .l	s .f :m .
.dr	d d :d ,d .d	t, .r :s	r' .d',d' :t .l	s f :m .
Come,	trip it merri-ly	ho, ho, ho,	List to the li - ly	bell's sweet sound,

.l ,t	*f* d' .d' :d' ,r'.m'	r' .t :s	*p* r' .t :s .l ,t	m' .r' :d'
Come,	trip it merri-ly,	ho, ho, ho,	Lightly trip it	round and round.
.f	m .m :m ,f .s	s .s :s	f .f :f .f	f .f :m
.r	d .d :d ,d .d	t, .r :s	t, . :t, .	t, .t, :d
Come,	trip it merri-ly,	ho, ho, ho,	Trip it	round and round.

A. t.m.l.

:	*p* :ld,- ,r	m :m	m :- ,re ,m	s :- ,- ,f
pp	Wea-ry	mor - tals	now are	sleep - -
m s,. :s, .	s, . : s, .	s, . :s, .	s, . :s, .	t, . :t, .
La la,	la, la,	la, la,	la, la,	la, la,
dem,. :m, .	m, . : m, .	d, :d, .	d, . :d, .	s, . :s, .

m .l, ,- ,t,	d :d	d :- ,t,.d	m :- ,- ,r	d *f* :s .,fe	s :—
ing Sil -ver	stars the	watch are	keep -	ing, Fays and	fair -
d . :l, .	s, . :s, .	s, . :s, .	se,. :se,.	l, . :m .,re	m :—
la, La,	la, la,	la, la,	la, la,	la,	Come, come,
d, . :f, .	m, . :m, .	m, . :m, .	m, . :m, .	l, . :	d . :d .

St. Co. (New.)

m :m .,re	m :—	d :	r .t,,d:r .	:
ies, Fays and	fair - -	ies,	Come from the glen,	
d :	d . :d .	d . :d .	t, . :t, .	t, . :t, .
	Come, come,	come, come	Come, come,	come. come,
d . :s, .,fe,	s, :—	m, . :d, .	s, . :s, .	s, . :s, .
come, Fays and	fair - -	ies, come,		

m .d,r :m .	:s .,fe	s :—	m :m .,re	m :—
Come from the hill,	Fays and	fair -	ies, Fays and	fair -
d . :d .	d . :m .,re	m :—	d :	d . :d .
Come, come,	come,			Come, come,
d, . :d, .	d, . :	d . :d .	d . :s, .,fe,	s, :—
		Come, come,	come, Fays and	fair -

				f. D. D.S.
d :	r .t,,d :r .t,	:	m .d,r:m	d s :—
ies.	Come from the foun-tain,		Come from the rill,	yes.
d . :d .	t, . :t, .	t, . :t, .	d . :d .	ta,f :—
come, come,	Come, come,	come, come,	Come come,	yes.
m, . :d, .	s, . :s, .	s, . :s, .	d, . :d, .	m,t, :—
ies, come,				

More Distant Removes are much used in modern music. They can be studied on the extended modulator. See also my "Construction Exercises," p. 154, and "The Staff Notation."

Effect of Speed and Force.—We all know that when we are excited our pulse moves quickly, and that when we are calm and meditative our pulse moves more gently and slowly. This is the general principle which must govern our speed of movement in singing. It should be regulated by the character of the emotion we are expressing. We may also notice, that the same state of our feelings, which naturally suggests that we should speak *quickly*, *generally* leads us, at the same time, to speak *aloud*. And the same emotions which lead us to speak *slowly*, *commonly* also suggest that we should speak *softly*. Hence the connection between *speed* and *force*. In this study, however, the following caution from Dr. Lowell Mason should be kept in mind. He says, "The very same words may be sung by different persons, or even by the same person at different seasons,—in different moods of mind, and so with a pervading difference of expression. The hymn commencing, "When I can read my title clear," would be sung by one man (looking at his Christian hopes through the tears of penitence and sorrow) with a subdued trembling confidence, and by another man (who has *long* taken 'Jesus' for 'the Christ,' in whom his soul trusts) with the free full triumph of gratitude and faith. The Israelites, before they crossed the Red Sea, might have sung such a hymn as that which begins—

I sing th' almighty power of God,
That made the mountains rise;
That spread the flowing seas abroad,
And built the lofty skies.

But they would have sung it, in a very different strain *after* they had crossed the Red Sea! It might be said, that, in both these cases, the second way of singing is *the right* way. But allowances must, nevertheless, be made for this difference in the *general style* and manner of delivery." The principles here laid down are necessarily incomplete; but they will serve the purpose of setting the pupil to think. Each case given below, should be brought before the class, and submitted to the judgment of the pupils. They should then be requested to find other cases illustrative of the same principles, or cases developing any new principle. Let the pupil remember that this exercise of independent thought and feeling is *the only exercise*, in connexion with this subject, *of any real value to him.* The mere learning of *rules* for expression, without apprehending and testing their meaning, and without trying to apply them for yourself, or to invent others if need be,—would be just the putting on of so many weights and shackles to hinder all free movement.*

Loud and Quick.—These principles will naturally suggest to us that passages of music expressing joyful praise, gladness of heart, and other excited emotions, should be delivered with force, and with quick and sometimes accelerated speed. Besides this, among the many passages where music seems to *act the words*, there are some in which this dramatic delivery naturally assumes the same qualities of loudness and quickness.

Joyful praise.—Illustrations of this will be found in "Jacksons," p. 2, v. 4, last line,—"Swiftly" p. 32 "Nature's," &c.,—and St. Co. Ex. 111.

Gladness.—See Sunshine, p. 45, last two lines of verses 1, 2,—"Spring life," p. 3, where full voiced gladness bursts out on the words "Hurrah," "grow away," &c.,—see also St. Co. Ex. 174, at the opening and at the close before "FINE."

Excited emotion.—By this we mean other exciting emotions besides those of praise and gladness; and any of these emotions when suddenly aroused. See the feeling of patriotism in p. 13, first 8 measures and last 8 measures,—see exulting confidence in "Rise my soul," p. 33, v. 1,—see a change to excited confidence in "Nearer my God," p. 34, v. 2, lines 1 to 5,—in "Hope will," p. 12, close of each verse, —in "Hear me," p. 18, third score, where the words are those of prayer but the feeling is that of exulting confidence,—and in "Saviour breathe," p. 91, third score, where even the depressing sentiment of confession is naturally overlooked in the rising urgency of passionate entreaty. See cases in which the excited emotion suggests also, accellerated speed, in "We fly," p. 20, through the whole, —and in "Awake," p. 62, end of second score, contrasted with the slow and sustained music which precedes it.

Dramatic effects.—Cases in which our mental associations naturally suggest loudness and quickness in the "picturing out" or acting of a musical passage may be found in "Quail," p. 14, score 2, "Ruthless the winter comes on,"—"Awake," p. 64, score 4,—see also St. Co. Ex. 175, accompaniment in Tenor and Bass "rushing along."

The student should here be cautioned against an unnatural straining after expression, against giving such expression to a single word, or to a single line of the poetry, as will distract the attention from the general sentiment—the pervading and predominating feeling of the piece.

The author of "Our Church Music" cites two striking illustrations of this. "The following stanza," he says:—

> Sinners rejoice, and saints be glad,
> Hosanna, let his name be blest;
> A thousand blessings on his head
> With peace, and joy, and glory rest:

"is evidently throughout a *jubilant* one; and the individual word *peace* does not change its character. I once heard a leader, with a powerful voice, singing this hymn. Catching at such words as '*rejoice*,' '*be glad*,' &c., he bounded on exultingly. But suddenly his eye fell upon the word '*peace*.' This 'gave him pause.' He was startled. But, with ready presence of mind, he checked his musical career, and sinking his voice to a whispering *pianissimo*, faintly articulated the word *peace*. This accomplished, however, he rallied manfully for the remainder of the line, to depict the 'JOY' and 'GLORY' of it." The following stanza:—

> See, the storm of vengeance gathering,
> O'er the path you dare to tread,
> Hark! the awful thunder rolling
> Loud and louder o'er your head:

our author heard sung with an AWFUL *crescendo* on the third line, and a great thundering of the organ-pipes. But the true feeling of the verse is that of subdued solemnity. The attitude both of speaker and hearer is that of quiet listening. "Would not an effective reader," he says, "sink his voice to a whisper, and turn the listener's ear inward, to the thunder of his own conscience, rather than stun it by material noise?"

Let the student always ask himself—"What should be *my own state of mind* (excited, or quiet, &c.), while uttering this sentiment?" Let him determine first to *feel* the sentiment quietly and fully, next to *speak* it feelingly, and then to *sing* it so as to make others feel. If he does this he will never be found labouring to bring out expression

* This subject is more fully treated in "Musical Theory," Book IV

from unimportant words, and forgetting the main sentiment which he is uttering.

Loud and Slow.—Passages which express some grand idea on which the mind delights to dwell should be sung loudly, and not only without quickened movement; but often in a delayed and sustained manner.

Grand Ideas.—See examples in "God speed," p. 1 —"Spring Life," p. 4, "praise and pray," where, in the same place, the other verses would be sung *loud and quick*,—and in "Quail," p. 15, end of third verse, where after trembling and fear, there comes a solemn confident utterance of thoughtful faith on the words "God for his creatures will care,"—"How lovely," p. 61, first score "throughout" to "tidings," expressing the universal triumph of the gospel. Musically considered, this *forte, rallentando* prepares the way, by contrast,—for the light *piano* which follows,—in "Sunshine," p. 45, where the singer is contemplating with strong satisfaction the blessings he has realised, and where, in the same place the previous verses would be sung loud and quick. See also St. Co. Ex. 139, last line v. 3 & 4.

Ex. 256. What musical expression is suitable to the words in "Morning prayer," p. 80, "I feel my being new created?"—in "May time," p. 5, opening of v. 1 and 3?

Ex. 257. What expression would you give to "Quail," p. 15, "God be thanked," and "Look she goes?"—to "Home," p. 76, "tell me heaven?"—and to "Saviour," p. 92, "for we are safe if thou."

Ex. 258. What expression would you give to "The stout limbed," p. 77, last score and p. 78, third score?—and to "How lovely," p. 58, last score. Give your reasons in both cases.

Ex. 259. What general musical expression would you give to the words in St. Co. Ex. 134,—and what special expression to Ex. 113, scores 1, 2, 3, 6, 7?—in Ex. 175, on the words "The sea," "The deep blue sea for me?"—what expression would you give to St. Co. Ex. 143, "Great is the Lord," "He makes his promise good."

Soft and Slow.—The principles stated at the commencement of this subject naturally suggest,—that words which express Worship, Sadness, or other Subdued Emotions as well as those which place the mind in the attitude of Meditation, Description, or Repose, should be sung more softly and often more slowly than other passages. There are also several Dramatic Effects which can be well expressed by soft and slow singing.

Worship.—See examples in "Hear me," p. 17, at the opening, where the second score, being a repetition section and expressive of rising urgency is naturally sung louder than the first; but still *piano*,—"Lord in this," p. 33, v. 2, where the worshipful feeling is deeper and humbler than in v. 1, and should be sung more softly and slowly. This expression prepares for rising urgency of prayer in v. 3. See also St. Co. Ex. 135, v. 1.

Sadness. — See illustrations in "Shepherds lament," p. 89, score 4, where the closed door, produces a sadness, which sobs in the words "and all, —all," and deepens into utter desolation, delaying the utterance of the words "me, a dream to me,"—and in St. Co. Ex. 188, v. 2, second and third scores, —Ex. 190, v. 2, last two lines.

Subdued Emotion.—See examples in "Jackson's" p. 2, v. 2, first and last lines, and v. 4, second line. Note that in this piece, the last line of the last verse would be sung with a contrasting expression,—"Quail call," p. 14, "Ah! but" to "defend,"—also the same, "cold" to "cries,"—and the subdued feeling of the listener, v. 1 and 4 of the same,—"Come freedom's," p. 13, v. 2, lines 1, 2,—"Fortune hunter," v. 5, last two lines,—"Hope will," p. 12, v. 1, line 1, and v. 2, line 1. See also St. Co. Ex. 139, v. 3, first line.

Meditation, Description, or Repose.—See examples in "If I had," p. 45, last score "But thoughts" to "here,"—"How lovely," p. 58, duet,—"Swiftly," p. 31, "sweet," &c.,—"My lady," p. 21, where soft respectful "description" mingles with "excited emotion," which, see above, requires a different treatment,—"Spring life," p. 3,—"Hear me," p. 18, "I will,"—where the singer anticipates the sense of repose. See also St. Co. Ex. 119, "oh, sweet content" "oh, punishment,"—Ex. 193, where, the whole is descriptive and subdued; but where, in the second and third verses, the second half is made softer and slower still by the "subdued emotion."

Dramatic Effect.— See illustrations in "Night around," p. 22. The accompaniment imitates the effect of a night breeze,—"The woods," p. 73, last score "and vanish," &c., when the *diminuendo, pianissimo* pictures the passing away of a dream,—"Ye spotted," p. 83, fourth score, "Beetles black," where the low voiced horror of the fairies, when thinking of the "beetles," is contrasted with their loud defiance of the spiders.

Soft and Quick.—On the same principles it is easy to see that passages expressing Gaity or the feeling of Cunning and Inuendo are naturally delivered in a soft, light, and quick manner.

Gaiety.—See examples in "Come let," p. 24, "trip it to and fro,"—"Fortune hunter," p. 5,—"Gipsies' tent," p. 35,—and "O the joy,"—"The woods," p. 71, where the light gaiety of the music is moderated by the descriptive character of the words. See also St. Co. Ex. 78, "Tra, la, la,"—Ex. 174 where the gaiety of the first half of the music is contrasted with the boldness of its opening and close, and with the more *legato* descriptive passage which follows.

Playful Cunning.—See examples in "Fortune hunter," p. 4, v. 8, "Without asking my lady," and v. 10, last line where the fun would be increased by a pause after "not,"—"Quail," p. 14, v. 3, "here I lie." See St. Co. Ex. 145 on the last words "my love loves me," as though playing with a pleasant secret,—Ex. 120, where after the importunate "Tell me," another set of voices seems to reply "Oh! no," and p. 42, from "all among" to "dwell," where the pretty little secret is let out.

Dramatic Effect.—See examples in "Swiftly," p. 29, where first the quick fleeting shadows and afterwards the quickly glinting sunbeams are imitated, See St. Co. Ex. 102, where the rise and fall of laughter is not only imitated but enacted.

Ex. 260. What expression would you give to "O Saviour," p. 86, 6 measures beginning "Save us?"—"Father my," p. 34, v. 1, lines 5, 6?—"Lord in this," p. 33, v. 4, line 2?—"Saviour," p. 92, "Though" to "fly?"—"Loud the storm wind," p. 95, "soft comes?"

Ex. 261. What expression should be given to St. Co. Ex. 97, v. 1, line 1, v. 3, lines 1 and 2?—to Ex. 194, v. 1, "In silence" to end,—and in what different manner should the mingled emotions of joy, and sustained, intensified agony, in "Jerusalem," &c., be expressed?—Ex. 137, first line of each verse?—Ex. 139, v. 3, "and quiet lie?"

Loud to Soft.—Passages which suggest "Excited emotion" at their opening, gradually changing to "Subdued emotion," will naturally be sung *diminuendo.* See "Spring," p. 51, "Cloe" to "gone,"—"Going home," p. 2, v. 2, last line,—"Morning prayer," p. 79, where the ma in the contralto twice hushes the outburst of greeting at the solemn sense of the Divine presence,—and where, on the repetition, the feeling, still more deepened, may be expressed by a *pianissimo, rallentando* finish to the *diminuendo.* The words of the second verse do not require such refined expression: but those of the third verse in the same place, demand all the feeling which conductor and singers can throw into them. See also St. Co. Ex. 79, score 4, v. 1.

Single tones may take the same shape, but in that brief and condensed form, which we call the explosive tone, when the singer wishes to express vigour and energy in a somewhat spasmodic manner. Let the pupils sing the scale upward and downward with a feeling of resolute determination, to the words, "No! I will not! No! I will not!" See also illustrations in the fairies saying "Hence, hence," to the spiders, p. 83,—"Where the gay," p. 65, score 4, the energetic climax of a remarkable *crescendo* passage,—"Hear me," p. 18, first and fourth scores,—"The Shepherd's," p. 88 in which a number of explosive tones must be excused on account of the state of passionate excitement which the singer has to impersonate,—"Harvest Home," p. 39.

Soft to Loud.—Passages which suggest "Subdued emotion" at their opening, gradually changing to "Excited emotion," will naturally be sung *crescendo.* See "At first," p. 54, first score, where the gathering force of a mountain stream is represented by *crescendo* and *accelerando;* and the same thing, p. 55, score 4,—"Loud the storm wind," pp. 94 and 95, "loud," &c., where the subdued feeling of description gradually changes into dramatic excitement. See also St. Co. Ex. 139, v. 2, "And in," to "to be,"—Ex. 175, "Beautiful" to "free," where contemplation rises into ecstasy.

Single tones may take the same shape but in that brief and condensed form which we call pressure tone, when the singer wishes to express the breathings of desire, entreaty, or any deepening emotion. Let the pupil sing the scale slowly upward and downward to the words "Oh! do, pray do! Oh! do, pray do!" See "Jackson," p. 3, on the words, v. 2, last line,—"Father," p. 34, v. 1, where a pressure tone on each syllable of "From human agony," would well express the deepening emotion,—"Hear me," p. 17, score 2, "O,"—ditto p. 18, second score, "prayer,"—"O Saviour," p. 86, score 2, "Save," "Help." It should here be noticed, however, that the same emotion is sometimes expressed violently and passionately by the explosive tone which in other moods would require the desireful pressure tone; see "Saviour," p. 87, "Save," "Help," and

"Home," p. 76, score 1, "shall." See also St. Co. Ex. 189,—Ex. 194, each syllable of "the anguish of our soul."

Ex. 262. Mark for expression the following stanza, first on the supposition that the poet wishes the mind strongly impressed with the contrast in the picture, for the sake (for example) of some lesson he means to draw from it,—and, secondly, supposing the sentiment to mean nothing more than a descriptive meditation:—

In winter, from the mountain,
The stream, like a torrent, flows,
In summer, the same fountain
Is calm as a child's repose.

Ex. 263. Mark the following—from Gersbach's "Little Singing Bird," translated by Mr. James Stallybrass:—

On airy wings
The skylark springs
To yonder cloud on high;
His thanks to God
He flings abroad,
And fills the wide blue sky.

O songster rare,
You swing up there—
Creation's morning bell!
My songs I'll blend
With yours, and send
Them up to heaven as well.

Ex. 264. Ditto, ditto.

Oh! never fear
Old Winter's cheer,
Though rude and sharp his greeting;
His coat is rough
His voice is gruff,
But warm his heart is beating.

He wears no smile
And for a while
He'll seem to hide our treasures;
But in the end
He'll prove a friend
And bring us back Spring pleasures."

Ex. 265. Ditto, ditto.

When Spring unlocks the frozen ground
And scatters all its treasures round,
How sharp and active then is found,
Old Master Spade the Gardener!

When 'mong the crops feeds hungry Bun,
Oh! who will rise before the sun
To scare the rogue and make him run!
Old Master Spade the Gardener!

Suppose the last line in each stanza repeated, what would be your feeling in the repetition, and how would you mark it?

St. Co. (New.)

Ex. 266. Ditto, ditto.

Oh! there's not a sweeter pleasure
Than to know a faithful heart.
Ye that own so rich a treasure
Never, never with it part!
Blest are we, in joy and woe,
If but one true heart we know.

Ex. 267. Ditto, ditto.

Your cage is nice and ready;
Though green boughs, pretty bird,
Are now your home delightful
And rightful,—
Yet spiteful
Is Winter, and he'll pinch hard.

The cage has long been ready:
What says the pretty bird!
I'm still to freedom clinging
And swinging
And winging
My flight o'er the bright green sward!

Ex. 268. Mark this from "Favourite Welsh Hymns," by Joseph Morris:—

Far on the ocean, one cold starless night
A small bark was sailing in pitiful plight;
The boom of the billows, as on rushed the storm,
O'ercame the stout hearts of the men with alarm.
But one in that lone boat was fearless the while,
The captain's bright boy,—looking round with a smile;
"The storm," he said, "threatens, but still do not fear,
We safely shall land, for my father doth steer."

Ex. 269. Mark this, by the Rev. W. B. R.:—

Never forget the dear ones,—
What songs, like theirs, so sweet?
What brilliant dance of strangers
Like their small twinkling feet?
Thy sun-lights on life's waters,
Thy rainbows on its foam;
Never forget the dear ones
Within thy house at home.

Ex. 270. Mark this, from Barry Cornwall:—

Oh! the summer night
Has a smile of light,
And she sits on a sapphire throne;
Whilst the sweet winds load her
With garlands of odour,
From the bud to the rose o'erblown.

But the winter night
Is all cold and white,
And she singeth a song of pain;
Till the wild bee hummeth
And warm spring cometh,
Then she dies in a dream of rain.

Ex. 271. How would you treat the last verse of "Oh! where and oh! where is your Highland laddie gone?" We once heard it sung all *in one piano.* Should question and answer be given alike?

Suppose, and suppose that your Highland lad should die!
The bagpipies should play o'er, him and I'd lay me down and cry;
And 'tis oh! in my heart I wish he may not die.

Will you take the first line as a simple thoughtless remark of the questioner, as a solemn fear seriously entertained, or as a heartless mocking suggestion? Is the opening of the second line the sad musing of sorrow as it pictures the parting scene? Or is it the earnest voice of a momentary triumphant feeling, claiming, even in death, some honour for the Highland lad? Does the last line imply hope, or a troubled heart near despair? Mark the verse according to all these various readings.

Finally, on this subject of expression, let pupils be always reminded, that, in the preceding exercises, we have only introduced them to certain general principles and *instruments* of ART. But, to use the memorable words of M. Fétis, "ART WITHOUT LOVE IS POWERLESS. To persuade we must BELIEVE in what we say. To MOVE WE MUST OURSELVES BE MOVED." If you want to see how this principle is forgotten, and how little the highest art can do without TRUTH and LOVE, go listen to the well-paid chorus in some first-rate opera-house of England or France, or to the unbelieving choir and organist in some of our greatest churches.

Phrasing of Words.—From the commencement of the course, as at pp. 9, 16, and 30, the attention of the student has been directed to the proper division of the melody into portions, marked by breathing places. At pp. 69, 70, instructions and exercises have been given in the art of quickly detecting the natural divisions of musical sections and phrases, and at p. 98, the principles of "Melodic Phrasing" are still further developed. But to the singer a yet more important art is that of dividing the *words* so as to give the *sense* most clearly and of making the hearer receive that sense as the singer feels it. When singers take breath in the middle of a word, or between words which so belong to one another as properly to make up a compound word, they commit an outrage on the poetry they sing. "Who would do so?" exclaims the irritable reader. "Let him listen attentively," says Mr. Wordsworth, "to the next ten singers and out of the number, nine shall be caught in what appears an impossible fault. Intelligent people have *sung* words thus punctuated,—

I saw the *vir*,—tuous man contend
With,—life's unnumbered,—woes.
And,—he was poor *with*,—out a friend.
Pressed,—*by* a thousand foes."

The singer should form the habit of looking on words not singly but *in groups* joined together naturally by the sense. In other languages than our own the little words are absorbed into the larger ones. Thus, in Latin or in Hebrew nearly all the "groups" marked in the verse below could be expressed by single words. Without studying deeply the details of grammatical analysis, the musical student will easily see, by his common sense, what words *belong to one another*. Let not such words be separated. When the smaller groups—the compound words—are readily distinguished, the student will begin to form these again into larger groups. Thus each line of the following verse may be divided into *two* larger groups as well as into three or four smaller ones. The stronger the retaining power of the lungs the larger the phrase they can easily deliver in one breath.

With all my powers of heart and tongue
I'll praise my Maker with my song
Angels shall hear the notes I raise
Approve the song and join the praise.

Mr. G. F. Root proposes that a verse, like the following, should be sung by the class to some familiar tune:—

While shepherds watched their flocks by night,
All seated on the ground,
The angel of the Lord came down,
And glory shone around.

Let the pupils be first required to take breath in the middle of the words "shepherds," "seated," "angel," and "glory." "All would feel," he says, "that taking breath between the syllables of a word is wrong, and thus one rule would be deduced. Next, the pupils might be asked to take breath after the words 'their,' and 'by' in the first line, and after 'the' in the second, &c. It would then be seen that the breath must not be taken after words that are *in close connexion* with other words. Finally, the pupils should sing the verse, taking breath where the stops occur, and after emphatic words. That will be found agreeable and expressive, and thus the rule for correct breathing would be established."

The musical and poetical phrases, in ordinary cases, coincide with each other. But where that is not the case, the words must rule. In the following illustration, from W. A. Wordsworth's "Treatise on Singing," the *musical* phrasing would suggest, as breathing places, those where the cross is placed. But such a phrasing would, in two places, be false to the sense. The other marking is therefore necessary. Sing the passage in both ways.

```
   KEY A.  †         ×                        ×
:s, |r  :-.m |f  :-.t, |d  :-.r |m  :-.d
 It  is   not that  its  meads  are green, It

          †          ×
|f  :-.r |m  :-.d |r  :f .m |r  :—  ||
 is   not that  its  hills are  fair.
```

In a chorus it is a point of special importance that all should be agreed as to the principal places of taking breath. It produces a delightful effect of unity and clear expression thus to make the "phrasing" *unanimous*.

Ex. **272.** Divide the words of Ex. 191, 144, 140, into smaller groups and mark them after the manner of the verse above.—"With all," &c.

Ex. **273.** Divide into larger groups, and mark in the same way, the words of "Hope will," p. 12, "Come freedom's," p. 13, "Lord in this," p. 33, "Father my spirit," p. 34.

Vowels.—The importance of vowel sounds to the singer has been shown, and the consonants have already been studied, pp. 59, 60. Whenever a class grows careless in the utterance of consonants, the "articulation exercises" Nos. 146 to 152 will have to be revived. This study of the consonants is sufficient to render intelligible the rapid recitations of a chant, or the quick speech of a comic song, but not to produce any lengthened tones with clearness and beauty. It is to the vowels that we owe the chief charm of speech in song. Unfortunately also it is the vowels in which the dialects of the different parts of the country principally differ. The local teacher may not always think it advisable to fight against an accepted and well confirmed local habit of speech. But he should at least know what the received sounds are, and how to produce them. Again, those vowels which are commonly short in speech have often to be sung to a long note, but few speakers have been accustomed to notice the exact formation of these vowels, or to sustain them, except for a passing moment. Now these vowels in English are rarely shortened utterances of the corresponding well known long vowels. They generally require some parts of the vocal organs to be differently arranged. Hence the power of sustaining them has to be learnt as a new art. So difficult are they that Kollmann and some other writers on musical pronunciation, misled by the word short, and not noticing that these vowels really differ from others in quality, take for granted that "the short vowel, cannot be prolonged." But to hear the quality of a vowel altered in singing, as for example steal, sate, cart, fool, substituted for still, set, cat, full, produces a most disagreeable, often painful effect even on the uncultivated hearer,—whereas a pure vowel is a pure delight. The following explanations will help to make the subject clear to the pupil's mind.

Mechanism of the Vowels.—Vowels are produced by giving certain fixed forms to the cavities between the larynx and the lips. Those cavities act as a "resonator" to the tones produced in the larynx, just as the body of the violin acts as a resonator to the tones generated by its strings. By their varying shapes they modify the quality, and tend also to modify the pitch, of the vowels. Not only are some vowels of a much pleasanter quality than others, but some vowels are more easily and clearly produced at a low or a high pitch than others. As any fixed shape of the vocal cavities will produce a new vowel, the number of possible vowels is practically infinite, and the number acknowledged in various languages and dialects, without reckoning individual peculiarities, is very great. We shall of course confine our attention to the principal English vowels, indicating their commonest dialectic varieties.

The following diagram is a kind of vowel modulator, the vowels being for convenience expressed in glossic letters. The arrangement is according to natural pitch. If the vowels *oo, oa, au, aa, ai, ee*, are pronounced in a whisper, without any effort to give them any particular musical character, and run up quickly, the rise in pitch will be as perceptible, and much of the same character, as the rise in pitch produced by pouring water from a height into a jug till it is full. The exact relation of vowel quality to absolute pitch is still under investigation, but it is believed that when the change of register does not interfere, the character of the whispered vowel system is generally maintained, *ee* being best adapted to the higher, and *oo* to the lower pitches, and so on.

SCALE OF ENGLISH VOWELS.*

	GENERALLY LONG.	GENERALLY SHORT.
Open lips.	EE, in b*ee*t.	———
	———	I, in b*i*t.
	AI, in b*ai*t.	———
	———	E, in b*e*t.
	———	A, in b*a*t.
	———	U, in b*u*t.
	AA, in b*aa*, baz*aa*r.	———
Rounded lips.	AU, in P*au*l.	———
	———	O in pol.
	OA, as *o* in pole.	———
	OO, in p*oo*l.	———
	———	UO, as *u* in p*u*ll.

In speaking of the vowels it will be most convenient not to call them by their sounds, but by the usual alphabetic or spelling names of the letters composing their glossic form: *ee* will be "double-e," i will be "eye," *ai* will be "a-eye," and so on. The teacher will thus be able to call for a sound without first pronouncing it.

The open Italian *aa* forms the centre of this vowel scale. Proceeding upwards from *aa* the middle of the tongue is raised for each higher vowel. The lips are open throughout this series. Below *aa* the lips are gradually more and more rounded, being closest for *oo* or *uo*. At *oo* or *uo* the *back* of the tongue is highest, and the tongue is altogether lowest at *au* or *o*. The tongue is in precisely the same position for *oa* and *aa*, but for *aa* the lips are not rounded, and the larynx is lower.

Just as in studying tune we took the boldest tones of the modulator first, so in studying the vowels we commence with those most readily produced by the singer or most familiar as separate sounds to the speaker. The vowels will therefore be studied in five groups in the following order, first *aa*; second *au, oa, oo*; third *ai, ee*; fourth *u, a, e, i*; fifth *uo, o*. Here the first group stands alone; the second are all spoken with rounded lips; the third are the less sonorous long vowels; the fourth are all short vowels with open lips; and the fifth are peculiar vowels with rounded lip.

First Group: AA.

aa—in baa, papa, father, harp, calf, ass, chance, aunt, laugh, guard, heart. This sound is formed with the lips well open, and the teeth considerably separated. The tongue is depressed, lying almost flat, and quite free in the lower jaw. Pouting the lips, or closing the corners, so as partly to cover the teeth, much injures this, and all the upper vowels. If the tongue is lowered too much as for *au* (the lips not being rounded) a deeper, thicker, lower sound is formed, the glossic *ah*, which is much used in Scotland in place of both *aa* and *au*. A short form of *aa* or *ah* is used in the North in place of *a*, and in the West a long form of *a* is used for long *aa*. All these variations materially injure *the quality of tone* in singing. The *ah* is felt to be uttered in the throat, the long *a* is almost a bleat, driving the sound against the palate. Obtain the pure *aa* by keeping a medium position of the tongue, and endeavouring to drive the breath against the upper teeth, but keeping the teeth well opened. A still finer sound, the glossic *a'*, is made by keeping the tongue flat but altogether raising it in the mouth to the same position as for *u*, and is heard now in Paris and very much in London, in place of *aa* (in *ask, grant, pass, path*, and such words not containing *r*) but its use detracts from the pureness of the quality of tone.

As this Italian *aa* has been so much used in previous exercises, it is not necessary to give new exercises upon it here, but if from not perceiving the importance of pure vowels the pupils have been allowed to change *aa* into *au, ah, oa*, or *a*, they must now go through the klang and tuning exercises of this step over again with exclusive attention to the vowel *aa*. If there remains any difficulty in producing the Italian *aa*, let the plan recommended by Fredrick Wiek, of Dresden, and Madame Seiler be adopted, of beginning with *oo*, and then changing the vowel into *aa*, thus: *oo-aa*. The *oo* puts the mouth in a forward position and so prepares it for the best quality of tone that can be got on *aa*. Of course the teacher will be careful not to stop at *oa* or *au* on the road.

As *aa* is the central vowel we do not expect any marked difference to arise from the change in the pitch. Its tendency however to alter into *au* in the

* For pictorial diagrams, see Teacher's Manual, p.198.

lower part of men's voices is very noticable. Try with the class such passages as second part of St. Co., Ex. 78, ms. 11 and 13, Ex. 136, sc. 2, m. 8. Add. Ex. p. 2, sc. 4, m. 3, v. 2, Bass, p. 9, sc. 1, m. 3, Bass. And it sometimes has a tendency to alter into *u* at the top of the soprano voice. Try such cases as St. Co. Ex. 172, last "Amen" 1st part,—and Add. Ex. p. 5, m. 1, soprano.

Second Group, AU, OA, OO.

au—as in Paul, daub, cause, caught, laud, law, all, talk, broad, brought, cord, fork, &c. The tongue is much lower than for *aa*, the back of it being as much depressed as possible. The middle parts of the lips are widely separated, but they are slightly rounded at the corners. The jaw is depressed.

As, in the North, deep *ah* is used for *au*, so in the West *aa* is substituted for *au*, as *kaard* for "cord." The sound of *ao* (see Diphthongs p. 143) is frequently confused with *au* by people in the South, who for "more" (properly maor), will say *maur*, or even *mau!*, and even confuse "court," (properly kaort) with "caught." Sometimes *au* is used provincially for *aa*, and *ao* or *oa* for *au*.

Ex. 274. After striking the tonic chord of Key G. sing the vowel *au* in lengthened tones, first downwards from G, then upwards from G, and always piano till the sound is securely struck at all pitches. The teacher will find it necessary to set a pattern for his pupils. He should guide them in the beginning and ending of the tones by means of the "manual signs." The pupils should take breath before each vowel, and deliver it with that clear and perfect attack (without breathiness, force, or hollowness), that "good touch," on which the quality of tone so much depends. Even on this almost invariably long vowel the pupils will soon perceive how difficult it is to hold a vowel position without change, for even a second of time. They will feel the constant tendency to relax the rounding of the lips so changing into *ah*, to rise into *aa*, to fall into *oa*, or to end with a slight *u*, representing a final *r*. If there is any difficulty in getting a good quality of tone on this vowel it should be practised on Wiek's plan described above. The singer will feel that this, like all other vowels, is more difficult to produce at certain pitches than at others. At no moment must his attention be withdrawn from the purity of the vowel sound. As high pitched and low pitched voices have different difficulties to contend with in producing vowel sounds with purity the women's and children's and the men's voices should be practised separately and alternately; the alternation will give them rest and opportunity for self-improving criticism. As this is not an exercise in strength of lungs or compass of voice, certain voices will be allowed to drop out when the majority of the class has gone beyond their reach.

The tendency to change this vowel in the high part of the Sopr. voice may be studied in such cases as Add. Exs. p. 45, sc. 4, "thoughts."

oa.—as in load, shoal, coat, blow, hoe, globe, grove, most, folk, though. The tongue lies flat and free in the lower jaw, in the same position as for *aa*. The lips are much more rounded than for *au*, a considerable portion about the corners being quite closed. But the teeth inside the lips should be kept well apart, and the lips should not be pursed or outwardly rounded into the shape of an O, as either error much impairs the quality of the tone. In the South of England there is a tendency to finish the vowel by closing the lips still more and raising the back of the tongue, producing a final *oo*; this should be avoided in singing. In many places the larynx is too much depressed, producing the broader sound *ao*, which too closely resembles *au*: this is particularly unpleasant to a Southerner. Care must also be taken not to commence the vowel with a sound resembling *u* and then finish with *oa*; this arises from not rounding the lips at the moment of striking the vowel; it is very common and should be carefully avoided. The Cockney fault of almost confusing *oa* with the diphthong *ou*, making "no hoe" into "now how," (which is also the practice in Ireland, when the sound of long *ou* should be heard before *l*, as in "cold soul,") must of course never be tolerated. We may say the same of stain and bain or steen and been, sometimes heard in the far North for stone and bone.

Ex. 275.—Practise this vowel in key F♯, and in the manner described Ex. 274. Guard against the tendency towards *ah* or *au* in the lower, and *u* in the higher pitches. Study it at high pitches in St. Co. Ex. 175, last sc. m. 2, "home," and Add Exs. p. 41, sc. 4, m. 4, "home." See it at low pitches in St. Co. Ex. 136, 2nd verse, last word, 2nd part. Add. Exs. p. 17, sc. 3, m. 2, bass, and p. 24, sc. 4, m. 3, bass, "fro."

Ex. 276.—Sing the following words to long sounds. Each pair should be sung to the same tone and the same breath: bought boat, caught coat, groat

Grote, abroad road, flawed flowed, sawed sowed, gnawed node, naught note, sought creosote.

oo.—as in fool, cool, whose, lose, you, soup, two, rheum, wooed, rude, rule, blue. The back of the tongue is raised nearly into the position required for *k*, and quite conceals the uvula, but the tongue is thick and not wide, the back part of it lies between, but does not touch the back teeth, and the tip presses gently below the lower gum. The opening of the lips is much more contracted than for *oa*, but the teeth must be kept wide apart to secure a good quality of tone. Be careful not to pout the lips, making a funnel of them, and thus muffling the tone. Be careful also not to raise the *middle*, instead of the *back* of the tongue, for if you approach the *ee* position with the tongue while the lips are rounded, you will get one of those French sounds so common in Scotland (glossic *eo*, *oe* or *ue*, French *eu eû* or *u*), and sounding like *ai* or *i* to English ears. Thus, as Mr. Melville Bell observes, when a Scotchman says "John has gone out to *cool* himself," an Englishman is apt to hear "to *kill* himself." As this vowel has been so much used in the klang exercises it is not necessary to practise it here except by way of comparison. Its natural changes at high pitches may be tested by the sopranos in such cases as St. Co. Ex. 175, sc. 9, 1st note. See instructions under *uo*.

Ex. **277**.—Comparison exercises as above, Ex. 276: groove grove, coot coat, doom dome, room roam, tool toll, gloomy gloaming, boon bone, noose nose, stool stole, whom home, hoop hope, loof loaf, poop pope.

THIRD GROUP, AI, EE.

ai.—as in paid, ail, aim, ale, flame, hay, they, weigh, great, gauge. For this vowel the lips are wide open; any contraction of the opening spoils the sound. The teeth are wide apart, the *middle* (and *not* the back) of the tongue is raised. No part of it presses against the palate, though the edges lightly touch the back teeth, the tip of the tongue lies loosely near and slightly higher than the lower teeth, but must not touch them. There is a great tendency in the South to raise the middle of the tongue still higher towards the end of the sound, thus making it taper into *i*. Some elocutionists consider that this tapering *ai-i* gives a softness and a beauty to the speech; others think it may well be dispensed with. In singing, endeavour to produce *ai without* the tapering. In the North the tapering is not used, but there is a contrary tendency to broaden the sound into that heard in the South only before *r*, as in "air, care, pear, pair, pare," which is the long sound of *e* explained below. The indefinite article *a* is commonly spoken of as *ai*, but it has this sound only when emphatic; otherwise it is *e*, *u*, *a*, *a'* or *aa*, according to the habits of the speaker, and *u*, *aa*, are best adapted for singing. Notice the tendency of *ai* to change at low pitches, while the Basses sing Add. Ex. p. 33, sc. 2, last note "Face," and p. 45, sc. 1, last pulse "rain."

Ex. **278**.—Practise these vowels in Key E and in the manner of Ex. 274.

Ex. **279**.—Sing the following pairs of words on any tone, each pair to the same breath, and dwelling on the important syllables: pay-er pair, obey-er O bear, a stay-er a stair, decay-er care, lay-er lair, pray-er prayer, array-er rare, sway-er swear.

ee.—as in meet, meat, mete, me, tea, grief, seize, quay, people. The *middle* of the tongue is brought close to the middle of the palate, against which and the teeth it is pressed close on each side, leaving a narrow channel at the top for the breath to pass through. The tip of the tongue is directed down towards the back of the lower teeth, against which it is pressed in ordinary speaking, but in singing it should be kept free, as it will have to assume slightly different positions for different pitches, and as the tight pressure injures the quality of the tone. The teeth must be kept open, but cannot be opened so widely as for *ai*, without impairing the pureness of the tone. The larynx must be as high as possible, but as this cannot be maintained for low pitches, there is a constant tendency for this vowel to sink into a lengthened *i*. Notice this tendency while the Basses sing St. Co. Ex. 136, 4th verse last word, Add. Ex. p. 1, m. 3, "speed" and p. 74, m. 3, "dream." It can only be sung in great purity at high pitches, Before *r* it always falls into *i*, as in "*ear*, m*ere*, p*ier*." Singers must be careful not to let "leap, steal, feel, seen, green," sound the same as "lip, still, fill, sin, grin" lengthened. When, however, short or "brief" *ee* does not run on to the following consonant, it may be always sung as *i*, if more convenient.

Ex. **280**.—Practise this vowel in Key B and in the manner described above. Men should guard against this sound descending into *i* (as in still) only lengthened.

FOURTH GROUP, U, A, E, I.

u.—short, in but, brush, judge, tun, sun, dun, blood, rough, money. For this vowel the tongue is almost flat, and altogether higher in the mouth than for *aa*, but it is quite free from all the teeth, loose and unrestrained, filling nearly the middle of the hollow of the mouth. Many persons drop the tongue too deep, which destroys the beauty of this simple natural sound and gives it a disagreeable roughness or thickness. Care must be taken not to round the lips in the least. The teeth must be wide apart. If the larynx is lowered, as in the low pitches, the sound naturally approaches *aa*, but all approach to *oa* can be avoided by keeping the lips open. Notice this vowel at low pitches in the Bass, St. Co. Ex. 119, m. 8. "punish," and Ex. 145, m. 10, joy*ous* thr*u*sh." Add. Ex. p. 47, sc. 4, m. 3, "shuts." Try to sustain it purely although not at low pitch in Add. Ex. p. 58, scs. 1 and 2, "lovely," St. Co. Ex. 98, last word, 1st v. "*done*," and Ex. 99, ms. 6 and 8, "bove" and "love." The deeper vowel (glossic *uu*) is common in North Wales and in the Provinces.

As a short vowel it is the commonest of conversational sounds and all our unaccented vowels have a tendency to fall into it. But notwithstanding this, many writers on elocution condemn it as slovenly and obscure. In the South of England this vowel is long before R in accented syllables, the R being generally omitted, as in mirth, earth. In none of these should *e* long (the modified *ai* of air) be tolerated. Other examples are in nurse, purse, murmur, word, world. In these a deeper sound, made by lowering the back of the tongue and much heard in the West, should be avoided. No approach to *aa* should be allowed. In both these sets of words the singer must learn to insert the *r* as a very slight rapid trill following the vowel. In Scotland these sets of words are pronounced with different short vowels before a trilled *r'*.

Ex. 281.—Practise this vowel in Key D and in the manner described as above, Ex. 274. In order to guard against its great tendency to change, let the pupil think, while he sings, of one of the above words containing this vowel.

Ex. **282.**—Comparison exercise as above. Ton tone, nuns nones, run roan, pup pope, sup soap, sun sewn, rut rote, rum roam, stirring starring, bird bard, occurred card, deterring tarring, serve salve, firm farm, gird guard, herd hard, girl garland, pearl parlance, further farther, serge sarjeant.

Ex. **283.***—Sing on any tone each pair to the same breath :—buck book, luck look, cud could, tuck took, knuckle nook, rush push, gullet bullet, pulp pulpit, null pull, hull bull, hulk bulk (*u* in both)

a.—in tap, pat, pant, sad, mash, flax, plaid, plait, bade. The whole tongue is greatly higher than for *aa*, and the middle of the tongue is more raised than for *u*. It is however much lower than for *ai*, and should be quite free of the back teeth, below which it hangs freely, the tip of the tongue being slightly higher than the lower teeth, but not obstructing the free opening of the mouth. Both teeth and lips must be wide open. Persons who mince their words in England pronounce the word man almost as though it were men. Mr. Bell accuses the mincers of saying "the ettidude is edmirable." The sound which they really use is the open sound of *ai* (glossic *ae*) so much heard in France, Italy, and Germany, (*é*, *ä*,) and frequently in some English provinces in place of *e*. The larynx is lower for *a* than for *ae*; partly for this reason, there is a natural tendency to convert *a* into *ae* at high pitches, which require the larynx to be raised. See *a* at high pitches in St. Co. Ex. 134, m. 3, v. 3, "happy," and Ex. 137, m. 7, "manfully." Foreigners always confuse *a* and *ae*. It is heard as a long vowel in the West and in Ireland in place of *aa*, and in Ireland it is the name of the first letter of the alphabet. In Scotland short *ah* (the deeper sound of *aa*) is constantly substituted for *a*, and the teacher should carefully correct any tendency to say *aa* for *a*, except in such words as "pass, glass, ask, path, lath, aunt, haunt, gauntlet, grant, sha'n't," *aa* is commonly used in these cases; the use of *a* is only common in the West and among the educated classes in the North. See cases St. Co. Ex. 133. v. 4, last line, "everlasting." Add. Ex. p. 21, sc. 3, m. 3, "glass." The unaccented *a* in ide*a*, Chin*a*, *a*gainst, pass*a*ble, is generally pronounced *u* and may be so sung, but the effect of *a'* (see *aa*,) or *aa*, is much finer in singing and is always admissible. See Add. Ex. p. 47, sc. 1, "alone," and p. 34, sc. 4. m. 4, "around." Any final trilled *r* in such cases must be avoided most sedulously, especially before a following vowel. In *-al*, *-an*, final, an *u* sound is generally used in speaking, but an *a* sound is admissible in singing. See Add. Ex, p. 32, sc. 4, "universal," p. 34, sc. 1, "human." Singers should never sing *l*, *n*, without any vowel when there is the least excuse for their inserting one, as the quality of their tones is so bad.

Ex. 284.—Practise this vowel in the Key D and in the manner described above, Ex. 274.

* This exercise should be introduced later, as 290*b*.

Ex. 285.—Comparison exercises as above: pat pate, pad paid, bat bate, back bake, ban bane, tap tape, tack take, dally dale, cap cape, can cane, gap gape, fat fate, fan fain, sat sate, sham shame, lack lake, mat mate, nap nape.

e.—short, in threat, dead, health, friend, said, heifer, leopard, any, many; long, before *r* and tapering into *u*, in there, where, ere, e'er, stair, stare, pear, bear, bare. The tongue is precisely in the same position as for *ai*, but the larynx is lowered. Hence in high pitches *e* has a tendency to become *ai*, or else the tongue is lowered into the position of *a*, and *ae* is substituted. See St. Co. Ex. 133, v. 4, "commend," Ex. 171, m. 4, "Amen," Ex. 144, v, 4, "where," Ex. 145, m. 3. v. 3, "ere." The sound of *ae* is so commonly used for *e* in Scotland (where *e* is reserved for our *i*, the Scotch *pin* being sounded like our *pen*) and in the provinces, and even by many Southern speakers, that the use of *ae* for *e* need not be corrected, but care must be taken to avoid *a* for *e*, as is sometimes heard in Scotland. When *e* is written brief in unaccented syllables either *i* or *e* may be spoken but *e* is generally the best for the singer. See St. Co. Ex. 137, last note. The singer must be very careful not to prolong such words as "kept, set, met, wed, ell, Ben," into "caped, sate, mate, wade, ail, bane, &c., and hence must practise the prolongation of this vowel sound.

Ex. 286.—Practise this vowel in Key D. in the manner described above.

Ex. 287.—Comparison exercises as above: pet pate pat, bet bate bat, tell tale tallow, dell dale dally, kennel cane can, get gate gat, fell fail fallow, sell sale Sall, shell shale shall, let late lattice, met mate mat, neck snake knack.

i.—as in hip, pit, bid, cliff, his, gild, lynx. The tongue and lips are precisely in the same position as for *ee*, but the larynx is lowered, so that the voice naturally sinks from *ee* to *i* in lowering pitch and great care is required to sing both *ee* and *i* to the same pitch. The vowel *i* is very characteristic of English, and although it does not occur as a recognised long sound, it has to be constantly prolonged in singing. All meaning is lost if "lip, sit, grit, bid, hid, sick, sin," are prolonged into "leap, seat, greet, bead, heed, seek, scene." Such words as "happy, vanity, unity," have constantly a long tone to their last syllables, which must never be called *ee*. See prolonged *i* in St. Co. Ex. 116, sc. 2, "kill," Ex. 139, m. 2, "little," Ex. 140, v. 3, "fill," Ex. 174, m. 12, "hill," Add. Ex. p. 30, sc. 3, "village." The great fault of English speakers is to use *i* long for *ee*, and of foreigners to use *ee* short for *i*. Before *r*, *i* long is always used for *ee* long, and after *r* many speakers find the pure *ee* difficult. Most bass voices take *i* for *ee*. In the Comparison exercises prolong the final *y* as in baby, etc, singing it to a note as long as that for the following *e* or *ee*, etc.

Ex. 288.—Practise this vowel in Key E in the manner described above.

Ex. 289.—Comparison exercises as above: let baby be, a palfry free, with ugly glee, a tiny knee, the glassy sea, make worthy thee, a wintry tree, thy enemy me, a flashy she, best city tea, they chiefly flee, cried gruffly flee, the lucky key, fit feet, sit seat, mill meal, knit neat, whip weep.

Fifth Group, UO, O.

uo.—as in full, wool, could, book and foot. The tongue, teeth and lips are in precisely the same position as for *oo*, but the larynx is lower. Most elocutionists consider *uo* to be the same as *oo* short, but the Scotch pronounce "book, look, cook," with a real *oo* short, and the effect is so different from the English, that they are wrongly supposed to say *oo* long. Compare Yorkshire *bôok*, with *oo* long; Scotch *bòok*, with *oo* short, and Southern *bùok*, with *uo* short. Also compare English *pôol*, French *pòol*, written "poule," and English *pùol*, written "pull." The distinction between *oo* and *uo* is precisely the same as between *ee* and *i ai* and *e*, *au* and *o*. But a good imitation of *uo* (not of *oo*) can be made with widely opened lips, and sung at any high pitch on the scale, where *oo* cannot be touched. This sound is therefore valuable to singers. It is a common fault to say *rùom*, *sùon*, and even *fùod*, with *uo* short, in place of *rôom*, *sôon*, *fôod*, with *oo* long. But when "pull, full, could, would" are prolonged, the singer should never say "pool, fool, cooed, wooed." The words "*wool, woman, would,*" present great difficulties to Scotch and Welsh, and even many English speakers. The pure *wuo* should be heard in each. In the provinces *u* and *uo* are constantly interchanged, so that "bull" is pronounced "bul" instead of "buol," and "foot" is pronounced "fut" instead of "fuot." Observe that *uo* and not *u* should be heard in bull, full, pull, (and their derivatives, bullace, bullet, bulwark, bullion, fuller, fullage, fullers, Fulham, pulpit, pullet, butcher, cushion, cushat, sugar, cuckoo, huzzar, huzzay! hurrah! push, bush, to put.

The game of *put* has *u*. The word *fulsome* is pronounced both ways. All other words with *u* short have *u* not *uo*. In bl*oo*d fl*oo*d, *oo* is sounded *u*; in *soot* both *u* and *uo* are heard.

Ex. 290.—Comparison exercises, as above: pool pull, fool full, cooed could, wooed would, shooed should, food good, who'd hood, shoot put, goose puss. Ex. 290*b*—see above, Ex. 283.

o.—as in nod, pond, stock, odd and dog. The tongue, teeth and lips are precisely in the same position as for *au*, but the larynx is lower. Hence this sound has often been thought to be the same as *au* short, and most elocutionists put it down as such But if any singer inadvertently prolonged the name of God into *gaud*, he would feel ashamed of the irreverence. The following exercise will shew how the sense may be utterly destroyed by not attending to this distinction. The difference between *au* and *o*, is of precisely the same nature as that between *ee* and *i*, *ai* and *e*, *oo* and *uo*. Let the student prolong *odd*, he will find it distinct from *awed*. Next let him shorten *awed* as much as possible, and he will not get *odd*. Foreigners usually say *ao* short in place of *o*, which is a peculiarly *English* vowel. The accented syllable *or* when no vowel follows is nearly always *aur'*; the *au* is long and the *r'* should be slightly trilled for distinctness, though it is frequently altogether omitted. The words "soft, often, office, broth, groat, gone, cross," and sometimes "dog, long," especially in America, are pronounced with *au*, but either *o* long, or *ao* long are preferable, and *o* short is much used, and is indispensable in "dog, long." See prolonged *o* in St. Co. Ex. 68, m. 2, "song," Add. Ex. p. 1, m. 3, "God," p. 4, sc. 3, m. 2, "spot," p. 14, sc. 4, m. 2, "on."

Ex. 291.—Comparison exercises as above: odd awed, pod pawd, sod sawed, holiday haul, Moll maul, stock stalk, yon yawn, nod gnawed, fond fawned, God gaud, pollard pall, rot wrought, hockey hawk, solid salt, totter taught.

Ex. 292.—Error exercises on the vowels. The teacher sings on G the wrong pronunciation, and the pupils immediately (on the same tone, and prolonging the syllables) sing the *correct* pronunciation of that word, and of the other words like it. "*ai*tone" atone, adore, among, alone, amaze, alarm, awake, above, about, amidst. "D*ei*vert," divert, digress, direct, divulge, engine. "Testim*oa*ny," migratory, patrimony, dilatory, and matrimony. "Cummand," command, complete, comply, commend, correct, and corrupt. "Goodn*i*ss," goodness, endless, matchless, boundless, anthem, forget, yes and instead. "Evid*u*nce," evidence, silence, prudence, ardent, excellent, providence, influence, contentment, judgment. "Regelar," regular, educate, singular, articulate, perpendicular, particular. "Fee-aar," fear, near, their, more. "*Ai* house," a house, a mile, a town. "Thee bee," thu bee, thu house, thu mile, thu town. "Thu evening," thee evening, thee upper, thee open, thee apple, thee autumn. "Aimen," aamen. "Jeroosailum," Jeroosalem. "A nice house," an ice house. "A nox," an ox. "This sour," this hour. "Our roan," our own. "This sage," this age. "On neither side," on either side. "Bear u sonward," bear us onward. "Tai kit," take it. "Ree din," read in. "Glory yand honour," glory and honour. "The glory, coand the power," the glory and.

Note that in the solemn style of music, the word "my" is pronounced fully, but in the familiar style, as it is in the last syllable of "clammy," "mummy," "Tommy,"—that the termination "ed" is in sacred music sung as a separate syllable,—that the word "wind" is sometimes in poetry pronounced weind,—that the word "heaven" is sometimes pronounced as one syllable, and sometimes as two, and that when pronounced in two syllables, the second should be very lightly dwelt upon.

Diphthongs.—There are four principal diphthongs in the English language; *ei* as in height, *oi* as in foil, *ou* as in foul, and *eu* as in feud. It will be convenient to treat along with the Diphthongs the vowel *ao*, as in pore, because although it is not a diphthong it is used in English only as the first element of one. A diphthong is not merely two vowels put close together. The word "cawing" might be repeated ever so quickly without its two vowels producing the sound of *oi* as in "coin." The two vowels must be cemented and bound together by the Glide already explained, p. 61. Thus in the phrase "pap*a* *i*s a Tonic Sol-*fa*ist," we have two cases of vowels put close together. The second vowel in each case has a clear separate "attack." If we allowed the voice to continue while the organs are passing from one vowel position to another, we should make these double vowels into diphthongs, thus, "papeiz a Tonic Solfeist." Let it be noticed that the common letters *i* and *u*, as usually pronounced, are really diphthongs though single letters, and that the sounds *au*, *ee*, etc., are simple vowels although they have two letters, and are hence properly distinguished as Digraphs. One of the vowels which form a Diphthong is much shorter than the other. In a Diphthong, the Glide which is the characteristic part should always be longer than the shorter of the two vowels, and one of the two vowels should be formed by a closer approach of the lips or of the tongue and palate to each other. It is important to notice that the accent is generally laid on that vowel which has the widest opening.

ei.—as in I, eye, isle, buy, tie. This diphthong is very variously pronounced in speaking. The second element is always the same, *i*, not the foreign sounding *ee*. The first element, although it has the principal stress, is extremely short and difficult to catch, but is generally *u*, *a'* (not *a*) or *aa*. The stress suggests to the singer that the first vowel should be dwelt upon, but its indefiniteness, as spoken, leaves him to chose his own vowel, and he selects the beautiful *aa*. The Glide between *aa* and *i* should be very marked. When *ei* has to be sustained, in singing, prolong the pure *aa* sound, and finish rapidly, clearly and distinctly with the glide and *i*. See St. Co. Ex. 65, sc. 2, Ex 116, last word.

Ex. 293. Sing the following pairs of words on any tone, being careful not to raise the pitch on the final sounds. Sing the first word of each pair as short, and the second as long as possible. Pie pipe, buy bribe, tie tight, die died, fie fife, thy scythe, sigh size, sly slice, my mine, nigh nine.

oi in boil, boy, buoy, buoyed, toy, toyed, quoit, coin, joy. The proper first element of this diphthong is *o*, not *au*, and those who have learnt to prolong *o* will find a great refinement from its use, but others may use *au*. Even in speaking, the first element is somewhat prolonged; much more so in singing. Avoid the vulgarity of singing *oi* as *ei*. See cases in St. Co. Ex. 134, 174. When *oi* occurs before a vowel as in "toying," sing *oi* distinctly and commence the next syllable with *y* thus *toi-ying*.

Ex. 294. Sing on any tone or group of tones the following words. Anoint, ointment, oil, boil, broil, coil, foil, foist, froise, groin, hoise, hoist, join, joint, joist, loin, moil, point, poise, poison, soil, spoil; destroy, decoy, loyal, royal, voyage.

ou as in thou, how, now, cow, out, down, town, plough, round, house. This diphthong resembles *ei* in character. The first element is the same as in *ei*, and is always short in speech, having the stress. The second element is always *uo*, and may be lengthened in speech. Do not use the foreign *oo* for *uo*. In singing select *aa* as the first element, and when the diphthong has to be sustained, prolong the pure *aa* (taking great care not to round the lips before the glide), and finish rapidly, clearly, and distinctly with the glide and *uo*. Be careful not to lower the pitch in finishing off with *uo*. The rule of making *aa* always the first element will prevent all sorts of vulgarities and provincialisms. See cases in St. Co. Ex. 80, 134.

Ex. 295. Sing as in Ex. 267, descending on *ei* and ascending on *ou*: how hound, now noun, cow cowed, about out, found out, round about, round sound, thou doubt'st, cow house.

eu in pew, imbue, tune, dew, cue, few, view. This diphthong is always preceded by a consonant. In *u*nite, *u*nion, *u*se, &c., a *y* is always prefixed in speech. The first element is *i* which is always short and *without* stress. The second element is *oo* and in accented syllables, is long, having the stress, but in unaccented syllables, as doc*u*ment, may be short. The glide from *i* to *oo* is very short, but longer than the *i* which is just touched. To make the first element long, as *ee* with the stress, in *tree-oo See-oo-zun* for "true Susan," is a great vulgarism, especially offensive in singing. This diphthong always becomes *oo* after *r'*, as rue, imbrue, crew, etc., but not after *l*, *n*, *s*, *z*. In singing, dwell on the *second* element. See cases St. Co. Ex. 145, score 2, Ex. 174, score 9. Be careful not to change *t* and *d* into *ch* and *j* before *eu*, and not to pronounce - *ture*, - *dure*, - as in *nature*, *verdure*, either as - *chur*, - *jur*, or as - *tur*, - *dur*, but keep the *t*, *d* and the diphthong *eu* quite pure in singing, whatever may be your practice in speaking.

Ex. 296. Sing as above: lieu, lute, illumine, new, news, nuisance, newt; sue, consume, resume, pew, tune, dew, cue, few, view.

ao as in roar, tore, ore, more, four, is never used in received English except before *r*, forming part of a diphthong, and is hence placed here. But it is a pure vowel in itself. The tongue, teeth and lips are precisely in the same position as for *oa*; but the larynx is more depressed and hence the pitch is naturally deeper. It may be obtained by pronouncing *oa* and thinking of *aa*. If the student will sing *aa* to a very prolonged tone, and first round his lips and then open them successively, without interrupting the tone or in any way changing the position of his other organs, he will pronounce *aa*, *ao*, *aa*, *ao*, alternately, and gain much knowledge of the effect on vowel quality produced by rounding the lips. When clearly produced, *ao* is a very beautiful vowel, much finer than either *au* or *oa*. It is very common in the provinces in place of *oa*, it is the true Welsh *o* long, it is the Italian open *o*, and is in general use on the continent. It may be used to replace *oa* in low pitches, but never when pure *oa* can be produced. It always replaces *oa* before *r*, and is sometimes used in place of *o* or *au* in such words as "soft, often, office, broth, gone, cross." It will require some practice for the pupil to hold the fixed position of this vowel. The learner will be assisted by remembering some familiar word in which it occurs. It is important to distinguish such words as *mow-er*, one who mows, from *more*, as in the Comparison exercises; the first words have *oa* and two syllables; the second *ao* and only one syllable.

Ex. 297. Practise this vowel in the key of F♯ in the manner described above.

Ex. 298. Comparison exercises as above: blore blower, ore ower, tore tow-er (one who tows), gore goer, roar rower, hoar hoer, shore shewer, lore lower, sore sower, more mower, store stower.

Other Diphthongs such as *ai-i* in day, *oa-uo* in known, *i-u* in beer, *e-u* in bear (see Ex. 279), *ao-u* in boar (with the above vowel *ao* in place of *oa*), *uo-u* in boor, need not be separately practised. The singer should in the four last cases always trill the *r* even when final, at least slightly. And when *r* comes between two vowels as in *weary*, *Mary*, *glory*, he should be careful never to omit the glide to *u*; *wee-r'i* is Scotch, *Mai-r'i* is very vulgar, and *gloa-ri* is old fashioned.

The South of England custom of ending *ai* with a vanishing *i* and *oa* with vanishing *uo*, rather spoils the vocal effect. Hence it is best to practise avoiding it in singing.

Special Forms of vocal music.* Of the various forms of vocal music adapted to special purposes, the simplest is,—

The Response.—This may be only the word "Amen," on one tone and in unison, or the same harmonized, or it may be a more lengthened sentence like the responses after the commandments. In any case, if a response is intended to be really sung by the *whole* mass of a congregation it must be as simple and natural as the "Gregorian tones," and must have a pitch and range easy to all kinds of voices. A humble full-voiced unisonous "Amen" cannot be got at a higher pitch than E or F.

The Chant.—The practice of reciting a verse of a Psalm on one tone and ending each recitation with a natural cadence was older than Gregory or even Ambrose. It is the "form" of every excited speaker. Its essentials are a reciting-tone and a cadence. The length of the reciting-tone depends on the length of the words. The cadence may be of one, two, three or more tones. The regular form of the Anglican Chant (a reciting-tone with a two-measure cadence, followed by another with a three-measure cadence), p. 35, originated in England at the time of the Reformation. It has as much variety and beauty as can be desired in so elemental a form, but the reciting-tone is often placed too high or too low for the common voices of the people and the cadence is often made too wide in its intervals to be smoothly sung,—thus unfitting it for its proper use. Instructions in chanting are given, pp. 36, 27, 59, 63, 47, 82, 93.

Hymn Tunes.—There were metrical hymns, as distinguished from prose chants, in the earliest ages of the christian church, and although "time" and "measure" were not then *written* in music the tunes for these hymns were necessarily *sung* with the accents and measure of the hymns. At the time of the Reformation many of the old Latin hymn-tunes were revived, and others made. The attempt to sing them with large masses of voices, in simple people's harmony, encouraged musicians to study the progression of plain sustained chords, and so helped to form modern harmony. It is still this march of plain chords which is the glory of the hymn-tune. The introduction of chromatic resolution—of unprepared discords other than those which (like ^{7}S, ^{7}T, ^{7sc}*M*, and ^{7}*SE*) are familiar to the common ear—of difficult transitions and modulations like those in the Tonic-minor,—of the sharp sixth of the minor bah, except when moving from and to the seventh se,—of extreme compass for the "parts,"—and of difficulties in time—is ruinous to the *congregational* character of a psalm or hymn-tune. Let not the precentor be misled by the great names of composer, or harmonist attached to such tunes. Very few great composers ever taught a psalmody class or took the trouble to make themselves acquainted with the capacities and incapacities of the common people's voice. We have many hymn-tunes for the Organ and many for the Choir, but only a few for the People.

* "Musical Theory," Book III., treats this subject more fully.

The speed at which a hymn-tune is sung affects its harmonic character—its rhythmical impression—and its adaptation to the emotion of the hymn. When a tune—before sung at moderate speed—is sung very quickly, every *two* pulses (in two and four-pulse measures) or every *three*-pulses (in three and six-pulse measures) become practically to the ear, *one-pulse*, and the harmony should be altered accordingly;—the chords being made to change less frequently, and many "passing tones" allowed. Thus if "Jackson's," p. 2, were meant to be sung rapidly, as a *la, la, la* tune, the chords would have to be changed once in a measure (as they do in dances or quick marches) instead of twice;—and if the "Waits," p. 8, were altered, by exceedingly slow singing, into a mournful hymn-tune, the chords should be made to change twice or three times as frequently as now—so as to suit the slow and solemn tread of the music. To sing at great speed a tune harmonized for slow singing, and changing its chords at every pulse, produces a heavy jogging effect. To sing slowly a tune harmonized for speed, produces a drawling effect. The precentor must look to his harmonies.

The more rapidly a tune is sung the more marked is the rhythm, and the greater necessity for Rhythmical Balance and proportion between the lines. The popular ear demands this balance. Witness its delight in dance-tunes and marches. If the tune books do not make the lines of equal length, it will be easy for the Precentor or Organist to do so, because "balance of rhythm" comes naturally to the people.

In selecting a tune for a hymn, the Precentor will have to consider what is the general sentiment of the hymn. He will find it convenient to classify hymns as first, the bold and spirited, second those expressive of cheerful emotion, third those which are didactic and varied in character, and fourth those which are solemn and prayerful. To the first class of hymns, tunes in two or four-pulse measure, moving somewhat quickly, and having *doh, me*, and *soh* placed in effective positions in the melody, are well adapted. Tunes of this character when sung very slowly and firmly, change their effect into the grandly solemn. To the second class of hymns, tunes in three or four-pulse measure having *te, ray, fah* and *lah* placed in the most effective positions, are well adapted. These cheerful tunes can be changed by slow and firm singing, not into grand tunes, but into prayerfully solemn tunes, of the fourth class. To the third class of hymns, tunes must be adapted which give no special effectiveness in their melody either to the *strong* or to the *leaning* tones of the scale. These non-emotional tunes have generally a step-wise melody, and they cannot be much altered in mental effect by speed of movement.

Different speeds are used for the same tune in different places, but the natural force of habit prevents any great change of speed in the same tune at the same place. To some extent however change of sentiment from verse to verse may be indicated by change of speed. If the congregation are accustomed to the ways of their precentor, a bold tone or two from his voice will rouse them into spirited expressions as by electric sympathy; and a pause after a verse will easily suggest that the precentor desires the next verse to be sung softly and more slowly. This art of adapting music well to the words is a great secret of *spiritual* success in the precentor's office.

Anthems differ from hymn tunes in giving musical expression to particular words rather than to the general sentiment of a hymn of many verses. See "Hear me when I call" p. 17, and "O Saviour" p. 85. The anthem is free to introduce repetitions of music and words, the silencing of parts, and fugal imitations, which are inadmissible in a hymn of many verses. Although these contrivances are essentially characteristic of an Anthem, they must be carefully used in one which is intended to be sung by a whole congregation. It will be well not to leave the tenors or contraltos, who are often weak in a congregation, to take the lead in a fugal passage, and it is unwise to attempt a fugal entry on a half-pulse, or to introduce any other perplexity of the time. *The Motet* is the ancient form of the anthem. Anthems often consist of various distinct movements, with changes of key and measure and speed,—one movement being so contrived as to set off by contrast the other movements. Cathedral anthems are written for choirs which are seated in two divisions, one on the Dean's side (that is on the right hand as you enter from the nave) called *Decani*; and the other opposite on the Precentor's side called *Cantoris*. Some parts of the anthems are sung by the full choir (marked "Full"), and other parts antiphonally, that is alternately by the two halves of the choir. Portions marked "verse" are to be sung by one voice to each part. These anthems also include solos, duets, &c., and bold recitations in unison, which are called choral recitatives. Anthems are generally intended to be sung with organ accompaniment, though many of the full anthems may be well performed without it.

The Madrigal is the oldest form of secular vocal music in parts. It partakes of the old style of harmony, abounding in fugal entry and imitation. No one part predominates over the others, but each takes its turn in specially claiming the ear of the listener. Any number of voices may join in a madrigal. The same style of music was used in the old anthems, of which "Bon accord," p. 11, is a short example. Some quaint point of sentiment at the close often characterizes the madrigal. There is no good example of a madrigal in the Additional Exercises. "The time for joy" p. 15, is the nearest. See however examples in the Tonic Sol-fa Reporter—"In going to my lonesome bed" No. 68, "The Silver Swan" No. 274, and "Flora gave me" No. 287. Many pieces are called madrigals which are only harmonized airs, such as "My lady" p. 21. A light form of the madrigal is the *Ballet*, which was sung chiefly to "fal-la," as an accompaniment to dancing. Instrumental accompaniment is out of place in this class of music.

The Glee is a musical form of English birth. It is meant for single voices, and therefore gives each an opportunity of display, and develops every nicety of time and tune. It is commonly extended, like the anthem, into several distinct movements, one relieving, by its variety of style, the general effect of the others. See "Swiftly" p. 29, "Come let us all" p. 24, "The Spring" p. 50, "Awake" p. 62, "The Stout limb'd oak" p. 77, and "Ye spotted snakes" p. 81. *These* glees will bear a number of voices on each part, though great care should be taken to secure unity and delicacy. But many glees contain too minute divisions of time for this. Instrumental accompaniment was never intended for such glees and would defeat their object in displaying the voices. But accompanied glees have been written by Sir Henry Bishop and others, in which the instruments play special parts and produce special effects.

The *Part Song* differs from the glee as the Hymn tune differs from the Anthem. The Part Song and Hymn-Tune repeat the same music to several verses, which the Glee and Anthem never do. The Part Song is claimed as of German birth. It is intended to bear many voices on each part. It differs from the madrigal in not admitting so much of the fugal style, in depending more upon modern choral effects, and in permitting the upper part generally to predominate. Specimens of the German part songs are to be found on pp. 1, 3, 4, 5, 13, 14, etc. The Part Song as naturalized in England, is to be seen in "Sunshine after rain" p. 44, and "Harvest Home" p. 39. The greatest refinement of this style is to be found in the compositions of Mendelssohn (pp. 71 and 79) and Henry Smart (pp. 45 and 88). The *Harmonized Air* is practically a part song, but from the nature of its origin a greater comparative interest attaches to the melody. See the examples on p. 12 and pp. 57 and 65. The plainer part songs, like those first named, would bear accompaniment, but are better without it; such part-songs as those of Mendelssohn and Smart with their fine development of voice and expression, would be injured by it.

Oratorio Choruses are meant to be sung by *large masses* of voice, and to receive full band accompaniment, though the harmonies are generally complete without it. See "Hallelujah" p. 26, "How lovely" p. 58, and "Theme Sublime" p. 66.

Operatic Choruses are generally of a light style requiring accompaniment, but not a great mass of voices. See examples in the *Tonic Sol-fa Reporter*, "Market Chorus," No. 487 and "Carnovale," No. 142.

A Canon is a fugal imitation in which the music of the leading part is imitated through its whole length in the other parts. A fine example is "Thou shalt shew me" p. 7. It has *four* voices engaged on *two* subjects and is called a Canon "four in two." The *leading subject* is announced by the soprano, and continued to the first note of the second score of p. 8, after which it is repeated as far as its first cadence. This leading subject is again taken up by the tenor, but not till after six measures, and is carried on to the end, the tenor having time only just to commence its repetition. Meanwhile the *counter subject* has been announced by the contralto in the third measure. This is carried on to the end of the first measure of the second score, p. 8, the contralto having time to repeat nearly half of it. This counter subject is imitated by the bass, also after six measures. The bass has no time for repetition. The Counter Subject in this case closely resembles the leading subject itself, and may be called a "fugal imitation" of it. *A Round* is a canon with one subject, and in one "part" which is taken up successively by the different voices.

A Fugue does not require its subjects to be imitated exactly as in a Canon, or through their whole length. But it is a more lengthened piece and is more varied in the treatment of its subjects. It allows the parts which are not engaged upon the subject to sing beautiful phrases, as Accompaniments, which should be delivered in a subdued manner. It also permits short interludes or distinct Episodes, and various kinds of Closes, in which the Subject does not necessarily play any part.

The essentials of a Fugue are—that there shall be a Subject and a Response, carried through the various parts of which the music consists, and that this Subject shall be the main point of interest in the whole movement. Some make a counter subject essential to the Fugue. Others say that there is no Fugue without a Stretto (see p. 105), and others again require for their true Fugue an Organ-point or Pedal. But the strict definitions are practically inconvenient. It is difficult to exclude from the category of Fugues any piece or movement the whole frame work of which is evidently built on some one Subject and Response. According however to our own definition, "Hallelujah, Amen," p. 26 is not a Fugue; for though it has a Subject in the first two measures which is simply repeated in the next two, and has a proper Response starting from a fifth above in the Soprano, and although the same subject is again announced in the Bass of sc. 4, and has again a Response a fifth above in the Tenor, and once more re-appears at the bottom of p. 27, yet the Subject is not carried through the parts in turn, and it is not made the principal point of interest in the greater part of the Chorus. Such pieces may be called Fugal passages or movements, but not Fugues. Two smaller passages of the same kind are in "Bon Accord" p. 11, and "Hear me" p. 19.

The Subject is a Phrase (seldom extending to a Section) of melody, which is imitated (more or less perfectly) in its rhythm or melodial waving or both in the after parts of the Fugue. It is of such character as can be easily recognised by the ear when it re-appears in different parts and in different keys. In the more complete Fugues it is imitated by the several parts successively, and that several times over in different ways. Each time of its being "carried through" the parts is called a new "Unfolding" of the Subject.

The Response or Answer is an exact or nearly exact Imitation of the Subject. It generally commences, the first time it is made, on the fifth above or the fourth below, or in the octave. Afterwards it may commence on the same tone as the Subject or on the 1st, 2nd, 3rd, &c., either above or below. It may be by contrary or similar motion. It may be in equal length of tones, or expanded or contracted. It may also be with contrary accents (*per arsin et thesin*), the Subject and Response beginning one on the weak and the other on the strong pulse.

The Counter Subject is really an Accompaniment to the Subject or to the Response or to both. There is often however no distinct Counter-subject, but the Accompaniment varies. On the other hand there are sometimes several Counter-subjects in different parts. A good illustration of the Counter-subject is in the first movement of "Theme sublime," p. 66. The Subject (of three and a half measures) is announced in the Contralto, with a Counter-subject in the Soprano. The Response is immediately given an octave below by the Bass, with the same Counter-subject *above* it in the Tenor, Next the Subject appears in the Soprano, sc. 2, with the Counter-subject *below* it in the Contralto. The two are inverted. Then comes the Subject in the Bass again altered in its first interval, with the Counter-subject in the Tenor. And lastly the altered Subject comes in the Soprano again with the Counter-subject under it in the Contralto. This is not quite a perfect "carrying" of the Subject "through" all the parts, and several other elements of Fugue are wanting; but as, with the exception of a little play of the Accompaniment and a cadence, there is nothing else in the movement but Subject, Counter-subject and Response, we prefer to call this a Fugue.

The Stretto.—The Response generally commences the first time it is made, *after* the Subject is completed, but it often commences with the last pulse of the Subject and sometimes earlier. In the latter parts of a Fugue it greatly adds to the excitement and beauty of the music when the Response appears in one part before the Subject has come to a close in the other. This *drawing closer* of the answer to the beginning of the Subject is called Stretto. Sometimes there is more than one Stretto, the Response coming each time closer to the beginning of the Subject.

Organ Point or Pedal,—Complete Fugues, after employing a vast variety of contrivances for shewing off in various lights their Subjects and Counter-subjects, often conclude with a long holding tone, commonly in the Bass, called an Organ Point, which floods with its grand sound the last parting phrases of their various themes. There is such an Organ Point in the close of "How lovely" p. 61, but it is placed in the instrumental part.

No Complete Fugue is to be found in Additional Exercises, but there are interesting illustrations of the less regular forms which should be carefully studied, each student being able to answer questions upon them. In the second movement of "Theme Sublime" p. 67, the Subject is "carried through" all the parts twice, first in the order,—Bass, Tenor, Soprano, Contralto; then in the order,—Soprano, Bass, Tenor, Contralto. It then occurs again, p. 68, sc. 1, m. 6, in the Bass and is answered in the Soprano.

In the third movement p. 69, sc. 1, m. 7, a Subject (of six and a half measures) is announced in the Contralto. The Response comes (with a Stretto of one pulse) in the Soprano sc. 3. It is taken up again (with a Stretto of one pulse) in the Tenor, sc. 4, but here the close is altered to accommodate the Bass which wishes to enter at the fifth instead of the seventh measure. After being thus "carried through" once, the subject re-appears slightly altered in the Soprano at the end of sc. 5, with the same Stretto which the Bass secured. Then follows a digression or episode of sixteen measures, containing the first four tones of Subject and Response fugally treated in Tenor, Contralto and Soprano. At the bottom of p. 70, the contracted Subject re-appears in the Contralto, and is again "carried through" the Bass, Soprano and Tenor, but with ever shortening proportions,—the close of its melody being broken off to make way for the cadence

In "How lovely" p. 58, a Subject of eight measures commences in the Contralto, and after a full measure's interval the Bass takes up the Response an octave below. After a measure of interlude there enters p. 58, last score, an Episode of ten measures containing imitative passages, and passing into the first sharp key. Then p. 59, end of sc. 2, the Subject re-appears in the Tenor, but only the first half of it. Before this is concluded the Soprano takes up the Subject for the same length, but omitting the middle part gives only the first and last portions. With a very close Stretto (after only one measure) the Tenor again introduces the Subject in the same way as the Soprano. At the bottom of p. 59, is a brief interlude. On p. 60 a new Subject is introduced in the Soprano with a Counter-subject in the Tenor; to which there is immediately a response in the Contralto with the same Counter-subject in the Bass. Then follows an Episode of fourteen measures containing phrases imitating those of the previous Episode. Once more softly and alone p. 61, sc. 2, about three quarters of the original Subject is delivered by the Contralto, but before it is finished the Soprano takes up its closing phrases, and the Tenor re-echoes them. A short cadence concludes the piece. In singing music of this kind it would be well for the Singer to mark in his own part, all those passages or phrases which contain the Subject, the Response, or the Counter-subject, and to sing them with clearness and vigour; singing everything else except the Episodes in a very soft and subdued manner.*

Recitative is a sort of artificial declamation, in which the singer endeavours to imitate the inflections, accents, and emphasis of natural speech. It differs from the recitation of a chant, chiefly in changing its key frequently, more frequently indeed than is common even in the wildest and most impassioned speech that is unconnected with music. Instruments (one or more) are employed to announce, and sometimes sustain the chords of each new key. The length of the notes in a Recitative are intended by the composer only as approximations. The singer delivers them absolutely according to his own fancy. He makes them long or short, quiet or impassioned, just as he thinks best. He must avoid the regular rhythm of an air. He must simply express with energy and propriety, whatever passion there is in the words. Recitatives serve to connect the different parts of an Opera, an Oratorio or a Cantata, by the narration of events or the suggestion of sentiments which carry on the story.

An Opera is a play in which the actors sing instead of speaking their parts, and which is accompanied throughout by a band. While developing some exciting story, it gives opportunity for the introduction of a great variety of musical forms. It might be supposed that this union of four arts, poetry, music, painting, and acting, to excite lively

 * See other examples of Fugue analysed in "Musical Theory," Book III, pp. 223 & 226

interest and illusion, would elevate all the arts thus employed. But it is not so, because the human mind cannot appreciate the highest excellence in a number of arts at the same time, and the arts of acting and singing sadly interfere with one another. Hence, neither the best poetry, the best painting, the best acting, nor (except in solo singing) the best music are to be found in the Opera. For the best music we must look to

The Oratorio.—This is a sacred opera, without scenery or acting, in which music enjoys its full and undisputed sovereignty. It develops some sacred story by means of recitatives, songs, duets, trios, quartets, and single and double choruses. Choruses are more used, and solo voices, less than in the Opera. The attempt to bring an ordinary Opera into this pure sphere of music by singing it without the action and the scenery, only tends to shew how much exciting Operas are dependent on sensuous effects for their popularity.

The Cantata.—This, if a sacred one, is a short Oratorio,—if on a secular theme a short Opera, commonly without scenery or action.

Music for equal voices.—In England and in the United States most part singing is done by Mixed Voices—that is, by Male and Female voices together. This is best, both socially aud musically; but it cannot always be attained. It is therefore desirable that women in their work-shops and men in theirs should have music specially harmonized for them. Our Tonic Sol-fa composers are rapidly using their skill to supply this want. Mr. Callaway has done our young men great service; and his investigations and historical enquiries on the subject have contributed much to the value of this work.

Choral Contrivances.—As we have often had occasion to notice that some even of the great composers are quite cruel in their demands on the vocal compass,—it is equally fair for a Chorus-leader to borrow a few voices from one part to assist another for a phrase or two. Thus the Tenors may aid the Contraltos when their part lies too low, and the Contraltos may assist the Tenors when their part is too high, and so on.

The Resonances.—If one takes a wide organ pipe or a wide brass instrument, which is of the same length as a narrow one, the *pitch* of the two will be the same, but that quality which arises from the resonance of air in the tube will be different. The *wide* resonator will give a pure but somewhat dull and *sombre* tone. The *narrow* resonator will give a more marked and *clear* sound. So does the shape of the human mouth, in singing, affect the character of the sound. A *full* distended mouth gives the *Sombre* Resonance, fit for wailing awe and lamentation. A *narrowed* mouth gives the *Clear* Resonance, well suited to aid the expression of joy and exultation. A *medium* shape given to the mouth adapts it for quiet peaceful songs. Sing the following phrase, 1st to the words, "Hark, the voice of Rachel weeping," 2nd to "See the conquering hero coming," 3rd to "Sweet and peaceful is our meeting."

|d :s |f :r |r :f |m :d ||

It is important to cultivate the medium resonance as *a habit*, from which to vary as the sentiment requires. Some persons *always* use the sombre resonance, and utter every sentiment with the same dull face and tone.

Ex. **299.**—Say, with which Resonance each of the following songs should be sung, and give your reasons for the decision,—"Night around" p. 22, "Angel of hope" p. 48, and "Home" p. 74.

Breathing Places.—In addition to the suggestions already made for the choice of breathing places, pp. 16 and 30, it should be noticed that the little step of the scale **f m, t d', fe s, de r, ta l**, etc., is always most effectively delivered when the first tone glides into the second; we should therefore never take breath between two such tones. For a similar reason we should not take breath between a dissonating tone and its resolution. It is absolutely *necessary* to take breath before a crescendo or swell passage, or before any long holding-tone, or before a passage of quick tones—"a division," as it is called. Care must be taken always to do this *rapidly* and *easily*, so as to interfere as little as possible with the preceding rules.

"The mouth," says Dr. Mason, "should *retain the position* it had while performing the previous note, and by no means form itself into the shape necessary for the following note; neither must the mouth be, at all, closed while taking breath." There should be no sobbing or catching noise in the inhalation. "Emission of breath," says Sabilla Novello, in her "Voice and Vocal Art,"—"should be made as tardily as possible, and the student will do well to consider breath more as a propellant power which sends forth sound *by remaining behind it*, than as the sound itself. . . . . The chest and the muscles below it should be kept *permanently expanded.* Fresh supplies of air will thus be *more readily* admitted, and subsequently *remain longer* than if the walls of the chest are suffered to collapse."

Portamento, or the *carrying* of the voice from one tone to another, is made by a rapid and connected glide, or more properly by a slur, see p. 96. The voice passes through all the tones of the interval, but with a *relaxation*, in the emission of breath. This, in solo singing, and after a long and careful practice, may be made a very beautiful ornament; but the lazy imitations of it common among chorus singers, are discordant and disagreeable to all except the self-satisfied singer. It will be useful, however, to the chorus singer in cases in which the musical phrasing differs from the verbal. By a careful Portamento the musical connection may be retained while the verbal distinction is made. There can however be no breathing place in a Portamento.

Voice Training.—It is only to a small extent that voice training can be carried out in class,—but the experience gained in a well trained class will encourage many pupils to seek additional practise under the watchful ears of a master. The difficulty of voice exercises in a mixed class arises from this,—that each of the Seven "Parts" (See p. 106) requires to cultivate a different compass, and that voices singing the same exercises, an octave apart, must use different registers at the same time. It would therefore be necessary, (if breaks and registers are to be watched) to divide the class into Seven or at least Four parts, and the rest of the parts would have to sing "a second" *softly* while the teacher was attending to the one which performed the exercise. Only where the pupils themselves are *intelligent and observant students* of their own voices can voice-training in class be profitable. In ignorant and careless hands it may destroy voices by forcing them up into unnatural registers. No teacher should attempt to carry pupils far in these studies who has not patiently examined and reported on every voice in the manner described at the last step. It is well for the student to know at once that the secret of success will not be in the particular form of his exercises, or in the multitude of them, or in their being written by this man or the other,—but in their being frequently used and perfectly worked through. Gustave Nauenburg, in his "Daily Sing-studies for all Voices," says "The celebrated singer, Farinelli, was already reaping the first fruits of his fame, when he visited the singing master Pistocchi, to ask his unfettered judgement on his past performances. Pistocchi said, 'Nature has lent you all the qualities of an artist in song; with properly conducted *Voice-forming Studies* you would become a truly great singer.' This was not the answer Farinelli had expected; but inspired with a wish to attain the highest point in his art, he begged that he might pursue his studies with the worthy master. Pistocchi accepted the anxious scholar. The studies which Farinelli daily practised with persevering zeal, were all written *on a single sheet.* In a year's time the master dismissed his pupil with the character of an accomplished singer. 'What can the exercises on that sheet have been?' has often been asked." This question Herr Nauenburg answers by saying that doubtless they were such as would daily, 1st, *Tune* the voice to the different chords. 2nd, *Strengthen* it (securing equal strength for all its tones), and 3rd, *Give it Flexibility.* To these objects of Voice Training M. Seiler has taught us how to add *Quality.* Herr Nauenburg published *on a single sheet* a few simple and *easily remembered* exercises with these ends in view, and the exercises of this work, seeking strength and flexibility, are chiefly copied from his.

Manner of using voice exercises in class. The exercises used thus far have not had a range above F♯ for males and one-F♯' for females; so that none of them except the Register Exercises themselves have passed over any difficult points of breakage in the registers. But the pupil has now learnt how to study his own voice more minutely, and wishes to cultivate it to the fullest extent. He will see (p. 106) that the range of tones to be cultivated and the registers and breaks to be studied differ with each kind of voice, and for each new key he will have to "Sol-fa his breaks" (p. 110) afresh. If the pupil stands in front of a large Voice Modulator,* he cannot miss *seeing*, while he sings, the Register he is in and his place of break; but it may be useful to state distinctly what are the keys through which each of the following exercises should be worked by each different sort of voice, and what are the Sol-fa notes just below each break in each key. Although the use of a Voice Modulator *renders all this unnecessary*, it will serve to show what minute care is required even when we make the imperfect division of voices into only four "parts." Notice that the lower voices in each

* "Voice Modulator," price 1s.

part will have to be excused the highest tones, and the higher voices must not be forced to the lowest tones. It may also be noticed that each of these exercises can be made into "flying exercises,"—passing upwards or downwards through all the parts. For an upward flight, it is started low in the Bass, caught up by the Tenors the instant the Basses have finished, taking s for d, and sung in the new key,—caught up again by the Contraltos in the *new* dominant,—and once again, in the same way, flung to the top of the scale by the Sopranos. For a downward flight the exercise will be started by the Sopranos, and caught up by each lower part in the *Sub*dominant key.

Exercises with Range of a Tenth (Ex. 301 to 303), have to be thus worked.

Basses. Keys from F-two (F_2) to C-one (C_1). In F_2 f' is the tone below the break; in G_2 r'; in A_2 d'; in B_2 t; in C_1 l.

Tenors. Keys from C-one (C_1) to G-one (G_1). In C_1 l; in D_1 s; in E_1 f and r' are tones below breaks; in F_1 f and d'; in G_1 r and t.

Contraltos. Keys from E-one (E_1) to B♭-one (B♭$_1$). In E_1 s and r'; in F_1 s and d'; in G_1 f and t; in A_1 r and l; in B♭$_1$ r, s and r'.

Sopranos. Keys from B_1 to F♯. In B_1 d, s and r'; in C d, f and d'; in D m, t and m'; in E r, l and r'; in F d, s and d'; in F♯ d, s and d'.

Exercises with Range of an Octave (Ex. 304 to 307), may be worked each in two higher keys, as well as those given above.

Basses. Keys from F_2 to E_1. In D_1 s; in E_1 f.

Tenors. Keys from C_1 to B_1. In A_1 d and l; in B_1 s.

Contraltos. Keys from E_1 to D. In C d, f and d'; in D m and t.

Sopranos. Keys from B_1 to B♭. In G f and t; in A m and l; in B♭ r and s.

Exercises with Downward Range may be worked thus:

Basses. Ex. 308. Range a *tenth.* Keys C down to A♭$_1$; Ex. 309 down to F_1; and Ex. 310 from C down to D♭$_1$. No break.

Tenors. Ex. 308. Range a *tenth.* Keys G down to E♭; Ex. 309 down to B_1; no break; and Ex. 310 from G down to A♭$_1$. In D m'.

Contraltos. Ex. 308. Range a *tenth.* Keys B♭ down to G. In B♭ s_1 and r_1; in A l_1 and r_1; in G t_1 and f_1; Ex. 309, down to E♭. In F d and s_1; in E♭ l; Ex. 310, from B♭ down to C. In F s_1; in E f_1; in D m, s_1.

Sopranos. Ex. 308. Range a *tenth.* Keys G down to E. In G t_1, f_1; in F d and s_1; in E s_1; Ex. 309, down to C. In D l; in C d; and Ex. 310, from F' down to G. In F d', s; in D m', m; in C d', f; in B s; in A m'; in G f_1.

Agility of Voice.—Ease and flexibility of the voice are commonly regarded as natural gifts, but Madame Seiler has shown that they are really dependent on the formation of certain habits in the action of the vocal organs. In all groups of tones rapidly succeeding each other, the vocal membranes have to be set vibrating in short, quick impulses, and after each impulse there is a natural recoil like that of a gun after the discharge. The breath retreating expands the windpipe, and thereby draws down the larynx. These momentary motions can plainly be seen outside the throat, so that the voice-trainer can watch and see whether his pupil is forming the habit on which is built agility of voice. This will suggest the reason why it is important that all exercises in agility should at first be practised slowly and piano—except in the case of the Italians generally, and of individuals in other nations, to whom the proper movements of the larynx have already grown into a habit, and seem to be natural and instinctive. Madame Seiler recommends the employment of simple exercises, using at first *koo.*—See p. 14 and 33. Let each of the following exercises, therefore, be first sung to the syllable *koo* without slurs, softly and slowly,—second more rapidly and more loudly,—third more so still,—fourth to the open and more beautiful vowel *aa*, on the word *skaa-laa*, with slurs and expression as marked:—

Ex. 300. KEYS B♭$_1$ up to F. M. 60 to 132.

:d ,r ,m	r ,m ,f :m ,f ,s |f ,s ,l :s,l ,t	l ,t ,d' :t,d',r' |d' ‖	m',r',d'	r',d',t :d',t,l |t ,l ,s :l,s ,f	s ,f ,m :f ,m ,r |d ‖
Skaa	- - -	- laa.	Skaa	- - -	- laa.
:d	t_1 :d |r :m	f :s |d ‖	d'	t :l |s :f	m :t_1 |d ‖

St. Co. (New.)

Ex. 301. KEYS **B** up to **E**. M. 60 to 132.

cres - cen - do. *dimin - uen - do.*

:d ,t₁,d	r ,d ,r :m ,r ,m	f ,m ,f :s ,f ,s	l ,s ,l :t ,l ,t	d'		d',r',d'	t ,d',t :l ,t ,l	s ,l ,s :f ,s ,f	m ,f ,m :r ,m ,r	d	
Skaa	- -	- -	- -	laa.		Skaa	- -	- -	- -	laa.	
:d	t₁ :d	r :m	f :s	d		l	s :f	m :r	d :t₁	d	

Ex. 302. KEYS **B** up to **E**. M. 60 to 160.

p *cres - cen - do.*

d .m :r .d	r .f :m .r	m .s :f .m	f .l :s .f	s .t :l .s	l .d' :t .l	t .r' :d'.t	d' :—	
Skaa	- -	- -	- -	- -	- -	- -	laa.	
d :—	t₁ :—	d :—	r :—	m :—	f :—	s :—	d :—	

f *di - min - - - u - en - - do.*

d'.m' :r'.d'	t .r' :d'.t	l .d' :t .l	s .t :l .s	f .l :s .f	m .s :f .m	r .f :m .r	d :—	
Skaa	- -	- -	- -	- -	- -	-	laa.	
l :—	s :—	f :—	m :—	r :—	d :—	t₁ :—	d :—	

Ex. 303. KEYS **B** up to **E**. M. 60 to 160.

:d .m	r .f :m .s	f .l :s .t	l .d' :t .r'	d'		m'.d'	r'.t :d'.l	t .s :l .f	s .m :f .r	d	
Skaa	- -	- -	-	laa.		Skaa	- -	- -	-	laa.	
:d	t₁ :d	r :m	f :s	d		d'	t :l	s :f	m :r	d	

Ex. 304. KEYS **B** up to **F**. M. 80 to 160.

d :r ,d ,t₁ :d	r :m ,r ,de :r	m :f ,m ,re :m	f :s ,f ,m :f
Skaa - -	- - -	- - - -	- - -
d :— :—	t₁ :— :—	d :— :—	r :— :—

s :l ,s ,fe :s	l :t ,l ,se :l	t :d',t ,le :t	d' :— :—
- - -	- - -	- - - -	la,
m :— :—	f :— :—	s :— :—	d :— :—

d' :r',d',t :d'	t :d',t ,le :t	l :t ,l ,se :l	s :l ,s ,fe :s
Skaa - -	- - -	- - -	- - - -
l :— :—	s :— :—	f :— :—	m :— :—

f :s ,f ,m :f	m :f ,m ,re :m	r :m ,r ,de :r	d :— :—	
- - -	- - -	- - -	laa.	
r :— :—	d :— :—	t₁ :— :—	d :— :—	

St. Co. (New.)

Strength of Voice.—The following three exercises are extremely difficult to perform well. They are intended to strengthen the *volume* of pure vocal klang—to increase the *retaining* power of the chest in holding a steady breath for about *thirty* seconds—and to cultivate the faculty of passing from *Forte* to *Piano* and *vice versa* without losing pitch. The Teacher will test the pitch of each exercise as it concludes. The pupil will bear in mind the remark on p. 33 that strength is obtained by somewhat forceful exercise, and by the careful use of the crescendo passage and the explosive tone, but always be it remembered, with *as little breath* as possible.

Ex. 305. KEYS B♭ up to A. M. 60 to 132.

```
:d   |r    :m   |f .s :l .t |d'   :—   |t .l :s,f.m,r |d   :d'  |d
Skaa                                                             laa.
:d   |t,   :d   |f    :—    |m    :—   |r    :—       |d   :—   |—

:d'  |t .l :s,f.m,r |d   :—   |r    :m   |f .s :l .t |d'  :d  |d'
Skaa                                                           laa.
:d   |—    :—       |—   :—   |t,   :d   |f    :—    |m   :—  |—
```

Ex. 306. KEYS B♭ up to A. M. 40.

```
|d  :—  |—  :—  |m  :—  |s  :—  |d'  :—  |—  :—  |t  :—  |l  :—
Skaa
|d  :—  |—  :—  |—  :—  |—  :—  |—   :—  |—  :—  |—  :—  |—  :—

|s  :f,m,r |d  :—  ||d  :—  |—  :—  |f  :—  |l  :—  |d's :—  |—  :—
           laa.      Skaa
|—  :—     |d  :—  ||f  :—  |—  :—  |—  :—  |—  :—  |f d :—  |—  :—

|f  :—  |m  :—  |r   :d .t,.l, |s,  :—  ||s,  :—  |—  :—
                         laa.            Skaa
|—  :—  |—  :—  |s,  :—        |—   :   ||s,  :—  |—  :—

|t,  :—  |r  :—  |f  :—  |—  :—  |m  :—  |r  :—  |d  :t,.l, |s,d  :—
                                                            laa.
|—   :—  |—  :—  |—  :—  |—  :—  |—  :—  |—  :—  |—  :—     |s,d  :—
```

Ex. 307. KEY B♭ to A. M. 72, 60 & 50.

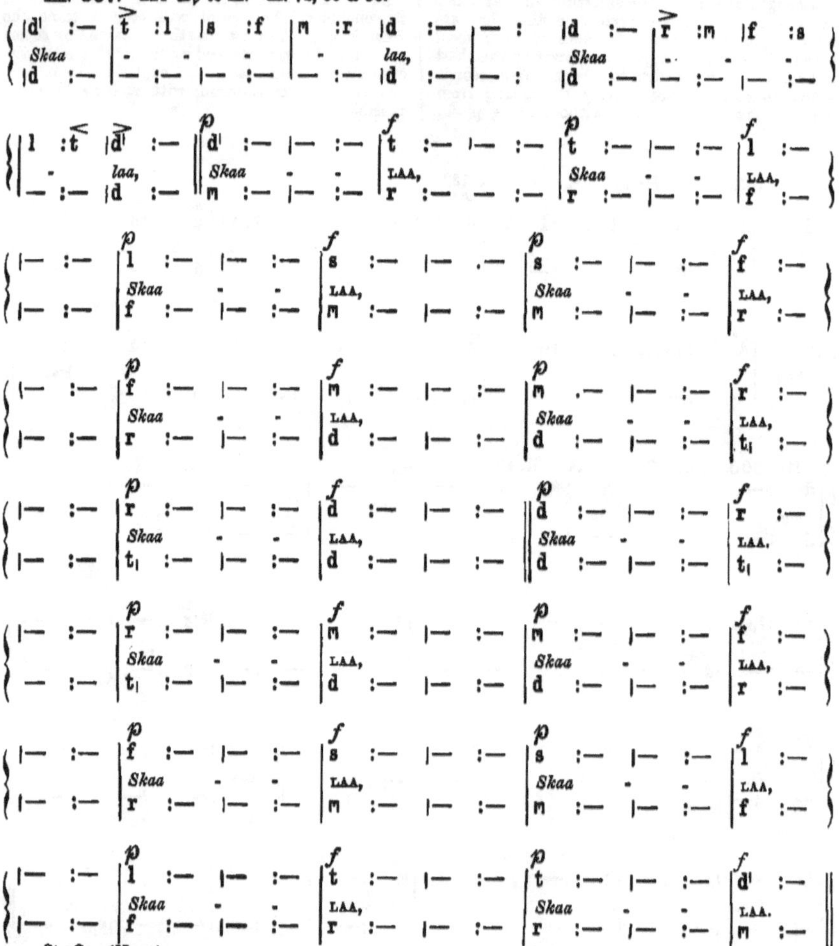

|d' :— |t :l |s :f |m :r |d :— |— : |d :— |r :m |f :s
Skaa - - - - laa, Skaa - - -
|d :— |— :— |— :— |— :— |d :— |— : |d :— |— :— |— :—

|l :t |d' :— ||*p* d' :— |— :— |*f* t :— |— :— |*p* t :— |— :— |*f* l :—
- laa, Skaa - - LAA, Skaa - - LAA,
|— :— |d :— ||m :— |— :— |r :— |— :— |r :— |— :— |f :—

|— :— |*p* l :— |— :— |*f* s :— |— .— |*p* s :— |— :— |*f* f :—
Skaa - - LAA, Skaa - - LAA,
|— :— |f :— |— :— |m :— |— :— |m :— |— :— |r :—

|— :— |*p* f :— |— :— |*f* m :— |— :— |*p* m .— |— :— |*f* r :—
Skaa - - LAA, Skaa - - LAA,
|— :— |r :— |— :— |d :— |— :— |d :— |— :— |t$_1$:—

|— :— |*p* r :— |— :— |*f* d :— |— :— ||*p* d :— |— :— |*f* r :—
Skaa - - LAA, Skaa - - LAA.
|— :— |t$_1$:— |— :— |d :— |— :— ||d :— |— :— |t$_1$:—

|— :— |*p* r :— |— :— |*f* m :— |— :— |*p* m :— |— :— |*f* f :—
Skaa - - LAA, Skaa - - LAA,
— :— |t$_1$:— |— :— |d :— |— :— |d :— |— :— |r :—

|— :— |*p* f :— |— :— |*f* s :— |— :— |*p* s :— |— :— |*f* l :—
Skaa - - LAA, Skaa - - LAA,
|— :— |r :— |— :— |m :— |— :— |m :— |— :— |f :—

|— :— |*p* l :— |— :— |*f* t :— |— :— |*p* t :— |— :— |*f* d' :— ||
Skaa - - LAA, Skaa - - LAA.
|— :— |f :— |— :— |r :— |— :— |r :— |— :— |m :— ||

St. Co. (New.)

Downward Cultivation of Voice.—Nearly all the exercises in voice training books are adapted for the extension of the voice upward but the lower tones equally require cultivation with regard to strength, if not to flexibility. Mr. Proudman found the following exercise very useful in training Contraltos and Basses for the Paris Prize Choir. To it are added two exercises from other teachers. These exercises have added to them, here, an accompanying *upper* part to be sung *piano*.

Ex. 308. *cres - - - cen - do. dim.* *J. P.*

| d' :— \|— :— \|m :s \|f :— \|m :r \|d :— ‖
| Skaa - - - - - - - - laa.
| d' :t .l \|s .f :m .r \|d :t_1 \|l_1 :- .t_1 \|d :r \|m :— ‖

Ex. 309.

| d' :— \|t :— \|d' :— \|— :— ‖
| d' :t .l \|s .f :m .r \|d :— \|— :— ‖

Ex. 310.

‖ m :— \|— :f \|r :— \|d :— ‖
‖ d :m \|d :s_1 \|f_1 :— \|m_1 :— ‖

The Shake or Trill is an ornament much cultivated by the solo singer. When performed with great evenness and accuracy it produces a very delightful effect upon the hearer. It consists in rapidly alternating the principal tone with the tone *above it* in the scale. When a shake is introduced in a close, it is usual to commence it by accenting the *principal* tone. Thus if the cadence is **r. r | d** the singer would strike **r m r m r m** &c., accenting the **r**, and ending thus:—**m r d e r**. When a Shake is introduced in the course of a song, for mere ornament, it is usual to commence it by accenting the higher tone thus:—**m r m r m r** &c., accenting the **m** and closing thus:—**m r de m r**. Mdme. Seiler says that the most beautiful trill is formed by practising triplets, thus:—**m r m r m r**, accenting first the higher and next the lower tone. She recommends that the trill should be practised at first *always piano*, to the syllable *koo* on each tone, and afterwards with other syllables slurred. The mouth, she says, must continue immovably open and the tongue must lie perfectly still. The trill must be sung very slowly at first; afterwards quicker and quicker. But it is no trill directly the two tones lose their distinctness.

The Swell, that is the practice of a lengthened *Crescendo* and *Diminuendo* on each tone of the scale, was at one time much practised by voice trainers, but it has been found injurious to many voices. Garcia speaks of it as a last acquirement. Mdme. Seiler condemns it in the early steps and even Cruvelli has abandoned it in the first part of his course. It is exceedingly difficult to perform this exercise with perfect evenness, that is without giving a jagged shake to the tone; and it is especially difficult to make the *diminuendo* as good as the *crescendo*. It was common, in a swell on the optional tones, to allow the singer to change register, so as to get the middle part of the swell on the lower and stronger of the two registers; this also required much art. Those however who wish to attain that magic power—a perfect control of the voice on every tone, in all its gradations of force, are commended to careful daily practice and a voice trainer.

The Appoggiatura (appod·jyatoo·ra) is a grace note placed before a principal note, and occupying the place immediately above or below it. The long Appoggiatura occupies half the time properly belonging to the note before which it is placed, which time it takes from that note. Thus Haydn writes, :m | f :— :s | m :— ‖. But by means of appoggiaturas he directs us to sing thus, :m | f :— :l.s | f :m ‖. In the Tonic Sol-fa Notation there is no sign for the long Appoggiatura, it being thought much better to write the notes in the time in which they are to be sung. The *short Appoggiatura* can scarcely be said to take any time from the note before which it is placed. It only gives a kind of "fillip" to the accent. It is expressed in the Sol-fa Notation by a note like a bridge note of transition, distinguished from that however, by being in italic type, thus ʳd.

The Turn.—The direct Turn which is most common, consists of a triplet of notes beginning with that above the principal tone. Thus | f : f | m :— with a direct Turn on the second f would be sung thus, | f :sfm.f | m :— ||. (3 over sfm) As the writing of this Turn would spread out the music too much it is better to employ the sign of the common notation, thus ~. The *inverted Turn* consists of a triplet of notes beginning below the principal note. Thus | d : d with an inverted Turn of the second note would be | d :$t_1$dr.d ||. (3 over $t_1$dr) The sign for this is ≀. When either the first or last note of the triplet has to be sharpened, this will be expressed by writing, in small size, the altered note under or over the ~. Thus re (fe over, m under the ~) would be sung | femre.m ||. Both these Turns when used in a cadence may sometimes be allowed to delay the time, but not when they occur in the course of a piece. They should be delivered with subdued voice, but with great clearness. The direct turn gives spirit to the expression, the inverted turn gives tenderness.

"**The natural voice,**" says Nauenburg, "is merely the raw material, which has to be *elaborated* into an instrument of art. Even in the most favourable organization, if the voice be uncultivated, there will be found side by side with healthy and powerful tones, others that are sickly, feeble, shrill, in short, unavailable for the purposes of art, until they are trained and beautified. Indeed, the greatest irregularities come to light in voices in which the natural development of the organ has already been disturbed by unregulated singing and various physical influences. High tones, wrested from nature, will by-and-bye rob the lower tones of that clear ring of true *voice* which we call *Klang*, and of *fulness*. So long as the body, and with it the vocal organs, are yet growing, the voice will doubtless stand a good deal of mismanagement, but it is sure to collapse when the physical strength can no longer withstand unnatural treatment. The forced tones below as well as above, often lose their fulness and energy, nay, there occasionally happens quite a new break of the voice. Such results plainly prove that those tones *were forced*, and not founded in the nature of the organ."

Voice exercises should be repeated every year, and at the opening of every season of singing practice meetings. Every one should seek to have a *cultivated* voice. The cultivated voice is known from another by its first sound. There is no mistaking *the master of his instrument*.

Finally, let us remember two things. First, that even music must be enjoyed "soberly," and the more steadily and soberly it is pursued the more *fresh* will be our desire for its pleasures and the more keen the enjoyment they bring. And last, that all this vocal culture only puts into our hands a delicate but effective *instrument*. See, reader, that you use it nobly. Exercise yourself to win a humble, true, and joyous soul, and let your heart be heard singing in your voice. Use that voice for social recreation—innocent and elevating. But use it most rejoicingly for "the service of song in the house of the Lord." If the singing at your place of worship does not satisfy you, try to improve it; but first of all show that you mean *cheerfully* to fulfil *your own personal duty* of vocal praise, whoever leads the singing, whatever tunes are used and howsoever the organ is played.

THE CERTIFICATES.

The Tonic Sol-fa movement has been distinguished from all other efforts to promote music among the people by its System of Certificates for practice and theory. These certificates have grown into common use and general acceptance, partly through the good will of teachers and pupils towards the method and their desire to testify a grateful love—a proud fealty to it,—but chiefly because of their proved advantages. For the true pupil they find out (what he wants to know) his *weak places*, shew him in what direction *self-teaching* is specially demanded, and give him the *confidence* of knowing that he has really and satisfactorily reached a certain stage. When some unloving, unsocial pupil boasts that "he *could* take the certificate if he *would*," the surest way to destroy his boast is to try him. For the true teacher (who knows how easy it is to obtain merely one-sided or merely collective results and how deceptive) they offer the *only* practicable means of guaging his real work. The ambition to obtain them also promotes such an amount of home work that fully four-folds (as has been ascertained) the usefulness of the class.

All faithful teachers of our method "put honour" on the certificates, by definitely preparing the class, lesson by lesson, for each of the requirements, by making them necessary for admission to their higher classes, and above all by *inflexibly* refusing to allow uncertificated singers—pupils ungrateful to the method and careless of their own progress and their teacher's honour—to take part in any public Demonstration or Concert. This is commonly the strongest power with which the teacher can enforce self-drill at home. Woe to the teacher who, by weakly yielding, throws this power away.

Our Certificates have been already accepted by other societies than our own as grounds of admission to Crystal Palace choirs, to Choral Societies, and to Precentorships. The more faithful we are to ourselves, in this matter, the more will our higher certificates grow in public acceptance and usefulness.

QUESTIONS FOR WRITTEN AND ORAL EXAMINATION.

DOCTRINE.

1. What is meant by transition of two removes? In going to the second sharp key, what tones of the old key are blotted out, and what tones of the new key are introduced? How does this move the key tone? In going to the second flat key, what tones of the old key are blotted out and what of the new introduced? How does this move the key tone? p. 117.

2. What emotion does the second sharp remove express?—what the second flat? For what purpose is a *principal* second remove chiefly used? How is a *subordinate* second remove commonly employed?

3. What are the three points to be observed in helping pupils to master Transitions? What are the points which make some transitions easier than others? What points make them more difficult?

4. In transition of three flat removes what Modulation generally takes place? What Modulation usually accompanies three sharp removes? What physical changes may, or may not be made in a transition of three removes? What is the common mental effect of three flat removes?—of three sharp removes?

5. What are the general principles which should guide us in fixing the speed of movement and the degrees of Force in singing? Which should be more studied—the actual words or the mood of mind in which they are uttered? Give an illustration. What is the exercise, in connection with this subject, which is of chief value? p. 130.

6 What kinds of passages should be sung loudly and quickly? Mention four kinds with illustrations to each.

7. What kind of passages should be sung loudly and slowly?

8. What kinds of passages should be sung softly and slowly? Mention five kinds with illustrations to each.

9. What kinds of passages should be sung softly and quickly? Mention three kinds with illustrations to each.

10. What kind of passages should be sung with a gradual change from loud to soft? Give illustrations from memory.

11. What is the mental effect of a sudden change from loud to soft on single tones? Give illustrations.

12. What kind of passages should be sung with a gradual change from soft to loud? Give illustrations.

13. What is the mental effect of a change from soft to loud on a single tone? Give illustrations.

14. What kind of Phrasing is more important than the proper division and marking out of the parts of a melody? What habit should the singer form in order to perceive quickly the proper phrasing of words? When musical and poetical phrasing do not agree, which of the two should yield? In Chorus singing, what is important in reference to phrasing? p. 135.

15. How often should the use of the articulation exercises of this step be revived? In what circumstances will a mastery of the consonants render singing intelligible without much study of the vowels? In what kind of singing is a study of the vowels absolutely necessary for clearness and beauty? In what elements of speech do the local differences and vulgarisms chiefly shew themselves? In what respects do the vowels commonly called short, in English, differ from the long vowels? What is the new art of vowel utterance which the singer has to learn but which the speaker does not require? p. 136.

16. If the cavities of the throat and mouth are held open steadily in any one fixed form while voice is produced, what element of speech will result? How many vowels are possible? Name the six principal vowels going upward in the order of natural pitch?

17. In what manner in speaking do we name the vowel sounds? What vowel forms the centre of the vowel scale? In proceeding upwards what change takes place with the middle of the tongue? In proceeding downwards how do the lips change their position? For which vowels is the back of the tongue highest and for which vowels is the tongue altogether lowest? Give the letter names (not the sounds) of the three principal descending vowels,—of the two principal less sonorous ascending vowels,—of the four ascending vowels that are commonly short in speech,—of the three more obscure descending vowels.

18. Mention three words in which *aa* occurs, without being so spelt. How is this sound formed? Give the position of the lips, teeth and tongue. How is the deeper, thicker, *ah* formed? What defects in pronouncing this vowel are common in your neighbourhood?

19. Mention three words in which *au* occurs without being so spelt. What is the position of the tongue and lips in forming this sound? What difficulties are found in sustaining *au*? In what pitch of what voice is there a tendency to change this vowel? What wrong pronunciation of this vowel are you familiar with? p. 138.

20. Mention three words in which the sound *oa* occurs, without being so spelt. What are the positions of the tongue, lips and teeth in forming this vowel? What are the tendencies of this vowel in the lower pitches and in the higher pitches? What faults in sounding this vowel are you practically acquainted with?

21. Mention three words in which *oo* occurs, though not so spelt. What is the position of the tongue, lips and teeth in producing this vowel? In which voice, and in what pitch of it has this vowel a tendency to change? Name any defects in sounding *oo* with which you are familiar.

22. Mention three words in which the sound *ai* occurs, but not so spelt. What is the position of the lips, teeth and tongue for this vowel? In which voice and at what pitch has it a tendency to change? How is this vowel commonly mispronounced?

23. Mention three words in which the sound *ee* occurs, though not so spelt. What is the position of the tongue and teeth in producing *ee*? In which voice and at what part of its pitch is this vowel likely to alter?

24. Mention three words in which the sound *u* occurs, though not so spelt. What is the position of tongue, lips and teeth in holding this vowel? In what voice and at what part of its pitch is this vowel most likely to change? What defective pronunciation of it do you know? p. 139.

25. Mention two words in which the sound *a* occurs, though not so spelt. What is the position of the tongue, teeth and lips for this vowel? What is the natural change of *a* at high pitches? What defective pronunciations of this vowel are you personally acquainted with?

26. Mention three words in which the sound *e* occurs, though not so spelt. What is the difference between the positions of the organs in *ai* and in *e*? What is *e* likely to change into at high

pitches? What defects do you notice in the pronunciation of this vowel?

27. Mention three words in which the sound *i* occurs, in one of them at least the *i* being differently spelt. What is the difference of the position of the organs for *ee* and for *i*? What faults do you know of in the pronunciation of this vowel?

28. Mention three words in which the sound *uo* occurs, though not so spelt. What is the difference in the position of the organs for *oo* and for *uo*? What wrong pronunciation of this vowel are you acquainted with? p. 141.

29. Mention three words in which the sound *o* occurs. What is the difference between the position of the organs for *au* and *o*? What three other cases are there in which vowel positions differ in the same way, though otherwise alike? Have you noticed any mispronunciation of *o*?

30. How is *the* pronounced before a vowel?—how before a consonant? How is *my* pronounced?

31. What are the four principal diphthongs in the English Language? What vowel is treated along with the diphthongs, and why? What is the difference between two vowels put close together and a diphthong? Give an illustration. What is the difference between a diphthong and a digraph? Of the three elements of a diphthong, which is neither the longest nor the shortest? Of the two vowel elements, which generally has the accent? p. 142.

32. Mention three words in which the diphthong *ei* occurs, though not so spelt. On which vowel element does the stress fall, and what sound should be given to that element in singing? How should the glide be treated?

33. Mention three words in which the sound *oi* occurs, though not so spelt. What is the proper first vowel element and which of the two should be prolonged? What error in pronouncing this diphthong have you noticed?

34. Mention three words in which the sound *ou* occurs, though not so spelt. What is the second vowel element, and which of the two should be prolonged in singing and with what sound?

35. Mention three words in which the sound *eu* occurs, though not so spelt. What is the second element, what is the first? Which has to be prolonged in singing? What error has to be avoided in pronouncing *t* and *d* before *eu*?

36. What other diphthongs can you describe?

37. Mention three words in which the sound *ao* occurs, though not so spelt. What is the difference in the position of the organs for *oa* and for *ao*? How may the pronunciation of this vowel be easily attained?

38. What are the musical properties proper to a Response? p. 144.

39. What are the essentials of a Chant? Describe the form of an Anglican Chant. What are two of the common faults in the construction of an Anglican Chant?

40. How did the modern hymn tune originate? What are some of the defects of structure which often unfit it for the voice of a Congregation?

41. How does the speed of a hymn tune affect its harmonic character?

42. How does the speed of a tune affect the rhythmical impression it produces, and what sort of speed demands the closer attention to rhythmical proportion and balance? p. 145.

43. What sort of tunes are best adapted to the bold and spirited hymns, and how do tunes of this character change their mental effect when sung slowly? What kind of tune is best adapted to hymns of cheerful emotion, and how do such tunes alter their mental effect when sung slowly?

44. What is the sort of tune which best suits hymns of didactic and varied character?

45. How can a precentor best remind a Congregation of a change of sentiment in the hymn, and secure the proper expression?

46. How do Anthems essentially differ from Hymn tunes in their aim and in their musical character? When Anthems are meant for congregational use, what musical difficulties should be avoided? Explain the words Decani, Cantoris, Full, Verse.

47. What are the musical characteristics of a Madrigal? What kind of sentiment often characterises a Madrigal? What is a Ballet?

48. For what peculiarities of vocal arrangement was the English Glee specially adapted? What sort of Glees will bear a number of voices on each part?

49. How does the Part-Song differ from the Glee, and how does it differ from the Madrigal? How does the Harmonised Air differ from the Part-Song? p. 146.

50. Whence arises the importance of music for equal voices? p. 149.

51. For what vocal arrangement are Oratorio Choruses specially adapted?

52. What is the style of Operatic Choruses? p. 146.

53. What is a Canon, and what is meant by "a Canon four in two"?

54. How does a Fugue differ from a Canon? p. 147.

55. What are the essentials of a Fugue, and what other musical contrivances are necessary to a fully developed Fugue? What sort of pieces may be called Fugal Passages or movements rather than Fugues?

56. What is a Subject in Fugue, and what is meant by its various expositions?

57. What is a Response in Fugue? Where does it commence the first time it occurs, and what are some of the various ways in which it is treated?

58. What is the Counter-subject in Fugue? What other forms often take the place of one distinct Counter-subject?

59. What is Stretto, and what is its emotional effect?

60. What is an Organ-point, and what is its effect?

61. How does a Recitative differ from the good recitation of a Chant? How should Recitative be sung and what is the chief use of it? p. 148.

62. What is an Opera, and why does a combination of arts fail to produce the highest developement in any one of them?

63. What is an Oratorio, and how does it differ from the Opera?

64. What is a Cantata?

65. What choral contrivances are allowable when Composers write "parts" which are beyond the fair limits of a chorus voice? p. 149.

66. In what respect does a wide musical pipe differ in its effect from a narrow one? What kind of Resonance or Timbre is produced by a full distended mouth,—what by a narrow mouth,—what by a mouth of medium shape and size?

67. In what places of melody ought we not to take breath, and in what places are we obliged to do so?

68. How is the Portamento made? In what cases should it be used in Solo singing and in Chorus singing?

69. Whence arises the difficulty of carrying out voice exercises in a mixed class? In what cases only can voice training in a class be profitable? In what cases is it likely to be injurious? What is the secret of success in voice exercises? What, according to Nauenburg, are the three objects of voice training? What other object should be kept in view?

70. What is the use of the large Voice Modulator? p. 150.

71. How is flexibility of voice secured?

72. By what kind of practice is strength of voice maintained?

73. What is the special use of downward voice cultivation exercises?

74. In what does the Shake or Trill consist? In what case does the singer usually accent the principal tone, and how does he close?—in what case the upper tone, and how does he then close? How does Madame Seiler recommend that the Trill should be practised?

75. What is a Swell? Why has it been abandoned in the early steps?

76. What is the long Appoggiatura, and how is it expressed in the Sol-fa notation? What is the short Appoggiatura, and how is it expressed in the Sol-fa notation? p. 155.

77. What is the direct Turn and how is it written? What is the inverted Turn and how is it written?

78. What irregularities are commonly found in the natural uncultivated voice? What injury is produced by high tones wrested from nature?

79. What two things must we constantly bear in mind if we would gather the highest possible enjoyment from music?

PRACTICE.

80. Sing your part in Exs. 243 to 248, whichever the Examiner chooses.

81. Ditto Exs. 249 to 255.

82. Work Exs. 256 to 259, whichever the Examiner selects.

83. Work Exs. 260, 261, whichever the Examiner selects.

84. Work Exs. 262 to 271, whichever the Examiner selects.

85. Work Exs. 272, 273, whichever the Examiner selects.

86. Sing any one of the Exs. 274 to 280 which the Examiner may select.

87. Sing any of the Exs. 281 to 291, which the Examiner may select.

88. Sing Ex. 292.

89. Sing any of the Exs. 293 to 298 which the Examiner may select.

90. Sing (if your voice is bass) *to the correct vowel* "passing by" Add. Ex. p. 79, sc. 3, m. 4, second bass,—"go" Add. Ex. p. 33, sc. 2, last note, bass,—"amain," Add. Ex. p. 64, sc. 1,—"be" Add. Ex. p. 71, 1st pulse,—"love" Add. Ex. p. 61, sc. 3, m. 3.

91. Sing (if your voice is soprano) *to the correct vowel*, "la" Add. Ex. p. 8, sc. 5, m. 3, 1st note,—"storm" Add. Ex. p. 96, sc. 2, m. 3,—"roar" Add. Ex. p. 64, sc. 4, m. 1, 2, 3, and 4,—"troops" Add. Ex. p. 20, m. 4,—"shadows" Add. Ex. p. 43, sc. 3, m. 6,—"Amen" the last syllable St. Co.. Ex. 172.

92. Sing (whatever your voice) *to the correct vowel*, "love loves" St. Co., Ex. 145,—"rills" Add. Ex. p. 62, sc. 4, m. 4,—"along" St. Co., Ex. 175.

93. Sing, first using the vowel *aa* and then *a*, "last" Add. Ex. p. 39, sc. 3, m. 2, and "path" Add. Ex. p. 7, sc. 4, m. 4. Sing also first using *u* and then *aa* to the first syllable "away" Add. Ex. p. 53, sc. 2.

94. Find words in Add. Ex. p. 34 and 53 in which *ai* is sometimes sounded instead of *a*.

95. Find cases in St. Co. Ex. 144 in which *ai* is sometimes sounded for the article *a*.

96. Find words in St. Co Exs. 78 and 113 in which *ei* is sometimes sounded instead of *i*. See Ex. 299.

97. Find a word in St. Co. Ex. 143 in which *oa* is sometimes sounded instead of the sound *u*.

98. Find a word in St. Co. Ex. 98 in which *u* is sometimes sounded instead of *o*.

99. Find a word in St. Co. Ex. 115 in which *i* is sometimes sounded instead of *e*.

100. Find a word in St. Co. Ex. 77 in which *u* is sometimes sounded instead of *e*.

101. Find a word in Add. Ex. p. 77 in which *e* is sometimes sounded instead of *u*.

102. Find words in Add. Ex. p. 3 in which *ee-aa* is sometimes sounded before *r* instead of *ee* with the mere vanishing *u*.

103. Find cases in St. Co. Ex. 144 and 145 in which "the" before a consonant is sometimes sounded *thee* instead of *thu*.

104. Find cases in St. Co. Ex. 144 and 145 in which "the" before a vowel is sometimes sounded *thu* instead of *thee*.

105. Find four cases in St. Co. Ex. 175 of the diphthong which is sounded *ei*, and sing them as directed.

106. Sing the diphthong *oi* in Ex. 113 as directed.

107. Sing the diphthong *ou* in Ex. 69 as directed.

108. Sing the diphthong sounded *eu* in St. Co. Ex. 145, v. 3, m. 2, dwelling on the second element.

109. Without referring to St. Co. write an analysis of "Thou shalt shew me," Add. Ex. p. 7.

110. Write an analysis of the fugal imitations in "Hallelujah Amen," Add. Ex. p. 26.

111. Write a fugal analysis of the first movement in "Theme sublime," Add. Ex. p. 66.

112. Write a fugal analysis of the second and thi rd movements of "Theme sublime," Add. Ex. p. 67.

113. Write a fugal analysis of "How lovely," Add. p. 58.

114. Answer the question in Ex. 299.

APPENDIX.—CHROMATIC TONES.

Accidental Sharps and Flats.—The notes of the Chromatic Scale, which lie between the notes of the ordinary scale, are as follows :—

Flat.	Scale.	Sharps.
	t	
ta		le
	l	
la		se
	s	
		fe
	f	
	m	
ma		re
	r	
ra		de
	d	

The commonest and easiest use of Chromatic notes is as waving tones coming from and returning to the note a little step above or below.

Example of First Presentation: Sharps.—Teacher sings to *laa*, and points on modulator **d t_1 d** several times. He then does the same with **s fe s**. Without pointing he then sings, also to *laa*, **m re m** several times, questioning the class, varying it with **m r m**, and making them feel the resemblance to **d t_1 d** and **s fe s**, and the contrast with **m r m**. He elicits the fact gradually that the new note is higher than **r**; then names it, and gets the class to sing it. He then explains the names for all the sharps of the scale, **de re fe se le**, and gives copious exercises on them, always waving from and to the tone next above.

Flats.—These must be taught by comparison with **m f m**. Unlike the sharps they are most easily approached from the tone below. Thus :—

l ta l   r ma r

s la s   d ra d

Exercise on Waving Chromatics.

| d' :t :d' | t :le :t | l :se :l | s :fe:s |
| f :m :f | m :re :m | r :de :r | d :- :- ||

Stepwise Motion.—The Chromatic sounds must also be mastered in the form of stepwise progression in an upward or downward direction, thus :—

d	de	r	t	ta	l
r	re	m	l	la	s
f	fe	s	s	fe	f
s	se	l	m	ma	r
l	le	t	r	ra	d

There is no model in the common scale for this. The notes may first be introduced as an ear exercise, the teacher singing to *laa* **d r**, and then **d de r**, and getting the class to perceive the new tone.

Leaps.—When both the Flats and the Sharps are familiar as waving tones and in stepwise motion, they may be approached and quitted by leaps, as frequently happens in modern music. All the exercises on leaps should be formed upon one pattern, namely, first giving the intervening note, and then omitting it. For example :—

Sharps.

m r de r m de r	d r re m d re m
f m re m f re m	f s se l f se l
l s fe s l fe s	s l le t s le t
d' t le t d' le t	s l le t s le t
f r de r f de r	r re m f r re f

Flats.

d r ma r d ma r	d' t ta l d' ta l
t_1 d ra d t_1 ra d	t l la s t la s
f s la s f la s	f m ma r f ma r
s l ta l s ta l	m r ra d m ra d
d' l la s d' la s	d r ma r d ma r
d' ta l s d' ta s	s la s f s la f

If the Voluntaries be all constructed on this principle, power over these chromatic leaps will gradually be gained.

Transitional Models.—It will be noticed that some of the above progressions of notes have already been studied under Transition (imperfect method) or the Minor Mode, and many difficult intervals which occur, such as **m ta, fe d', l de r, ta de'**, &c., are best referred to their prototypes in the key in which they really are.

Hints for teaching difficult intervals in the Minor Mode, by R. Dunstan, Mus.Bac.

Fah, Se.—This interval may easily be mastered by singing the following exercises from the modulator :—

| m :— | l :— | — ‖

:m | f :m | f :l | se :— | — ‖

:l | se :— | se :l | f :— | l :— | f :— | — ‖

| f :— | l :— | f :— | — ‖

:l | se :l | f :l | se :l | f ‖

:l | se :— | f :— | m ‖

:m | f :— | se :— | l ‖

Doh' Se—

| l :— | d' :— | l :d' | l :se | l :d'

| d' :l | se :— | d' :— | se :— | l :— ‖

If the pupil "thinks of *laa*" he will readily be able to attack *se* (a little step below it) from any other note.

Intervals.—The Chromatic tones may also be studied from the point of view of intervals. Without going into the subject of Intervals generally, we may explain that for the purposes of Intervals the scale is divided into twelve little steps, each of which, roughly speaking, is of the distance between **d** t_1. The following table shows the number of semi-tones which each interval contains :—

	Semi-tones.	Example.
Minor Second	1 ———	d t_1
Major Second..............	2 ———	s f
Augmented Second	3 ———	d re
Minor Third	3 ———	l d'
Major Third	4 ———	d m
Diminished Third	2 ———	f re
Perfect Fourth	5 ———	s d'
Augmented Fourth, or Pluperfect ..	6 ———	f t
Diminished Fourth	4 ———	se d'
Perfect Fifth	7 ———	d s
Diminished Fifth, or Imperfect	6 ———	t_1 f
Augmented Fifth	8 ———	d se
Major Sixth	9 ———	s m'
Minor Sixth	8 ———	m d'
Augmented Sixth	10 ———	f re'
Major Seventh	11 ———	d t
Minor Seventh	10 ———	s_1 f
Diminished Seventh	9 ———	t_1 l
Octave	12 ———	d d'

It matters not whether the Intervals be comprised within the notes of the common scale or not. A Minor Third is the same Interval whether it occurs as l_1 **d** or as **d ma**. The teacher may, therefore, point Voluntaries which exhaust any one interval, presenting it in all its forms in the scale, both ascending and descending. For example, a succession of Minor Seconds :—

d t_1 r de m re f m s fe l se t le d' t d'

In reverse order :—

t d' le t se l fe s m f re m de r t_1 d

These two exercises, it will be observed, also comprise Minor and Diminished Thirds. Another exercise on Minor Thirds would be :—

l_1 d t_1 t_1 r d d ma r r f

m m s f f la s s ta l

Which could be shortened afterwards to :—

l_1 d t_1 r d ma r f m s f la s ta l

This process can be continued with the easier intervals, but with the wider and more difficult ones it would involve melodies which would be practically unsingable. The best practical course is for the teacher to follow, in his Voluntaries, the actual habits of composers, and present Chromatics interspersed with Diatonic notes.

Naming of Intervals.—Notice that intervals formed by two adjoining notes are seconds, however either of the two may be inflected; those formed by three adjoining notes, thirds, and so on. Thus **d ra, d r,** and **d re** are all seconds (Minor, Major, and Augmented), as also are **f fe, f s,** and **f se**. On the pianoforte **d re** is the same as **d ma**, and **f se** the same as **f la**. But in the language of intervals they are different. Thus **d re** is a second (augmented) because the sounds from which it is derived (**d r**) are two adjoining notes, and **d ma** is a third (minor) because the interval from which it is derived (**d** and **m**) is formed by *three* adjoining notes.

Flats or Sharps.—The teacher who wishes to point chromatic voluntaries may fairly ask, should I point sharps or flats, **d ra** or **d de**; **l le t** or **l ta t**; **s la l** or **s se l**. The notes being the same on the pianoforte, composers are often indifferent as to which they write. Some theorists hold that flats should generally be preferred to sharps, **r ma m** instead of **r re m**, &c. In music, however, especially of a popular kind, sharps are much more common than flats, and flats (because they are less often encountered) are more difficult to singers. The best way is for the teacher to point both by turns, and when he wishes his voluntary to be specially searching and difficult, to prefer flats.

The Extended Modulator.—It is to be wished that the Extended Modulator, which gives the complete range of keys, may become more common, and supersede, for advanced pupils, the small sectional modulators. It affords far better practice to the pupils, and gives much greater scope to a teacher whose fancy for the invention of melody is active. In using the Extended Modulator the teacher should always observe absolute pitch. Each column represents a key, and in the proper key the teacher should start. As a rule it is best to begin in C and return to it at the close of the voluntary. The loss of pitch, if any, can then be ascertained. The following will serve as a specimen of a somewhat advanced voluntary on the Extended Modulator:—

St. Co. (*New*).

C. E♭.
d' s m d m s d' — $^{d'}$l m d l, d m l —

C. D♭. E♭.
l se t l — ^{l}d' t r' d' $^{d'}$t l d' t ^{t}l s

G. A♭.
t l ^{l}f m s f m r f t, d — ^{d}t, d r m

G♭. A♭.
d ^{d}r m f s m — s, l, t, d l, ^{l,}s, l, t, d

B♭. C. D.
l, ^{l,}s, l, t, d l, ^{l,}s l t d' l ^{l}s l t d'

C.
l s f ^{f}s l t d' l s f m r s t, s d

In this voluntary the changes of key are made in the easiest way, by passing horizontally to a note of the same pitch in the new key. The more difficult exercise is to leap obliquely to a note of different pitch in the new key. The following is an example:—

C. A♭.
s m' d' t d' r' — l $^{d'}$m f r l, t, d — s,

E♭. F.
^{l,}r t, d r ^{m}r t, d r f m l s — d f m —

B♭. E♭. C.
^{r}l, d f m ^{l,}m se t l d' — d' — $^{de'}$m' m' r' l

r' r' d' s l s t l d' — t — d' — —

The principles on which all Voluntaries on the Extended Modulator should be constructed are these:—

1. Take a phrase of six or eight notes, and having pointed it in one key seek to get imitations of it in other keys, and in their relative Minors.
2. Never change key without introducing promptly the distinguishing tones of the new key. A change of column without the new tones is merely a change of notation.
3. Do not be afraid to repeat a note. All good melodies repeat notes.
4. If possible, let your phrases fall into measures and become rhythmical. This makes the singing more spirited.

A VOCABULARY OF MUSICAL TERMS.

NOTE.—Mr. ALEXANDER J. ELLIS, who has kindly added the pronunciations to the following words, states that they are mere English imitations of Italian, but that a very near approach to the true Italian pronunciations will be made, if in those given *ai* is never allowed to vanish into *ee*, or *oa* into *oo*; if *aa* be used always for *a*, and *ee* for *i*; the broad *ae* (St. Co., p. 140) for *e*, and the broad *ao* (St. Co., p. 143) for *o*; if also the consonants which are here doubled, be really doubled in speech, as in "book-keeping," "boot-tree," "mis-sent," "un-noticed"; and *r'* be *always* very strongly trilled. Italians do not generally pronounce their vowels so short as English short vowels, or so long as English long vowels. The full stop turned upwards (·) in the middle of a word, throws the accent on what precedes. If there are two such in one word, the first one has less weight than the second.

Abbandono, con (*koan abbandoa·noa*), with self-abandonment.

Accelerando (*atchel·air'an·doa*), more and more quickly.

Accelerato (*atchel·air'aa·toa*), increased in rapidity.

Acciaccatura (*at·chiak·katoo·r'a*), a short appoggiatura.

Adagio (*adaa·jioa*), very slow and expressive.

Adagio Assai or **Molto** (*adaa·jioa assaa·i, moal·toa*), extremely slow and expressive.

Adagio Cantabile e Sostenuto (*adaa·jioa kantab·ilai ai sostenoo·toa*), slow, sustained, in a singing manner.

Adagissimo (*adaajis·simoa*), slower than *adagio*.

Ad libitum (*ad lib·itum*), Latin, at will or discretion.

Affettuoso (*affet·too-oa·soa*), with tenderness and pathos.

Afflizione, con (*koan afflee·tsioa·nai*), in a manner expressive of grief.

Agilità, con (*koan ajee·litaa·*), with lightness and agility.

Agitato (*aj·itaa·toa*), with agitation.

Alla Breve (*al·aa brev·ai*), a quick species of common time used in Church music.

Alla Cappella (*al·laa kapel·laa*), in the Church style.

Alla Stretta (*al·laa str'ait·taa*), increasing the time.

Allargando (*al·laar'gan·doa*), with free, broad style.

Allegretto (*al·legr'ait·toa*), cheerful. Not so quick as *Allegro*.

Allegro (*alleg·r'oa*), quick, lively. Sometimes modified by the addition of other words, as follows:

Allegro Assai (*alleg·r'oa assaa·i*), very quick.

Allegro con moto (*alleg·r'oa koan mo·toa*), with a quick lively movement.

Allegro con Spirito (*alleg·r'oa koan spee·r'itoa*) quick. With spirit.

Allegro di Molto (*alleg·r'oa dee moal·toa*), exceedingly quick.

Allegro veloce (*alleg·r'oa velo·chai*), quick, to absolute rapidity.

Allegro vivace (*alleg·r'oa veevaa·chai*), with vivacity.

Allegrissimo (*allegr'ees·simoa*), superlative of *Allegro*.

Amabile (*amaa·bilai*), amiably.

Amoroso (*am·oar'oa·soa*), lovingly, tenderly.

Andante (*andan·tai*), "going" easily and rather slowly

Andante Affettuoso (*andan·tai affettoo-oa·soa*), slow, with much pathos.

Andante Cantabile (*andan·tai kantab·ilai*), slow and in a singing style.

Andante con Moto (*andan·tai koan mo·toa*), slow and with emotion.

Andante grazisoso (*andan·tai gr'aa·tsioa·soa*), slow and gracefully.

Andante Maestoso (*andan·tai maa·estoa·soa*), slow and with majesty.

Andante non troppo (*andan·tai non tr'op·poa*), slow but not in excess.

Andantino (*an·dantee·noa*), a little slower than *Andante*,—moving gently.

Animato (*an·imaa·toa*), with animation.

Anima con (*koan an·imaa*), with soul, with fervour.

A plomb (*aa ploan'*), French,—*n'* indicating French nasality,—in a decisive, firm, steady manner.

Appassionato (*appas·sioanaa·toa*), with fervid, impassioned emotion.

Appoggiatura (*appod·jiaatoo·r'aa*), a forestroke.

Ardito (*aar'dee·toa*), with ardour.

A tempo (*aa tem·poa*), after a change in speed, to return to the original rate of movement.

A tempo giusto (*aa tem·poa joos·toa*), in strict and equal time.

A tempo ordinario (*aa tem·poa or'dinaa·r'ioa*), in an ordinary rate of time.

Audace (*oudaa·chai*), better (*aaoo-daa·chai*), bold, fearless, impudent.

Al, All', Alla, Alle, Allo, Ai (*al, all, al·laa, al·lai, al·loa, aa·i*), to the, or, in the style of.

Basso Primo (*bas·soa pree·moa*), First Bass.

Basso Secondo (*bas·soa saikoan·doa*), Second Bass.

Bene Placito (*ben·ai plaa·chitoa*), at will.

Ben Marcato (*ben maar'kaa·toa*), in a clear, distinct, strongly marked manner.

Bis (*bees*), or (*bis*) as Latin; twice. A passage indicated by a stroke to be performed twice.

Bravura (*bravoo·r'aa*), with vigour, with boldness.

Brioso (*bree-oa·soa*) with spirit.

Brillante (*br'illan·tai*), in a showy, sparkling style.

Burlesco (*boor'lai·skoa*), with comic humour.

Cacophony (*kakof·uni*), English. A discordant combination of sounds.

Cadence (*kai·dens*), English. A close in melody or harmony. Also an ornamental passage at the end of a piece of music.

Cadenza (*kaden·tsaa*), Italian. An ornamental series of notes at the close of a piece of music.

Calando (*kalan·doa*), becoming softer and slower by degrees.

Cantabile (*kantab·ilai*), in a smooth, melodious, graceful, singing style.

Canticle (*kan·tikl*), English, **cantico**, pl. **cantici** (*kan·tikoa, kan·tichee*), Italian. Devotional song.

Canto (*kan·toa*), the highest part in a piece of vocal music.

Cantor (*kan·taur'*), Latin, **cantore** (*kantoa·r'ai*) Italian. A singer.

Cantoris (*kantaor·r'is*), Latin. A term used in Cathedral music, to distinguish the singers on the left side, where the Cantor or Precentor sits.

Canzonet (*kanzoanet·*), English, **canzonetto** (*kan·tsoanait·toa*), Italian. A short song.

Capriccio (*kapr'eet·chioa*), in a fanciful style

Celerità (*cheler'itaa·*), with celerity, quick.

Cavatina (*kav·atee·naa*), an air of one movement only, sometimes preceded by recitative, of a dramatic character, and generally employed in Opera.

Chorus (*kaor·r'us*), Latin, **coro** (*ko·r'oa*), Italian. A band or company of singers.

Chiaroscuro (*kyaa·r'oskoo·r'oa*), light and shade in *piano* and *forte*.

Comodo (*ko·modoa*), with composure, quietly.

Con (*koan*), with.

Con moto (*koan mo·toa*), with motion, or a spirited movement.

Con Spirito (*koan spee·r'itoa*) with quickness and spirit.

Coi, Col, Coll', Colla, Collo, (*koa·i, koal, koall, koal·laa, koal·loa*), with the.

Corale (*kor'aa·lai*), the plain chant.

Crescendo (*kr'aishen·doa*), becoming louder. Sometimes expressed thus <

Da Capo, or **D.C.** (*daa kaa·poa*), from the beginning.

Da (*daa*), from, **dal** (*daal*), from the.

Decani (*deekai·nei*), Latin. A term used in Cathedral music, to distinguish those singers who are placed on the right side of the building, (entering the choir from the nave), where the Dean sits.

Decrescendo (*dai·kr'aishen·doa*), gradually decreasing in power of tone.

Dell', Della, Dello, (*daill, dail·lau, dail·loa*) of the.

Detaché (*daitaashai*) French, make each syllable short and accent equally. French term for staccato.

Deliberato (*dailee·ber'aa·toa*) adj., **deliberatamente** (*dailee·ber'aa·tamain·tai*), adv., deliberately.

Demi (*dem·i*), English, (*du-mee*), after a consonant, (*d-mee*) after a vowel, French. A half.

Diluendo (*dee·loo-en·doa*), a washing away, a dissolving. Passages so marked to diminish in force, until they vanish into silence.

Diminuendo (*deemee·noo-en·doa*), diminishing the force.

Di Molto (*dee moal·toa*), much or very.

Dolce (*doal·chai*), in soft and sweet style.

Dolorosa (*do·loar'oa·saa*),
Dolente (*dolen·tai*), with an expression of pain, —dolorously.

Duett(*deu-et'*), English, **Duetto** (*doo-ait'toa*), Italian. A composition for two performers.

E, Ed, (*ai, aid*), and.

Eco, Ecco, (*ek'oa, ek'koa*) Italian, echo (*ek'oa*, English. A repetition or imitation of a previous passage, with some modification of tone.

Elegante (*el'aigan'tai*), with elegance.

Energico (*ener'jikoa*), con **energia** (*koan en'er'jee'aa*) **energicamente** (*ener'jikaamain'tai*), with energy.

Enharmonic (*en-haar'mon'ik*), English, **enarmonico** (*en'aar'mon'ikoa*), Italian, proceeding by quarter tones.

Espressivo (*es'pr'essee'voa*), or con **espressione** (*koan espr'es'sioa'nai*), with expression.

Extempore (*eks-tem'puri*), Latin, unpremeditated.

Facilmente (*fach'ilmain'tai*), easily, with facility.

Fermato (*fair'maa'toa*), with firmness and decision.

Fine (*fee'nai*), the end.

Forte (*for''tai*), loud.

Fortissimo (*for'tees'simoa*), very loud.

Forzando (*for'tsan'doa*), **forzato** (*for'tsaa'toa*), with peculiar emphasis or force.

Forza (*for''tsaa*), force, vehemence.

Fugato (*foogaa'toa*) in the fugue style.

Furioso (*foo'r'ioa'soa*), with rage, furiously.

Gajamenta (*gaa'yaamain'tai*), Italian, **Gaiement** (*gemon'*), French, *n'* nasal, **Gai, Gaio, Gajo,** with gaity.

Giocoso (*jokoa'soa*), humorously, with sportiveness.

Giustamente (*joo'staamain'tai*), justly, with precision.

Giusto (*joo'stoa*), in just and exact time.

Glissando (*gleessan'doa*), in a gliding manner.

Grande (*gran'dai*), great.

Grandioso (*gran'dioa'soa*), in grand and elevated style.

Gravamente (*gr'aa'vamain'tai*), with gravity, dignified, and solemn.

Grave (*gr'aa'vai*), a very slow and solemn movement.

Grazia, con (*koan gr'aa'tsiaa*), **graziosamente,** (*gr'aa'tsioa'saamain'tai*), **grazioso** (*gr'aa'tsioa'soa*), in a flowing, graceful style.

Gusto (*goo'stoa*), **gustoso** (*goostoa'soa*), con **gusto,** (*koan goo'stoa*), with taste, elegantly.

Il, (*eel*), the, as *il violino* the violin.

Impeto (*im'petoa*), con **impetuosità,** (*koan impet'oo-oa'sitaa'*), **impetuoso** (*impet'oo-oa'soa*), adj., **impetuosamente** (*impet'oo-oa'samain'tai*), adv., with impetuosity.

Imponente (*im'ponen'tai*), with haughtiness

Impromptu (*impr'om'teu*), Latin, an extemporaneous production.

Improvvisamente (*im'pr'ovvee'samain'tai*), extemporaneously.

Innocentemente (*in'noachen'taimain'tai*), **innocente** (*in'noachen'tai*), con **innocenza,** (*koan in'noachen'tsaa*), in artless simple style.

La (*laa*), the, as *la voce* (*laa vo'chai*), the voice.

Lagrimoso (*lag'r'imoa'soa*), in a mournful dolorous style.

Lamentabile (*laa'mentab'ilai*), **lamentoso** (*laa'mentoa'soa*), plaintively, mournfully.

Languente (*lan-gwen'tai*), **languido** (*lan'gwidoa*), with languor.

Largamenta (*laar'gamain'tai*), very slowly.

Larghetto (*laar'gait'toa*), a slow and measured time; but less slow than *Largo*.

Larghissimo (*laar'gees'simoa*), extremely slow.

Largo (*laar''goa*), a very slow and solemn degree of movement.

Le (*lai*), the, as *le voci* (*lai vo'chee*), fem. pl. the voices.

Legatissimo (*lai'gatees'simoa*), very smoothly connected.

Legato (*laigaa'toa*), bound or tied, in a smooth gliding manner.

Leggiero (*led'jier''oa*), with lightness.

Leggierissimo (*led'jier'ees'simoa*), with the utmost lightness and facility.

Lentando (*lentaan'doa*), with increased slowness.

Lento (*len'toa*), in slow time.

Ma (*maa*) but; as *allegro ma non troppo* (*alleg'r'oa maa non tr'op'poa*), quick, but not too much so.

Maestà, con, (*koan maa-aistaa'*), **maestoso** (*maa'aistoa'soa*), with majesty and grandeur.

Marcato (*maar'kaa'toa*), in a marked and emphatic style.

Meno (*mai'noa*), less, as *meno forte*, less loud.

Mesto (*mes'toa*), **mestoso** (*mestoa'soa*), mournfully, sadly, pathetically.

Mezza voce (*med·dzaa voa·chai*), observe *not* (*met·tsaa*), in a gentle, flute-like voice.

Mezzo (*med·dzoa* observe *not met·tsoa*), half, as *mezzo-piano*, rather soft; *mezzo-forte*, rather loud.

Moderato (*mod·air'aa·toa*), adj., **moderatamente** (*mod·air'aa·taamain·tai*), **con moderazione**, (*koan mod·air'aa·tsioo·nai*), with a moderate degree of quickness.

Moderatissimo (*mod·air'atees·simoa*), in very moderate time.

Molto (*moal·toa*), very, extremely; as *molto allegro*, very quick.

Molta voce, con (*koan moal·taa voa·chai*) with full voice.

Morendo (*mor'en·doa*), gradually subsiding, dying away.

Moto, or **con moto** (*mo·toa, koan mo·toa,* almost *mau·toa*), with agitation.

Nobile (*nob·ilai*), **nobilmente** (*nob·ilmain·tai*), with nobleness, grandeur.

Non (*non*) an adverb of negation, generally associated with *troppo* as,—

Non troppo allegro (*non tr'op·poa alleg·r'oa*), **non troppo presto** (*non tr'op·poa pr'es·toa*), not too quick.

Non molto (*non moal·toa*), not very much; as *non molto allegro*, not very quick.

Non tanto (*non tan·toa*), not too much; as *allegro non tanto*, not too quick.

Nuovo, di (*dee nwo·voa*), newly, again.

O (*o*, nearly *au*), or; as *flauto o violino* (*flaa·ootoa o vee·olee·noa*, nearly *flout·toa au v.*), flute or violin.

Obbligato (*ob·bligaa·toa*), a part to be performed by some particular instrument in conjunction with the principal part, and *indispensable* to the harmony and proper effect.

Obbligati (*ob·bligaa·tee*), pl., two or more indispensable parts to be performed by different instruments in conjunction with the principal part.

Oppure (*oppoo·r'ai*), or else.

Ordinario (*or'dinaa·r'ioa*), usual; as *a tempo ordinario*, in the usual time.

Parlando (*paar'lan·doa*), in a speaking manner.

Passionatamente (*pas·sioanaa·tamain·tai*), **passionato** (*pas·sionaa·toa*), in an impassioned manner.

Pianissimo (*pyaanees·simoa*), extremely soft.

Piano (*pyaa·noa*), soft. The opposite of *forte*.

Piano piano or **più piano** (*pyaa·noa pyaa·noa, pyeu pyaa·noa*), more soft or very soft.

Più (*pyeu*), almost like the English *pew*) an adverb of augmentation, as *più forte* louder, *più lento* slower.

Piacere al (*al pyaachai·r'ai*), at pleasure in regard to time.

Piu mosso (*pyeu mos·soa*), with more motion.

Più tosto (*pyeu tos·toa*), or **piuttosto** (*pyeuttos·toa*), rather; meaning "in preference," as *allegretto o piuttosto allegro* (*al·legr'ait·toa o pyeuttos·toa alleg·r'oa*), rather quickly, or in preference, quickly.

Placido (*plaa·chidoa*), calm, quiet.

Poco (*po·koa*, almost *pau·koa*), a little.

Poco meno (*po·koa mai·noa*), somewhat less.

Poco più mosso (*po·koa pyeu mos·soa*), a little faster.

Poco a Poco (*po·koa aa po·koa*,) nearly (*pauk aa pau·koa*) by degrees, gradually.

Poggiato (*pod-jyaa·toa*), dwelt on, struck impressively.

Poi (*po·ee* almost *poi*), then; *adagio, poi allegro*, slow, then quick.

Pomposo (*poampoa·soa*), in a grand and pompous manner.

Portamento (*por'tamen·toa*), sustaining the voice, gliding from note to note.

Precipitamente (*pr'echee·pitamain·tai*), **precipitato** (*pr'echee·pitaa·toa*), **con precipitazione**, (*koan pr'echee·pitaa·tsioa·nai*), **precipitoso** (*pr'echee·pitoa·soa*), in a hurried manner.

Prestamente (*pr'es·tamain·tai*), hastily, rapidly.

Prestezza (*pr'estait·tsaa*), with haste and vivacity.

Prestissimo (*pr'estees·simoa*), exceedingly quick, quicker than *presto*.

Presto (*pr'es·toa*), very quickly.

Primo (*pr'ee·moa*), first; as *primo tempo*, return to the original time.

Quasi (*kooaa·zee*, nearly *kwaa·zee*), in the manner or style of; as if; almost; as *quasi allegretto*, like an *allegretto*.

Quieto (*kooee-et·oa*), nearly (*kwee-et·oa*), usual form *cheto* (*ket·oa*), with calmness and repose.

Rabbia (*r'ab·byaa*), with rage, furiously.

Raddolcendo (*r'ad·dolchen·doa*), **raddolcente** (*r'ad·-dolchen·tai*), with augmented softness.

Rallentando (*r'al·lentan·doa*), more and more slowly

Rapidamente (*r'apee·damain·tai*), **con rapidità** (*koan r'apee·ditaa·*), **rapido** (*r'aa·pidoa*), rapidly with rapidity.

Rattenendo (*r'att·enen·doa*), restraining or holding back the time.

Ravvivando (*r'av·vivan·doa*), reviving, re-animating, accelerating, as *ravvivando il tempo*, animating or quickening the time.

Recitando (*r'eoh·itan·doa*), declamatory, in the style, of recitation.

Recitativo (*r'ech·itatee·voa*), a species of musical recitation.

Religiosamente (*r'ailee·jioa·samain·tai*), **religioso** (*r'ailee·jioa·soa*). in a solemn style.

Rinforzando (*r'in·fortsan·doa*), **rinforzato** (*r'in·-for'tsaa·toa*) **rinforzo** (*r'infor'·tsoa*), with additional tone and emphasis.

Risolutamente (*r'ee·soaloo·tamain·tai*), **risoluto** (*r'ee·-soaloo·toa*), **risoluzione con** (*koan r'ee·soaloo·tsioa·nai*) in a bold decided style.

Risolutissimo (*r'eesoa·lootees·simoa*), with extreme resolution.

Ritardando (*r'ee·taardan·doa*), **ritardato** (*r'ee·taar-daa·toa*), a gradual delaying of the pace, with corresponding diminution in point of tone.

Ritenendo (*r'ee·tenen·doa*), holding back in the time,—slackening.

Ritenente (*r'ee·tenen·tai*), **ritenuto** (*r'ee·tenoo·toa*), slackening the time. The effect differs from Ritardando, by being done at once, while the other is effected by degrees.

Scherzando, scherzante, scherzo, scherzevolmente, scherzosamente, scherzoso, (*sker'tsan·doa*, *sker'-tsan·tai*, *sker'·tsoa*, *sker'tsai·voalmain·tai*, *sker'tsoa·-samain·tai*, *sker'tsoa·soa*), in a light, playful, and sportive manner.

Segno (*sai·nyoa*), a sign; as dal segno, repeat from the sign.

Segue, seguito (*seg·wai*, *seg·witoa*), now follows or as follows. As **segue il coro** (*seg·wai eel ko·roa*), the chorus following. Sometimes means, in similar or like manner, to show that a passage is to be performed like that which precedes it.

Semplice, semplicemente, semplicità, con, (*saim·-pleechai*, *saimplee·chaimain·tai*, *koan saimplee·-chitaa·*), with simplicity, artlessly.

Sempre (*sem·pr'ai*), always; as **sempre staccato** (*sem·pr'ai stakkaa·toa*), always staccato, or detached.

Serioso (*ser'·ioa·soa*), in a grave and serious style.

Senza (*sain·tsaa*), without.

Siciliana (*seechee·liaa·naa*), a movement of slow, soothing, pastoral character, in six-pulse time, resembling a dance peculiar to the people of Sicily.

Sforzando (*sfor'tsan·doa*), **sforzato** (*sfor'tsaa·toa*), imply that a particular note is to be performed with emphasis and force.

Sincopato (*sin·kopaa·toa*), to connect an unaccented note with the accented one which follows.

Slegato (*slaigaa·toa*), separately or disconnectedly.

Slentando (*slentan·doa*), a gradual diminution in the time or speed of the movement.

Sminuendo (*smee·noo-en·doa*), gradually diminishing the sound.

Smorzando (*smor'tsan·doa*), **smorzato** (*smor'tsaa·toa*), diminishing the sound, dying away by degrees.

Soave (*soa-aa·vai*), nearly (*swaa·vai*,) in soft, sweet, delicate style.

Soavemente (*soa-aa·vaimain·tai*), with great sweetness.

Solennemente (*soalen·naimain·tai*), solemnly.

Solennità con (*koan soalen·nitaa·*), with solemnity.

Soli (*soa·lee*), pl., implies that two or more different principal parts play or sing together *i.e., one* voice or one instrument of each part only.

Solo (*soa·loa*), sing., a passage for a single voice or instrument, with or without accompaniments.

Sonorammente (*sonor'·amain·tai*), **sonorità con** (*koan sonor'·itaa·*), sonorously; with a full vibrating kind of tone.

Sostenuto (*soas·tenoo·toa*), **sostenendo** (*soas·tenen·doa*), with tones sustained to their full length.

Sotto (*soat·toa*), under; as **sotto voce** (*soat·toa vo·chai*), in a soft subdued manner, in an under tone.

Spirito con (*koan spee·r'itoa*), **spiritosamente** (*spee·r'itoa·samain·tai*), **spiritoso** (*spee·r'itoa·soa*), with spirit, animation.

Staccatissimo (*stak·katees·imoa*), very detached.

Staccato (*stakkaa·toa*), distinct, short, detached. The tones separated from each other by short rests.

Stentando (*stain-tan·doa*), with difficulty or distress,

Strepito con, Strepitoso (*koan str'ep·itoa, str'ep·-itoa·soa*), in an impetuous boisterous style; noisy manner.

Suave, suavemente, suavità con (*soo-aa·vai, soo-aa·vaimain·tai, koan soo-aa·vitaa·*), the usual form is *soave*, with sweetness and delicacy of expression.

Subitamente, subito (*soobee·tamain·tai, soo·bitoa*), quickly, as volti subito, turn over quickly.

Tace (*taa·chai*), **Tacet** (*tai·set*), Latin. Silent.

Tacia si (*see taa·chiaa*), let it be silent.

Tanto (*tan·toa*), so much, as **non tanto** (*non tan·toa*) not so much.

Tardo (*tar·doa*), slowly, in a dragging manner.

Tasto solo (*tas·toa soa·loa*), indicates that certain bass notes are not to be accompanied by chords.

Tempo A, or In (*aa, in tem·poa*), in time, an expression used after some change in the time, to indicate a return to the original degree of movement.

Tempo a piacere (*tem·poa aa pyaachai·r'ai*), the time at pleasure.

Tempo Commodo (*tem·poa kom·odoa*), at a convenient and moderate speed.

Tempo frettoloso (*tempoa fr'ait·toaloa·soa*), accelerated time.

Tempo guisto (*tem·poa joos·toa*), in exact or strict time.

Tempo ordinario (*tem·poa or'·dinaa·r'ioa*), at an ordinary and moderate rate.

Tempo perduto (*tem·poa per'doo·toa*), a gradual decrease of time.

Tempo primo (*tem·poa pr'ee·moa*), return to the original time.

Tenuto (*tenoo·toa*), held on, the tones sustained for their full time.

Timoroso (*tee·moar'oa·soa*), with timidity, awe.

Tosto (*tos·toa*), swift, soon.

Tranquillo (*tr'ankooeel·loa*), nearly (*tr'ankwil·loa*), **tranquillamente** (*tr'ankooeel·lamain·tai*), **tranquillità con** (*koan tr'ankooeel·litaa·*), with tranquillity.

Tremando (*tr'eman·doa*), **tremolando** (*tr'em·oalan·doa*), **tremolato** (*tr'em·oalaa·toa*), **tremolo** (*tr'em·oaloa*), a tremolous effect produced by rapid reiteration of a sound.

Troppo (*tr'op·poa*), too much; generally preceded by the negative **non**; as, **adagio non troppo** (*adaa·jioa non tr'op·poa*), not too slow.

Tutta, tutte, tutti, tutto (*toot·taa,-ai,-ee,-oa*), all; as, **con tutta forza** (*koan toot·taa for'·tsaa*), with all possible force. **Tutti** (*toot·tee*), the entrance of all the instruments after a solo.

Tutta forza con (*koan toot·taa for'·tsaa*), with the utmost vehemence; as loud as possible.

Un, uno, una (*oon, oo·noa, oo·naa*), a, as **un poco** (*oon po·koa*), a little.

Un poco ritenuto (*oon po·koa ree·tenoo·toa*), gradually slower.

Va (*vaa*), goes on; as, **va crescendo** (*vaa kr'ai·shen·doa*), continues to increase in loudness.

Veloce, or con velocità (*velo·chai, koan velo·chitaa·*), in a rapid time. Sometimes signifying as rapid as possible.

Velocissimo (*vai·loachees·simoa*), with extreme rapidity.

Vigoroso (*vee·goar'oa·soa*), **vigorosamente** (*vee·goar'oa·samain·tai*), boldly, vigourously.

Vivace, vivacemente (*veevaa·chai, veevaa·chaimain·tai*), quick and lively.

Vivamente, vivacità con (*vee·vaamain·tai, koan veevaa·chitaa·*) with briskness and animation.

Vivacissimo (*vee·vaachees·simoa*), with extreme vivacity.

Voce (*voa·chai*), the voice.

Volti subito (*vol·tee soo·bitoa*), turn over quickly.

Volante (*volan·tai*), in a light and rapid manner

GRADED TIME EXERCISES.

For Pupils preparing for the Elementary Certificate.

1.

| d :— | d :d | d :d | d :— | d :d | d :d | d :d | d :— ||

2.

| d :d | d :d .d | d :d | d :— | d :d | d .d :d | d :d | d :— ||

3.

| d :— | d :d | d :— | — :d | d :d .d | d :d | d :— | d :—

| d :— | — :d | d :— | d :d | d :d | d .d :d | d :— | — :— ||

4.

| d :— | d :— .d | d :— | d :d | d :d .d | d :d | d :— | — :d

| d :— | d :d | d :— .d | d :d | d .d :d | d :d | d :— | — : ||

5.

| d :— :d | d :d :d | d :— .d :d | d :— :

| d :d :d | d :— :d | d :d :d .d | d :— :— ||

6.

:d | d :d | d :— .d | d :— | — :d | d :d .d | d :d | d :— |

:d | d :— .d | d :d | d :d .d | d :d | d .d :d | d :— .d | d :— | — ||

7.

:d |d :— |d : |d :d .d |d :— | :d |d :d .d |d :— |

:d |d :— | :d |d :— | :d |d :d .d |d :d |d : |d ||

8.

:d |d :— :d |d :d :d .d |d :- .d :d |d :—

:d |d :- .d :d |d : :d |d :d :d .d |d :— ||

9.

|d :d |d ,d .d ,d :d |d :d |d ,d .d ,d :d

|d :d .d |d ,d .d ,d :d .d |d :d .d |d :— ||

10.

|d :— :d,d.d,d |d :— :d |d :d .d :d |d :— :

|d :- .d :d |d :— :d .d |d :d,d.d,d:d .d |d :— :

11.

|d :- :- |d :d :d |d :- :- |d :- :- |d :- :d |d :d :d |d :- :- |- :- :-

|d :- :d |d :- :d |d :- :d |d :- :- |d :d :d |d :- :d |d :- :- |- :- :- ||

St. Co. (New).

12.

{ :d |d :d |d,d.d,d:d .d |d :d .d,d|d :— |d .d,d:d .d |d,d.d,d }

{ :d |d .d,d:d .d |d ||

13.

{ |d :d .d |d :d |d :d .d,d|d :— |d .,d :d .d |d .,d :d .d }

{ |d :d,d.d,d|d :— |d :d .d |d .,d :d |d :d .d |d,d.d,d:d }

{ |d .,d :d .d |d .,d :d .d |d .d,d:d .d |d :— ||

14.

{ |d :- :d |d :- :d |d :d :d |d :- :- |d :- :d |d :d :d |d :- :- |d :- :- }

{ |d :d :d |d :- :d |d :d :d |d :- :- |d :d :d |d :- :d |d :- :- |- :- :- ||

15.

{ |d :— |d :- .d |d :d .d |d :— |d :d .d |d .,d :d .d }

{ |d .d,d:d .d |d :— |d :d |d,d.d,d:d .d |d :d .,d |d : }

{ |d : |d :d .,d |d :d .,d |d :— ||

St. Co. (New).

16.

|d :— :d .,d |d :d :d .,d |d :d :d .d |d :— :

|d :- .d :d,d.d,d |d : :d |d :- .d :d .d |d :— :

17.

|d :d :d |d :- :d |d :- :d |d :d :d |d :- :d |d :d :d |d :- :- | : :

|d :- :d |d :d :d |d :d :d |d :- :d |d :d :d |d :- :d |d :- :d |d :- :-

18.

|d :- .d :d .d |d :— :d .,d |d :d :d .d,d |d : :d

|d :- .d :d .,d |d :— :d |d,d.d,d :d .d :d .,d |d :— :

19.

:d |d .,d :d ,d .d ,d |d :- .d |d :d .,d |d

:d .d |d ,d .d :d d |d ,d .d :d .d |d :d ,d .d ,d |d

20.

:d |d :— | :d .d |d :- .d |d : |d .d :d,d.d |d .d

:d,d.d |d :d |d :— | :d | :d | :d .d |d

:d,d.d,d |d :d .d |d :d .,d |d : |d ||

For Pupils preparing for the Intermediate Certificate.

These exercises are to be sung on *one tone* as well as in tune.

No. 1. KEY **G**. M. 72, twice.

| d :- :d | d :r :m | r :- :- | s_1 :- :- | m :r :d | m :-.r:d | s :- :- | - : :s_1 |

| d :- :d | d :r :m | f :- :m | r :- :s_1 | l_1 :-.t_1:d | t_1 :-.d:r | d :- :- | - :- : ||

No. 2. KEY **E♭**. M. 72, twice.

| m :m :m | m :r :d | f :- :- | - :m :r | d :- :- | - :t_1 :d | r :- :- | : : |

| m :r :m | f :- :s | l :- :- | - :s :f | m :-.r:d | m :- :r | d :- :- | - :- : ||

No. 3. KEY **B♭**. M. 96, twice.

:s_1 | d :- :d | d :t_1 :l_1 | s_1 :- :f_1 | m_1 :- :s_1 | l_1 :-.l_1:l_1 | l_1 :-.t_1:d | t_1 :- :- | - : |

:s_1 | m :- :- | - :r :d | f :- :- | - :m :r | d :t_1 :l_1 | t_1 :- :s_1 | d :- :- | - :- ||

No. 4. KEY **D**. M. 66, twice.

| s :- :f | m :r :d | l :- :- | s :- :- | f :- :m.r | s :- :f.m | r :- :- | : : |

| m :- :- | f :- :m | l :s :fe | s :- :s | l :t :d^1 | m :- :r | d :- :- | - :- : ||

No. 5. KEY **A**. M. 80, twice.

:s_1 | d :- :d | m :r :d | f :- :- | m :- :r | d :- :t_1.d | r :- :d.r | m :- :- | - |

:m_1 :f_1 | s_1 :- :- | - :l_1 :t_1 | d :- :- | - :t_1 :d | r :- :s_1 | m :- :r | d :- :- | - :- ||

St. Co. (New).

No. 6. KEY **D**. M. 72, twice.

:s |s : :s |m :f :s |l :- :- |- : :l |l : :l |r :m :f |s : :d |d :

:d' |t :- :- |- :l :s |f :- :- |- :m :r |m :-.f:s |s : :t_1 |d :- :- |- :- ||

No. 7. KEY **G**. M. 112.

|d :s_1 |d .r :m .f |s :- .f |m : .m |r :d |f :m |m :— |r :s

|l :— :s : .s |f :— |m : .m |r :d |t_1 :r |d :— |— : ||

No. 8. KEY **E♭**. M. 80.

:m .r |d :d .,d |d :m |s :— |— : .d' |t :— |d' : .s |fe :— |s

: .d |f :- .m |r :d |t_1 :— |— : .s |s : .s |m :d |r :— |d ||

No. 9. KEY **C**. M. 72.

|d' :s .,s |m :s |d .r :m .f |s : .m |l .l,l:l .l |s :- .s

|d' .d',d':d' .d' |t :- .d' |m' .r',d':t .l |s .f :m .f |m :r .,d |d :— ||

No. 10. KEY **A♭**. M. 80.

|s_1 :l_1 .t_1 |d : .r |m .r,d:r .d,t_1 |d : .s_1 |l_1 :t_1 .d |r : .m

|f .m,r:m .fe |s : .s_1 |d :- .t_1 |l_1 :— |f .m :r .d |t_1 :- .m

|m :- .r |d .t_1,d:l_1 .r |d :t_1 |d :— ||

St. Co. (New).

No. 11. KEY **F**. M. 72.

| d :d | d .s_1 : | m :- .r | d :— | s .f,m:r .f | m .r,d:t_1 .r |

| d,t_1,d,r:m .d | r : | m :m .,m | m .d : | s .,l :s .f | m : .d |

| r,d.r,m:f .l | s .f,m:r .d | m :r .,d | d :— ||

No. 12. KEY **E♭**. M. 84.

| m :- .f | s .,s :s .s | m :- .d | l :— | s :- .s | f :f .f | m :- .,m | r : |

| l .s :l .s | d' :- .d | r :m .,m | f : | .r :m .f | s :d | r :- .m | d :— ||

No. 13. KEY **G**. M. 88.

:m .,r | d . :d . | d :t_1.d | r :— | :d .,r | m :— | - .,r:d .t_1 | d : | .s_1:fe_1.s_1 |

| t_1.,l_1:s_1 | .d :t_1.d | m .,r:d | .s :f .m | r . :d . | t_1 :-.l_1,t_1 | d :— | — ||

No. 14. KEY **A**. M. 66.

.s_1 :s_1 .s_1 | m :— | :- .,r | d : .d :t_1 .d | m .,r :r | : .d | t_1 :- . |

.d :m_1 .f_1 | s_1 :- .l_1,t_1:d .s_1 | l_1 :- .t_1,d:r .s_1 | m .r :f .m,r:d .t_1 | d :- . ||

No. 15. KEY **B♭**. M. 72.

| s_1 .s_1,s_1 :m_1 .s_1 | d : .s_1 | l_1,l_1.l_1,l_1 :s_1 .f_1 | m_1 : .s_1 |

| d .d ,d :t_1,l_1 .s_1 | m .,r :d ,t_1 .l_1 ,s_1 | l_1 :t_1 | d :— ||

No. 16. KEY **C**. M. 96.

:d .,r | m :d | s :- .m | l,d'.-:d' .,r' | d' :d .,r | m :s | l,s.- :s,m.- | r :- .m | r |

:d .,r | m :d | s :- .m | l,d'.-:d' .,r' | d' :l | s :- .s | l,s.- :d | r :— | d ||

St. Co. (New).

No. **17**. KEY **E**. M. 104. (A beat for every pulse.)

{ :m ,,f | s :m :d' | t :- .l :s | f .l :s .f :m .r | m :- :m ,,f | s :- .l :s .f | m :-

{ :d | s :m :- .d | t_1 :- : | s :- .l :s | s : :f | m :- .r :d ,,r | m :-

{ :l | s :d'.t :l .s | s :m :d ,,m | r :- :- | d :- ||

No. **18**. KEY **F**. M. 88.

{ :m .r | d :- .d :r .m | f :m :s ,fe,s | l :s :d ,t_1 ,d | r :—

{ :s ,,f | m :d :s ,f ,m | l :— :l ,,t_1 ,d | f :- .m :r ,,m | d :—

No. **19**. KEY **D**. M. 80. [Tripletted three-pulse measure=nine-pulse measure.]

{ :m ,- ,r | d :- ,- ,m :s ,- ,f | m : :d' ,- ,t | t ,l ,s :s ,- ,f :m ,- ,r | f :m

{ : , ,s | l ,- ,s :s : , ,d | f ,- ,m :m :- ,r ,m | s ,f ,m :m :- ,- ,r | d :- ,- ,

No. **20**. KEY **E♭**. M. 108.

{ :d ,,r | m :m | m .r :d .m | s :— | — :s ,,l | s :f | — :f ,,s | f :m | —

{ :d' | t :l | s :fe | s :— | :d | f ,,f :f | :m .f | m :— | r

{ :s | — :f | — :m | — :f | m :r .d | d :— | t_1 :— | d :— | —

No. **21**. KEY **G**. M. 96.

{ | d :s_1 | m :d | s :f .m | r :- .r | m .m :- .m | f .f :- .m | r :m .fe | s :—

{ | l :l | s .d :- .m | f :f ,,f | m :— | r .r :- .r | d .s_1 :- .s_1 | l_1 :t_1 | d :—

ADVANCED RHYTHMS,

For pupils preparing for the Matriculation and Advanced Certificates.

For the Time Exercise of the MATRICULATION CERTIFICATE (requirement 2) Nos. 1 to 17 should be practised to *laa* on one tone, also in correct time and tune. They must be sung at the rate marked. The key may be changed when necessary. The test used in the examination is sent from the College and not seen before, but it contains no greater difficulties than these.

For the Time Exercise of the ADVANCED CERTIFICATE (requirement 1) any one of Nos. 18 to 42 is chosen by lot in the examination, and sung on one tone at the rate marked. The candidate also sings to *laa* a test sent by the College to the examiner, and also writes from ear two or three measures of "Elementary Rhythms" sung to him.

1. KEY **A.** M. 88. *Bishop.*

:m_1 .,f_1 | s_1 :- .,d :r .,t_1 | t_1,d.- : :d .,r | m :- .m :f .,r
Na - tive land, I'll love thee ever, Let me raise the wel-come

| d .t_1 :t_1 .,d | r :- .t_1 :m .,r | r,d.- : :d.,r.,m | m.,s_1.,s_1 :t_1 :l_1
strain, Mine were ban - ish'd feet that never Hop'd to press thy turf a -

| s_1 :— :s_1 .,t_1 | r :- .m,r :t_1 .s_1 | s_1 .,d :d :m .,r
gain! Now these eyes il - lum'd with glad - ness, As they

| d :- .l_1 :t_1,m.- | l_1 :— :s_1 .,f_1 | m_1 :- .f_1 :s_1 .l_1
scan thy beauties o'er, Ne'er a - gain shall melt in

| t_1 .,d :d :d .,t_1 | t_1,l_1.f,r :d :t_1 .,d | d :— :d .,d
sad - ness, Part - ing to re - turn no more. O Bri-

| d :- .s_1 :l_1,d.- | s_1 :— :m_1 .,f_1 | s_1 :- .d :t_1 .,r | r,d.- :— ||
tan - nia! native land, na - tive land, I'll love thee ever.

J. CURWEN & SONS, 8 & 9 Warwick Lane, E.C. Price One Penny. Where also may be had Elementary Rhythms (½d.) and Intermediate Rhythms (½d.)

2. KEY D. M. 80. **SAAte-ene. TAAsefe.** *Bishop.*

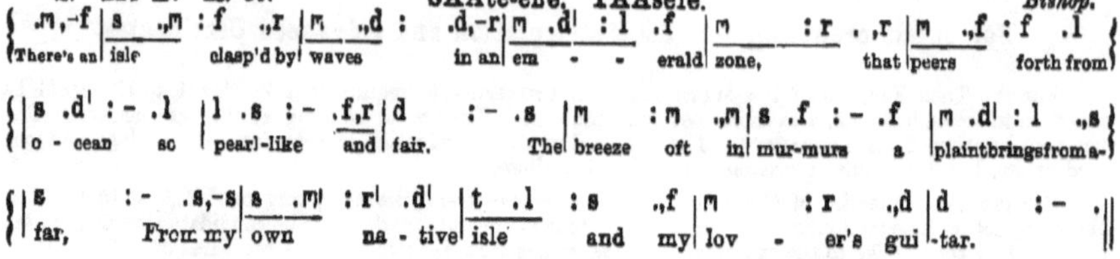

.m,-f | s .,m : f .,r | m .,d : .d,-r | m .d' : l .f | m : r . ,r | m .,f : f .l
There's an | isle clasp'd by | waves in an | em - - erald | zone, that | peers forth from

| s .d' : - .l | l .s : - .f,r | d : - .s | m : m .,m | s .f : - .f | m .d' : l .,s
| o - cean so | pearl-like and | fair. The | breeze oft in | mur-murs a | plaint brings from a-

| s : - .s,-s | s .m' : r' .d' | t .l : s .,f | m : r .,d | d : - . ||
| far, From my | own na - tive | isle and my | lov - er's gui | -tar. ||

3. KEY G. M. 60. **ta-ana-te-ene. taralaterele. tafaterele.** *Rossini.*

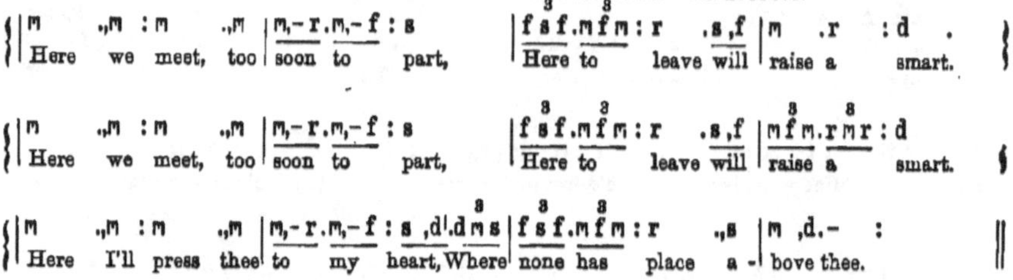

| m .,m : m .,m | m,-r.m,-f : s | fsf.mfm : r .s,f | m .r : d . |
| Here we meet, too | soon to part, | Here to leave will | raise a smart. |

| m .,m : m .,m | m,-r.m,-f : s | fsf.mfm : r .s,f | mfm.rmr : d |
| Here we meet, too | soon to part, | Here to leave will | raise a smart. |

| m .,m : m .,m | m,-r.m,-f : s ,d'.dms | fsf.mfm : r .,s | m ,d.- : ||
| Here I'll press thee | to my heart, Where | none has place a - | bove thee. ||

4. KEY D. M. 72. **TAAte-ene. ta-anatefe.** *Bishop.*

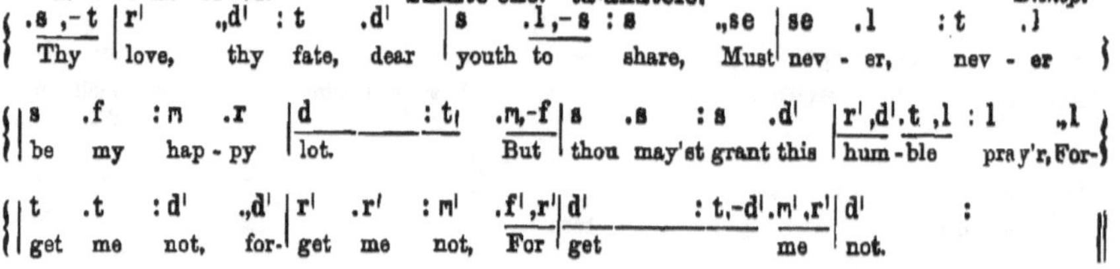

.s ,-t | r' .,d' : t .d' | s .l,-s : s .,se | se .l : t .l
Thy | love, thy fate, dear | youth to share, Must | nev - er, nev - er

| s .f : m .r | d : t, .m,-f | s .s : s .d' | r',d'.t ,l : l .,l
| be my hap - py | lot. But | thou may'st grant this | hum - ble pray'r, For-

| t .t : d' .,d' | r' .r' : m' .f',r' | d' : t,-d'.m',r' | d' : ||
| get me not, for- | get me not, For | get me | not. ||

5. KEY A. M. 96. **afatefe.** From *Handel's* "Samson," p. 5.

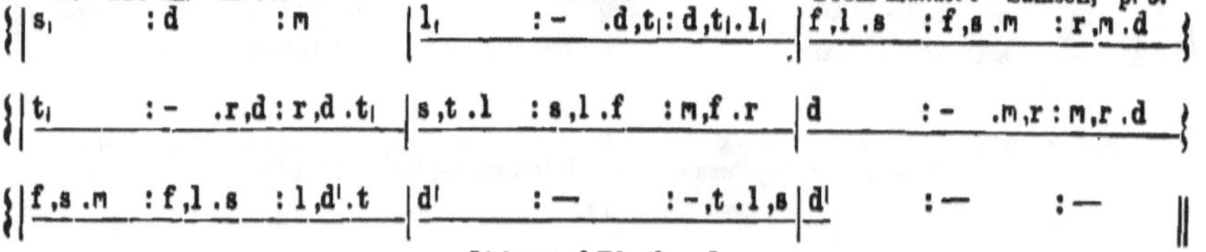

| s, : d : m | l, : - .d,t, : d,t,.l, | f,l .s : f,s .m : r,m .d

| t, : - .r,d : r,d .t, | s,t .l : s,l .f : m,f .r | d : - .m,r : m,r .d

| f,s .m : f,l .s : l,d'.t | d' : — : -,t .l,s | d' : — : — ||

[Advanced Rhythms.]

6. KEY F. M. 58. From *Handel's* "Samson," p. 95.

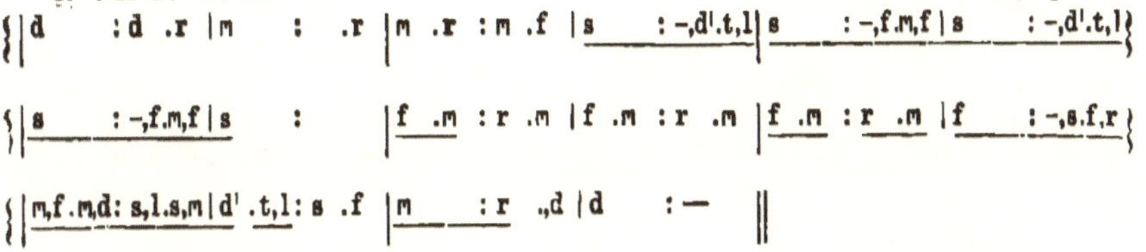

{|d :d .r |m : .r |m .r :m .f |s :-,d'.t,l|s :-,f.m,f |s :-,d'.t,l}

{|s :-,f.m,f |s : |f .m :r .m |f .m :r .m |f .m :r .m |f :-,s.f,r}

{|m,f.m,d: s,l.s,m|d' .t,l: s .f |m :r .,d |d :— ||

7. KEY F. M. 66. **TAA-efene.** From *Handel's* "Samson," p. 21.

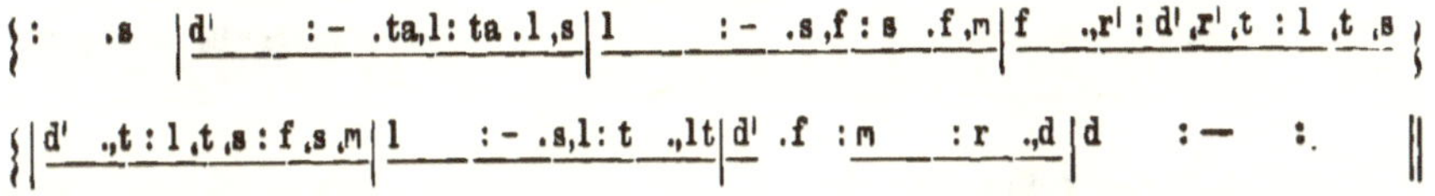

{: .s |d' :- .ta,l: ta .l ,s|l :- .s ,f : s .f ,m|f .,r' : d' ,r' ,t : l ,t ,s}

{|d' .,t : l ,t ,s : f ,s ,m|l :- .s,l: t .,lt|d' .f :m :r .,d|d :— : ||

8. KEY D. M. 84. From *Handel's* "Samson," p. 35.

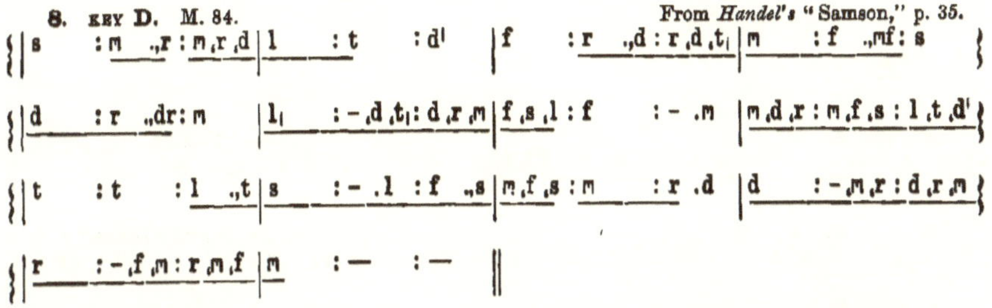

{|s :m .,r : m ,r ,d|l :t :d' |f :r .,d : r ,d ,t,|m :f .,mf: s}

{|d :r .,dr: m |l, :- ,d ,t,: d ,r ,m|f ,s ,l : f :- .m |m ,d ,r : m ,f ,s : l ,t ,d'}

{|t :t :l .,t|s :- .l :f .,s|m ,f ,s : m :r .d |d :- ,m ,r : d ,r ,m}

{|r :- ,f ,m : r ,m ,f |m :— :— ||

9. KEY F. M. 88. From *Handel's* "Messiah," p. 65.

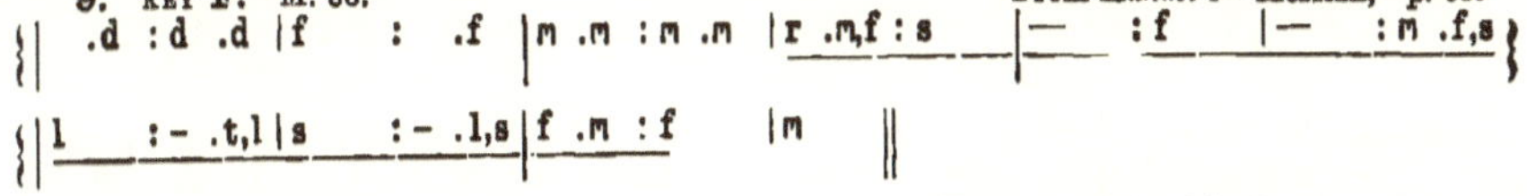

{| .d :d .d |f : .f |m .m :m .m |r .m,f : s |— :f |— :m .f,s}

{|l :- .t,l |s :- .l,s|f .m :f |m ||

10. KEY F. M. 88. From *Handel's* "Messiah," pp. 64, 65.

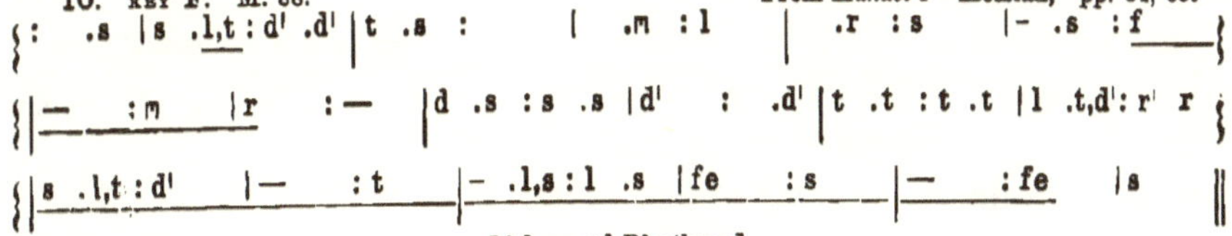

{: .s |s .l,t : d' .d' |t .s : | .m :l | .r :s |- .s :f}

{|— :m |r :— |d .s :s .s |d' : .d' |t .t :t .t |l .t,d': r' r}

{|s .l,t : d' |— :t |- .l,s : l .s |fe :s |— :fe |s ||

[Advanced Rhythms.]

11. KEY F. M. 96. TAI-AA. From *Handel's* "Jephtha," p. 1.

{| .s : f .m : r .d | t,.fe : - .s : - .m | s,.m : - .f : - .r | s,.r : - .m : - .d | s : .d : t,.l, | s, ||

12. KEY C. M. 104. From *Mozart's* "Twelfth Mass," p. 66.

{| .l : - .s | fe.s : - .f | m : | .s : - .f | m : | .s : - .f | m : d .d | d : ||

13. KEY B♭. M. 72. From *Handel's* "Acis and Galatea," p. 11.

{| m : - .f | s .r : - .m | f .d : - .r | m .t, : - .d | r .l, : - .t, | d : r .m | f : - .f | m : ||

14. KEY D. M. 116. From *Handel's* "Samson," p. 9.

{| m' : l : l | l.t : d'.t : l | -.t : d'.t : l | -.t : d'.t : l | f' : t : t | t.d' : r'.d' : t }

{| -.d' : r'.d' : t | -.d' : r'.d' : t | r' : m' : f' | m' : r'.d' : t.l | r' : t : - | l : - : s }

{| f : s.f : m.f | r : - : s | f.s : f : m | r : - : - ||

15. KEY A. M. 60. From *Handel's* "Samson," pp. 33, 34.

{: .s, | l, .l, : - .s,,l, | t, .t, : - .l,,t, | d .d : - .t,,d | r,d.t,,l, : s, .f, | m, ||

16. KEY G. M. 126. From *Graun's* "Te Deum," p. 9.

{: .s | s : f .m | s : f .m | l .l,l : l .l | l .s : - .d' | - .t : - .l | - .s : - .l | s : f | m ||

17. KEY D. M. 80. From *Graun's* "Te Deum," p. 21.

{| m' : r' | - .de' : r' .m' | f',m'.r' : - .d' | - .t : d' .r' | m',r'.d' : - .t | l ||

18. KEY E. M. 60. From *Graun's* "Te Deum," p. 27.

{| m' : -,r'.r',d' : r',d'.d',t | d' : — : — | - .de' : - .r' : m' .f' | t : - .t : d' ||

19. KEY A. M. 80. From *Graun's* "Te Deum," p. 29.

E. t.

{: .m | m .de : r | - .t, : d .m | f : — | - .r : ml.t | d' .s,l : s | - .f : - .m,r }

{| m .s,l : s | - .f : - .m,r | m .f,s : f .s,l | s .l,t : d' .f | m : — | r ||

[Advanced Rhythms.]

20. KEY G. M. 80. From *Handel's* "Acis and Galatea," p. 39.

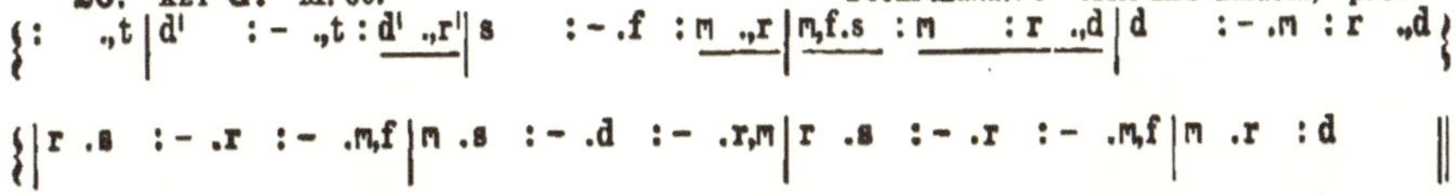

{: ,,t |d' :- ,,t : d' .,r' |s :- .f :m .,r |m,f.s :m :r .,d |d :- .m :r ,,d }

{ |r .s :- .r :- .m,f |m .s :- .d :- .r,m |r .s :- .r :- .m,f |m .r :d ||

21. KEY E. M. 66. From *Handel's* "Messiah," p. 3.

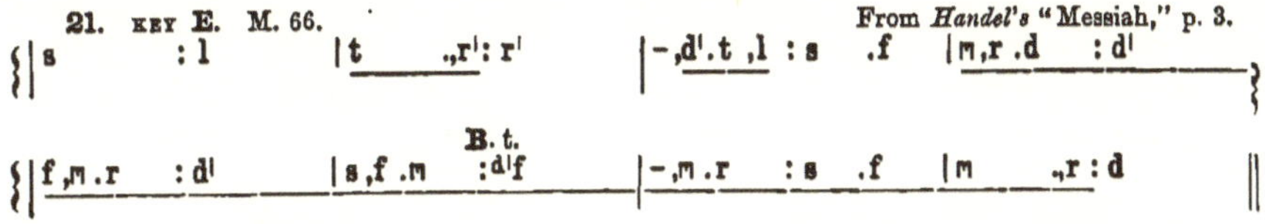

{ |s :l |t .,r' : r' |- ,d'.t ,l :s .f |m,r .d :d' }

B. t.

{ |f ,m .r :d' |s ,f .m :d'f |- ,m .r :s .f |m .,r :d ||

22. KEY G. M. 72. From *Mozart's* "Twelfth Mass," p. 2.

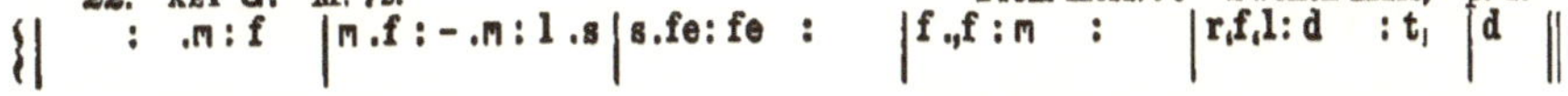

{ | : .m :f |m .f :- .m :l .s |s.fe: fe : |f .,f :m : |r,f,l: d :t, |d ||

23. KEY D. M. 84. A. t. From *Handel's* "Samson," p. 34.

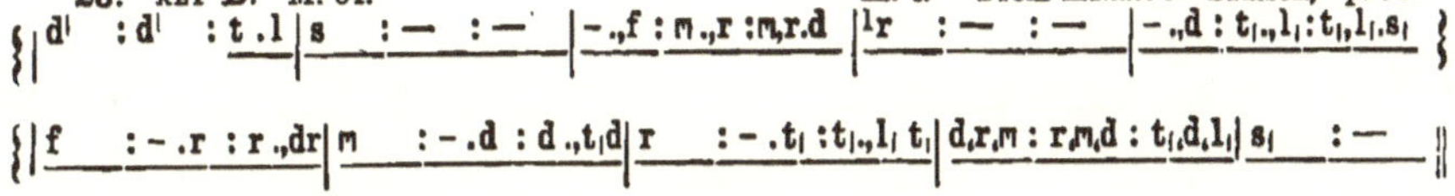

{ |d' :d' :t .l |s :— :— |- .,f :m .,r :m,r.d |[l]r :— :— |- .,d :t,.,l, :t,,l,.s, }

{ |f :- .r :r .,dr |m :- .d :d .,t,d |r :- .t, :t,.,l, t, |d,r,m :r,m,d :t,.d,l, |s, :— ||

24. KEY G. M. 80. Fae. From *Graun's* "Te Deum," p. 35.

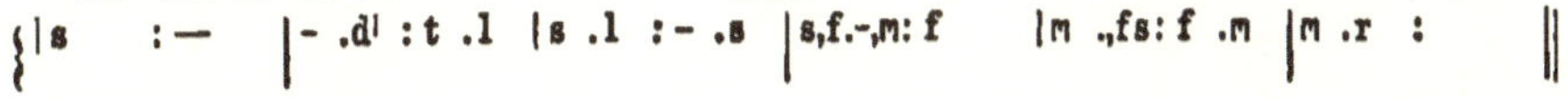

{ |s :— |- .d' :t .l |s .l :- .s |s,f.-,m: f |m .,fs: f .m |m .r : ||

25. KEY F. M. 120. From *Haydn's* "Creation," p. 12.

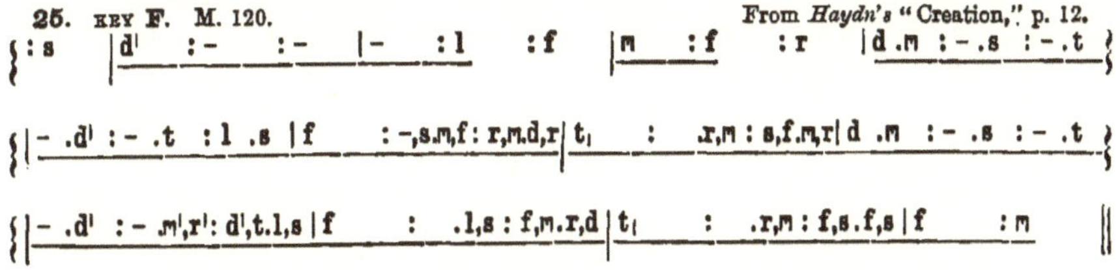

{: s |d' :- :- |- :l :f |m :f :r |d .m :- .s :- .t }

{ |- .d' :- .t :l .s |f :-,s.m,f: r,m.d,r |t, : .r,m :s,f.m,r |d .m :- .s :- .t }

{ |- .d' :- .m',r': d',t.l,s |f : .l,s :f,m.r,d |t, : .r,m :f,s.f,s |f :m ||

26. KEY G. M. 50. te-ene. From *Weber's* "Mass in G," p. 32.

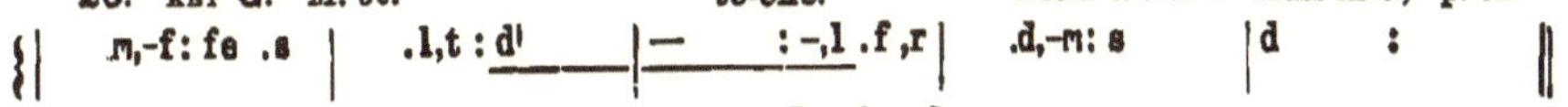

{ | .m,-f: fe .s | .l,t :d' |— :-,l .f ,r | .d,-m: s |d : ||

27. KEY B♭. M. 60. ta-ene. From *Handel's* "Messiah," p. 37.

{: .s₁ |d ,,r : m .r,d |s : -,l .s ,l |f,-m.f ,-s : f ,s .f ,s |m,r .d : .f }

{|m,r .d : - .l |s,f .m : .s₁ |l₁,t₁.d : .s |f .m,r : r ,,d |d ||

28. KEY B♭. M. 80. -aataitee. From *Handel's* "Jephtha," pp. 17, 18.

{|f :m ,,r : m |- ,d ,r : m ,d ,r : m |- ,f ,d : r ,m ,d : r |- ,t₁,d : r ,t₁,d : r }

F. t.

{|-,m ,t₁: d,r ,t₁: ᵈf |- .t : - .r' : - .f |m,f ,s : s : s |-,m ,f : s,f ,m : f ,m ,r |d ||

taralaterele. ene-fe. a-ana-terele.

29. KEY A. M. 60. From *Handel's* "Samson," p. 83.

{: d |d : — |— : — |— : - .t₁l₁,s₁}

{|m : -,-r.d t₁l₁|s₁l₁t₁.d r m : f .r |t₁ : - .d |d : — ||

30. KEY G. M. 80. tana-a. tene-e. From *Graun's* "Te Deum," p. 35.

{| .lf,- : sm,-.fr,- |d : r ,,mf|m .lf,- : sm,- .fr,- |d : r |d ||

Tanafa-AI.

31. KEY A. M. 72. From *Handel's* "Samson," p. 56.

{: .s |s,r.- :m,d.- |t₁ : .s |s,r.- :m,d.- |l : d |d : d |d :mr,d.- }

{|d :mr,d.- |d' : - .t |l .s : f .m |rd,t₁.- : d .f |m : r ,,d |d ||

[Advanced Rhythms.]

TAAtefene. TAAte-ene. SAAte-ene.

32. KEY E♭. M. 30. From *Handel's* "Samson," p. 42.

: .s₁ |m :- .r,d|s :- .f,m|r :d .,t₁|t₁ : - | :

|l .l :s .f,-m|m .,s :l,s.f,m|r : .m |d : .f |r : .s

|m .d,-t₁: d .,ls|s :— |— : .f,-m|m : .r |d .t₁ :d .r,mf|r ||

33. KEY G. M. 80. From *Graun's* "Te Deum," p. 35.

|s :s |s .l,-ta: l .s |fe .sl,td': r' |-,d' .t,l : s,f .m,r

|m .fs,lt: d' | : ||

SAAtene-fe.

34. KEY D. M. 66. From *Handel's* "Jephtha," p. 70.

| :d' :- .t,-l|l :— : | .d' :m .,s :fe

f. G.

|s : :ˢr .,m |f : .mf,s: f .m |r : : ||

Safatefe.

35. KEY E. M. 100. From *Handel's* "Jephtha," p. 105.

|s :s |s :- .m |f :- .s |m .d :m |,m.r,m: f,m.r,m|r .f :—

| ,f.m,f: s,f.m,f|m .s :— | ,s.f,s: l,s.f,s|f .l :- .r' |r' .d' :d' .t |d' :— ||

TAI-AAte-ene.

36. KEY D. M. 80. From *Graun's* "Te Deum," p. 35.

|s :— |- .d',-r': d' .m' |- .t ,-d': t .r' |- .d',-r': d' .m'

|- .t ,-d': t .r' |d' .,r'm': r' ||

SAAte-ene. TAAtene-e.

37. KEY G. M. 80. From *Graun's* "Te Deum," p. 36.

|s :— |- .d',-r': d' .t | .l ,-t : l .s | .f ,-s : f .m

|r .sr,- : ts,- .r't,- |d' .,tl : s ||

38. KEY D. M. 80. From *Graun's* "Te Deum," p. 35.

| .f'r',- : m'd',- .r't,- | d' : r' .,m'f'| m' .f'r',- : m'd',- .f'r',- | d' ||

39. KEY D. M. 84. **AA-efene.** From *Handel's* "Samson," p. 97.

: s | m .,rm : m .,rm | f .,mf : f .,mf | s .,fs : s .,fs | l .f : s .l | t, : - .t, | d : ||

To be sung in two parts, the Examiner or some other person taking one part.

40. KEY G. M. 120. From *Handel's* "Dettingen Te Deum," p. 16.

| : s | - .f ,m : f | f .m ,r : m | - .r ,d : f |
| s, : - .l,,t, | l, : - .t, ,d | t, : - .l, ,s, | d : - .t,,l, |

| f .s : m .r | m : r .,d | d ||
| t, .s, : d | — : t, | d ||

In two parts, as above.

41. KEY G. M. 120. From *Handel's* "Dettingen Te Deum," p. 17.

| m : - .fe,s | fe : - .se,l | se : - .l ,t | m : l .s |
| : m | - .r ,d : r | - .d ,t, : m .r | d .t, : l, |

| f .m : r | - .m : d .t, | d : t, .,l, | l, : — ||
| l : - .t ,l | se .m : l | — : se | l : — ||

In two parts, as above.

42. KEY B♭. M. 120. From *Handel's* "Dettingen Te Deum," p. 28.

: s, : d, | l, : - .s, : l, .f, | r, : s, : - .f, | m, : l, : - .ta, |
: m : s, | l, .d : r : - .l, | t, .r : m : - .t, | d .m : f : - .r |

F. t.

| s, .m, : l, : - .r, | s, : - .d, : d | df.r : m .d : r .t, | d : - .m : r .d | t, : t, ||
| m : - .d : f | - .r : m : - .d | rs : — : — | - .m : f : - .m | r : r ||

[Advanced Rhythms.]

Elementary Transitions.

These Exercises are intended for students or classes preparing for the Intermediate Certificate. Requirement 4.

Cadence Transitions to First Sharp Key.

1. KEY F.

{ :s |f :r |m :s |s :fe |s :s |f :r |m :d |d :t_1 |d ||

2.

{ :m |r :s |f :r |m :fe |s :m |r :s |f :r |m :r |d ||

3.

{ :s |m :f |r :s |l :fe |s :r |f :s |m :d |r :t_1 |d ||

4.

{ :d |r :f |m :s |fe :l |s :m |f :l |s :d' |m :r |d ||

5.

{ :d |t_1 :s_1 |d :s |fe :r |s :s |l :f |s :m |r :r |d ||

6.

{ :s |f :m |r :d |r :fe |s :r |m :f |s :m |f :r |d ||

7.

{ :s |f :s |l :m |f :fe |s :s |r :m |f :r |d :t_1 |d ||

8.

{ :m |d :f |m :l |d' :fe |s :s |m :l |s :d |m :r |d ||

9.

{ :d |m :s |d' :l |t :fe |s :m |s :l |f :r |m :t_1 |d ||

Passing Transitions to First Flat Key.

10. KEY D.

{ |m :r |m :d |m :f |s :— |d' :ta |l :s |d' :t |d' :— ||

11.

{ |d' :t |d' :s |m :l |s :— |l :ta |l :t |d' :r' |d' :— ||

Price One Halfpenny. London: J. Curwen & Sons, 8 & 9, Warwick Lane, E.C.

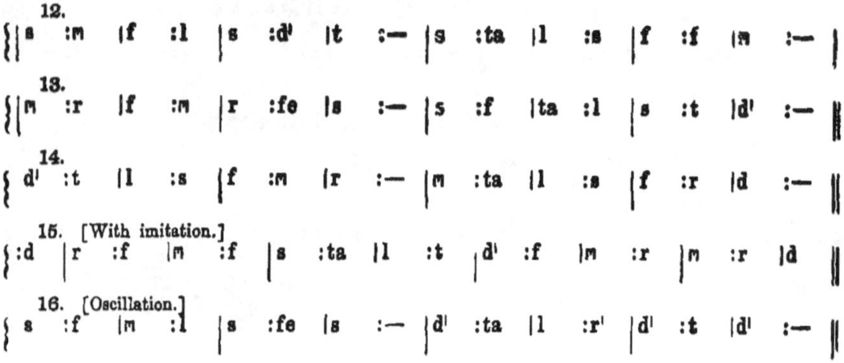

12.
| s :m | f :l | s :d' | t :— | s :ta | l :s | f :f | m :— |

13.
| m :r | f :m | r :fe | s :— | s :f | ta :l | s :t | d' :— ||

14.
d' :t | l :s | f :m | r :— | m :ta | l :s | f :r | d :— ||

15. [With imitation.]
:d | r :f | m :f | s :ta | l :t | d' :f | m :r | m :r | d ||

16. [Oscillation.]
s :f | m :l | s :fe | s :— | d' :ta | l :r' | d' :t | d' :— ||

Extended Transitions—Better Method.

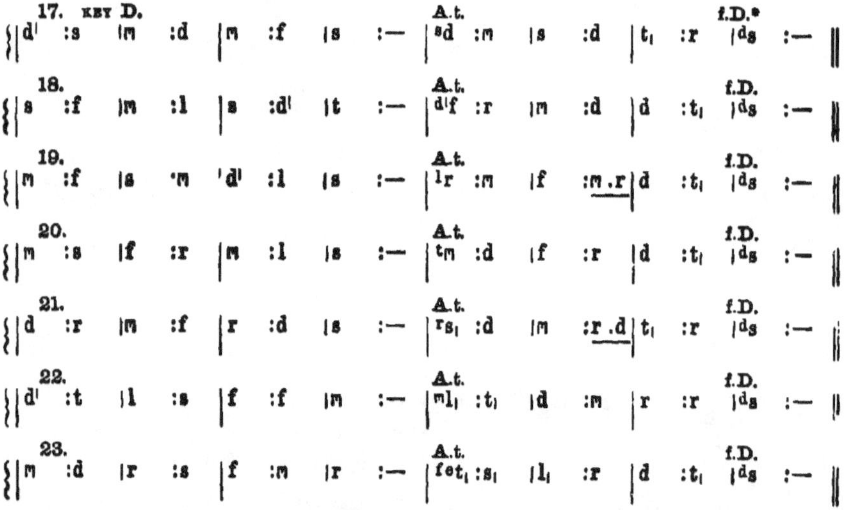

17. KEY D. ... A.t. ... f.D.*
| d' :s | m :d | m :f | s :— | ^{s}d :m | s :d | t_1 :r | ^{d}s :— ||

18. ... A.t. ... f.D.
| s :f | m :l | s :d' | t :— | $^{d'}$f :r | m :d | d :t_1 | ^{d}s :— ||

19. ... A.t. ... f.D.
| m :f | s :m | d' :l | s :— | ^{l}r :m | f :m.r | d :t_1 | ^{d}s :— ||

20. ... A.t. ... f.D.
| m :s | f :r | m :l | s :— | ^{t}m :d | f :r | d :t_1 | ^{d}s :— ||

21. ... A.t. ... f.D.
| d :r | m :f | r :d | s :— | $^{r}s_1$:d | m :r.d | t_1 :r | ^{d}s :— ||

22. ... A.t. ... f.D.
| d' :t | l :s | f :f | m :— | $^{m}l_1$:t_1 | d :m | r :r | ^{d}s :— ||

23. ... A.t. ... f.D.
| m :d | r :s | f :m | r :— | $^{fe}t_1$:s_1 | l_1 :r | d :t_1 | ^{d}s :— ||

* The return transition is made on the last note so that the Exercise can be repeated or the next one taken without pause.

First Sharp Transitions. shewing Cadential forms of Bass.

24. KEY E. S.B.

```
:d  |m  :s  |d' :l  |s  :fe |s  :f  |m  :d  |s  :m  |r  :r  |d  ||
:d  |s  :f  |m  :d  |r  :r  |s, :t, |d  :l, |t, :d  |f, :s, |d  ||
```

25.

```
:m  |m  :r  |d  :m  |m  :fe |s  :m  |f  :s  |l  :d' |m  :r  |d  ||
:d  |d  :r  |m  :d  |l, :r  |s, :d  |l, :s, |f, :l, |s, :s, |d  ||
```

26.

```
:m  |r  :f  |m  :s  |l  :fe |s  :m  |f  :l  |s  :m  |f  :r  |d  ||
:d  |t, :s, |d  :t, |l, :l, |s, :d  |l, :f  |m  :d  |r  :s  |d  ||
```

27.

```
:m  |f  :m  |r  :m.fe |s  :fe |s  :f  |m  :d'  |t  :l .s |f  :f  |m  ||
:d  |t, :d  |r  :d    |t, :l, |s, :s, |l, :fe, |s, :l,   |t, :s, |d  ||
```

First Flat Key, Imitation, and Oscillation.

28. KEY E.

```
:m  |d  :r  |m  :fe |s  :—  |—  :m  |f  :s  |l  :t  |d' :—  |—
:d  |m  :r  |d  :l, |s, :—  |—  :d  |l  :s  |f  :r  |d  :—  |—

:s  |d' :ta |l  :l  |r' :d' |t  :s  |f  :m  |m  :r  |d  :—  |—  ||
:m  |m  :d  |f  :f  |fe :r  |s  :m  |r  :d  |s  :s, |d  :—  |—  ||
```

Extended Transitions, without Distinguishing Tone.

29. KEY F.

```
                                    C.t.                      f.F.
:d  |m  :s  |d  :r  |m  :—  |—  :s d'  |f' :m' |m' :r' |d's  :—  |—  ||
:d  |d  :t, |m  :r  |d  :—  |—  :t,m   |r  :d  |s  :s, |d s, :—  |—  ||
```

30.

```
                                    C.t.                      f.F.
:m  |d  :r  |m  :d  |t, :d  |r  :t,m   |s  :d' |m' :r' |d's  :—  |—  ||
:d  |m  :r  |d  :m  |r  :d  |t, :s,d   |m  .d  |s  :s, |d s, :—  |—  ||
```

With Distinguishing Tone.

31. KEY F.

```
                                    C.t.                      f.F.
:m  |s  :f  |m  :r  |d  :—  |—  :ml    |s  :d' |d' :t  |d's  :—  |—  ||
:d  |t, :s, |l, :t, |d  :—  |—  :df    |m  :l  |s  :s  |d s, :—  |—  ||
```

32.

```
                                    C.t.                      f.F.
:m  |r  :d  |t, :d  |r  :f  |m  :r s   |l  :r' |d' :t  |d's  :—  |—  ||
:d  |f  :m  |r  :d  |t, :s, |d  :t,m   |f  :r  |l  :s  |d s, :—  |—  ||
```

33. C.t. f.F.

{ :d |m :f |s :m |f :s |l :t m' |f' .m' |r' :t |d's :— |— ‖
{ :d |d :r |m :d |l_1 :s_1 |f_1 :^{s}d |t_1 :d |f :s |d s_1 :— |— ‖

34. C.t. f.F.

{ :s |m :r |d :m |s :f |m :^{r}s |l .t :d' |d' :t |d's :— |— ‖
{ :d |d :r |m :d |t_1 :s_1 |d :t_1m |f :m |r :s |d s_1 :— |— ‖

35. C.t. f.F.

{ :m |s :f |m :d |m :r |d :^{r}s |m' :r' |d' :t |d's :— |— ‖
{ :d |m :r |d :m |s :s_1 |l_1 :t_1m |d :r |m .f :s |d s_1 :— |— ‖

Sudden Extended Transition and Chromatic fe in Bass.

36. KEY D. A.t.

{ |d' :t |l :s |f :r |m :d |d'f :r |t_1 :r |s :f |m :— }
{ |d :m |f :m |r :t_1 |d :m |fet_1 :r |s_1 :f_1 |m_1 :s_1 |d :— }

f.D.

{ |^{f}d' :s |m :ta |l :s |f :r |s :f |m :r |m :r |d :— ‖
{ |$^l{}_1$m :m |d :m |f :m |f :s |m :l |s :fe |s :s_1 |d :— ‖

Sudden Passing Transition.

37. KEY D. A.t. f.D.

{ :s |s :d' |t :ta |l :d' |s :^{s}d |t_1 :d |m – .r |ds :— |— ‖
{ :d |m :d |r :m |f :f |s :t_1m |r :d |s_1 :– .s_1 |ds :— |— ‖

Chromatic fe and ta (in Air), and Cadence Transition to First Flat Key in Better Method.

38. KEY D. A.t.

{ |s :fe |f :m |r :l |s :— |fet_1 :d |r :f |m :r |d :— ‖
{ |d :r |s_1 :l_1 |f_1 :f_1 |s_1 :— |$^r s_1$:m_1 |f_1 :r_1 |s_1 :s_1 |d_1 :— ‖

f.D. f.G. D.t.

{ |l_1m :f |s :^{l}m |f :s |m :— |ml :ta |t :d' |m :r |d :— ‖
{ |f_1d :r |m :^{f}d |l_1 :t_1 |d :— |df :m |r :d |s :s_1 |d :— ‖

[Elementary Transitions.]

Intermediate Transitions from the Classics.

Selected from the works of Bach, Handel, Graun, Haydn, Mozart, &c.

These selections are intended to give exercise to classes which are preparing for the study of difficult music, and especially to aid pupils in obtaining the Matriculation or the Advanced Certificates. The keys may be changed to suit the voice.

J. C.

Two Removes.

1. KEY A♭. B♭. t.m. *Bach's* "Blessing and Glory," p. 11, 12.

| s :r :f | m .r :d .t_1 :d | ^{l}s :r :f | m .r :d .t_1 :d ||
His name is | ex - cel - lent, | His name is | ex - cel - lent.

2. KEY C. d.f. B♭. "Samson," p. 95.

: .m' | m' .m' :r' .d' | f' : | $^{f}s_1$:t_1 .r | f : .r | t_1 .s_1 :s .r | m ||
Je- | ho-vah's glo-ry known; | Their i - dol gods shall | from his presence fly.

3. KEY F. G. t.m. "Jephtha," p. 4.

:s | s :- :f | m :- :r | d :- :t_1 | l_1 :- :l | ^{l}s :- :f | m :- :r | d :- :t_1 | l_1 :- ||
No more to | Am - mon's God and | King, fierce Mo - loch, | shall our cym - bals | ring.

4. KEY D. E. t.m. "Jephtha," p. 4, 5.

:r' | r' :- :d' | t :- :l | s :- :f | m :- :m' | $^{m'}$r' :- :d' | t :- :l | s :- :f | m :- ||
No more to | Am - mon's God and | King, fierce Mo - loch, | shall our cym - bals | ring.

5. KEY C. D. t.m. "Jephtha," p. 92.

| t :r' .t :l .s | d' .t :d' : | $^{de'}$t :r' .t :l .s | d' .t :d' : ||
And their | tri - bute, | And their | tri - bute.

6. KEY D. "Samson," p. 83, 84.

E. t.m.

| :r' :m' | d' .t :d' .l :t .d' | r' .d' :r' .m' :r' .d' | t .l :^{t}l .t :d' |
Rules the | world

| — :r' :d' | t :t :r' | s :— :s | d' :— :— ||
rules the | world, rules the | world in | state.

Price One Penny. London: J. Curwen & Sons, 8 & 9, Warwick Lane, E.C.

7. KEY G. "Samson," p. 94.

d.f. F.

|m .m : .m |d : | .d :d .r |t₁ .t₁ : |t₁ .d :r .d |l₁ : |ᵈr :r .m
Brethren, fare- well your kind at- tendance now I pray for- bear, Lest it of-

G. t.m.

|f : .f |f .f :f .m |d : .d |m : .m |l : .ˡs |f .f :f .m |d : ||
fend to see me girt with friends, Ex-pect of me you'll nothing hear im- pure.

8. KEY E♭. f. A♭. "Acis and Galatea." p. 52.

|r :- .r |m :f |m .r :s .m |d :— |ˢr :- .r |m :f |m .r :s .m
Mur - m'ring still his gen - tle love, Mur - m'ring still his gen - tle

B♭. t.m.

|d :— |ᵐr :- .r |m :f |m .r :s .m |d :— |— :— ||
love, Mur - m'ring still his gen - tle love.

9. KEY B♭. "Come let us sing," p. 20.

d.f. A♭.

| : | :m₁ |l₁ :— |t₁ :— |d :l₁ |ᶠs :f
And his hands form - ed and pre -

B♭. t.m.

|m :— |m :- .m |s :— |s :s₁ |ᵐr :— |d :t₁
par - - ed the dry land. For His is the

f. E♭.

|m :— | :m |f :- .f |m :r |taf¹ :— |— :— ||
sea, and he hath fash - ion'd it.

10. KEY F. "Israel," p. 26.

:m .r :m |- .r :m :m .r |f .m :r .d :t₁ .l₁ |s₁ : :
Mingled with the hail, ran a- long up - on the ground,

G. t. m.

:m .d :r |- .r :r :ʳd .d |d .t₁ :l₁ .s₁ :f₁ .d |r :m .t₁ :d
mingled with the hail, ran a- long up - on the ground, mingled with

|- .t₁ :d :m .r |d :- .d :t₁ .d |t₁ :— : ||
the hail, ran a- long up - on the ground.

[Intermediate Transitions.]

11. KEY E. "Jephtha," p. 15.

| s :f :- | m :- :s | l :r :- | s.f :m.r :d | d' :r' :m' | l.r' :t :- |
Take the heart you fond - ly gave; lodged in your breast with

d. f. D.

| d' :- :- | - :- :- | fs :f :- | m :- :s | m' :r'.d' :t.d' | r' :- :- ||
mine; Take the heart you fond-ly gave.

12. KEY B♭. d. f. A♭. "Song of the Bell," p. 36.

:s, | m, :d, | t₂ :s₂ | d, :s₂ | r,m, :l₂ | f, :r, | r :d | t, :m, | l, ||
But woe! when burst - ing un - con - troll'd, The glow - ing me - tals fierce ex - pand.

13. KEY B♭. d. f. A♭. "Blessing and Glory," p. 10, 11.

:d | t, .d :r .t, :l, .d | r .l, :t, .d :r .t, | dr :— :s | d :— :r
His won - drous frame to raise, Whose glo - rious

E♭. t.

| df :— :f | s :— :d' | d' .s :l .t :d' .l | s :— :f | m :— ||
name a - lone de - serves our end - less praise.

14. KEY E♭. **Three Removes.** *Haydn's* "First Mass," p. 52.

s. d. f. G♭.

:s .s | s :s | :l | s :s | :s | s :— | — :— | — :— | fr :d
He is bless-ed that com - eth, O Lord. in thy

| t, :— | r :d | t, :- .d | r :d | t, :— | : | : | : |
Ho - - - - - ly name.

E♭. t. m. l.

| ms :d' | t :r' | d' :— | s :l | r :— | r .,m :f .,s | f :— | m ||
He is bless - ed, is bless - ed that com - eth.

15. KEY C. A. t. m. l. "Samson," p. 1.

.m :t .t | t : .t | t .t :t .d' | r' . : .d' | ld : | .d :d .r
Un-will-ing-ly their super - sti - tion yields this rest; To breathe heav'n's

| m : .m | f .r :r .d | l, : | : ||
air; fresh blowing, pure and sweet.

[Intermediate Transitions.]

16. KEY D. d. f. C. "Jephtha," p. 4.

:s |s :- :s |l :- :- | s :l t |r' :- :r' |r' :- .d' :r'
In dis - mal dance a - round the fur - nace

f. F. s. d. f. A♭.

m' :- :- | : : | : :s r |f :- :r |m :- :- |- :- :s m
blue, In dis - mal dance a-

f :- :- |m :- :- |m :- :- |d :- :r |m :- ||
round the fur - - nace blue.

17. KEY A♭. "Song of the Bell," p. 36.

f. D♭.

:s |s :d |t, :t, |f :f |m :- .m t |r' :r'
De - signed for joy and peace, is made, The toc - sin

B♭. t. m. l.

r f :m |r :r |d :— ||
to re - volt and crime.

18. KEY C. *Macfarren's* "May-day," p. 30. 31.

A. t.m.l.

m' :— |s' :— |f' :— |m' :— |t :— |d' :— |r' :— |— :m s,
Sport up - on en - chant - ed ground; A

m :— |— :d .r |m :— |— :d .r |m :d |s :m |l :— |s : ||
joy - - ous, joy - - ous throng now comes a - long.

19. KEY B♭. "Judas Maccabæus," pp. 98, 99.

: |d :d .r |m .m : |m .t, : t, .d |r : | .r :m .f |r .r : |r .r :r .d
Come, then, my daughters, choicest art be - stow, To weave a chaplet for the victor's

G. t. m.l. E. t. m. l.

l, : | .l, d :d .r |m : .m |m s .s :s .l |t : .t |r' .t :l .s |d' : | : ||
brow, And in your songs for ever be con - fess'd The valour that pre - serv'd.

20. KEY F. **Two Removes. More difficult rhythms.** "Jephtha," p. 40.

G. t. m.

:f |f .f :s .r |m .m : .t, ,t, |m .r :m .t, |d : .m r |t, .t, :l, .s,
He made a bloody slaughter, and pur - sued the fly - ing foe till night bade sheathe the

[Intermediate Transitions.]

|d : | .d :m .d |f : .d |f .,f : f .m |d ||
sword, And taste the joys of vic - to - ry and peace.

21. KEY A "Jephtha," p. 33.
d. f. G.

| .s :s .s :s .s |l :m : |f .,s :f .,m :f .,r |s .,l :s .,f :s .,^{r}m
In vain they roll their foam - ing tide,

|f .,l :s .,f :s .,f |m :- .m :m .m |m : : ||
their foam-ing tide.

22. KEY E♭. "Jephtha," p. 61.

| : .d |m : .m |t_1 : .t_1 |r .r :r .d |l_1 .l_1 :
Be - gone, my child! Thou hast un - done thy fa - ther.

F. t.m.
|^{m}r : .s_1 |m : .s_1 |f .r : .l_1,l_1 |r .r :r .d |l_1 : ||
Fly be - gone, And leave me to the rack of wild des-pair.

23. KEY B♭. "Judas Maccabæus," p. 56. C. t. m.

|m .d : .s_1 |d :m |s : .m |d .d : | .d :d .r |m : .^{m}r^1
Saying, The sword of "God and Gideon." It was the Lord that

|t .t :r^1 .t |s : | .d^1 :m^1 .d^1 |l,l.l : ,d^1.t,d^1 |s : | : ||
for his Is - rael fought, And this their wonderful salvation wrought.

24. KEY C. "Samson," p. 68.

|r^1 : .s,s |t .,t :r^1 .s |d^1 .,d^1 :d^1 | .s :s .l |t .t :t,d^1.r^1,d^1
Ha! dost thou, then, al - rea - dy sin - gle me? I thought that labour and thy chains had

D. t. m.
|l .l : ,m .m,m |^{l}s .s :s,s .s ,l |t .,l :l .t |s .s :s ,f .s ,r
tam'd thee. Had fortune brought me to that field of death, where thou wrought'st wonders with an ass's

|m : ,s.d^1,s |l .l :l,l.t ,d^1 |s : ||
jaw, I'd left thy carcase where the ass lay dead.

25. KEY C. D. t. m. "Israel," p. 133.

|s .s :s .s |d^1 .d^1 : .d^1 |d^1 :d^1 .r^1 |^{m}r^1.r^1 : ,r^1.d^1,r^1 |t .t :t .d^1,r^1 |s ||
For the horse of Pharoah went in with his chariots and with his horsemen in - to the sea.

[Intermediate Transitions.]

26. KEY G♭. **Three Removes. More difficult Rhythms.** "Samson," p. 44, 45.

.t, :m .t, |d .t, : .t, |d .t, :m .t, |r :- .r |r :- .r |r :—
Be - hold thy servant, Thy servant in dis-tress, O God! be - hold,

E♭. t.m.l.
.dem :r .d |t, .l,.s, :d .t,.l, |r .d,t, :m .r,d |f .m,r :s .f,m |r : .l,s
To dust his glo - ry they would tread, To dust his glo - ry they would tread, And

|s :f .,m |m : .r,d |t, :- .t, |d :— | :
num - ber him a - mongst the dead.

27. KEY B♭. "Samson," p. 74.
d :d .d |l, : .m, |l, .l, :l, .t, |d : | .d :d .r |t, .t, :
Here lies the proof: If Da-gon be thy God, With high devo - tion

f. E♭. C. t. m. l.
t, .d :r .s, |d : .rl |f .f :f .m |d : | .d :d .r |m .,ms :s .l
in - vo - cate his aid, His glo-ry is con-cern'd. Let him dis-solve those magic

t : .t |t .t :l .s |d' : .s |d' : | .m :f . ,s |d :
spells that gave our hero strength, Then know whose God is God.

28. KEY B♭. G. t.m.l. "Jephtha," p. 31.
:s |r .m :f .m |d : | .d :d .r |ms .,r :r .m |f .f :
Sound then the last a - larm! And to the field ye sons of Is - rael!

D. t.
f .f :s .r |m : .d |m .m :r .df |t .,t :t .d' |s : | :
with in - trepid hearts; De - pendent on the might of Israel's God.

29. KEY E. *Macfarren's* "Christmas," p. 21.
: |m .,r :m |r :d |s .m :r .d |f :- .f |s :l |l :r
Taught by great Al - fred, never from your door, will you re - lent - less

s. d. f. G.
|f :m .,r |d :t, | :sm |t, .,t, :t, .t, |f :- .m |r .,d :d .d |d :
thrust the poor. No tale can to the time more fitt - ing be than one

30. KEY B♭. "Samson," p. 43.
: .l, |l, :- .l, |r :- .r, |f, .,f, :t, .,f, |m, : | .m, :m, .m,
His migh - ty griefs, His mighty griefs re - dress, His mighty

[Intermediate Transitions.]

s. d. f. D♭.

| l₁ : | .l₁ : l₁ .t₁ | d :— | — :— .d l | t .r : f .m | d : |
griefs, His mighty griefs, His mighty griefs re-dress,

E♭. t. m. F. t. m.

| .ls : r .m | f .f : f .m | d . | .ls : r .m | f .f : f .m | de : ||
Nor by the hea-then be they told, Nor by the heathen be they told.

Two and Three Removes. Advanced Rhythms.

31. KEY G. A. t.m. "Jephtha," p. 102.

| r : r ,m ,f : r ,m ,f | m ,r ,d : r ,d ,t₁ : d | mr : r ,m ,f : r ,m ,f | m ,r ,d : r ,d ,t₁ : d ||
Still I'm of thee pos - sess'd Such is kind heav'ns de - cree.

32. KEY G. *Macfarren's* "Christmas," p. 26.
s.d.f. B♭.

| s₁ :— ,fe₁,s₁ : l₁ ,t₁ ,d | m ,,d : s : m₁ | f₁ :— .f₁ : s₁m₁ ,,m₁ |
Blood of Dan - ish war - riors Is red up - on the

| f₁ :— : .l₁ | l₁ :— .r : d ,,l₁ | d ,,t₁ : d : ||
snow, A - mid the conqu'ring Sax - ons.

33. KEY G♭. "Samson," p. 42, 43.

| : .t₁ | d .t₁ : m .t₁ | d .t₁ : .t₁ | d .t₁ : m .t₁ | r :— | — :— |
Be-hold, be-hold Thy ser-vant, Thy ser-vant in dis- tress,

E♭. t. m. l.

| — .dem : r .d | t₁l₁,s₁. : .d | r ,d .t₁ : .m | f .m ,r : s .f ,m |
Re - turn, re - turn, O God! Re - turn, O God of

| r : .l,s | s :— .f,m | m : .r | s₁ :— .f | m : r ,,d | d :— ||
hosts! be - hold, be - hold Thy ser - vant in distress.

34. KEY B♭. *Macfarren's* "Christmas," p. 22.
G. t.m.l.

| : l₁ | l₁ :— .r : d .l₁ | d ,,t₁ : d : l₁ | l₁ :— .r : d,l₁.— | m :— : m₁s₁.,f₁ |
And breath - ing forth his sor - rows, Lifts up his withered hands: "The

| m₁ :— : s₁ | d :— : d | s₁ : d :— | m :— :— |
heav'n - ly King who reigns on high,

| l : r : m | l₁ : s :— .f | m : r :— | d :— : ||
Bless him who hears the poor man's cry."

[Intermediate Transitions.]

35. KEY B♭. *L is G.* **Minor Mode.** "As the Hart," p. 8.

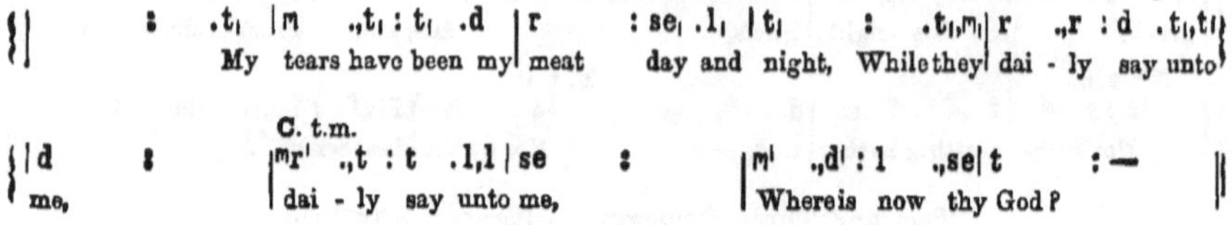

:.t,	m .,t, : t, .d	r :se, .l,	t, : .t,,m,	r .,r : d .t,,t,
My	tears have been my	meat day and night,	While they	dai - ly say unto

d :	C. t.m. ^m^r' .,t : t .l,l	se :	m' .,d' : l .,se	t : — ‖
me,	dai - ly say unto me,		Where is now thy God?	

36. KEY F. *L is D.* *Rossini's* "Stabat Mater," p. 16.

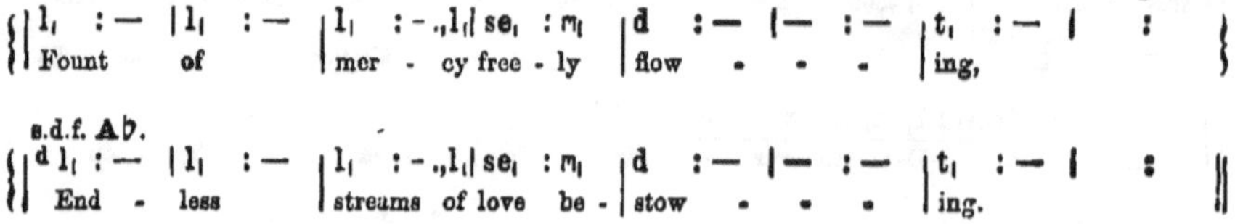

l, :—	l, :—	l, :-.,l,	se, :m,	d :—	— :—	t, :—	:
Fount	of	mer - cy free - ly		flow -	- -	ing,	

s.d.f. A♭.

^d^l, :—	l, :—	l, :-.,l,	se, :m,	d :—	— :—	t, :—	: ‖
End -	less	streams of love be -		stow -	- -	ing.	

37. KEY B♭. **More than Three Removes.** "Song of the Bell," p. 27.

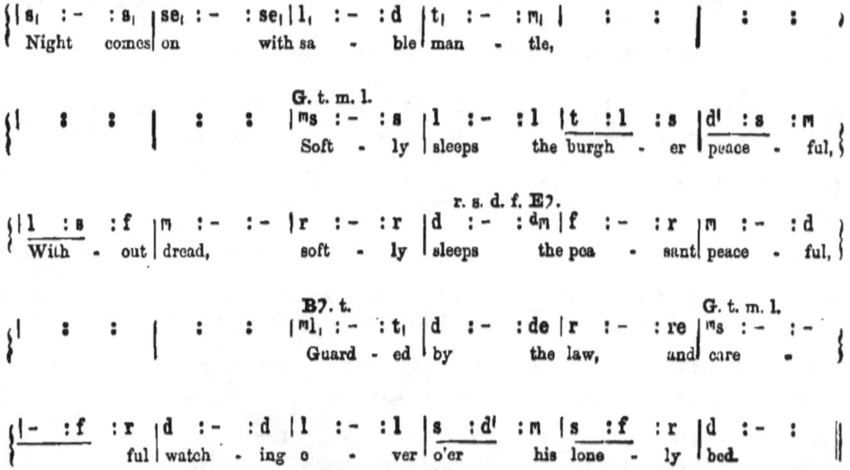

s, :- :s,	se, :- :se,	l, :- :d	t, :- :m,	: :	: :
Night comes	on with sa -	ble	man - tle,		

G. t. m. l.

: :	: :	^m^s :- :s	l :- :l	t :l :s	d' :s :m
		Soft - ly	sleeps the	burgh - er	peace - ful,

r. s. d. f. E♭.

l :s :f	m :- :-	r :- :r	d :- :^d^m	f :- :r	m :- :d
With - out	dread,	soft - ly	sleeps the pea	- sant	peace - ful,

B♭. t. ... G. t. m. l.

: :	: :	^m^l, :- :t,	d :- :de	r :- :re	^m^s :- :-
		Guard - ed	by the	law, and	care -

- :f :r	d :- :d	l :- :l	s :d' :m	s :f :r	d :- : ‖
ful	watch - ing	o - ver	o'er his	lone - ly	bed.

[Intermediate Transitions.]

Advanced Transitions from the Classics.

More than Three Removes.

38. KEY E. r.s.d.f. C. "Jephtha," p. 42.

| .s :s .s | :l .t | d' .d :d'm' .r' :d' .t | d' : : |
Of swift-er flight, of | swift-er flight and sub - tler | frame,

d.f.B♭.
| : : | d'r :r :m | r : .r :r .r | d : : ||
| Of swift - er | flight and subtler | frame.

39. KEY C. *Beethoven's* "Mass in C," p. 23.
s.d.f. E♭.

: .l | t .s :d' .m' | d' .t,d':r' .s | - .d' :d' | d' : | :r't
A | - - - - | - - - - | - men, A - | men, | A -

d.f.D♭. C. t.m.l.r.s.
| d' : | :lt | d' :d' | — :— | de'r' :— | m' :— | r' :— | d' . ||
| men, | A - | men, A | - - | - - | men, | A - | men.

40. KEY A♭. *Rossini's* "Stabat Mater," p. 9.

:d ,,d | d :t, | ,,f :f ,,f | f :m . | :d ,,d | d :t, . | :f ,,f
When she | saw Him, | the Lord of | glo - ry, | All his | vis - age | marr'd and

r.s.d.f. F♭.
| fl :s . | t :- .t | d' :- .d' | de' :- .de' | r' :- .r' | re' :- .re'
| go - ry, all | His | vis - age marr'd | and | go - ry, Smart - | ing

A♭. t.m.l.r.
| m' :— | f' :— | — :m'd' | - .s :fe.s | l :- .t, | l :- .s | d : ||
| from | | | the | Fa - | ther's | rod.

41. KEY G. "Creation," p. 42.

| : | :s | l :l | s .f :m .r | s :— | m : | f :— | :f | m : |
And | in his | eyes with | bright - ness | shines | The | soul,

l.r.s.d.f. A♭.
| :m | lse :— | — :se | l :— | — :f .r | d :— | r :d | d :— | : ||
the | breath | and | im - | - age | of | his | God.

Price ONE PENNY. J. CURWEN & SONS, 8 & 9, WARWICK LANE, E.C.

42. KEY D. *Graun's* "Te Deum," p. 9.

: s | s : f .m | s : f .m | l .l : l .l | l ,,s : s .d' | - .t : - .l | - .s : - .l
The good - ly fel - lowship of the prophets praise Thee, praise

s. d. f. F.

s : f,m.f | m : | : | d'l : l, .m | f .f : f .f,f | f .m :
Thee, praise Thee, The no - ble army of martyrs

G. t. m.

sf .m : | l .s : | d' : t,l .s,f | m : — | r : | ||
praise Thee, praise Thee, praise Thee, praise Thee.

43. KEY G. **Transitional Modulation. Two Removes.** "Israel," p. 100, 101.

A. t. m. f. D. *L* is *B*.

: .s | m : d .d | l,s, : s, .s | m : d .d | l,m. : m .m' | d' : l .l | se : m ||
The depths were congeal - ed, the depths were con-geal - ed, the depths were congeal - ed.

44. KEY A. "Samson," p. 49.

: d | s : — | — : f .m | r : — | : r | m : — | — : r .d | t, : — | : r
Like me, a - verse to each de - light, She

r : — | — : r | se : — | — : t | r : — | — : m | d : — | : l,
wears the te - - dious wid - - ow'd night, She

d. f. G.

dr : — | — : r | se : — | — : t | r : — | — : m | d : — | ||
wears the te - - dious wid - - ow'd night.

45. KEY B♭. "Acis and Galatea," p. 15.

m : d : l | r : — : — | — : m : f | m : r : d | t, .r : d : t, .l,
Melt - ing mur - - - - - murs, last - ing

C. t. m. *L* is *A*.

l, : — : — | det : — : t | d' : s : d' | r' : t : s | m' : — : —
love. Melt - ing mur - murs fill the grove.

f' : l : f' | m' : l : d' | t : d' : l | se : — : — ||
Melt - ing mur - murs, last - ing love.

[Advanced Transitions.]

46. KEY F. G. t. m. *L* is *E*. "Samson," p. 14.

| m :m .m | l .l : | m .m :m .ba | se :^m r | s : | .t, :t, .l, | t, .t, :t, .d |
In the warm sunshine of our prosp'rous days, friends swarm! But in the winter of ad-

| r .r :r | .r :f .m | d : ||
ver-si - ty, draw in their head.

47. KEY C. *L* is *A*. "Israel," p. 152.

| :m .ba | se .l :t .d' | r' :— | — :r' | d' :t .l |
till Thy peo - ple pass o - - - - - - ver, which Thou hast

D. t. m.

| m :- .m | l,s, .l, :t, .d | r .m :f .s | l .t :d' .r' | t :— ||
pur - chas ed, till Thy peo - ple pass o - ver, O Lord.

48. KEY A. "Israel," p. 128. 129.
d. f. G. *L* is *E*.

| :r .d | t, .r :d .t, | l, :r, .r, | m, :- .m, | l, :l, | l, :s, | fe,se, :se, .l, |
Thy peo - ple which Thou hast pur - chas- ed, they shall be still, till Thy

| t, .d :r .m | f :— | f :m | l, :— | — :— | — :— | — :— ||
people pass o - - ver, O Lord.

49. KEY D. "Israel," p 103.

| s :d' .r' :m' | d' :— : | s' :m' :d' | s :— : |
The en - e - my said, I will pur - sue,

d. f. C. *L* is *A*.

| d' :s :m .r | dr .m :ba .se :l .t | d' .r' :m' .r' :d' .t | d' : : ||
I will ov-er - take,

50. KEY A♭. **Transitional Modulation. Three Removes.** "St. Paul," p. 21.

| s :f | m :- .m | m :r .l, | t, : | :s | f :m | :l |
Lord! lay not this sin to their charge. Lord Je - sus! re -

pp s.d.f. C♭. *L* is *A♭*.

| l :s .f | m :r | .d l :l .l | l .t :d' .d' | — :t .l | se :- .l | l :— ||
ceive my spi - rit! And when he had said this he fell a - sleep.

[Advanced Transitions.]

51. KEY B♭. *L* is *G*. C. t. m. *L* is *A*. "Creation," p. 40, 41.

| :t₁ :t₁ .t₁ | d :- .t₁ :d .se₁ | l₁ :det :t .t | d' :- .t :d' .se |
But all the | work was not com | -plete, But all the | work was not com-

f. F. *L* is *D*.

| l : : | : :ˡm | l :— :m | d :- .d :t₁ .l₁ |
| plete, | There | want - ed | yet that wondrous

D. t. m. l.

| m :— :m | ˡ₁d :m :s | l :— :f | t :— :t | d' :— : ||
| be - ing, | That grate - ful | should God's | pow'r ad - | mire.

52. KEY A♭. *L* is *F*. *Haydn's* "First Mass," p. 4.

F. t.m.l.

:m | d :m :se | l :l₁ :t₁ | d :l₁ :— | t₁ :— : | ʳf :— :m |
The | works of thine | own | hands. | Hide not

| r : :r | s :— :f | m :d' :t | d' :— :d' | d' ||
| thou thy | face from | us, Hide not | thou thy | face.

53. KEY F. *Beethoven's* "Mass in C," p. 40, 41.

:t₁ | d :— | — :d | r :— | r :r | m :- .m | m :m |
Re - | joice, re - | joice in the | Lord and mag - ni -

C. t.

| ᶠᵉt :t | t .t :t .t | d' :- .d' | d' : | :d' | d' :d' .d' | t :— | r' :r' |
fy him all ye seed of | Is - ra-el, How plen - ti-ful, | Lord, is thy

s. d. f. E♭. *L* is *C*.

| ᵐᵃd' :— | t :— | l :l | s :s | f :m | re :- .re | re :m | ||
good - ness | which thou hast laid | up for them that | fear thee.

54. KEY E♭. *Romberg's* "Bell," p. 41.

| :r | s :— | — :l₁ | f :— | — :s₁ | m :— | — :r | r :d |
Its voice to sor - - row it shall

F. t. m.

| d :t₁ | :f | f :m | :ʳd | d :t₁ | f :— | — :t₁ | m : .r |
lend, it - self not feel - ing joy or pain, And

[Advanced Transitions.]

| r .d : t₁.l₁ | m : m .m | r : d | t₁ : l₁ | se₁ : | .m : se.m | l : l₁ |
with its va - ry-ing notes at - tend, On life's e-vent - ful,

D. t. m. l.
| d :re₁.re₁ | m₁ : — | — : — | : | : | : | m₁s₁ : d .m |
va - ry-ing scene; And as its

| s : — .m | s .f : r .t₁ | r .d : .d | s : — .m | l : — .s | f .s : l .t | d' : — | — : — ||
tones, which first so clear, Soon fade, and on the ear de - cay.

Transitional Modulation. More difficult Rhythms.

55. KEY E♭. "Acis and Galatea," p. 24.

B♭. t. d.f. A♭. *L* is *F*.
| .t : d' | — .r' : t ,.t | d' .s : .r's | l .f : r .s | m ,.d : sl |
No show'rs to larks so pleasing, Not sunshine to the bee, Not sleep

E♭. t.
| — .t : se ,.se | l .l : .tm' | f' .r' : t .m' | d' : | : ||
to toil so cas - ing, As these dear smiles to me.

56. KEY F. "Israel," p. 16.
: s | fe : f .f | m .f : s .l | r : s | — : f | f : m .s | l : l .t |
They loa - thed, they loa-thed to drink of the ri - ver: He turn -ed their

d. f. E♭. *L* is *G*.
| d' .s : d'r' | — .d',t : d' | — .ta : l .se | l ||
wa - - - - - ter in - to blood.

57. KEY B♭. *L* is *G*. "Judas Maccabæus," p. 9.
| r : t₁ .t₁ | se₁ : .se₁ | se₁.se₁ : l₁ .t₁ | d : .l₁ | f₁ .f₁ : .m₁,r₁ | se₁ .se₁ : se₁ .l₁ |
Wretch-ed in - deed! But let not Ju - dah's race Their ru-in with desponding arms em-

C. t. m. *L* is *A*.
| m₁ : | l₁s : s .s | d' : | .s : s .l | t .t : | t .r' : f |
brace. Dis - tractful doubt and desper- a - tion Ill be - come

D·. t. m. *L* is *B*.
| .f : l .s | m .m : | m .m : m .ba | se : .m | l : .ls | t : .s |
the cho-sen na - tion, Chosen by the Great I AM! The Lord of

| d' : | m : m .ba | se : .m | l : .l | d'.l : l .m | f : ||
Hosts! who still the same, We trust, will give at- ten-tive ear.

58. KEY E♭. f. A♭. *L* is *F*. *Haydn's* "First Mass," p. 59, 60.

|d :— :d |t₁ .,r :s : |ᵗᵃ₁f₁ :— :f₁ |m₁ .,se₁ :t₁ : |
|Hal - le - |lu - jah. |A - men, |A - men, |

B♭. t. m. *L* is *A*.

|l₁ :— :l₁ |se₁ .,t₁ :m : |ˢ₁f₁ :— :f₁ |m₁ .,se₁ :t₁ : ||
|Hal - le - |lu - jah. |A - men, |A - men. ||

59. KEY A. *L* is *F*♯. Beating thrice to the measure. "Jephtha," p. 49.

|m .,f :s .,f |s :m |l :- .s |f .m :r .d |t₁ :l₁ |se₁ :- .l₁ |t₁ .l₁ :t₁ .de |
|Singing great Jeho - vah's praise, The ho - ly choir em - ploy, |

f. D. *L* is *B*.

|ʳl.se :l .t |se.ba :m.ba |se.l :t .d' |r'.t :m'.r' |d'.t :d'.r' |m' :l |t :l.,se |l :— |
| - - | - - - - The | ho - ly choir em - ploy. |

E. t. m.

| : | : | : |ˡs.,l :t .,d' |r' :f |m :— |s .,f :m .,r |d :ta |l :— ||
| Such as on our so-lemn days, | Singing great Jehovah's praise. ||

60. KEY G. "Israel," p. 100, 101.

A. t. m.

| : .d |t₁ .l₁ :t₁ .s₁ |d .,d :d .m |ᵈᵉt₁ .l₁ :t₁ .s₁ |
| The wa - ters were | gath - er - ed, the wa - ters were |

f. D. *L* is *B*.

|d .,d :d .m |ᵈᵉse.ba :se .m |l .,l :l .d |t₁ .t₁ : ||
|gath - er - ed, the wa - ters were | gath - er - ed to - geth-er. ||

61. KEY E♭. "Acis and Galatea," p. 42.

B♭. t. d. f. A♭.

| : .s |l .f :r .s |m .r,d :ˢd |- .r :t₁ .,d |d : .ʳm |f .r :t₁ .m |
| No show'rs to larks so | pleasing, Not sun - shine to the | bee, Not sleep to toil so |

E♭. t. *L* is *C*.

|d .t₁,l₁ :ᵐl |- .t :se .,l |l ||
|eas - ing As these dear smiles to | me. ||

[Advanced Transitions.]

62. KEY D♭. *L* is *B*♭. *Haydn's* "First Mass," p. 21, 22.

|m' :— |d' :l |se.,l : t . | :l |se :t .t |d' :l |se :t |d' :l |
Thou, Lord, art God a-lone, al - migh - ty and e - ver - last - ing. A - men.

B♭. t. m. l.

|m' :— |- :— |m : | : | : | : |m's :— |m :d .d |
A - - men, O praise ye the

|l, .t, :d .r,m |f :— |m :s .f,m |r :- .r |m :r |d .r :m .fe |s ||
Lord for e - ver. A - - men, A - - - - - men.

63. KEY F. *L* is *D*. "Israel in Egypt," p. 112.

|m .r :d .t, :d,t,.l, |f .m :f :- .m |r .de :r :— |
Thou in thy mer - - - - cy

G. t. m. s.d.f. B♭. *L* is *G*.

|r .r :m .f :mr .d |t, :- .r :s, .t, |d .t, :d :- .ta,s, |
hast led forth thy peo - ple, which thou hast re -

|f, .m, :r, .l, :se, .t, |l, :— :se, |l, :— : ||
deem - - - - - - - - ed.

Transitional Modulation. More than three Removes.

64. KEY A♭. "As the hart," p. 28.

f. D♭.

|:d |r :l |s :f |m :— |— :— |mt :f' |m' :r' |
From hence - forth and for ev - - - - - - - -

A♭. t. *L* is *F*.

|d' :— |— :t |l :— |— :m'l |se :m |l :— |
- - - - - - - - - - - - -

C. t. m. l. r.

|lf' :r' |t :s |d' :— | :d' |t : |f' :— |m' :— | ||
- - er - more. for ev - er - more.

65. KEY C. r.s.d.f. A♭. *L* is *F*. "Song of the Bell," p. 22.

|:s .s |d' :m |f :r |d : |dm, .se, :t, .se, |l, : |m, .l, :d .l, |
All our art and toil re - pay. Should the mould be wrong, Or the "gush" too

F. t. m. l.

|m : | : | : |ms :- .f |m :- .r |d :r .m |
strong. Ah! per - haps, while joy we

s.d.f. A♭.

|s .fe :f | :rt, .t, |m :d |l, :- .d |d :s, | : ||
cher - ish, All our hopes and wish - es per - ish.

66. KEY D. *L* is *B*. "Israel," p. 121.

| d' :- .d' | d' ,,d': d' .d' | d' ,,t : l | : .t | d' .l : .se | l : .t |
All th' inhab-i - tants of Ca - naan shall melt a - way, shall

| d' .l : .se | l : | .r' : m' .de' | r' :- .d' | t :- .l | l :— |
melt a - way, shall melt a - way, shall melt a - way;

f. G. s. d. f. B♭. D. t. m. l. r. B. t. m. l.

| :d's |— :s | d'l :— | l :— | fe r' :- .r' | r' :— | r'f :- .f | m :— ||
by the great - ness of Thy arm, of Thy arm.

67. KEY C. *L* is *A*. *Rossini's* "Stabat Mater," p. 14.

| l ,,t : d' ,,t : l ,,f | m ,,d : l, : | d ,,r : m ,,f : s ,,f | m ,,r : d : |
For His peo - ple's sin He suf - fer'd,

l. r. s. d. f. D♭.

| l ,,t : d' ,,t : l ,,f | m ,,re : m :— | fm ,,f : s ,,l : s ,,f | m ,,r : d :— ||
His own pre - cious life He of - fer'd.

68. KEY B♭. "Come, let us sing," p. 23.

r. s. d. f. G♭. *L* is *E*♭.

| d :d :d | d :- .d : r | m :— : | m :— :m | mse :- .l : se.l |
As at Mer - i - bah they did, and at Mas - sa in the

A♭. t. m.

| t :— :r | :det, : r | f :— :f | m :f :- .f | f :m .t, : d .r |
des - ert, Af - ter for - ty years grief at this diso-bedient

| d : :l | r :— :d .t, | m :d :t, .l, | r :d :t, .f | m :- .d : l, |
race, I said: 'Tis a peo - ple that do err, and in their hearts re - bel,

B♭. t. m. *L* is *G*. f. E♭. *L* is *C*.

| :m :m | s :— :sf | m :f :- .f | f :m .t, : de.r | dese : :m |
Af - ter for - ty years grief at this dis-obedient race, I

f. A♭. *L* is *F*. B♭. t. m. *L* is *G*.

| l : :lm .m | f :f :m .r | de :— :sf | — :f .f :m .r |
said: 'Tis a peo - ple that do err, and in their hearts re -

| de :s .s :f .m | r :r : | m :m :- .l, | f :l : ||
bel, and that of my sta - tutes are still un - mind - ful.

[Advanced Transitions.]

NEW EDITION.

MINOR MODE PHRASES,

SELECTED FROM WELL-KNOWN COMPOSERS.

For the 5th requirement of the Intermediate Certificate, any one of Nos. 11 to 22, taken by lot must be Sol-faad in correct tune and time. Two attempts allowed. The key may be changed when necessary.

No. 1. KEY G. *L* is *E*. SIR H. BISHOP. From "Tis when to sleep."

l, :l,.t,	d :r	m :f	t, :m	l .l :d	r :m	l, :—	:l,
Still as un-daunt-ed		on we	stray, Thro'	many a	tan - gled	brake,	We

m :-.r	d .r :d .t,	l, :d	t, :m,	l, :t,	d :r	m :—	— :—
pause to	mark the	si - lent	way The	cau - tious	trav'l - lers	take.	

No. 2. KEY B♭. *L* is *G*. MENDELSSOHN. From the "Turkish Drinking Song."

l, :m,.,m,	l, :m,	t, :m,	t, :m,.,m,	d :l,.,t,	d :l,.,d	m :—	d :
Bump not the flask, thou		churl-ish	clown, On the	board as	tho' you would	break	it!

No. 3. KEY A. *L* is *F*♯. W. BOYD. From a Part-Song.

:m .r	d :l,	t, :m,	l, :-.t,	d :d	r :r	f :f	m :—	—
At	Christmas -	time, when	frost is	out, The	year is	grow-ing	old,	

:m,	l, :-.t,	d :r	m :f	m :r	d :t,.l,	t, :se,	l, :—	—
But	sure - ly,	soon as	A - pril	comes, 'Twill	wake and	bloom a -	gain.	

No. 4. KEY C. *L* is *A*. WELSH AIR. From "The Dawn of Day."

:l	l :m	m :d'	d' :—	t :t	l :d'	t :l	l :—	se
Sweet	Spring a -	gain re -	turn -	ing, Makes	ev - 'ry	bo - som	glad,	

:l	m :f	r :m	d :r	t, :-.d	l :l	d'.t :l.se	l :—	—
The	birds are	sing - ing	from each	spray, 'Tis	I a -	lone am	sad.	

PRICE ONE HALFPENNY. LONDON: J. CURWEN & SONS, 8 & 9, WARWICK LANE, E.C.

No. 5. KEY A. *L is F* J. R. THOMAS. From "There are good fish in the sea."

:m .r | d :d | t_1.l_1 :t_1.d | l_1 :— | :l_1.t_1 | d .t_1 :l_1.t_1 | m_1 :se_1 | l_1 :— |

:m | m .f :m .f | m :l_1 | m :— | :m | m :r .d | t_1 :m | l_1 :— ‖

No. 6. KEY D♭. *L is B♭.* WELSH AIR. From "Of noble race was Shenkin."

:l .t | ${d^1}$:t .l | se.l :t .se | l :l_1 | :l_1.t_1 | d .l_1 :r .t_1 | m :m | d :l_1 |
From his | cave in | Snow-don's | moun-tains, | Hath the | pro - phet | min - strel | spo - ken;

:l .t | ${d^1}$.${m^1}$:${r^1}$.${d^1}$ | t .${r^1}$:${d^1}$.t | l .${d^1}$:t .l | se :- .m | f .m :f .r | m :se | l :l_1 ‖
It | o - mens | great suc - | cess in | war, Of | con - quest the | sure | to - ken.

No. 7. KEY C. *L is A.* H. LAHEE. From a Part-Song.

:m | l :m | f :m .r | l :m | f :m .r | l :l .se | l :l .t | ${d^1}$:— | — |
We | all must | work, it | is our | lot, Each | one must | take his | part,

:${m^1}$.${r^1}$ | ${d^1}$:d | ${d^1}$:${d^1}$.t | l :l | l .l.se | l :l.se | l :l.se | l :— | — ‖
There's | no - thing | done, There's | no - thing | won, With- | out the | earn - est | heart.

No. 8. KEY A. *L is F♯.* C. G. ALLEN. From a Part-Song.

:m_1 | d :— | t_1 :l_1 | t_1 :— | m_1 :m_1 | m :— | r :d | t_1 :— | — |
The | sad | leaves are | dy - | ing, the | sweet | birds have | flown,

:m_1 | l :— | t_1 :d | t_1 :se_1 | m_1 :m_1 | d :— | r :d | t_1 :— | — |
O'er | ev - | 'ry fair | blos - | som once | bloom - | ing and | bright,

:t_1 | m :— | r :d | r :— | d :l_1 | m_1 :— | l_1 :se_1 | l_1 :— | — ‖
The | frost | spi - rit | lays | her cold | fin - | gers to - | night.

No. 9 KEY B♭. HANDEL. From "Judas."

:d.r | m :se_1 | l_1 :t_1.d | r :d .t_1 | d :r .m | f :m .r | m :r.d | t_1 :l_1 | m :— | — ‖
Where warlike | Ju - - | das | wields | his | right - - | eous | sword.

(Minor Mode Phrases.)

No. 10. KEY F. *L* is *D*. J. R. THOMAS. From "The Owl."

:m | l :m .,m | d :m .,m | t_1 :m | l_1 : .,t_1 | d :d .,r | m :m | l_1 : |
Mourn | not for the owl, nor his | gloomy plight; The | owl hath his share of | good;

:m | m :t_1 .,d | l_1 :m .,m | m :t_1 .,d | l_1 :t_1 | d :m .,m | l :- r | m :— |
Nor | lone - ly the bird, nor his | ghast-ly mate, They're | each un-to each a | pride,

:se | l :s .s | f :m .m | r :d | f :- .m | l :f .r | m :m | l_1 :— ||
Thrice | fond - er, perhaps, since a | strange dark fate Has | rent them from all be - | side.

No. 11. KEY B♭. *L* is *G*. HENRY SMART. From "Good night, thou glorious sun."

:m_1 | m_1 :- .m_1 | ba_1 :se_1 | l_1 :l_1 | t_1 :t_1 | d :m | r :l_1 | d :— | t_1 ||
Veil'd | by thy cloak of | crim - son gold, Thy | day's high du - ty | done.

No. 12. KEY C. *L* is *A*. P. LA TROBE. From the Tune "Hereford."

:l | se :l | se :m | m :re | m :m | ba :se | l :t | d^1 :t | l ||
On | thee a - lone our | spi - rits stay, While | held in life's un - | e - ven way.

No. 13. KEY D. *L* is *B*. HANDEL. From "Jephtha."

:m | l :m | ba :se | l :— | :t | d^1 :se | l :t |
Or | heav'n, earth, seas and | sky In | one con - fu - sion

| d^1 :— | :f | m :r | d :t_1 | l_1 :— | — ||
lie, Ere | in a daugh - ter's | blood

No. 14. KEY D. *L* is *B*. HENRY SMART. From "The Lady of the Lea."

| m :m | ba :se | l :t | d^1 :— | d :d | r :- .d | d :— | — :— ||
Cold with - in the | grave lies she, | Sleep-ing peace - ful - | ly.

No. 15. KEY D. *L* is *B*. LEVERIDGE. From "Black-eyed Susan."

.m :l .t | d^1 :t .l :se .l | m :- .f :m .r | d :t_1 .l_1 :d .,r | m :- . |
All in the | downs the fleet was | moor'd, The streamers | wav - ing in the | wind,

.d :m .ba | se :m .m :l .t | d^1 :m^1 : | m .,l :d^1 .t :l .se | l :- . ||
Does my sweet | William, Does my sweet | Wil - liam | Sail a - mong your | crew?

(Minor Mode Phrases.)

No. 16. KEY C. *L* is *A*. HENRY SMART. From "Now May is here."

{ :l.se | l :t | se.ba:se.l | t :se | m :l.se | l :se | t :m | d' :— | — ||

No. 17. KEY A. *L* is *F*♯. From the same.

{ :l, | m :— | t, :se, | m, :— | — :m, | ba, :se, | l, :t, | d :— | — ||

No. 18. KEY C. *L* is *A*. HAYDN. From "Achieved is the glorious work."

{ | m :m | ba :m | ba :se | l : | l :se | l :s | f :— | m : {

{ | l :t | d' :d' | l :t | se : | se :se | l :l | m :— | m : ||

No. 19. KEY C. *L* is *A*. HANDEL. From "Esther."

{ :m | se :m | l :— | se :m | ba :se | l :— | se :l | t :se | d' :— | t ||
For | ev - er | bless - | ed, For | ev - er | bless - | ed, For | ev - er | bless - | ed.

No. 20. KEY B♭. *L* is *G*. J. L. HATTON. From "Jack Frost."

{ | d :t, | se, :m, | ba, :se, | l, :t, | d :r | t, :se, | l, :t, | se, :— {

{ | m, :se, | l, :l, | d :t, | t, :l, | m :se, | l, :d | t, :se, | l, :— ||

No. 21. KEY C. *L* is *A*. G. A. MACFARREN. From "The Three Fishers."

{ | m :ba | m :ba | se :l | se :l | t :d' | t :d' | r' :d' | r' :t | l :— | — :— ||

No. 22. KEY E♭. *L* is *C*. HANDEL. Phrases from "Israel in Egypt."

{ :se | l :m | ba :se | l :f | m :— | l :— | — :se | ba :se | l {

{ :se | l .t :d'.l | se :— | m :— | :d' | l :se | m m | ba :ba | se {

{ :se | l :— | :m | se :ba | m :ba | se :l t | d' :l | se :— | ||

(Minor Mode Phrases.)

FIRST EXERCISES FOR MIXED VOICES.

TO BE USED AS AN INTRODUCTION TO "ADDITIONAL EXERCISES."

FIRST STEP.

Ex. 1. KEY D.

| d :— | m :— | s :— | d' :— | d' :— | s :— | m :— | d :— ||

Ex. 2. KEY E♭. † *(Sopr. and Bass.)*

:s | s :— | m :d | s :— | s :s † | m :— | d :m † | s :— | m ||
:d | d :— | d :d | d :m | s :d | d :— | d :d | m :s | d ||

Ex. 3. KEY C.

| d :m | s :m † | d :— | — :— † | m :s | d' :s † | m :— | — :— ||
| d :— | — :— | d :m | s :m | d :— | m :— | s :s | d :— ||

Ex. 4. KEY F.

| d :s_1 | m :d † | s :— | — :— † | m :— | d :m † | s :— | d :— ||
| : | : | d :s_1 | m :d | s :— | — :— | s_1 :— | d :— ||

Ex. 5. KEY G.

| d :s_1 :d | m :— :— † | s :m :d | s_1 :— :— † |
| : : | d :s_1 :d | m :— :— † | s :m :d |

| s :s :s | m :— :d | m :— :s | d :— :— ||
| s_1 :— :— † | d :— :d | s_1 :— :s_1 | d :— :— ||

Ex. 6. KEY F.

| d .s_1 :d | m .d :m † | s :m | d :— † | s .m :s | m .d :m † | s :s | d :— ||
| : | : | d .s_1 :d | m .d :m | s :m | d :— | s_1 :— | d :— ||

SECOND STEP.

Ex. 7. KEY G. **SWELL THE ANTHEM.** A.L.C.

s_1 :s_1	d :d	m :d	s :—	d :m
1.Swell the	an - them, †	raise the	song;	Prais - es †
s_1 :s_1	s_1 :s_1	d :d	t_1 :—	d :d

m :m	m :m	s :m	r :—	m :s
2.Hark! the	voice of	na - ture	sings,	Prais - es †
d :d	d :d	d :d	s_1 :—	d :d

London: J. Curwen & Sons, 8 & 9, Warwick Lane, E.C. Price 1d.
St. Co. (New).

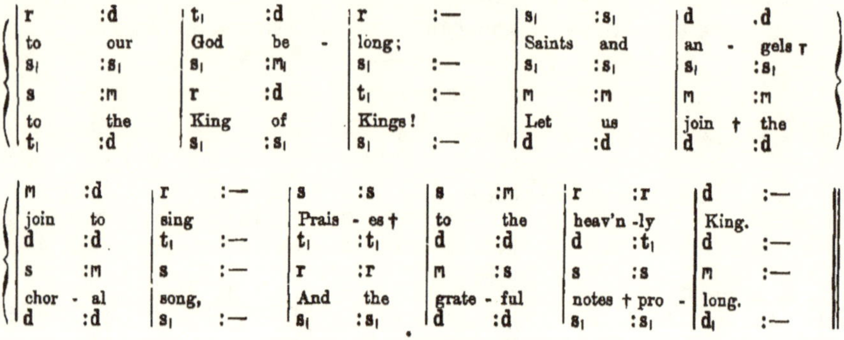

r :d	t, :d	r :—	s, :s,	d .d
to our	God be -	long;	Saints and	an - gels †
s, :s,	s, :m,	s, :—	s, :s,	s, :s,
s :m	r :d	t, :—	m :m	m :m
to the	King of	Kings!	Let us	join † the
t, :d	s, :s,	s, :—	d :d	d :d

m :d	r :—	s :s	s :m	r :r	d :—
join to	sing	Prais - es †	to the	heav'n -ly	King.
d :d	t, :—	t, :t,	d :d	d :t,	d :—
s :m	s :—	r :r	m :s	s :s	m :—
chor - al	song,	And the	grate - ful	notes † pro -	long.
d :d	s, :—	s, :s,	d :d	s, :s,	d, :—

SWEET SUMMER-TIME.

Ex. 8. KEY C. A.L.C.

s .m :m	d' .s :s	t .d' :r' .t	d' .r' :m'	s .m :m
1. Summer-time,	Summer- time,	Mer-ry, mer-ry	Summer- time;	Gai-ly sing,
m .d :d	m .m :m	s .m :s .s	s .s :s	m .d :d
2. Summor-time,	Summer- time,	Mer-ry, mer-ry	Summer- time;	Sing a - gain,
d' .s :s	s .d' :d'	r' .d' :t .r'	m' *.r' :d'	d' .s :s
3. Summer-time,	Summer- time,	Mer-ry, mer-ry	Summer- time;	Sing a - gain,
d .d :d	d .d :d	s .s :s .s	d .d :d	d .d :d

d' .s :s	m' .m' :m' .r'	d' :—	t .r' :t .s	d' .m' :s
gai- ly sing,	'Tis sweet Summer-	time.	Brightly now the	sun's gay beam,
m .m :m	s .s :s .s	m :—	s .s :s .s	s .s :s
sing a - gain,	'Tis sweet Summer-	time.	Sweetly scent-ed	is the air,
s .d' :d'	d' .d' :d' .t	d' :—	r' .t :r' .t	d' .d' :t
sing a - gain,	'Tis sweet Summer-	time.	Now the birds on	ev - 'ry tree,
d .d :d	d .m :s .s	d :—	s .s :s .s	m .d :s

t .r' :t .s	d' .m' :s	s .m :m	d' .s :s	m' .m' :m' .r'	d' :—
Glances o'er the	crys-tal stream,	Summer- time,	Summer- time,	'Tis sweet Summer	-time.
s .s :s .s	s .s :s	m .d :d	m .m :m	s .s :s .s	m :—
Beauteous flow'rs bloom	ev - 'ry - where,	Summer- time,	Summer- time,	'Tis sweet Summer	-time.
r' .t :r' .t	d' .d' :t	d' .s :s	s .d' :d'	d' .d' :d' .t	d' :—
Warble their sweet	mel - o - dy,	Summer -time,	Summer- time,	'Tis sweet Summer	-time.
s .s :s .s	m .d :s	d .d :d	d .d :d	d .m :s .s	d :—

* In marking the Tenor Registers (as p. 68), study the optional tones (pp. 32, 110), the phrasing (pp. 69, 70, 98), and the need for piano or forte in each case.

St. Co. (New).

MUSIC IN THE VALLEY.

Ex. 9. KEY A♭. A. L. C.

d :s_1 |d :r	m :— |r :—	d :s |d :r	m :— |— :—
1. Mu- sic in the	val - ley,	Mu - sic on the	hill,
s_1 :s_1 |s_1 :s_1	s_1 :— |s_1 :—	m_1 :m_1 |s_1 :s_1	s_1 :— |— :—
2. Mu- sic by the	fire - side,	Mu - sic in the	hall,
m :m |m :r	d :— |t_1 :—	d :d |d :t_1	d :— |— :—
3. Sing with joy - ful	voi - ces,	Friends and lov'd ones	dear;
d :d |d :d	d :— |s_1 :—	d_1 :d_1 |m_1 :s_1	d :— |— :—

r :r |r :s	m :— |d :—	t_1 :d |r :t_1	d :— |— :—
Mu - sic in the	wood - land,	Mu - sic in the	rill;
t_1 :t_1 |t_1 :t_1	d :— |s_1 :—	s_1 :m_1 |s_1 :s_1	s_1 :— |— :—
Mu - sic in the	school - room,	Mu - sic for us	all;
s :s |s :s	s :— |m :—	r :d |t_1 :r	m :— |— :—
Dis - cord and vex-	a - tion,	Ne'er shall en - ter	here,
s_1 :s_1 |s_1 :s_1	d :— |d :—	s_1 :s_1 |s_1 :s_1	d_1 :— |— :—

s :m |d :m	s :— |m :—	r :t_1 |s_1 :t_1	r :— |— :—
Mu - sic on the	moun - tain,	Mu - sic in the	air,
d :d |d :d	d :— |s_1 :—	s_1 :s_1 |s_1 :s_1	s_1 :— |— :—
Mu - sic in our	sor - row,	Mu - sic in our	care,
m :s |m :s	m :— |d :—	t_1 :r |t_1 :r	t_1 :— |— :—
Join the hap - py	cho - rus	Of all na - ture	fair,
d :d |d :d	d :— |d :—	s_1 :s_1 |s_1 :s_1	s_1 :— |— :—

d :s_1 |d :r	m :— |d :—	t_1 :d |r :t_1	d :— |— :—
Mu - sic in the	true heart,	Mu - sic ev - 'ry -	where.
m_1 :m_1 |s_1 :s_1	s_1 :— |s_1 :—	s_1 :m_1 |s_1 :s_1	m_1 :— |— :—
Mu - sic in our	glad - ness,	Mu - sic ev - 'ry -	where.
d :d |d :t_1	d :— |m :—	r :d |t_1 :r	d :— |— :—
Swell the glo - rious	an - them,	Mu - sic's ev - 'ry -	where.
d_1 :d_1 |m_1 :s_1	d :— |d :—	s_1 :s_1 |s_1 :s_1	d_1 :— |— :—

HIGHER, HIGHER WILL WE CLIMB.

Ex. 10. KEY D. A.L.C.

s :s | d' :d'	m' :-.r' | d' :—	s :m | s :d'	d' :t | :
1.Higher, high - er †	will we climb †	Up the mount of	glo - ry,
m :m | m :m	s :-.s | m :—	m :d | m :m	m :r | :
2.On - ward, on - ward†	may we press †	Through the path of	du - ty;
d' :d' | s :s	d' :-.t | d' :—	d' :s | d' :s	s :s | :
3.Clos-er, clos - er, †	let us knit †	Hearts and hands to -	ge - ther,
d :d | d :d	d :s, | d :—	d :-.d | d :m	s :s | :

s :s | d' :d'	m' :-.r' | d' :—	s :m | s :d'	d' :t |
That our names † may	live thro' time, †	In our coun - try's	sto - ry;
m :m | m :m	s :-.s | m :—	m :d | m :m	m :r | :
Vir - tue is true	hap - pi-ness, †	Ex - cel - lence, true	beau - ty;
d' :d' | s :s	d' :-.t | d' :—	d' :s | d' :s	s :s | :
Where our fire - side -	com - forts sit, †	In the wild - est	wea - ther;—
d :d | d :d	d :s, | d :—	d :-.d | d :m	s :s |

r :-.m | r :r	r :-.m | s :	s :-.m | s :d'	d' :-.t | t :
Hap - py,† when her	wel - fare calls,	He who conquers,†	he who falls,
t, :d | s, :t,	t, :d | r :	m :-.d | m :m	m :-.r | r :
Minds are of ce -	les - tial birth,	Make we then † a	heav'n of earth,
s :-.s | s :s	s :-.s | s :	d' :-.d' | d' :s	s :-.s | s :
O, they wan - der	wide † who roam	For the joys of	life † from home,
s, :d | t, :s,	s, :d | t, :	d :-.d | d :m	s :-.s | s :

d' :s | m :d	d' :— | d' :d'	d' :t | m' :r'	d' :— | — :
1.He who con - quers, 2.Make we then a 3.For the joys of	he who heav'n, make we life, for the	con - quers, he who then a heav'n of joys of life from	falls. earth. home.
d :s | m :d	m :— | m :m	m :r | s :s	m :— | — :
: | :	d' :s | m :d	s :— | d' :t	d' :— | — :
	1.He who con - quers, 2.Make we then a 3.For the joys of	he who heav'n of life from	falls. earth. home.
: | :	d' :s | m :d	s :— | s, :—	d :— | — :

St. Co. (New).

HEAVEN IS MY HOME.

Ex. 11. KEY A♭. A.L.C.

s_1 :d :t_1	d :- .r :m	s :m :d	r :— :—
1.I'm but a	stran - ger here,	Heaven is my	home;
s_1 :s_1 :s_1	s_1 :- .s_1 :s_1	s_1 :m_1 :d	s_1 :— :—
2.What though the	tempests rage?	Heaven is my	home;
m :m :r	d :- .t_1 :d	s :m :d	t_1 :— :—
3.There at my	Sav - iour's side,	Heaven is my	home;
d :d :s_1	m_1 :- .s_1 :d_1	s_1 :m_1 :d_1	s_1 :— :—
4.There-fore I	mur - mur not,	Heaven is my	home;

s_1 :d :t_1	d :- .r :m	s :m :d	s_1 :— :—
Earth is a	de - sert drear,	Heaven is my	home,
m_1 :s_1 :s_1	s_1 :- .s_1 :s_1	s :m :d	s_1 :— :—
Short is my	pil - grimage,	Heaven is my	home;
d :m :r	d :- .t_1 :d	s :m :d	s_1 :— :—
I shall be	glo - ri - fied,	Heaven is my	home;
d :d :s_1	m_1 :- .s_1 :d_1	s_1 :m_1 :d_1	s_1 :— :—
What - e'er my	earth - ly lot,	Heaven is my	home;

d :d :d	t_1 :- .d :r	r :r :r	d :- .r :m
Dan - ger and	sor - row stand	Round me on	ev - 'ry hand;
s_1 :s_1 :s_1	s_1 :- .m_1 :s_1	t_1 :t_1 :t_1	d :- .t_1 :d
And time's wild	win - try blast	Soon will be	o - ver-past:
m :m :m	r :- .d :t_1	s :s :s	m :- .r :d
There are the	good and blest,	Those I loved	most and best;
d :d :d	s_1 :- .s_1 :s_1	s_1 :s_1 :s_1	d :- .s_1 :d
And I shall	sure - ly stand	There at my	Lord's right hand;

s :m :d	r :- .m :r	d :m :r	d :— :—
Heaven is my	Fa - ther-land,	Heaven is my	home.
d :d :d	t_1 :- .d :s_1	m_1 :s_1 :s_1	m_1 :— :—
I shall reach	home at last,	Heaven is my	home.
m :s :m	r :- .d :t_1	d :d :t_1	d :— :—
And there I,	too, shall rest,	Heaven is my	home.
d :d :d	s_1 :- .s_1 :s_1	d :s_1 :s_1	d_1 :— :—
Heaven is my	Fa - ther-land,	Heaven is my	home.

St. Co. (New.)

SWEETEST, FAIREST.

Ex. 12. KEY F. A.L.C.

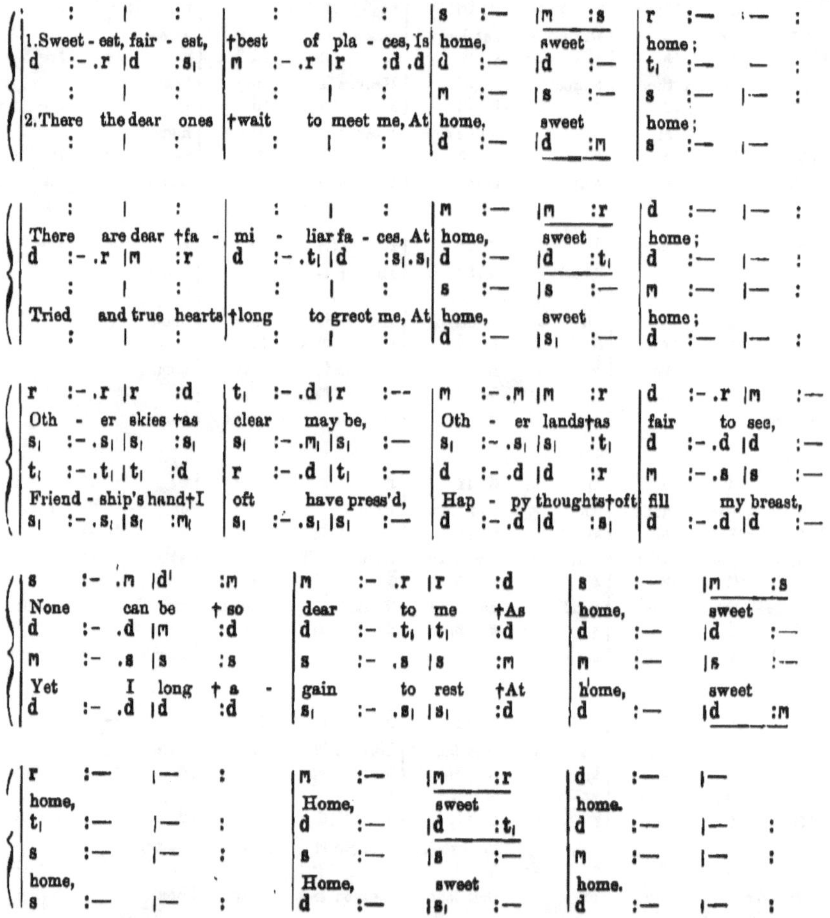

```
|  :    |  :    |  :    |  :     |s  :—    |m  :s    |r  :—   |—  :
1.Sweet - est, fair - est, †best of pla - ces, Is home, sweet home;
|d :-.r |d :s,  |m :-.r |r :d.d  |d  :—    |d  :—    |t, :—   |—  :
|  :    |  :    |  :    |  :     |m  :—    |s  :—    |s  :—   |—  :
2.There the dear ones †wait to meet me, At home, sweet home;
|  :    |  :    |  :    |  :     |d  :—    |d  :m    |s  :—   |—

|  :    |  :    |  :    |  :     |m  :—    |m  :r    |d  :—   |—  :
There are dear †fa - mi - liar fa - ces, At home, sweet home;
|d :-.r |m :r   |d :-.t,|d :s,.s,|d  :—    |d  :t,   |d  :—   |—  :
|  :    |  :    |  :    |  :     |s  :—    |s  :—    |m  :—   |—  :
Tried and true hearts †long to greet me, At home, sweet home;
|  :    |  :    |  :    |  :     |d  :—    |s, :—    |d  :—   |—  :

|r :-.r |r :d   |t, :-.d |r :--  |m :-.m |m :r   |d :-.r |m :—
Oth - er skies †as clear may be, Oth - er lands †as fair to see,
|s, :-.s, |s, :s, |s, :-.m, |s, :— |s, :-.s, |s, :t, |d :-.d |d :—
|t, :-.t, |t, :d |r :-.d |t, :— |d :-.d |d :r |m :-.s |s :—
Friend - ship's hand †I oft have press'd, Hap - py thoughts †oft fill my breast,
|s, :-.s, |s, :m, |s, :-.s, |s, :— |d :-.d |d :s, |d :-.d |d :—

|s :- .m |d' :m |m :- .r |r :d |s :— |m :s
None can be †so dear to me †As home, sweet
|d :- .d |m :d |d :- .t, |t, :d |d :— |d :—
|m :- .s |s :s |s :- .s |s :m |m :— |s :—
Yet I long †a - gain to rest †At home, sweet
|d :- .d |d :d |s, :- .s, |s, :d |d :— |d :m

|r :— |— : |m :— |m :r |d :— |—
home, Home, sweet home.
|t, :— |— : |d :— |d :t, |d :— |— :
|s :— |— : |s :— |s :— |m :— |— :
home, Home, sweet home.
|s :— |— : |d :— |s, :— |d :— |— :
```

St. Co. (New).

MAY IS COMING.

Ex. 13. KEY G. A.L.C.

d :d :d |r :- :r |m :- :- |r :- :- |d :d :d |t_1 :- :d

1.Coming thro' clouds † and | dark - ness, | Com-ing thro' sleet † and

d :d :d |t_1 :- :t_1 |d :- :- |t_1 :- :- |s_1 :s_1 :s_1 |s_1 :- .m_1

m :m :m |s :- :s |s :- :- |s :- :- |m :m :m |r :- :d

2.Coming † a morn of | glo - ry, | Com-ing † a day of

d :d :d |s_1 :- :s_1 |d :- :- |s_1 :- :- |d :d :d |s_1 :- :s_1

r :- :- |- :- : |s_1 :t_1 :r |s :- :m |m :- :- |r :- :-

rain, | Beau-ti - ful month of | flow - ers,

s_1 :- :- |- :- : |s_1 :s_1 :s_1 |s_1 :- :d |d :- :- |t_1 :- :-

t_1 :- :- |- :- : |s_1 :t_1 :r |s :- :s |s :- :- |s :- :-

rest, | Faith sees its gold - en | pro - mise

s_1 :- :- |- :- : |s_1 :s_1 :s_1 |s_1 :- :d |s_1 :- :- |s_1 :- :-

d :d :d |m :- :r |d :- :- |- :- : |r :r :r |r :- :d

Hast'ning to us a - | gain; | Thought of the win - try

d :d :d |d :- :t_1 |d :- :- |- :- : |t_1 :t_1 :t_1 |t_1 :- :d

m :m :m |s :- :s |m :- :- |- :- : | : : | : :

Break thro' the cloud - ed | west; | Star of the dark - est

d :d :d |s_1 :- :s_1 |d_1 :- :- |- :- : | : : | : :

t_1 :- :- |- :- : |m :m :m |m :- :r |d :- :- |- :- : |s :s :s

hour— | Cheer of the dark - est | day— | Coming,†tho'

s_1 :- :- |- :- : |d :d :d |d :- :t_1 |d :- :- |- :- : |m :m :m

: : | : : | : : | : : | : : | : : |s :s :s

hour, | Beaming with death - less | ray— | Coming,†tho'

: : | : | : : | : : | : : | : : |d :d :d

|s :- :m |m :- :- |r :- :- |d :d :d |m :- :r |d :- :- |- :- :

tem - pests | low - er, | Beauti - ful month of | May.

|m :- :d |d :- :- |t_1 :- :- |d :d :d |d :- :t_1 |d :- :- |- :- :

|s :- :s |s :- :- |s :- :- |m :m :m |s :- :s |m :- :- |- :- :

tem - pests | low - er, | Blessed e - ter - nal | May.

|d :- :d |s_1 :- :- |s_1 :- :- |d :d :d |s_1 :- :s_1 |d_1 :- :- |- :- .

St. Co. (New).

THIRD STEP.*

Ex. 14. KEY F. BRAILSFORD.

m	m :f	s :-	s	f :m	r :r	m :-
d	d :d	t_1 :-	d	t_1 :d	d :t_1	d :-
s	s :d	r :-	m	f :s	l :s	s :-
d	d :l_1	s_1 :-	m	r :d	f_1 :s_1	d :-

Ex. 15. KEY A. NARES.

m	f :r	t_1 :-	d	l_1 :f	m :r	d :-
s_1	l_1 :l_1	s_1 :-	s_1	f_1 :l_1	s_1 :f_1	m_1 :-
d	d :f	r :-	d	d :d	d :t_1	d :-
d	l_1 :f_1	s_1 :-	m_1	f_1 :r_1	s_1 :s_1	d_1 :-

Ex. 16. KEY G. GREGORIAN.

d	m :r	d :-	r	m :f	m :r	d :-
s_1	d :t_1	l_1 :-	t_1	d :d	d :t_1	d :-
m	s :f	m :-	s	s :l	s :f	m :-
d	d :s_1	l_1 :-	s_1	d :f_1	s_1 :s_1	d_1 :-

Ex. 17. KEY G. J.S.S.

m	f :m	l :-	f	m :r	d :t_1	d :-
d	r :d	d :-	l_1	s_1 :f_1	m_1 :f_1	m_1 :-
s	s :s	f :-	d	d :t_1	d :r	d :-
d	t_1 :d	f_1 :-	f_1	s_1 :s_1	s_1 :s_1	d :-

FOURTH STEP.†

Ex. 18. KEY F. E. J. HOPKINS.

s	m :l	s :-	s	d :m	r :d	d :t_1	s	m :l	s :-	s	d :m	r :r	d :-
d	d :d	d :-	t_1	d :d	l_1 :s_1	s_1 :-	t_1	d :d	t_1 :-	d	l_1 :d	d :t_1	d :-
m	s :f	m :-	r	d :s	f :m	m :r	s	s :fe	s :-	s	m :s	l :s.f	m :-
d	d :f_1	d :-	s_1	l_1 :m_1	f_1 :d	s_1 :-	m_1	l_1 :r_1	s_1 :-	m_1	l_1 :s_1	f_1 :s_1	d :-

Ex. 19. KEY E♭. G.O.

B♭.t. — f.E♭.

m	l :s	f :-	^{s}d	l_1 :t_1	d :r	m :-	r	d :t_1	d :-	^{l}m	l :s	f :r	d :-
d	r :m	d :-	$^{r}s_1$	l_1 :f_1	s_1 :s_1	s_1 :-	s_1	s_1 :s_1	s_1 :-	^{f}d	r :m	d :t_1	d :-
s	f :m	f :-	$^{r}s_1$	d :r	d :t_1	d :-	t_1	d :r	m :-	^{d}s	f :m	l :s.f	m :-
d	t_1 :d	l_1 :-	$^{t_1}m_1$	f_1 :r_1	m_1 :s_1	d :-	s_1f_1	m_1 :r_1	d_1 :-	^{f_1}d	t_1 :d	f_1 :s_1	d :-

Ex. 20. KEY F. DR. CHIPP.

d	m :r	d :-	l	s :f	m :r	d :-
s_1	d :t_1	l_1 :-	d	d :d	d :t_1	d :-
m	s :f	m :-	f	ta:l	s :f	m :-
d	d .s_1	l_1 :-	f_1	m_1 :f_1	s_1 :s_1	d :-

Ex. 21. KEY G. G.O.

m	r :r	s :-	m	f :s	r :r	d :-
d	t_1 :t_1	d :-	d	d :d	d :t_1	d :-
s	s :s	s :-	s	d :d	f :r	m :-
d	s_1 :f_1	m_1 :-	ta_1	l_1 :m_1	f_1 :s_1	d :-

* To be introduced before page 1 of "Additional Exercises."

† To be introduced before page 12 of "Additional Exercises."

ADDITIONAL EXERCISES, PART I.

NOTE.—In teaching to sing, these exercises should be preceded by at least a selection from the Exercises of the 1st, 2nd, and 3rd steps in "Standard Course," or by the "First Exercises for Mixed Voices." And before the Ex. on p. 12 is commenced, either the St. Co. Ex. of the Fourth Step, or those on the last page of "First Exercises," &c., should be introduced. For style of singing see "Hints on the Tunes."

Words by *W. E. Hickson.* By permission.

GOD SPEED THE RIGHT.

Music from the *German.*

KEY D. M. 66.

| s :s | d' :-.s | m :m | s :m | m :— | r :-.r | m :— | :
1.Now to heav'n our pray'rs as - cend - ing, God speed the right!
| s :s | d' :-.s | m :m | s :m | d :— | t, :-.t, | d :— | :
2.Be that pray'r a- gain re - peat - ed, God speed the right!
| s :s | d' :-.s | m :m | s :m | s :— | s :-.s | s :— | :
3.Pa - tient, firm, and per - se - ver - ing, God speed the right!
| s :s | d' :-.s | m :m | s :m | d :— | s, :-.s, | d :— | :
4.Still their on - ward course pur - su - ing, God speed the right!

| s :s | d' :-.s | m :m | s :m | m :— | r :-.r | m :— | :
In a no - ble cause con - tend - ing, God speed the right!
| s :s | d' :-.s | m :m | s :m | d :— | t, :-.t, | d :— | :
Ne'er des - pair - ing, though de - feat - ed, God speed the right!
| s :s | d' :-.s | m :m | s :m | s :— | s :-.s | s :— | :
Ne'er th'e - vent nor dan - ger fear - ing, God speed the right!
| s :s | d' :-.s | m :m | s :m | d :— | s, :-.s, | d :— | :
Ev - 'ry foe at length sub - du - ing, God speed the right!

| d' :t | l :s | l :s | f :m | r :m | f :r | s :f | m :r
Be their zeal in heav'n re - cord - ed, With suc - cess on earth re - ward - ed,
| m :s | f :m | f :m | r :d | t, :d | r :t, | m :r | d :t,
Like the good and great in sto - ry If they fail, they fail with glo - ry,
| d' :d' | d' :d' | d' :d' | s :s | s :s | s :s | s :s | s :s
Pains, nor toils nor tri - als heed - ing, And in heav'n's own time suc - ceed - ing,
| d :d | d :d | d :d | d :d | s, :s, | s, :s, | s, :s, | s :f
Truth! thy cause, what - e'er de - lay it, There's no pow'r on earth can stay it,

| d' :— | r' :-.r' | m' :— | — : | s :— | s :-.s | d :— | — :
God speed the right! God speed the right!
| d :— | s :-.s | s :— | — : | s :— | s :-.s | d :— | — :
God speed the right! God speed the right!
| s :— | t :-.t | d' :— | — : | s :— | s :-.s | d :— | — :
God speed the right! God speed the right!
| m :— | r :-.r | d :— | — : | s :— | s :-.s | d :— | — :
God speed the right! God speed the right!

LONDON: J. CURWEN & SONS, 8 & 9, WARWICK LANE, E.C. In three parts, 4d. each.

GOING HOME.

KEY F. M. 88. *Gersbach.*

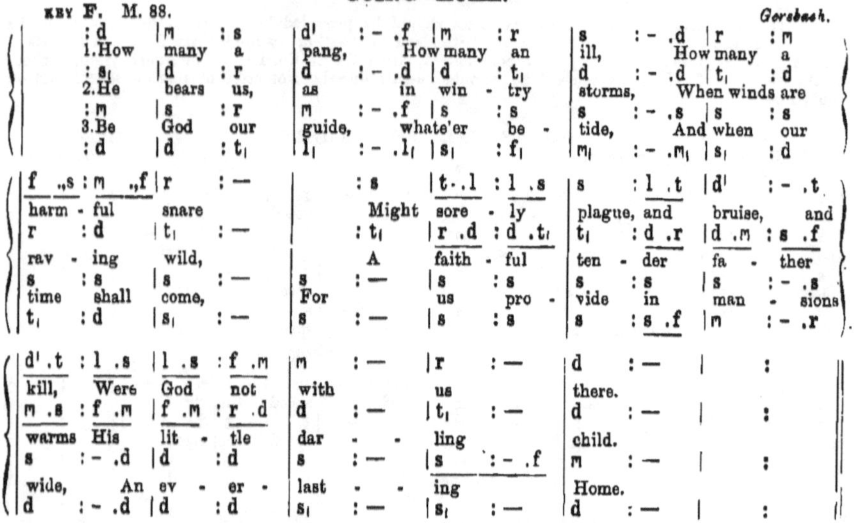

: d |m : s |d' : - .f |m : r |s : - .d |r : m
1.How many a | pang, How many an | ill, How many a
: s, |d : r |d : - .d |d : t, |d : - .d |t, : d
2.He bears us, | as in win - try | storms, When winds are
: m |s : r |m : - .f |s : s |s : - .s |s : s
3.Be God our | guide, whate'er be - | tide, And when our
: d |d : t, |l, : - .l, |s, : f, |m, : - .m, |s, : d

f .,s : m .,f |r : — | : s |t .,l : l .s |s : l .t |d' : - .t
harm - ful snare | Might sore - ly | plague, and bruise, and
r : d |t, : — | : t, |r .d : d .t, |t, : d .r |d .m : s .f
rav - ing wild, | A faith - ful | ten - der fa - ther
s : s |s : — |s : — |s : s |s : s |s : - .s
time shall come, | For us pro - | vide in man - sions
t, : d |s, : — |s : — |s : s |s : s .f |m : - .r

d' .t : l .s |l .s : f .m |m : — |r : — |d : — | :
kill, Were God not | with us | there.
m .s : f .m |f .m : r .d |d : — |t, : — |d : — | :
warms His lit - tle | dar - - ling | child.
s : - .d |d : d |s : — |s : - .f |m : — | :
wide, An ev - er - | last - - ing | Home.
d : - .d |d : d |s, : — |s, : — |d : — | :

JACKSON'S EVENING HYMN. *

KEY E♭. M. 72. *W. Jackson.*

m : — : m |f : — : m |m : r : d |t, : d : |f : — : m |r : — : m
1.Fa - ther, in high | hea - ven | dwell-ing, | May our | eve - ning
d : — : d |r : — : d |l, : — : l, |s, : s, : |d : r : d |t, : — : d
2.This day's sins, O | par - don, | Sa - viour, | E - vil | thoughts, per-
s : — : s |s : — : s |l : — : f |f : m : |l : s : s |s : — : s
3.From en - tice - ments | of the | De - vil. | From the | might of
d : — : d |t, : — : d |f, : — : f, |s, : d : |l, : t, : d |f : — : m
4.Whilst the night - dews | are dis - | till - ing, | Ho - ly | Ghost, each

s : f : m |m : r : |d' : f : l |s : d : f |m : — : r |d : — : —
song be | tell - ing | Of thy | mer - cy | large and | free.
s, : — : s, |s, : s, : |f : — : d |d : — : d |d : — : t, |d : — : —
verse be - | ha - viour, | En - vy, | pride, and | van - i - | ty;
t : — : d' |d' : t : |d' : — : d' |s : — : l |s : — : f |m : — : —
spi - rits | e - vil, | Be our | shield and | pan - o - | ply;
r : — : d |s, : s, : |l : — : f |m : — : f |s : — : s, |d : — : —
heart be | fill - ing, | With thine | own se - | ren - i - | ty;

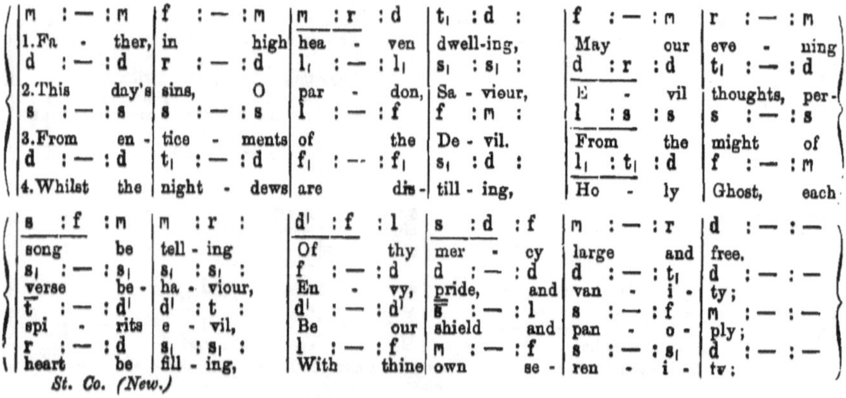

St. Co. (New.)

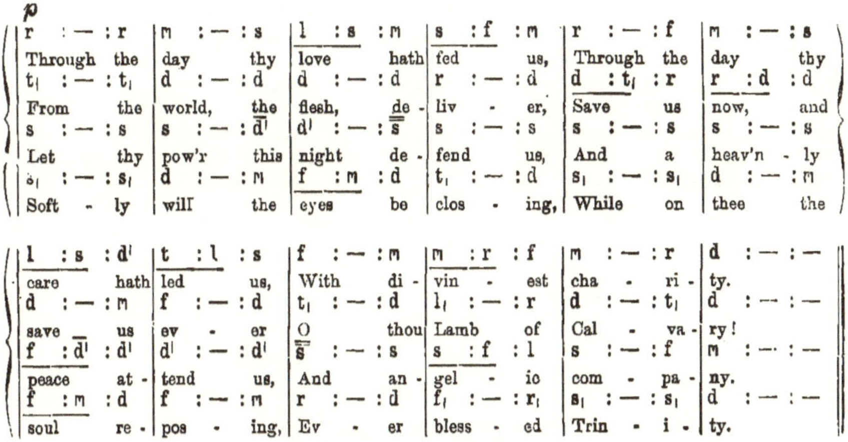

p

r :— :r	m :— :s	l :s :m	s :f :m	r :— :f	m :— :s
Through the	day thy	love hath	fed us,	Through the	day thy
t_1 :— :t_1	d :— :d	d :— :d	r :— :d	d :t_1 :r	r :d :d
From the	world, the	flesh, de -	liv - er,	Save us	now, and
s :— :s	s :— :d'	d' :— :s	s :— :s	s :— :s	s :— :s
Let thy	pow'r this	night de -	fend us,	And a	heav'n - ly
s_1 :— :s_1	d :— :m	f :m :d	t_1 :— :d	s_1 :— :s_1	d :— :m
Soft - ly	will the	eyes be	clos - ing,	While on	thee the

l :s :d'	t :l :s	f :— :m	m :r :f	m :— :r	d :— :—
care hath	led us,	With di -	vin - est	cha - ri -	ty.
d :— :m	f :— :d	t_1 :— :d	l_1 :— :r	d :— :t_1	d :— :—
save us	ev - er	O thou	Lamb of	Cal - va -	ry!
f :d' :d'	d' :— :d'	s :— :s	s :f :l	s :— :f	m :— :—
peace at -	tend us,	And an -	gel - ic	com - pa -	ny.
f :m :d	f :— :m	r :— :d	f_1 :— :r_1	s_1 :— :s_1	d :— :—
soul re -	pos - ing,	Ev - er	bless - ed	Trin - i -	ty.

SPRING LIFE.

(Words translated from E. M. ARNDT, by J. S. STALLYBRASS.)

KEY D. M. 144. *Gersbach.*

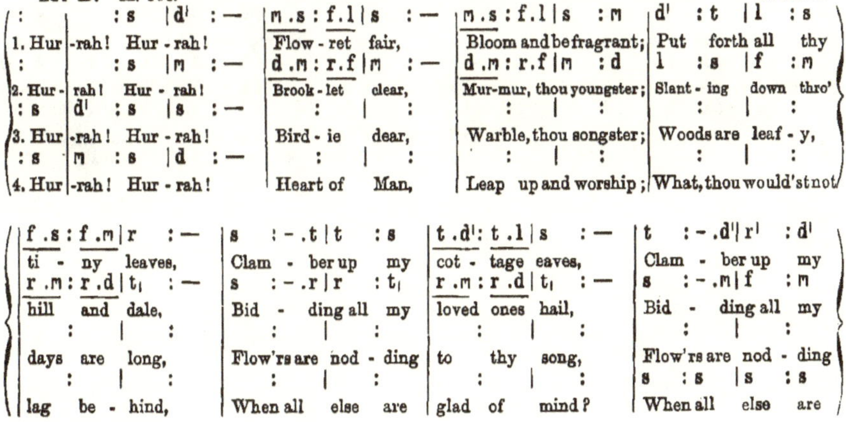

: :s	d' :—	m.s :f.l | s :—	m.s :f.l | s :m	d' :t | l :s
1. Hur	-rah! Hur - rah!	Flow - ret fair,	Bloom and be fragrant;	Put forth all thy
: :s	m :—	d.m :r.f | m :—	d.m :r.f | m :d	l :s | f :m
2. Hur -	rah! Hur - rah!	Brook - let clear,	Mur-mur, thou youngster;	Slant - ing down thro'
:s	d' :s | s :—	: | :	: | :	: | :
3. Hur	-rah! Hur - rah!	Bird - ie dear,	Warble, thou songster;	Woods are leaf - y,
:s	m :s | d :—	: | :	: | :	: | :
4. Hur	-rah! Hur - rah!	Heart of Man,	Leap up and worship;	What, thou would'st not

f.s :f.m | r :—	s :-.t | t :s	t.d' :t.l | s :—	t :-.d' | r' :d'
ti - ny leaves,	Clam - ber up my	cot - tage eaves,	Clam - ber up my
r.m :r.d | t_1 :—	s :-.r | r :t_1	r.m :r.d | t_1 :—	s :-.m | f :m
hill and dale,	Bid - ding all my	loved ones hail,	Bid - ding all my
: | :	: | :	: | :	: | :
days are long,	Flow'rs are nod - ding	to thy song,	Flow'rs are nod - ding
: | :	: | :	: | :	s :s | s :s
lag be - hind,	When all else are	glad of mind?	When all else are

St. Co. (New.)

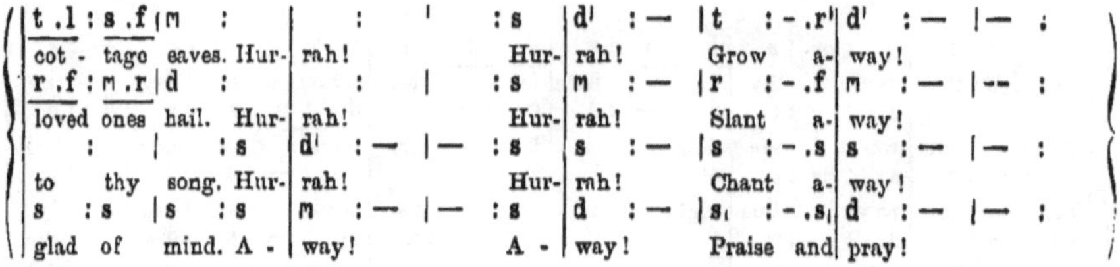

| t .l : s .f | m : | : | : s | d' : — | t : - .r' | d' : — | — : |
cot - tage eaves. Hur- | rah! Hur- | rah! Grow a- | way!
| r .f : m .r | d : | : | : s | m : — | r : - .f | m : — | — : |
loved ones hail. Hur- | rah! Hur- | rah! Slant a- | way!
| : | : s | d' : — | — : s | s : — | s : - .s | s : — | — : |
to thy song. Hur- | rah! Hur- | rah! Chant a- | way!
| s : s | s : s | m : — | — : s | d : — | s, : - .s, | d : — | — : |
glad of mind. A - | way! A - | way! Praise and | pray!

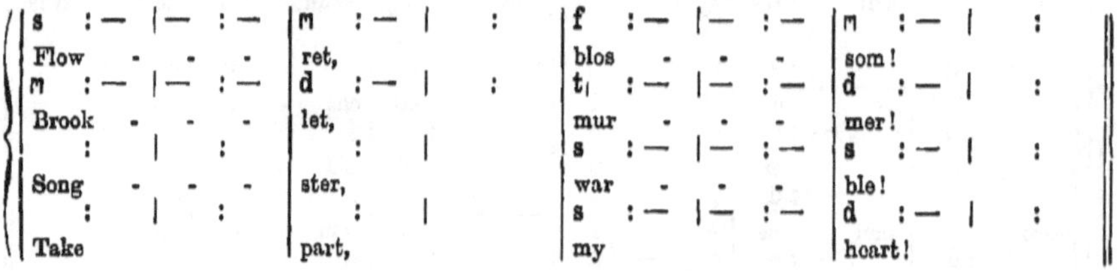

| s : — | — : — | m : — | : | f : — | — : — | m : — | : ||
Flow - - - | ret, | blos - - - | som!
| m : — | — : — | d : — | : | t, : — | — : — | d : — | : ||
Brook - - - | let, | mur - - - | mer!
| : | : | : | | s : — | — : — | s : — | : ||
Song - - - | ster, | war - - - | ble!
| : | : | : | | s : — | — : — | d : — | : ||
Take | part, | my | heart!

THE FORTUNE HUNTER.

(Words translated from RUCKERT, by J. S. STALLYBRASS.)

KEY F. M. 60, twice. *Gersbach.*

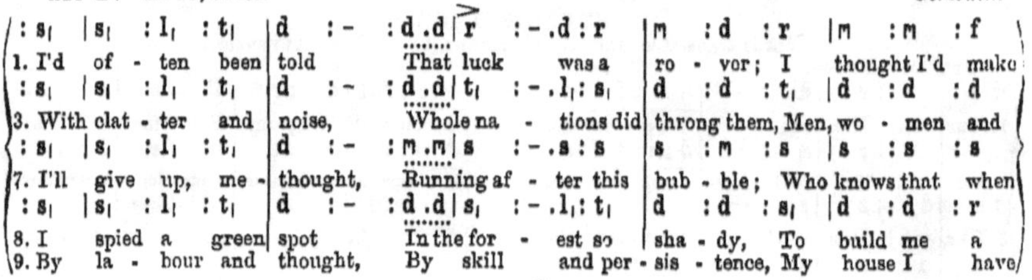

: s, | s, : l, : t, | d : - : d .d | r : - .d : r | m : d : r | m : m : f
1. I'd of - ten been | told That luck was a | ro - ver; I | thought I'd make
: s, | s, : l, : t, | d : - : d .d | t, : - .l, : s, | d : d : t, | d : d : d
3. With clat - ter and | noise, Whole na - tions did | throng them, Men, | wo - men and
: s, | s, : l, : t, | d : - : m .m | s : - .s : s | s : m : s | s : s : s
7. I'll give up, me - | thought, Running af - ter this | bub - ble; Who | knows that when
: s, | s, : l, : t, | d : - : d .d | s, : - .l, : t, | d : d : s, | d : d : r
8. I spied a green | spot In the for - est so | sha - dy, To | build me a
9. By la - bour and | thought, By skill and per - | sis - tence, My | house I have

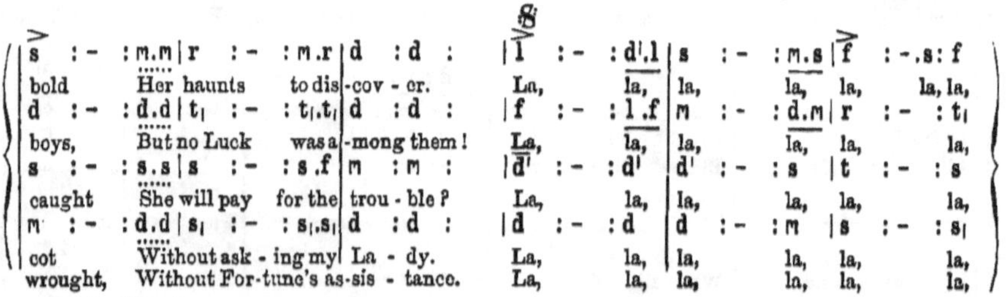

𝄋
| s : - : m .m | r : - : m .r | d : d : | l : - : d' .l | s : - : m .s | f : - .s : f
bold Her haunts to dis- | cov - er. La, la, | la, la, la, la, la,
| d : - : d .d | t, : - : t, .t, | d : d : | f : - : l .f | m : - : d .m | r : - : t,
boys, But no Luck was a- | mong them! La, la, | la, la, la, la,
| s : - : s .s | s : - : s .f | m : m : | d' : - : d' | d' : - : s | t : - : s
caught She will pay for the | trou - ble? La, la, | la, la, la, la,
| m : - : d .d | s, : - : s, .s, | d : d : | d : - : d | d : - : m | s : - : s,
cot Without ask - ing my | La - dy. La, la, | la, la, la, la,
wrought, Without For - tune's as - sis - | tance. La, la, | la, la, la, la,

St. Co. (New.)

FINE.

m :d :d d' :- :d' | d'.t :l.s :f.m | r :- :s | d :- || s, | s :l, :t,
la, la, la, la, | la, la, la, la, la, | la! || 2.I left my own
d :- : | f :- :l.f | m :- :d | t, :- :t, | d :- || s, | s, :l, :t,
la, la, la, | la, la, la, la, | la! || 4.I ask'd of those
s :- :m | l :- :f.l | s :- :s | f :- :f | m :- || s, | s, :l, :t,
la, la, la, la, | la, la, la, la, | la! || 5.At one place I
d :- : | :d :d | d :- : | s, :- :s, | d :- || s, | s, :l, :t,
la, la, la, | la, la, la, | la! || 6.At a great ci - ty's
la, la, la, | la, la, la, | la! || 10.Here, Luck, is my

D.S.

d :-.t,:d | r :d :r | m :- :r | m :m :f | s :-.f :m | r :m :r | d :- :- ||
gate - way, And wander'd a - | broad, Went this way and | that way, And tried ev'ry | road.
d :-.s,:s, | t, :l, :s, | s, :- :t, | d :d :d | d :-.t,:d | t, :t, :t, | d :- :-
near me, Where was the shy | elf; But none seem'd to | hear me, Each sought for him | -self.
d :-.r :m | s :s :s | s :- :s | s :s :s | s :-.s :s | s :s :f | m :- :-
ask'd them If For - tune was | near; They said she had | past them Full ma-ny a | year.
d :-.d :d | s, :l, :t, | d :- :s, | d :d :r | m :-.r :d | s, :s, :s, | d :- :-
gate - way I ask'd, had she | been? They answer'd "here | wait we, To wel - come her | in."
dwell - ing, And here will I | stay; Come in, if you're | wil - ling; If not, keep a - | way!

THE MAY-TIME.

Words translated from the German by J. S. STALLYBRASS.

KEY G. M. 66, twice. *Gersbach.*

:s | s :d' :m | m :s :d | m :m.s :f.l | s :- :s, | d :d.m :r.f | m :d :f.m
The | May-time, the May-time, how | love - ly and fair, What | pas - time and plea - sure is
:d | d :- :- | - :m :d | d :d.m :r.f | m :- : | : :s, | s, :d :d
The | May - - time, how | love - ly and fair, | What pleasure is
:m | m :- :s | s :- : | : : | : : | : :r | m :s :s
The | May - time, | What pleasure is
:d | d :- :- | d :- : | : : | : :s | m :d :t,.r | d :m :d
The | May - time, | What | pas - time and plea - sure is

r :- :- | - :- :s | s :-.f :m | r :t, : | : : | : :s,.s,
there; The | night - in - gale sing - eth, | Over
t, :- :- | - :- :m | m :-.r :d | t, :s, : | : : | : :
s :- :- | - :- : | : : | : :s | s :-.f :m | r :t, :
there; | The | lark it up - springeth,
s :- :- | - :- : | : : | : :m | m :-.r :d | t, :s, :

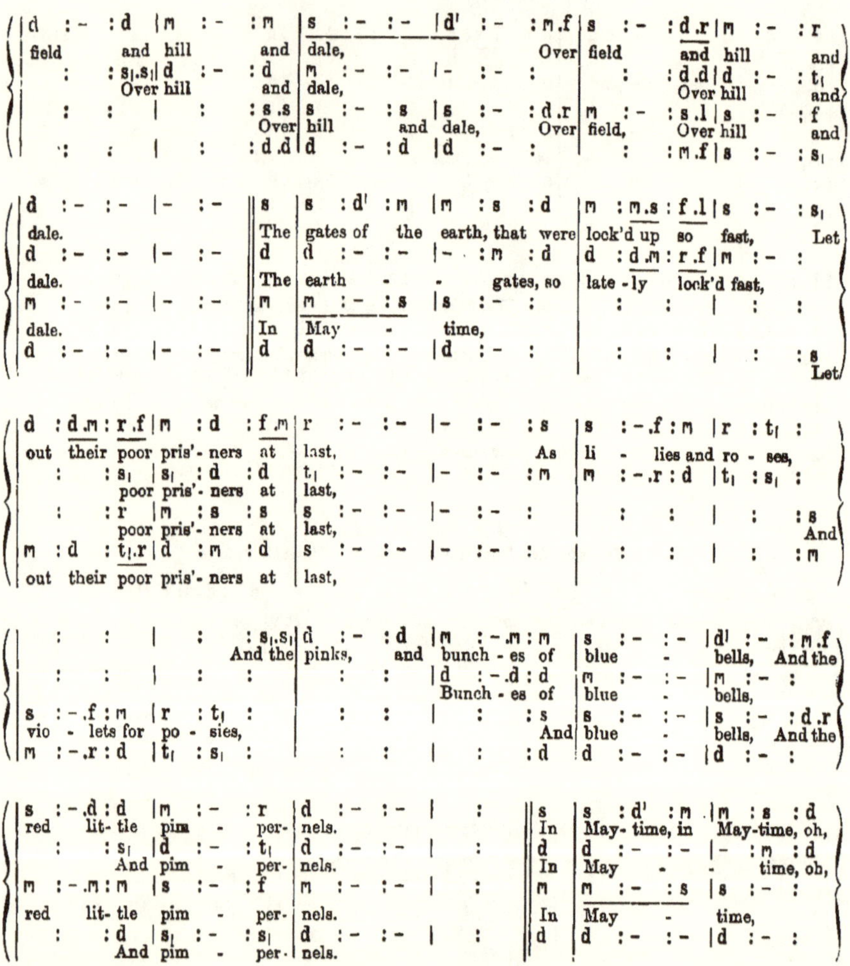

| d :- :d | m :- :m | s :- :- | d' :- :m.f | s :- :d.r | m :- :r |
field and hill and dale, Over field and hill and
| : :s₁.s₁ | d :- :d | m :- :- | - :- : | : :d.d | d :- :t₁ |
Over hill and dale, Over hill and
| : : | : :s.s | s :- :s | s :- :d.r | m :- :s.l | s :- :f |
Over hill and dale, Over field, Over hill and
| : : | : :d.d | d :- :d | d :- : | : :m.f | s :- :s₁ |

| d :- :- | - :- ‖ s | s :d' :m | m :s :d | m :m.s :f.l | s :- :s₁ |
dale. The gates of the earth, that were lock'd up so fast, Let
| d :- :- | - :- ‖ d | d :- :- | - :m :d | d :d.m :r.f | m :- : |
dale. The earth - - gates, so late - ly lock'd fast,
| m :- :- | - :- ‖ m | m :- :s | s :- : | : : | : : |
dale. In May - time,
| d :- :- | - :- ‖ d | d :- :- | d :- : | : : | : :s |
Let

| d :d.m :r.f | m :d :f.m | r :- :- | - :- :s | s :-.f :m | r :t₁ : |
out their poor pris'- ners at last, As li - lies and ro - ses,
| : :s₁ | s₁ :d :d | t₁ :- :- | - :- :m | m :-.r :d | t₁ :s₁ : |
poor pris'- ners at last,
| : :r | m :s :s | s :- :- | - :- : | : : | : :s |
poor pris'- ners at last, And
| m :d :t₁.r | d :m :d | s :- :- | - :- : | : : | : :m |
out their poor pris'- ners at last,

| : : | : :s₁.s₁ | d :- :d | m :-.m :m | s :- :- | d' :- :m.f |
And the pinks, and bunch - es of blue - bells, And the
| : : | : : | : : | d :-.d :d | m :- :- | m :- : |
Bunch - es of blue - bells,
| s :-.f :m | r :t₁ : | : : | : :s | s :- :- | s :- :d.r |
vio - lets for po - sies, And blue - bells, And the
| m :-.r :d | t₁ :s₁ : | : : | : :d | d :- :- | d :- : |

| s :-.d :d | m :- :r | d :- :- | : ‖ s | s :d' :m | m :s :d |
red lit- tle pim - per- nels. In May- time, in May-time, oh,
| : :s₁ | d :- :t₁ | d :- :- | : ‖ d | d :- :- | - :m :d |
And pim - per- nels. In May - - time, oh,
| m :-.m :m | s :- :f | m :- :- | : ‖ m | m :- :s | s :- : |
red lit- tle pim - per- nels. In May - time,
| : :d | s₁ :- :s₁ | d :- :- | : ‖ d | d :- :- | d :- : |
And pim - per- nels.

St. Co. (New).

m :m.s :f .l |s :- :s, |d :d.m :r.f |m :d :f.m |r :- :- |- :- :s
waste not the hours, Go twine you sweet gar - lands of flow'rs; Oh!
d :d.m :r.f |m :- : | : :s, |s, :d :d |t, :- :- |- :- :m
sweet gar - lands of flow'rs;
: : | : | : :r |m :s :s |s :- :- |- :- :
sweet gar - lands of flow'rs;
: : | :s |m :d :t,.r |d :m :d |s :- :- |- :- :
Go twine you sweet gar - lands of flow'rs;

s :-.f :m |r :t, : | : : | : :s,.s, |d :-.d :d |m :- :m
far on the mea - dows, There is ful - ness of life and
m :-.r :d |t, :s, : | : : | : : | : :s,.s, |d :- :d
There is life and
: : | : :s |s :-.f :m |r :t, : | : : | : :s.s
And deep in the sha - dows There is
: : | : :m |m :-.r :d |t, :s, : | : : | : :d.d

s :- :- |d' :- :m.f |s :d :d.r |m :- :r |d :- :- |- :-
joy, And there reach-eth us no an- noy.
m :- :- |- :- : | : :s, |d :- :t, |d :- :- |- :-
joy, And no an- noy.
s :- :- |- :- :d.r |m :m :m.f |s :- :f |m :- :- |- :-
joy, And there reach-eth us no an- noy.
d :- :- |- :- : | : :d |s, :- :s, |d :- :- |- :-
And no an- noy.

THOU SHALT SHOW ME.

KEY D. M. 96. Canon, four (voices) in two (subjects). *S. Webbe.*

: |s :— |— :s |d' :— |— :t |d' :— |l :— |— :t
Thou shalt show me the path of
: | : | : | : | : :d :— |— :d |f :—
Thou shalt show
: | : | : | : | : | : | : | :
: | : | : | : | : | : | : | :

d' :— |d' :— |— :— |t :— |d'.,t :d'.,r' |d' :d' |t :— |d' :d'
life in Thy pre - sence is ful - ness of
f :m |f :— |r :— |— :s.f |m :— |— :— |r :— |m :—
me the path of life; in Thy
: | : | : | : | : |s :— |— :s |d' :—
Thou shalt show
: | : | : | : | : | : | : | :

St. Co. (New).

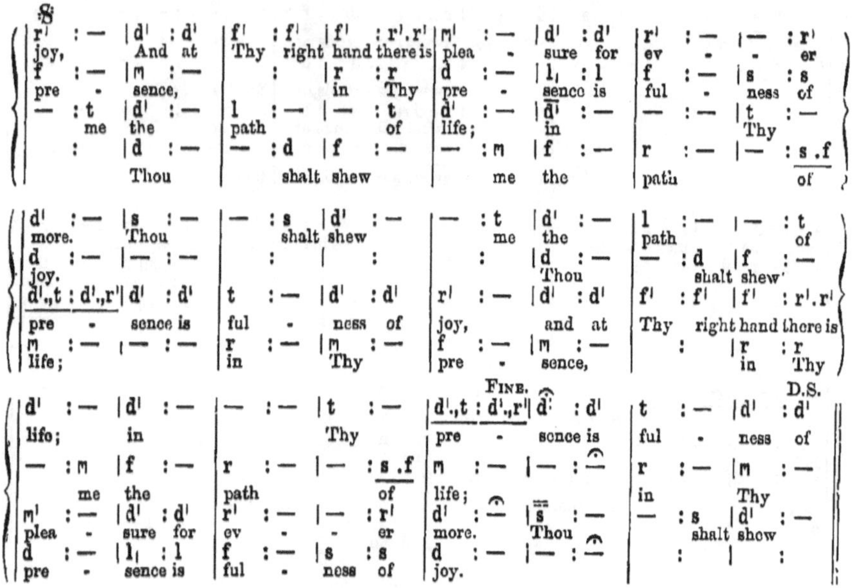

𝄋

| r' :— | d' :d' | f' :f' | f' :r'.r' | m' :— | d' :d' | r' :— | — :r' |
joy, And at Thy right hand there is plea - sure for ev - - er
| f :— | m :— | : | r :r | d :— | l, :l | f :— | s :s |
pre - sence, in Thy pre - sence is ful - ness of
| — :t | d' :— | l :— | — :t | d' :— | d' :— | — :— | t :— |
me the path of life; in Thy
| : | d :— | — :d | f :— | — :m | f :— | r :— | — :s .f |
Thou shalt shew me the path of

| d' :— | s :— | — :s | d' :— | — :t | d' :— | l :— | — :t |
more. Thou shalt shew me the path of
| d :— | — :— | : | : | : | d :— | — :d | f :— |
joy. Thou shalt shew
| d'.,t :d'.,r' | d' :d' | t :— | d' :d' | r' :— | d' :d' | f' :f' | f' :r'.r' |
pre - sence is ful - ness of joy, and at Thy right hand there is
| m :— | — :— | r :— | m :— | f :— | m :— | : | r :r |
life; in Thy pre - sence, in Thy

FINE. D.S.

| d' :— | d' :— | — :— | t :— | d'.,t :d'.,r' | d' :d' | t :— | d' :d' |
life; in Thy pre - sence is ful - ness of
| — :m | f :— | r :— | — :s .f | m :— | — :— | r :— | m :— |
me the path of life; in Thy
| m' :— | d' :d' | r' :— | — :r' | d' :— | s :— | — :s | d' :— |
plea - sure for ev - - er more. Thou shalt shew
| d :— | l, :l | f :— | s :s | d :— | — :— | : | : |
pre - sence is ful - ness of joy.

THE WAITS.

KEY C. M. 72, twice. 1st time *p.*, 2nd *f.*, 3rd *ff.*, 4th *f.*, 5th *p.*, 6th *pp.* *Jeremiah Saville*, 1667.

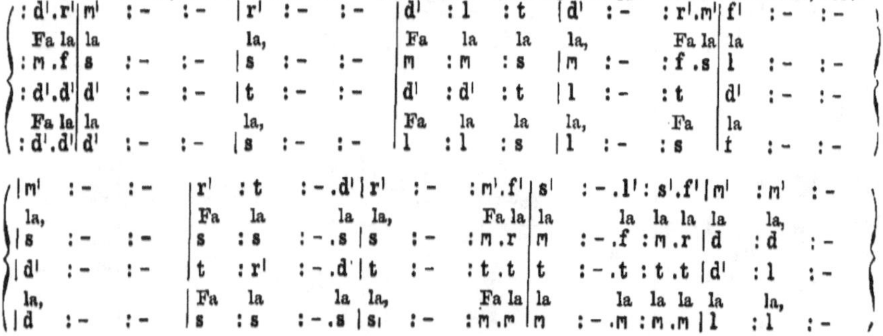

| :d'.r' | m' :- :- | r' :- :- | d' :l :t | d' :- :r'.m' | f' :- :- |
Fa la la la, Fa la la la, Fa la la
| :m .f | s :- :- | s :- :- | m :m :s | m :- :f .s | l :- :- |
| :d'.d' | d' :- :- | t :- :- | d' :d' :t | l :- :t | d' :- :- |
Fa la la la, Fa la la la, Fa la
| :d'.d' | d' :- :- | s :- :- | l :l :s | l :- :s | f :- :- |

| m' :- :- | r' :t :-.d' | r' :- :m'.f' | s' :-.l' :s'.f' | m' :m' :- |
la, Fa la la la, Fa la la la la la la la,
| s :- :- | s :s :-.s | s :- :m .r | m :-.f :m .r | d :d :- |
| d' :- :- | t :r' :-.d' | t :- :t .t | t :-.t :t .t | d' :l :- |
la, Fa la la la, Fa la la la la la la la,
| d :- :- | s :s :-.s | s, :- :m .m | m :-.m :m .m | l :l :- |

St. Co. (New.)

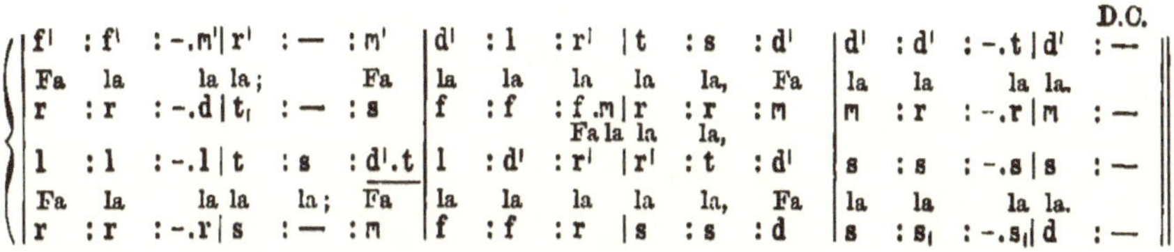

D.C.

| f' :f' :-.m'\|r' :— :m' \| d' :l :r' \|t :s :d' \| d' :d' :-.t\|d' :— ||
Fa la la la; Fa la la la la la, Fa la la la la.
| r :r :-.d\|t, :— :s \| f :f :f.m\|r :r :m \| m :r :-.r\|m :— ||
Fa la la la,
| l :l :-.l\|t :s :d'.t \| l :d' :r' \|r' :t :d' \| s :s :-.s\|s :— ||
Fa la la la la; Fa la la la la la, Fa la la la la.
| r :r :-.r\|s :— :m \| f :f :r \|s :s :d \| s :s, :-.s,\|d :— ||

THE CUCKOO.

KEY F. M. 96. SOLI. *J. Gersbach.*

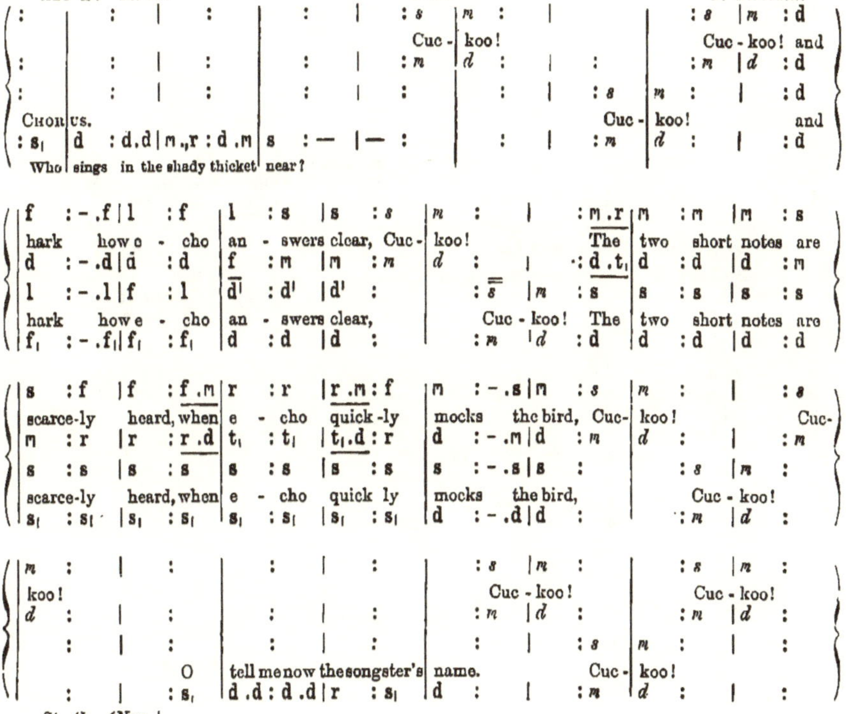

| : \| : \| : \| : \| :*s* \| *m* : \| \| :*s* \|*m* :d
Cuc - koo! Cuc - koo! and
| : \| : \| : \| : \| :*m* \| *d* : \| : \| :*m* \|*d* :d
| : \| : \| : \| : \| : \| : \| :*s* \| *m* : \| :d
CHORUS. Cuc - koo! and
| :s, \| d :d.d\|m.,r :d.m \| s :— \|— : \| : \| :*m* \| *d* : \| :d
Who sings in the shady thicket near?

| f :-.f\|l :f \| l :s \|s :*s* \| *m* : \| :m.r \| m :m \|m :s
hark how e - cho an - swers clear, Cuc - koo! The two short notes are
| d :-.d\|d :d \| f :m \|m :*m* \| *d* : \| :d.t, \| d :d \|d :m
| l :-.l\|f :l \| d' :d' \|d' : \| :*s* \|*m* :s \| s :s \|s :s
hark how e - cho an - swers clear, Cuc - koo! The two short notes are
| f, :-.f,\|f, :f, \| d :d \|d : \| :*m* \|*d* :d \| d :d \|d :d

| s :f \|f :f.m \| r :r \|r.m:f \| m :-.s\|m :*s* \| *m* : \| :*s*
scarce-ly heard, when e - cho quick - ly mocks the bird, Cuc - koo! Cuc-
| m :r \|r :r.d \| t, :t, \|t,.d:r \| d :-.m\|d :*m* \| *d* : \| :*m*
| s :s \|s :s \| s :s \|s :s \| s :-.s\|s : \| :*s* \|*m* :
scarce-ly heard, when e - cho quick ly mocks the bird, Cuc - koo!
| s, :s, \|s, :s, \| s, :s, \|s, :s, \| d :-.d\|d : \| :*m* \|*d* :

| *m* : \| : \| : \| : \| :*s* \|*m* : \| :*s* \|*m* :
koo! Cuc - koo! Cuc - koo!
| *d* : \| : \| : \| : \| :*m* \|*d* : \| :*m* \|*d* :
| : \| : \| : \| : \| : \| :*s* \| *m* : \| :
O tell me now the songster's name. Cuc - koo!
| : \| :s, \| d.d:d.d\|r :s, \| d : \| :*m* \| *d* : \| :

St. Co. (New.)

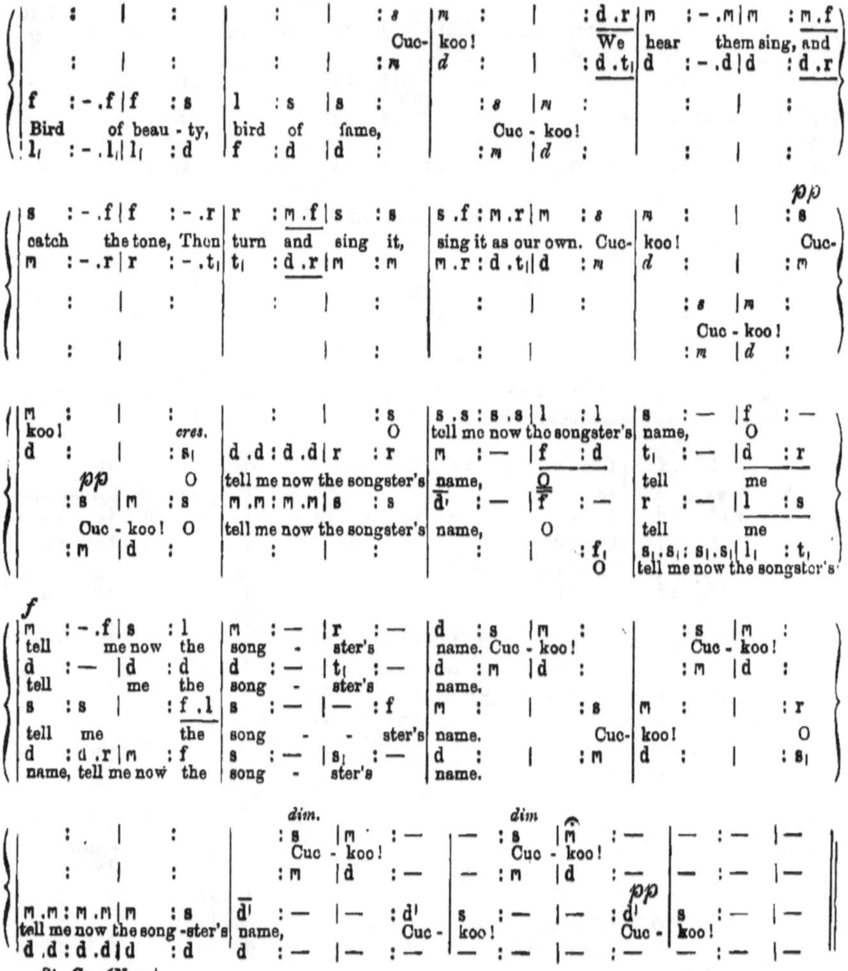

: | : | : | :s |m : | :d .r |m :-.m|m :m .f
Cuc- koo! We hear them sing, and
: | : | : | :m |d : | :d .t_1|d :-.d|d :d .r
f :-.f|f :s |l :s |s : | :s |m : | : | :
Bird of beau - ty, bird of fame, Cuc - koo!
l_1 :-.l_1|l_1 :d |f :d |d : | :m |d : | : | :

pp
s :-.f|f :-.r|r :m .f|s :s |s .f :m .r|m :s |m : | :s
catch the tone, Then turn and sing it, sing it as our own. Cuc- koo! Cuc-
m :-.r|r :-.t_1|t_1 :d .r|m :m |m .r :d .t_1|d :m |d : | :m
: | : | : | : | : | :s |m :
Cuc - koo!
: | | : | : | | :m |d :

m : | : | : | :s |s .s :s .s|l :l |s :— |f :—
koo! *cres.* O tell me now the songster's name, O
d : | :s_1 |d .d :d .d|r :r |m :— |f :d |t_1 :— |d :r
pp O tell me now the songster's name, O tell me
:s |m :s |m .m :m .m|s :s |d' :— |f :— |r :— |l :s
Cuc - koo! O tell me now the songster's name, O tell me
:m |d : | : | : | : | :f_1 |s_1 .s_1 :s_1 .s_1|l_1 :t_1
O tell me now the songster's

f
m :-.f|s :l |m :— |r :— |d :s |m : | :s |m :
tell me now the song - ster's name. Cuc - koo! Cuc - koo!
d :— |d :d |d :— |t_1 :— |d :m |d : | :m |d :
tell me the song - ster's name.
s :s | :f .l |s :— |— :f |m : | :s |m : | :r
tell me the song - - ster's name. Cuc- koo! O
d :d .r|m :f |s :— |s_1 :— |d : | :m |d : | :s_1
name, tell me now the song - ster's name.

dim. *dim*
: | : | :s |m :— |— :s |m :— |— :— |—
Cuc - koo! Cuc - koo!
: | : | :m |d :— |— :m |d :— |— :— |—
pp
m .m :m .m|m :s |d' :— |— :d' |s :— |— :d' |s :— |—
tell me now the song -ster's name, Cuc - koo! Cuc - koo!
d .d :d .d|d :d |d :— |— :— |— :— |— :— |— :— |—

St. Co. (New.)

BON ACCORD.

KEY G. M. 80. (Music from the old Scottish Psalters.)

s :— |s :d |t_1 :-.d|r :m |r :s |m :d |r :r |d :
Lord, bless our fel - lowship this hour, And bless the food we eat;
d :— |s_1 :s_1 |s_1 :-.l_1|t_1 :d |r :t_1 |d :s_1 |l_1 :t_1 |d :
m :— |m :m |r :-.r|s :s |s :s |d :d |f :r |m :s
Lord, bless our fel - lowship this hour, And bless the food we eat; Oh,
d :— |d :d |s_1 :-.s_1|s_1 :d |t_1 :s_1 |l_1 :m_1 |f_1 :s_1 |d_1 :

: | : | : | :s |f :m |r :d |t_1 :-.d|r :m
Oh, grant us by Thy sav - ing power, A -
| :d |t_1 :l_1 |s_1 :d |t_1 :d |s_1 :s_1 |s_1 :-.s_1|s_1 :s_1
Oh, grant us, by Thy sav - ing power, A - round Thy throne, a-
f :m |r :d |s :f |m :s |s :s |s :m |r :-.r|r :s
grant us, by Thy sav - ing power, Oh! grant us by Thy sav - ing power, A -
:d |t_1 :l_1 |s_1 :l_1.t_1|d :m |r :d |t_1 :d |s_1 :-.l_1|t_1 :d
Oh, grant us, by Thy sav - ing power, A - round Thy throne to meet,

r :d |d :t_1 |d :— |— :— ||s :— |s :d |t_1 :-.d|r :m
round Thy throne to meet. On ev - 'ry soul as-sem - bled
t_1 :d |l_1.s_1:f_1.s_1|m_1 :— |— :— ||d :— |s_1 :s_1 |s_1 :-.l_1|t_1 :d
f :m |r :r |d :— |— :— ||m :— |m :m |r :-.r|s :s
round Thy throne to meet. On ev - 'ry soul as-sem - bled
s_1 :l_1 |f_1 :s_1 |d_1 :— |— :— ||d :— |d :d |s_1 :-.s_1|s_1 :d

r :s |m :d |r :r |d : | : | : | : | :s
here, Oh, make Thy face to shine, Thy
r :t_1 |d :s_1 |l_1 :t_1 |d : | : | :d |t_1 :l_1 |s_1 :d
Thy good - ness more our
s :s |d :d |f :r |m :s |f :m |r :d |s :f |m :s
here, Oh, make Thy face to shine, Thy good - ness more our hearts can cheer, Thy
t_1 :s_1 |l_1 :m_1 |f_1 :s_1 |d_1 : | :d |t_1 :l_1 |s_1 :l_1.t_1|d :m
Thy good - ness more our hearts can

f :m |r :d |t_1 :-.d|r :m |r :d |d :t_1 |d :— |— :—
good - ness more our hearts can cheer, Than rich - est food or wine.
t_1 :d |s_1 :s_1 |s_1 :-.s_1|s_1 :s_1 |t_1 :d |l_1.s_1:f_1.s_1|m_1 :— |— :—
hearts can cheer, Than rich - est food, Than rich - est food or wine.
s :s |s :m |r :-.r|r :s |f :m |r :r |d :— |— :—
good - ness more our hearts can cheer, Than rich - est food or wine.
r :d |t_1 :d |s_1 :-.l_1|t_1 :d |s_1 :l_1 |f_1 :s_1 |d_1 :— |— :—
cheer, Than rich - est food or wine, Than rich - est food or wine.

St. Co. (New.)

* HOPE WILL BANISH SORROW.

KEY F. M. 72. Words by GEO. BENNETT. *Swabian Melody.*

p *p*

s :-.m : l.s | s ,,f : m :— | r.m : f.l : s.f | f :m : | s :-.m : l.s | s ,,f : m :—
1.Once again we're doom'd to part, Deem not 'tis for ev - er; Love if rooted in the heart,
d :-.d : d.d | r ,,r : d :— | t₁.d : r.f : m.r | r :d : | d :-.d : d.d | r ,,r : d :—
2.When I'm far a -way from thee, O'er the o - cean sail - ing, You will often muse of me,
m :-.s : f.m | s ,,s : s :— | s.s : s :s | s :s : | m :-.s : f.m | s ,,s : s :—
3.Faith and trust in heav'n we have, God is ev - er near - est, He can still the stormy wave,
d :-.d : d.d | t₁,,t₁ : d :— | f.m : r.s₁ : l₁.t₁ | t₁ :d : | d :-.d : d.d | t₁,,t₁ : d :—

f *p*

r.s : t.l : s.fe | l :s : | f :-.m : r.d | t₁ ,,d : r :— | l :-.s : f.m
Time nor tide can sev - er; 'Tis the sad a- dieus that chill, Make the parting
t₁.r : m :r | r :r : | r :-.d : t₁.l₁ | s₁ ,,l₁ : t₁ :— | f :-.m : r.d
Tears & sighs pre - vail - ing, But ne'er think of me with fear, Check at once the
s.t : r'.d' : t.l | d' :t : | t₁ :-.d : r.m | f ,,m : r :— | r :-.m : f.s
Bear me safe - ly, dear - est. Then, farewell my na- tive shore, Clasp me to thy
s₁.s₁ : d :r | fe :s : | s₁ :-.l₁ : t₁.d | r ,,d : t₁ :— | t₁ :-.d : r.m

cres. *f* *ff*

r ,,m : r :— | s :-.m : f.s | l.t : r'.d' : t.l | s :-.m : f.r | r :d :
sadder still, Say "we'll meet to -mor - row," Hope will banish sor - row.
d ,,d : s₁ :— | s₁ :-.d : d.d | d :— :d | d :-.d : t₁.t₁ | t₁ :d :
ris-ing tear, Sing "we'll meet to -mor - row," Hope will banish sor - row.
l ,,l : t :— | d' :-.s : s.s | f.s : t.l : s.f | m :-.s : r.s | f :m :
heart once more, Sing "we'll meet to -mor - row," Hope will banish sor - row.
f ,,f : f :— | m :-.d : r.m | f :— :f₁ | s₁ :-.s₁ : s₁.s₁ | s₁ :d :

HOW BEAUTIFUL THE SUNSHINE.

KEY D. M. 80. Words by GEO. BENNETT. *German Air.*

mf *cres.*

: .s | s ,,d' : d' :- .s | s ,,r' : r' : .s | m' ,,r' : d' .t :l .r' | s :—
1. How beau ti-ful the sun - shine gleams In glorious summer's golden prime,
: .m | m ,,m : m :- .m | f ,,f : f : .f | m ,,s : s .s :s .fe | r :—
2. But oft the sun - shine brighter glows, And dear-er seems to heart & eye,
: .s | s ,,s : s :- .s | s ,,s : s : .r' | d' ,,t : d' .r' :m' .r' | t :—
3. 'Tis thus in life, the cares and clouds But make the pleasures sweeter still,
: .d | d ,,d : d :- .d | t₁ ,,t₁ : t₁ : .t₁ | d ,,r : m .r :d .r | s :—

p A.t. *mf*

:s | s ,,m : m .s :d' ,,s | l :— :l | r's ,,f : m .r :d .r | m :—
On all a - round it sheds its beams, From ear - ly morn to ev - en- time;
:r | m ,,d : d .m :s ,,s | f :— :f | l r ,,t₁ : d .t₁ :l₁ .t₁ | d :—
When sparkling o'er the wintry snows, Or glowing o'er the autumn sky;
:t | d' ,,s : s .d' :d' ,,d' | d' :— :d' | r's ,,r : m .s :s .s | s :—
When twilight sorrow's vale en- shrouds, Hope shines more bright on sun-kiss'd hill;
:s | d ,,d : d .d :m ,,m | f :— :f | fet₁ ,,s₁ : s₁ .s₁ :s₁ .s₁ | d :—

St. Co. (New.) *In teaching, introduce here St. Co. Ex. 133 to 145, or "First Exercises" 18 to 21.

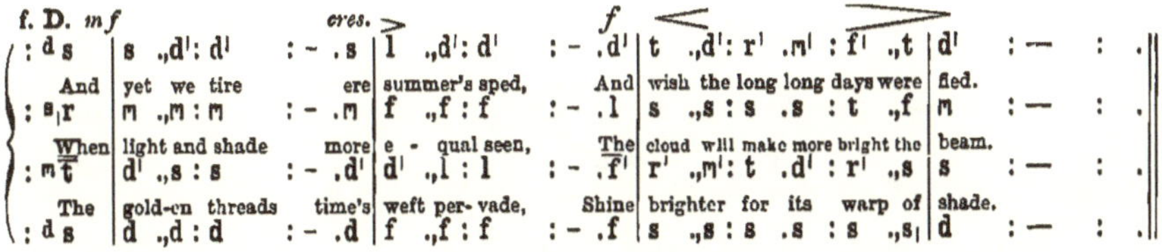

f. D. *mf* *cres.* > *f* < >

:^{d}s | s .,d^1 : d^1 :- .s | l .,d^1 : d^1 :- .d^1 | t .,d^1 : r^1 .m^1 : f^1 .,t | d^1 :— : . ||
And | yet we tire ere | summer's sped, And | wish the long long days were | fled.
:^{s_1}r | m .,m : m :- .m | f .,f : f :- .l | s .,s : s .s : t .,f | m :— : . ||
When | light and shade more | e - qual seen, The | cloud will make more bright the | beam.
:^{m}t | d^1 .,s : s :- .d^1 | d^1 .,l : l :- .f^1 | r^1 .,m^1 : t .d^1 : r^1 .,s | s :— : . ||
The | gold-en threads time's | weft per- vade, Shine | brighter for its warp of | shade.
:^{d}s | d .,d : d :- .d | f .,f : f :- .f | s .,s : s .s : s .,s_1 | d :— : . ||

COME, FREEDOM'S SONS.

KEY B♭. M. 72. *Schultz.*

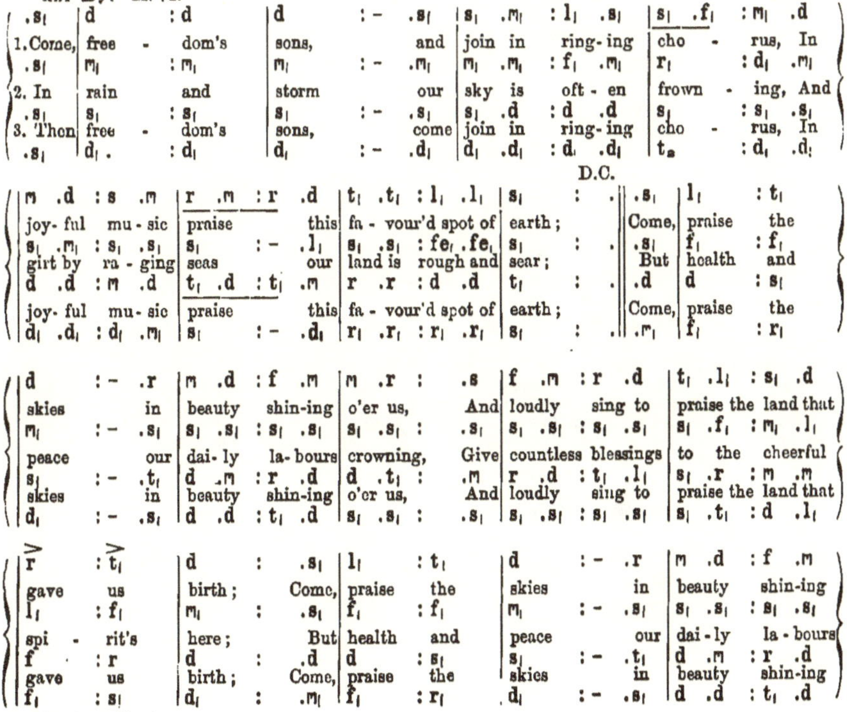

.s_1 | d : d | d :- .s_1 | s_1 .m_1 : l_1 .s_1 | s_1 .f_1 : m_1 .d
1. Come, | free - dom's | sons, and | join in ring- ing | cho - rus, In
.s_1 | m_1 : m_1 | m_1 :- .m_1 | m_1 .m_1 : f_1 .m_1 | r_1 : d_1 .m_1
2. In | rain and | storm our | sky is oft - en | frown - ing, And
.s_1 | s_1 : s_1 | s_1 :- .s_1 | s_1 .d : d .d | s_1 : s_1 .s_1
3. Then | free - dom's | sons, come | join in ring- ing | cho - rus, In
.s_1 | d_1 . : d_1 | d_1 :- .d_1 | d_1 .d_1 : d_1 .d_1 | t_2 : d_1 .d_1

D.C.

m .d : s .m | r .m : r .d | t_1 .t_1 : l_1 .l_1 | s_1 : . || .s_1 | l_1 : t_1
joy- ful mu - sic | praise this | fa - vour'd spot of | earth; || Come, | praise the
s_1 .m_1 : s_1 .s_1 | s_1 :- .l_1 | s_1 .s_1 : fe_1 .fe_1 | s_1 : . || .s_1 | f_1 : f_1
girt by ra - ging | seas our | land is rough and | sear; || But | health and
d .d : m .d | t_1 .d : t_1 .m | r .r : d .d | t_1 : . || .d | d : s_1
joy- ful mu- sic | praise this | fa - vour'd spot of | earth; || Come, | praise the
d_1 .d_1 : d_1 .m_1 | s_1 :- .d_1 | r_1 .r_1 : r_1 .r_1 | s_1 : . || .m_1 | f_1 : r_1

d :- .r | m .d : f .m | m .r : .s | f .m : r .d | t_1 .l_1 : s_1 .d
skies in | beauty shin-ing | o'er us, And | loudly sing to | praise the land that
m_1 :- .s_1 | s_1 .s_1 : s_1 .s_1 | s_1 .s_1 : .s_1 | s_1 .s_1 : s_1 .s_1 | s_1 .f_1 : m_1 .l_1
peace our | dai- ly la- bours | crowning, Give | countless blessings | to the cheerful
s_1 :- .t_1 | d .m : r .d | d .t_1 : .m | r .d : t_1 .l_1 | s_1 .r : m .m
skies in | beauty shin-ing | o'er us, And | loudly sing to | praise the land that
d_1 :- .s_1 | d .d : t_1 .d | s_1 .s_1 : .s_1 | s_1 .s_1 : s_1 .s_1 | s_1 .t_1 : d .l_1

\> \>
r : t_1 | d : .s_1 | l_1 : t_1 | d :- .r | m .d : f .m
gave us | birth; Come, | praise the | skies in | beauty shin-ing
l_1 : f_1 | m_1 : .s_1 | f_1 : f_1 | m_1 :- .s_1 | s_1 .s_1 : s_1 .s_1
spi - rit's | here; But | health and | peace our | dai - ly la - bours
f : r | d : .d | d : s_1 | s_1 :- .t_1 | d .m : r .d
gave us | birth; Come, | praise the | skies in | beauty shin-ing
f_1 : s_1 | d_1 : .m_1 | f_1 : r_1 | d_1 :- .s_1 | d .d : t_1 .d

St. Co. (New).

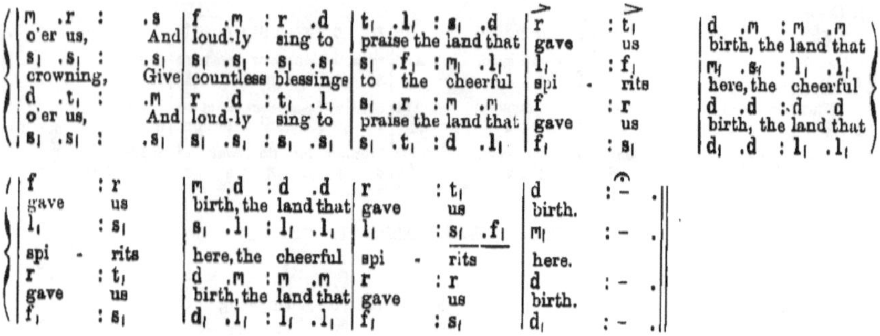

| m .r : .s | f .m : r .d | t_1 .l_1 : s_1 .d | r : t_1 | d .m : m .m |
o'er us, And | loud-ly sing to | praise the land that | gave us | birth, the land that
| s_1 .s_1 : .s_1 | s_1 .s_1 : s_1 .s_1 | s_1 .f_1 : m_1 .l_1 | l_1 : f_1 | m_1 .s_1 : l_1 .l_1 |
crowning, Give | countless blessings | to the cheerful | spi - rits | here, the cheerful
| d .t_1 : .m | r .d : t_1 .l_1 | s_1 .r : m .m | f : r | d .d : d .d |
o'er us, And | loud-ly sing to | praise the land that | gave us | birth, the land that
| s_1 .s_1 : .s_1 | s_1 .s_1 : s_1 .s_1 | s_1 .t_1 : d .l_1 | f_1 : s_1 | d_1 .d : l_1 .l_1 |

| f : r | m .d : d .d | r : t_1 | d : - . ||
gave us | birth, the land that | gave us | birth.
| l_1 : s_1 | s_1 .l_1 : l_1 .l_1 | l_1 : s_1 .f_1 | m_1 : - . ||
spi - rits | here, the cheerful | spi - rits | here.
| r : t_1 | d .m : m .m | r : r | d : - . ||
gave us | birth, the land that | gave us | birth.
| f_1 : s_1 | d_1 .l_1 : l_1 .l_1 | f_1 : s_1 | d_1 : - . ||

THE QUAIL CALL.

(Words translated from the German by J. S. STALLYBRASS.)

KEY G. M. 66, twice. *p* *f* *Gersbach.*

| m : - : m.m | m : -.m : m | f : -.s : f | m : — : s.,s | s : — : | : :
1.Hark to the Quail how she | pipes at | morn, "Come a- | long! Come a-long!
| d : - : d.d | d : -.d : d | r : -.r : r | d : — : | : s.,s | s : — :
2.Cool on the hea - ther the | dew yet | lies; "Cold the | night! Cold the night!"
| s : - : s.s | s : -.s : s | s : -.s : s | s : — : | : : | : :
3.Now come the huntsmen with | horn and | hound; "Get you | gone! Get you gone!
| d : - : d.d | d : -.d : d | t_1 : -.t_1 : t_1 | d : — : | : : | : :
4.Hark, when the reaping is | ov - er and | done, "I'll be- | gone! I'll be-gone!

| d' : d' : d' | d' : -.r' : d' | t : - : | s : -.s : s | s : l : t | d' : -.r' : d' |
come let us hide in the | corn." | Look at her, | steal- ing through yonder green
| m : s : l | s : -.s : s | s : - : | s : -.s : s | s : fe : s | l : -.l : l |
flutt'-ring and shiv - 'ring she | cries; | Runs to the | sand, where she mak - eth her
| d' : d' : d'.r' | m' : -.f' : m' | r' : - : | t : -.t : t | r' : d' : t | l : -.l : l |
here I lie safe in the | ground; | While the wheat | stands and the leaves are yet
| d : m : f | s : -.s : s | s : - : | s : -.s : s | t : l : s | fe : -.fe : fe |
ruth - less the win - ter comes | on." | Hi - ther and | thi - ther she flits and she

| t : - : - | s : l : t | d' : r' : m' | f' : -.f' : f' | m' : - : | d' : d' : d' |
field, Tell-ing of | sweets that the | har - vest will | yield, Sing-ing the
| s : - : - | s : s : s | s : s : s | s : -.s : s | s : - : | s : s : s |
bed, Pa - tient-ly | waits till the | shades are all | fled, Wist-ful - ly
| r' : - : - | t : d' : r' | d' : t : d' | r' : -.r' : r' | d' : - : | m' : r' : d' |
green, I by the | hun - ter shall | nev - er be | seen; Ah, but the
| s : - : - | s : s : f | m : r : d | t_1 : -.t_1 : t_1 | d : - : | d : r : m |
flies, But not a | glean-ing of | har - vest she | spies, Tho' in the

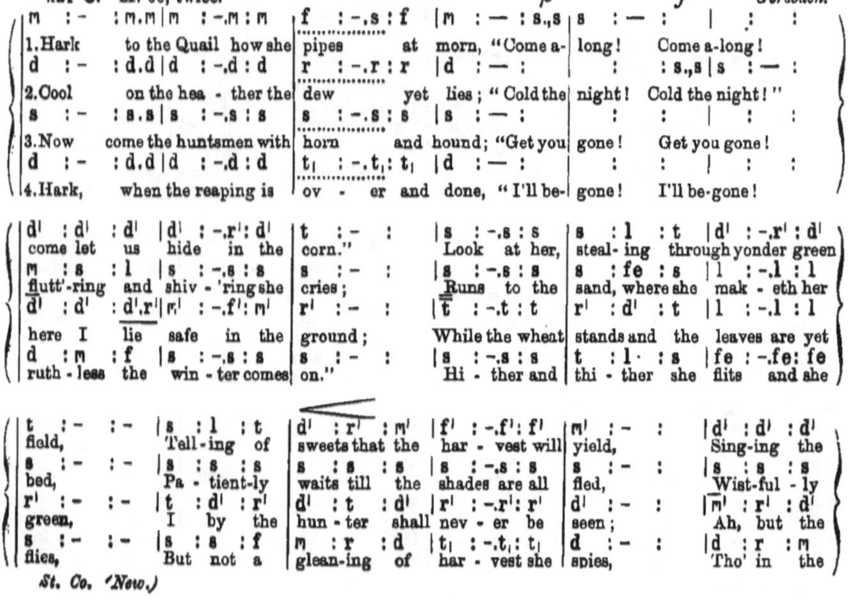

St. Co. (New.)

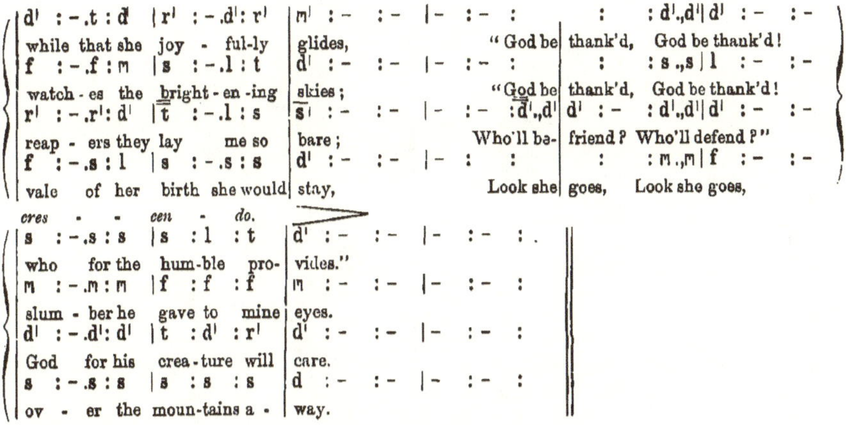

d' :-.t :d' |r' :-.d':r' |m' :- :- |- :- : | : :d'.,d'|d' :- :-

while that she joy - ful-ly | glides, "God be | thank'd, God be thank'd!

f :-.f :m |s :-.l :t |d' :- :- |- :- : | : :s.,s|l :- :-

watch-es the bright-en-ing | skies; "God be | thank'd, God be thank'd!

r' :-.r':d' |t :-.l :s |s :- :- |- :- :d'.,d' |d' :- :d'.,d'|d' :- :-

reap - ers they lay me so | bare; Who'll be- | friend? Who'll defend?"

f :-.s :l |s :-.s :s |d' :- :- |- : : | : :m.,m|f :- :-

vale of her birth she would | stay, Look she | goes, Look she goes,

cres - - cen - do.

s :-.s :s |s :l :t |d' :- :- |- :- :.

who for the hum-ble pro- | vides."

m :-.m :m |f :f :f |m :- :- |- :- :

slum - ber he gave to mine | eyes.

d' :-.d':d' |t :d' :r' |d' :- :- |- :- :

God for his crea-ture will | care.

s :-.s :s |s :s :s |d :- :- |- :- :

ov - er the moun-tains a - | way.

Words by *J. S. Stallybrass.*

THE TIME FOR JOY.

("Soldiers, brave and gallant be")

Gastoldi.

f KEY B♭. S.S.C.T.B. M. 144.

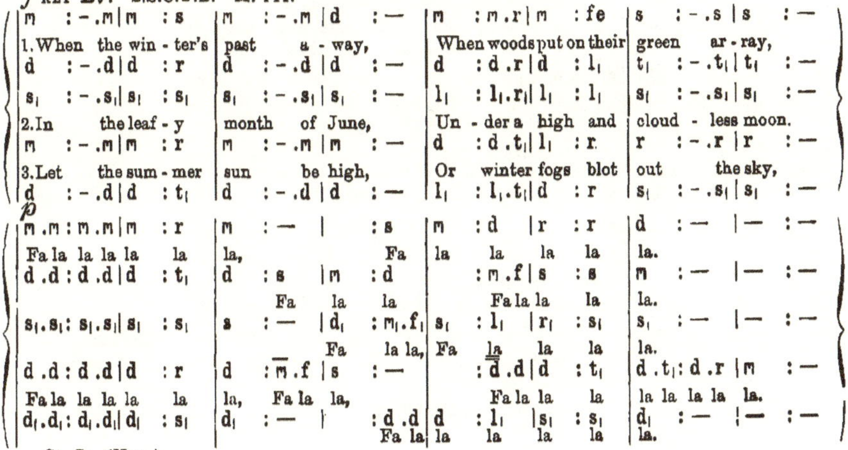

m :-.m|m :s |m :-.m|d :— |m :m.r|m :fe |s :-.s|s :—

1.When the win - ter's | past a - way, | When woods put on their | green ar - ray,

d :-.d|d :r |d :-.d|d :— |d :d.r|d :l, |t, :-.t,|t, :—

s, :-.s,|s, :s, |s, :-.s,|s, :— |l, :l,.r,|l, :l, |s, :-.s,|s, :—

2.In the leaf - y | month of June, | Un - der a high and | cloud - less moon.

m :-.m|m :r |m :-.m|m :— |d :d.t,|l, :r |r :-.r|r :—

3.Let the sum - mer | sun be high, | Or winter fogs blot | out the sky,

d :-.d|d :t, |d :-.d|d :— |l, :l,.t,|d :r |s, :-.s,|s, :—

p

m.m:m.m|m :r |m :— | :s |m :d |r :r |d :— |— :—

Fa la la la la la | la, Fa | la la la la | la.

d.d:d.d|d :t, |d :s |m :d | :m.f|s :s |m :— |— :—

Fa la la | Fa la la la | la.

s,.s,:s,.s,|s, :s, |s :— |d, :m,.f, |s, :l, |r, :s, |s, :— |— :—

Fa la la, Fa | la la la | la.

d.d:d.d|d :r |d :m.f |s :— | :d.d|d :t, |d.t,:d.r|m :—

Fa la la la la la | la, Fa la la, | Fa la la la | la la la la la.

d,.d,:d,.d,|d, :s, |d, :— | :d.d |d :l, |s, :s, |d, :— |— :—

Fa la | la la la la | la.

St. Co. (New.)

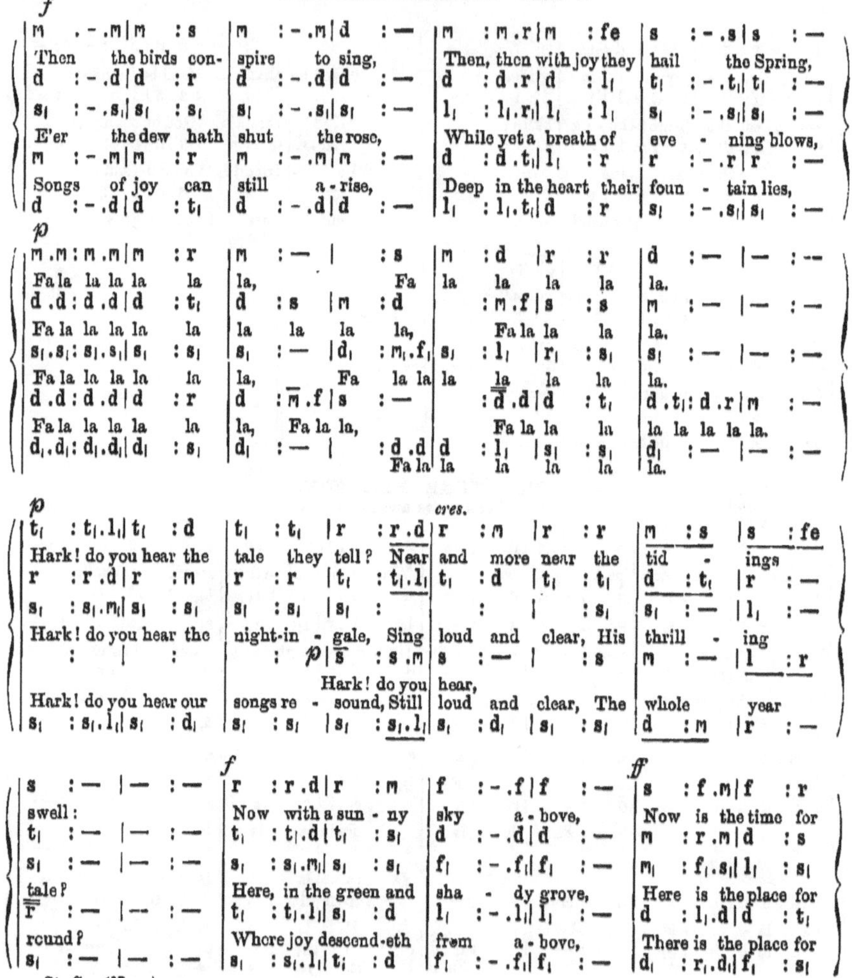

f

m .-.m|m :s |m :-.m|d :— |m :m.r|m :fe |s :-.s|s :—

Then the birds con- spire to sing, Then, then with joy they hail the Spring,

d :-.d|d :r |d :-.d|d :— |d :d.r|d :l, |t, :-.t,|t, :—

s, :-.s,|s, :s, |s, :-.s,|s, :— |l, :l,.r,|l, :l, |s, :-.s,|s, :—

E'er the dew hath shut the rose, While yet a breath of eve - ning blows,

m :-.m|m :r |m :-.m|m :— |d :d.t,|l, :r |r :-.r|r :—

Songs of joy can still a - rise, Deep in the heart their foun - tain lies,

d :-.d|d :t, |d :-.d|d :— |l, :l,.t,|d :r |s, :-.s,|s, :—

p

m.m:m.m|m :r |m :— | :s |m :d |r :r |d :— |— :—

Fa la la la la la la, Fa la la la la la.

d.d:d.d|d :t, |d :s |m :d | :m.f|s :s |m :— |— :—

Fa la la la la la la la la la, Fa la la la la.

s,.s,:s,.s,|s, :s, |s, :— |d, :m,.f, |s, :l, |r, :s, |s, :— |— :—

Fa la la la la la la, Fa la la la la la la la.

d.d:d.d|d :r |d :m.f|s :— | :d.d|d :t, |d.t,:d.r|m :—

Fa la la la la la la, Fa la la, Fa la la la la la la la la.

d,.d,:d,.d,|d, :s, |d, :— | :d.d |d :l, |s, :s, |d, :— |— :—

Fa la la la la la.

p *cres.*

t, :t,.l,|t, :d |t, :t, |r :r.d |r :m |r :r |m :s |s :fe

Hark! do you hear the tale they tell? Near and more near the tid - ings

r :r.d|r :m |r :r |t, :t,.l, |t, :d |t, :t, |d :t, |r :—

s, :s,.m,|s, :s, |s, :s, |s, : | : | :s, |s, :— |l, :—

Hark! do you hear the night-in - gale, Sing loud and clear, His thrill - ing

: | : | : *p*|s :s.m |s :— | :s |m :— |l :r

Hark! do you hear,

Hark! do you hear our songs re - sound, Still loud and clear, The whole year

s, :s,.l,|s, :d, |s, :s, |s, :s,.l, |s, :d, |s, :s, |d :m |r :—

s :— |— :— |*f* r :r.d|r :m |f :-.f|f :— |*ff* s :f.m|f :r

swell: Now with a sun - ny sky a - bove, Now is the time for

t, :— |— :— |t, :t,.d|t, :s, |d :-.d|d :— |m :r.m|d :s

s, :— |— :— |s, :s,.m,|s, :s, |f, :-.f,|f, :— |m, :f,.s,|l, :s,

tale? Here, in the green and sha - dy grove, Here is the place for

r :— |— :— |t, :t,.l,|s, :d |l, :-.l,|l, :— |d :l,.d|d :t,

round? Where joy descend-eth from a - bove, There is the place for

s, :— |— :— |s, :s,.l,|t, :d |f, :-.f,|f, :— |d, :r,.d,|f, :s,

St. Co. (New.)

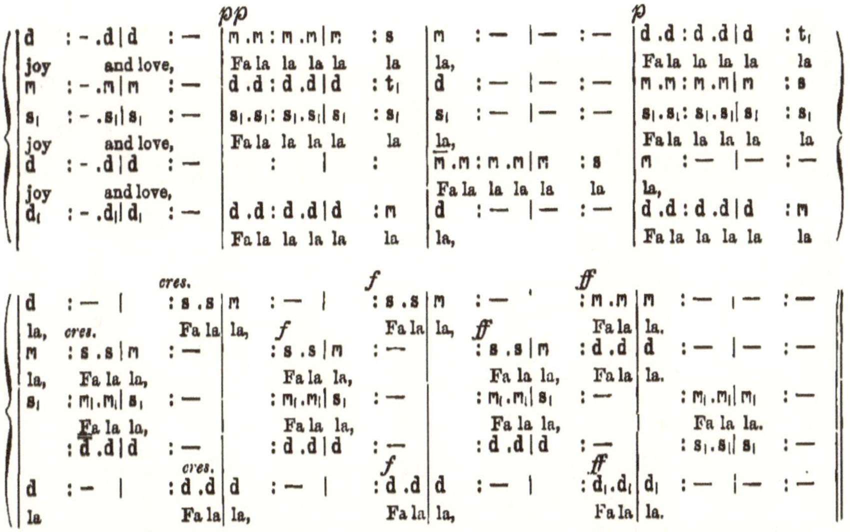

```
                                  pp                                                  p
| d    :-.d | d    :-    | m.m : m.m | m    :s    | m    :-  | -  :-    | d.d : d.d | d    :t,   |
  joy   and love,          Fa la  la la  la   la     la,                   Fa la  la la  la   la
| m    :-.m | m    :-    | d.d : d.d | d    :t,   | d    :-  | -  :-    | m.m : m.m | m    :s    |

| s,   :-.s, | s,  :-    | s,.s, : s,.s, | s,  :s, | s,  :-  | -  :-    | s,.s, : s,.s, | s,  :s, |
  joy   and love,          Fa la  la la  la   la     la,                   Fa la  la la  la   la
| d    :-.d | d    :-    |      :     |     :     | m.m : m.m | m  :s    | m    :-  | -  :-    |
  joy   and love,                                    Fa la  la la  la  la  la,
| d,   :-.d, | d,  :-    | d.d : d.d | d    :m    | d    :-  | -  :-    | d.d : d.d | d    :m    |
                           Fa la  la la  la   la     la,                   Fa la  la la  la   la
```

```
            cres.                        f                         ff
| d    :-  |      :s.s | m    :-  |      :s.s | m    :-  |      :m.m | m    :-  | -  :-    ||
  la,  cres.      Fa la  la,  f           Fa la  la,  ff          Fa la  la.
| m    :s.s | m    :-   |      :s.s | m    :-   |      :s.s | m    :d.d | d    :-  | -  :-    ||
  la,   Fa la  la,              Fa la  la,              Fa la  la,  Fa la  la.
| s,   :m,.m, | s,  :-  |      :m,.m, | s,  :-  |      :m,.m, | s,  :-  |      :m,.m, | m,  :-  ||
        Fa la  la,              Fa la  la,              Fa la  la,              Fa la  la.
|      :d.d | d    :-   |      :d.d | d    :-   |      :d.d | d    :-   |      :s,.s, | s,  :-  ||
            cres.                       f                          ff
| d    :-  |      :d.d | d    :-  |      :d.d | d    :-  |      :d,.d, | d,  :-  | -  :-    ||
  la              Fa la  la,              Fa la  la,              Fa la  la.
```

HEAR ME WHEN I CALL.

KEY F. *pp* *G A Macfarren.*

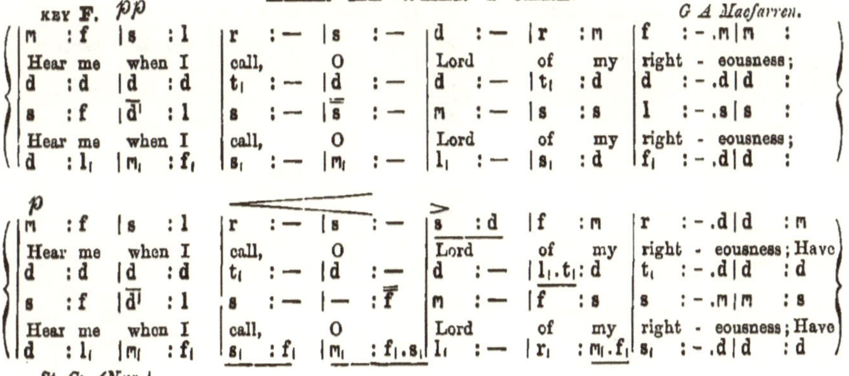

```
| m    :f    | s    :l    | r    :-   | s    :-   | d    :-   | r    :m    | f    :-.m | m    :    |
  Hear me      when I       call,        O           Lord         of   my      right - eousness;
| d    :d    | d    :d    | t,   :-   | d    :-   | d    :-   | t,   :d    | d    :-.d | d    :    |

| s    :f    | d'   :l    | s    :-   | s    :-   | m    :-   | s    :s    | l    :-.s | s    :    |
  Hear me      when I       call,        O           Lord         of   my      right - eousness;
| d    :l,   | m,   :f,   | s,   :-   | m,   :-   | l,   :-   | s,   :d    | f,   :-.d | d    :    |
```

```
  p                                              >
| m    :f    | s    :l    | r    :-   | s    :-   | s    :d   | f    :m    | r    :-.d | d    :m    |
  Hear me      when I       call,        O           Lord         of   my      right - eousness; Have
| d    :d    | d    :d    | t,   :-   | d    :-   | d    :-   | l,.t, :d   | t,   :-.d | d    :d    |

| s    :f    | d'   :l    | s    :-   | -    :f   | m    :-   | f    :s    | s    :-.m | m    :s    |
  Hear me      when I       call,        O           Lord         of   my      right - eousness; Have
| d    :l,   | m,   :f,   | s,   :f,  | m,   :f,.s, | l,  :-   | r,   :m,.f, | s,  :-.d | d    :d    |
```

St. Co. (New.)

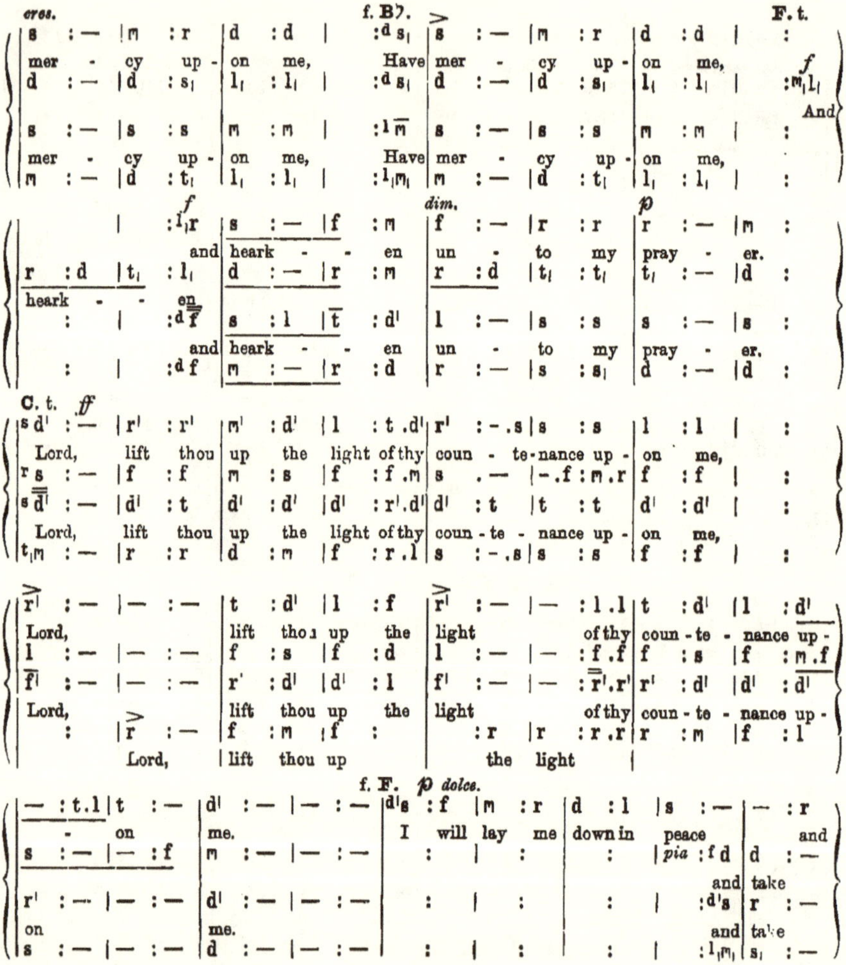

cres. f. B♭. > F. t.

|s :— |m :r |d :d | :ᵈs₁ |s :— |m :r |d :d | :
mer - cy up - on me, Have mer - cy up - on me, *f*
|d :— |d :s₁ |l₁ :l₁ | :ᵈs₁ |d :— |d :s₁ |l₁ :l₁ | :m₁l₁
And
|s :— |s :s |m :m | :ˡm |s :— |s :s |m :m | :
mer - cy up - on me, Have mer - cy up - on me,
|m :— |d :t₁ |l₁ :l₁ | :ˡ₁m₁ |m :— |d :t₁ |l₁ :l₁ | :

f *dim.* *p*
| | :ˡ₁r |s :— |f :m |f :— |r :r |r :— |m :
and heark - - en un - to my pray - er.
|r :d |t₁ :l₁ |d :— |r :m |r :d |t₁ :t₁ |t₁ :— |d :
heark - - en
| : | :ᵈf |s :l |t :d' |l :— |s :s |s :— |s :
and heark - - en un - to my pray - er.
| : | :ᵈf |m :— |r :d |r :— |s :s₁ |d :— |d :

C. t. *ff*
|ˢd' :— |r' :r' |m' :d' |l :t .d' |r' :- .s |s :s |l :l | :
Lord, lift thou up the light of thy coun - te - nance up - on me,
|ʳs :— |f :f |m :s |f :f .m |s .— |- .f :m .r |f :f | :
|ˢd' :— |d' :t |d' :d' |d' :r'.d' |d' :t |t :t |d' :d' | :
Lord, lift thou up the light of thy coun - te - nance up - on me,
|t₁m :— |r :r |d :m |f :r .l |s :- .s |s :s |f :f | :

|r' :— |— :— |t :d' |l :f |r' :— |— :l .l |t :d' |l :d'
Lord, lift thou up the light of thy coun - te - nance up -
|l :— |— :— |f :s |f :d |l :— |— :f .f |f :s |f :m .f
|f' :— |— :— |r' :d' |d' :l |f' :— |— :r'.r' |r' :d' |d' :d'
Lord, lift thou up the light of thy coun - te - nance up -
| : |r :— |f :m |f : | :r |r :r .r |r :m |f :l
Lord, lift thou up the light

f. F. *p dolce.*
|— :t .l |t :— |d' :— |— :— |ᵈ's :f |m :r |d :l |s :— |— :r
- on me. I will lay me down in peace and
|s :— |— :f |m :— |— :— | : | : | : |*pia* :ᶠd |d :—
and take
|r' :— |— :— |d' :— |— :— | : | : | : | :ᵈ's |r :—
on me. and take
|s :— |— :— |d :— |— :— | : | : | : | :ˡ₁m₁ |s₁ :—

St. Co. (New.)

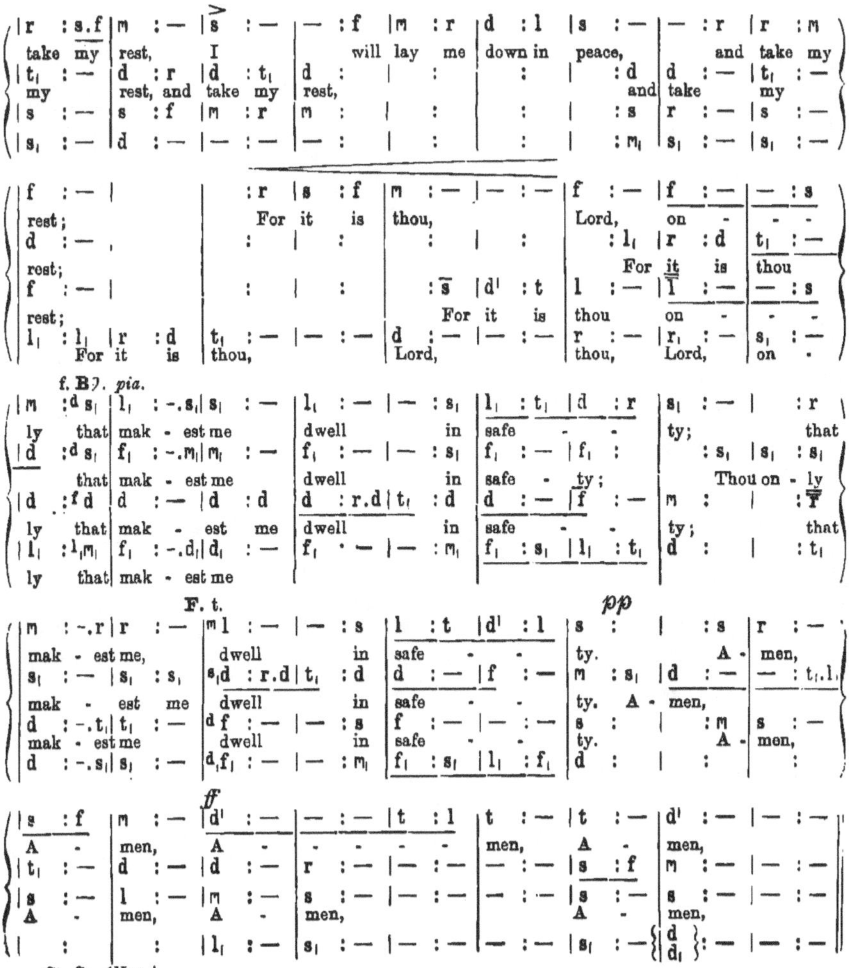

|r :s.f |m :— |s :— |— :f |m :r |d :l |s :— |— :r |r :m

take my | rest, I | will lay me | down in | peace, | and take my

|t_1 :— |d :r |d :t_1 |d : | : | : | :d |d :— |t_1 :—

my | rest, and take my | rest, | and | take | my

|s :— |s :f |m :r |m : | : | : | :s |r :— |s :—

|s_1 :— |d :— |— :— |— : | : | : | :m_1 |s_1 :— |s_1 :—

|f :— | | :r |s :f |m :— |— :— |f :— |f :— |— :s

rest; For it is thou, Lord, on - - -

|d :— | : | : | : | : | :l_1 |r :d |t_1 :—

rest; For it is thou

|f :— | | : | : | :s |d^1 :t |l :— |l :— |— :s

rest; For it is thou on - - -

|l_1 :l_1 |r :d |t_1 :— |— :— |d :— |— :— |r :— |r_1 :— |s_1 :—

For it is thou, Lord, thou, Lord, on -

f. B♭. *pia.*

|m :$^d s_1$ |l_1 :-.s_1 |s_1 :— |l_1 :— |— :s_1 |l_1 :t_1 |d :r |s_1 :— | :r

ly that mak - est me dwell in safe - - ty; that

|d :$^d s_1$ |f_1 :-.m_1 |m_1 :— |f_1 :— |— :s_1 |f_1 :— |f_1 : | :s_1 |s_1 :s_1

that mak - est me dwell in safe - ty; Thou on - ly

|d :^{f}d |d :— |d :d |d :r.d |t_1 :d |d :— |f :— |m : | :f

ly that mak - est me dwell in safe - - ty; that

|l_1 :$^{l}m_1$ |f_1 :-.d_1 |d_1 :— |f_1 :— |— :m_1 |f_1 :s_1 |l_1 :t_1 |d : | :t_1

ly that mak - est me

F. t. *pp*

|m :-.r |r :— |^{m}l :— |— :s |l :t |d^1 :l |s : | :s |r :—

mak - est me, dwell in safe - - ty. A - men,

|s_1 :— |s_1 :s_1 |^{s}d :r.d |t_1 :d |d :— |f :— |m :s_1 |d :— |— :t_1.l_1

mak - est me dwell in safe - - ty. A - men,

|d :-.t_1 |t_1 :— |^{d}f :— |— :s |f :— |— :— |s : | :m |s :—

mak - est me dwell in safe - - ty. A - men,

|d :-.s_1 |s_1 :— |$^d f_1$:— |— :m_1 |f_1 :s_1 |l_1 :f_1 |d : | : | :

ff

|s :f |m :— |d^1 :— |— :— |t :l |t :— |t :— |d^1 :— |— :—

A - men, A - - - - - men, A - men,

|t_1 :— |d :— |d :— |r :— |— :— |— :— |s :f |m :— |— :—

|s :— |l :— |m :— |s :— |— :— |— :— |s :— |s :— |— :—

A - men, A - men, A - men,

| : | : |l_1 :— |s_1 :— |— :— |— :— |s_1 :— |{d d_1} :— |— :—

St. Co. (New.)

WE FLY BY NIGHT.

KEY F. M. 108. C. t. *Matthew Locke.*

| d' :d'.t \| l : | r' :r'.d' \| t : | d'f' :r'.d' \| t :s' | r'.f' :m'.r' \| m'.d' :— |
We fly by night, we fly by night, we fly by night 'mong troops of spirits,
| : \| d :d.d | f :-.m \| r : | m l :l.l \| s :s | s :-.s \| s.s :— |
We fly by night, we fly by night 'mong troops of spirits,
| : \| f :f.s | l : \| s :s.s | s d' :f' \| r' :d' | d' :t \| d'.d' :— |
We fly by night, we fly by night, by night 'mong troops of spirits,
| : \| f :f.m | r : \| s :s.f | m l :f \| s :m | s :s \| d.d :— |

f. F.

| : \| : | d's :s.f \| m : | d' :d'.t \| l.t :l.s | f.s :f.m \| r : |
We fly by night, we fly, - - - - -
| s r :r.d \| t, : | d :d.t, \| d : | d :d.d \| d : | r :r.r \| r : |
We fly by night, We fly by night, we fly by night, we fly by night,
| m't :t.l \| s : | s :s.s \| s : | l :l.l \| l : | l :l.f \| s : |
| : \| d's :s.f | m : \| d :d.t, | l, : \| f :f.m | r.m :r.d \| t,.d :t,.l, |
We fly by night, we fly by night, we fly - - - -

| s :s.f \| m.f :m.r | d.r :m.d \| r.m :f.r | m.f :s.m \| f.s :l.f |
we fly - - - - - - - - - - - - -
| r :r.r \| d : | d :d.d \| t, :-.t, | d :— \| f :f.f |
we fly by night, We fly by night, by night, we fly by
| t :t.t \| d' : | m :m.m \| s :-.s | s :d' \| d' :d'.t |
| s, : \| d :d.t, | l,.t, :d.t,.l, \| s, :s, | d.r :m.d \| r.m :f.r |
- we fly, - - - we fly - - -

D.C.

| s.l :ta.s \| l.t :d' | t :d' \| d' :t | d'.d' :— \| : |
- - - by night 'mong troops of spi- rits.
| m :-.m \| d :f | r :m \| r :r | m.m :— \| : |
night, we fly by night 'mong troops of spi- rits.
| d' :-.d' \| d' :-.l | s :s \| s :s | s.s :— \| : |
| m.f :s.m \| f.s :l.f | s :d \| s, :s, | d.d :— \| : |
- - - by night 'mong troops of spi- rits.

St. Co. (New).

MY LADY IS AS FAIR AS FINE.

KEY B♭. M. 90. *p* F. t. *John Benet,* 1614.

```
:d .r |m   :-.m |m   :f   |m   :r .d |f   :r   |m   :r .d |ˢs  :d'  |d'  :t   |d'  :d .r
 My    la   -  dy is  as    fair  as  fine, With milk - white hands and gold - en  hair; Her
:m,.f,|s,  :-.s,|s,  :l,  |s,  :f,.m,|r,  :t,  |s,  :d   |ᵗ,m :d   |r   :-.r |d   :d
:s,   |d   :-.d |d   :d   |d   :s,   |s,  :s .f|m   :s   |ˢd' :s   |l   :s .f|m .f :m .r
 My    la   -  dy is  as    fair  as  fine, With milk - white hands and gold - en  hair; Her
:d,   |d,  :-.d,|d,  :f,  |d,  :d,   |s,  :s,  |d,  :d,  |ˢ,d :m,  |f,  :s,  |d   :—
```

cres. f. B♭. *f*

```
|m   :r .m |r .d :t,.d |ʳl,.t,:d .m |r   :—   |m   :-.s |f   :d   |r   :r   |m   :
 eyes the  ra  -  diant  stars  out - shine,    Light - ing all things far   and  near:
|d   :t,.d |t,.l,:s,.l,|ᵗᵃ,f, :s,.l,|t,  :—   |s,  :-.s,|l,  :d   |d   :t,  |d   :
|d   :r    |r   :-.r   |ˢr   :m .d  |r   :—   |d   :m   |r   :d   |s   :s   |s   :
 eyes the  ra  -  diant  stars  out - shine,    Light-ing all  things far  and  near:
|    :s,   |s,  :-.s,  |ˢ,r, :d,    |s,  :—   |m,  :-.m,|f,  :l,  |s,  :s,  |d,  :
      Her   eyes   the   stars  out - shine,
```

pp

```
|d   :-.r |m   :d .s,|l,.t,:d   |d .t, :—  |d   :-.r |m   :d   |d   :t,  |d .d :—
 Fair  as Cyn - thia,  not   so   fickle;    Smooth as glass, tho' not  so   brittle.
|m,  :-.f,|s,  :s,   |f,   :m,  |r,.r, :—  |l,  :-.l,|s,  :m,  |r,  :r,  |d,.d,:—
|d   :d   |d   :s,   |r    :s   |s   :r .m |f   :d   |d .r :m .f|s  :-.f |f .m :—
 Fair as   Cyn - thia, not   so   fickle;    Smooth as glass, tho'  not  so   brittle.
|d,  :-.d,|d,  :m,   |r,   :d,  |s,.s, :—  |f,.s,:l,.t,|d  :d,  |s,  :s,  |d,.d,:—
```

p F. t.

```
|  :  |  :d .r |m   :-.m |m   :f   |m   :r .d |t,  :r   |m   :r .d |ˢs  :d'
           My    heart  is like  a   ball  of   snow, Fast melt - ing  at  her
|  :  |  :m,.f,|s,  :-.s,|s,  :l,  |s,  :f,.m,|r,  :t,  |s,  :d   |ᵗ,m :d
|  :  |  :s,   |d   :-.d |d   :d   |d   :s,   |s,  :s .f|m   :s   |ˢd' :s
           My    heart  is like  a   ball  of   snow, Fast melt - ing  at  her
|  :  |  :d,   |d,  :-.d,|d,  :f,  |d,  :d,   |s,  :s,  |d,  :d,  |ˢ,d :m,
```

cres. f. B♭. *f*

```
|d'  :t   |d'  :d .r |m   :r .m |r .d :t,.d |ʳl,.t,:d .m |r   :—   |m   :-.s |f   :d   |r   :r
 glan-ces bright; Her ru  -  by  lips   like  nightworms glow,       Spark - ling thro' the pale twi-
|r   :-.r |d   :d    |d   :t,.d |t,.l,:s,.l,|ᵗᵃ,f, :m,.d,|r,  :—   |s,  :-.s,|l,  :d   |d   :t,
|l   :s .f|m .f :m .r|d   :r    |r   :-.r   |ˢr   :s,.l,|t,  :-.r |d   :m   |r   :d   |s   :s
 glan-ces bright; Her ru  -  by  lips   like  nightworms glow,       Spark - ling thro' the pale twi-
|f,  :s,  |d   :—    |    :s,   |s,  :-.s,  |ˢ,r, :d,    |s,  :—   |m,  :-.m,|f,  :l,  |s,  :s,
                           Her   lips   like  nightworms glow,
```

St. Co. (New).

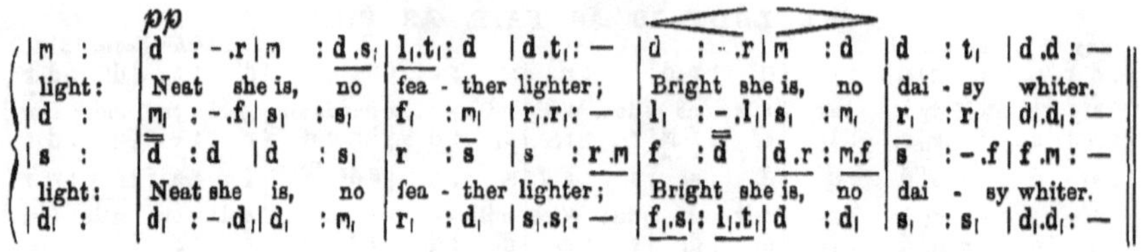

pp

|m : |d :-.r|m :d.s_1|l_1.t_1:d |d.t_1:— |d :-.r|m :d |d :t_1 |d.d:— ||
light: Neat she is, no fea - ther lighter; Bright she is, no dai - sy whiter.
|d : |m_1 :-.f_1|s_1 :s_1 |f_1 :m_1 |r_1.r_1:— |l_1 :-.l_1|s_1 :m_1 |r_1 :r_1 |d_1.d_1:— ||
|s : |d :d |d :s_1 |r :s |s :r.m |f :d |d.r :m.f |s :-.f|f.m:— ||
light: Neat she is, no fea - ther lighter; Bright she is, no dai - sy whiter.
|d_1 : |d_1 :-.d_1|d_1 :m_1 |r_1 :d_1 |s_1.s_1:— |f_1.s_1:l_1.t_1|d :d_1 |s_1 :s_1 |d_1.d_1:— ||

NIGHT AROUND.

Air by *Weingand.*

KEY F. M. 72, thrice. (Arranged for this work by GEO. OAKEY).

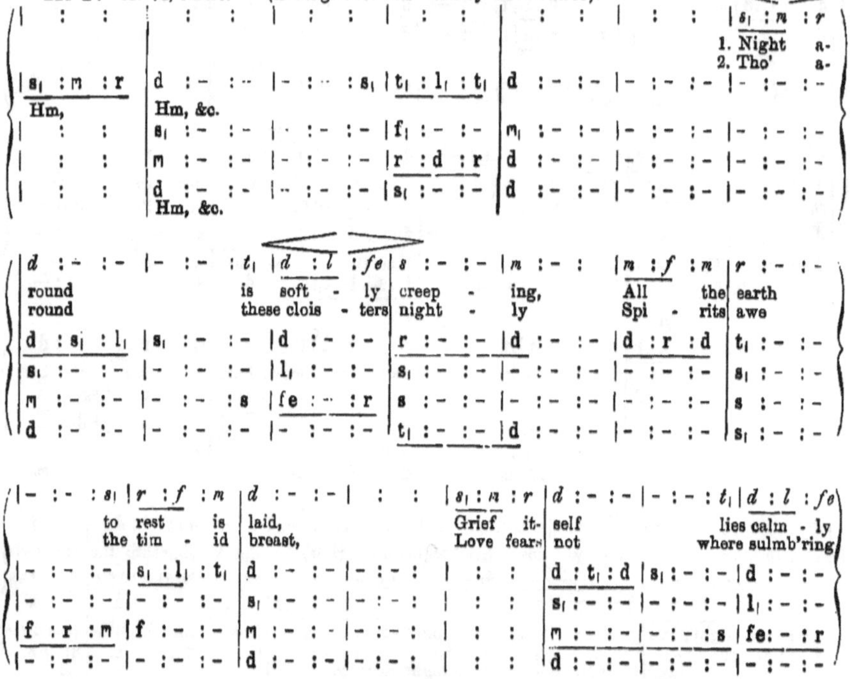

| : : | : : | : : | : : | : : | : : |*s_1 :m :r*
1. Night a-
2. Tho' a-
|s_1 :m :r |d :- :- |- :- :s_1 |t_1 :l_1 :t_1 |d :- :- |- :- :- |- :- :-
Hm, Hm, &c.
| : : |s_1 :- :- |- :- :- |f_1 :- :- |m_1 :- :- |- :- :- |- :- :-
| : : |m :- :- |- :- :- |r :d :r |d :- :- |- :- :- |- :- :-
| : : |d :- :- |- :- :- |s_1 :- :- |d :- :- |- :- :- |- :- :-
Hm, &c.

|*d :- :- |- :- :t_1 |d :l :fe |s :- :- |m :- : |m :f :m |r :- :-*
round is soft - ly creep - ing, All the earth
round these clois - ters night - ly Spi - rits awe
|d :s_1 :l_1 |s_1 :- :- |d :- :- |r :- :- |d :- :- |d :r :d |t_1 :- :-
|s_1 :- :- |- :- :- |l_1 :- :- |s_1 :- :- |- :- :- |- :- :- |s_1 :- :-
|m :- :- |- :- :s |fe :- :r |s :- :- |- :- :- |- :- :- |s :- :-
|d :- :- |- :- :- |- :- :- |t_1 :- :- |d :- :- |- :- :- |s_1 :- :-

|*- :- :s_1 |r :f :m |d :- :- | : : |s_1 :m :r |d :- :- |- :- :t_1 |d :l :fe*
to rest is laid, Grief it- self lies calm - ly
the tim - id breast, Love fears not where sulmb'ring
|- :- :- |s_1 :l_1 :t_1 |d :- :- |- :- : | : : |d :t_1 :d |s_1 :- :- |d :- :-
|- :- :- |- :- :- |s_1 :- :- |- :- : | : : |s_1 :- :- |- :- :- |l_1 :- :-
|f :r :m |f :- :- |m :- :- |- :- : | : : |m :- :- |- :- :s |fe :- :r
|- :- :- |- :- :- |d :- :- |- :- : | : : |d :- :- |- :- :- |- :- :-

St. Co. (New.)

C. t. *cres.*

s :- :- | *m* :- :- | ˢ*d'* : *t* : *d'* | *s* :- :- | - :- : *m'* | *f'* : *m'* : *r'* | *d'* :- :- | - : :
sleep - ing, Sleep - est thou be- lov - ed maid?
light - ly I - da lies in heav'n - ly rest.
r :- :- | d :- :- | t_1m : r : m | s :- :- | - :- : d' | t :- :- | d' :- :- | - : :
s_1 :- :- | - :- :- | : : | t_1m : f : m | r :- : d | r : m : f | m :- :- | - : :
s :- :- | - :- :- | : : | ˢd' : t : d' | s :- :- | - :- :- | s :- :- | - : :
t_1 :- :- | d :- :- | ˢ$_1$d :- :- | - :- :- | d : t_1 : d | s :- :- | d :- :- | - : :

dolce. f.F. *cres.*

d' : *t* : *d'* | r'*l* :- :- | - :- : *s* | *f* : *m* : *r* | *m* :- :- | *s* :- :- | *s* : *fe* : *s* | *l* :- :-
I - da hear my lute's soft num - bers, Float - ing on
Play - ful ze - - - phyrs gent- ly steal - ing, Up - ward waft
: : | taf :- :- | - :- : m | r : d : t_1 | d :- :- | - :- :- | : : | f : m : f
: : | mt_1 :- :- | d : t_1 : d | s_1 :- :- | - :- :- | - :- :- | : : | t_1 :- :-
: : | sr :- :- | - :- : m | f : s : f | m :- :- | - :- :- | : : | r :- :-
: : | ds_1 :- :- | - :- :- | - :- :- | d :- :- | - :- :- | : : | s_1 :- :-

Poco rit.

- :- : *s* | *f* : *m* : *r* | *m* :- : *d'* | *s* :- :- | *s_1* : *m* : *r* | *d* :- :- | - :- : *t_1* | *d* : *l* : *fe*
the balm - y air, Yet, my lute if I - da
my song to thee, May its tones my love re-
r :- : m | r :- :- | d :- : m | s :- :- | : : | d : s_1 : l_1 | s_1 :- :- | d :- :-
- :- :- | s_1 : l_1 : t_1 | d :- :- | - :- :- | : : | s_1 :- :- | - :- :- | l_1 :- :-
- :- :- | s :- :- | - :- :- | m :- :- | : : | m :- :- | - :- : s | fe :- : r
- :- :- | - :- :- | d :- :- | - :- :- | : : | d :- :- | - :- :- | - :- :-

dim.

s :- :- | *m* :- : | *l* : *t* : *d'* | *m* :- :- | - :- : *s* | *f* : *m* : *r* | *d* :- :- | - : :
slum - bers, Hush! nor wake my la - dy fair.
veal - ing, Fill thy dreams with thoughts of me.
r :- :- | d :- :- | r :- :- | m :- :- | - :- : d | r : d : t_1 | d :- :- | - : :
s_1 :- :- | d :- :- | - :- :- | - : t_1 : d | s_1 :- :- | - :- :- | s_1 :- :- | - : :
s :- :- | - :- :- | fe :- :- | s :- :- | - : r : m | f :- :- | m :- :- | - : :
t_1 :- :- | d :- :- | l_1 :- :- | s_1 :- :- | - :- :- | - :- :- | d :- :- | - : :

St. Co. (New.)

COME, LET US ALL A MAYING GO.

Arranged for mixed voices by Geo. Oakey. *L. Atterbury.*

KEY E♭. *Vivace.* M. 132.

f | s :s .s | s :s | l :s | s : .s | *p* l .f :f .l | s .m :s | r .m :f .m | r :

Come, let us all a May - ing go, And light - ly trip it to and fro; *f*

| m :m .m | r :m | f :r | m : .m | f :d | d :m | t, .d :r .d | t, :r .d

Let us

| d' :d' .d' | t :d' | d' :t | d' : .s | f .l :l .f | d' :d' | r' .d' :t .d' | s :r .r

Come, let us all a May - ing go, And light - ly trip it to and fro;

| d :d .d | s, :d | f, :s, | d : .d | f :- .f | m .s :d' | s :s | s :

p B♭. t. :ᵗm .d | l, : | *p* :f .r | t, :- . | *cres - cen - do.* d :d .d | r :- .r | m :m

Let us go, *f* let us go. Come, let us all a May - ing

| t, : | :ᵐl, .s, | f, :f, .l, | s, :- . | s, :s, .s, | s, :- .s, | s, :l,

go, let us go,

| s : | :ᵐl, .l, | r :l, .l, | r :- . | m :m .m | r :- .r | d :d

p let us go. Come, let us all a May - ing

:ˢd, .m, | f, : | :r, .f, | s, :- . | d :d .d | t, :- .t, | d :l,

Let us go,

ff | f :- .f | f :r | m .d :f .r | m .r :d .t, | d :— | | : | *p* r .t, :t, .s,

go, And light - ly trip it to and fro, trip it to and

| t, :- .l, | s, :t, | d .d : | s, :s, | s, :— | *p* s, .m, :m, .d, | l, : | :

trip it to and fro,

| r :- .r | r :s | s :l | s .f :m .r | m :— | : | f .r :r .t, | s, :s, .s,

go, And light - ly trip it to and fro, trip it to and fro, to and

| r :- .d | t, :- .s, | d :f, | s, :- .s, | d :— | : | : | :

| d :— | *f* f :r | m .d :f .r | m .r :d .t, | 1st time. f. E♭. D.C. ᵈs :— || 2nd time. d : .s, | 𝄋 d .m . r .d | t, .l, :s, .f,

fro, light - ly, light - ly trip it to and fro. fro. The bells shall

| m, d, :s, .m, | s, :t, | d .d : | s, .s, :s, .s, | ˢ,r :— | s, : .s, | d, .d :t, .l, | s, .f, :m, .r,

trip it, trip it, light - ly trip it,

| s, :— | r :s | s :l | s .f :m .r | ᵐt :— | m : | s :m | :

fro, light - ly, light - ly, trip it to and fro, fro. Cuc - koo,

| s, .m, :m, .d, | t, :s, | d, .d :f, | s, .s, :s, .s, | ᵈ,s, :— | d, : .d | d :— | d :—

trip it, trip it, The bells shall

St Co. (New.)

f. E♭.

```
m,.m : r .d | t,.l,. s,.f, | m,.m : r .d | t,.l, : s,.f, | m,  :—  |      :    | ds :m  |   :
ring,            and the | cuc   -   -   koo       | sing,                  | Cuc-koo,
d,.d : t,.l,| s,.f, : m,.r, | d,.d : t,.l,| s,.f, : m,.r, | d,  :—  |  :m,t, | d  :—  | d  :—
ring,            and the | cuc   -   -   koo       | sing,           The | bells      shall
s   :m  |    :      | s   :m  |   :      | s   :m  |   :s r' | d'.m': r'.d'| t .l : s .t
Cuc - koo,            | Cuc - koo,           | Cuc - koo.      The | bells              shall
d   :—  |   :d .d   | d   :—  | d  :—     | d   :—  |   :d s  | d .d': t .l | s .f : m .r
ring,          and the | cuc   -   koo       | sing,           The | bells              shall
```

pp

```
s   :m  |   :      | s   :m  |   :      | s   :m  |   :      |    :   |  :d'.d'
Cuc - koo,          | Cuc - koo,           | Cuc - koo,           |          And the
d   :—  |   :d .s,  | d   :—  | d  :—     | d   :—  | — :      |    :   |  :m .m
ring,        and the | cuc   -   koo       | sing,                f
d'.m': r'.d'| t .l : s .t | d'.m': r'.d'| t .l : s .t | d'  :—  | — :d'  | s  :d'  | s  :
ring,            and the | cuc   -   -   koo     | sing,          The | drum shall beat,
d .d': t .l | s .f : m .r | d .d': t .l | s .f : m .r | d   :—  |   :    |    :    |    :
ring,            and the | cuc   -   -   koo     | sing,
```

```
                      f                          p                               ff
t     :d'   | t    :s    | s    :- .s | s    :s .d'   | t    :d'   | t    :  .t
fife  shall  play,  The  | drums   shall beat, and the | fife  shall  play,   And
r     :m    | r    :m    | r    :- .m | r    :s .s    | s    :s    | s    :  .s
      :     |      :d'   | t    :- .d'| t    :m' .m'  | r'   :m'   | r'   :  .r'
                   The   | drums   shall beat, and the | fife  shall  play,   And
      :     |      :d    | s,   :- .d | s,   :d' .d'  | s    :d'   | s    :  .s,
```

```
                          | 1ST TIME.   B♭. t.    D.S. || 2ND TIME.
d'    :s    | s    :f .m  | r    :s     | m l,  : .s,   || r    :s     | m    :—
so    we'll   pass   our  | time   a  -   way.    The   || time   a  -   way.
s     :- f  | m    :d     | d    :- .t, | d f,  : .s,   || d    :- .t, | d    :—
d'    :r    | d'   :l .s  | s    :s     | s d   :       || s    :s     | s    :—
so    we'll   pass   our  | time   a  -   way.    The   || time   a  -   way
l,    :t,   | d    :f,    | s,   :s,    | d f,  : .d    || s,   :s,    | d    :—
```

St. Co. (New.)

HALLELUJAH, AMEN.

KEY D. *Allegro.* M. 88. (From "Judas Maccabæus.") *Handel.*

```
| :  |  :          | :  |  :            |     :  |  :
| :  |  :          | :  |  :            | f :d .r |m,f.s :l .s
                                        |   Hal-le - lu - jah, A-men,
| :  |  :          | :  |  :            |   :d' .t |d',r'.m' :f' .m'
f
d :- .r |m,f.s :l .s |l .s :f .m |f .m :r |d  :  |  :
Hal - le - lu - jah, A-men, | A - men, Halle - lu- jah, A - | men.
```

```
|       |  :        | f A. t. :s d .r |m,f.s :l .s      |l .s :f .m |f .m :r
                    |     Halle - lu - jah, A-men,      | A - men, Halle - lu- jah, A -
|l .s :f .m |r .m :f |m  :s d .t, |d  :d                 |- .d :t, d |s, .d :- .t,
 A - men, Halle - lu- jah, A - | men, Halle - lu - jah,  |  Hal-le - lu - jah, Hal - le-
|f' .m' :r' .d' |t .d' :r' |d' :r's .f |s .s :f .s       |f .s :  .s |s  :- .s
                    |     Halle - lu - jah, Hal-le-     | lu - jah,  Hal-le  -  lu-
|  :  |  :          |  :t m .r |d,r.m :f .m              |f .m :r .d |t, .d :s,
                    |     Halle - lu - jah, A-men,      | A - men, Halle - lu- jah, Hal -
```

```
                 f. D.
|d  :f  |—  :m t       |l  :—  |s  :d'         |d'  :f'  |f'  :m' .r'
 men, A  -  -  men,    | A  -  -  men, Hal -    | le - lu - jah,  Hal -
|d  :- .t,,l, |s,  :- .s, r |m  :f .m |r  :s    |s  :f ,m.r |s  :—
 lu - jah, Hal - le-   | lu - jah,  Hal -       | le - lu - jah,
|s  :f  |s  :- .s r'   |d'  :r' .d' |t .l :s    |d'  :- .r' |d' .s :d'
 jah, Hal - le - lu-   | jah,  Hal -            | le - lu - jah,
|l,  :- .s,,l, |t, .s, :d s |- .d :f |—  :m     |l  :- .t |d'  :
 le - lu - jah, -      | -  -  Hal -            | le - lu - jah,
```

```
                                                  A. t.
|m'  :- .r' |d'  :- .d' |d'  :—  |—  :t        |d' f  :m .r |d,r.m :f .m
 le - lu - jah, Hal-    | le - - - - lu -      | jah, Hal-le - lu - jah, A-men,
|s  :- .t, |d,r.m :f .m |f .m :l .s |l .s :f   |m l,  :  |  :
 Hal - le - lu - jah, A-men, | A - men, Halle - lu- jah, A - | men.
|s  :- .f |s  :d'       |  :  |  :            |s d  :- .r |m,f.s :l .s
 Hal - le - lu - jah,   |                      | Hal - le - lu - jah, A-men,
|d  :- .r |m,f.s :l .s  |l .s :f .m |f .m :r   |d f,  :  |  :
 Hal - le - lu - jah, A-men, | A - men, Halle - lu- jah, A - | men.
```

f. D.
f m :l .s |l .s :f |m :fd' |r' :r' .r' |s : .d' |r' .,m':f' .m',r'
A - men, Halle - lu- jah, A - men. O Ju - dah, re- joice, re - joice, - -
: | : | :ds |f :f .f |m : .s |l :s
O Ju - dah, re- joice, re - joice, re -
l .s :f .m |f .m :r |d :lm' |r' :r' .r' |d' : .m' |f' .,m':r' .m',f'
A - men, Halle - lu- jah, A - men. O Ju - dah, re- joice, re - joice, - -
: | : | :fd' |d' :t .t |d' : .d' |d' .r',d':t .l ,t

m' : .d' |r' .,m':f' .m',r' |m',r'.d' : .s |l :- .t |d' : .m' |f' .f' :f' .f'
- Re-joice, O Ju - dah, in songs di- vine, With cherubim and
s : .s |l :s |s .s : .s |f :- .f |m : .s |l .l :l .l
joice, Re-joice, O Ju - dah, in songs di- vine,
m' : .m' |f' .,m':r' .m',f' |m' .m' : .m' |r' :- .r' |d' : .s |f .s :l .t
- Re-joice, O Ju - dah, in songs di- vine, With cherubim and
d' : .d' |d' .r',d':t .l ,t |d' .d : .d' |f :- .s |l : | :

m' .m' :m' .m' |r' :- .t |s : .t |d' .d' :d' .d' |t .t :t .t |d' :- .d'
se - ra - phim harmo - nious join, With cheru-bim and se - ra - phim harmo - nious
s .s :s .s |f :- .f |m : .s |s .s :s .s |s .s :s .s |s :- .s
d' .r' :m' .d' |r' .d' :t .s |d' : .r' |m' .m' :m' .m' |r' .r' :r' .r' |m' :- .m'
se - ra - phim harmo - nious join, With cheru-bim and se - ra - phim harmo - nious
: | : | : .s |d .r :m .f |s .l :t .s |d' :- .d

A. t. f. D.
t :sd .r |m,f.s :l .s |l .s :f .m |f .m :r |s :— |lm' :r'
join. Halle - lu - jah, A-men, A - men, Halle - lu - jah, A - men, and in
s :rs, |s, :f, |d :d |d :t, |d :— |ds :s
Har - mo - nious join. Hal - le - lu - jah, and in
r' :tm .r |d ,r.m :f .m |f .m :l .s |l .s :f |m :— |mt :t
join. Halle - lu - jah, A-men, A - men, Halle - lu - jah, A - men, and in
s :sd |d :— |— :— |— :r |d :— |ds :s
Har - mo - - - - - - nious join,

St. Co. (New.)

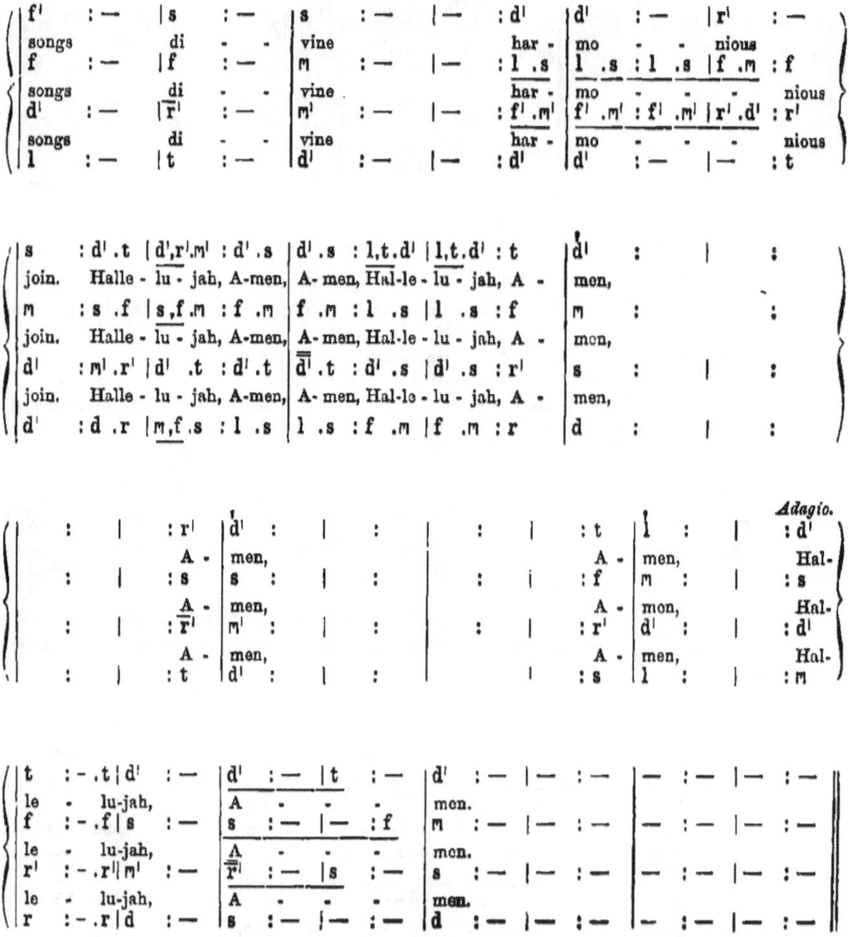

```
f'    :—  |s    :—  |s    :—  |—    :d'     |d'    :—     |r'    :—
songs      di   -  - vine                 har - mo   -  -   nious
f     :—  |f    :—  |m    :—  |—    :l .s   |l .s  :l .s  |f .m  :f
songs      di   -  - vine                 har - mo   -   -   -   nious
d'    :—  |r'   :—  |m'   :—  |—    :f' .m' |f' .m' :f' .m' |r' .d' :r'
songs      di   -  - vine                 har - mo   -   -   -   nious
l     :—  |t    :—  |d'   :—  |—    :d'     |d'    :—     |—     :t
```

```
s     :d' .t  |d',r'.m' :d' .s |d' .s :l,t.d' |l,t.d' :t  |d'  :  |  :
join.  Halle - lu - jah, A-men, A- men, Hal-le - lu - jah, A - men,
m     :s .f   |s,f.m   :f .m   |f .m  :l .s   |l .s   :f  |m   :  |  :
join.  Halle - lu - jah, A-men, A- men, Hal-le - lu - jah, A - men,
d'    :m'.r'  |d' .t   :d'.t   |d' .t :d' .s  |d' .s  :r' |s   :  |  :
join.  Halle - lu - jah, A-men, A- men, Hal-le - lu - jah, A - men,
d'    :d .r   |m,f.s   :l .s   |l .s  :f .m   |f .m   :r  |d   :  |  :
```

```
                                                      Adagio.
  :  |  :r'  |d'  :  |  :  |  :  |  :t   |l   :  |  :d'
        A -   men,                 A -   men,        Hal-
  :  |  :s   |s   :  |  :  |  :  |  :f   |m   :  |  :s
        A -   men,                 A -   men,        Hal-
  :  |  :r'  |m'  :  |  :  |  :  |  :r'  |d'  :  |  :d'
        A -   men,                 A -   men,        Hal-
  :  |  :t   |d'  :  |  :  |  :  |  :s   |l   :  |  :m
```

```
t   :-.t |d'  :—  |d'  :—  |t   :—  |d'  :—  |—  :—  |—  :—  |—  :—
le  -  lu-jah,     A    -    -    -    men.
f   :-.f |s   :—  |s   :—  |—   :f  |m   :—  |—  :—  |—  :—  |—  :—
le  -  lu-jah,     A    -    -    -    men.
r'  :-.r'|m'  :—  |r'  :—  |s   :—  |s   :—  |—  :—  |—  :—  |—  :—
le  -  lu-jah,     A    -    -    -    men.
r   :-.r |d   :—  |s   :—  |—   :—  |d   :—  |—  :—  |—  :—  |—  :—
```

St. Co. (New.)

Words by *Cunningham.*

SWIFTLY FROM THE MOUNTAIN'S BROW.

Music by *Samuel Webbe.*

KEY E♭. *Allegretto.* M. 80.

d' :s	d' :d'	.r',d' :t .d'	r' :r .f	:l .f	:s .d'
Swift - ly,	swift - ly	from the mountain's	brow, Shadows,	shadows	nurs'd by
:	m :d	.t_1,d :r .m	f :—	m .d :	t_1 .r :r .m
	Swift - ly,			Shadows	shadows
:	d :m	.s ,s :s .s	f :—	:	r .t_1 :t .s
		from the mountain's	brow,		nurs'd by
d :m	:m .d	f .f :f .m	r :t_1 .s_1	d :f_1 .l_1	s_1 :– .m_1
Swift - ly,	swiftly	from the mountain's	brow, Shadows	nurs'd, shadows	nurs'd by

	dim.	*p*			
d' :t	d' :—	— :t	d' :—	d' :s	s :d'
night re -	tire,	re -	tire,	Swift - ly,	swift - ly
r :r	m :—	— :r	m :—	— :—	m :d
l :s	s :—	— :s	s :—	— :—	s :m
night re -	tire,	re -	tire,		swift - ly
f_1 :s_1	d :—	— :s_1	d :—	— :—	— :—

.r',d' :t .d'	r' :r .f	:l .f	:s .d'	d' :t	d' :—
from the mountain's	brow, Shadows,	shadows	nurs'd by	night re -	tire,
.t_1,d :r .m	f :—	m .d :	t_1 .s_1,l_1 :t_1,r.d,m	l_1 :s_1	s_1 :—
		shadows,	shadows		
.s ,s :s .s	f :—	:	r .t_1,d :r .m	r :r .m,f	m :—
from the mountain's	brow,		Shadows nurs'd by	night re -	tire,
f .f :f .m	r :t_1 .s_1	d :f_1 .l_1	s_1 :– .m_1	f_1 :s_1	d :—
	Shadows	nurs'd, shadows	nurs'd,		

p		*Dolce.* M. 80, twice.					
— :t	d' :—	:m :m	f :– :s	l :– :–	s :– :–	d' :– :–	– :– :–
re -	tire.	And the peep -	ing	sun -	beams	now,	
— :r	m :—	:d :d	r :– :m	f :– :–	m :– :–	d :– :–	– :– :–
— :s	s :d'	d' :– :–	– :– :–	– :– :–	– :– :–	:m :m	f :– :s
re -	tire, re -	tire.				And the peep -	ing
— :s_1	d :—	– :– :–	– :– :–	– :– :–	– :– :–	:d :d	r :– :m

St. Co. (New.)

B♭. t.

| - :- :- | - :- : | :s | ^s d :- :d | t, :- :- | s :- :- | f :- :- |
Now paint with gold, now paint
| - :- :- | - :- : | : :m | ^m l, :- :l, | s, :- :- | s, :- :- | - :- :s, |
now
| l :- :- | s :- :f | m :- :- | ^l r :- :- | r :- :- | m :- :- | r :- :- |
sun - beams now paint with gold, now paint
| f :- :- | m :- :r | d :- :- | ^d f, :- :- | s, :- :- | - :- :- | - :- :s, |
now

| m :- :- | r :- :- | m :- :- | r :- :- | d :- :- | t, :- :- | d :- :d |
with gold, now paint with gold the
| s, :- :s, | s, :- :- | - :- :- | - :- :s, | s, :- :s, | s, :- :- | - :- :l, |
paint with gold, now paint with gold the
| d :- :- | t, :- :- | s :- :- | f :- :- | m :- :- | r :- :- | m :- :r |
with gold, now paint with gold the
| s, :- :s, | s, :- :- | - :- :- | - :- :s, | d, :- :d, | s, :- :f, | m, :- :f, |
paint with gold, now paint with gold the

f. E♭.

| d :- :- | t, :- :- | ^d s :- :- | - :- :- | :m :m | f :- :s | l :- :- |
vil - - lage spire, And the peep - ing sun -
| s, :- :- | - :- :f, | ^m t, :- :- | - :- :- | :d :d | r :- :m | f :- :- |
| m :- :- | r :- :- | ^d s :- :- | - :- :- | - :- :- | : : | : : |
vil - - lage spire,
| s, :- :- | s, :- :- | ^d s, :- :- | - :- :- | :d :d | d :- :d | f :- :- |
And the peep - ing sun -

B♭. t

| s :- :- | d' :- :- | - :- :- | - :- :- | - :- : | : :s | ^s d :- :d |
beams, now, now paint with
| m :- :- | d :- :- | - :- :- | - :- :- | - :- : | : :m | ^m l, :- :l, |
| : : | :m :m | f :- :s | l :- :- | s :- :f | m :- :- | ^l r :- :- |
And the peep - ing sun - beams now paint with
| d :- :- | :d :d | r :- :m | f :- :- | m :- :r | d :- :- | ^d f, :- :- |
beams,

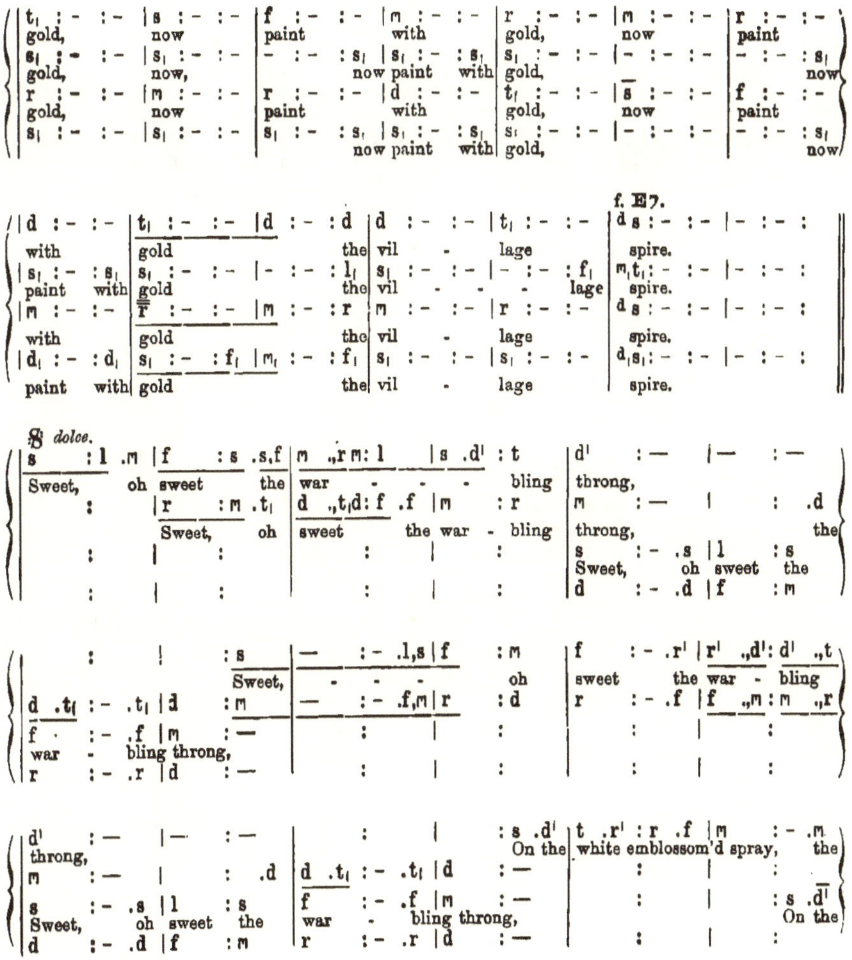

| t, :- :- | s :- :- | f :- :- | m :- :- | r :- :- | m :- :- | r :- :-
gold, now paint with gold, now paint
s, :- :- | s, :- :- | - :- :s, | s, :- :s, | s, :- :- | - :- :- | - :- :s,
gold, now, now paint with gold, now
r :- :- | m :- :- | r :- :- | d :- :- | t, :- :- | s :- :- | f :- :-
gold, now paint with gold, now paint
s, :- :- | s, :- :- | s, :- :s, | s, :- :s, | s, :- :- | - :- :- | - :- :s,
now paint with gold, now

f. E7.
| d :- :- | t, :- :- | d :- :d | d :- :- | t, :- :- | d s :- :- | - :- :
with gold the vil - lage spire.
| s, :- :s, | s, :- :- | - :- :l, | s, :- :- | - :- :f, | m,t, :- :- | - :- :
paint with gold the vil - - - lage spire.
| m :- :- | r :- :- | m :- :r | m :- :- | r :- :- | d s :- :- | - :- :
with gold the vil - lage spire.
| d, :- :d, | s, :- :f, | m, :- :f, | s, :- :- | s, :- :- | d,s, :- :- | - :- :
paint with gold the vil - lage spire.

dolce.
| s :l .m | f :s .s.f | m .,r m :l | s .d' :t | d' :— | — :—
Sweet, oh sweet the war - - - bling throng,
| : | r :m .t, | d .,t,d :f .f | m :r | m :— | :.d
Sweet, oh sweet the war - bling throng, the
| : | : | : | : | s :- .s | l :s
Sweet, oh sweet the
| : | : | : | : | d :- .d | f :m

| : | :s | — :- .l,s | f :m | f :- .r' | r' .,d' :d' .,t
Sweet, - - - oh sweet the war - bling
| d .t, :- .t, | d :m | — :- .f,m | r :d | r :- .f | f .,m :m .,r
| f :- .f | m :— | : | : | : | :
war - bling throng,
| r :- .r | d :— | : | : | : | :

| d' :— | — :— | : | :s .d' | t .r' :r .f | m :- .m
throng, On the white emblossom'd spray, the
| m :— | :.d | d .t, :- .t, | d :— | : | :
| s :- .s | l :s | f :- .f | m :— | : | :s .d'
Sweet, oh sweet the war - bling throng, On the
| d :- .d | f :m | r :- .r | d :— | : | :

St. Co. (New.)

| r .f :f .r | s : | : | f :f | f .s : l,t.d' | d' :t
white emblossom'd spray, On the white emblossom'd spray,
: | d :d | d .m :m .m | f :— | : | :
On the white emblossom'd spray,
t .r' : r .f | m :s .l | ta.ta : ta.s | l :— | : | s :s
white emblossom'd spray, on the white emblossom'd spray, Na - ture's
: | :d .f | m .s :s, .ta, | l, :l .s | f .m :r .d | s, :—
on the white emblossom'd spray,

f p
: | m :m | m .r,d: r,m.f,s | l :l .l | t .d',t: d' .d' | t :t .s
Na - ture's u - ni - ver-sal song, Nature's u-ni - ver-sal song Echoes
: | : | : | :f .f,m | r .m,f: m .m | r :r .t,
s .f,m: f,s.l,t | d' :— | — :— | — :d' .d' | r' .s :s .s | s :—
u - ni - ver-sal song, Nature's u-ni - ver-sal song
: | : | : | f :f | f .m,r : d,r.m,f | s :—

f
:s .m | : | : | :d' .s | :d' .s | l .t :d' .r'
echoes, echoes, echoes, echoes to the
:m .d | :t, .d | l, .t, :d .r | m :— | d .s, : | d .r :d .d,f
to the ris - ing day, echoes,
r' .t : | s .m :r .m | f .s :l .t | d' :— | d .m : | l .f :s .l
Echoes, echoes to the ris - ing day, echoes, echoes, echoes to the
t .s : | m .d : | : | :d .m | :d .m | f .r :m .f

p
| d' :t | d' :— | m .s,f :m .m | f .l,s :f .f,m | r .r',d': t .d',r'
ris - ing day, Na - ture's u - - ni - ver - sal
| m :r | m :— | d .m,r :d .ta, | l, .d,ta, : l, .r,d | t, .,d :r m,f
| s :s | s :— | s :- .s | l :- .l | t .s :s
ris - ing day, Na - ture's u - - ni - ver - sal
| s :s, | d :— | d :- .d | f :- .r | s :s,

f D.S.
| d' :— | d' .s : | d' .s : .r',r' | d' :t | d' :—
song, Echoes, echoes to the ris - ing day.
| m :— | d .m,r :d .t, | d .m,r :d .f | m :r | m :—
Ech - oes to the ris - ing day.
| s :— | m :f | s :l | s :s | s :—
song, Ech - oes to the ris - ing day.
| d :— | d :r | m :f | s :s, | d :—

St. Co. (New.)

ADDITIONAL EXERCISES, PART 2.

NOTE.—The Standard Course Exercises, 188, 189, 191, and 192, may precede these,—but it is not essential that they should do so. For style of singing see "Hints on the Tunes."

LORD, IN THIS THY MERCY'S DAY.

KEY A♭. *L* is *F*. By permission from Anglican Hymn Book. *J. Crüger.*

l_1 :d	t_1 :m	r :d	t_1 :—	d :r	m :f
1.*Lord, in*	*this thy*	*mer - cy's*	*day,*	*Ere it*	*pass* for
m_1 :l_1	se_1 :l_1	l_1 :l_1	se_1 :—	l_1 :t_1	d :d
2.*By thy*	*night of*	*a - gon -*	*y,*	*By thy*	*sup - pli -*
d :m	m :m	f :m	m :—	m :s	s :l
3.By thy	tears of	bit - ter	woe	For Je -	ru - sa -
l_1 :l_1	m_1 :d_1	r_1 :l_2	m_1 :—	l_1 :s_1	d :f_1
4.Grant us	'neath thy	wings a	place,	*Lest we*	*lose this*

r :r	d :—	m :d	t_1 :l_1	l_1 :se_1	l_1 :—
aye A -	WAY,	ON OUR	knees we	*fall and*	*pray.*
d :t_1	d :—	s_1 :l_1	f_1 :f_1	m_1 :m_1	m_1 :—
ca - ting	*cry,*	*By thy*	*wil - ling -*	*ness to*	*die.*
s :s	m :—	d :d	r :— .d	t_1 :t_1	d :—
lem be -	low,	Let us	not thy	love fore -	go.
s_1 :s_1	d :—	d_1 :f_1	r_1 :r_1	m_1 :m_1	l_2 :—
day of	*grace,*	*Ere we*	*shall* be -	hold THY	FACE.

RISE MY SOUL, ADORE THY MAKER.

KEY G. By permission from Anglican Hymn Book. D. t. *G. E. Monk.*

m :f	s :r	d :r	m :t_1	${}^{m}l$:l	t :—
1.RISE MY	SOUL, A -	DORE THY	MA - KER!	AN - GELS	PRAISE
d :d	t_1 :t_1	l_1 :l_1	se_1 :se_1	${}^{l_1}r$:f	r :—
2.*Nev - er*	*cast me*	*from thy*	*pre - sence*	*Till my*	*soul*
s :f	r :s	m :r	t_1 :m	${}^{m}l$:l	s :—
3.Thou the	night wast	my Pro -	tec - tor:	With me	stay
d :l_1	s_1 :s_1	l_1 :f_1	m_1 :m_1	${}^{d}f$:r	s :—
4.*Ho - ly,*	*ho - ly,*	*ho - ly*	*Giv - er*	*Of all*	*good,*

		f. G.			
t :t	d' :—	${}^{f}d$:f	m :d	r :—	d :—
JOIN THY	LAYS;	WITH THEM	BE PAR -	TAK -	ER.
m :s	m :—	${}^{r}l_1$:d	d :d	t_1 :—	d :—
Shall be	*full*	*Of thy*	*bles - sed*	*es - -*	*sence.*
t :t	l :—	${}^{r'}l$:l	s :s	s :f	m :—
All the	day,	Ev - er	my Di -	rect -	or.
s :m	l :—	${}^{ta}f$:f_1	d :m_1	s_1 :—	d_1 :—
Life and	food,	REIGN, A -	DOR'D FOR	EV - -	ER!

FATHER, MY SPIRIT OWNS.

KEY E♭. *L is C.* "O mourn," in Anglican Hymn Book, by per. *G. A. Macfarren.*

:m | l :-.m | d.r :m | r :— | — :f | l :-.f | r.m :f | m :— | —
1.Fa- | ther, my spi - rit | owns Thy | right to mine and | me;
:d | m :-.d | l_1.t_1 :d | r :— | — :r | f :-.r | l_1 :r | t_1 :— | —
2.A- | las! the brit - tle | reed, On | hu - man life to | lean!
:l | d^1 :-.l | m :l | l :— | — :l | r^1 :-.l | f.s :l | t :— | —
3.In | deep submis - sion, | aid The | brok - en heart to | lie,
:l_1 | l_1 :-.l_1 | l_1 :l_1 | f :— | — :r | r :-.r | r :r | se_1 :— | —

B♭. t. f. E♭.

:m | f :f | $^{m}l_1$:se_1 | m :— | — :d | d :t_1 | l_1 :se_1 | l_1 :-.^{l_1}m | f
Yet | par - don hu - man | groans From | hu - man a - go - | ny; The eye's
:d | d :d | $^{l_1}r_1$:m_1 | m_1 :— | — :l_1 | f_1 :f_1 | r_1 :m_1 | m_1 :-.$^{m_1}t_1$ | r
A | so - lace frail in - | deed, 'Tis | gone as soon as | seen! Then who
:l | l :l | ^{l}r :t_1 | l_1 :— | — :m | r :r | r :t_1 | d :-.^{d}s | l
Nor, | when the stroke is | made, To | mur - mur or re - | ply; Great grace
:l_1 | l_1 :l_1 | $^{d}f_1$:m_1 | d_1 :— | — :l_2 | r_1 :r_1 | f_1 :m_1 | l_1 :-.^{l_1}m | r

:l | se :l | t :m.r | d :-.l | se :l | f :r | d :t_1 | l_1 :— | —
de - | sire, the soul's de - | light, Thy wis - dom | hath seen good to | blight.
:m | r :d | m :t_1 | d :-.d | r :d | ta_1 :ta_1 | l_1 :se_1 | l_1 :— | —
shall | fill the cheer - less | void, Or stay the | soul 'mid hopes de - | stroyed?
:l | t :d^1 | t :t | l :-.l | r :m | f :f | m :-.r | d :— | —
for | great - est need be - | stow, And strong sup - | ports for deep - est | woe.
:d | t_1 :l_1 | se_1 :se_1 | l_1 :-.l_1 | t_1 :d | r :r | m :m_1 | l_1 :— | —

NEARER, MY GOD, TO THEE.

KEY F. From Anglican Hymn Book, by per. *Henry Smart.*

| d :— | d :f | m :r | s :— | d :— | r :r | m :— | — :—
| 1.*Near - er, my* | *God, to thee,—* | *Hear thou my* | *prayer;*
| s_1 :— | l_1 :r | d :t_1 | d :— | d :— | d :t_1 | d :— | — :—
| 2.Though the great | bat - tle rage | Hot - ly a - | round,
| m :— | f :l | s :s | s :— | m :— | l :s | s :— | — :—
| 3.*When, my course* | *fin - ished, I* | *Breathe my last* | *breath,*
| d :— | f_1 :r_1 | s_1 :-.f_1 | m_1 :— | l_1 :— | f_1 :s_1 | d :— | — :—
| 4.And when thou, | Lord, once more, | Glo - rious shalt | come,

St. Co. (New.)

C. t.

ᵐl :—	l :t	d' :r'	m' :—	l :—	d' :t	l :—	— :—
E'en	though a	hea - vy	cross,	Faint -	ing, I	bear,	
ᵈf :—	f :s	s :f	m :—	f :—	m :-.r	d :—	— :—
Still	where my	cap - tain	fights	Let	me be	found;	
ˢd' :—	r' :r'	s :l .t	d' :t	l :—	l :se	l :—	— :—
Ent -	*'ring the*	*sha - dow - y*		*Val* -	*ley of*	*death;*	
ᵈf :—	r :s .f	m :r	d :—	r :—	m :m	l_1 :—	— :—
Oh!	for a	dwell-ing	place.	In	thy bright	home!	

f. F.

d' :—	f' :m'	r' :r'	d' :—	ˡm :—	l :s
Still	all my	prayer shall	be,	*Near* -	*er,* my
m :—	f :s	l :s .f	m :—	ᶠd :—	d :t_1
Through	toils and	strife to	be	*Near* -	*er,* my
·l :—	l .t :d'	d' :t	d' :—	ᶠd :—	f .m :r
E - -	ven there	shall I	be	*Near* -	*er,* my
l :—	r :m	f :s	d :—	ʳl_1 :—	f_1 :s_1
THROUGH	ALL E -	TER - NI -	TY	*Near* -	*er,* my

f :f	m :—	r :—	d :t_1	d :—	— :—
God, TO	THEE,	*Near* -	*er to*	*thee.*	
l_1 :t_1 .l_1	se_1 :—	l_1 :—	s_1 :s_1	s_1 :—	— :—
God, TO	THEE,	*Near* -	*er to*	*thee.*	
r :r	t_1 :—	l_1 :f	m :r	m :—	— :—
God, TO	THEE,	*Near* -	*er to*	*thee.*	
r_1 :r_1	m_1 :—	f_1 :—	s_1 :s_1	d :—	— :—
God, TO	THEE,	*Near* -	*er to*	*thee.*	

THE GIPSY'S TENT.

KEY A. M. 120. *Allegro Vivace.* Bohemian Air arranged by *W. H. Birch.*
mf SOLO S. or T. (By permission.)

	s_1 :d :r	*m :-.r :d*	*s_1 :d :m*	*r :— :—*
Eight measures	1.We live so 2.Come to our	mer - ry, so green - wood home	hap - py and and blithe-some	free, be,
	:d :d	:d :d	:d :d	:r :r
	La, la.			
	:s_1 :s_1	:s_1 :s_1	:s_1 :s_1	:l_1 :l_1
Symphony.	:m :m	:m :m	:m :m	:f :f
	d_1 : :	d_1 : :	d_1 : :	f_1 : :
	La.	la.		

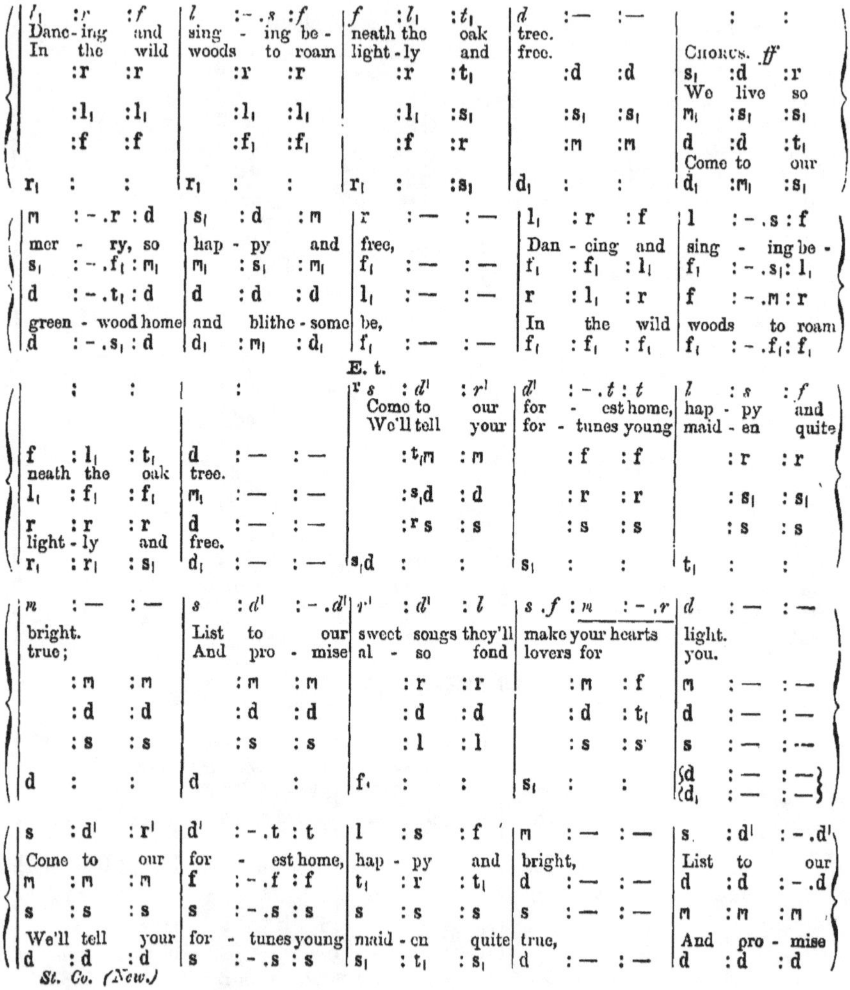

l, :r :f	l :-.s :f	f :l, :t,	d :— :—	: :
Danc-ing and	sing - ing be -	neath the oak	tree.	
In the wild	woods to roam	light - ly and	free.	CHORUS. *ff*
:r :r	:r :r	:r :t,	:d :d	s, :d :r
				We live so
:l, :l,	:l, :l,	:l, :s,	:s, :s,	m, :s, :s,
:f :f	:f, :f,	:f :r	:m :m	d :d :t,
				Come to our
r, : :	r, : :	r, : :s,	d, : :	d, :m, :s,

m :-.r :d	s, :d :m	r :— :—	l, :r :f	l :-.s :f
mer - ry, so	hap - py and	free,	Dan - cing and	sing - ing be -
s, :-.f, :m,	m, :s, :m,	f, :— :—	f, :f, :l,	f, :-.s, :l,
d :-.t, :d	d :d :d	l, :— :—	r :l, :r	f :-.m :r
green - wood home	and blithe - some	be,	In the wild	woods to roam
d :-.s, :d	d, :m, :d,	f, :— :—	f, :f, :f,	f, :-.f, :f,

E. t.

: :	:	r s :d' :r'	d' :-.t :t	l :s :f
		Come to our	for - est home,	hap - py and
		We'll tell your	for - tunes young	maid - en quite
f :l, :t,	d :— :—	:t,m :m	:f :f	:r :r
neath the oak	tree.			
l, :f, :f,	m, :— :—	:s,d :d	:r :r	:s, :s,
r :r :r	d :— :—	:r s :s	:s :s	:s :s
light - ly and	free.			
r, :r, :s,	d, :— :—	s,d : :	s, : :	t, : :

m :— :—	s :d' :-.d'	r' :d' :l	s .f :m :-.r	d :— :—
bright.	List to our	sweet songs they'll	make your hearts	light.
true;	And pro - mise	al - so fond	lovers for	you.
:m :m	:m :m	:r :r	:m :f	m :— :—
:d :d	:d :d	:d :d	:d :t,	d :— :—
:s :s	:s :s	:l :l	:s :s	s :— :—
d : :	d :	f, : :	s, : :	{d :— :— / d, :— :—}

s :d' :r'	d' :-.t :t	l :s :f	m :— :—	s :d' :-.d'
Come to our	for - est home,	hap - py and	bright,	List to our
m :m :m	f :-.f :f	t, :r :t,	d :— :—	d :d :-.d
s :s :s	s :-.s :s	s :s :s	s :— :—	m :m :m
We'll tell your	for - tunes young	maid - en quite	true,	And pro - mise
d :d :d	s :-.s :s	s, :t, :s,	d :— :—	d :d :d

St. Co. (New.)

f. A. *ff*

r' :d' :l	s :l :-.t	d' :— :—	$^{d}s_1$:d :r	m .-.r :d
sweet songs they'll	make your hearts	light.	We live so	mer - ry, so
l_1 :l_1 :l_1	d :d :-.r	d :— :—	$^{l_1}m_1$:s_1 :s_1	s_1 :-.f_1 :m_1
f :f :f	m :s :-.f	m :— :—	^{f}d :d :t_1	d :-.t_1 :d
al - so fond	lov - ers for	you.	We live so	mer - ry, so
f_1 :f_1 :f_1	s_1 :s_1 :-.s_1	d :— :—	$^{f_1}d_1$:m_1 :s_1	d :-.s_1 :d

s_1 :d :m	r :— :—	l_1 :r :f	l :-.s :f	f :l_1 :t_1
hap - py and	free,	Dan - cing and	sing - ing be -	neath the oak
m_1 :s_1 :m_1	f_1 :— :—	f_1 :f_1 :l_1	f_1 :-.s_1 :l_1	l_1 :f_1 :f_1
d :d :d	l_1 :— :—	r :l_1 :r	f :-.m :r	r :r :r
hap - py and	free,	Dan - cing and	sing - ing be -	neath the oak
d_1 :m_1 :d_1	f_1 :— :—	f_1 :f_1 :f_1	f_1 :-.f_1 :f_1	r_1 :r_1 :s_1

	Solo C. or B.			
: :	*m_1 :l_1 :t_1*	*d :-.t_1 :l_1*	*m_1 :l_1 :d*	*t_1 :— :—*
	Taste of our	Gip - sy fare,	whole-some and	plain,
	Come, where the	song - thrush and	lin - net holds	sway,
d :— :—	:l_1 :l_1	:l_1 :l_1	:l_1 :l_1	:t_1 :t_1
m_1 :— :—	:m_1 :m_1	:m_1 :m_1	:m_1 :m_1	:f_1 :f_1
tree.				
d :— :—	:d :d	:d :d	:d :d	:r :r
d_1 :— :—	l_1 : :	l_1 : :	l_1 : :	r_1 : :

t_1 :r :m	*f :-.m :r*	*m :d :t_1*	*l_1 :— :m_1*	*m_1 :l_1 :t_1*
And if you	like it then	pray come a -	gain. With	rich foam - ing
Come where they	war - ble their	well tun - ed	lay, Oh	come with a
:t_1 :t_1	:t_1 :r	:d :t_1	:l_1 :l_1	:l_1 :l_1
:f_1 :f_1	:f_1 :l_1	:l_1 :se_1	:m_1 :m_1	:m_1 :m_1
:r :r	:r :f	:m :r	:d :d	:d :d
r_1 : :	r_1 : :	m_1 : :m_1	l_2 : :	l_1 : :

d :-.t_1 :l_1	*m :-.r :d*	*t_1 :— :f_1*	*f_1 :t_1 :r*	*f :-.m :r*
ale in large	bum - pers of	horn, We'll	toast our brown	beau - ties till
light - some heart,	cheer - ful and	gay, We'll	sing, feast, and	dance till the
:l_1 :l_1	:l_1 :l_1	:t_1 :t_1	:t_1 :t_1	:t_1 :r
:m_1 :m_1	:m_1 :m_1	:f_1 :f_1	:f_1 :f_1	:f_1 :t_1
:d :d	:d :d	:r :r	:r :r	:r :f
l_1 : :	l_1 : :	r_1 : :	r_1 : :	r_1 : :

St. Co. (New.)

| *m* :*d* :-.t_1 | l_1 :— :— | 𝄋 | | |
dawn's the bright morn.
close of the day.
ff
| :d :t_1 | l_1 :— :— | s_1 :d :r | m :-.r :d | s_1 :d :m |
We live so mer - ry, so hap - py and
| :l_1 :se_1 | l_1 :— :— | m_1 :s_1 :s_1 | s_1 :-.f_1 :m_1 | m_1 :s_1 :m_1 |
| :m :{m/r} | {m/d} :— :— | d :d :t_1 | d :-.t_1 :d | d :d :d |
We live so mer - ry, so hap - py and
| m_1 :m_1 | l_2 :— :— | d_1 :m_1 :s_1 | d :-.s_1 :d | d_1 :m_1 :d_1 |

D.S.
| r :— :— | l_1 :r :f | l :-.s :f | f :l :t_1 | d :— :— |
free, Dan - cing and sing - ing be - neath the oak tree.
| f_1 :— :— | f_1 :f_1 :l_1 | f_1 :-.s_1 :l_1 | l_1 :f_1 :f_1 | m_1 :— :— |
| l_1 :— :— | r :l_1 :r | f :-.m :r | r :r :r | d :— :— |
free, Dan - cing and sing - ing be - neath the oak tree.
| f_1 :— :— | f_1 :f_1 :f_1 | f_1 :-.f_1 :f_1 | r_1 :r_1 :s_1 | d :— :— |

| s :f :— | f :m :— | r :l :s.f | m :— :m | f :s :l |
Gai - ly, hap - py, jol - ly and free, No life e - quals
| l_1 :l_1 :— | s_1 :s_1 :— | t_1 :t_1 :t_1 | d :— :d | d :d :d |
| d :d :— | d :d :— | s :s :s | s :— :d | d :d :d |
Gai - ly, hap - py, jol - ly and free, No life e - quals
| f_1 :f_1 :— | s_1 :s_1 :— | s_1 :f :m.r | d :— :ta_1 | l_1 :s_1 :f_1 |

| s :— :d.r | m :f :r | d :— :— | s :f :— | f :m :— |
ours 'neath the old oak tree. Gai - ly, hap - py,
| d :— :l_1.l_1 | d :— :t_1 | d :— :— | l_1 :l_1 :— | s_1 :s_1 :— |
| d :— :m.f | s :— :f | m :— :— | d :d :— | d :d :— |
ours 'neath the old oak tree. Gai - ly, hap - py,
| m_1 :— :l_1.l_1 | s_1 :— :s_1 | d :— :— | f_1 :f_1 :— | s_1 :s_1 :— |

rall. *adagio.*
| r :l :s.f | m :— :{s/m} | {d'/f} :{t/s} :l | s :—𝄐 :d.r | m :f :r | d :— :—𝄐 ||
jol - ly and free, No life e - quals ours 'neath the old oak tree.
| t_1 :t_1 :t_1 | d :— :d | d :d :d | d :— :m_1.f_1 | s_1 :l_1 :f_1 | m_1 :— :— ||
| s :s :s | s :— :d | d :d :d | d :— :d.d | d :— :t_1 | d :— :— ||
jol - ly and free, No life e - quals ours 'neath the old oak tree.
| s_1 :f :m.r | d :— :ta_1 | l_1 :s_1 :f_1 | m_1 :— :l_1.l_1 | s_1 :— :{s_1/s_2} | d :— :— ||

St. Co. (New.)

"HARVEST HOME."

KEY D. M. 80, twice. Chorus from "Helvellyn." *G. A. Macfarren.*

f

| s :s | d' :— | l :l | d' :— | t :d' | r' :t | l :— | s :
Har - vest home, har - vest home, har - - vest home,
| m :m | m :— | f :f | f :— | f :— | — :f | m :— | — :
| d' :d' | s :— | d' :d' | l :— | r' :d' | t :s | d' :— | — :
Har - vest home, har - vest home, har - - vest home,
| d :d | d :— | d :d | d :— | d :— | — :d | d' :— | — :

| s :s | d' :— | l :l | d' :— | t :d' | r' :t | d' :— | *p* :d'
Har - vest home, har - vest home, har - - vest home. We
| m :m | s :— | f :f | f :— | f :— | — :f | m :— | :s
| d' :d' | d' :— | d' :d' | d' :— | r' :d' | t :r' | d' :s | s :—
Har - vest home, har - vest home, har - - vest home. We come, We
| d :d | m :— | f :f | l :— | s :— | — :s | d :— | :m

| t :l | s :l .f | m :s | d' :— | t :d'.l | s :l .f | f :— | m :
come, we come, And we bring the last load of our gol - den grain.
| f :m | r :f .r | d :m | s :— | f :s .m | r :f .r | r :— | d :
| — :— | — :s .s | s :s | s :— | s :s .s | s :t | t :— | d' :
come, we come, And we bring the last load of our gol - den grain.
| r :d | t, :s,.s, | d :d | m :— | r :m .d | t, :s, | d :— | — :

A. t. *cres.*

| ^s d :— .d | l, :— | r :— .r | t, :— .t, | m :— .m | d :— .d | f :— |
Loud - ly shout, loud - ly shout, a- gain, a- gain, a- gain. *ff*
: | ^m l, :— .l, | l, :— | t, :— .t, | t, :— .t, | d :— .d | d :— | d :— .d
Loud - ly shout, loud - ly shout, a- gain, a- gain. Har - vest
: | ^d' f :— .f | r :— | s :— .s | m :— .m | l :— .l | f :— | :
Loud - ly shout, loud - ly shout, a- gain, a- gain.
| ^d f, :— .f, | f, :— | s, :— .s, | s, :— .s, | l, :— .l, | l, :— |

ff

| m :— .r | s :— | : | | m :— .r | s :— |
Har - vest home, har - vest home,
| d :— | — :— | — :— | d :— .d | d :— | — :— | — :— | d :— .d
home, Har - vest home, loud - ly
: | s :— .l | s :— | : | : | s :— .l | s :— | :
Har - vest home, har - vest home,
: | s, :— .f, | m, :— | : | : | s, :— .f, | m, :— | :

St. Co. (New).

f. D.

|d :-.r |m :— |— :— |r :— |— :-.d |d :— | :
Loud - ly shout, har - - vest home.
d :— |d :-.d |d :— |— :— |t, :— |— :-.d |d :— | :
shout,
: |m :-.f |s :— |— :— |f :— |— :-.m |m :— | :d s'
Loud - ly shout, har - - vest home. The
: |l, :-.l, |s, :— |— :— |s, :— |— :-.d |d :— | :d s,

dolce.

: | : | : | :d s |s :— |l .t :d'.r' |m' :d' |s :l
The The fields board once more have will groan with
: | : | : | :d s |f :— |— :— |m :m |m :m
f :s |f :s |m :s |m :s |r :s |r :s |m :s |m :s
fields once more have boun - teous been, O'er them the wa - vy wealth was seen, The
board will groan with Eng - lish cheer, In hon - our of the fall - ing year, The
t, :s, |t, :s, |d :s, |d :s, |r :s, |r :s, |d :s, |d :s,

|s :— |r :l |s :— |m : |s :— |l .t :d'.r' |m' :f'.m' |r'.d' :t .l
boun - - teous been, O'er them the wa - - vy
Eng - - lish cheer, Hon - 'ring the brave de -
r :— |— :f |m :— |d : |f :— |f :f |m :— |— :m
f :s |f :s |m :s |m :s |r :s |r :s |m :s |m :s
fields once more have boun -teous been, O'er them the wa - vy wealth was seen, O'er
board will groan with Eng - lish cheer, In hon - our of the fall - ing year, In
t, :s, |t, :s, |d :s, |d :s, |r :s, |r :s, |d :s, |d :s,

f. G. *cres.*

|s :— |r :l |s :— |m t, :f |m :— |t, :f |m :— |d :l
wealth was seen, But now they are robb'd of their
clin - ing year, Which thus has en - rich'd us with
r :— |— :f |m :— |d s, :t, |t, :— |t, :r |d :— |l, :d
f :s |f :s |m :s |m t, :r |r :m |r :m |d :m |d :m
them the wa - vy wealth was seen, But now they've lost their am - ple store, they've
hon - our of the fall - ing year, Which thus has shed its gold - en store, has
t, :s, |t, :s, |d :s, |d s, :r, |se, :m, |se, :m, |l, :m, |l, :m,

St. Co. (New.)

f

s :— |r :l	s :— |m :-.d	s :— |— :—	— :— |m :-.d
am - - ple	store. Shout once	more,	shout once
gold - - en	store.		
r :— |— :f	m :— |m :-.d	s :— |— :—	— :— |m :-.d
f :s |f :s	m :— | :	: |m :-.d	s :— |— :—
lost their am - ple	store.	Loud - ly	shout,
shed its gold - en	store.		
t_{1} :s_{1} |t_{1} :s_{1}	d :— | :	: | :	: | :

D. t. *piu cres.*

$^{1}r^{1}$:— |— :—	— :— |— :—	— :— |— :—	s :— |— :—
more,			once
$^{1}r^{1}$:— |— :—	— :— |— :—	— :— |— :—	s :— — :—
$^{s}d^{1}$:— |t :-.s	f^{1} :— |— :—	— :— |— :—	s :— |— :—
loud - ly	shout, loud - ly	shout,	once
: | :	: |$^{1}{}_{1}r$:-.s_{1}	s :— |— :—	s :— |— :—

poco rit. *ff a tempo.*

s :— |s :—	s :— |s :—	s :s |d^{1} :—	l :l |d^{1} :—
more, shout	once more,	Har - vest home,	har - vest home,
s :— |s :—	s :— |s :—	m :m |s :—	f :f |f :—
s :— |s :—	s :— |s :—	d^{1} :d^{1} |d^{1} :—	d^{1} :d^{1} |d^{1} :—
more, shout	once more,	Har - vest home,	har - vest home,
s :— |s :—	s :— |s :—	d :d |m :—	f :f |l :—

t :d^{1} |r^{1} :t	l :— |s :	s :s |d^{1} :—	r^{1} :r^{1} |m^{1} :—
har - - vest	home,	Har - vest home,	har - vest home,
f :— |— :f	m :— |— :	m :m |m :—	l :l |se :—
r^{1} :d^{1} |t :r^{1}	d^{1} :— |— :	d^{1} :d^{1} |d^{1} :—	l :l |t :—
har - - vest	home,	Har - vest home,	har - vest home,
s :— |— :s	d^{1} :— |— :	d^{1} :d^{1} |l :—	f :f |m :—

sf

f^{1} :— |— :—	t :— |— :-.d^{1}	d^{1} :— |— :—
har - -	- - - vest	home.
l :— |— :—	s :— |— :-.s	s :— |— :—
r^{1} :— |— :—	f^{1} :— |— :-.m^{1}	m^{1} :— |— :—
har - -	- - - vest	home.
r :— |— :—	s :— |— :-.d	d :— |— :—

St. Co. (New).

AWAY TO THE FOREST.

Words for this work by *George Bennett.*

Music by *Franz Abt.*

KEY C. *Alla Marcia.*

f
.m'	m' :d' .l	s :d' .s	s :r' .s	s :- .s	m' :d' .l	s :d' .m
1. A-	way to the	for - est, fair	Na - ture in	-vites, With	fra - grance and	beau - ty and
.s	s :s .f	m :m .m	f :f .f	m :- .m	s :s .f	m :m .m
.d'	d' :d' .d'	d' :d' .d'	d' .,t :l .t	d' :- .d'	d' :d' .d'	d' :d' .d'
2. We'll	sit on a	moss - bank and	spread out our	fare, The	lov'd and the	lov - ing our
.d	d :m .f	s :s .s	s :s .s	d :- .d	d :m .f	d :d .l_1

p *poco rit.* *f* *f*
fe .,s :l .r'	s : .s	s :s .s	s :s .s	t .,d' :r' .m'	f' :- .f'
syl - van de-	lights; The	sun in its	splendour shines	lov - ing-ly	down, And
r :r .fe	s : .s	t_1 .,d :r .m	m .f :t_1 .s	s :s .s	s :- .s
d' :d' .d'	t : .s	s :s .s	s :s .s	s .,l :t .d'	r' :- .r'
dain - ties shall	share; We'll	troll the gay	car - ol or	tune - ful quar-	-tet, Our
r .,m :fe .r	s : .s	s_1 .,l_1 :t_1 .d	de .r :s_1 .s	s :s .s	s :- .s

a tempo.
m' :m' .m'	m' :l .r'	d' .,t :l .s	s :- .m	f .,s :l .t	d' .de' :r' .m'
glad - ly we'll	has - ten from	ci - ty and	town, And	glad - ly we'll	has - ten from
s :s .s	s :f .f	f :f .f	m :- .d	r .,m :f .f	s .ta :l .l
d' :t .ta	l :l .l	s .,r' :d' .t	d' :- .m	f .,s :l s	s .m' :r' .de'
cares and our	trou - bles for	ONE day for-	get, Our	cares and our	trou - bles for
d :d .d	de :r .r	s :s .s	d :- .d	r .,m :f .r	m .s :f .m

sf *rit.* *f* *rit.* *pp*
f' :l .t	d' :		: .m'	l' :		: .m'
ci - ty and	town.		la	la!		la
l :f .f	m : .d,m	s .fe,l :s .d'		t : .d,m	s .fe,l :s .d'
	f Tra la	la la la la la		la!	*pp* Tra la	la la la la la
r' :r' .r'	d' : .d,m	s .fe,l :s .d'		s' : .d,m	s .fe,l :s .d'
ONE day for-	get. Tra la	la la la la la		la! Tra la	la la la la la
r :r .s_1	d : .d,m	s .fe,l :s .s		s : .d,m	s .fe,l :s .s

f *a tempo.*
r' .s	d' :d' .d'	d' :l .r'	s :l .t	d' :
la! And	glad - ly we'll	has - ten from	ci - ty and	town.
t : .s	m :f .s	l :f .f	m :f .f	m :
s' : .s	d' :d' .d'	d' :d' .r'	d' :s .s	s :
la! Our	cares and our	trou - bles for	ONE day for -	get.
s : .s	d :r .m	f :f .r	s :s .s_1	d :

St. Co. (New.)

f

.m' |m' :d'.l |s :d'.s |s :r'.s |s :-.s |m' :d'.l |s :d'.m
3. We'll | hie through the | for - est with | laugh - ter and | shout, Its | glades and its | clois - ters we'll
.s |s :s.f |m :m.m |f :f.f |m :-.m |s :s.f |m :m.m
.d' |d' :d'.d' |d' :d'.d' |d' .,t :l.t |d' :-.d' |d' :d'.d' |d' :d'.d'
4. A - | way to the | for - est, a - | way and a - | way, Our | hol - i-day | bright-ens a
.d |d :m.f |s :s.s |s :s.s |d :-.d |d :m.f |d :d.l,

p *poco rit.* *f* *f*

fe .,s :l.r' |s : .s |s :s.s |s :s.s |t .,d' :r'.m' |f' :-.f'
wan - der a - | bout; While | gold-beams are | glint - ing o'er | pil - lar and | arch, We'll
r :r.fe |s : .s |t, .,d :r.m |m.f :t,.s |s :s.s |s :-.s
d' :d'.d' |t : .s |s :s.s |s :s.s |s .,l :t.d' |r' :-.r'
"red - let-ter | day!" This | life has not | man - y, then | wel - come the | few, With
r .,m :fe.r |s : .s |s, .,l, :t,.d |de.r :s,.s |s :s.s |s :-.s

a tempo.

m' :m'.m' |m' :l.r' |d' .,t :l.s |s :-.m |f .,s :l.t |d'.de' :r'.m'
roam 'neath the | sha - dows of | lin - den and | larch, We'll | roam 'neath the | sha - dows of
s :s.s |s :f.f |f :f.f |m :-.d |r .,m :f.f |s.ta :l.l
d' :t.ta |l :l.l |s .,r' :d'.t |d' :-.m |f .,s :l.s |s.m' :r'.de'
souls that are | grate - ful, and | hearts that are | true, With | souls that are | grate - ful, and
d :d.d |de :r.r |s :s.s |d :-.d |r .,m :f.r |m.s :f.m

sf *rit.* *f* *rit.* *pp*

f' :l.t |d' : | : .m' |r' : | : .m'
lin - den and | larch. | la | la! | la
l :f.f |m : .d,m |s .fe,l :s.d' |t : .d,m |s .fe,l :s.d'
Tra la | la la la la la | la! Tra la | la la la la la
r' :r'.r' |d' : .d,m |s .fe,l :s.d' |s' : .d,m |s .fe,l :s.d'
hearts that are | true. Tra la | la la la la la | la! Tra la | la la la la la
r :r.s, |d : .d,m |s .fe,l :s.s |s : .d,m |s .fe,l :s.s

a tempo. *f*

r' : .s |d' :d'.d' |d' :l.r' |s :l.t |d' :
la! We'll | roam 'neath the | sha - dows of | lin - den and | larch.
t : .s |m :f.s |l :f.f |m :f.f |m :
s' : .s |d' :d'.d' |d' :d'.r' |d' :s.s |s :
la! With | souls that are | grate - ful and | hearts that are | true.
s : .s |d :r.m |f :f.r |s :s.s, |d :

St. Co. (New.)

SUNSHINE AFTER RAIN.

KEY B♭. *Firmly and in moderate time.* (Copyright.) *Henry Lahee.*

mf F. t.

: .s,	d .s, : m .r,d	d : s, .s,	m .d : s .f,m	r s .s : d'
1. I	left my love in	Eng - land, In	pov-er - ty and	pain, The tears
.m,	s, .m, : s, .f,	m, : s, .f,	m, .f, : s, .l,	t,m : - .d
2. I	left my love in	Eng - land, And	sailed the stormy	sea, To
: .d	d .d : d .t,	d .t,,l, : s, .l,.t,	d .d : d .d	t,m : - .s
3. I	sought my love in	Eng - land, And	brought her o'er the	sea; A
.d,	m, .d, : s, .s,	l, .s,,f, : m, .r,	d, .r, : m, .f,	s,d - .m

f. B♭. *p*

- .t,l : s .l	l .s,f : m .s	s .f,m : m .r	d s, : - .s,	l, .l, : l, .t,,d
hung hea- vy	in my eyes, But	hers came down like	rain. I 2. I	gave her half of / wrought & strove from
f .f : f .f	f .m,r : d .ta,	l, .r,d : t, .t,	d s, .s, : s,	— : fe,
earn my bread by	dai- ly toil, An	hon-est man and	free. {I gave / I wrought / My farm	her / and / is
f .,m : r .t,	d .r : m .d	d .l : s .f	m t, : - .t,	d .d : d .d
hap - py man, a	hap-py wife, To	bless my home and	me. My	farm is large, my
r .,d : t, .s,	l, .t, : d .m,	f, .r, : s, .s,	d s, .s, : s,	— : —

cres -

r .t, : s, .s,	l, .l, : l, .t,,d	r : - .s,	m .m : m .r,d	d .d : d .r.m
all I had, Re- / morn till night, And	press'd the ris - ing / sav'd my lit - tle	sigh, For, / store;	thinking of the	days to come, I
f, : - .m,,r,	de, : d,	d, : t₂ .s,	s, .se, : l, .m,	m, .m, : f, .f,
half of / strove from / large, my	all I / morn till / wants are	had, / night, / small, } And	ev -'ry sum-mer	gave me wealth, And
d .t,,l, : t, .s	s : - .fe	f : - .f	m .r : d .t,	d .ta, : l, .s,
wants are small, I	bid (my care) de-	part; And	sit be - neath my	own oak tree, With
— : —	— : —	— : - .l,,t,	d .t, : l, .se,	l, .s, : f, .m,

cen - do. *f*

f .r,m : f .r,m	f̂ : s .,f	m,f .r,m : d .r	t,,d .l,,t, : s, .l,,t,	d .d : f,-s .m,-f
kept my cour-age	high. "O! fare-	well," I said, "if	sea - sons pass, And	sun- shine fol - lows
f, .s, : l, .la,	s, : s, .,s,	s, .t, : d .fe,	s, .fe, : s, .s,	s, .s, : s, .s,
made the lit - tle	more. Oh! at	length I bought the	field I ploughed, The	sun- shine fol-lowed
f, .f : f .m	r : t, .,t,	d .f : m .r	r .d : t, .r	d .m : r .d
proud, yet grate-ful	heart. Oh! the	children smil-ing	round the board, Ne'er	ask for bread in
r, .r : r .d	t, : s, .,s,	d .s, : l, .r,	s, .r, : s, .f,	m, .m : t, .d

St. Co. (New.)

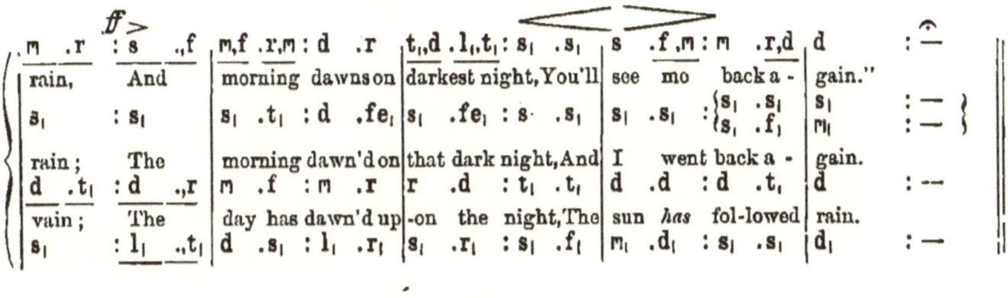

ff >

.m .r :s .,f | m,f .r,m : d .r | t,,d .l,,t, : s, .s, | s .f ,m : m .r,d | d :—
rain, And | morning dawns on | darkest night, You'll | see me back a - | gain."
s, : s, | s, .t, : d .fe, | s, .fe, : s .s, | s, .s, : {s, .s, / s, .f, } | {s, / m,} :—
rain; The | morning dawn'd on | that dark night, And | I went back a - | gain.
d .t, : d .,r | m .f : m .r | r .d : t, .t, | d .d : d .t, | d :—
vain; The | day has dawn'd up | -on the night, The | sun *has* fol-lowed | rain.
s, : l, .,t, | d .s, : l, .r, | s, .r, : s, .f, | m, .d, : s, .s, | d, :—

Words by *Coleridge.*

IF I HAD BUT TWO LITTLE WINGS.

(COPYRIGHT.)

Music by *Henry Smart.*

p KEY E♭. *Con moto.* M. 88.

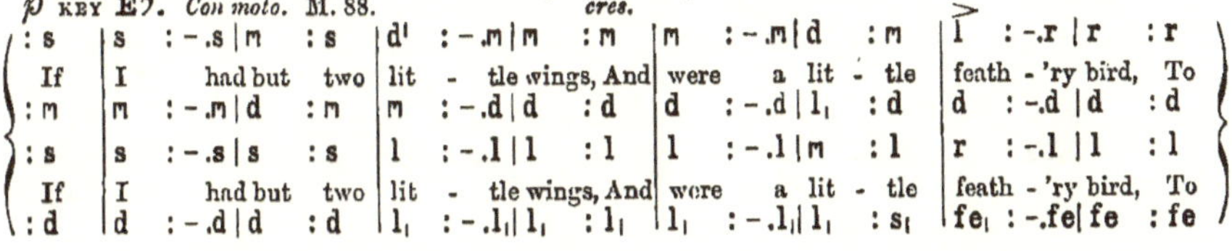

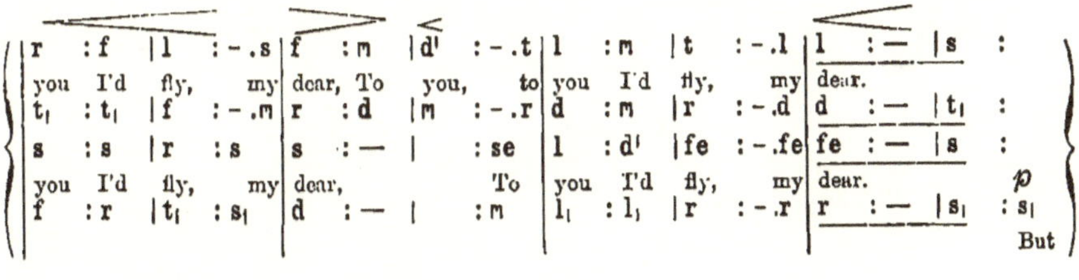

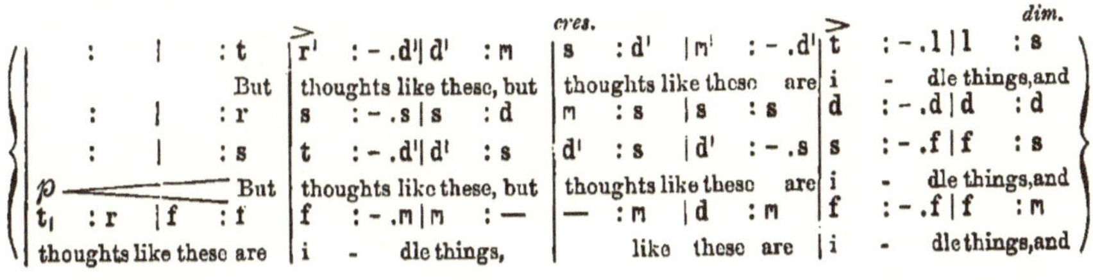

:s | s :-.s | m :s | d' :-.m | m :m | m :-.m | d :m | l :-.r | r :r
If | I had but two | lit - tle wings, And | were a lit - tle | feath - 'ry bird, To
:m | m :-.m | d :m | m :-.d | d :d | d :-.d | l, :d | d :-.d | d :d
:s | s :-.s | s :s | l :-.l | l :l | l :-.l | m :l | r :-.l | l :l
If | I had but two | lit - tle wings, And | were a lit - tle | feath - 'ry bird, To
:d | d :-.d | d :d | l, :-.l, | l, :l, | l, :-.l, | l, :s, | fe, :-.fe | fe :fe

r :f | l :-.s | f :m | d' :-.t | l :m | t :-.l | l :— | s :
you I'd fly, my | dear, To you, to | you I'd fly, my | dear.
t, :t, | f :-.m | r :d | m :-.r | d :m | r :-.d | d :— | t, :
s :s | r :s | s :— | :se | l :d' | fe :-.fe | fe :— | s :
you I'd fly, my | dear, To | you I'd fly, my | dear.
f :r | t, :s, | d :— | :m | l, :l, | r :-.r | r :— | s, : s,
p But

: | :t | r' :-.d' | d' :m | s :d' | m' :-.d' | t :-.l | l :s
But | thoughts like these, but | thoughts like these are | i - dle things, and
: | :r | s :-.s | s :d | m :s | s :s | d :-.d | d :d
: | :s | t :-.d' | d' :s | d' :s | d' :-.s | s :-.f | f :s
p But | thoughts like these, but | thoughts like these are | i - dle things, and
t, :r | f :f | f :-.m | m :— | — :m | d :m | f :-.f | f :m
thoughts like these are | i - dle things, | like these are | i - dle things, and

cres. *dim.*

St. Co. (New.)

poco ritard. p

| s :— | f :— | m :— | — :f | m :— | — :r | d :— | — || s
I stay here, and I stay here, But
| r :— | r :— | d :r | d :r | d :— | t, :— | d :— | — || m
I stay here, and I, and I stay here,
| l :— | t :— | s :se | l :— | s :— | — :— | s :— | — || s
I stay here, and I stay here, But
| r :— | s, :— | d :m, | l, :f, | s, :s, | s :f / s, :s, | m :— | — / d :— | — || d
I stay here, and I stay here, And I stay here,

cres.

| s :-.s | m :s | d' :-.m | m :m | m :-.m | d :m | l :-.r | r :r
in my sleep to you I'd fly; I'm al - ways with you in my sleep! The
| m :-.m | d :m | m :-.d | d :d | d :-.d | l, :d | d :-.d | d :d
| s :-.s | s :s | l :-.l | l :l | l :-.l | m :l | r :-.l | l :l
in my sleep to you I'd fly; I'm al - ways with you in my sleep! The
| d :-.d | d :d | l, :-.l, | l, :l, | l, :-.l, | l, :s, | fe, :-.fe | fe :fe

| r :f | l :-.s | f :m | d' :-.t | l :m | t :-.l | l :— | s :
world is all one's own, The world, the world is all one's own,
| t, :t, | f :-.m | r :d | m :-.r | d :m | r :-.d | d :— | t, :
| s :s | r :s | s :— | :se | l :d' | fe :-.fe | fe :— | s :
world is all one's own, The world is all one's own. p
| f :r | t, :s, | d :— | :m | l, :l, | r :-.r | r :— | s, :s,
But

cres.

| | :t | r' :-.d' | d' :m | s :d' | m' :-.d' | t :-.l | l :s
But then one wakes, but then one wakes, And where am I? All,
| : | :r | s :-.s | s :d | m :s | s :-.s | s :-.f | f :d
| : | :s | t :-.d' | d' :s | d' :s | d' :-.d' | d' :-.d' | d' :s
But then one wakes, but then one wakes, And where am I? All,
| t, :r | f :f | f :-.m | m :— | — :m | d :m | f :-.f | f :m
then one wakes, and where am I? One wakes, And where am I? All

St. Co. (New.)

dim. *poco ritard.* B♭. t.

s :— |— :f |m :— |— :f |m :— |— :r |d :— |— || $^m l_1$
all a - | lone, All, | all a - | lone, || Sleep
r :— |r :— |d :r |d :r |d :— |t_1 :— |d :— |— || $^s d_1$
all, all a - | lone, a - | lone.
l :— |t :— |s :se |l :l |s :— |— :s |s :— |— || $^m l_1$
all a - | lone, all, all a - | lone, all, all a - | lone. || Sleep
r :— |s_1 :— |d :m_1 |l_1 :f_1 |{s_1 :s_1 |s :f / s_1 :— |— :s_1} |{m :— |— / d :— |—} || $^d f_1$
all a - | lone, all, all a - | lone, a - | lone.

cres.

l_1 :s_1 |s_1 :-.d |d :-.t_1|t_1 :l_1.s_1 |m :-.r|d :t_1 |r :d |s :f
stays not though a | mon - arch bids; So I | love to wake e'er | break of day; For
r_1 :m_1 |s_1 :-.s_1 |f_1 :-.f_1|f_1 :f_1.f_1 |m_1 :-.f_1|l_1 :se_1 |t_1 :l_1 |l_1 :l_1
t_1 :d |d :-.s_1 |s_1 :-.s_1|s_1 :l_1.t_1 |d :-.t_1|m :m |m :m |m :r
stays not though a | mon - arch bids; So I | love to wake e'er | break of day; For
f_1 :m_1 |m_1 :-.m_1 |r_1 :-.r_1|r_1 :r_1.r_1 |d_1 :-.r_1|m_1 :m_1 |l_1 :l_1 |f_1 :f_1

f. E♭.

m :-.d|m :r |d :— |— :t_1 |l_1 :l_1 |d.t_1 :l_1.t_1 |^{d}s :— |— :
though my sleep be | gone, For | though my sleep be | gone,
d :-.s_1|d :t_1 |d :m_1 |d :se_1 |l_1 :f_1 |f_1 :f_1 |$^m t_1$:— |— :s
For though my | sleep, my sleep be | gone, yet
s :-.m|s :f |m :d |m :r |d :r |r :r |^{d}s :— |— :t
though my sleep be | gone, For though my | sleep, my sleep be | gone, yet
s_1 :-.s_1|s_1 :s_1 |l_1 :— |m_1 :— |f_1 :r_1 |s_1 :s_1 |$^d s_1$:r |s :—
For | though my sleep be | gone, yet while

p

: | :l |s :-.f|f :— |— :r^1|d^1 :t |l :-.s|s :-.l
yet | while 'tis dark, | 'tis dark one | shuts one's lids, And
f :m |r :de |r :-.r|r :-.d |d :t_1 |l_1 :s_1 |r :-.m|m :d
while 'tis dark one | shuts one's lids, yet | while 'tis dark one | shuts one's lids, And
d^1 :t |l :s |l :-.l|r :— |r :f |r^1 :r^1 |t :-.d^1|d^1 :s
while 'tis dark one | shuts one's lids, | while 'tis dark one | shuts one's lids, And
l :s |f :m |r :d |t_1 :l_1 |s_1 :— |f :— |f :-.m|m :m
while 'tis dark one | shuts one's lids, one | shuts, one | shuts one's lids, And

St. Co. (New.)

dim. *p* *poco ritard.*

s :—	f :—	m :—	— :f	m :—	— :r	d .:—	—
still	dreams	on,	And	still	dreams	on.	
r :—	r :—	d :r	d :r	d :—	t_1 :—	d :—	—
still	dreams	on, and	still, and	still	dreams	on.	
l :—	t :—	s :se	l :—	s :—	— :—	s :—	—
still	dreams	on, and	still	dreams		on.	
r :—	s_1 :—	d :m_1	l_1 :f_1	s_1 :s_1	{s :f / s_1 :s_1}	{m / d} :—	—
still	dreams	on, and	still dreams	on, and	still dreams	on.	

Words by *Geo. Bennett.*

ANGEL OF HOPE.

(Arranged for mixed voices by ALFRED STONE.)

Music by *G. Reichardt.*

KEY D. *Sostenuto con espressione.*

SOLO—CONTRALTO.

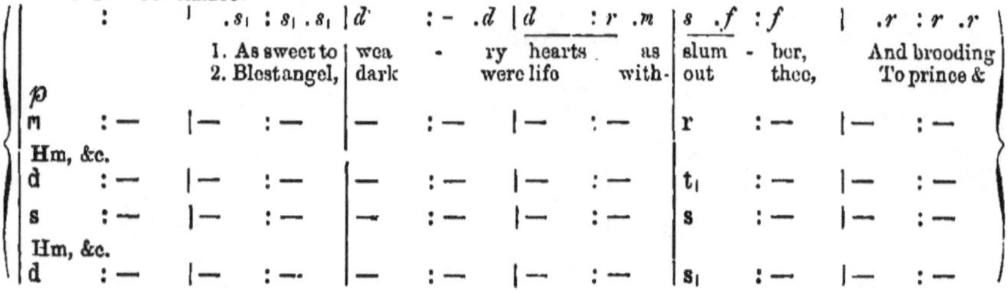

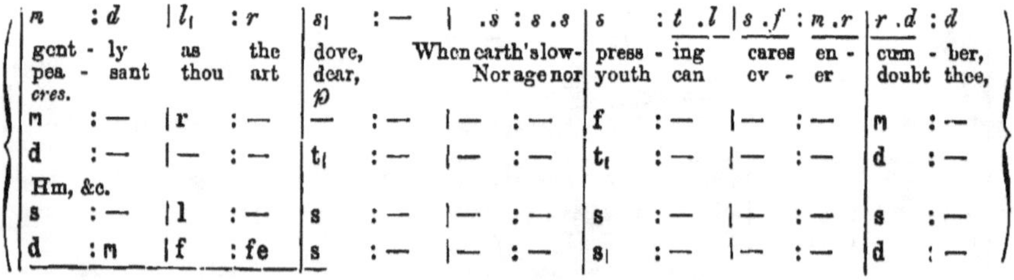

:	.s_1 :s_1 .s_1	d' :- .d	d :r .m	s .f :f	.r :r .r
	1. As sweet to / 2. Blest angel,	wea - / dark	ry hearts as / were life with-	slum - ber, / out thee,	And brooding / To prince &
p m :—	— :—	— :—	— :—	r :—	— :—
Hm, &c.					
d :—	— :—	— :—	— :—	t_1 :—	— :—
s :—	— :—	— :—	— :—	s :—	— :—
Hm, &c.					
d :—	— :—	— :—	— :—	s_1 :—	— :—

m :d	l_1 :r	s_1 :—	.s :s .s	s :t .l	s .f :m .r	r .d :d
gent - ly / pea - sant	as the / thou art	dove, / dear,	When earth's slow- / Nor age nor	press - ing / youth can	cares en - / ev - er	cum - ber, / doubt thee,
cres. m :—	r :—	*p* — :—	— :—	f :—	— :—	m :—
d :—	— :—	t_1 :—	— :—	t_1 :—	— :—	d :—
Hm, &c.						
s :—	l :—	s :—	— :—	s :—	— :—	s :—
d :m	f :fe	s :—	— :—	s_1 :—	— :—	d :—

St. Co. (New.)

| .d : r .m | r : - .r | d' : t .l | s : — | .s : s .s | d' : - .s | m : l .s |
Bright Hope comes | mis - sion'd from a- | bove. Where gloom'd the | cloud, a glo - ry
Thy radiant | pres - ence all must | cheer. Sweet Seraph, | who, when E - den's
cres. *p*
| — : — | r : — | fe : — | s : — | — : — | — : — | l : — |
| — : — | t, : — | d : — | t, : d | r : f | m : — | — : — |
Hm, &c.
| — : — | s : — | l : — | s : l | t : r' | d' : — | de' : — |
| — : — | r : — | — : — | s, : — | : | : | l : — |

| s .f : f | .f : s .l | t, : - .r | s : - .f | m : — | .s, : s, .s, | d .r : m .r | d .m : s .ta |
brightens, Where sorrow | wept, there glad - ness | smiles; While trusting | faith the spi - rit
por - tals Shut in those | scenes so fair and | bright, Still deign'd to | so - lace fal - len
| l : — | — : — | s : — | — : — | s : — | — : — | s : — | — : — |
| f : — | — : — | f : — | — : — | m : — | — : — | m : — | — : — |
Hm, &c.
| r' : — | — : — | r' : — | — : — | d' : — | — : — | d' : — | — : — |
| r : — | — : — | s : — | — : — | d : — | — : — | d : — | — : — |

| ta.l : l | .l : l .l | d'.s : m .d | s, : m .r | d : — | : | : | : |
light- ens, And aimless | doubt no more be- | guiles.
mor - tals, And ha-lo | earth with heav'n's de- | light.
f Quicker.
| f : — | re : — | m : — | f : — | m : — | .s : s .s | se : - .se | se : - .se |
1. While trusting | faith the spi - rit
| d : — | — : — | d : — | t, : — | d : — | .m : m .m | m : - .m | m : - .m |
Hm, &c.
| d' : — | l : — | s : — | — : — | s : — | .d' : d' .d' | r' : - .r' | r' : - .r' |
2. Still deign'd to | so - lace fal - len
| f : — | fe : — | s : — | s, : — | d : — | .d' : d' .d' | t : - .t | t : - .t |

ten.

| t .l : l | .d' : t .l | s : - .s | s : - .f | m : — | .m : m .m | l : - .l | l : s .f |
light - ens, And aimless | doubt no more be- | guiles, And aimless | doubt no more be-
| m : m | .l : s .f | m : - .m | r : - .r | r : — | .d : d .d | d : f .m | r : - .r |
| d' : d' | .d' : d' .d' | d' : - .d' | t : - .t | t : — | .l : l .l | d' : - .d' | t : - .t |
mor - tals, And ha-lo | earth with heav'n's own | light, And ha-lo | earth with heav'n's own
| l : l | .f : f .f | s : - .s | s : - .s | se : — | .l : l .l | f : - .f | s : - .s |

St. Co. (New.)

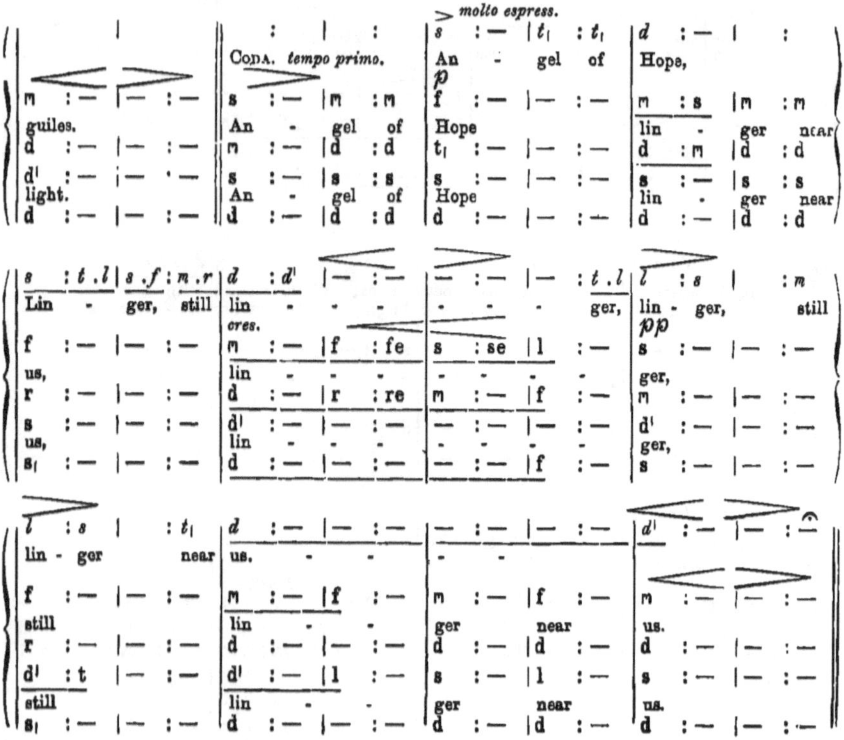

> *molto espress.*

| : | : || : | : | s :— | t_1 :t_1 | d :— | : |
CODA. *tempo primo.* An - gel of Hope,
p
m :— |— :— || s :— |m :m | f :— |— :— | m :s |m :m
guiles. An - gel of Hope lin - ger near
d :— |— :— || m :— |d :d | t_1 :— |— :— | d :m |d :d
d' :— |— :— || s :— |s :s | s :— |— :— | s :— |s :s
light. An - gel of Hope lin - ger near
d :— |— :— || d :— |d :d | d :— |— :— | d :— |d :d

s :t .l |s .f :m .r | d :d' |— :— | — :— |— :t .l | l :s | :m
Lin - ger, still lin - - - - - - ger, lin - ger, still
cres. *pp*
f :— |— :— | m :— |f :fe | s :se |l :— | s :— |— :—
us, lin - - - - - - - ger,
r :— |— :— | d :— |r :re | m :— |f :— | m :— |— :—
s :— |— :— | d' :— |— :— | — :— |— :— | d' :— |— :—
us, lin - - - - - - - ger,
s_1 :— |— :— | d :— |— :— | — :— |f :— | s :— |— :—

l :s | :t_1 | d :— |— :— | — :— |— :— | d' :— |— :—
lin - ger near us. - - - -
f :— |— :— | m :— |f :— | m :— |f :— | m :— |— :—
still lin - - ger near us.
r :— |— :— | d :— |— :— | d :— |d :— | d :— |— :—
d' :t |— :— | d' :— |l :— | s :— |l :— | s :— |— :—
still lin - - ger near us.
s_1 :— |— :— | d :— |— :— | d :— |d :— | d :— |— :—

p KEY G. M. 88. **THE SPRING, THE PLEASANT SPRING.** *R. Spofforth.*

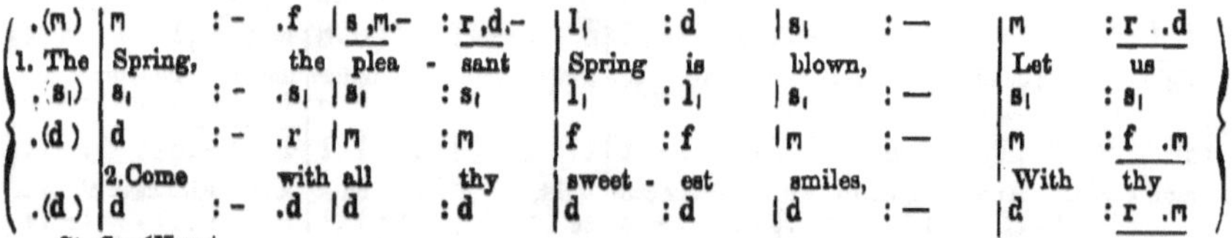

.(m) | m :- .f |s ,m.- :r ,d.- | l_1 :d |s_1 :— | m :r .d
1. The Spring, the plea - sant Spring is blown, Let us
.(s_1) | s_1 :- .s_1 |s_1 :s_1 | l_1 :l_1 |s_1 :— | s_1 :s_1
.(d) | d :- .r |m :m | f :f |m :— | m :f .m
2. Come with all thy sweet - est smiles, With thy
.(d) | d :- .d |d :d | d :d |d :— | d :r .m

St. Co. (New.)

D. t.

| t, .r :- .d | s ,f .- : f ,m .- | m : r | m :- .m | r s :- .d' |
leave the smo - ky town, From the mall and
| s, :- .s, | s, : s, | s, :— | s, :- .s, | s,d :- .m |
| r :- .m | r : d | d : t, | d :- .d | r s :- .s |
gra - ces, with thy wiles, Come and we will
| f :- .m | t, : d | s, :— | d :- .d | t,m :- .m |

cres.

| t .d' : r' .t | d' .t : d' .r' | m',f'.- : r',t .- | d' :- .l | s ,f .- : m .,r |
from the ring, Ev' - ry one has ta - ken
| s : s | s :— | s : s | s :- .f | m ,r .- : d .,t, |
| s : s | s :— | s : s | s :- .d' | d',r'.- : s |
mer - ry be, Who shall be so blest as
| r .m : f .r | m .f : m .r | d ,t,.- : r ,f .- | m :- .f | s : s, |

f

| m : m .,f | s : l .,t | d' :- .r' | m',f'.- : r',t .- | d' : s |
wing, Ev' - ry one, ev' - ry one has ta - ken wing, has
| d : m .,r | d : f .,f | s :- .l | s : s | s : s |
| s : s .,s | s : d' .,r' | d' :- .l | d',r'.- : t .r'.- | m' : d' |
we, Who shall be, who shall be so blest as we, so
| d : d .,r | m : f .,r | m :- .f | s : s | d' : m |

f. G. *ff* *Much slower.*

| l : f' | r' : t | d' :— | — :— || s r .r :— | r .r :— |
ta - - ken wing. Clo-e, Strephon,
| f :— | f :— | m :— | — :— || m t,.t, :— | l, .r :— |
| d' : l | t : s | s :— | — :— || d's .s :— | l .l :— |
blest as we? Clo-e, Strephon,
| f :— | s :— | d :— | — :— || d's .s :— | f .f, :— |

| m : m | f :— | d :- .d | d :- .d | r : r | m :— ||
Co - ry - don, All are fled and all are gone;
| r : de | r :— | d :- .d | d :- .d | d : t, | d :— ||
| l : l | l :— | l :- .l | s :- .s | s : s | s :— ||
Co - ry - don, All are fled and all are gone;
| m, : l, | r :— | f :- .f | m :- .m, | r, : s, | d :— ||

St. Co. (New.)

p Original time. *cres.*

f,m.- :f,s.- |l :- .f |m,r.- :m,f.- |s :— |r :- .de |r .f :l .s
What is left's not worth your stay, Come, Au-re - lia,
d :d |d :- .d |d :l_1 |s_1 :— |l_1 :- .l_1 |l_1 :l_1
d :d |d :- .d |d :d |d :— |r :- .m |r :de
What is left's not worth your stay, Come, Au-re - lia,
l_1 :l_1 |l_1 :- .l_1 |s_1 :f_1 |m_1 :— |f_1 :- .s_1 |f_1 :m_1

f .m :r .d |t_1 :s .s |s : | :s .s |s | :
come, come a- way, come a- way, come a- way,
l_1 :l_1 .l_1 |t_1 : | :t_1 .t_1 |d : | :r .r |m :
come a - way, come a - way,
r .de :r .r |r : | :r .r |d : | :t_1 .t_1 |d :
come, come a- way, come a - way, come a - way,
r_1 .m_1 :f_1 .fe_1 |s_1 : | :f_1 .f_1 |m_1 : | :r_1 .r_1 |d_1 :

p

s :- .m |f :m |f :s .s |l :— |l,s.- :f,m.- |r :- .r
Come, Au-re - lia, come, come a- way, What is left's not
d :- .d |d :d |d :d .d |d :— |l_1 :l_1 |t_1 :- .t_1
m :- .s |l :s |f :m .m |f :— |f :f |s :- .s
Come Au-re - lia, come, come a- way, What is left's not
d :- .ta_1 |l_1 :ta_1 |l_1 :s_1 .s_1 |f_1 :— |f :f |f :- .f

cres.

s,f.- :m,r.- |d :— |f .m :f .r |m :f |m :r .m |f :—
worth your stay, Come, come, Au-re - lia, come, come a - way,
t_1 :t_1 |d :— |t_1 .d :t_1 .r |d :r |d :t_1 .t_1 |d :—
s :s |s :— |s :s .s |s :l |s :s .s |f :—
worth your stay, Come, come, Au-re - lia, come, come a - way,
f :f |m :— |r .d :r .t_1 |d :f_1 |s_1 :s_1 .s_1 |l_1 :—

f

f .l :s .f |m .f :s .f |m :— |r :- .r |m .f :s .l |s .f :m .r
Come, come, Au-re - lia, Come, come a- way, - - -
d :r .r |m .r :d .r |d :— |t_1 :- .t_1 |d :d .d |d :d .r
Come a- way, come a-
f :r .r |s :s .l |s :— |s :- .s |s :s .f |s :s .s
Come, come, Au-re - lia, Come, come a- way, - - -
l_1 :t_1 .t_1 |d .r :m .f |s :— |s_1 :- .s_1 |d .r :m .f |m .r :d .t_1

St. Co. (New.)

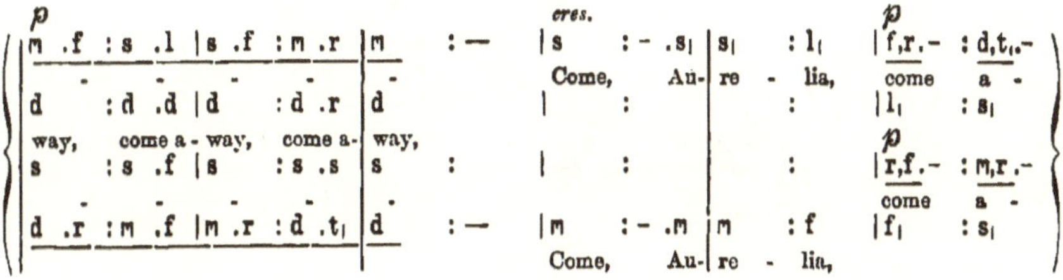

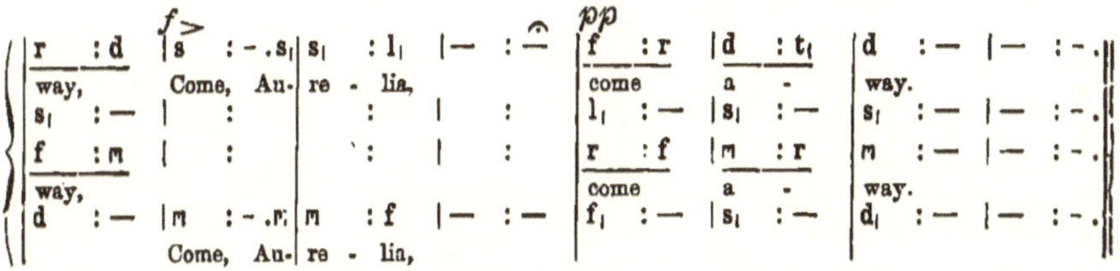

p cres. p
| m .f : s .l | s .f : m .r | m : — | s : — .s, | s, : l, | f,r.— : d,t,.—
- - - - - Come, Au- re - lia, come a -
| d : d .d | d : d .r | d | : | : | l, : s,
way, come a - way, come a- way,
p
| s : s .f | s : s .s | s : | : | : | r,f.— : m,r.—
- - - - - come a -
| d .r : m .f | m .r : d .t, | d : — | m : — .m | m : f | f, : s,
Come, Au- re - lia,

f> pp
| r : d | s : — .s, | s, : l, | — : — | f : r | d : t, | d : — | — : — . ||
way, Come, Au- re - lia, come a - way.
| s, : — | : | : | : | l, : — | s, : — | s, : — | — : — . ||
| f : m | : | : | : | r : f | m : r | m : — | — : — . ||
way, come a - way.
| d : — | m : — .m | m : f | — : — | f, : — | s, : — | d, : — | — : — . ||
Come, Au- re - lia,

Words by *John Oxenford.*

AT FIRST THE MOUNTAIN RILL.

(Part-song from "Jessy Lea.")

(T. S. Copyright.)

Music by *G. A. Macfarren.*

KEY D. *Andante.*

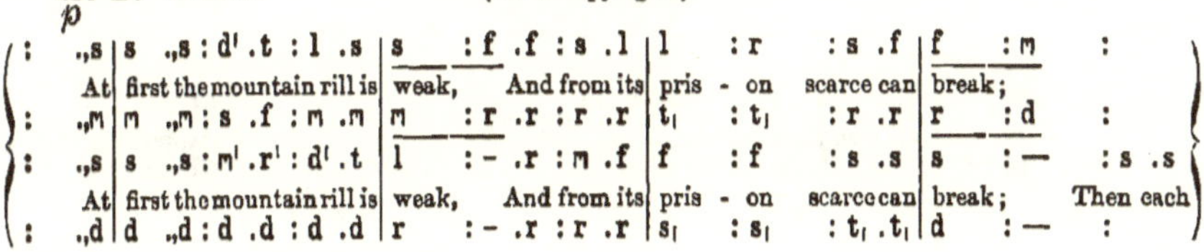

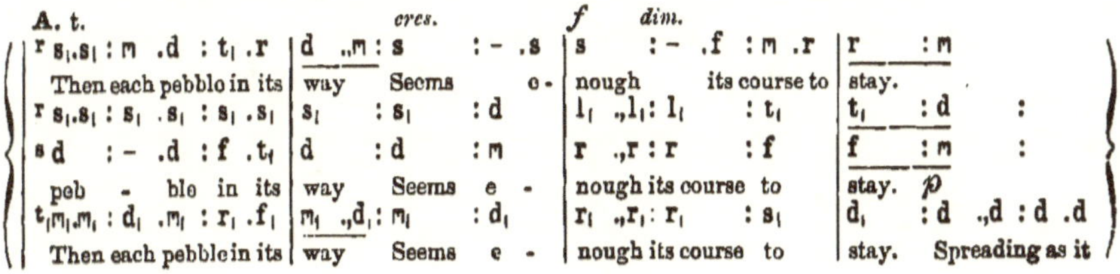

p
: ,,s | s ,,s : d' .t : l .s | s : f .f : s .l | l : r : s .f | f : m :
At first the mountain rill is weak, And from its pris - on scarce can break;
: ,,m | m ,,m : s .f : m .m | m : r .r : r .r | t, : t, : r .r | r : d :
: ,,s | s ,,s : m' .r' : d' .t | l : — .r : m .f | f : f : s .s | s : — : s .s
At first the mountain rill is weak, And from its pris - on scarce can break; Then each
: ,,d | d ,,d : d .d : d .d | r : — .r : r .r | s, : s, : t, .t, | d : — :

A. t. cres. f dim.
| r s,.s, : m .d : t, .r | d ,,m : s : — .s | s : — .f : m .r | r : m
Then each pebble in its way Seems e - nough its course to stay.
| r s,.s, : s, .s, : s, .s, | s, : s, : d | l, ,,l, : l, : t, | t, : d :
| s d : — .d : f .t, | d : d : m | r ,,r : r : f | f : m :
peb - ble in its way Seems e - nough its course to stay. p
| t, m,.m, : d, .m, : r, .f, | m, ,,d, : m, : d, | r, ,,r, : r, : s, | d, : d ,,d : d .d
Then each pebble in its way Seems e - nough its course to stay. Spreading as it

p f. D. *mf*

ˢr' ,,d' : t .l : s .f	m : :	f' ,,m' : r' .d' : t .l	s : :
Spreading as it glides a-	long,	Soon it is a torrent	strong;
ᵐt ,,l : s .f : m .r	d : :	r' ,,d' : t .l : s .f	m : :
: :	*mf* ˡm' ,,r' : d' .t : l .s	s : :	*f dim.* s' ,,f' : m' .r' : d' .t
	Spreading as it glides a-	long,	Soon it is a torrent
cres. ᵈs : — : s	s : — : —	s : - .s : s .s	s ,,s : s : —
glides a -	long,	Soon it is a	tor - rent strong,

p

s ,,s : fe .s : l .m'	m' ,,f' : l : m' .r'	r' : s .l : s .f	m : :
And its path is broad and	free, As it	bounds in - to the	sea.
r ,,r : r .r : de.de	r : — : f .f	m : - .f : m .r	d : :
ta : — : l .l	l ,,l : l : l .l	d' : - .s : l .t	d' : :
strong; And its	path is free, As it	bounds in - to the	sea.
s ,,s : s .s : s .s	f : — : f .f	s : — : —	l ,,s : f .m : r .d
And its path is broad and	free, As it	bounds,	Soon it is a torrent

f dim. *p* *cres.*

s ,,s : fe .s : l .m'	s' .f' : se .l : m' .r'	r' : s .d' : t .d'	m' ,,r' : s
And its path is broad and	free, As it	bounds in - to the	sea.
r ,,r : r .r : de.de	r : — : f .f	m : - .m : m .m	s : — :
s ,,s : s .s : s .s	l : r' : l .l	d' : - .d' : - .d'	f' : - .r' : t ,,l
And its path is broad and	free, As it	bounds, as it	bounds in - to the
ta, : — : l, .l,	r ,,r : f : r .r	s : - .l : l .l	t : — :
strong; And its	path is free, As it	bounds in - to the	sea.

p *cres.*

: .r : m .f	s ,,s : d' .t : l .s	s : f	,,l : r' .d' : t .l
At first, at	first the mountain rill is	weak,	But spreading as it
: .t, : d .r	m ,,m : s .f : m .m	m .l :	,,f : l .s : f .f
l : s :	: : *p* ,,s	d' : - .t : l .s	f : : ,,l
sea.	At	first the rill is	weak, But
: .f : m .r	d ,,d : m .r : d .t,	l, : - .d : f .m	r ,,r : f .m : r .d
At first, at	first the mountain rill is	weak, the rill is	weak, But spreading as it

mf *cres.*

l ,,s : s :	,,d' : f' .m' : r' .d'	t .l : s .f : f .m	s ,,f : t : l
glides a-long,	A torrent strong, its	path is broad and free,	As it bounds,
f ,,s : s :	,,d : d' .t : l .s	f .f : m .r : r .d	m ,,f : f : —
r' : - .d' : t .l	s : ,,d' : f' .m'	r' .t : d' .r' : s	ta ,,l : r : —
spread - ing as it	glides, A torrent	strong, its path is broad,	As it bounds,
t, ,,t, : t .r : s .f	m ,,m : l .s : f ,,r	s .s, : l, .t, : d	de ,,r : f : —
glides a-long, as it	glides, A torrent strong, its	path is broad and free,	As it bounds,

St. Co. (*New.*)

p

t .,l : m' : r'	f' .,m' : s' .m' : d' .l	s .l : t : m' .r'	d' : —
as it bounds,	bounds	in - to the	sea.
f .,f : l : —	s .,s : d' : s .m	f .f : t : - .f	m : —
	As it bounds	in - to the	sea.
r' .,r' : f' : —	d' .,d' : m' .d' : m' .d'	t .d' : r' : t .t	d' : —
as it bounds,	As it bounds	in - to the	sea.
f .,f : r : —	s .,s : s : —	- .s : s : s, .s,	d : —

p

: s	s .,s : d' .t : l .s	s : f .f : s .l	l : r .r : s .f	f : m	
Thus	love is oft so weak at	first, That e'en the	heart in which 'tis	nurs'd	
: m	m .,m : s .f : m .m	m : r .r : r .r	t, : - .t, : r .r	r : d	:
: s	s .,s : m' .r' : d' .t	l : - .r : m .f	f : - .f : s .s	s : —	: s .s
Thus	love is oft so weak at	first, That e'en the	heart in which 'tis	nurs'd	Scarcely
: d	d .,d : d .d : d .d	r : - .r : r .r	s, : - .s, : t, .t,	d : —	:

A. t. *cres.* *f* *dim.*

r s,.s, : m .d : t, .r	d .,m : s : - .s	s : - .f : m .r	r : m :
Scarcely can its presence	feel; But its	pow'r 'twill soon re	-veal;
r s,.s, : s, .s, : s, .s,	s, : s, : d	l, .,l, : l, : t,	t, : d :
s d : - .d : f .t,	d : d : m	r .,r : r : f	f : m :
can its presence	feel; But its	pow'r 'twill soon re -	veal; *p*
t,m,.m, : d, .m, : r, .f,	m, .,d, : m, : d,	r, .,r, : r, : s,	d, : d .,d : d .d
Scarcely can its presence	feel; But its	pow'r 'twill soon re -	veal; And so mighty

f. D. *mf*

s r' .,d' : t .l : s .f	m : :	f' .,m' : r' .d' : t .l	s : :
And so mighty is its	force,	Nothing can re-strain its	course;
m t .,l : s .f : m .r	d : :	r' .,d' : t .l : s .f	m : :
	mf		*f dim.*
: :	l m' .,r' : d' .t : l .s	s : :	s' .,f' : m' .r' : d' .t
	And so mighty is its	force,	Nothing can restrain its
d s : — : s	s : — : —	s : - .s : s .s	s .,s : s : —
is its	force,	No - thing can re-	strain its course;

p

s .,s : fe .s : l .m'	m' .,f' : l : m' .r'	r' : s .l : s .f	m : :
Riches, honours, what are	they? Love thro'	all will find a	way;
r .,r : r .r : de.de	r : — : f .f	m : - .f : m .r	d : :
ta : — : l .l	l .,l : l : l .l	d' : - .s : l .t	d' : :
course, Riches,	what are they? Love thro'	all will find a	way;
s .,s : s .s : s .s	f : — : f .f	s : — : —	l .,s : f .m : r .d
Riches, honours, what are	they? Love thro'	all.	Nothing can re-strain its

St. Co. (New).

f dim. *p* *cres.*

s ,,s : fe .s : l .m'	s' .f' : se .l : m' .r'	r' : s .d' : t .d'	m' ,,r' : s :
Nothing can re- strain its	course, Love thro'	all will find a	way.
r ,,r : r .r : de.de	r : — : f .f	m : - .m : m .m	s : — :
s ,,s : s .s : s .s	l : r' : l .l	d' : - .d' : - .d'	f' : - .r' : t ,,l
Nothing can re- strain its	course, Love thro'	all, Love thro'	all will find a
ta_1 : — : l_1 .l_1	r ,,r : f : r .r	s : - .l : l .l	t : — :
course, can re-	strain its course, Love thro'	all will find a	way.

p *cres.*

: .r : m .f	s ,,s : d' .t : l .s	s : f :	,,l : r' .d' : t .l
Thus love, thus	love is oft so weak at	first;	But soon it will its
: .t_1 : d .r	m ,,m : s .f : m .m	m : f :	,,f : l .s : f .f
l : s :	: : ,,s	d' : - .t : l .s	f : : ,,l
way.	Thus	love is weak at	first, But
: .f : m .r	d ,,d : m .r : d .t_1	l_1 : - .d : f .m	r ,,r : f .m : r .d
Thus love, thus	love is oft so weak at	first, so weak at	first, But soon it will its

mf *cres.*

l ,,s : s :	,,d' : f' .m' : r' .d'	t .l : s .f : f .m	s ,,f : t : l
pow'r reveal,	so mighty, Nothing	can re - strain its course,	Love thro' all,
f ,,s : s :	,,d : d' .t : l .s	f .f : m .r : r .d	m ,,f : f : —
r' : - .d' : t .l	s : ,,d' : f' .m'	r' .t : d' .r' : s	ta ,,l : r' : —
soon re - veals its	pow'r, so mighty,	Nothing can re - strain,	Love thro' all,
t_1 ,,t_1 : t_1 .r : s .f	m ,,m : l .s : f ,,r	s .s_1 : l_1 .t_1 : d	de ,,r : f : —
pow'r re-veal, its	pow'r so mighty, Nothing	can re - strain its course,	Love thro' all,

f

t ,,l : m' : r'	f' ,,m' : s' .m' : d' .l	s .l : t : m' .r'	d' : — ‖
love thro' all,	love thro'	all will find a	way.
f ,,f : l : —	s ,,s : d' : s .m	f .f : f : - .f	m : — ‖
	Love thro' all	will find a	way.
r' ,,r' : f' : —	d' ,,d' : m' .d' : m' .d'	t .d' : r' : t .t	d' : — ‖
love thro' all,	love thro' all	will find a	way.
f ,,f : r : —	s ,,s : s : —	- .s : s : s_1 .s_1	d : — ‖

St. Co. (New.)

O THE JOY OF SPRING.

Words by *J. S. C.* *Styrian Air.*

KEY F.

mf

:d .r |m .s, :m :r .d |r .l, :r :f .l |s .r :s .l :r .f |m :— :d .r

1. O the joy of Spring, Let us gaily sing, While the sunshine on the mead is bright, While the

:d .d |d .s, :d :t, .d |l, .l, :l, :l, .r |t, .t, :t, .t, :t, .t, |d :— :d .t,

2. Now the primrose pale Greets the daf-fo - dil, And the vio-let - scented air is sweet, Birds in

:m .f |s .m :s :s .s |f .f :f :r .f |f .f :f .r :s .s |s :— :s .s

3 Then com-panions, ho! To the fields we go, And in harmo - ny be - guile the hours, Now in

:d .d |d .d :d :r .m |f .f, :f, :f, .f, |s, .s, :s, .s, :s, .s, |d :— :m .r

C. t. *cres.* *f* f. F. *p*

m .s, :m :r .d |t,m.s :m' :r' .d' |t .d' :r' .m' :f' .,t |d' :— :d's .se

lambkins play, And the earth is gay, And all na-ture keeps a hol - i- day. La la

d .s, :d :t, .d |s,d.m :s :s .s |s .s :t .d' :t .,s |s :— :l m.m

ev-'ry tree Make a melo - dy, Singing welcome to the sun- ny May. La la

s .m :s :f .m |r s.d' :d' :f' .m' |r' .m' :f' .m' :r' .,f' |m' :— :f'd'.d'

softest trill; Now in music shrill, Shall our song the joy-ful wel-kin fill. La la

d .d :d :d .d |r s.s :s :s .s |s .s :s .s :s .,s |d :— :f d.d

dim. *f*

l .f :d' :t .l |l .,s :m :s .se |t .,l :s .l :f .r |m :— :s .se

la la la, La la la la la, La la la la la la la la la, While the

f .f :f :d .d |d .,d :d :d .d |r .,d :t, .t, :t, .t, |d :— :m .m

la la la, La la la la la, La la la la la la la la la, Birds in

d' .l :l :s .f |f .,m :s :m .m |f .,f :f .f :r .s |s :— :d' .d'

la la la, La la la la la, La la la la la la la la la, Now in

f .f :f :f, .f, |d .,d :d :d .d |s, .,s, :s, .s, :s, .s, |d :— :d .d

molto. rit. e dim.

rit.

l .s :f :t .,l |fe .s :d' :t .l |l .,s :l .,s :f .t, |d : ||

lambkins play, And the earth is gay, And all na - ture keeps a hol - i - day.

f .d :d :f .,f |re .m :m :f .f |f .,f :f .,f :t, .s, |s, :

ev-'ry tree, Make a mel-o - dy, Singing wel - come to the sun-ny May.

d' .ta :l :s .,s |l .s :s :d' .d' |t .,t :t .,t :s .f |m :

softest trill; Now in mu-sic shrill, Shall our song the joy - ful wel-kin fill.

f .f :f :r .,r |d .d :d .f, f, |s, .,s, :s, .,s, :s, .s, |d :

St. Co. (New)

HOW LOVELY ARE THE MESSENGERS.

(Chorus from "St. Paul.") *Mendelssohn.*

KEY G. *Andante con moto.* M. 132. ALTO.

p
| : : | : : s, | d :- : t, | l, :- : s, | f :- : m | r :- : d | t, : d : r | s, : s, : s, |
How | love - ly are the | mes - sen-gers that | preach us the gos-pel of

| s, :- :- | : : s, | l, :- : t, | d :- : r | t, :- : d | r :- : f |
peace; How | love - ly are the | mes - sen-gers that

| m : r : d | r : l, : t, | d :- :- | : : d | s, :- :- | s, :- : f, |
preach us the gos - pel of | peace; The | gos - pel of
| : : | : : | : | : : | : : | : BASS. : s, |
How

| m, :- : | : : s, | l, :- : s, | t, :- : d | r :- :- | - : m : f |
peace; the | mes - sen - gers that | preach us the
| d :- : t, | l, :- : s, | f :- : m | r :- : d | t, : d : r | s, : s, : s, |
love - ly are the | mes - sen - gers that | preach us the gos - pel of

| m : m : r | d :- : | : : | : : | : d | d :- :- |
gos - pel of peace! How love -
| s, :- :- | : : s, | l, :- : t, | d :- : r | t, :- : d | r :- : f |
peace, How | love - ly are the | mes - sen - gers that

| - :- :- | s, :- :- | : d | d :- : f | m : r : d | r : l, |
- - ly are they that | preach us the gos - pel
| m : r : d | r : l, : t, | d :- :- | : : d | s, :- :- | - :- |
preach us the gos - pel of | peace! the | words

f S.C.T.B.
| : s, | s :- :- | - :- : m | m :- :- | r :- : d | t, : d : r | r : m : f |
To | all *f* the | na - tions is | gone forth the sound of their
| : t, | d :- : s, | d :- : d | d :- :- | t, :- : d | s, : l, : t, | t, : d : r |
of | peace; To all the | na - tions is | gone forth the sound of their
| : s, | m :- :- | - :- : s | s :- :- | s :- : s | f : m : r | r : d : t, |
To | all *f* the | na - tions is | gone forth the sound of their
| : s, | d, :- : d | m :- : d | s :- :- | f :- : m | r : d : t, | t, : l, : s, |
of | peace; To all the | na - tions is | gone forth the sound of their

St. Co. (New).

D. t.

| m :- :- | : :m | l :- :- | - :- :d' | d' :- :- | t :- :t,m | f :s :l |
words, to | all the | na - tions is | gone forth the
| d :- :- | : :m | m :- :- | - :- :- | - :- :- | - : :r s | f :- :- |
words, the | sound is | gone,
| d :- :m | m :- :- | - :- :- | - :- :l | l :- :- | se :- : | : : |
words, to all the | na - tions
| d :- : | : :m | d :- :- | - :t, :l, | m :- :- | m, :- :m,l, | r :- :- |
words, to | all the | na - tions is | gone,

| t :d' :r' | s :- :- | - :- :s | l :t :d' | r' :m' :f' | f' :- :- | - :- : |
sound of their | words, is | gone forth the sound of their | words,
| - :- :f | f :- :- | m :- :s | s :- :- | f :- :- | - :- :r | s :- :f |
is | gone forth, the | sound of their
| : :df | s :l :t | d' :r' :m' | m' :- :- | r' :- :d' | t :- :- | :s |
is | gone forth the sound of their | words, their | words, How
| - :- :r | m :f :s | l :t :d' | f :- :- | - : :f | s :- :- | - :- :- |
is | gone forth the sound of their | words. the | sound.

f

| : : | : : | : : | : : | : : | : :s | d' :- :t |
How | love - ly
f
| m :- :- | : | : : | : : | : :s, | s :- :f | m :- :- |
words. How love - ly | are
| d' :- :t | l :- :s | f' :- :m' | r' :- :d' | t :d' :r' | s :s :s | s :- :- |
love - ly are the | mes - sen - gers that | preach us the gos - pel of | peace,
| - :- :- | - :- :- | - :- :- | : :s, | s :- :f | m :- :r | m :- :d |
How | love - ly are the | mes - sen-

| l :- :s | f' :- :m' | r' :- :d' | m' :r' :d' | r' :l :t | d' :- :- | s :- : |
are the | mes - sen - gers that | preach us the gos - pel of | peace,
| : :s | f :- :s | l :- :f | m :- :- | f :- :r | s :f :m | f :d :r |
the | mes - sen - gers that | preach us, that | preach us the gos - pel of
| : :s | d' :- :t | l :- :r' | d' :- :- | s :- :f' | m' :r' :d' | r' :l :t |
the | mes - sen - gers that | preach us, that | preach us the gos - pel, the
| f :- :m | l :- :s | f :- :r | s :- :- | - :- :- | s :- :- | - : :s |
gers, the | mes - sen - gers that | preach us, that

dim. *p* f. G.

| s :- :- | - :- :f | m :- :- | m :- :f | m :- :- | r :- :d | ds, :- :- |
they that | preach us the | gos - pel of | peace.
| m :- :- | : :r | r :- :- | d :- :d | d :- :- | t, :- :d | ds, :- :- |
peace, that | preach us the | gos - pel of | peace.
| d' :s :ta | l :- :l | se :- :- | l :- :f | s :- :- | f :- :m | mt, :- :- |
gos - pel of peace, that | preach us the | gos - pel of | peace.
| s :f :m | f :d :r | m :- :- | l, :- :- | s, :- :- | s, :- :s, | ds, :- :- |
preach us the gos - pel of | peace, the | gos - pel of | peace.

St. Co. (New).

f. C. *L* is *A*.

| : :r | s :- :f | ᵐt :- :l | se :- :- | se :- :l | se :l :t | t :d' :r' |
To all the na - tions is gone forth the sound of their
| : : | : : | : : | : : | : : | : : | : : |
| : : | : : | : :ᵐt | m' :- :- | - :- :- | - :- :- | m' :- :- |
To all the
| : : | : : | : : | : : | : : | : : | : : |

G. t. *L* is *E*. *cres.*

| d'f :- :- | : : | : : | : : | : : | : : | : : |
words.
| : : | : :l, | r :- :d | t, :- :l, | se, :- :- | se, :- :l, | se, :l, :t, |
To all the na - tions is gone forth the
| ᵐ'l :- :f | r :- :- | : : | : : | : : | : : | : : |
na - tions, *cres.*
| : : | : : | : : | : :t, | m :- :- | - :- :- | - :- :- |
To all,

f f. C.

| : | : : | : :ᵈs | s' :- :- | - :- :m' | m' :- :- | r' :- :s |
To all the na - tions is
| t, :d :r | d :- :- | : :ᵈs | d' :- :- | - :- :d' | d' :- :- | t :- :s |
sound of their words;
| : : | : : | : :ᵈs | m' :- :- | - :- :d' | s' :- :- | s :- :s |
To all the na - tions is
| m :- :- | m :- :d | l, :- : | : : | : : | : : | : : |
the na - tions

G. t.

| m' :m' :r' | ᵈ'f :m :r | t :- :- | : :s | d' :d' :t | l :s :f | r' :- :- |
gone forth the sound of their words, is gone forth the sound of their words,
| m :ba :se | ˡr :m :f | f :- :- | : :m | d :r :m | f :s :l | r :- :- |
| s :l :t | ᵈ'f :s :l | r :- :- | : :d | m :f :s | l :t :d' | s :- :- |
gone forth the sound of their words, is gone forth the sound of their words,
| : : | : :f, | s, :l, :t, | d :r :m | m :- :- | : :l, | t, :l, :s, |
is gone forth the sound of their words, is gone forth the

f

| - : :s | s :- :- | - :- :m | m :- :- | r :- :d | t, :d :r | r :m :f |
To all the na - tions is gone forth the sound of their
| - : :f | m :- :- | - :- :d | d :- :- | t, :- :d | s, :l, :t, | t, :d :r |
| - : :s, | s :- :- | - :- :s | s :- :- | s :- :s | f :m :r | r :d :t, |
To all the na - tions is gone forth the sound of their
| f :m :r | d :- :s, | d :- :m | s :- :- | f :- :m | r :d :t, | t, :l, :s, |
sound of their words to all the na - tions is gone forth the sound of their

St. Co. (New).

m :- :- | :d :d | l :- :- | s :- :- | f :- :- | m :- :r | r :- :-
words, throughout all the lands their glad tid -
d :- :- | ta, :- :ta, | l, :- :- | t, :- :- | d :- :- | d :- :d | d :- :-
through - out all the lands their glad tid -
m :- :- | :d :d | f :- :- | r :- :- | l :- :- | s :- :l | s :- :-
words, throughout all the lands their glad tid -
d :- :- | :d :d | f, :- :- | s, :- :- | l, :- :- | d :- :f, | s, :- :-

|- :- :- | d :- :- | : : | | : : | | : :
- - dings.
p
t, :- :- | d :- :- | :s, | d :- :t, | l, :- :s, | f :- :m | r :- :d
- - dings. How love - ly are the mes - sen - gers that
|- :- :- | s :- :- | - :- : | : : | : : | : : | : :
- - dings.
|- :- :f, | m, :- :- | - :- : | : | : | : : | :

p
: : | : | : : | : :s | s :- :- | f :- :- | - :- :-
How love - ly
t, :d :r | s, :s, :s, | s, :- :- | :s, | l, :- :t, | d :- :r | t, :- :-
preach us the gos - pel of peace, How love - ly are the mes -
: : | : : | : : | :m | l :- :- | - :- :- | s :- :-
How love - - - ly
: | : | | : :d, | f, :- :- | - :- :- | s, :- :-
How love - - - ly

p
m :- :r | m :r :d | r :l, :t, | d :- :- | s, :- : | d :- :- | - :- :f
they that preach us the gos - pel of peace, they that
d :- :- | - :- :- | s, :- :s, | s, :f, :m, | f, :f, :f, | m, :- : | l, :- :-
sen - - - gers that preach us the gos - pel of peace, that
d :- :l | s :- :- | f :- :f | m :r :d | r :l, :t, | d :- :- | : :t,
they that preach, that preach us the gos - pel of peace, that
l, :- :f, | s, :- :- | - :- :- | - :- :- | - :- :- | - :f, :m, | f, :d, :r,
they that preach us the gos - pel of

m :- :- | m :- :r | d :- :- | t, :- :d | d :- :- | : || *Four measures*
preach us the gos - pel of peace.
se, :- :- | l, :- :l, | s, :- :- | f, :- :m, | m, :- :- | :
t, :- :- | d :- :f | m :- :- | r :- :d | d :- :- | :
preach us the gos - pel of peace.
m, :- :- | - :- :f, | s, :- :- | s, :- :s, | d, :- :- | : || *Symphony.*
peace, the gos - pel of peace.

St. Ca. (New).

"AWAKE ÆOLIAN LYRE."

KEY D. M. 50. *Largo e sostenuto.* *J. Danby.*

cres. *f*

:s	m :-.s	d' :—	— :—	— :—	:d'	d' :d'	t :—	— :t
A -	wake, a - wake,				Æ - o - lian		lyre,	a -
:t,	d :—	— :—	— :-.m	s :—	:m	m :m	r :—	— :r
				a - wake,				
:r	m :—	— : .d'	m' :—	— :—	:s	s :s	s :—	— :s
A -	wake,	a-	wake,		Æ - o - lian		lyre,	a -
:s,	d :—	— :—	— :—	— :—	:d	d :d	s, :—	— :—

Quicker. M. 100.

ff *f*

d' :m'	r' :t	d' :—	— :d'	t :—	— :		
wake, Æ - o - lian		lyre,	a -	wake,			
m :s	f :r	m :—	— :m	r :—	— :	:	:
s :d'	t :r'	d' :—	— :s	s :—	— :s	s :f	m.f :s.m
wake, Æ - o - lian		lyre,	a -	wake,	and	give to	rap - ture,
— :—	— :s,	d :—	— :d	s, :—	— :	*f* .s,: l,.t,	d.r :m.d
	a -	wake,				and give to rap - ture,	

f *mf* *mf*

.l :t.d'	r' :d'	t.d' :t.d'	t :			:d'
and give to rap - ture		all thy trembling strings;				From
.d :r.m	f :m	r.m :r.m	r :r	s .,s :s.f	m :s	f :
			From	Hel-i - con's harmo - nious		springs,
l :-.s	f :s	s.s :s.s	s :	:s	d'.,d': d'.ta	l :d'
give to rap - ture		all thy trembling strings;		From Hel-icon's har		-mo - nious
f :-.m	r :m.d	s,.d :s,.d	s, :	:	:d	f .,f :f.m
					From	Helicon's har-

dim. *p* *f*

f' .,f': f'.m'	r' :-.d'	s :—	— :—	— : .t	d' :m'	d' :—
Helicon's har	-mo - nious springs,			A	thou - sand	rills
: .d	s.f :f.m	m.r : .t,	d.t, :t,.d	d.t, : .r	m :s	m :-.m
har	-mo - nious springs,	har	-mo - nious springs,			
t :	:	: .s	s.f :f.m	m.r : .s	s :s	s :-.s
springs,		har	-mo - nious springs,	A	thou - sand	rills their
r :-.d	t, :-.d	d.t, :d.r	m.r :r.d	s, : .s,	d :d	d :-.d
mo - nious	springs, har-monious,	har	-mo - nious springs,			

St. Co. (New).

— :— |— :d'.s | l .s : f .m | d' : | .f' : m'.r' | d' : t | d' :— |— :

a | thou - sand rills | their mazy pro - gress | take,

f .m : f .m | f : m | f .m : r .d | l : | .l : s .f | m :.r | m :— |— : s,

mazy progress take,

l .s : l .s | l : d' | d'.m : f .s | l : | .d' : d'.l | s : s | s :— |— : s

mazy progress take, a | thou - sand rills | their mazy pro - gress | take, The

f .d : f .d | f : d | d : r .m | f : | .f : d .f | s : s, | d :— |— :

mf *dim* *p* *rall.*

: | : | : | : m'.d' | t :- .r'| d' : t.l | l : se | l :—

Drink | life and fragrance | as they flow.

d .m : - .r | r .d : t,.d | r : m | f : | : | : | : | :

laugh - ing flow'rs that | round them blow.

m : s | s : - .l | t : d' | r' : | : | | : | :

laugh-ing flow'rs that | round them blow.

: | : | : | : d'.l | se : - .t | l : r | m : - .m | l, :

Drink | life and fragrance | as they flow.

Largo e sostenuto.

f M. 60.

s : - .s | s :— | m : f | s : l | s :— | s : t | l : t | d' : - .d'

Now the rich | stream of | Mu - sic | winds a-

m : - .s | s :— | s : f | m : - .m | m : r | d : t, | d : r | m : fe

d' : - .m'| m' :— | m' : r' | d' : - .d' | d' : t | m' : r' | d' : t | l : - .l

Now the rich | stream of | Mu - sic | winds a-

d : - .d | d :— | d : r | m : fe | s :— | s, :— | l :— |— : l

p *f* *p* *ff*

t :— |— :— | s :— |— : t | d' :— | t :— | t : l |— : l

long | Deep, ma - | jes - tic, | smooth and

s :— |— :— | s, :— |— : r | m :— | r :— | r :— |— : r

r' :— |— :— | s :— |— : s | s :— | s :— | s : fe |— : fe

long; | Deep, ma - | jes - tic, | smooth and

s :— |— :— | s, :— |— : s, | d :— | s, :— | r :— |— : r

𝄋 *Spiritoso.* M. 152. *dolce.*

t :— |— || : | : | : | : m' | m' : - .f'| m' : r'

strong. | And | Ce - res' gold - en

r :— |— || *dolce.* : | : | : | : s | s : - .l | s : f

s :— |— || s | s : - .l | s : f | f : m | : | : | :

strong. | Thro' | ver - dant | vales,

s, :— |— || m | m : - .f | m : r | r : d | : | : | :

St. Co. (New).

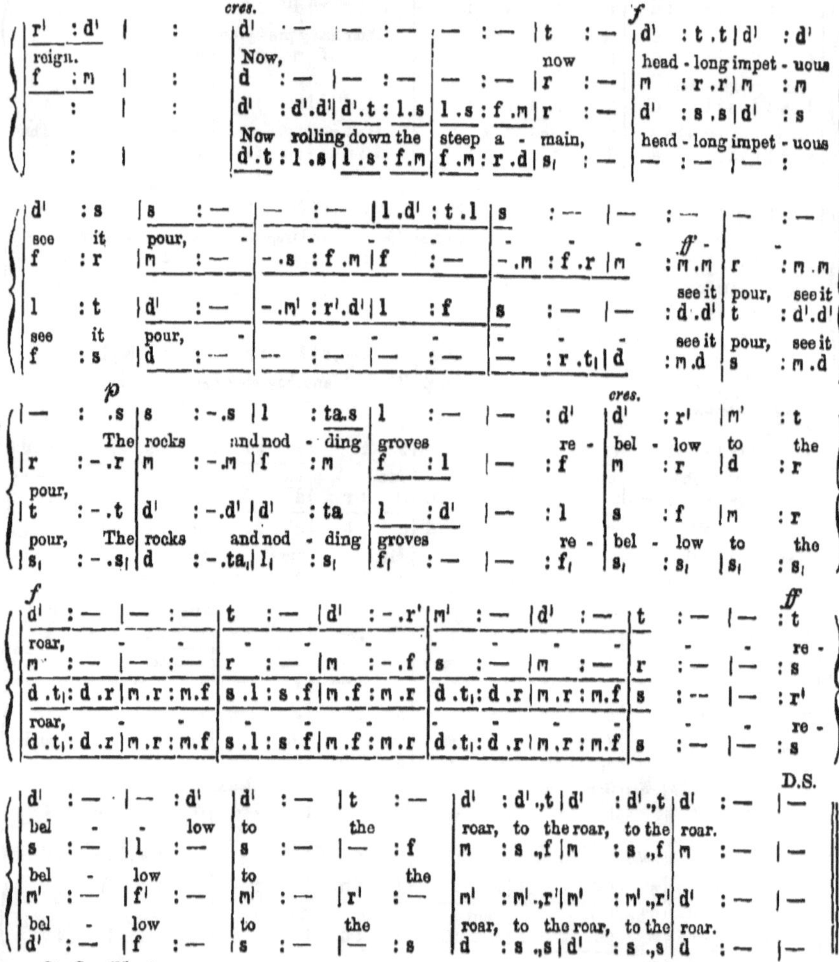

cres. *f*

r' :d'	:	d' :—	— :—	— :—	t :—	d' :t .t	d' :d'
reign.		Now, now	head - long impet - uous
f :m	:	d :—	— :—	— :—	r :—	m :r .r	m :m
:	:	d' :d'.d'	d'.t :l.s	l .s :f .m	r :—	d' :s .s	d' :s
		Now rolling down the	steep a - main,	head - long impet - uous
:		d'.t :l .s	l .s :f.m	f .m :r .d	s, :—	— :—	— :

d' :s	s :—	— :—	l .d' :t .l	s :—	— :—	— :—
see it pour, -	- - - -	- - - -	*ff* - -
f :r	m :—	— .s :f .m	f :—	— .m :f .r	m :m .m	r :m .m
			see it	pour, see it
l :t	d' :—	— .m' :r'.d'	l :f	s :—	— :d'.d'	t :d'.d'
see it pour, -	- - - -	- - -	see it	pour, see it
f :s	d :—	— :—	— :—	— :r .t,	d :m .d	s :m .d

p cres.

— : .s	s :— .s	l :ta.s	l :—	— :d'	d' :r'	m' :t
The	rocks and nod - ding	groves re -	bel - low to the
r :— .r	m :— .m	f :m	f :l	— :f	m :r	d :r
pour,
t :— .t	d' :— .d'	d' :ta	l :d'	— :l	s :f	m :r
pour, The	rocks and nod - ding	groves re -	bel - low to the
s, :— .s,	d :— .ta,	l, :s,	f, :—	— :f,	s, :s,	s, :s,

f *ff*

d' :—	— :—	t :—	d' :— .r'	m' :—	d' :—	t :—	— :t
roar, - -	- - - -	- - - -	- - re -
m :—	— :—	r :—	m :— .f	s :—	m :—	r :—	— :s
d .t, :d .r	m .r :m.f	s .l :s .f	m .f :m .r	d .t, :d .r	m .r :m.f	s :—	— :r'
roar, - -	- - - -	- - - -	- - re -
d .t, :d .r	m .r :m.f	s .l :s .f	m .f :m .r	d .t, :d .r	m .r :m.f	s :—	— :s

D.S.

| d' :— |— :d' | d' :— |t :— | d' :d' .,t |d' :d' .,t | d' :— |— ‖
| bel - - low | to the | roar, to the roar, to the | roar. |
| s :— |l :— | s :— |— :f | m :s .,f |m :s .,f | m :— |— ‖
| bel - low | to the |
| m' :— |f' :— | m' :— |r' :— | m' :m' .,r' |m' :m' .,r' | d' :— |— ‖
| bel - low | to the | roar, to the roar, to the | roar. |
| d' :— |f :— | s :— |— :s | d :s .,s |d' :s .,s | d :— |— ‖

St. Co. (New).

ADDITIONAL EXERCISES, PART 3.

For style of singing see "Hints on the Tunes."

Words by **WHERE THE GAY DREAMS OF CHILDHOOD?**
George Bennett. (Copyright.) *German Air.*
KEY G. *Moderato.* Harmonised by *Kücken.*

p	<	>	< >	> D. t.
: s, .,s,	s, .,m :.m :- .f	s :r :r .,m	f :l :- .s	m :— :ml
1 Where the	gay dreams of	child - hood, With the	love - light of	truth? The
: s, .,s,	s, .,d :d :- .d	t, :t, :t, .,d	t, :t, :- .t,	d :— :df
2 Where the	bright dreams of	man-hood, That would	seem not like	dreams, But
: m .,m	m .,s :s :- .f	r :s :f .,m	r :f :- .f	m :— :sd'
3. Let us	live for the	re - al, There's no	truth in our	dreams, They
: d .,d	d :d :- .l,	s, :s, :s, .,s,	s, :s, :- .s,	d :— :df

<	>	*mf* *dim.*	*p* f. G.	
l :- .s :s .t	r' :d' :t .,l	l :- .s :r .,m	d : :ds,	s, .,r :r :- .m
vi - sion of	beau - ty That	daz - zled our	youth? They	pass'd like the
f :- .f :f	f :m :re	m :- .m :t,	d : :ds,	s, .,t, :t, :- .t,
pre - sent and	cer - tain, The	sur - est of	schemes? We	near the temp-
t :- .t :t	t :d' :d'	d' :- .d' :f .,s	m : :ds,	s, .,f :f :- .s
melt like the	rain - bow, With	fair - est of	beams, In	youth's morn of
r :- .r :s	s :l :fe	s :- .s, :s,	d : :ds,	s, :s, :- .s,

		p f. C.	*poco accell.*	> D. t.m.
r :d :- .s,	s, .,f :f :- .s	m :— : .ds	s :l :t	r' :d' : .ls
cloud- lets By	morn - ing un-	roll'd, All	touch'd with the	glo - ries, All
s, :s, :- .s,	s, .,r :r :- .t,	d :— : .ds	s :fe :f	s :s : .ls
ta - tion, It	fades at the	touch, We	grasp at the	bub - ble, We
f :m :- .m	r .,s :s :- .s	s :— : .mt	t :d' :r'	f' :m' : .ls
beau - ty In	man - hood or	age, The	true and the	last - ing, The
d :d :- .d	t, :t, :- .s,	d :— : .ds	s :s :s	d :d : .ls

	> f. G.	*p* > > >	>	*f* >
s :l :t	r' :d' : .d's	s :l :t	r' :d' : .s	t :l :- .f
touch'd with the	glo - ries, All	touch'd with the	glo - ries Of	crim - son and
s :fe :f	s :s : .mt,	t, :d :r	d :d : .d	t, :t, :- .t,
grasp at the	bub - ble, We	grasp at the	bub - ble, It	bursts at the
t :d' :r'	f' :m' : .d's	s :fe :f	m :m : .m	r :r :- .s
true and the	last - ing, The	true and the	last - ing, Our	thoughts should en-
s :s :s	d :d : .ds,	s, :s, :s,	s, :s, : .s,	s, :s, :- .s,

LONDON: J. CURWEN & SONS, 8 & 9 WARWICK LANE, E.C. PRICE FOURPENCE.

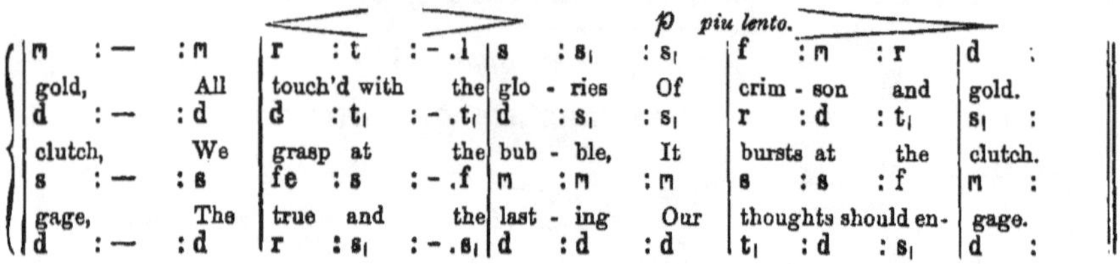

p piu lento.

m :— :m	r :t :-.l	s :s, :s,	f :m :r	d :
gold, All	touch'd with the	glo - ries Of	crim - son and	gold.
d :— :d	d :t, :-.t,	d :s, :s,	r :d :t,	s, :
clutch, We	grasp at the	bub - ble, It	bursts at the	clutch.
s :— :s	fe :s :-.f	m :m :m	s :s :f	m :
gage, The	true and the	last - ing Our	thoughts should en-	gage.
d :— :d	r :s, :-.s,	d :d :d	t, :d :s,	d :

THEME SUBLIME OF ENDLESS PRAISE.

KEY B♭. M. 60. *Handel.*

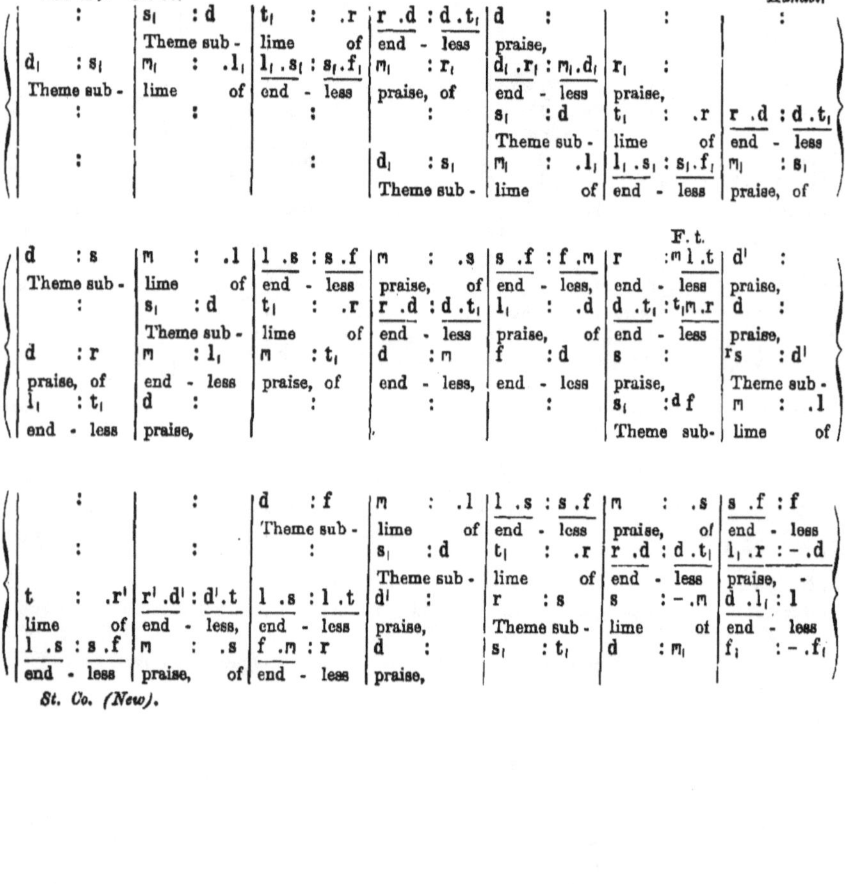

:	s, :d	t, : .r	r .d :d .t,	d :	:	:
	Theme sub -	lime of	end - less	praise,		
d, :s,	m, : .l,	l, .s, :s, .f,	m, :r,	d, .r, :m, .d,	r, :	
Theme sub -	lime of	end - less	praise, of	end - less	praise,	
:	:	:	:	s, :d	t, : .r	r .d :d .t,
				Theme sub -	lime of	end - less
:		:	d, :s,	m, : .l,	l, .s, :s, .f,	m, :s,
			Theme sub -	lime of	end - less	praise, of

					F. t.	
d :s	m : .l	l .s :s .f	m : .s	s .f :f .m	r :ᵐl .t	d' :
Theme sub -	lime of	end - less	praise, of	end - less,	end - less	praise,
:	s, :d	t, : .r	r .d :d .t,	l, : .d	d .t, :t,ᵐ.r	d :
	Theme sub -	lime of	end - less	praise, of	end - less	praise,
d :r	m :l,	m :t,	d :m	f :d	s :	ʳs :d'
praise, of	end - less	praise, of	end - less,	end - less	praise,	Theme sub -
l, :t,	d :	:	:	:	s, :ᵈf	m : .l
end - less	praise,				Theme sub-	lime of

:	:	d :f	m : .l	l .s :s .f	m : .s	s .f :f
		Theme sub -	lime of	end - less	praise, of	end - less
:	:	:	s, :d	t, : .r	r .d :d .t,	l, .r :- .d
			Theme sub -	lime of	end - less	praise, -
t : .r'	r' .d' :d' .t	l .s :l .t	d' :	r :s	s :- .m	d .l, :l
lime of	end - less,	end - less	praise,	Theme sub -	lime of	end - less
l .s :s .f	m : .s	f .m :r	d :	s, :t,	d :m,	f, :- .f,
end - less	praise, of	end - less	praise,			

St. Co. (New).

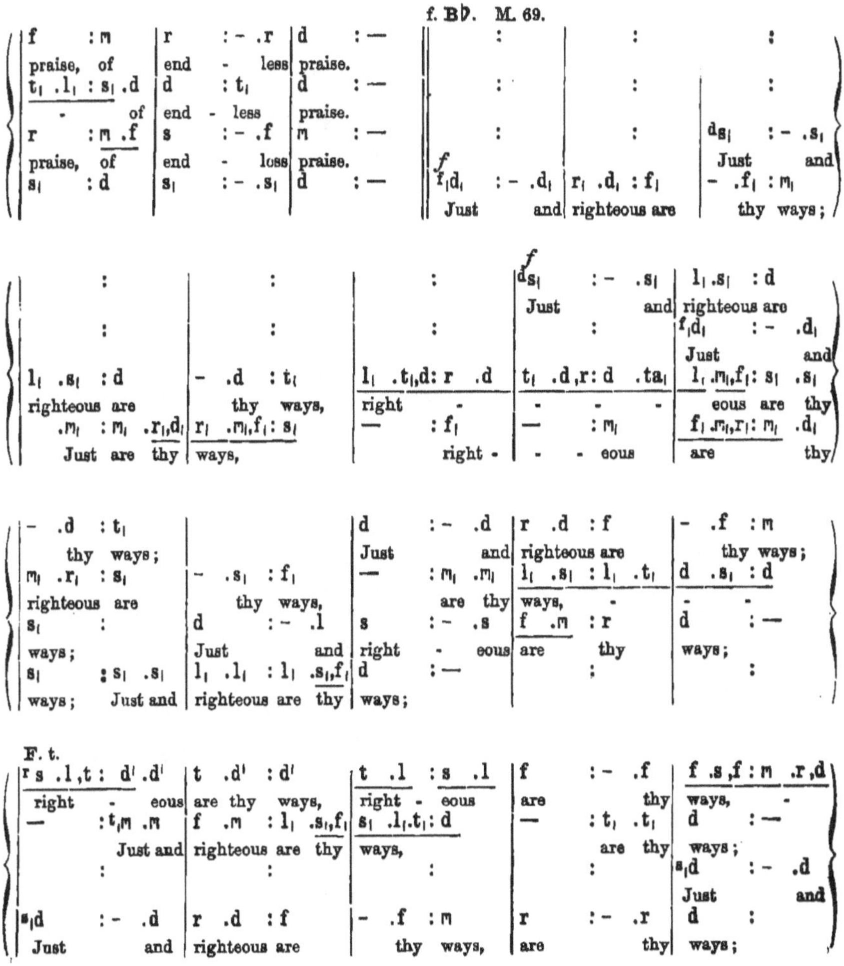

f. B♭. M. 69.

| f :m | r :- .r | d :— || : | : | : |
praise, of | end - less | praise.
| t₁ .l₁ : s₁ .d | d : t₁ | d :— || : | : | : |
- of | end - less | praise.
| r :m .f | s :- .f | m :— || : | : | ᵈs₁ :- .s₁ |
praise, of | end - less | praise. | | | Just and
| s₁ :d | s₁ :- .s₁ | d :— || *f* ᶠ₁d₁ :- .d₁ | r₁ .d₁ : f₁ | - .f₁ : m₁ |
|| Just and | righteous are | thy ways;

| : | : | : | *f* ᵈs₁ :- .s₁ | l₁ .s₁ : d |
| | | Just and | righteous are
| : | : | : | : | ᶠ₁d₁ :- .d₁ |
| | | | Just and
| l₁ .s₁ : d | - .d : t₁ | l₁ .t₁,d: r .d | t₁ .d ,r: d .ta₁ | l₁ .m₁,f₁: s₁ .s₁ |
righteous are | thy ways, | right - | - - - | eous are thy
| .m₁ : m₁ .r₁,d₁ | r₁ .m₁,f₁: s₁ | — : f₁ | — : m₁ | f₁ .m₁,r₁: m₁ .d₁ |
Just are thy | ways, | right - | - - eous | are thy

| - .d : t₁ | | d :- .d | r .d : f | - .f : m |
thy ways; | | Just and | righteous are | thy ways;
| m₁ .r₁ : s₁ | - .s₁ : f₁ | — : m₁ .m₁ | l₁ .s₁ : l₁ .t₁ | d .s₁ : d |
righteous are | thy ways, | are thy | ways, - | - -
| s₁ : | d :- .l | s :- .s | f .m : r | d :— |
ways; | Just and | right - eous | are thy | ways;
| s₁ : s₁ .s₁ | l₁ .l₁ : l₁ .s₁,f₁ | d :— | : | : |
ways; Just and | righteous are thy | ways;

F. t.
| ʳs .l ,t : d' .d' | t .d' : d' | t .l : s .l | f :- .f | f .s ,f : m .r ,d |
right - eous | are thy ways, | right - eous | are thy | ways, -
| — : t,m .m | f .m : l₁ .s₁,f₁ | s₁ .l₁,t₁ : d | — : t₁ .t₁ | d :— |
Just and | righteous are thy | ways, | are thy | ways;
| : | : | : | : | ˢ₁d :- .d |
| | | | Just and
| ˢ₁d :- .d | r .d : f | - .f : m | r :- .r | d : |
Just and | righteous are | thy ways, | are thy | ways;

St. Co. (New).

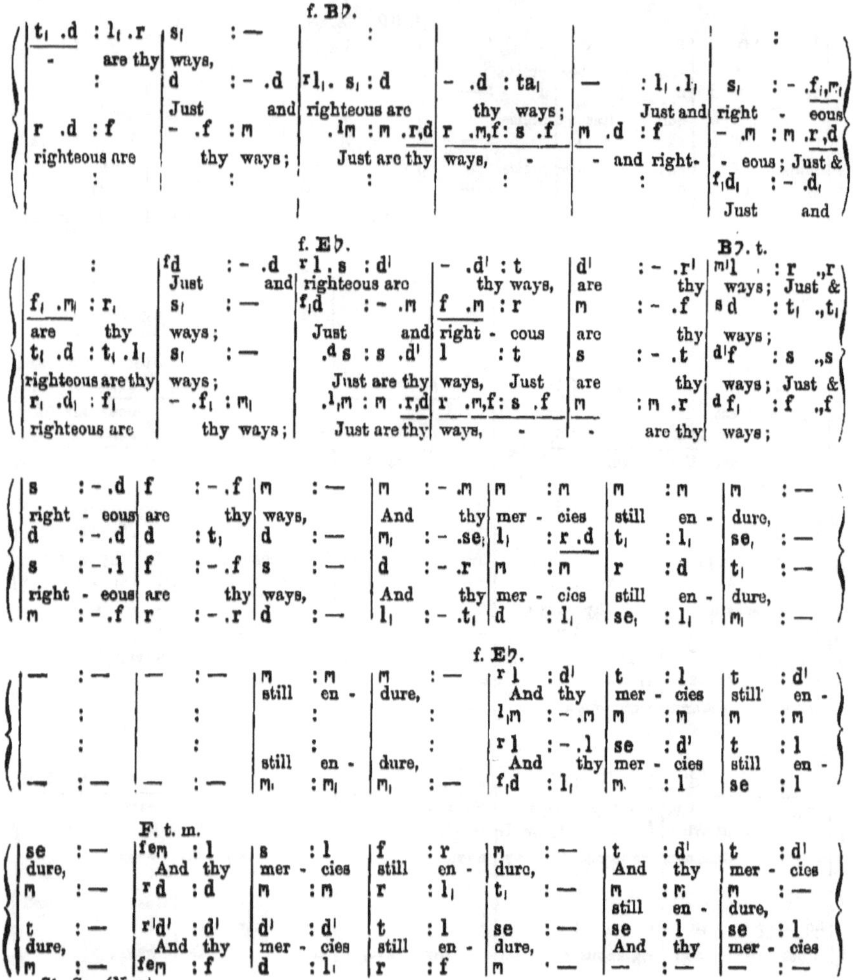

f. B♭.

t, .d : l, .r	s, :—	:			:
- are thy	ways,				
:	d :- .d	ʳl, . s, : d	- .d : ta,	— : l, .l,	s, :- .f,.m,
	Just and	righteous are	thy ways;	Just and	right - eous
r .d : f	- .f : m	.ˡm : m .r,d	r .m,f : s .f	m .d : f	- .m : m .r,d
righteous are	thy ways;	Just are thy	ways, -	- and right-	- eous; Just &
:	:	:	:	:	ᶠ,d, :- .d,
					Just and

f. E♭. B♭. t.

:	ᶠd :- .d	ʳl . s : d'	- .d' : t	d' :- .r'	ᵐ'l : r .,r
	Just and	righteous are	thy ways,	are thy	ways; Just &
f, .m, : r,	s, :—	ᶠ,d :- .m	f .m : r	m :- .f	ˢd : t, .,t,
are thy	ways;	Just and	right - eous	are thy	ways;
t, .d : t, .l,	s, :—	.ᵈs : s .d'	l : t	s :- .t	ᵈ'f : s .,s
righteous are thy	ways;	Just are thy	ways, Just	are thy	ways; Just &
r, .d, : f,	- .f, : m,	.l,m : m .r,d	r .m,f : s .f	m : m .r	ᵈf, : f .,f
righteous are	thy ways;	Just are thy	ways, -	- are thy	ways;

s :- .d	f :- .f	m :—	m :- .m	m : m	m : m	m :—
right - eous	are thy	ways,	And thy	mer - cies	still en -	dure,
d :- .d	d : t,	d :—	m, :- .se,	l, : r .d	t, : l,	se, :—
s :- .l	f :- .f	s :—	d :- .r	m : m	r : d	t, :—
right - eous	are thy	ways,	And thy	mer - cies	still en -	dure,
m :- .f	r :- .r	d :—	l, :- .t,	d : l,	se, : l,	m, :—

f. E♭.

— :—	— :—	m : m	m :—	ʳl : d'	t : l	t : d'
		still en -	dure,	And thy	mer - cies	still en -
:	:	:	:	ˡ,m :- .m	m : m	m : m
:	:	:	:	ʳl :- .l	se : d'	t : l
		still en -	dure,	And thy	mer - cies	still en -
— :—	— :—	m, : m,	m, :—	ᶠ,d : l,	m : l	se : l

F. t. m.

se :—	ᶠᵉm : l	s : l	f : r	m :—	t : d'	t : d'
dure,	And thy	mer - cies	still en -	dure,	And thy	mer - cies
m :—	ʳd : d	m : m	r : l,	t, :—	m : m	m :—
					still en -	dure,
t :—	ʳ'd' : d'	d' : d'	t : l	se :—	se : l	se : l
dure,	And thy	mer - cies	still en -	dure,	And thy	mer - cies
m :—	ᶠᵉm : f	d : l,	r : f	m :—	— :—	— :—

St. Co. (New).

f. B♭.

r :d' | t :— | l :-.t | d' :t.l | l :se.l | l :— | :
still en - | dure, | And thy | mer - cies | still en - | dure, |
— :— | — :— | m :-.r | d :f | m :-.m | m :— | fd :l1
 | | | | | | Ev - er
se :l | t :— | d' :-.t | l :r'.d' | t :-.t | d' :— | :
still en - | dure, | And thy | mer - cies | still en - | dure, |
m :l | se :— | l :f | d :r | m :-.m | l1 :— | :

: | : | : | : | .
s1 :f1 | m1,r1.m1,f1:s1 .t2 | d1 .d1,r1:m1,f1.s1,m1 | l1,s1.l1,t1:d,s1.l1,s1 | f1,s1.m1,f1:r1,s1.f1,s1
faith - ful, | ev - - er | sure, Ev - | - - | - - -
: | : | : | : | :
: | : | : | : | :

F. t.

d's :m | r :d f | m,r.m,f:s .t1 | d .d,r :m,f.s,m | l,s.l,t:d',s.l,s
Ev - er | faith - ful, | ev - - er | sure, Ev - | - -
m1 .d1 :s1 .d | t1 .s1 :m l1 .t1 | d,t1.d,r:m .s1 | l1 :d .m | f :m .d
- er, ev - er | faithful, ev- er, | ev - - er | sure, ev - er | sure, Ev - er
: | : | : | : | :
: | : | : | : | :

f,s.m,f:r,s.f,s | m .d :m .fe | s,fe.s,l:t,s.l,t | d' .t,l :s,f.m,r | m :s .m
- - | - er, ev - er | faith - - | - ful, ev - er | sure, ev - er
r .d :t1 .l1,t1 | d :d .r | t1,l1.t1,d:r,t1.d,r | s1 .s1,l1:t1 .r | s1 :d .m
faithful, ev - er | sure, Ev - er | faith - - | - ful, ev - er | sure, ev - er
: | d' :l | s :f | m,r.m,f :s .t1 | d .d,r :m,f.s,m
 | Ev - er | faith - ful, | ev - er | sure, Ev -
 | : | : | : | :

f. B♭.

d :f .r | mt1 : | | | d :l
sure, ev - er | sure, | | | Ev - er
f :l1 .f1 | sr1 :t1 t1 | d .t1,l1:s1,f1.m1,r1 | m1,r1.m1,f1:s1,l1.t1,s1 | d .l1 :d1 .f1
sure, ev - er | sure, Ev - er | faith - | - - - | - ful, ev - er
l,s.f,m:f,s.l,t | d's .f,m:r,d.t1,l1 | s1,f1.s1,l1:t1,r.s1 | s :m | f,m.f,s:l,s.f,s
- - - | - er, ev - er | faith - ful, | ev - er | faith - -
f :r | ds1 :f1 | m1,r1.m1,f1:s1 .t2 | d1 .d1,r1:m1,f1.s1,m1 | l1,s1.f1,m1:f1,s1.l1,t1
Ev - er | faith - ful, | ev - er | sure, Ev - | - - er

St. Co. (New).

s :f	m,r.m,f :s .t_1	d .d,r :m,f.s,m	l,s.f,m :f .s	m :—
faith - ful,	ev - - er	sure, ev - -	- - er	sure,
d :l_1 .r	d :t_1 .t_1	l_1 :s_1 .s_1	f_1 :d .s_1	s_1 :—
sure, ev - er	sure, ev - er	sure, ev - er	sure, ev - er	sure,
m,f.s,m :l .s	s :– .m	m :m .m	d :d .r	m :—
- - ful,	ev - - er	sure, ev - er	sure, ev - er	sure,
d,r.m,d :r .t_1	d,t_1.d,r :m .s_1	l_1,s_1.l_1,t_1 :d .d_1	f_1,m_1.f_1,s_1 :l_1 .t_1	d :—
ev - - er,	ev - - er	faith - ful,	ev - - er	sure,

:	:	:	:	:	d :l_1	s_1 :f_1
					Ev - er,	ev - er
:	:	:	:	d :l_1	s_1 :f_1	m_1 :d_1
				Ev - er	faith - ful,	ev - er
:	:	d :l	s :f	m :f	m :	d :l
		And thy	mer - cies	still en -	dure,	ev - er
d :d	d :–.d	d :d	d :—	— :—	— :—	— :—
And thy	mer - cies	still en -	dure,			

m_1 :—	s :m	r :d	s :m	r :—	s :m	r :—
sure,	Ev - er	faith - ful,	ev - er	sure,	ev - er	sure,
d :—	d :s_1	t_1 :s_1	t_1 :d	t_1 :—	d :s_1	t_1 :—
sure,						
s :—	d :m	s :m	r :d	s :—	m :d	s :—
sure,	Ev - er	faith - ful,	ev - er	sure,	ev - er	sure,
— :—	m_1 :d_1	s_1 :s_1	s_1 :s_1	s_1 :—	— :—	— :—
	And thy	mer - cies	still en -	dure,		

s :m	r :—	:	:	:
ev - er -	sure,			
t_1 :d	t_1 :—	d :l_1	s_1 :f_1	m_1,r_1.m_1,f_1 :s_1 .t_2
		Ev - er	faith - ful,	ev - er
r :d	s :—	f :d .r	m .s_1 :l_1 .t_1	d,t_1.d,r :m .s_1
ev - er	sure,	Ev - er	faith - ful,	ev - er
— :—	— :—	l_1 :f_1	d :	:
		ev - er	sure,	

St. Co. (New).

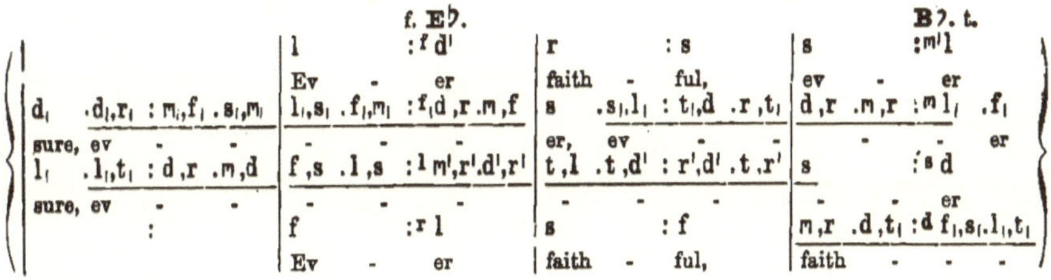

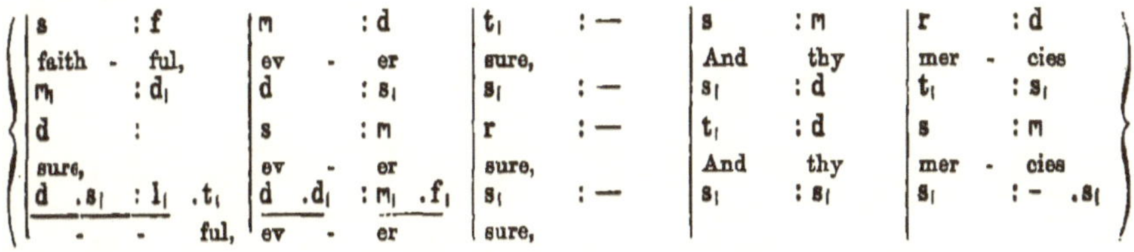

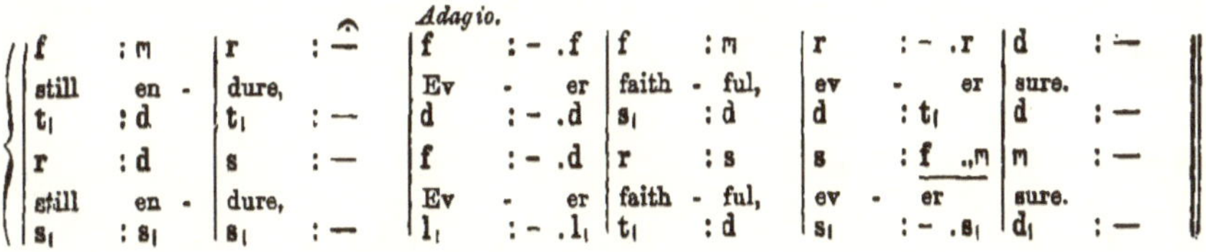

f. E♭. B♭. t.

	l :ᶠd'	r :s	s :ᵐ'l
	Ev - er	faith - ful,	ev - er
d, .d,r, :m,f, .s,m,	l,s, .f,m, :ᶠ,d ,r .m ,f	s .s,l, :t,d .r ,t,	d ,r .m ,r :ᵐl, .f,
sure, ev - -	- - - -	er, ev - -	- - er
l, .l,t, :d ,r .m ,d	f ,s .l ,s :ˡm',r'.d',r'	t ,l .t ,d' :r',d' .t ,r'	s :ˢd
sure, ev - -	- - -	- - -	- - er
:	f :ʳl	s :f	m ,r .d ,t, :ᵈf,s,.l,t,
	Ev - er	faith - ful,	faith - - -

s :f	m :d	t, :—	s :m	r :d
faith - ful,	ev - er	sure,	And thy	mer - cies
m, :d,	d :s,	s, :—	s, :d	t, :s,
d :	s :m	r :—	t, :d	s :m
sure,	ev - er	sure,	And thy	mer - cies
d .s, :l, .t,	d .d, :m, .f,	s, :—	s, :s,	s, :- .s,
- - ful,	ev - er	sure,		

Adagio.

f :m	r :— (pause)	f :- .f	f :m	r :- .r	d :—
still en -	dure,	Ev - er	faith - ful,	ev - er	sure.
t, :d	t, :—	d :- .d	s, :d	d :t,	d :—
r :d	s :—	f :- .d	r :s	s :f .,m	m :—
still en -	dure,	Ev - er	faith - ful,	ev - er	sure.
s, :s,	s, :—	l, :- .l,	t, :d	s, :- .s,	d, :—

THE WOODS.

KEY A. *Andante con moto.* M. 80. *Mendelssohn.*

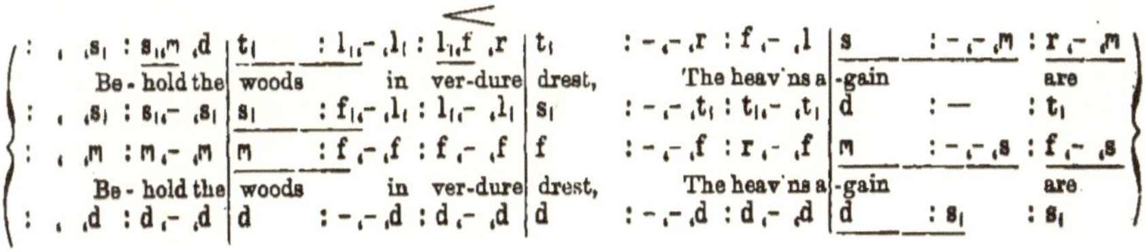

: ,s, :s,.,m ,d	t, :l,.- ,l, :l,.f ,r	t, :- .- ,r :f .- ,l	s :- .- ,m :r .- ,m
Be - hold the	woods in ver-dure	drest, The heav'ns a	-gain are
: ,s, :s,.- ,s,	s, :f,.- ,l, :l,.- ,l,	s, :- .- ,t, :t,.- ,t,	d :— :t,
: ,m :m .- ,m	m :f .- ,f :f .- ,f	f :- .- ,f :r .- ,f	m :- .- ,s :f .- ,s
Be - hold the	woods in ver-dure	drest, The heav'ns a	-gain are
: ,d :d .- ,d	d :- .- ,d :d .- ,d	d :- .- ,d :d .- ,d	d :s, :s,

St. Co. (New).

p E. t. *cres.*
d :-.,-. :ᵐl	l .-.s : l .-.s : l .-.s	s :— : s	f .-.m : f .-.f : l .-.f
bright: Re -	turn - ing Spring inspires the	breast, Re -	turn - ing Spring inspires the
d .-.s₁ : s₁.-.s₁ :ˢ₁d.-.d	r :— : r	s .-.d : d .-.d : d .-.d	d :— : t₁
bright: Return-ing Spring in	-spires the	breast, Return - ing Spring in	-spires the
m .-.m : m .-.m :ᵐl.-.l	t :— : t	d'.-.s : s .-.s : s .-.s	l :— : f
bright: Return-ing Spring in	-spires the	breast, Return - ing Spring in	-spires the
d₁.-.d : d .-.d :ᵈf.-.f	f :— : f	m .-.m : m .-.m : m .-.m	r :— : r

d. f. D. *L is B.* *dim.*
ᶠs : fe .-.r' : d' .-.t	l : t : m	d' :- .-.t : l .-.s
breast With hope and	calm de -	light, With hope and
ᵈr :- .-.f : m .-.f	m :— : r	d :- .-.r : m .-.m
ˡt : l .-.se : l .-.r'	d' : r' : se	l :- .-.se : l .-.d'
breast With hope and	calm de -	light, With hope and
ᵈr :- .-.t₁ : d .-.r	m :— : m	l₁ :- .-.t₁ : d .-.d

A. t.
ˢd : m .-.r : d .-.t₁	d :— :—	- .-.t₁ : f .-.r : d .-.t₁	d
calm de -	light,	With hope and calm de -	light.
ʳs₁ :— : s₁	s₁ .-.s₁ : l₁ .-.s₁ : l₁ .-.s₁	f₁ :— :—	m₁
calm de -	light, With hope and calm de -	light.	
ᵗm :— : f	m .-.m : f .-.m : f .-.m	r :— : s	—
calm de -	light, With hope and calm de -	light.	
ʳs₁ :— : s₁	d .-.d₁ : d₁ .-.d₁ : d₁ .-.d₁	d₁ :— :—	—

: .s₁ : s₁.m .d	t₁ : l₁.-.l₁ : l₁.f .r	t₁ :- .-.r : f .-.l	s :- .-.m : r .-.m
For-sake the	bus - y haunts of	men, Thou child of	toil and
: .s₁ : s₁.-.s₁	s₁ : f₁.-.l₁ : l₁.-.l₁	s₁ :- .-.t₁ : t₁.-.t₁	d :— : t
: .m : m .-.m	m : f .-.f : f .-.f	f :- .-.f : r .-.f	m :- .-.s : f .-.s
For-sake the	bus - y haunts of	men, Thou child of	toil and
: .d : d .-.d	d :- .-.d : d .-.d	d :- .-.d : d .-.d	d : s₁ : s₁

p E. t. *cres.*
d :-.,-. :ᵐl	l .-.s : l .-.s : l .-.s	s :— : s	f .-.m : f .-.f : l .-.f
care, Come,	roam the shady woodland	glen, Come,	roam the shady woodland
d .-.s₁ : s₁.-.s₁ :ˢ₁d.-.d	r :— : r	s .-.d : d .-.d : d .-.d	d :— : t₁
care, Come, roam the shady	wood - - land	glen, Come, roam the shady	wood - - land
m .-.m : m .-.m :ᵐl.-.l	t :— : t	d'.-.s : s .-.s : s .-.s	l :— : f
care, Come, roam the shady	wood - - land	glen, Come, roam the shady	wood - - land
d₁.-.d : d .-.d :ᵈf.-.f	f :— : f	m .-.m : m .-.m : m .-.m	r :— : r

St. Co. (New).

d. f. D. *L* is *B*. *dim.*

fs :fe ,– ,r' :d' ,– ,t | l :t :m | d' :– ,– ,t :l ,– ,s
glen, And breathe the | balm - - - y | air, And breathe the
dr :– ,– ,f :m ,– ,f | m :— :r | d :– ,– ,r :m ,– ,m
lt :l ,– ,se :l ,– ,r' | d' :r' :se | l :– ,– ,se :l ,– ,d'
glen, And breathe the | balm - - - y | air, And breathe the
dr :– ,– ,t_1 :d ,– ,r | m :— :m | l_1 :– ,– ,t_1 :d ,– ,d

A. t.

sd :m ,– ,r :d ,– ,t_1 | d :— :— | – ,– ,t_1 :f ,– ,r :d ,– ,t_1 | d
balm - - y | air, | And breathe the balmy | air.
rs_1 :— :s_1 | s_1 ,– ,s_1 :l_1 ,– ,s_1 :l_1 ,– ,s_1 | f_1 :— :— | m_1
balm - - y | air, And breathe the balmy | air.
tm :— :f | m ,– ,m :f ,– ,m :f ,– ,m | r :— :s | —
balm - - y | air, And breathe the balmy | air.
rs_1 :— :s_1 | d ,– ,d_1 :d_1 ,– ,d_1 :d_1 ,– ,d_1 | d_1 :— :— | —

: , ,s_1 :s_1,m ,d | t_1 :l_1,– ,l_1 :l_1,f ,r | t_1 . – ,– ,r :f ,– ,l | s :– ,– ,m :r ,– ,m
Here o-dours | float, and zephyrs | play, On morning's | gold - - en
: , ,s_1 :s_1,– ,s_1 | s_1 :f_1,– ,l_1 :l_1,– ,l_1 | s_1 :– ,– ,t_1 :t_1,– ,t_1 | d :— :t_1
: , ,m :m,– ,m | m :f ,– ,f :f ,– ,f | f :– ,– ,f :r ,– ,f | m :– ,– ,s :f ,– ,s
Here o-dours | float, and zephyrs | play, On morning's | gold - - en
: , ,d :d ,– ,d | d :– ,– ,d :d ,– ,d | d :– ,– ,d :d ,– ,d | d :s_1 :s_1

p E. t. *cres.*

d . – ,– , :m l | l ,– ,s :l , . ,s :l ,– ,s | s :— :s | f ,– ,m :f ,. ,f :l ,– ,f
beam; With | them thy griefs will pass a | -way, With | them thy grief will pass a-
d ,– ,s_1 :s_1,– ,s_1 :sd_1,– ,d | r :— :r | s ,– ,d :d ,– ,d :d ,– ,d | d :— :t_1
beam; With them thy griefs will | pass a - | way, With them thy griefs will | pass a -
m ,– ,m :m ,– ,m :m l ,– ,l | t :— :t | d' ,– ,s :s ,– ,s :s ,– ,s | l :— :f
beam; With them thy griefs will | pass a - | way, With them thy griefs will | pass a -
d_1,– ,d :d ,– ,d :d f , ,f | f :— :f | m ,– ,m :m ,– ,m :m ,– ,m | r :— :r

d. f. D. *L* is *B*. *dim.*

fs :fe ,– ,r' :d' ,– ,t | l :t :m | d' :– ,– ,t :l ,– ,s
way, And van - ish | like a | dream, And van - ish
dr :– ,– ,f :m ,– ,f | m :— :r | d :– ,– ,r :m ,– ,m
lt :l ,– ,se :l ,– ,r' | d' :r' :se | l :– ,– ,se :l ,– ,d'
way, And van - ish | like a | dream, And van - ish
dr :– ,– ,t_1 :d ,– ,r | m :— :m | l_1 :– ,– ,t_1 :d ,– ,d

St. Co. (New).

A. t.

sd :m ,- ,r :d ,- ,t,	d :— .—	- ,- ,t, :f ,- ,r :d ,- ,t,	d
like a	dream,	And van - ish like a	dream.
rs, :— :s,	s, ,- ,s, :l, ,- ,s, :l, ,- ,s,	f, :— :—	m,
like a	dream, And van-ish like a	dream.	
tm :— :f	m ,- ,m :f ,- ,m :f ,- ,m	r :— :s	—
like a	dream, And van-ish like a	dream.	
rs, :— :s,	d ,- ,d, :d, ,- ,d, :d, ,- ,d,	d, :— :—	—

HOME, O WHERE IS THY BLEST HAVEN.

Words by *George Bennett.*

Music by *G. Reichardt.*

Arranged for mixed voices* by ALFRED STONE.

KEY C. M. 64. TENOR SOLO.

:	: | :	: |	: | :	: | :
:m	d' :- .t | t .l :l .s	s :f | — :m	re : | re :	m :m | — :f .,m
Hm.				
:m	m :— | — :m	r :— | d :—	— : | l, :	d : | t, :—
:m	d' :— | — :l	l :— | — :—	— :d' | — :t .l	l : | l :se
Hm.				
:m	l :— | — :d	r :— | m :—	f : | f :	m : | m :—

l :- .t | d' :r'	m' :- .f' | m' .r' :d' .t	l :- .t | d' .,d' :r' .,r'	m' :— | — :—
Home, O where is	thy blest hav-en!	Sever'd now from all I	love,
pp			
m :— | — :—	— :— | — :—	— :— | — :—	— :— | se :t
Hm.			
d :— | — :—	r :— | — :—	d :— | — :—	t, :— | m :se
l :— | — :—	se :— | — :—	l :— | — :—	se :— | t :m'
Hm.			
m :— | — :—	— :— | — :—	— :— | — :—	— :— | — :—

*May be sung in key A♭. by A.T.B.B., and Baritone Solo.

f' :-.m' | r'.r' : s'.,f' | m' :— | — :— | m' :-.r' | r'.r' : m'.r' | r' : d' | — : t
All that with dear life is wove, Far away I toil with spi - - rit
pp
t :— | — :— | d' :— | s :m | l :— | — :— | s :— | — :—
s :— | — :— | s :— | m :d | r :— | — :— | m :— | f :—
Hm.
r' :— | f' :r' | m' :— | d' :s | l :— | — :— | s :d' | r' :—
s :— | — :— | d :— | — :— | f :— | — :— | s :— | — :—

r' :— | d' : | | | | : | : | :
crav - en. *mf*
t :— | d' :s | m' :-.r' | r'.d' : d'.t | t :l | — :— | s :-.l | t.,d' : r'.,m'
f :— | m :s | m :— | — :s | f :— | — :— | — :— | — :—
Hm.
s :— | — : | s :— | — :d' | d' :— | — :— | t :-.d' | r'.,d' : t
— :— | d : | d :— | — :m | f :— | — :— | s :— | — :—

: | :m' | m' :-.r' | r'.d' : d'.t | t :l | :l | s :- l | t.d' : r'.,m'
In fo - reign lands I am a stran - ger, No lov'd ones here with kindly
pp
r' :d' | : | s :— | — :— | l :— | — :— | s :— | — :—
Hm.
m :— | — :— | m :— | — :— | r :— | — :— | f :— | — :—
s :— | — :— | d' :— | — :— | — :— | — :— | t :— | — :—
Hm.
d :— | — :— | d :— | — :— | f :— | — :— | s :— | — :—

r' :d' | : | m' :-.m' | m'.f' : m'.r' | r' :d' | | d' :-.t | l.l : t.l
greet - ing, Words of welcome are re- peat - ing, Coldness haunts the unknown
— :— | — :s | se :— | — :— | l :— | — :— | — :— | — :—
Hm.
m :— | — :m | r :— | — :— | m :— | — :— | re :— | — :—
d' :— | — :d' | t :— | — :— | d' :— | — :— | — :— | — :t
Hm.
d :— | — :d | m :— | — :— | — :— | — :— | f :— | — :—

St. Co. (New.)

m' :— |— :— |m' :— | | : | : |l :-.t |d' :-.r'
ran - - - ger. Shall I ev - er
se :t |— :se |m :f.,m |m :— |— :f.,m |m :f.,m |m :m |— :m
Hm.
m :se |— :m |t, :d.,t, |t, :r |d :— |r :— |d :d |— :d
t :m' |— :t |se :l.,se |se :t |l :— |se :— |l :l |— :l
Hm.
m :m |— :— |m :— |— :— |m :— |— :— |m :m |— :m

m' :-.f' |m'.r' :d'.t |l :-.t |d'.,d' :r'.,r' |m'.,f' :m' |— :— |f' :-.m' |r'.,r' :s'.,f'
have to cheer me, One sweet form I lov'd so well? Tell me, heav'n, my spirit
pp
— :m |— :m |— :m |— :m |m :— |se :t |t :— |— :—
Hm.
r :r |— :r |d :d |— :d |t, :— |m :se |s :— |— :—
se :se |— :se |l :l |— :l |se :— |t :m' |r' :— |f' :r'
Hm.
— :m |— :m |— :m |— :m |m :— |— :— |s :— |— :—

m' :— |— :— |m' :-.r' |r'.r' :m'.r' |r' :d' |— :t |m'r' :— |d' :
tell, Point the home that I may have her near me.
mf
d' :— |s :m |l :— |— :— |s :— |— :— |t :— |d' :s
Hm.
— :— |m :d |r :— |— :— |m :— |f :— |f :— |m :m
m' :— |d' :s |l :— |— :— |s :d' |r' :— |s :— |— :d'
Hm.
d :— |— :— |f :— |— :— |s :— |— :— |s :— |d :d'

: | : | : | : | : | : | *pp* : | : | *ppp* : |
dim.
— :m' |-.r' :d'.t |r' :d' |— :t |— :l |— :se |l : |m : |d :— |—
Hm.
s :— |se :— |m :— |f :— |m :— |r :— |d : |d : |l, :— |—
m' :— |r' :— |d' :— |r' :— |d' :— |t :— |l : |l : |m :— |—
Hm.
d' :— |m :— |l :— |r :— |m :— |— :— |l, :— |— :— |l, :— |—

St. Co. (New.)

KEY D. **THE STOUT-LIMB'D OAK.** *J. Danby.*

:s |s :l |s :-.s |d'.t :l.s |f :— |— :-.f |m.m :s.s |d' :-.r' |t :—
The stout-limb'd oak that long has borne Th' unnumber'd shocks of win - try skies,
:m |m :f |m :-.m |l.s :f.m |r :— |— :-.r |d.d :r.r |m :fe |s :—
:d' |d' :d' |d' :— |— :-.m' |f'.m' :r'.d' |t :-.s |s.s :s.s |s :l |s :—
The stout-limb'd oak that long has borne Th' unnumber'd shocks of win - try skies,
:d |d :f |d :— |— :-.d |r.d :t,.l, |s, :-.s, |d.d :t,.t, |l, :r |s, :—

|d' :d'.d' |d'.t,l :t.s |d' :m' |l :-.r' |A. t. tm :m |r :-.r
Lift - ing its head with dauntless scorn, The wind's tu - mul - tuous rage de -
: | : | : | : |sd :d.d |d .t,,l, :t,.s,
Lift - ing its head with dauntless
: |r' :r'.r' |m' :d' |f' :r' |sd :-.m |s :f
Lift - ing its head with daunt - less scorn, The wind's tu -
: | : | : | : | : | :

|d :-.d |d :f |f :m |r .m,f :s .f |f. D. mt :— | .r' :r'.r'
fies, The wind's tu - mul - tuous rage de - fies, The winds tu-
d :m |l, :-.r |t, :d |d :t,. |ds :— | .t :t.t
scorn, The wind's tu - mul - tuous rage de - fies,
m :d |f :r |s :— |— :— | : | :
mul - tuous rage de - fies, Lift - ing its head with dauntless
: | : | : | : |s :s.s |s,f.s,l :s,f.m,r

|m' :m' |f' :r' (tr) |d' :— |— : |A. t. r's :s.s |s,f.s,l :s,f.m,r
mul - tuous rage de - fies, Lift - ing its head with dauntless
d' :s |f :-.f |s :— | : |t m :m.m |m,r.m,f :m,r.d,t,
fd' :d'.d' |d'.t,l :t.s |d' :m' |l :-.r' |t m :d |s, :-.s,
Lift - ing its head with dauntless scorn, The wind's tu - mul - tuous rage de -
d : |r :r.r |m :d |f :r |s d :— | :
scorn, Lift - ing its head with daunt - less scorn,

|m :-.m |f :-.f |m :— |f :— |f :m |r :-.r
scorn, The wind's tu - mul - tuous rage de -
d :-.d |r :-.r |d :— |— :r |r :d |— :t,
d :— | : | .s |l :-.f |s :s |s :-.s
fies, The wind's tu - mul - tuous rage de -
d :d.d |d .t,,l, :t,.s, |d :m |l, :-.r |t, :d |s, :-.s,
Lift - ing its head with dauntless scorn,

St. Co. (New).

```
 1st time.          D.C.|| 2nd time.  𝄋                          tr
|mt   :—   |—          ||mt   :—    ||m'.r':d'.t  |l   :s   |f   :-.f  |m    :-.d' |t .d' :r'.d'
 fies                    fies.        And should it fall, and should it fall, its buoyant, buoyant
|mt   :—   |—          ||mt   :—    ||m'.r':d'.t  |l   :s   |f   :-.f  |m    :-.l  |se.l  :t .l
|sr'  :—   |—          ||sr'  :—    ||m'.r':d'.t  |l   :s   |f   :-.f  |m    :—    |—     :—
 fies.                   fies.        And should it fall, and should it fall,
|ds   :—   |—          ||ds   :—    ||m .r :d .t, |l,  :s,  |f,  :-.f, |m,   :—    |—     :—

|t    :t   |d'.t  :d'.m' |m'.r',d':r'  |-.d',t:d'.r' |d'.t :l .se |l    :-.
 course, its buoyant course It guides a-long   the roll - ing waves,
|se   :se  |l .se :l .se |l    :-.l    |se.m  :-.f   |m .r :d .t, |d    :-.
|—    :    |      :      |     :       |      :      |     :      |     : .d'
                                                                          the
|—    :m   |l .m  :l .m  |f    :-.f    |f .se :l .r  |m    :-.m   |l,   :-.l,
      its   buoyant course It guides a-long   the roll - ing waves,

|     :      |      : .d' |r'.m':f'.m'|r'.d':t .l |s    :     |     : .s  |l .t :d'.t |l .s :f .m
                     the   roll  -  -  ing         waves,             the   roll  -  -  ing
|     :      |      : .s  |t .d':r'.d'|t .l :s .f |m    :     |     : .m  |f .s :l .s |f .m :r .d
|l .t :d'.t  |l .s  :f .m |r    :     |     : .r  |m .f :s .f |m .r :d .t,|l,   :-.l  |l    :l
 roll  -  -   ing          waves,            the   roll  -  -  ing         waves, the roll - ing
|f .s :l .s  |f .m  :r .d |t,   :     |     : .t, |d .r :m .r |d .t,:l,.s,|f,   :-.f, |f,   :f,

 tr
|m    :—   |r    :𝄐—   |d'   :d' .,d' |d'   :f'   |m'   :d'   |d'   :f'
 waves,                 And   though assail'd with e  -  qual   force The
|d    :—   |t,   :—    |d    :d  .,d  |m    :f    |s    :f    |d    :r
|s    :—   |—    :—    |m    :l  .,l  |s    :t    |d'   :l    |s    :t
 waves,                 And   though assail'd with e  -  qual   force The
|s,   :—   |—    :—    |d    :f  .,f  |m    :r    |d    :f    |m    :r

                                                s. d. f. F.
|m'   :-.m' |r'   :r'  |d'   :-.t,l |t    :t    |d'l.s :f .m |f,m r,d:r,d.t,,l,
 roar  - ing tem - pest still    it   braves, The roar - ing  tempest still it
|m .s :-.d' |t    :s   |s    :fe    |s    :t    |d'l.s :f .m |f,m.r,d:r,d.t,,l,
|d'   :-.d' |s    :t   |l    :-.r'  |r'   :r'   |d'l.s :f .m |f,m.r,d:r,d.t,,l,
 roar  - ing tem - pest still    it   braves, The roar - ing  tempest still it
|d,t,.d.r:m,r.m,fe|s :s|d    :r     |s,   :s    |d'l.s :f .m |f,m.r,d:r,d.t,,l,
```

St. Co. (New).

D. t. m. l. tr D.S.

ms :—	— :r'	m' :m'	m' :r'	d' :—	t :—	d' :—
braves,	The	roar - ing	tem - pest	still	it	braves.
se,t, :—	— :t	d' :d'	d' :l	s :—	— :s	s :—
t,r :—	— :r'	d' :m'	s' :f'	m' :—	r' :—	m' :—
braves,	The	roar - ing	tem - pest	still	it	braves.
m,s, :—	— :s	d' :l	m :f	s :—	— :s,	d :—

MORNING PRAYER.

Words by *J. S. Stallybrass.*

Music by *Mendelssohn.*

KEY C. *Adagio.* M. 69.

f :s	m' :-.m'|r' :d'	f' :-.f'|m' :r'	*p* s :l.,f|f :m	*pp* f :f |m :-.m
A	sol - emn calm, a	si - lence ho - ly,	Now lies on all things	far and nigh; The
:m	s :-.s|f :m	l :-.l|s :s	s :l.,f|f :m	m :r.,d|t, :-.r
:d'	m' :-.m'|t :d'	d' :-.d'|d' :t	s :l.,f|f :m	l :t.,l|se :-.se
A	sol - emn calm, a	si - lence ho - ly,	Now lies on all things	far and nigh; The
:d	d' :-.d'|s :l	r :-.r|s :s	s :l.,f|f :m	r :r |m :-.m

cres. l :l |l :se	d' :d' |d' :t .l	*sf* *dim.* r' :-.t|s :l	s :-.s|s :—
woods a - lone are	bend - ing low - ly, To	greet their Ma - ker	pass - ing by,
d .r :m .f|m :-.r	d .m :l .s|fe :fe.l	s :f |m :ma	r :f |m :—
l .t :d'.r'|d' :-.t	l .t :d'.m'|l :r'.fe	s :-.s|s :d'	d' :t |d' :-.m'
woods a - lone are	bend - ing low - ly, To	greet their Ma - ker	pass - ing by. To
l, :l, |m :-.m	l .s :fe.m|r :r .d	t, :-.t,|d :{fe / fe,}	{s / s,} :{s / s,} |d :-.d'

— : |	*f* :.d'|d' :t.,l	*p* s :-.s|s :s	s :— |—	*f* s
	To greet their	Ma - ker pass - ing	by.	I
f :.f|f :m.,r	d :ta |l :ma	r :-.m|f :f	m :— |—	m
f' To greet their	Ma - ker, greet their	Ma - ker pass - ing	by.	
m' :r'.,d'|t :-.s'	s' :f'.,m'|f' :d'	d' :-.d'|d' :t	d' :— |—	d'
greet their Ma - ker	pass - ing by, their	Ma - ker pass - ing	by.	I.
d' :t.,l|s :-.f	m :r.,d|f :fe	s :-.{s / s,}|{s / s,} :{s / s,}	d :— |—	d

St. Co. (New).

p pp
m' :-.m'|r' :d' |f' :-.f'|m' :r' |s :l.,f|f :m |f :f |m :-.m
feel my be - ing new - cre-a - ted, Where is the care, the tor - ment gone? The
s :-.s|f :m |l :-.l|s :s |s :l.,f|f :m |m :r.,d|t, :-.r
m' :-.m'|t :d' |d' :-.d'|d' :t |s :l.,f|f :m |l :t.,l|se :-.se
feel my be - ing new - cre-a - ted, Where is the care, the tor - ment gone? The
d' :-.d'|s :l |r :-.r|s :s |s :l.,f|f :m |r :r |m :-.m

cres. sf dim.
l :l |l :se |d' :d' |d' :t.l |r' :-.t|s :l |s :-.s|s :—
fears that late - ly o - ver - weighted, Re -tire a - bash'd be - fore the Dawn,
d.r :m.f|m :-.r |d.m :l.s|fe :fe.l |s :f |m :ma |r :f |m :—
l.t :d'.r'|d' :-.t |l.t :d'.m'|l :r'.fe |s :-.s|s :d' |d' :t |d' :-.m'
fears that late - ly o - ver - weighted, Re -tire a - bash'd be - fore the Dawn, Re-
l, :l, |m :-.m |l.s :fe.m|r :r.d |t, :-.t,|d :{fe / fe,} |{s / s,} :{s / s,} |d :-.d'

f p f
— : ¦ | : .d'|d' :t.,l |s :-.s|s :s |s :— |— || s
Re-tire a- bash'd be-fore the Dawn. The
f
: .f|f :m.,r |d :ta |l :ma |r :-.m|f :f |m :— |— || m
Re-tire a- bash'd, re - tire a - bash'd be-fore the Dawn.
m' :r'.,d'|t :-.s' |s' :f'.,m'|f' :d' |d' :-.d'|d' :t |d' :— |— || s
tire a - bash'd be -fore the Dawn, a - bash'd be-fore the Dawn. The
d' :t.,l|s :-.f |m :r.,d|f :fe |s :-.{s|s :s / s,|s, :s,} |d :— |— || d

p pp
m' :-.m'|r' :d' |f' :-.f'|m' :r' |s :l.,f|f :m |f :f |m :-.m
world, with all its joy and sor - row, Is but a bridge o'er time's deep flood, That
s :-.s|t :d' |l :-.l|s :s |s :d.,t,|d :d.m |m :r |de :-.de
d' :-.d'|f' :m' |f' :-.f'|d' :t |d' :d'.,s|s :s |l :l |l :-.l
world, with all its joy and sor - row, Is but a bridge o'er time's deep flood, That
d :m |s :l |r :-.r|s :-.f |m :f.,r|r :d |f, :f,.s,|l, :-.s

cres. f cres. sf
l :l |l :se |d' :d' |d' :t.l |r' :f' |m' :-.r' |d' :r'.t|s' :—
I, a cheer-ful pil - grim, bor - row, To bear me to my home and God.
de.r :m.f|m :-.r |d.m :l.s|fe :fe.fe |s :-.s|s :l |s :-.s|s :—
f
l :l.r'|t :-.t |l.t :d'.m'|l :r'.r' |r' :-.r'|m' :d'.r' |m' :t.r'|d' :-.m'
I, a cheer - ful pil - grim, bor - row, To bear me to my home and God. To
f .:m.r|m :-.m |l.s :fe.m|r :r.d' |t :-.t|d' :f |s :f |m :-.d'

St. Co. (New).

— :	:	: .d'	d' : t .,l	s : - .s	s : s	s : —	—	
	To bear me	to my home and	God.
f — : .f	f : m .,r	d : ta	l : ma	r : - .m	f : f	m : —	—	
To bear me	to my home, my	home, my home and	God.
m' : r' .,d'	t : - .s'	s' : f' .,m'	f' : d'	d' : - .d'	d' : t	d' : —	—	
bear me to my	home and God, my	home, my home and	God.
d' : t .,l	s : - .f	m : r .,d	f : fe	s : - .{s, s₁}	{s, s₁} : {s, s₁}	d : —	—	

YE SPOTTED SNAKES.

KEY A. *Andante.* M. 96. *R. J. S. Stevens.*

mf
: d : t₁ .d | l₁ .t₁ : d : r : m .f | f : m | m : - .m | m .r : d .t₁ | t₁ : l₁ | s₁ : | :
Ye spotted | snakes with dou - ble | tongue, Thor - ny | hedge-hogs be not | seen;
| s₁ : s₁ .s₁ | f₁ : s₁ | l₁ : s₁ | s₁ : — | s₁ : s₁ | s₁ : l₁ .s₁ | s₁ : fe₁ | s₁ : *p* | :
| m : r .d | d : d | d : t₁ | d : — | d : d | r : m | r : - .d | t₁ : s | — : f
Ye spotted | snakes with dou - ble | tongue, Thor-ny | hedge-hogs be not | seen; Newts and
| d₁ : r₁ .m₁ | f₁ : m₁ | r₁ : s₁ | d₁ : — | d : - .d | t₁ : d | r : r₁ | s₁ : *p* | l₁ : - .r

| : | : | *p* : r | — : d f | f : m | s : s | s : — | *cres.* l : - .l
Newts and | blind worms do no | wrong; Come not
p : d | — : ta₁ | ta₁ : l₁ | ta₁ : l₁ r | r : d | f : m | m : r | f : - .d
Newts and | blind worms, newts
f : m | f : r | s : f | s : m l | t : d' | r' : d' | d' : t | d' : - .d'
blind worms, newts and | blind worms, newts and | blind worms do no | wrong; Come not
t₁ : d | r : - .s₁ | m₁ : f₁ | m₁ : l₁ r | s : l | t : d' | s : — | f : - .f

| s .m : r .d | f : m | m : r | s : r | m .fe : s | s : fe
near our fai - ry | queen, Come not | near our fai - ry
| d : d | t₁ : d | d : t₁ | r : r | d : r | d .r,m : r .d
| s : s | s : s | s : — | s : - .s | s : s | l : l
near our fai - ry | queen, Come not | near our fai - ry
| m : m | r : d | s₁ : — | t₁ : - .t₁ | d : t₁ | l₁ : r

St. Co. (New).

| s :— | : | : | . | : | : | : | :
queen, *Con espres.* *p*
| d :t₁ | s₁ :–.s₁ | l₁.t₁:d | r :m.f | f :m | | : *p* | d.t₁:d.l₁
Phi - lo- mel with mel - lo - dy, Sing in
| s :— | : | : | : | : *p* | m.r:m.d | r :s | — :fe
queen, Sing in your sweet
| s₁ :— | : | : | : | : | *p* :d | — :t₁ | l₁ :—
Sing in your

p *cres.*
| : | f.m:f.r | m.fe:s | s :fe | s :— | f.m:f.r | m.f:s.l | m :r
Sing in your sweet lul - la - by, sing in your sweet lul - la -
| t₁ :d | — :t₁ | d :r | m :r | f.r:m.d | l₁ :s₁ | d :–.d | d :t₁
your sweet lul - la - by, sing, sing in your,
cres.
| s.f:m | r :s | — :— | d'.t:d'.l | t :d' | — :t | d' :m.l | s :–.f
lul - la - by, sing, sing in your sweet lul - la, lul - la-
cres.
| s₁ :— | — :— | d :t₁ | l₁ :— | s₁ :— | r :— | d.r:m.f | s :s₁
sweet lul - la - by, sing in your sweet lul - la -

p *pp* *mf*
| d :m.m | f.f:r.r | s :d.d | r.r:t₁.t₁ | d : 𝄐 | s :f.m | l :t.d' | r :m.f
by, lul-la, lul-la, lul-la- by, lul-la, lul-la, lul-la- by. Nev - er harm, nor spell, nor
| d :s₁.s₁ | l₁.l₁:t₁.t₁ | d :*pp* | :s₁.s₁ | s₁ : | d :r.m | f :d | d :t₁
| m : | *p*:s.s | s :m.m | f.f:r.r | m : | s.l:t.d' | d' :t.l | s :s
by, lulla- by, lul-la, lul-la, lul-la- by. Nev - er harm, nor spell, nor
| d : | :s.s | m : | *pp*:s₁.s₁ | d : | m :r.d | f :f | s :s

un poco cres. *dim.*
| f :m | s :f.m | l :–.s | f.m:r.d | r :— | s :f.m | l :— | r :s
charm, Come our love - ly la - dy nigh, So good night, so good
| d :— | d :r.m | f :d | t₁.d:s₁.l₁ | d :t₁ | d :d | d :— | d :t₁
| l :— | m.s:t.d' | d' :–.s | s :–.fe | s :— | m :f.s | f :— | s :s
charm, Come our love - ly la - dy nigh; So good night, so good
| l₁ :— | m :r.d | f :–.m | r.d:t₁.l₁ | s₁ :— | m :r.d | f :— | s :s

St. Co. (New).

```
        p                                               pp                              dim.
f  :m̂  |d'. :d'. |d'  :-.m.f .r :d .t₁|d  :m .m|f .f :r .r |s   :d .d|r .r :t₁.t₁
night,   so  good |night, with lulla, lulla-|by, lul-la, lul-la, lul-la-|by, lul-la, lul-la, lul-la-
d  :—  |d . :d . |d   :-.d|d .r :s₁    |s₁  :s₁.s₁|l₁.l₁:t₁.t₁|d   :    |    :s₁.s₁
                    with lul - la -    |by,        pp              dim.
l  :—  |s . :l . |s   :-.s|l .f :m.r   |m   :    |    :s .s |s   :m .m|f .f :r .r
night,   so  good |night, with lulla, lulla-|by,            lulla-|by, lul-la, lul-la, lul-la-
l₁ :—  |m . :f . |m   :-.d|f    :s     |d   :    |    :s .s |m   :    |    :s₁.s₁
                    with lul - la -    |by,

f. A.  D.C. 𝄋                                              f. D. mf
ds₁ :—  ||    :        |      |        |    |s₁r  :m .f |s .f :s .m|f .m :r .s
by.     || mf                                Weav-ing    |spi - ders come not
s₁r₁ :— ||r₁  :m₁.f₁ |s₁  :m₁  |f₁  :r₁ |m₁  :—  |m₁t₁ :d .r |m  r :m .d|r .d :t₁.r
           Weav-ing    spi - ders come not here,
mt₁ :—  ||t₁  :d .r  |d   :-.d |d   :t₁ |d   :—  |ds  :-.f |m   :l   |r   :s
by.     ||Weav-ing    |spi - ders come not |here,      Weav- ing|spi - ders come not
ds₁ :—  ||s₁  :-.f₁  |m₁.r₁:m₁.d₁|r₁ :s₁ |d   :—  |    :     |    :    |    :

          f                                               ff
f  :m   |t   :     |d'  :-.t|l   :s   |l   :s   |    :s   |l   :l   |s   :f
here,     Hence,    |hence, ye long-legg'd |spin - ners,   ye |long- legg'd spin - ners
r  :d   |f   :     |m   :-.m|d   :d   |d   :d   |d   :-.d |d   :r   |m   :r
                                                   hence,
d  :—   |r'  :     |d'  :-.s|l   :d'  |d'  :d'  |    :m   |f   :f   |d'  :s
here,     Hence,    |hence, ye long-legg'd |spin - ners,   ye |long- legg'd spin - ners
   :    |ds  :     |d   :-.d|f   :m   |f   :m   |    :d   |f   :r   |s   :s₁

        d. f. C. L is A.                                 cres.       f
m  :—p|sl  :l   |t   :t   |d'  :r'  |m'  :—  |t   :t   |d'  :—  |t   :—
hence!   Bee-tles |black ap - proach not |near;    Worm and |snail     do
d  :—  |rm  :l   |l   :se  |l   :l   |l   :se  |m   :f   |m   :—  |f   :—
s  :—  |tad' :d' |t   :m'  |m'  :r'  |d'  :t   |s   :s   |s   :—  |t   :r'
hence!   Bee-tles |black ap - proach not |near;    Worm and |snail     do
d  :—  |sl  :l   |m   :m   |l   :f   |m   :—  |m   :r   |d   :—  |s   :—

                                        cres.
l  :—  |—   :l   |l   :se  |t   :t   |d'  :r'  |m'  :l .t |d'  :—  |t   :—
no           of - |fence,     worm and |snail          do |no        of -
m  :—  |m   :—   |m   :—   |m   :se  |l   :s .f|m   :f   |m   :—  |—   :r
d' :—  |d'  :—   |t   :—   |se  :m'  |m'  :r'  |d'.t :l |l   :—  |se  :—
no       of  -    |fence,     worm and |snail          do |no        of -
l  :—  |—   :l   |m   :—   |m   :m   |l₁  :t₁  |d   :r   |m   :—  |—   :m
```

St. Co. (New).

A. t.m.l. *Con espressione.*

```
|¹d :— p|s, :-.s,|l,.t,:d |r :m.f |f :m | | : | :
 fence. Phi - lo- mel with mel - o - dy,
|ᵈᵉm :— | : | : | : | : | | : p|d.t,:d.l,
                                                          Sing in
|¹d :— | : | : | | : p|m.r:m.d |r :s |— :fe
 fence.                                 Sing in your sweet
|¹,d, :— | : | : | | p:d |— :t, |l, :—
                                            Sing in your

      p                 cres.                  mf
| : |f.m:f.r |m.fe:s |s :fe |s :— |f.m:f.r |f.m:r.d |d :t,
      Sing in your sweet lul - la - by, sing in your sweet lul - la -
|t, :d |— :t, |d :r |d.t,:d.l, |t, :d |— :t, |d :l, |s, :-.f,
 your sweet lul - la - by, in your sweet lul - la, lul - la-
|s.f:m |r :s |— :— |m :r |f.r:m.d |r :-.s |l.s:f.m |m :r
 lul - la - by, sing, sing in your sweet lul - la- by, sweet lul - la -
|s, :— |— :— |d :t, |l, :— |s, :— |— :s, |d :f, |s, :s,
 sweet lul - la - by, sing in your sweet lul - la -

    p              pp                        mf
|d :s,.s,|l,.l,:t,.t,|d :s,.s,|l,.l,:t,.t,|d :— |d :r.m |r :r |s :-.f
 by, lul-la, lul-la, lul-la- by, lul-la, lul-la, lul-la- by. Nev - er harm, nor spell, nor
|m, :m,.m,|f,.f,:s,.s,|m, :m,.m,|f,.f,:s,.s,|m, :— |s, :s, |l, :l, |t, :t,
 by,          p                 pp
|d : | :r.r |d : | :r.r |d :— |m :r.d |f :f |r :r
 by, lulla- by, lulla- by. Nev - er harm, nor spell, nor
|d, : | :s,.s, |d, : | :s,.s, |d, :— |d :d |d :d |t, :s,

                                            p           dim.
|f :m |d :d |d :r.m|f :m |m :r |s :f.m |l :— |r :s |f :m
 charm, Come our love- ly la - dy nigh; So good night, so good night,
|d :— |s, :l, |s, :t,.d|r :d |d :t, |d :d |d :— |s, :t, |d :—
|l :— |m :f |m :s |s :s |s :— |s :s |f :— |s :r |d :—
 charm, Come our love- ly la - dy nigh; So good night, so good night,
|l, :— |d :d |d.m:r.d|t, :d |s, :— |m :r.d |f :— |t, :s, |l, :—

                       pp                                               D.S.
|s. :l. |s :-.m|f.r:d.t,|d :s,.s,|l,.l,:t,.t,|d :s,.s,|l,.l,:t,.t,|d :—
 so good night, with lulla, lulla- by, lul-la, lul-la, lul-la- by, lul-la, lul-la, lul-la- by.
|d. :d. |d :-.s,|l, :s, |s, :m,.m,|f,.f,:s,.s,|m, :m,.m,|f,.f,:s,.s,|m, :—
 lul - la - by,              pp                    dim.
|s. :f. |s :-.d|d.f:m.r |m : | :r.r |d : | :r.r |d :—
 so good night, with lulla, lulla- by, lulla- by, lulla- by.
|m. :f. |m :-.d|f, :s, |d : | :s,.s, |d, : | :s,.s, |d, :—
 lul - la - by,
```

St. Co. (New).

O SAVIOUR OF THE WORLD.

KEY A♭. *Andantino.* M. 60. (COPYRIGHT.) *John Goss.*

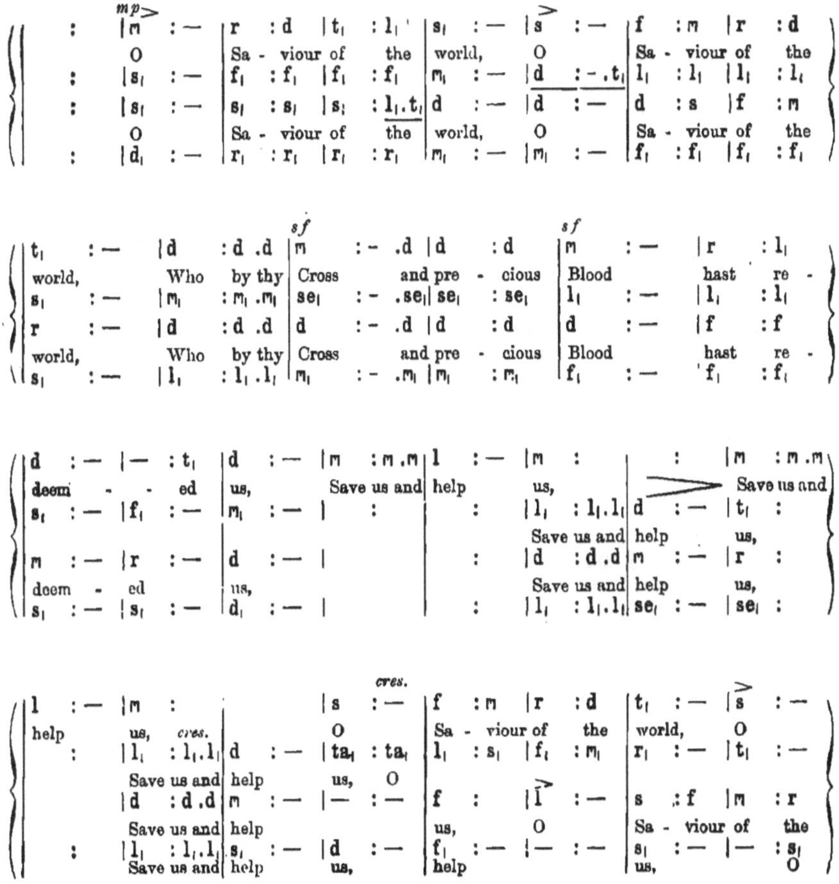

mp

: |m :— |r :d |t, :l, |s, :— |s :— |f :m |r :d
O Sa - viour of the world, O Sa - viour of the
: |s, :— |f, :f, |f, :f, |m, :— |d :-.t, |l, :l, |l, :l,
: |s, :— |s, :s, |s, :l,.t, |d :— |d :— |d :s |f :m
O Sa - viour of the world, O Sa - viour of the
: |d, :— |r, :r, |r, :r, |m, :— |m, :— |f, :f, |f, :f,

sf *sf*

t, :— |d :d .d |m :- .d |d :d |m :— |r :l,
world, Who by thy Cross and pre - cious Blood hast re -
s, :— |m, :m, .m, |se, :- .se, |se, :se, |l, :— |l, :l,
r :— |d :d .d |d :- .d |d :d |d :— |f :f
world, Who by thy Cross and pre - cious Blood hast re -
s, :— |l, :l, .l, |m, :- .m, |m, :m, |f, :— |f, :f,

d :— |— :t, |d :— |m :m .m |l :— |m : | : |m :m .m
deem - - ed us, Save us and help us, Save us and
s, :— |f, :— |m, :— | : | : |l, :l,.l, |d :— |t, :
Save us and help us,
m :— |r :— |d :— | | : |d :d .d |m :— |r :
deem - ed us, Save us and help us,
s, :— |s, :— |d, :— | | : |l, :l,.l, |se, :— |se, :

cres.

l :— |m : | |s :— |f :m |r :d |t, :— |s :—
help us, *cres.* O Sa - viour of the world, O
: |l, :l,.l, |d :— |ta, :ta, |l, :s, |f, :m, |r, :— |t, :—
Save us and help us, O
|d :d .d |m :— |— :— |f : |l :— |s :f |m :r
Save us and help us, O Sa - viour of the
: |l, :l,.l, |s, :— |d :— |f, :— |— :— |s, :— |— :s,
Save us and help us, help us, O

St. Co. (New).

s. d. f. G♭. *L* is *E♭*.

E♭. t. *mf* *cres.*

ᵈf :m |r :d	t₁ :— |ᵗse :—	l :l |l :l .l	l :- .l |l :l
Sa - viour of the	world, O	Sa - viour, Who by thy	Cross and pre - cious
ᵐ₁l₁ :l₁ |l₁ :l₁	s₁ :— |ʳt₁ :—	d :l₁ |l₁ :l₁ .l₁	d :- .l₁ |l₁ :l₁
ᵈf :s |f :m	r :— |ˢm :—	m :m |m :m .m	f :- .f |f :f
world, of the	world, O	Sa - viour, Who by thy	Cross and pre - cious
ˡ₁r :r |f₁ :f₁	s₁ :— |ᶠr :—	d :d |d :d .d	r :- .r |r :r
Sa - viour			

E♭. t. m. l.

f *dim.* *p*

ˡd' :— |t :l	l :- .s |s :	f :— |m :m	l :— |r :r
Blood hast re -	deem - ed us,	Save us and	help us, we
ᵈma :— |ma :ma	r :- .r |r :	r :— |d :d	d :— |d :d
ᶠᵉl :— |t :d'	d' :- .t |t :	se :— |l :l	r :— |r :r
Blood hast re -	deem - ed us,	Save us and	help us, we
ʳᵉfe :— |fe :fe	s :- .s |s :	: | :	f₁ :— |f₁ :f₁

f. A♭.

s :f .m |m :r .d	ᵈs₁ :— | :s	s :m .d |t₁ :l₁ .s₁
hum - bly be - seech thee, O	Lord, we	hum - bly be - seech thee, O
d :d .d |t₁ :t₁ .d	ᵈs₁ :— |f₁ :—	ᵐ₁ :d .l₁ |s₁ :fe₁ .s₁
	we	
m :l .s |f :f .f	ᵐt₁ :s₁ |s₁ :s₁ .s₁	s₁ :s₁ .m |r :d .t₁
hum - bly be - seech thee, O	Lord, we hum - bly be-	seech Thee, be-seech thee, O
s₁ :s₁ .s₁ |s₁ :s₁ .s₁	ˡ₁m₁ :— |t₂ :—	d₁ :d₁ .d₁ |r₁ :r₁ .r₁
	we	hum - bly be - seech thee, O

p

s₁ :— | :	: | :	| m :—	r :d |t₁ :l₁
Lord,		O	Sa - viour of the
s₁ :— | :	: | :	: |s₁ :—	f₁ :m₁ |r₁ :t₂
t₁ :— | :	: | :	: | :	: *p*|f :—
Lord,		*p*	O
s₁ :— |s₁ :—	f₁ :m₁ |r₁ :d₁	t₂ :— |d₁ :—	r₁ :— |— :—
Lord, O	Sa - viour of the	world, O	save

St. Co. (New).

cres. *sf* *cres - cen-*

| s :— | s :— | f :m | r :d | t, :— | m :— | m :l, | m :m.m |
world, O Sa - viour of the world, O Sa - viour, Who by thy
| d, :— | s, :— | l, :s, | f, :m, | r, :— | t, :— | d :d | l, :l,.l, |
| m :r | d :t, | l, :— | l :— | s :f | m :r | d :— | d :d.d |
Sa - viour of the world, O Sa - viour of the world, Who by thy
| m, :— | m, :— | f, :— | — :— | s, :— | se, :— | l, :l, | l, :l,.l, |
us and help us, O Sa - viour,

- - *do.* *al.* *f* f. D♭. A♭. t.

| f :-.f | f :f | ^f d' :— | r' :r' | m' :— | — :m' | m' :— | :
Cross and pre - cious Blood hast re - deem - - ed us, *p*
| l, :-.l, | l, :l, | ^r l :— | l :l | l :— | se :ba | se :— | ^m l, :—
Save
| d :-.d | d :d | ^r l :— | l :l | d' :— | t :l | t :— | :
Cross and pre - cious Blood hast re - deem - - ed us,
| f, :-.f, | f, :f, | ta,f :— | f :f | m :— | — :m | m :— |

p *sf*

| ^d f :— | m :r | d :— | t, :l, | l, :s,.s, | t, :l,.s, | s, :— | s :— |
Save us and help us, we hum-bly beseech thee, O Lord, O
| — :— | l, :l, | s, :— | f, :f, | f, :f,.f, | f, :f,.f, | m, :— | m, :— |
us and help us, O
| ^l r :— | s :f | m :— | r :d | t, :t,.t, | t, :t,.t, | d :— | d :— |
Save us and help us, we hum-bly beseech thee, O Lord, O
| ^l r, :— | m, :f, | s, :— | s, :s, | s, :s,.s, | s, :s,.s, | d, :— | ta, :— |

pp *Rather slower.* *p*

| f :m | r :d | t, :la, | — :la,.la, | la, :s, | :s, |
Sa - viour of the world, Save us, and help us, we
| f, :— | — :— | f, :la, | — :la,.la, | la, :s, | :s, |
save us,
| d :— | — :— | r :la, | — :la,.la, | la, :s, | :s, |
save us, Save us, and help us, we
| l, :— | la, :— | s, :la, | — :la,.la, | la, :s, | :s, |

cres. *dim.*

| m :r.r | f :t,.t, | d :— | — :— | — :— | d :— | d :— | — :— ||
hum-bly beseech thee, O Lord, A - men.
| f, :f,.f, | f, :f,.f, | m, :— | l, :— | s, :— | f, :— | m, :— | — :— ||
A - men,
| t, :t,.t, | t, :r.r | d :— | f :— | m :— | l, :— | s, :— | — :— ||
hum-bly beseech thee, O Lord, A - men.
| s, :s,.s, | s, :s,.s, | d, :— | — :— | — :— | f, :— | d, :— | — :— ||

St Co (New).

THE SHEPHERD'S LAMENT.

KEY E♭. *Andante lento.* M. 63. *Henry Smart.*

p

:m .,m	s :- .f :r .l	l :s :s .d'	m' :- .d' :t .l
On the	brow of yon-der	moun - tain A	thou - sand times I
:d .,d	d :- .t, :t, .r	r :m :s	m :m :m .m
:s .,s	s :- .s :s .t	t :d' :d' .s	s :d' .m' :r' .d'
On the	brow of yon-der	moun - tain A	thou - sand times I
:d .,d	m :- .r :f .f	f :m :m	d :l, .l, .l,

s :f : .l	l :- .f :m .s	f :r :d .t,	d .m :s .,s :s .f
stand, And	on my crook re-	pos - ing, Gaze	down on the ver-dant
r :— : .f	f :- .r :de.de	r :l, :s,	s, :s, .,d :d .d
t :l : .l	l :- .l :s .ta	l :f :r	d :d .,m :m .f
stand, And	on my crook re-	pos - ing, Gaze	down on the ver-dant
r :— : .r	r :- .r :r .r	r :f, :f,	m, :m, .,m, :l, .l,

cres. B♭. t.

m :r : .s	ˢd :- .t, .d :m .,r	d :— :t, .t,	l, :- .d :t, .d .r
land. The	flocks as they graze I	fol - - low, My	dog he guardeth them
d :t, : .r	ʳs, :- .s, .s, :s, .,s,	s, :— :se, .se,	l, :m, .l, :se, .l, .t,
s :— : .t	ᵗm :- .re .m :s .,f	m :— :r .r	d :- .m :m .m .m
land. The	flocks as they graze I	fol - - low, My	dog he guardeth them
s, :— :	: :	.t, m, :m, .m, .m, :m,	— .m, :m, .m, :m, .m, .m,
		The flocks as they graze,	My dog he guardeth them

f f. E♭ *dim.* *p*

d :— :ᵈs .,s	r' :t .t :d' .l	s :f :m .	r . : :m .
well, From the	moun - tain have I de-	scend - ed, Yet	how, yet
l, :— :ˡm .,m	f :f .f :m .m	r :r :d .	l, . : :ta, .
m :— :ᵐt .,t	t :r' .r' :s .d'	t :— :d' .d	d :d d :d .d
well; From the	moun - tain have I de-	scend - ed, Yet	how, I can scarcely
l, :— :ˡm .,m	s, :s, .s, :s, .s,	s, :s, :l, .	f, . : :s, .
well; From the	moun - tain have I de-	scend - ed, Yet	how, yet

ritard. *p*

f . : :fe	s :d' .t :l .s	fe.s :f . :r	d :— ‖ m
how, yet	how I can	scarcely, scarce - ly	tell. ‖ The
d . : d	d :m :d .d	d .d :d . :t,	d :— ‖ d
d :r :ma	m :s :m .m	re.m :l . :s	s :— ‖ s
tell, yet	how I can	scarcely, scarce - ly	tell. ‖ The
l, . : :la,	s, :— :s, .s,	s, .s, :s, . :{f/s,}	{m/d} :— ‖ d
how,			

St. Co. (New).

m :s ,,s : f ,r ,l | l :s :s ,,d' | m' :-,r' ,d' : d' ,t ,l | s :f : .f
mea-dows are sweetly en- | am - ell'd With | flow - ers so lovely and | gay, I
d :d ,,d : t, ,t, ,r | r :m :s | m :m ,,m : m ,m ,m | r :— .r
s :s ,,s : s ,s ,t | t :d' :d' ,,s | s :-,se,l : m' ,r' ,d' | t :l .l
mea-dows are sweetly en- | am - ell'd With | flow - ers so lovely and | gay, I
d :m ,,m : r ,f ,f | f :m :m | d :d ,,d : l, ,l, ,l, | r :— .r

f :-,m ,f : l ,s ,m | r :l, :t, | d .m :s .s :s ,f ,d | m :r : .s (*f*)
ga - ther them but without | know - ing To | whom I shall give them a- | way. In
r :-,de,r : de,de,de | l, :l, :s, | s, :s, .d :d ,d ,d | d :t, : .r
l :-,l ,l : m ,m ,s | f :r :r | d :d .m :m ,f ,f | s :— : .t
ga - ther them but without | know - ing To | whom I shall give them a- | way. In
r :-,r ,r : r ,r ,r | r :f, :f, | m, :m, .m, :l, ,l, ,l, | s, :—

B♭. t.

sd :- .d :r ,d ,t, | d :— :t, ,,t, | l, :l, ,,l, :t, ,d ,t,
rain, in rain, in storm, and in | tem - - - pest, I | stand there be - neath the
rs, .s, :s, .s, :la, ,la, ,la, | s, :— :se, ,,se, | l, :m, ,,l, :se, ,,se,
tm :- .m :f ,f ,f | m :— :r ,,r | d :d ,r ,m :m ,,m
rain, in storm, and in | tem - - - pest, I | stand there be - neath the
: : | .t,m, :m, .m, :m, ,m, ,m, | m, ,ba, ,se, : l, ,t, ,d :r ,m ,r
In rain, in storm, & in | tempest, I stand there beneath the

p f. E♭. *pp*

l, :— :l, .l, | l,m ,,r :r :d .l | s :f :m . | r . : :m .
tree; But yon | door re-mains clos'd a- | gainst me, And | all, And
l, :m, :m, | m,t, ,,t, : t, :d .d | t, :t, :d . | l, . : :s, .
m :d :d | ds ,,f :f :m .m | r :— :d .d | d :d .d :d ,,d
tree; But yon | door re-mains clos'd a- | gainst me, And | all is a dream to
d :— :d, .d, | d,s, ,,s, :s, :s, .s, | s, :se, :l, . | f, . : :ta, .
tree; But yon | door re-mains clos'd a- | gainst me, And | all, And

ritard.

f . : :fe | s .l :t .r' :d' .m | s :- .f :r .m | d :— :—
all, and | all is a dream to | me, a dream to | me.
d . : :d .d | d : : | .d :t, . :t, | d : .s, :l, .l,
all, is a | dream, | a dream to | me, a dream to
d :r :ma.ma | m : | .s :s . :s | s : .m :f .f
me, is a | dream, | a dream to | me, a dream to
l, . : :la, .la, | s, : | {.m :r . :f / .s, :s, . :s,} | {m / d} : .d :f, .f,
all is a | dream, | |

St. Co. (New).

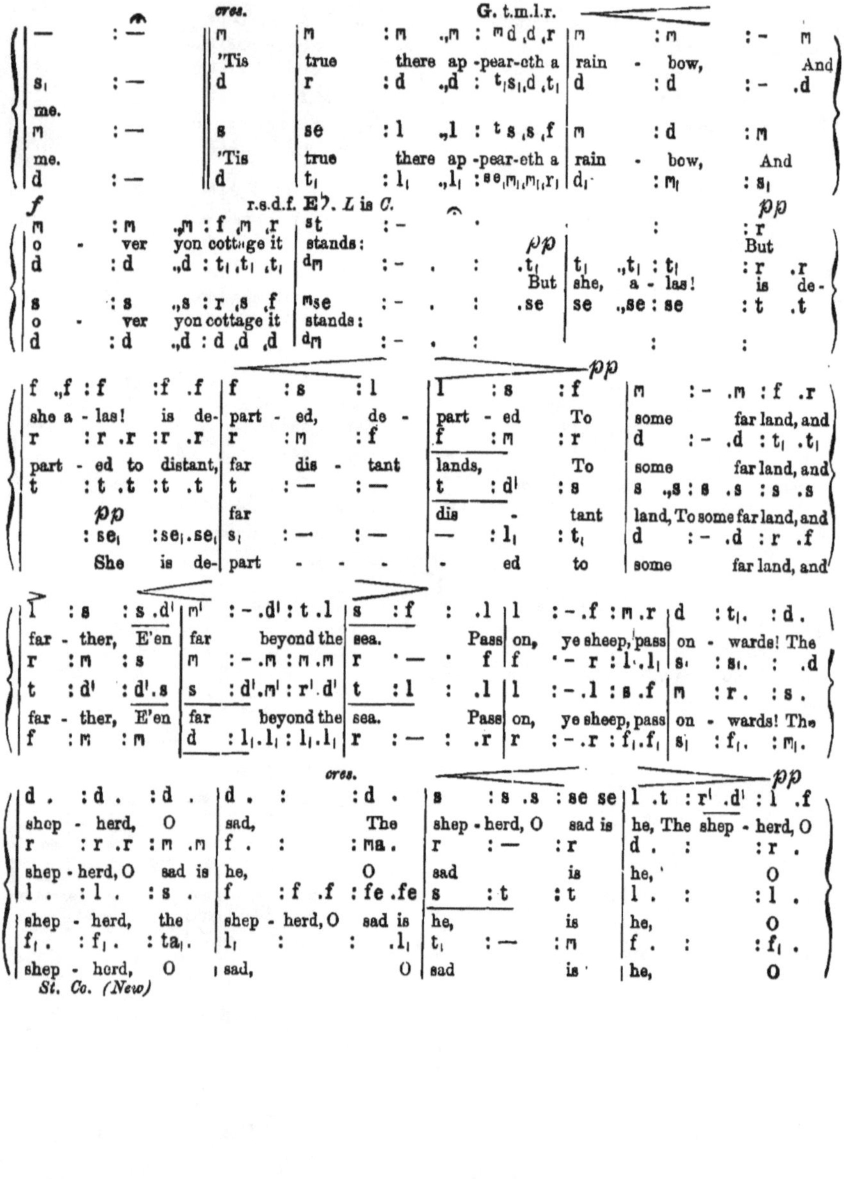

cres. G. t.m.l.r.

— :— ‖ m	m :m .,m : m d .d .r	m :m :— m
	'Tis	true there ap - pear-eth a	rain - bow, And
s_1 :— ‖ d	r :d .,d : t_1 s_1 .d .t_1	d :d :— .d
me.
m :— ‖ s	se :l .,l : t s .s .f	m :d :m
me.	'Tis	true there ap - pear-eth a	rain - bow, And
d :— ‖ d	t_1 :l_1 .,l_1 :se_1 .m_1 .m_1 .r_1	d_1 :m_1 :s_1

f r.s.d.f. E♭. L is C. pp

m :m .,m : f .m .r	st :— . :	: :r
o - ver yon cottage it	stands:	But
d :d .,d : t_1 .t_1 .t_1	dm :— . : .t_1	t_1 .,t_1 : t_1 :r .r
	But	she, a - las! is de-
s :s .,s : r .s .f	mse :— . : .se	se .,se : se :t .t
o - ver yon cottage it	stands:
d :d .,d : d .d .d	dm :— . :	: :

pp

f .,f :f :f .f	f :s :l	l :s :f	m :— .m :f .r
she a - las! is de-	part - ed, de -	part - ed To	some far land, and
r :r .r :r .r	r :m :f	f :m :r	d :— .d : t_1 .t_1
part - ed to distant,	far dis - tant	lands, To	some far land, and
t :t .t :t .t	t :— :—	t :d' :s	s .,s : s .s :s .s
pp	far	dis - tant	land, To some far land, and
:se_1 :se_1 .se_1	s_1 :— :—	— :l_1 :t_1	d :— .d :r .f
She is de-	part - - -	- ed to	some far land, and

l :s :s .d'	m' :— .d' :t .l	s :f : .l	l :— .f :m .r	d :t_1. :d.
far - ther, E'en	far beyond the	sea. Pass	on, ye sheep, pass	on - wards! The
r :m :s	m :— .m :m .m	r :— : f	f :— r :l .l_1	s_1 :s_1. : .d
t :d' :d' .s	s :d' .m' :r' .d'	t :l : .l	l :— .l :s .f	m :r. :s.
far - ther, E'en	far beyond the	sea. Pass	on, ye sheep, pass	on - wards! The
f :m :m	d :l_1 .l_1 :l_1 .l_1	r :— : .r	r :— .r :f_1 .f_1	s_1 :f_1. :m_1.

cres. pp

d. :d. :d.	d. : :d.	s :s .s :se se	l .t :r' .d' :l .f
shep - herd, O	sad, The	shep - herd, O sad is	he, The shep - herd, O
r :r .r :m .m	f. : :ma.	r :— :r	d. : :r.
shep - herd, O sad is	he, O	sad is	he, O
l. :l. :s.	f :f .f :fe .fe	s :t :t	l. : :l.
shep - herd, the	shep - herd, O sad is	he, is	he, O
f_1. :f_1. :ta_1.	l_1 : : .l_1	t_1 :— :m	f. : :f_1.
shep - herd, O	sad, O	sad is	he, O

St. Co. (New)

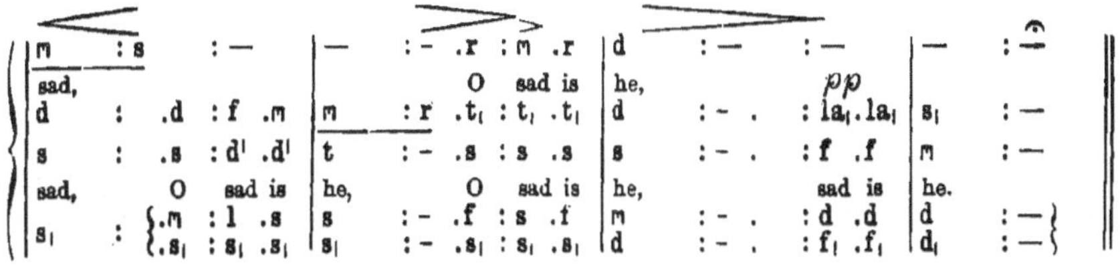

|m :s :— |— :— .r :m .r |d :— :— |— :— ||
sad, O sad is he,
d : .d :f .m |m :r .t, :t, .t, |d :— . :la, .la, |s, :— ||
s : .s :d' .d' |t :— .s :s .s |s :— . :f .f |m :— ||
sad, O sad is he, O sad is he, sad is he.
s, : {.m :l .s / .s, :s, .s,} |s :— .f :s .f / s, :— .s, :s, .s, |m / d :— . :d .d / :f, .f, |d / d, :— ||

pp

Words by *Edmeston.*

SAVIOUR, BREATHE.

"AVE VERUM."

Music by *Mozart.*

KEY D. *Adagio—sotto voce.* M. 72.

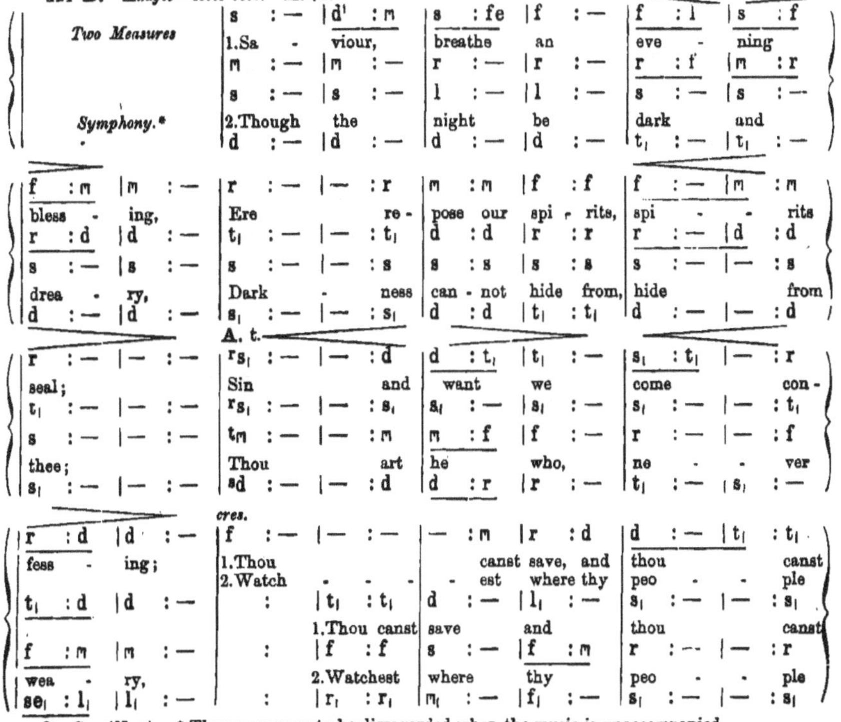

*Two Measures Symphony.**

|s :— |d' :m |s :fe |f :— |f :l |s :f |
1.Sa - viour, breathe an eve - ning
|m :— |m :— |r :— |r :— |r :f |m :r |
|s :— |s :— |l :— |l :— |s :— |s :— |
2.Though the night be dark and
|d :— |d :— |d :— |d :— |t, :— |t, :— |

|f :m |m :— |r :— |— :r |m :m |f :f |f :— |m :m |
bless - ing, Ere re - pose our spi - rits, spi - - rits
|r :d |d :— |t, :— |— :t, |d :d |r :r |r :— |d :d |
|s :— |s :— |s :— |— :s |s :s |s :s |s :— |— :s |
drea - ry, Dark - ness can - not hide from, hide from
|d :— |d :— |s, :— |— :s, |d :d |t, :t, |d :— |— :d |

A. t.
|r :— |— :— |rs, :— |— :d |d :t, |t, :— |s, :t, |— :r |
seal; Sin and want we come con -
|t, :— |— :— |rs, :— |— :s, |s, :— |s, :— |s, :— |— :t, |
|s :— |— :— |tm :— |— :m |m :f |f :— |r :— |— :f |
thee; Thou art he who, ne - - ver
|s, :— |— :— |sd :— |— :d |d :r |r :— |t, :— |s, :— |

cres.
|r :d |d :— |f :— |— :— |— :m |r :d |d :— |t, :t, |
fess - ing; 1.Thou canst save, and thou canst
2.Watch - - - - est where thy peo - - ple
|t, :d |d :— | : |t, :t, |d :— |l, :— |s, :— |— :s, |
1.Thou canst save and thou canst
|f :m |m :— | : |f :f |s :— |f :m |r :— |— :r |
wea - ry, 2.Watchest where thy peo - - ple
|se, :l, |l, :— | : |r, :r, |m, :— |f, :— |s, :— |— :s, |

St. Co. (New). * These measures to be disregarded when the music is unaccompanied.

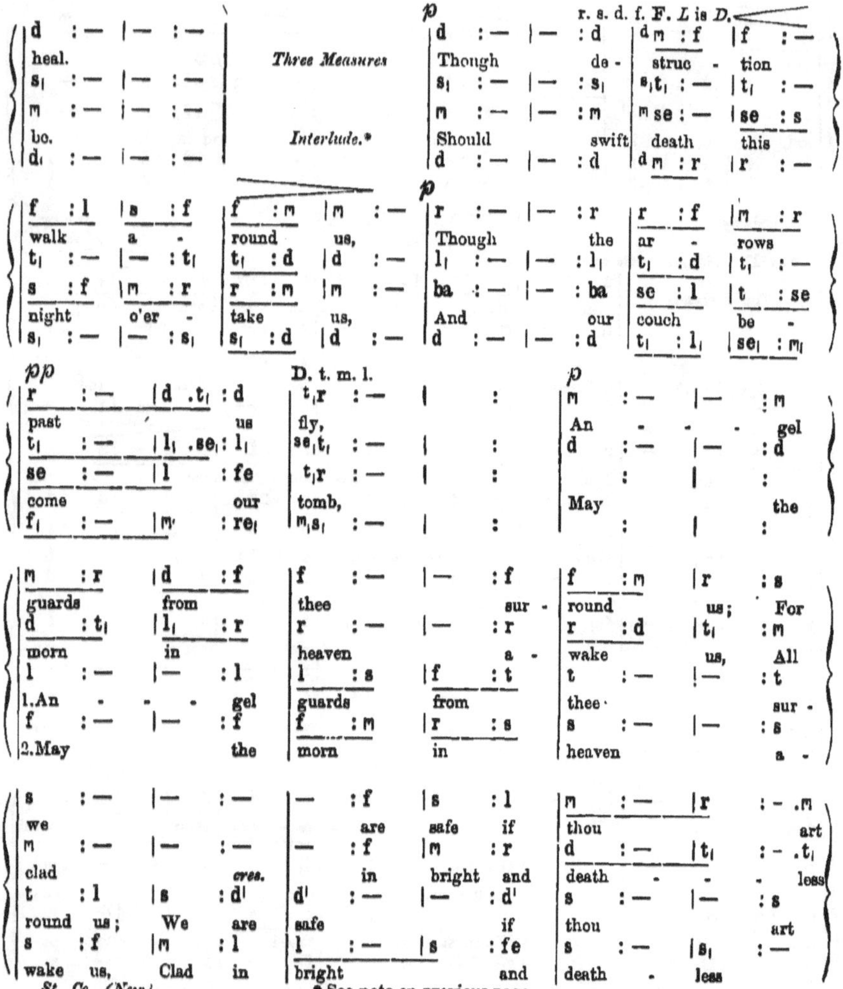

p r. s. d. f. F. *L* is *D.*

| d :— | — :— | *Three Measures* | d :— | — :d | ^d^m :f | f :— |
heal. Though de - struc - tion
| s, :— | — :— | | s, :— | — :s, | ^s^,t, :— | t, :— |
| m :— | — :— | | m :— | — :m | ^m^se :— | se :s |
bo. *Interlude.** Should swift death this
| d, :— | — :— | | d :— | — :d | ^d^m :r | r :— |

p

| f :l | s :f | f :m | m :— | r :— | — :r | r :f | m :r |
walk a - round us, Though the ar - rows
| t, :— | — :t, | t, :d | d :— | l, :— | — :l, | t, :d | t, :— |
| s :f | m :r | r :m | m :— | ba :— | — :ba | se :l | t :se |
night o'er - take us, And our couch be -
| s, :— | — :s, | s, :d | d :— | d :— | — :d | t, :l, | se, :m, |

pp D. t. m. l. *p*

| r :— | d .t, :d | ^t^,r :— | : | m :— | — :m |
past us fly, An - - - gel
| t, :— | l, .se, :l, | ^se^,t, :— | : | d :— | — :d |
| se :— | l :fe | ^t^,r :— | : | : | : |
come our tomb, May the
| f, :— | m, :re, | ^m^,s, :— | : | : | : |

| m :r | d :f | f :— | — :f | f :m | r :s |
guards from thee sur - round us; For
| d :t, | l, :r | r :— | — :r | r :d | t, :m |
morn in heaven a - wake us, All
| l :— | — :l | l :s | f :t | t :— | — :t |
1.An - - - gel guards from thee sur -
| f :— | — :f | f :m | r :s | s :— | — :s |
2.May the morn in heaven a -

| s :— | — :— | — :f | s :l | m :— | r :- .m |
we are safe if thou art
| m :— | — :— | — :f | m :r | d :— | t, :- .t, |
clad *cres.* in bright and death - - - less
| t :l | s :d' | d' :— | — :d' | s :— | — :s |
round us; We are safe if thou art
| s :f | m :l | l :— | s :fe | s :— | s, :— |
wake us, Clad in bright and death - less

St. Co. (New).

* See note on previous page.

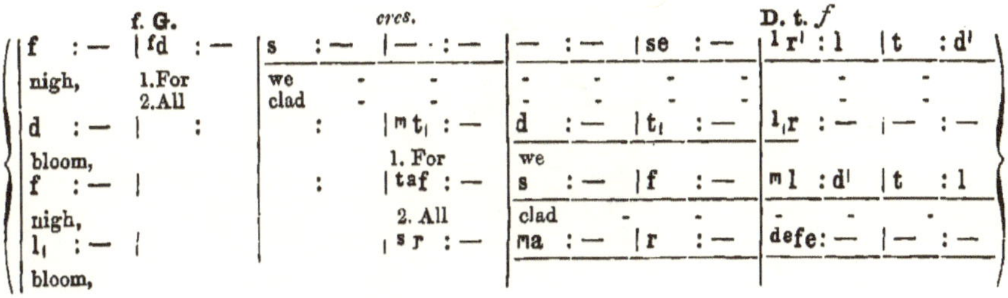

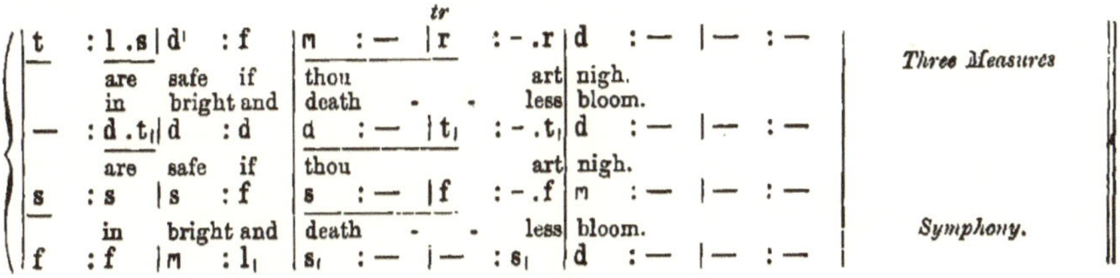

f. G.		cres.				D. t. *f*	
f :—	fd :—	s :—	— · :—	— :—	se :—	lr' :l	t :d'
nigh,	1.For 2.All	we clad	- -	- -	- -	-	-
d :—	:	:	mt, :—	d :—	t, :—	l,r :—	— :—
bloom,			1. For	we			
f :—		:	taf :—	s :—	f :—	ml :d'	t :l
nigh,			2. All	clad	- -	- -	-
l, :—			sr :—	ma :—	r :—	defe:—	— :—
bloom,							

		tr			
t :l .s	d' :f	m :—	r :-.r	d :—	— :—	*Three Measures*
are safe if in bright and		thou death - -	art less	nigh. bloom.		
— :d .t,	d :d	d :—	t, :-.t,	d :—	— :—	
are safe if		thou	art	nigh.		
s :s	s :f	s :—	f :-.f	m :—	— :—	
in bright and		death - -	less	bloom.		*Symphony.*
f :f	m :l,	s, :—	— :s,	d :—	— :—	

LOUD THE STORM-WIND DOTH HOWL.*

Words for this work by *J. S. C.* — Music by *Kreutzer.*

KEY E♭. *L* is *C.* *Allegro molto.*

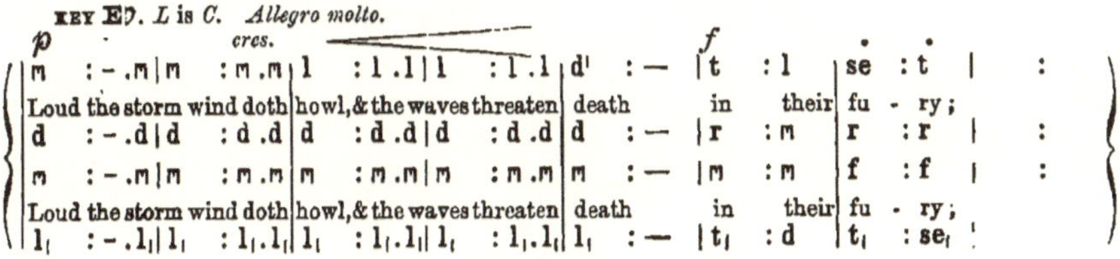

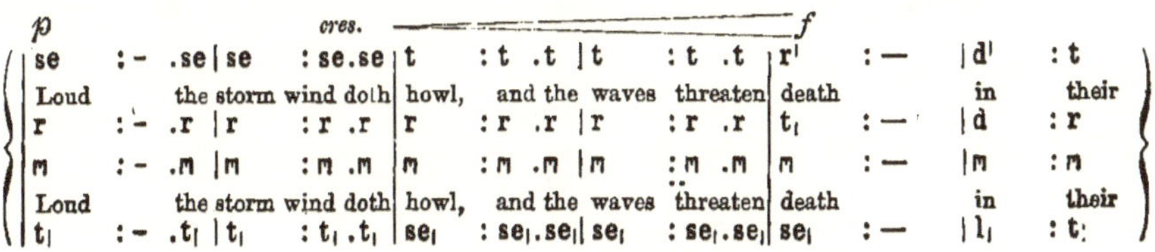

p cres.				*f*			
m :-.m	m :m .m	l :l .l	l :l .l	d' :—	t :l	se :t	:
Loud the storm wind doth		howl, & the waves threaten		death	in their	fu - ry;	
d :-.d	d :d .d	d :d .d	d :d .d	d :—	r :m	r :r	:
m :-.m	m :m .m	m :m .m	m :m .m	m :—	m :m	f :f	:
Loud the storm wind doth		howl, & the waves threaten		death	in their	fu - ry;	
l, :-.l,	l, :l, .l,	l, :l, .l,	l, :l, .l,	l, :—	t, :d	t, :se,	

p		cres.		*f*	
se :- .se	se :se .se	t :t .t	t :t .t	r' :—	d' :t
Loud	the storm wind doth	howl, and the	waves threaten	death	in their
r :- .r	r :r .r	r :r .r	r :r .r	t, :—	d :r
m :- .m	m :m .m	m :m .m	m :m .m	m :—	m :m
Loud	the storm wind doth	howl, and the	waves threaten	death	in their
t, :- .t,	t, :t, .t,	se, :se, .se,	se, :se, .se,	se, :—	l, :t,

* For T.T.B.B. by inverting the inner parts.

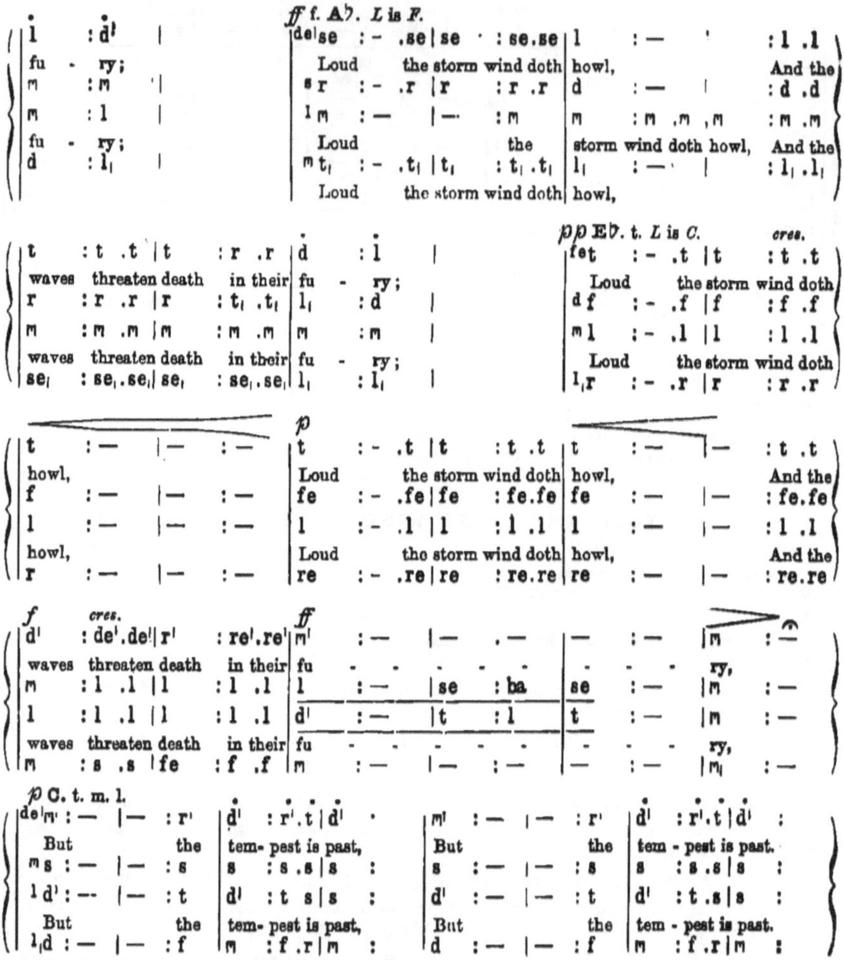

ff f. A♭. *L* is *F.*

| l' :d' | de|se :- .se | se : se.se | l :— | :l .l |
fu - ry; Loud the storm wind doth howl, And the
| m :m | s r :- .r | r : r .r | d :— | :d .d |
| m :l | l m :— | — :m | m :m .m ,m | :m .m |
fu - ry; Loud the storm wind doth howl, And the
| d :l, | m t, :- .t, | t, : t, .t, | l, :— | :l, .l, |
Loud the storm wind doth howl,

pp E♭. t. *L* is *C.* *cres.*

| t :t .t | t :r .r | d :l' | fe t :- .t | t :t .t |
waves threaten death in their fu - ry; Loud the storm wind doth
| r :r .r | r :t, .t, | l, :d | d f :- .f | f :f .f |
| m :m .m | m :m .m | m :m | m l :- .l | l :l .l |
waves threaten death in their fu - ry; Loud the storm wind doth
| se, :se, .se, | se, :se, .se, | l, :l, | l, r :- .r | r :r .r |

p

| t :— | — :— | t :- .t | t :t .t | t :— | — :t .t |
howl, Loud the storm wind doth howl, And the
| f :— | — :— | fe :- .fe | fe :fe.fe | fe :— | — :fe.fe |
| l :— | — :— | l :- .l | l :l .l | l :— | — :l .l |
howl, Loud the storm wind doth howl, And the
| r :— | — :— | re :- .re | re :re.re | re :— | — :re.re |

f *cres.* *ff*

| d' :de'.de' | r' :re'.re' | m' :— | — .— | — :— | m :— |
waves threaten death in their fu - - - - - - - - ry,
| m :l .l | l :l .l | l :— | se :ba | se :— | m :— |
| l :l .l | l :l .l | d' :— | t :l | t :— | m :— |
waves threaten death in their fu - - - - - - - - ry,
| m :s .s | fe :f .f | m :— | — :— | — :— | m, :— |

p C. t. m. l.

| de m' :— | — :r' | d' :r'.t | d' : | m' :— | — :r' | d' :r'.t | d' : |
But the tem- pest is past, But the tem - pest is past.
| m s :— | — :s | s :s .s | s : | s :— | — :s | s :s .s | s : |
| l d' :— | — :t | d' :t s | s : | d' :— | — :t | d' :t .s | s : |
But the tem- pest is past, But the tem - pest is past.
| l, d :— | — :f | m :f .r | m : | d :— | — :f | m :f .r | m : |

St. Co. (New).

SOLI. *dolce.*

| : | f' :— | s' :f' | m' :s' | s' : | f' :— | s' :f'
Soft comes the sun - shine, still - ing the
p
s :— | s :s | s :— | s : | s :— | s :s | s :— | s :s
Soft comes the sun - shine, peace - ful - ly still - ing the
d' :— | r' :d' | d' :— | t : | d' :— | r' :d' | d' :— | t :t
Soft comes the sun - shine, peace - ful - ly still - ing the
m :— | f :m | r :— | s, :— | d :m | f :m | r :— | s, :s,

r' :— | — :— | m' . | : | CHORUS. *pp* m' :- .m' | m' :m'.m' *cres.*
storm. - - - - - Loud the storm wind doth
s :— | — :— | — : | : | se :- .se | se :se.se
t :— | — :— | d' : | : | t :- .t | t :t .t
storm. - - - - - Loud the storm wind doth
s, :— | — :— | d : | : | m :- .m | r :r .r

m' :m' .m' | m' :m' .m' | *f* m' :— | m' :- .m' | m' :m' | :
howl, and the waves threaten death in their fu - ry,
l :l .l | l :l .l | se :— | l :- .l | l :se | :
d' :d' .d' | d' :d' .d' | r' :— | d' :- .d' | d' :t | :
howl, and the waves threaten death in their fu - ry,
d :d .d | d :d .d | t, :— | l, :- .d | m :m | :

p m' :- .m' | m' :m' .m' *cres.* | re' :re'.re' | re' :re'.re' | *f* r' :— | r' :- .r'
Loud the storm wind doth howl, and the waves threaten death in their
m :- .m | m :m .m | fe :fe .fe | fe :fe .fe | se :— | se :- .se
se :- .se | se :se.se | l :l .l | l :l .l | t :— | t :- .t
Loud the storm wind doth howl, and the waves threaten death in their
m :- .m | m :m .m | m :m .m | m :m .m | m :— | m :- .m

r' :d' | : | *pf.* F. *L* is *D.* f'd' :— | — :t | l :t .se | l : | *p* d' :— | — :t
fu - ry, But the tem- pest is past! But the
se :l | : | l m :— | — :f | m :m .m | m : | m :— | — :f
t :l | : | r'l :— | — :se | l :se.m | m : | l :— | — :se
fu - ry, But the tem- pest is past! But the
m :l | : | r l, :— | — :r | d :r .t, | d : | l, :— | — :r

St. Co. (New).

p C. t. SOLI. *dolce.*

| l :t .se \| l : | d'f' :— \| s' :f' | m' :s' \| s' : | f' :— \| s' :f' |
tem- pest is past! Soft comes the sun - shine, still - ing the
| m :m .m \| m : | r s :— \| s :s | s :— \| s :— | s :— \| s :s |
| l :se.m \| m : | fe t :— \| t :t | d' :— \| r' :d' | t :— \| t :t |
tem- pest is past! Soft comes the sun - shine, still - ing the
| d :r .t_{l} \| d : | l_{l}r :— \| s_{l} :s_{l} | d :m \| f :m | r :— \| s_{l} :s_{l} |

fp CHORUS.

| r' :— \| m' : | fe' :— \|— :s' | fe' :fe'.fe' \| fe' : |
storm. But the tem - pest is past!
| s :— \|— : | l :— \|— :l | l :l .l \| l : |
| t :— \| d' : | d' :— \|— :d' | d' :d' .d' \| d' : |
storm. But the tem - pest is past!
| s_{l} :— \| d : | r :— \|— :ma | r :r .r \| r : |

fp SOLI. *dolce.*

| f' :— \|— :f' | f' :f'.f' \| f' :— | m' :s' \| s' :d' | d' :m' \| m' :d' |
But the tem - pest is past! Soft comes the sun - shine,
| t :— \|— :d' | t :t .t \| t :— | s :— \| s :s | s :— \| s :— |
| r' :— \|— :r' | r' :r'.r' \| r' :— | d' :m' \| m' :m | m :d' \| d' :— |
But the tem - pest is past! Soft comes the sun - shine,
| s :— \|— :la | s :s .s \| s :— | d :— \| d :d | d :— \| d :— |

CHORUS. *p.*

| r' :s' — :f'.r' | r' :— \| m' : | m' :s' \| s' :d' | d' :m' \| m' :d' |
still - ing the storm, Soft comes the sun - shine, The
| s :t \|— :s | s :— \|— : | s :— \| s :s | s :— \| s :s |
| t :r' \|— :t | t :— \| d' : | d' :m' \| m' :m | m :d' \| d' :d' |
still - ing the storm, Soft comes the sun - shine, The
| s_{l} :s_{l} \|— :s_{l} | s_{l} :— \| d : | d :— \| d :d | d :— \| d :d |

cres. *f*

| r' :s' \|— :f'.r' | m' :— \|— :m' | r' :s' \|— :f'.r' | d' :— \|— :— |
sun - shine is here, The sun - shine is here.
| s :t \|— :s | s :— \|— :s | s :t \|— :t | s :— \|— :— |
| t :r' \|— :t | d' :— \|— :d' | t :r' \|— :r'.f' | m' :— \|— :— |
sun - shine is here, The sun - shine is here.
| s_{l} :s_{l} \|— :s_{l} | d :s \|— :m .d | s_{l} :s_{l} \|— :s | d :— \|— :— |

St. Co. (New).

HINTS ON THE TUNES IN

ADDITIONAL EXERCISES.

WITH REFERENCES TO INSTRUCTIONS IN "STANDARD COURSE."

GOD SPEED THE RIGHT, page 1, is treated of in "Standard Course" under the following topics:—Normal force, page 98; Breathing-places, page 98; Treatment of unison, page 103; Appropriate force and speed, page 132; Melodic phrasing and subordination of parts, Ex. 212; Degree of force in a cadence, page 103. See analysis of sectional relation in "How to Observe Harmony," page 63.

GOING HOME, page 2.—Delivery of repeated tones, page 99; Marked entrance of parts, page 100; Melodic Imitation, page 99. In scores 2 and 3 develope S. and C., running in thirds and sixths.

JACKSON'S EVENING HYMN, page 2.—Pervading force, page 98; Treatment of melodies, page 100; Study of congenial tones, page 102; Crescendo on single tones, page 103; Expression of joyful feeling, page 131; Contrition and supplication, page 132; Growing excitement, page 133. See analysis of sectional relation in "How to Observe Harmony," Study carefully the melodic phrasing of each part, pp. 69, 70. In harmony let S. and B. deliver well their *tertiary* dissonance in score 1, measure 3. They have the same in score 4, measure 4, where the Tenors also have to strike a primary dissonance against the C., and secondary as against the B. This double dissonance should be carefully done. There is a strong primary dissonance between S. and C., at score 3, measure 5, and another in the next measure. See "Standard Course," page 21, and "How to Observe Harmony," page 90.

SPRING LIFE, page 3.—Vigorous entry and unanimity, page 100; Outbursts of enthusiasm page 131; Didactic style mingled with emotion, page 132. Aim at perfect unity and blending of S. and C. in score 1 and 2.

THE FORTUNE HUNTER, page 4.—Ascending melodic imitations, page 99; Sympathetic singing in unison, page 103; Slyness and gaiety, page 133; Imitative sounds—laughter, page 101; Sad reflection, page 132. See analysis of sectional relation in "How to Observe Harmony," page 63. The changing expression suitable to every verse should be carefully attended to. In the last line deliver the word "not" *staccato*, and make a slight pause after it. Carefully attend to variations of both time and tune in verses 2, 4, 5, 6.

THE MAY-TIME, page 5.—Firm entry of parts, page 100; Ascending and descending phrases, Ex. 211. Should not exceed the rate of time marked. Clearness must not be sacrificed to rapidity. Sweet concord in the two-part passages is the essential feature.

THOU SHALT SHOW ME, page 7.—This should frequently be used as a test of steadiness in time and for the practice of syncopation and marked entry of parts. Let S., T., and B., hold firmly d against r in score 3, measure 4.

THE WAITS, page 8.—Example of soft singing, page 98; Increasing force in rising phrases, page 8; Representation of distance, page 101; The prominent and the subdued tones of a melody, Ex. 223. The highest part will prove very fatiguing if not sung in the upper thin register *without straining*. None but undoubted *first* sopranos should take this part. The *piano* singing of this piece will discover the presence of low and hard voices among the sopranos.

THE CUCKOO, page 9.—Imitative sounds, page 98; Cumulative force on repeated tones, page 99; Unanimous delivery of the bass voices is required in scores 1 and 4; Unity and good blending in S. and C., page 10, scores 1 and 2. The close *dim. pp* will require tenors to use their thin register gently. The word "cuckoo" should have its first syllable pronounced exactly like its last, and thus aid the imitation of the bird's cry.

BON ACCORD, page 11.—Entry of parts, page 100. This piece should be sung firmly, at a brisk rate and with fine round tone. It is one of the pieces which should be sung from memory in all its parts.

HOPE WILL BANISH SORROW, page 12.—General character of a piece, and appropriate force, page 98; Rising excitement, page 131; Depressing thoughts, page 132. The rhythm should be well practised. It is nearly the same in all the parts. Emotion ebbs and flows very much in this piece, and its phrasing is an interesting study. Transition analysis, score 2, measure 1, "How to Observe Harmony," page 57.

HOW BEAUTIFUL THE SUNSHINE, page 12.—See analysis of sectional relation in "How to Observe Harmony," page 63; Study the rhythm, which is varied and somewhat intricate; Three related phrases in scores 2 and 3, require increasing force; Transition analysis, score 1, measure 4, "How to Observe Harmony," page 57.

COME, FREEDOM'S SONS, p. 13.—Loud and bold delivery, page 98; Discouraging reflection, page 132; Poetic phrasing and expression, page 136.

THE QUAIL CALL, page 14.—Normal force, page 98; Imitative phrases in a melody, page 100; Dramatic expression of words, page 131; Effect of different expression in contrary motion, page 99; Excited exclamation, Ex. 257; Verbal expression, page 132; Proper rendering of cadences, page 103. The rhythm is not likely to be made perfect unless *each pulse* is distinctly beaten in learning the piece. Transition analysis, score 2, measure 3, "How to Observe Harmony," page 57.

THE TIME FOR JOY, page 15.—Appropriate force and speed, page 98; Notice alternate periods of *p* and *f*, and this order reversed at page 16, score 3; Develope tenor in last score, page 15, and score 2, page 16. The second S. must not cover up and obscure the first S. in those places where the second is the higher of the two, for even there the notes in the top line form the principal melody.

HEAR ME WHEN I CALL, page 17.—Subdued and prayerful effect, page 98; Exultation, page 131; Vowel sounds, page 138; Melodic and harmonic imitation, page 100; Marked entry of bass, page 100; Various contrasts of expression, page 132; Pressure tone, page 133; Bold delivery of fugal passage page 19; Triumphant affirmation, page 98. Transition analysis, "Additional Exercises," page 19, score 3, measure 1, "How to Observe Harmony," page 58. Let the bass, score 4, measure 4, hold its d well against the t and r of C and S.

WE FLY BY NIGHT, page 20.—Forceful delivery, Ex. 217; Acceleration of speed and force, page 131. Mark breathing places in the long run for S., scores 3 and 4, or still better, practise it till it can be sung easily to one breath. Marked entry is very important, especially in C. and T. For public performance this chorus may be preceded by the bass song in the Macbeth music, *Reporters* 520 and 521. Transition analysis, score 1, measure 3, "How to Observe Harmony," page 57.

MY LADY IS AS FAIR AS FINE, page 21.—Subdued general effect, page 98; Pronunciation, page 140; Develope the tenor in the 3rd score; Mark well the most effective part of the piece, which is at the beginning of 3rd score. Transition analysis, score 1, measure 4, "How to Observe Harmony," p. 57.

NIGHT AROUND, page 22.—How to produce h u m m i n g accompaniment, page 100; Dramatic effect, page 132. Obedience to the baton is imperative here. The conductor has to keep the chorus in time with the soloist. Transition analysis, score 2, measure 1, "How to Observe Harmony," page 57.

COME, LET US ALL A MAYING GO, page 24.—Expression of light-hearted gaiety, page 133; Imitation of the cuckoo and of bells, page 101. The piece must go freely and nimbly,—the quicker notes being struck neatly and somewhat *staccato*, especially in the downward runs imitating the sound of bells. Notice contrasted effect of *f* representing drums and *p* representing fifes. Transition analysis, score 2, measure 1, "How to Observe Harmony," page 58.

HALLELUJAH, AMEN, page 26.—Swell on prolonged tones, page 100. The rhythm of the principal subject must be perfect. Strongly marked accent is required at page 27, scores 1 to 3, beginning "O Judah." Tenors must use thin register in the higher passages, and this part must be well developed in measures 6 to 8, where it assumes the importance of an ascending bass. In the same way the bass part must be brought out when it imitates the same kind of ascent a fourth lower. The long silences are somewhat trying. The two "Amens," must be very bold.

SWIFTLY FROM THE MOUNTAIN'S BROW, page 29.—Expression changing in a new movement, page 98; Sunbeams and shadows, page 133; Warbling birds, Ex. 217; Prolonged tones, page 100; Normal force, page 98; Repose in nature, page 132; Expression rapidly changing, pp. 98, 99; Pronunciation, page 140. The two first movements of this glee represent the landscape, and the last one the music of nature at early morn. It abounds in melodial passages and fine effects. Transition analysis, "Additional Exercises," page 32, score 4, measure 2, "How to Observe Harmony," page 57.

LORD, IN THIS THY MERCY'S DAY, p. 33.—See "Standard Course," for proper expression of deepening emotion in v. 2, and increasing urgent supplication in v. 3, p. 132. Study of Verbal Expression, Ex. 260. Vowel *ai* low in pitch, p. 139. Preserve the subdued effect throughout, but study well the rise and fall of its three phrases. Tenors must use the thin register in the second phrase.

RISE, MY SOUL, ADORE THY MAKER, p. 33.—Tones to be developed as heightening the general effect, p. 102. Delivery of Cadences, p. 103. Give due effect to Harmonic Sequence, m. 7. The Verbal Expression requires great variety of speed and force. The chord ^{se}M, sc. 1, "How to Observe," pp. 76, 77.

FATHER, MY SPIRIT OWNS, p. 34.—Musical Expression, Ex. 215. Study of congenial tones, Ex. 224. Verbal E x p r e s s i o n—Resignation, Ex. 260. The vowel *a*, p. 140. Deep feeling expressed by p r e s s u r e tones, p. 133. Study the peculiarities of the rhythm in sc. 1, and mark well the change of rhythm in sc. 2. Chord *SE*, sc. 3. See "How to Observe," p. 78. Chord TA*b*, sc. 3, "How to Observe," p. 114. The bass part contains some difficulties. Practice the first line well, especially the octaves l₁ l, and r se. The S in sc. 2, m. 1, 2, 3, must be drilled also.

NEARER MY GOD, p. 34.—Tones to be emphasised, Ex. 225. Pure vowel sounds, p. 140. Melodic Imitations, p. 100. Get a pure quality of tone in the low passages for bass, sc. 1 and 4. Contraltos have to hold d against r in chord ^{7}R*b*, sc. 1. See "How to Observe," p. 26. T also has a Secondary Dissonance, p. 35, sc. 2, m. 2, in the same chord, ^{7}R*b*.

THE GIPSY'S TENT, p. 35.—Appropriate speed and force, p. 133. The proper singing of subordinate "parts," p. 100. When the S takes up the melody previously sung by the soloist, it should be done with great spirit, and be in strong contrast with the soft accompaniment which they were previously doing. A primary dissonance for the solo part (if soprano), occurs in chord ^{9}D*b*, m. 1. Also a tertiary dissonance in the same chord at p. 36, sc. 3, m. 3. See "How to Observe," p. 90, and pp. 4, 5. Also a secondary dissonance in the chord ^{6}D*c*. See "How to Observe." p. 100 Also a secondary and tertiary dissonance in the chord ^{9}F, p. 38, sc. 3.

HARVEST HOME, p. 39.—Characteristics of the "Part-Song," p. 146 Form of tones, p. 133. Sharp delivery of detached sounds, p. 103. Ascending and descending melody, and subordinate parts, p 101. Study of unison, uniform and equal emphasis, prolonged tones, "Vamping," Ex. 213, and p. 103. See that the correct tones are sung by T. and B. in this vamping accompaniment. The vowel *oa*, p. 138. Delivery of cadences, p. 103. The fine melody for S, p. 40, sc 2, should be well studied, and sung with perfect clearness. A pure, bright tone must be got at the f' (g'), last sc., which must not be attempted by any but *first* sopranos. Notice ^{4} ^{7} ^{9}D, p. 39, sc. 3., m. 4. See "How to Observe," p. 98. Tenors should use thin register in the three last tones.

AWAY TO THE FOREST, p. 42.—Staccato passages, p. 103 The lively, dancing effect of the rhythm, with alterations of *sforzando* and *staccato*, requires much practice. The piece is full of expression. Notice the echo effect in sc. 4, "Tra la," first *f* and then *pp*. Tenors must use thin register on s' at the close of the "Tra la."

SUNSHINE AFTER RAIN, p. 44.—Musical Form, p. 146. Emotion quickly changing, p. 132. Vowel *ai*, p. 139. Sc. 4, 5 contain some difficult rhythm. Develope tenor and bass, moving in thirds, sc. 3, 4. In these two parts the octaves, sc. 4, m. 1, should be clear. The S, in its turn, must be developed, sc. 4, m. 2. Bring out the *ff* at the close, which is intended to give great prominence to a repeated section.

IF I HAD BUT TWO LITTLE WINGS, p. 45. — Melodic Expression, Ex. 215. Musical Form, p. 146. Reflection, p. 132. Vowels *a* and *u*, p. 140. Melodic Imitation in sc. 1, should be studied, see p. 100. Give emphasis to d' m. 3, and l m. 5. The bass part, m. 5, 6, has some serious difficulties. Chromatic fe leaping up an octave and resolving on f in ^{7}S*d*. Tenors should use thin register at p. 47, sc. 4, m. 3, p. 3, to m. 4. p. 4.

ANGEL OF HOPE, p. 48.—How to produce humming accompaniment, p. 100. To avoid the danger of flattening, get the accompanying voices to *listen to the soloist*. The long sustained chords are, of themselves, difficult to hold in good tune without this kind of sympathy with the leading voice. Tenors should use the thin register wherever possible, and the closed lips assist them to do so. The rising passage, p. 49, m. 3, to sc. 2, m. 4, should be delicately sung in the thin, so as not to obscure the solo.

THE SPRING, p. 50.—Musical Form, p. 146. Excited emotion becoming subdued, p. 133. The rhythm is varied and difficult. Much practising together is required for unanimous delivery of tafa-AI which is of very frequent occurrence and is mingled with various other difficult forms. The piece abounds with melodial two-part passages, such as S and B, p. 51, sc. 2, where care must be taken to get good blending of these two parts while the C and T, in unison, must be quite subordinate. Tenors should use thin register on the notes d' r' m', p. 51, sc. 2, 3, 4.

AT FIRST THE MOUNTAIN RILL, p. 53. —Growing impetuosity descriptive of the gathering force of a stream, p. 133. The descending melodies in S and T alternately, starting each time a step higher are very dramatic, and must be commenced each one louder than the last. Tenors require to use the thin register for the higher notes in sc. 1, p. 54, and only *first* sopranos should attempt m' s' f' &c.. in sc. 3. The note se after f' is difficult. Other high passages will be found for sopranos and tenors in p. 54, sc. 5, and p. 55, sc. 1. Notice the dissonance 7 de*L*. See "How to Observe," p. 115. Tenors should use thin register in m. 2, p. 3, 4. Page 54, m. 2, 4, 11, 12, 18, 19, 21, 22, and corresponding parts of v. 2.

O THE JOY OF SPRING, p. 57.—Development of a principal melody, p. 100. Gay and tripping style, p. 133. Musical Form, p. 146. Pressure tones, p. 103. Subordination of parts should be attended to, see p. 100. Notice the chromatic part-pulse dissonances, fe and re, p. 57, sc. 4, m. 2. See "How to Observe," p. 119. The thin register should be employed by the tenors in m. 7, 8, 9, and on all following notes higher than s.

HOW LOVELY ARE THE MESSENGERS, p. 58.—Musical Form, p. 146 Vowel *u*, p. 140. Appropriate speed and force, p. 132. Bold and striking change of sentiment, Ex. 258. Fugal passages, p. 148. The proper rendering of "parts" in contrary motion, p. 99. Triumphant joy requiring the singer to dwell on the notes, p. 132. Changing emotion—triumph to repose—Ex. 219. Let each part study (in keys suited for each voice) the melody which opens this piece, and which becomes the subject. See "Melodic Phrasing," p. 98. Only *first* sopranos should sing the highest part, which abounds in high notes, often requiring small register. In pp. 59, 60, the thin register is constantly demanded from the tenors.

AWAKE, ÆOLIAN LYRE, p. 62.—Musical Form, p. 146. Smooth *legato*, p. 103. Downward rush of a stream, p. 99. The opening should have a well-sustained *cres.* the last chord being cut off sharply when the climax of force has been reached. The *ff* in sc. 2 is very important. Notice a little syncopation, p. 63, sc. 2. The last movement *spiritoso* should have very marked accent. Tenors should use thin register at the second "awake," at p. 63, first five measures of *Largo*, and in the *ff* close, except the last note which may be in the thick for the sake of effect.

WHERE THE GAY DREAMS, p. 65.—A series of *cres.* passages, rising each time higher. Standard Course, p. 133. Attend closely to the marks for *cres.* and *dim.* as they are intended to give form to the melody. Study "How to Observe Harmony," pp. 97, 101, 112, 113, for the dissonant and chromatic chords 4 9D, 9 7S, 9 4 feS, 7 feRE. Only *first* soprano voices should attempt the phrase commencing sc. 4, m. 2. Tenors must use thin register on the notes r' f' m in keys C and D, sc. 3, 4.

THEME SUBLIME, p. 66. — Study of fugal movements, subject, counter-subject, &c., p. 147. Development of parts, p. 148. Study of syncopated passages, and emphasis in a melody, Ex. 227. Fugal entry, p. 148. Form of prolonged tones, p. 100. Study of runs, and their accompaniment, Ex. 226, see also "Rapid Passages," p. 102. The "subject" and its variations, see p. 148. Delivery of cadences, p. 103. A very useful and invigorating practice piece, which ought to be often used. Study in "How to Observe," p. 103, the discord 7*L*. Tenors mark their books for thin register in the following passages: — First movement, m. 13-18. Second movement, m. 10-12, l s f m. Page 68, m. 11-15; score 5, m. 2-5. Page 69, sc. 1, m. 3-6; sc. 4, m. 2; sc. 5, m. 2, p. 1; m. 4 to p. 70, m. 1, 2; sc. 2, m. 3, p. 2. All the s's in sc. 2, 3, 4; p. 71, m. 2, 3. All the s's in sc. 2, 3, and the whole of the last 2 meas.

THE WOODS, p. 71.—Diverging sentiments in music and words. Gaiety in music and sober reflections in poetry, acting upon each other, p. 133. Structure of a part-song, p. 146. Dramatic effect—the fading away of a dream, p. 132. The vowel *ee*, p. 13. The normal force (see p. 98) of this piece should be *p* and the movement a gentle *legato*. The second verse may be *mf* for the sake of a little contrast, but the third must resume the *p*, and the close should be very soft and soothing. Study in "How to Observe," 7D, p. 103, 47D, p. 98.

HOME, O WHERE IS THY BLEST HAVEN, p. 74.—The study of vocal accompaniment, p. 100, and Ex. 218. Passionate utterance, explosive tone, p. 134, and Ex. 257. Where the soloist is silent, let the accompanying parts sing out with fuller voice, see "Subordination of parts," p. 100. Study in "How to Observe," 4R, p. 104, 4*L*, p. 95, 3R, p. 106, 4F, p. 104, 9D, p. 96, 6 7R (ornamentals) p. 109, 4*L*, p. 95. Tenor's to use thin register on m', p. 75, sc. 2, m. 2.

THE STOUT-LIMBED OAK, p. 77.—Musical form of a glee, p. 146. Delivery of cadences, p. 103. Delivery of bold passages, Ex. 258. Unison passages, p. 103. In the first movement of this glee all the "parts" claim in turn to be prominently heard. Notice in this way S, sc. 2, m. 1; C, sc. 2, m. 3; B, sc. 3, m. 3; T, sc. 4, m. 1. Then S and C together, sc. 4, m. 3; B, sc. 5, m. 1. The two-part passages on p. 78 must have both the voices perfectly together. Tenors should mark for thin register m. 3; sc. 2, m. 1, 2; the note m, sc. 4, m. 2; sc. 5, m. 2, to p. 78, m. 3, and all the last phrase.

MORNING PRAYER, p. 79.—Piano singing in unison, Ex. 230. See "piano passages," p. 98, and "unison passages," p. 103. Structure of a part song, p. 146. Solemn effect of ma introducing or invoking *p* in all the parts, p. 133. A shout of thankfulness, Ex. 256. Notice in verse 3 an alteration of the air, m. 8, 9; and of the harmony throughout. The s' should be sung by *first* sopranos only, and they should be careful to give it in the small register. The *forte* outburst at beginning of each verse should be finely delivered. Especially the bass, which in verses 1, 2, leaps an octave in the first two notes, thus d |d'. The expression is constantly varied, and should be carefully studied. See "How to Observe," maFE, p. 113, de*L*, p. 114, 7de*L* p. 115. Thin register should be used by T in the phrase beginning at the end of m. 9; in corresponding part of verse 2; also in fourth line of v. 3, p. 80, sc 5, m. 2.

YE SPOTTED SNAKES, p. 81.—Musical form—the glee, p. 146. *Legato* singing, p. 103. Soft and light *staccato*, p. 102 *Sforzando* for sudden exclamation, p. 133. Dramatic representation of terror. Secure marked entry (although *p*) in the syncopated notes, m. 5, 6, 7. The two transitions, p. 83, sc. 2, need careful practice, and still more does the transitional modulation, p. 83, sc. 4, and its return on the chord de*L*

(Picardy Third.) See "How to Observe," p. 114, and par. 98, p. 88. Tenors use thin register, m. 5, p. 2, to sc. 3, m. 1. Page 92, sc. 2, m. 1, p 3 to m. 4 p. 1. Page 83, sc. 4, m. 2; sc. 5, m. 2, p. 4 to m. 3, p. 3. Page 84, m. 4, p. 2 to sc. 2, m. 4, p. 3. Beginning of sc. 4 to m. 4, p. 3; and beginning of sc. 5 to m. 2, p. 2.

O SAVIOUR OF THE WORLD, p. 85.—Musical form of the anthem, p. 145. Prayerful utterance, Ex. 228. Increasing force on repeated tones, p. 99. Important words to be made prominent, p. 133. Humble supplication, Ex. 260. Unison passages *piano*, pp. 98 and 103. The transition to third flat, p. 86, sc. 1, is difficult, as it commences with an upward leap of an octave in S, and of a seventh in B. In the chromatic unison, p 87, sc. 4, nothing can help the singers but a strong sense of the note s, on which the repeated la resolves. Study in "How to Observe," 9 7F, p. 106, 7 *sE*, p. 78, 9 7 4S, p. 103 Tenors should use thin register on the word "O," p. 85, sc. 5, and p. 87. sc. 1.

THE SHEPHERD'S LAMENT, p. 88.—*Sforzando* tones expressive of passionate excitement, p. 133. Musical form of a part-song, p. 146. *pp* in detached notes expressive of deep sorrow, p. 132. The rhythm of sc. 3 should be well practised as a time-model of several passages following. The whole piece depends upon true intonation of chromatics. Study such chords as fe ma *La*, p. 89, sc. 5, in the light of "How to Observe," p. 118. In the transitional modulations, p. 90, practise each part separately, then two or more parts combined, and finally altogether in *slow time*. Study in "How to Observe," le ma LA, p. 118, m FE*b*, p. 118. Tenors should use thin register on the four last notes, sc. 1, and on a similar passage, p. 90. sc. 4, m. 2; also on the triplet, p. 89, sc. 1, m. 3.

SAVIOUR, BREATHE AN EVENING BLESSING, p. 91.—Subordination of parts, Ex. 216. Solemn thoughts, Ex. 260. Melody transferred to different parts, p. 100. Expression of a sense of safety in God's care, Ex. 257. Study the normal force of this piece. The time must be firmly kept, without drawling. In the transition to fourth flat minor, p. 92, m 4, the first chord has been already sung, which lessens the difficulty. Watch all the distinguishing tones as they appear. Look to the tenor, sc. 3. m. 1, 2. Study in "How to Observe," 7 4R, p. 103, 7 fe R, p. 58, 9 4D, p. 97, ma D. p. 116.

LOUD THE STORM WIND, p. 93.—Subdued description changing to the excitement of terror, p 133. The representation of calm after storm, Ex. 260. Form of repeated tones. Ex 214. See difficult intervals in S, p. 94, sc. 2, m. 1, 2, sc. 5, p. 1 (the latter will be most easily got by making the transition on previous note, ms.) Practise well the *p. cres*, *f*, p. 93, sc. 1, 2; page 94. sc. 3, 4. Try the parts separately at p. 95, sc. 4. *First* sopranos *only* should sing the highest part in this piece, using the "small register" for re' m p. 94, sc. 4. The continuous high passages, like that at page 95, sc. 2, 3, 4, are very trying, and good intonation is impossible if any but pure *first* sopranos take that part. Study the many discords and chromatic chords in the 12th and 13th steps of "How to Observe." On p. 93 will be found 7 *SE* On p 94 7 *T*, 7 de *L*, fe *R*, re *r*, 4 ba *M*. On p. 98 7 fe B

INDEX.

For Index to Music see page 320, *at end.*

INDEX TO STANDARD COURSE EXERCISES.

INDEX TO ADDITIONAL EXERCISES.

MUSIC FOR SCHOOLS.

COURSES OF LESSONS

ON THE TONIC SOL-FA METHOD.

The postage is given in brackets; those marked * can also be had in penny numbers.

The Standard Course.

	s. d.
The Complete Work, in cloth [3d.]	3 6
The Six Steps (instructions) [2d.]	1 6

The Exercises, Rhythms, &c., are also sold separately at prices from ½d. upwards, according to size.

Elementary Courses for Mixed Voices.

WITH INSTRUCTIONS AND TUNES.

*The Sunday School Singer [½d.]	0 6
*The Elementary Secular Course [1d.]	0 6
*The Elementary Sacred Course [1d.]	0 6

WITH EXERCISES AND TUNES ONLY.

THE SONG PRIMER [½d.] 4d.
A new course with exercises in unison and two-parts. A short cut to the Elementary Certificate. Concert pieces not provided. Aims at thorough drill. Pocket size (crown 8vo.) and stout cover.

VOICES IN SONG [1d.] 6d.
The latest course. The exercises are varied and comprehensive, and the pieces are carefully graded. In addition to other improvements, a number of specimen sight-tests are given for practice.

THE CHORUS SCHOOL [1d.] 6d.
Comprises several improvements on previous courses, and a large number of interesting exercises and pieces.

THE SONG HERALD [1d.] 6d.
Contains rounds, solfeggios, anthems, part-songs, elementary rhythms, &c., carefully graded.

CHOIR TRAINING [1d.] 6d.
The music is rather in advance of the other courses. The illustrative chants are a feature of this book.

*THE CHORAL SINGER [1d.] 6d.
A very popular course. Includes ninety-three exercises, rounds, part-songs, anthems, time and expression studies, illustrative chants, and the "Elementary Rhythms."

*THE SINGING CLASS [1d.] 6d
Contains several very popular anthems and secular pieces.

*HOURS OF SONG [½d.] 4d.
Shorter than the preceding courses. Has rounds and graded exercises.

VOCAL HARMONY [1d.] 4d.
The same length as "Hours of Song." Has proved a favourite course.

*THE TEMPERANCE COURSE [1d.] 6d.
This course now contains eighty part-songs, anthems, rounds, and exercises, all carefully graded according to the steps of Mr. Curwen's method.

THE TEMPLAR'S COURSE [1d.] 6d.
Containing a course of exercises, with Temperance part-songs, rounds, anthems, and choruses. May also be had in three 2d. numbers.

GRADED SIGHT TESTS [1d.] 6d.
A series of part-songs arranged according to the steps of the Tonic Sol-fa method for practice in sight-singing.

Elementary Courses for Schools.

WITH INSTRUCTIONS AND TUNES.

THE ACADEMY VOCALIST, Parts I and II [1d.] each 6d.
Suitable for High Schools, Academies, Middle Class and Private Schools. Part I comprises instructions for 1st to 3rd Steps. Part II, comprises 4th Step, including Transition, Six-pulse Measure, &c.

PUPIL-TEACHER'S ELEMENTARY CLASS BOOK [1d.] 4d.

THE PUPIL'S MANUAL [1d.] (Cloth, 9d.) 6d.
Ninety-one Exercises and Tunes in two-parts, with Rhythms and Bugle calls, and questions to be answered orally or in writing.

*THE FIRST HIGH SCHOOL VOCALIST [1d.] 6d.

THE YOUNG CHORISTER, Parts I to IV [1d.] each 3d.
By A. L. Cowley. In Parts, containing 40 pages, size of "Code Music Drill." Part I.—Steps I, II, and III. Part II.—Recapitulation of Steps I-III; Step IV as far as imperfect Sol-faing. Part III.—Steps IV and V. Part IV.—Additional Songs for Practice, and Introduction to the Staff Notation, Cloth complete, 1/-. Also EXAMINATION OR HOME LESSON SHEETS for above. A Series of Twenty Sheets of Questions, with spaces for writing the various answers. Price 1/6 per 100; 2/- assorted; the 20 sheets in wrapper, 6d.

THE EDUCATIONAL VOCALIST, Part I, for Div. 1, 1d.; Part II, for Div. II, 1½d.; Part III, for Div. III, 2d.; Part IV, for Div. IV, 3d. Complete, 8d. By A. ADAMSON.

AUXILIARY MUSIC CARDS, Packets I, II, III, & IV, 6d. each.

SCHOOL COURSES with Exercises and Tunes only.

For Standards I. to VI.

THE CALL TO SONG [½d.] 4d.
A pocket edition of the "Educational Music Charts," with an appendix of Voice Exercises, Elementary Rhythms, Certificate Requirements, &c.

For Infant Schools.

THE FIRST LINNET [½d.] 3d. | THE SECOND LINNET [½d.] 4d.

For Junior Schools.

THE IRISH TONIC SOL-FAIST [1d.]	6d.
GRADED ROUNDS [½d.]	3d.
THE FIRST BLACKBIRD [½d.]	2d.
THE ROYAL SONGSTER, Part VII [½d.]	1d.
YOUNG VOICES, Parts I to III [½d.]	each 2d.
CODE MUSIC DRILL, Parts I and II [1d.]	each 2d.

For Senior Schools.

THE SONG PRIMER [½d.]	4d.
THE FIRST NIGHTINGALE [½d.]	3d.
CODE MUSIC DRILL, Parts III and IV [1d.]	each 2d.
CROTCHETS AND QUAVERS, O.N., Pts. III & IV [1d.]	each 3d.
*SONGS AND TUNES FOR EDUCATION [2d.]	1s.

In cloth [2d.], 1s. 4d. First Course [1d. for 3], 3d. Second Course [1d. for 3], 4d.

*THE SECOND HIGH SCHOOL VOCALIST [1d. for 3]	4d.
*THE THIRD HIGH SCHOOL VOCALIST (Advanced) [½d.]	6d.
*THE FOURTH HIGH SCHOOL VOCALIST (Advanced) [1d.]	8d.
*ARRANGED REPORTERS, No. 1 [1d.]	6d.

Intermediate Courses.

INTERMEDIATE CLASS BOOK [1d.] 6d.
For pupils preparing for the Intermediate Certificate of the Tonic Sol-fa College.

INTERMEDIATE TRAINING [1d.] 6d.
Intended as a connecting link between the Elementary Class and the Choral Society.

*THE INTERMEDIATE SECULAR COURSE [1d.]	6d.
THE INTERMEDIATE STANDARD [1d].	6d.

Introductory Exercises.

INTRODUCTORY EXERCISES, No. I [½d.] ½d.
Rounds and two-part exercises, as far as the Fifth Step.

INTRODUCTORY EXERCISES, No. II [½d.] ½d.
Intended for psalmody purposes.

INTRODUCTORY EXERCISES, No. III [½d.] 1d.
Double the length of the preceding.

THE SHORT COURSE [½d.] 2d.
Its speciality is that all the exercises and tunes are printed in both old and new notations.

*** The first Number (1d.) of "The Choral Singer," "Hours of Song," or "The Singing Class," will also serve as introductory exercises.

STANDARD WORKS ON MUSIC.

BOY'S VOICE, THE. By J. Spencer Curwen. Price 2/6; postage 1½d. A book of practical information for choirmasters, with hints from choir-trainers.

CANDIDATE IN MUSIC, THE. By H. Fisher, Mus. D. Price, in paper, 2/-; in cloth, 2/6; post. 1½d. A text-book of Musical Elements for students.

CHORAL SOCIETY, THE. By L. C. Venables. Price 3/-; postage 2½d. A book of practical hints and experiences for the use of Conductors, Secretaries, &c.

COMPANION FOR TEACHERS. By J. S. Curwen. Price 1/-; postage 1½d. This work gives the school teacher all necessary information on the Tonic Sol-fa system.

COMPENDIUM OF HARMONY. By Geo. Oakey, Mus. B. Price 2/-; postage 2d. Comprises the subject matter of the first half of the author's "Textbook of Harmony," the examples in Sol-fa only.

FIGURED BASS. By Geo. Oakey, Mus. B. Price, limp cloth, 1/-; postage 1d. Explains figured bass in modern harmonies, and epitomises harmony.

HANDBELL RINGING. By C. W. Fletcher. Price 2/6; postage 2d. Explains the method on which the "Criterion" Handbell Ringers play; shows how to organise and train troupes of handbell ringers, and gives exercises and tunes arranged for the bells.

HANDBOOK OF ACOUSTICS. By T. F. Harris, B.Sc., F.C.S. Price 4/6; postage 3d. A handbook for the use of musical students.

HOW TO EARN THE MUSIC GRANT. By An Inspector of Schools. Pri e 4d., Sol-fa.

HOW TO OBSERVE HARMONY. By John Curwen. Tenth edition with appendix. Price 2/-; postage 2d.

HOW TO READ MUSIC. By John Curwen. Twenty-four chapters, pp. 128. Eighth edition. Price 1s.; postage 1½d. Teaches sight-singing by the Tonic Sol-fa system, then applies the knowledge gained to the Old Notation, and teaches that thoroughly.

HYMN LOVER, THE. By the Rev. W. Garrett Horder. Price 7/6; postage 4½d. An account of the rise and progress of English Hymnody.

MANUAL OF ORCHESTRATION. By Hamilton Clarke, Mus. B. With Appendix. Price 2/-; postage 2d. Gives much information that will help young conductors and enable amateurs to listen intelligently to the playing of an orchestra.

MECHANISM OF THE HUMAN VOICE. By Emil Behnke. Seventh edition, enlarged and revised. Price, cloth, 2/6; paper, 1/6; postage 2d. Illustrated.

MEMORIALS OF JOHN CURWEN. By his son, J. Spencer Curwen. Price 2/-; postage 3d.

MUSICAL INSPECTION, and How to prepare for it, The. By A School Inspector. Price 1/6; post. 2d. Lessons and instructions on the Tonic Sol-fa method, for teachers in elementary schools.

MUSICAL PROFESSION, THE. By H. Fisher, Mus. D. Price 6/-; postage 4½d. Contains advice for music teachers in every department of the art.

MUSICAL SELF-INSTRUCTOR. By J. Sneddon, Mus. B. Price 3/-; postage 2d. *Both* notations. Self-help in musical elements and vocal practice.

MUSICAL THEORY. By John Curwen. Price 3/6; post. 3d. Or in parts—I, 4d.; II, 4d.; III, 1/4; IV, 4d.; V, 1/-. All the musical examples are given in *both* notations.

MUSICIANS OF ALL TIMES. Compiled by David Baptie. Price 3/6. A biographical handbook of composers, &c., containing nearly 12,000 names.

ORGANS, ORGANISTS, AND CHOIRS. By E. Minshall. Price 1/6; post. 1½d. Hints and suggestions for all interested in Nonconformist Church Music.

PRONUNCIATION FOR SINGERS. By A. J Ellis, F.R.S. Price 4/6; postage 4d.

SCHOOL MUSIC TEACHER, THE. By J. Evans and W. G. McNaught. Third edition, revised and enlarged. Price 3/-; postage 3d.

SHORT DICTIONARY of MUSICAL TERMS By Arnold Kennedy, M.A. Price 1/-, postage 1d.; cloth, 1/6, postage 1½d. Includes about 2,700 terms.

SINGING IN ELEMENTARY SCHOOLS. By A. Watkins. Cloth, 1/-; postage 1d.

SOLO SINGER, THE. By Sinclair Dunn. Price 1/6; postage 1½d. A handbook giving hints to those who desire to become solo singers.

SPECIMEN LESSONS on the TONIC SOL-FA METHOD. Edited by J. Spencer Curwen. New and enlarged edition. Cloth limp, 1/6; post. 1d. Contains specimen first lessons on Time, Tune, Transition, &c.

STAFF NOTATION PRIMER, for Tonic Sol-fa Pupils. Price 6d.; postage 1d. Size and style of "Musical Theory," with 69 exercises.

STANDARD COURSE, THE. By John Curwen. Ninth edition of the re-written work. Price 3/6; post 3d. Lessons and exercises on the Tonic Sol-fa Method.

STUDENT'S MUSICAL HISTORY. By H. Davy. Price 1/-. In handy, popular, and modern style. A record of all the landmarks of musical history.

STUDIES in WORSHIP MUSIC, First Series By J. S. Curwen. Second edition, revised and enlarged. 7/6; postage 4½d. Contains articles and information on various matters relative to Worship music.

Studies in Worship Music, Second Series. By J. S. Curwen. Price 3/-; postage 2½d. A continuation of the above work.

TEACHER'S MANUAL, THE. By John Curwen. Fourth edition. A manual of the Art of Teaching in general, and especially as applied to music. Price 5/-; postage 5d.

TEXT-BOOK OF COUNTERPOINT. Sixth edition. By Geo. Oakey, Mus. B. Price 2/-, cloth; post. 1½d. All the examples are given in *both* notations. and a set of subjects for exercises are given at the end.

TEXT-BOOK OF HARMONY. By Geo. Oakey, Mus. B. Fifth edition, price 3/-; postage 2½d. Seventeen chapters, with about 150 Graded Exercises. All examples in *both* notations.

TEXT-BOOK OF MUSICAL ELEMENTS. By Geo. Oakey, Mus. B. Price, in paper, 1/-; cloth, 1/6; post. 1½d. All the usual topics arranged on a new plan, with an Appendix of questions and exercises.

TRAINING COLLEGE MUSIC COURSE. By E. Mills, Mus. B. Price 3/-; postage 2½d. O.N. Course, Vocal and Theoretical, to prepare directly for the various Examinations.

UNITED PRAISE. By F. G. Edwards. Price 3/6; postage 3d. A practical handbook of Nonconformist Church Music.

LONDON: J. CURWEN & SONS, 8 & 9 WARWICK LANE, E.C. 8/91